Introducing Language and Intercultural Communicati

Introducing Language and Intercultural Communication is a lively and accessible introduction for undergraduates who are new to the area of intercultural communication.

Incorporating real-life examples from around the world and drawing on current research, this text argues against cultural stereotyping and instead provides students with a skill-building framework to enhance understanding of the complexities of language and intercultural communication in diverse international settings. Readers will learn to understand and become aware of power relations, positioning and the impact of social and political forces on language choice and the intercultural communication process. This is the essential text for undergraduate students studying courses in intercultural communication for the first time.

Features include:

- clear learning objectives to structure your study
- end of chapter discussion questions to test your knowledge
- highlighted glossary terms to provide a strong understanding of the relevant vocabulary
- an array of photos including signs which make use of nonverbal codes and many examples that illustrate such issues as intercultural misunderstandings and the effects of culture shock
- substantial online resources for students including learning objectives, suggested readings, links to media resources and real-world intercultural scenarios and activities. Additional in-depth instructor resources feature test materials, powerpoints, key terms, extended chapter outlines and sample assignments and syllabi. The website can be found at www.routledge.com/cw/jackson.

Jane Jackson has many years of experience teaching intercultural communication and is Professor of Applied Linguistics at the Chinese University of Hong Kong.

Praise for this edition:

'*Introducing Language and Intercultural Communication* delivers a clear, accessibly written and above all comprehensive overview of the field. I know of no other single-author text that does this.'

Professor John Corbett, *University of Macau, China*

'*Introducing Language and Intercultural Communication* is a very well structured, well researched and impressively well informed course book with an in-depth elaboration of the different aspects of intercultural communication. In combination with the companion website, which offers a variety of identity narratives, interviews and critical incidents, it is a highly recommendable tool that will effectively facilitate intercultural teaching and learning at different levels and certainly compares very favourably with the textbooks I have used so far in my teaching.'

Professor Guido Rings, *Anglia Ruskin University, Cambridge, UK*

'*Introducing Language and Intercultural Communication* by Jane Jackson is a state of the art introductory textbook to intercultural communication that impresses with its comprehensiveness and convinces with its accessibility and ease of use. There is no doubt that this book will benefit instructors and students in equal measure.'

Professor Stefanie Stadler, *Nanyang Technological University, Singapore*

'With an emphasis on ethical Intercultural Communication (ICC) Jackson's book provides a chronology of the development in the field and gives a comprehensive overview of different research paradigms in the area of ICC, as well as their applications in other fields of scholarship. I would highly recommend this book to both students and researchers working in the field of ICC.'

Dr Maryam Jamarani, *University of Queensland, Australia*

'Intercultural communication is a notoriously complex phenomenon of immense importance in our contemporary and future worlds. This book succeeds in presenting that complexity in an elegant and simple approach while being neither simplifying nor reductive. For students new to the field, it introduces the crucial topics, concepts and theories in a logical sequence, but it also challenges them to think critically about what they read, in the best traditions of university education.'

Professor Michael Byram, *Professor Emeritus, University of Durham, UK*

Praise from students:

'As a student who is about to study abroad in Japan, reading this book has been of enormous help to me.

Not only does the book include different concepts related to intercultural communication, it is illustrated with various examples from different parts of the world. This offered me a brand new perspective on looking at culture and intercultural communication.

After reading this book, I now have a more comprehensive understanding of . . . how one can competently interact with people across cultures. I am convinced that what I have learnt from this book will contribute to making my study abroad experience even more valuable.'

Serena Kwok Ho Ching, *student at the Chinese University of Hong Kong*

'I can grasp the ideas and concepts quickly since the author illustrates them with short, straightforward daily-life examples. As for the rather complicated communication theories and models of other scholars, Professor Jackson explains them in a clear and understandable way and also applies them in intercultural situations.'

Flora Leung, *student at the Chinese University of Hong Kong*

Introducing Language and Intercultural Communication

JANE JACKSON

Routledge
Taylor & Francis Group

LONDON AND NEW YORK

First published 2014
by Routledge
2 Park Square, Milton Park, Abingdon, Oxon OX14 4RN

and by Routledge
711 Third Avenue, New York, NY 10017

Routledge is an imprint of the Taylor & Francis Group, an informa business

© 2014 Jane Jackson

British Library Cataloguing in Publication Data
A catalogue record for this book is available from the British Library

Library of Congress Cataloging in Publication Data
Jackson, Jane, 1954-
    Introducing language and intercultural communication / Jane Jackson.
        pages cm
    Includes bibliographical references and index.
    1. Intercultural communication. I. Title.
    P94.6.J33 2014
    302.2—dc23   2013027661

ISBN: 978-0-415-60198-6 (hbk)
ISBN: 978-0-415-60199-3 (pbk)
ISBN: 978-1-315-84893-8 (ebk)

Typeset in Akzidenz Grotesk and Eurostile
by Keystroke, Station Road, Codsall, Wolverhampton

MIX
Paper from
responsible sources
FSC   FSC® C013056
www.fsc.org

Printed and bound in Great Britain by
TJ International Ltd, Padstow, Cornwall

Contents

Plates

Figures

Tables

Preface

In recent decades, interaction between people from diverse linguistic and cultural backgrounds has never been greater. With advances in technology and transportation and increases in immigration quotas, more and more people are on the move and societies are becoming increasingly diverse. The number of students who are studying outside their home country is also on the rise. Consequently, there is a pressing need for better preparation for cross-cultural adjustment and intercultural relationship building, especially in a second language. Institutions of higher education across the globe now recognize the need to offer courses and experiences that foster the knowledge, skills and attitudes necessary for intercultural communicative competence and responsible, global citizenship. Introductory courses in intercultural communication are now being offered in baccalaureate degrees in a range of disciplines; however, few books are truly international in scope and the language dimension of intercultural communication is often given little attention.

This introductory book is written in an accessible, user-friendly style for undergraduates who are new to this area of study. It is designed to provide a basic skill-building framework to enhance understanding of the complexities of language and intercultural communication in diverse domestic and international settings. It raises awareness of the implications of English as a lingua franca in today's interconnected, globalized world and also underscores the benefits of mastering other languages.

The book begins by introducing foundational concepts of intercultural communication, drawing attention to historical developments in this exciting field of study. Throughout, readers are encouraged to engage, explore and dialogue with others as they develop a deeper understanding of what it means to be intercultural. Core issues related to language and the intercultural communication process are linked to real-life examples from around the world (e.g. photos of diverse cultural scenes, student narratives in different cultural/linguistic contexts, critical incidents involving study abroad students, excerpts from interviews with international exchange students). Readers are prompted to learn more about themselves (e.g. their values, beliefs, communication styles, attitudes towards different accents) and to challenge their assumptions and preconceived notions about other worldviews and ways of being. The text strives to avoid the essentialization of people and behaviours, that is, the tendency to overlook variations *within* cultures. The chapters aim to sensitize readers to power relations, positioning and the impact of social and political forces on language choice/use and the intercultural communication process (e.g. interpersonal relations, management styles, discourse, nonverbal communication). The text raises awareness of the cognitive, affective and behavioural dimensions of intercultural (communicative) competence and the qualities associated with global citizenship. Ultimately, *Introducing Language and Intercultural Communication* is intended to serve as a valuable resource for students both in their home environment and abroad. I hope that the readers will find the book useful and stimulating. My wish is that it will inspire more meaningful intercultural interactions and contribute to making the world more humane.

CHAPTER-BY-CHAPTER OVERVIEW OF THE BOOK

Chapter 1 introduces definitions of key terms and raises awareness of the imperatives of studying language and intercultural communication in today's globalized, interconnected world.

Chapter 2 provides a concise history of the multidisciplinary and interdisciplinary field of language and intercultural communication, largely focusing on the contributions of scholars in the United States, Europe and East Asia. Attention is also drawn to the need for more indigenous, localized research.

Chapter 3 examines the concept of culture and the process of language and cultural socialization, providing a foundation for the remainder of the text. Discussion centres on definitions and conceptions of culture, and the various qualities and dimensions that are associated with this construct (e.g. culture as learned, culture as shared, culture as relative, etc.).

Chapter 4 delves into the nature of communication and the many factors that can influence the communication process (e.g. culture, context, power). After describing the characteristics and properties of communication, discussion centres on variations in communication styles and the potential impact of culture. Suggestions are offered to become an effective intercultural communicator in situations where one's communication partner is a second language speaker.

Chapter 5 explores the vital role of nonverbal communication in intercultural encounters, whether in face-to-face interactions or online. Discussion centres on the forms and functions of nonverbal communication, with attention paid to both universal and culture-specific dimensions. The relationship between language and nonverbal codes is also explored. Suggestions are offered to enhance the nonverbal dimension of one's intercultural communication.

Chapter 6 explores identity in relation to language and intercultural communication. Discussion addresses such issues as the impact of socialization on identity formation; language as an emblem of identity; intercultural contact and identity change; multiple types of identity (e.g. social, personal, cultural, racial, global, hybrid); the relational, dynamic and sometimes contradictory nature of identity; and the complex relationship between language, identity and culture. The importance of recognizing and respecting the preferred self-identities of one's communication partners is emphasized.

Chapter 7 explores identity biases (e.g. ethnocentrism, stereotypes, discrimination, prejudice, racism) and their potential harmful impact on intercultural relations. Suggestions are offered for ways to cultivate a more open, inclusive perspective.

Chapter 8 focuses on intercultural transitions, that is, the movement of individuals from their home environment to an unfamiliar linguistic/cultural setting. After exploring different types of border crossers (e.g. immigrants, sojourners), discussion focuses on issues related to the challenges of adapting to a new environment. Several models of culture shock and adjustment are reviewed and critiqued. The chapter concludes with suggestions to optimize intercultural transitions.

Chapter 9 explores various types and dimensions of intercultural interpersonal relationships (e.g. interethnic, interfaith). Discussion centres on the benefits and challenges of forming and maintaining friendships and intimate relationships (e.g. romances, marriage) with individuals from another cultural and/or linguistic background. The chapter concludes with suggestions to enhance intercultural interpersonal relationships.

Chapter 10 explores intercultural conflict. After identifying multiple domains and types of conflict, discussion focuses on variations in the way conflict is viewed and managed. Intercultural conflict styles and taxonomies are examined, along with the role of face and facework in conflict resolution. The chapter concludes with suggestions to resolve language and intercultural conflict through peaceful dialogue and skilful intercultural communication/mediation.

Chapter 11 centres on intercultural communication in the global workplace and raises awareness of communication challenges that may occur in both domestic and international settings when people from different cultural backgrounds interact (e.g. divergent communication styles, a language barrier, discrimination, etc.). The use of cultural difference frameworks in intercultural business education is also examined and critiqued. The chapter concludes with suggestions to enhance intercultural communication in workplace contexts.

Finally, Chapter 12 discusses the characteristics of global citizenship and what it means to be globally and interculturally competent in today's increasingly diverse and interconnected world. Several models of intercultural (communicative) competence are reviewed and suggestions are offered to become a more effective intercultural communicator and ethical global citizen. This chapter serves as a review of key elements in the text and stresses that the road towards interculturality involves a life-long journey.

Throughout the text you will find key terms in bold. These terms are explained in the text and can also be found in the glossary at the end of the book.

ANCILLARY MATERIAL

Students may access the companion website (student pages), which has support material designed to deepen and extend learning related to issues and concepts presented in each chapter.

Instructors' resources are available online for qualified adopters of the book. Online materials include the following: additional discussion questions, Powerpoint presentations, suggested teaching resources (e.g. films, video/YouTube links, print material), 'real-world' excerpts (e.g. cultural identity narratives, critical incidents, interview excerpts), interactive student activities and a Testbank.

Acknowledgements

This book would not have been possible without the editorial assistance and encouragement provided by the Routledge team, especially Nadia Seemungul, Alexandra McGregor, Rachel Daw, Louisa Semlyen, Jenny Hunt, Sophie Jaques and the copy editor. I also wish to thank the anonymous reviewers who provided helpful feedback on the proposal for the text. Throughout the writing process, batches of chapters were sent to anonymous intercultural communication educators in Australia, Finland, Hong Kong, Lebanon, Singapore, South America, Spain, the United States and the United Kingdom. I am grateful for the careful readings and insightful criticisms of the reviewers. Their suggestions helped me to refine the content and sequence the material.

I also wish to express gratitude to some of the many scholars from various disciplines who have influenced my approach to language and intercultural communication: Janet Bennett, Michael Byram, Donal Carbaugh, Darla Deardorff, Fred Dervin, Alvino Fantini, Howard Giles, Manuela Guilherme, Adrian Holliday, Zhu Hua, Young Yun Kim, Claire Kramsch, Judith Martin, Thomas Nakayama, Ingrid Piller, Stella Ting-Toomey and Kathryn Sorells, to name a few. All of the interculturalists who contributed to *The Routledge Handbook of Language and Intercultural Communication,* which I edited, have enriched my understanding of the field and I very much appreciate their scholarship.

For many decades, I have taught intercultural communication courses at the undergraduate and postgraduate levels in several countries and am deeply indebted to my students who have willingly shared their intercultural stories and ideas with me both in and out of class. In particular, their cultural identity narratives and reflective intercultural journals offered a window into their language use/learning and intercultural understandings.

My research on education abroad has also helped to shape this book. In particular, I have drawn on my ethnographic investigations of short-term sojourners as well as mixed-method studies of the international exchange experiences of university students from Hong Kong and Mainland China who joined either a semester or year abroad international exchange programme. My research has been generously supported by the Research Grants Council of the Hong Kong SAR (Project nos. 444709, 445312).

With the support of Teaching Development Grants at my institution, I developed and researched an intercultural transitions course for students with recent or current international experience. The generous sharing of their sojourn and reentry experiences helped me to gain further insight into the intercultural learning of incoming international exchange students and local returnees. The intercultural challenges and triumphs of these participants, as well as other students who took part in my other investigations of education abroad, helped provide direction for the scope of this text. With their permission, some of their voices and photos are featured in some chapters as well as in the companion website.

I appreciate the support of my institution, the Chinese University of Hong Kong, especially the Department of English, throughout the writing of this book. Undergraduate and post-graduate students have conducted library research, processed student data and helped to gather examples of intercultural interactions. In particular, I would like to thank Chan Sin Yu (Cherry) for her valuable assistance with this project, as well as a number of junior research assistants who helped gather material for the website: Joyce Cheung, Serena Kwok Ho Ching, Flora Leung Yat Chi, Siu Ho Yan (Yancy), and Wong Po Yee (Bowie). Also, some local and international students at my institution kindly agreed to be photographed using common gestures in their home cultures. Their contribution is very much appreciated.

Finally, I wish to acknowledge the support of my extended multicultural family. Their enthusiasm, intercultural stories and photos have certainly enhanced my life as well as this book.

The author and publisher appreciate the permission granted to reproduce the copyright material in this book:

Table 1.1 Adapted from Internet World Stats – www.internetworldstats.com/stats.htm.
Table 1.2 Adapted from Internet World Stats – www.internetworldstats.com/stats7.htm 2000–10 Miniwatts Marketing Group
Table 1.3 Adapted from Internet World Stats – www.internetworldstats.com/stats7.htm
Figure 10.1 Taken from M. Hammer (2005) 'The intercultural conflict style inventory: A conceptual framework and measure of intercultural conflict resolution approaches', *International Journal of Intercultural Relations,* 29: 691.
Figure 12.1 Taken from D. B. Morais and A. C. Ogden (2011) 'Initial development and validation of the global citizenship scale', *Journal of Studies in International Education,* 15: 447.
Figure 12.2 Taken from B. Hunter, G. Godbey and G. P. White (2006) 'What does it mean to be globally competent?', *Journal of Studies in International Education,* 10(3): 278.
Figure 12.3 An updated version of an image that originally appeared in M. Byram (1997) *Teaching and Assessing Intercultural Communicative Competence,* Clevedon, UK: Multilingual Matters.
Figure 12.4 Taken from D. K. Deardorff (2006) 'Identification and assessment of intercultural competence as a student outcome of internationalization', *Journal of Studies in International Education,* 10(3): 256.

CHAPTER 1

Why study language and intercultural communication?

All of us are affected by the decisions and actions of people whose faces we may never see, whose language we may not speak, and whose names we would not recognize – and they, too, are affected by us. Our well-being, and in some cases, our survival, depends on recognizing this truth and taking responsibility as global citizens for it.

(Gerzon 2010: xii)

The key to community is the acceptance, in fact, the celebration of our individual and cultural differences. It is also the key to world peace.

(Peck 1978: 186)

learning objectives

By the end of this chapter, you should be able to:

1   define intercultural communication, interpersonal communication, and cross-cultural communication
2   identify and describe seven imperatives for studying language and intercultural communication today
3   explain how studying language and intercultural communication can lead to increased self-awareness and understanding of people who have a different linguistic and cultural background
4   describe the characteristics of an ethical intercultural communicator.

INTRODUCTION

This chapter begins by introducing various understandings of the terms 'intercultural communication', 'interpersonal communication' and 'cross-cultural communication'. We then examine seven imperatives for studying language and intercultural communication: globalization, internationalization, advances in transportation and communication technologies, changing demographics, conflict and peace, ethics and personal growth and responsibility. Finally, we review the characteristics of an ethical intercultural communicator.

DEFINITIONS

There are many definitions of intercultural communication. Each reflects the author's disciplinary roots and understandings of communication and culture, core elements that are explored in more detail in the next three chapters.

Intercultural and interpersonal communication

Rogers and Steinfatt (1999), communication specialists, define **intercultural communication** simply as 'the exchange of information between individuals who are unalike culturally' (p. 1). This is similar to Berry *et al*.'s (2011) conception. These social and cross-cultural psychologists refer to intercultural communication as the 'exchange of information (verbally or nonverbally) between members of different cultural populations' (Berry *et al*. 2011: 471).

For Müller-Jacquier (2004), an applied linguist, intercultural communication denotes 'a peculiar communication situation: the varied language and discourse strategies people from different cultural backgrounds use in direct, face-to-face situations' (p. 295). Zhu Hua offers a broader view, incorporating both cross-cultural and intercultural elements in her definition. For this applied linguist, intercultural communication refers to

> a situation where people from different cultural backgrounds come into contact with each other; or a subject of study that is concerned with interactions among people of different cultural and ethnic groups and comparative studies of communication patterns across cultures.
>
> (Zhu Hua 2011: 422)

Samovar, Porter and McDaniel, speech communication specialists, provide a more detailed definition than most and, not surprisingly, they emphasize elements in the communication process: 'Intercultural communication involves interaction between people whose cultural perceptions and symbol systems are distinct enough to alter the communication event' (Samovar *et al*. 2010: 12). For Jandt (2007), who is also a speech communication scholar, intercultural communication 'generally refers to face-to-face interactions among people of diverse cultures' (p. 36). In a later edition, he states that intercultural communication refers 'not only to the communication between individuals of diverse cultural identities but also to the communication between diverse groups' (Jandt 2010: 18). The relationship between language, culture and identity is explored in Chapter 6.

While some definitions focus on 'the exchange of information' between individuals from different cultural groups, Jack and Phipps (2005) understand intercultural communication to be 'a participatory set of actions in the world', that is, 'dialogical and material exchanges between members of cultural groupings' (p. 181). Their definition acknowledges the interpersonal, dynamic nature of intercultural dialogue and interaction. For these applied linguists, **cultural membership** is 'marked variously by race, ethnicity, nationality, language, class, age and gender' (p. 181).

Critical intercultural communication scholars (Rona Halualani, Adrian Holliday, Dreama Moon, Thomas Nakayama and Kathryn Sorrells, among others) sharply criticize static notions of culture and cultural groups. These interculturalists advocate a broader, more flexible conceptualization of culture than is evident in depictions of **'culture as nation'**, whereby nations or communities are viewed as homogeneous and the diversity within groups is largely ignored. We return to this contentious issue in later chapters.

For this text, **intercultural communication** generally refers to interpersonal communication between individuals or groups who are affiliated with different cultural groups and/or have been socialized in different cultural (and, in most cases, linguistic) environments. This includes such cultural differences as age, class, gender, ethnicity, language, race, nationality and physical/mental ability. **Interpersonal communication** is 'a form of communication that involves a small number of individuals who are interacting exclusively with one another and who therefore have the ability both to adapt their messages specifically for those others and to obtain immediate interpretations from them' (Lustig & Koester 2010: 19).

Nowadays, intercultural interaction may take place in face-to-face encounters, through written discourse or online (e.g. Skype, Facebook). Intercultural communication very often involves a second language, with either one or both interlocutors using a language that is not a mother tongue. Genuine intercultural communication goes beyond mere 'information-sharing' and narrow conceptions of cultural membership, whereby culture is reduced to nationality and variations *within* cultural groups are largely ignored. In conceptions of intercultural communication it is important to recognize the dynamic, interpersonal dimension inherent in relationship building between people from diverse backgrounds.

The difference between cross-cultural and intercultural communication

Although the terms 'cross-cultural' and 'intercultural' are sometimes used interchangeably, **cross-cultural communication** generally refers to the comparison of communication behaviours and patterns in two or more cultures, while **intercultural communication** involves interaction between people from different cultural backgrounds (Gudykunst 2003). **Cross-cultural communication research** typically compares and contrasts native discourse and communication behaviours (or styles) in different cultures. For example, the politeness norms or conflict negotiation strategies in Japanese management meetings may be compared with those in Irish management meetings. In another cross-cultural communication study, one might examine the behaviour of business students in case discussions in Riyadh, Saudi Arabia and compare it with the behaviour of business students in case discussions in Kuala Lumpur, Malaysia.

In contrast, **intercultural communication research** involves an investigation of interpersonal interaction between individuals (or groups) from diverse linguistic and cultural backgrounds. The form of this intercultural contact varies. It may be face-to-face or involve communication through written discourse. With advances in technology, more researchers are paying attention to intercultural interaction that is taking place online (e.g. Skype calls, chat groups, email, second language classes with online intercultural exchange). Intercultural communication studies may focus on the verbal or nonverbal behaviour, attitudes or perceptions of people from different cultural and linguistic backgrounds interacting with each other (e.g. face-to-face, online, through written discourse). The interlocutors may have a different first language and speak a second language that is common to all of them (e.g. an international language such as English). They may speak the native language of one of the participants or a combination of languages (e.g. code-mixing) as they interact with each other and build a relationship (Jenkins 2013; Mackenzie 2013).

An example of intercultural communication is a South Korean university student in Seoul interacting in English with an exchange student from Sweden. In this intercultural situation, neither of the speakers are using their first language and both have been socialized in a different linguistic and cultural environment. In another example, an American exchange student in Oxford is conversing on Skype with an Australian friend in Brisbane. While both speakers are using their first language, they are using different varieties of English and have been socialized in different cultural contexts, so this, too, is an intercultural encounter. In another scenario, an elderly Buddhist monk in Bangkok is conversing with a young, Thai female who is a Christian. While they share the same nationality and ethnicity, the interactants have a different religious background and also differ in terms of age, occupation and gender. This is another example of intercultural communication.

From an intercultural perspective, one might observe classroom interactions involving students from different linguistic and cultural backgrounds. For example, at a university in the Netherlands, one could investigate the communication behaviours and interaction of Chinese, Dutch and French business majors in English-medium tutorials. An intercultural researcher could focus on the language and intercultural learning experiences of students who move temporarily from one educational and geographic setting to another (e.g. international exchange students) or analyse the discourse of immigrants who are interacting with locals in their new country of residence. Culture shock, adjustment/adaptation, social networks, inter-cultural friendships/relations, identity shifts and culture/language-learning strategies in a new environment are just some of the interests and concerns of interculturalists. All of these topics (and many others) are explored in this text.

REASONS TO STUDY LANGUAGE AND INTERCULTURAL COMMUNICATION

There are many imperatives for learning more about intercultural communication, and the impact of language in intercultural relations. Because of globalizing forces, internationalization, transportation and technological advances, changing demographics and conflict situations, ethical intercultural communication is now more important than at any other time in the history of our planet. We need to learn how to adapt and thrive in unfamiliar environments, and con-tribute to our planet in a constructive, peaceful manner. Through interaction with people from diverse linguistic and cultural backgrounds, we can learn more about ourselves and discover respectful ways to build and nurture intercultural relationships.

Globalization

No matter where you live, you are impacted by globalizing forces. While the exchange of ideas, goods and people is not new, in the last few decades we have been experiencing an unprece-dented intensification of economic, cultural, political, linguistic and social ties (Fairclough 2006; Held *et al.* 1999). This phenomenon, **globalization**, involves 'a process of removing government-imposed restrictions on movements between countries in order to create an "open", "borderless" world economy' (Scholte 2000: 16). Rogers and Hart (2002: 12) charac-terize globalization as 'the degree to which the same set of economic rules applies everywhere in an increasingly interdependent world'. Europe's Maastricht Treaty and the North American Free Trade Agreement (NAFTA), for example, were signed to reduce tariffs and barriers to international trade among neighbouring countries.

Knight and deWit (1997: 6) offer a much broader conceptualization of globalization, defining it as 'the flow of technology, economy, knowledge, people, values, [and] ideas . . . across borders', while Appadurai (1990) simply refers to it as 'a dense and fluid network of global flows'. Inda and Rosaldo's (2006) understanding is particularly relevant to our study of language and intercultural communication. Acknowledging the cultural dimension, these social scientists characterize globalization as

> spatial-temporal processes, operating on a global scale that rapidly cut across national boundaries, drawing more and more of the world into webs of interconnection, integrating and stretching cultures and communities across space and time, and compressing our spatial and temporal horizons.
>
> (Inda & Rosaldo 2006: 9)

Due to this 'intensification of worldwide social relations', Giddens (1990: 64) observes that 'local happenings are shaped by events occurring many miles away and vice versa.' Gerzon (2010) concurs, noting that humans are affected by 'the decisions and actions' of people in other parts of the world that they may never meet. As well as closer ties in trade and commerce, globalizing forces are triggering profound changes in the social, cultural, political and linguistic dimensions of communities across the globe. For example, this interdependence is influencing language policies on all continents (e.g. the designation of English as the medium-of-instruction in educational institutions in non-English-speaking countries). It is also altering linguistic codes (e.g. increasing the mixing of English expressions with a local language, a process that is referred to as '**code-mixing**').

Due to colonialism and globalization, there are also more varieties of English in the world today, which is why most scholars now refer to **World Englishes**, rather than 'World English'. As Sharifian (2012: 310) explains, 'English has not "spread" as a monolithic code, but has become a pluricentric language: many new varieties have developed, and are still being developed . . .'. Around the world, the number of localized or indigenized varieties of English (e.g. Cameroon English, Indian English, Malaysian English, Nigerian English) continues to grow.

Further, Ryan (2006: 28) argues that 'globalization could not happen without its own language, and that language is unquestionably English.' According to David Crystal (2010), an English-language expert, non-native speakers of English now outnumber native speakers by three to one. In this age of rapid globalization, English has become a **lingua franca** in many parts of the world, that is, it is 'a language which is used in communication between speakers who have no native language in common' (Trudgill 2003: 80).

Globalizing forces are also creating more interest in other languages. For example, in the late 1970s, China's Open Door Policy and subsequent entry into the World Trade Organization (WTO) in 2001 have had a significant impact on the number of non-Chinese studying Mandarin (Putonghua) around the world. In 2004, the government of the People's Republic of China began establishing Confucius Institutes across the globe to encourage trade ties and promote Chinese culture and language abroad. As of October 2010, there were 322 Confucius Institutes and 337 Confucius Classrooms in 94 countries and regions (Xinhua 2010). China's Ministry of Education estimates that 100 million people overseas were learning Chinese in 2010; by 2020, the government aims to establish 1,000 Confucius Institutes worldwide so one can expect the number of second language speakers of Chinese to continue to rise along with China's increasing global influence in other spheres (e.g. global politics, trade and commerce, tourism).

When reflecting on the impact of globalization, McGrew (1992: 65) argues that these 'patterns of human interaction, interconnectedness and awareness are reconstituting the

Plate 1.1 Tourism in China has increased in recent years and there has also been a dramatic rise in the number of Mainland Chinese who are visiting other parts of the world © Jane Jackson

world as a single **social space**' (e.g. global community). On a personal level, this means that events, behaviours and values from far away are affecting many aspects of our daily habits or **'ways of being'** (e.g. the products we buy, the language and expressions we use in online chats, the clothes we wear, the food we eat, the music we listen to, the television programmes we watch, the Internet sites we access).

While some view this growing interdependence of societies and cultures as 'an opportunity to be embraced, allowing people to break free from the stifling restrictions of nationality and tradition' (Ryan 2006: 26), for others, globalization is 'a threat, removing the security of familiar local networks and imposing an unwanted external uniformity' (p. 26). Opponents argue that the process of **homogenization** is leading to the loss of linguistic and cultural distinctiveness (e.g. the McDonaldization and Anglicization of the world). For some, the global domination of American culture is at the expense of traditional, localized diversity. In response, in some regions there is an intensification of **localism**, that is, a range of political philosophies have emerged that prioritize the local (e.g. the local production and consumption of goods, local control of government, promotion of local culture and local identity) (O'Riordan 2001).

Critics also point to the widening gap between the 'haves' and the 'have-nots' and argue that the historical legacy of colonization and globalizing forces have exacerbated **inequality**, that is, unequal access to power and resources (e.g. cultural, economic, educational, linguistic, political, social, technological). For Sorrells (2013: 32), globalization is characterized by 'a magnification of inequities based on flows of capital, labor, and access to education and technology, as well as the increasing power of multinational corporations and global financial institutions'.

As noted by Canagarajah (2006), McKay (2010) and many other applied linguists, differential opportunities to learn English can divide societies. With better schooling, proficient speakers of this international language may gain admission to more prestigious institutions of higher education. They may then be offered better-paying jobs and rise to much higher ranks in their careers (e.g. civil service, business, education). Conversely, in some parts of the world, those who do not have access to quality English language education are left behind.

When the World Trade Organization (WTO) meets, loud and sometimes violent protests erupt, providing an outlet for deeply-felt concerns about growing inequality and poverty among people who have not benefited from globalization. This tension also provides enormous challenges for intercultural relations.

Whether one's conception of globalization is positive or negative it remains the most powerful force shaping our world today and in the foreseeable future. It is this interconnectedness that is bringing about more frequent intercultural contact. This, in turn, necessitates the development of effective intercultural communication skills as well as knowledge of more than one language, especially one with an international status. Whether your career path lies in applied linguistics, TESOL (Teaching English to Speakers of Other Languages), the civil service, business, international relations, health care or a completely different line of work, in

Plate 1.2 This McDonald's restaurant is situated in the heart of Beijing. Critics of globalization fear that the 'McDonaldization' of the world is leading to a lack of cultural diversity. What do you think?
© Jane Jackson

Plate 1.3 While some nations prosper and benefit from globalization, inequality and poverty persist in many regions © Jane Jackson

this new global world, intercultural understanding and skills are apt to be necessary for your future career as well as your personal life. In this highly competitive world, bilingualism or multilingualism is also a requirement for many and an advantage for most.

Internationalization

Accelerating globalization has resulted in increased investment in training for **knowledge industries** (organizations or industries dependent on a workforce with advanced scientific or technological knowledge and skills) and second or foreign language teaching. ELT (English language teaching), for example, has become a global industry. Higher levels of interconnectedness are also pushing educational institutions to devote more attention to international and intercultural dimensions of learning, teaching and research. There is now a high demand for well-educated, technologically advanced, bilingual or multilingual individuals who can interact effectively with people from diverse cultural backgrounds and perform successfully in the competitive, global marketplace.

Sensitive to increasing global interdependency and the new challenges facing graduates in all disciplines, institutions of higher education around the world have been revisiting their mission and responsibilities. In the process, most have found themselves confronting a range of challenging questions, including: How can they best prepare their students to become global citizens and professionals in today's diverse world? What steps can they take to help students become internationally knowledgeable, bilingual (or multilingual) and interculturally sensitive? How can they foster **intercultural competence**, that is, 'the ability to communicate effectively and appropriately in intercultural situations based on one's intercultural knowledge, skills and attitudes' (Deardorff 2006: 249)? How can institutions provide students with a transformative international education? What action is needed to attract students and faculty from other countries to their campus? What initiatives might help faculty develop an international, global perspective and enhance their intercultural competence?

Professional leaders in teacher education are asking how they can best ready pre-service teachers for classrooms with linguistically and culturally diverse learners. Those charged with the preparation of second language educators (e.g. TESOL professionals) seek the most effective ways to deal with the cultural and intercultural dimensions of language learning and teaching. Administrators in schools have also become more aware of the need for their staff to become interculturally competent. Whether in applied linguistics, general education, business, health care, law, science or other disciplines, educators are grappling with similar demands and issues.

The policy-based response of many tertiary institutions is **internationalization**, which Kälvermark and van der Wende (1997: 19) define as 'any systematic sustained effort aimed at making higher education more responsive to the requirements and challenges related to the globalization of societies, economy and labor markets'. More specifically, internationalization entails 'the process of integrating an international, intercultural or global dimension into the purpose, functions or delivery of post-secondary education' (Knight 2004: 11). In many parts of the world, primary and secondary schools are also incorporating international, intercultural learning into their curricula, especially in contexts where there is a large immigrant population.

Internationalization at home (IaH)

The term **internationalization at home (IaH)** refers to 'the embedding of international/intercultural perspectives into local educational settings' (Turner & Robson 2008: 15) to raise the global awareness, cultural understanding and intercultural competence of faculty and students. In fact, you are likely using this text in an intercultural communication course that is designed to help meet the IaH aims of your institution, faculty or department.

To provide local students with more exposure to other languages and cultures, many institutions of higher education are taking steps to draw international students to their home campus (e.g. semester- or year-long exchange students, full-degree students) (Jenkins 2013; Rumbley *et al.* 2012). Whether motivated by economic necessity or the desire for a more diverse, multicultural environment, tertiary institutions in non-English-speaking countries are increasingly offering courses and even full degrees in this international language in order to attract students from abroad. In Europe, for example, between 2002 and 2007 the number of English-taught degree programmes tripled (from around 700 to nearly 2,400) (Wächter & Maiworm 2008). At my university in Hong Kong, which has a bilingual (Chinese-English) policy, more courses are now being offered in English to accommodate incoming semester- and year-long exchange students who are unfamiliar with Cantonese. International students also have the opportunity to study Chinese languages and cultures.

Educators and administrators are discovering that increasing the number of international students on campus does not ensure meaningful intercultural interaction with local students. With this in mind, more educators and administrators are designing a range of innovative activities and events to encourage more interpersonal, intercultural contact (e.g. informal outings, social gatherings, international clubs, a 'buddy system' or mentorship scheme linking local and international students). On campus, administrators of student accommodation (e.g. hostels, dormitories) may also encourage local and international students to share rooms or common areas (e.g. lounges).

Ultimately, these IaH activities aim to prepare individuals for life in an interconnected world whereby interaction with people from diverse linguistic and cultural backgrounds is increasingly the norm.

Education abroad

As well as 'internationalization at home' (IaH) initiatives, there has been a dramatic increase in the number of students who are gaining some form of **education abroad**, that is, education outside their home country (e.g. study abroad, internships, work, volunteering, directed travel with learning goals) (Forum on Education Abroad 2011). According to a 2012 report issued by the Institute for Statistics of the United Nations Educational, Scientific and Cultural Organization (UNESCO), in 2010 at least 3.6 million students were enrolled in tertiary education abroad, up from two million in 2000.

At your institution, you may find a range of education abroad options to choose from. Perhaps you can join a year-abroad or semester-long exchange programme. If you have an advanced level of proficiency in the medium-of-instruction in the host institution you may study alongside host nationals in regular subject courses and then, with the necessary approval, transfer credits to your home institution.

Another option may be a language and cultural studies tour, an intensive summer language immersion programme, a regional or international conference for students (e.g. intercultural citizenship or global leadership forum, peace camp), or volunteering. You might also do a practicum or fieldwork abroad (e.g. anthropology, global health, language teacher education). More and more, university students are opting to take part in short-term sojourns, ranging from four to seven weeks, or micro-sojourns lasting three weeks or less (e.g. language enhancement programmes). If you have already participated in some form of education abroad, you can share your language and intercultural experiences with other students.

Following the emergence of English as the global language of internationalization, more non-English-speaking countries now offer study-abroad students exposure to local (and global) course content through English (Jackson 2012; Jenkins 2013; Rumbley et al. 2012). Business majors from Vietnam, for example, may take English-medium courses in management or marketing in Sweden or the Netherlands. In Hong Kong, incoming exchange students from Germany and Malaysia may do all of their coursework in English or, alternatively, study the local language (e.g. Cantonese) instead of or in addition to coursework in English. Whatever the language, intercultural interaction with host nationals or other international students (inside and outside the classroom) should be an important dimension of education abroad.

The amount of support provided to education abroad participants varies greatly. In faculty-led, short-term programmes, participants may receive pre-sojourn preparation, ongoing support during the sojourn (stay abroad) and guided debriefings when they return home. This level of support is not common, however, and longer-term sojourners usually receive even less guidance, if any. Most institutions offer only brief pre-departure orientation sessions for exchange students, which largely focus on logistics (e.g. the transfer of credits, safety and security). As educators and administrators become more familiar with recent education abroad research, they recognize the need for more intensive, systematic programming. For example, intercultural communication courses, like the one you may be taking now, are increasingly being offered to students in all disciplines to help optimize the time spent in a foreign country. Courses of this nature can also help participants develop the (inter)cultural knowledge and skills that are essential for successful intercultural interaction in one's home environment in all areas of life (e.g. academic, personal, professional). They can also help students to make sense of intercultural encounters that have not unfolded as expected.

As educational institutions play a central role in the formation of citizens and future professionals, **intercultural education** is vital to help prepare students for responsible intercultural citizenship in our global community, whether in the home setting or abroad. International, intercultural education and global citizenship are discussed in more detail in Chapter 12.

Advances in transportation and communication technologies

Recent developments in transportation and communication technologies now link the far corners of the globe, dramatically altering the world in which we live. By diminishing the physical barriers of time and distance, advances in both domains are greatly increasing the exchange of people, commodities, information and ideas. Today, modern transportation systems (e.g. air, rail, road, water, underground) facilitate movement of people and goods within countries, and from one country to another; vast geographic distances can be covered in far less time, with less cost, and with greater ease than in the past. Rapid trains, jet aircrafts, modern highways, high-speed ferries and other advanced forms of transport are all making it possible for travellers, services and products to move between countries and continents in record numbers. These transportation enhancements are bolstering economic growth, socio-political ties and intercultural contact (e.g. tourism, business, educational exchange).

This unprecedented population mobility is enabling more intercultural interaction both within nations and across borders. Technological developments in transport and communication are making it possible for people from diverse language and cultural backgrounds to interact more easily and frequently than ever before. Nowadays, we are in more contact with people from other cultural backgrounds than at any time in human history.

Telecommunication (e.g. communication through telephones, telegraphs, the Internet) and the mass media are also facilitating the dissemination and exchange of information over significant distances. **Mass media** refers to a message created by a person or a group of people sent through a transmitting device (a medium) to a large audience or market (e.g. books, newspapers, magazines, recordings, radio, television, movies, the Internet) (Campbell *et al.* 2011). The mass media and rapid advances in digital communication technology have enabled more and more people to connect in virtual space. The escalation of intercultural interaction, in both domestic and international settings, is no longer necessarily face-to-face.

In 1962, Marshall McLuhan, a Canadian educator, philosopher and scholar, coined the term **global village** to refer to the way the world is 'shrinking', as people become increasingly interconnected through media and other communication advances. He predicted that the ease and speed of electr(on)ic technology would have a profound impact on global communication and he was certainly right! Today, people from different parts of the world can interact with each other through instant messaging, Facebook, email, blogs and websites on the Internet, as well as through older technology such as fax machines and voice mail.

Information and communications technology (ICT) refers to the role of unified communications and the integration of telecommunication (e.g. wireless signals), computers,

Table 1.1   World Internet users and population statistics

World regions	Population (2012 est.)	Internet users latest data	Penetration (% population)	Users % of table
Africa	1,073,380,925	167,335,676	15.6	7.0
Asia	3,922,066,987	1,076,681,059	27.5	44.8
Europe	820,918,446	518,512,109	63.2	21.5
Middle East	223,608,203	90,000,455	40.2	3.7
North America	348,280,154	273,785,413	78.6	11.4
Latin America/ Caribbean	593,688,638	254,915,745	42.9	10.6
Oceania/Australia	35,903,569	24,287,919	67.6	1.0
WORLD TOTAL	7,017,846,922	2,405,518,376	34.3	100.0

Source: Adapted from Internet World Stats (www.internetworldstats.com/stats.htm)
(Accessed 15 April 2013)

Table 1.2   Top ten languages on the Internet

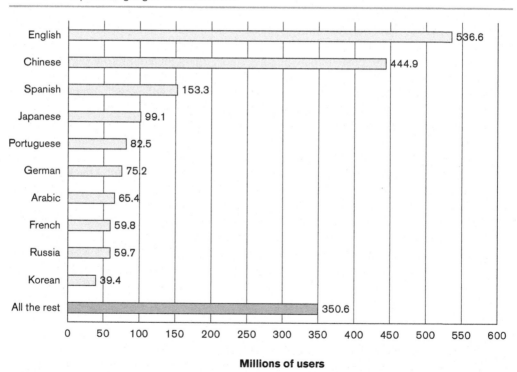

Millions of users

Source: Adapted from Internet World Stats (www.internetworldstats.com/stats7.htm) (Accessed 17 August 2013)

Estimated Internet users are 1,966,514,816 on June 30, 2010

Copyright © 2000–10, Miniwatts Marketing Group

middleware as well as necessary software, storage- and audio-visual systems, which allow users to create, access, store, transmit and manipulate information. ICT consists of **information technology (IT)** as well as telecommunication, broadcast media, all types of audio and video processing and transmission and network-based control and monitoring functions (Tuffley 2011).

In 2012 there were nearly 2.5 billion Internet users, more than 34 per cent of the world's population (Internet World Statistics 2012). As Table 1.1 illustrates, the most users were in developed countries, with other regions lagging far behind.

Table 1.2 shows the top ten languages used on the Internet in 2010. English was used most frequently (with much of the use involving non-native speakers of the language), followed by Chinese, as the number of users in Mainland China has grown exponentially in recent years. Globally, the majority of international websites are still in English and this has implications for information-sharing and intercultural interaction online. Even with the emergence of more multilingual websites as well as those in Chinese, Arabic, French and many other languages, a large number of academic/professional international sites remain in English. People who have limited (or no) proficiency in English or another international language have fewer opportunities to access information or interact online. This, in turn, may somewhat limit their international, intercultural contact in cyber space.

More and more, advances in digital communication technology are playing a critical role in educational, professional, social and personal settings, especially in countries that have benefited economically from globalization. The emergence of a range of new technologies is providing more opportunities for social interaction and collaboration. **Social media** is defined as 'a group of Internet-based applications that build on the ideological and technological foundations of Web 2.0, and that allow the creation and exchange of User Generated Content' (Kaplan & Haenlien 2010: 61). **Web 2.0** refers to 'the revolutionary new ways of creating, collaborating, editing and sharing user-generated content online. It's also about ease of use' (Discovery Education 2012). Recent computer-mediated interactive and social tools include Facebook, Myspace, Twitter, Google Groups, Windows Online, blogs, Wikis, Skype, LinkedIn and multimedia (such as YouTube), among others.

As Table 1.3 reveals, there were over 835 million active Facebook users in 2012, with more than 200 million added in 2011. Nearly all major universities are now on Facebook.

Table 1.3 Facebook users in the world

Geographic world regions	Population (2012 est.)	Facebook users Mar 31, 2012	Facebook penetration (%) Mar 31, 2012
Asia	3,922,066,987	195,034,380	5.0
Africa	1,073,380,925	40,205,580	3.9
Europe	820,918,446	232,835,740	28.5
South America	394,459,227	112,531,100	28.1
Central America	157,663,596	41,332,940	26.5
North America	348,280,154	173,284,940	49.9
Middle East	223,608,203	20,247,900	9.4
The Caribbean	41,565,815	6,355,320	15.3
Oceania/Australia	35,903,569	13,597,380	38.4
WORLD TOTAL	7,017,846,922	835,425,280	12.1

Source: Adapted from Internet World Stats (www.internetworldstats.com/facebook.htm) (Accessed 5 May 2013)

In 2011, over 48 per cent of young adults indicated that they relied on Facebook for news, and a similar number of people between the ages of 18 and 34 logged in as soon as they woke up (Digital Buzz Blog 2011). Increasingly, individuals are accessing Facebook through their mobile phones and, as technology becomes more affordable, more people in less affluent areas are gaining access to Facebook. In 2012, an average Facebook user had 130 'friends' and 'liked' 80 pages. On a weekly basis, more than 3.5 billion pieces of content were shared (Digital Buzz Blog 2012).

Another trend is the growing reliance on Twitter for sharing information. This instant messaging system allows a person to send brief text messages up to 140 characters in length to a list of followers. In 2012, Twitter had 100 million active users, while LinkedIn, the world's largest online professional network, had over 64 million users in North America alone (Digital Buzz Blog 2012).

Social networking sites are having a profound impact on contemporary social life and activity. With access to the Internet, mobile devices are enabling Facebook users and Twitter followers to continuously stay in touch with friends, family and other acquaintances wherever they are in the world. Interactive social tools are creating opportunities for the rapid dissemination and sharing of information and viewpoints both in one's home country and with people in different parts of the world. As the 'Arab Spring' unfolded, for example, Twitter, Facebook and other social media (e.g. online conversation boards, blogs) quickly spread news about demonstrations not only within Middle Eastern countries but in the outside world. Social tools are affording the exchange of diverse views about local and global issues and, in some cases, these technological tools are being credited with changing history.

Web 2.0 applications have also greatly facilitated collaborative learning and intercultural interaction in educational settings and beyond (Shelly & Frydenberg 2010). Social media allows users to collaborate in the creation and development of content (e.g. wikis, podcasts, blogs); nowadays, people from diverse linguistic and cultural backgrounds can share knowledge, information and opinions online using web-based applications and tools. Social media tools have radically changed our perceptions and use of communication. Web 2.0 is revolutionizing the way we interact with each other and opening up more possibilities for intercultural connections in education and other domains (e.g. business, health care, government).

Increased intercultural contact, facilitated by technological advances in transportation and communication, underscores the necessity of intercultural competence and the benefits of acquiring proficiency in more than one language, especially an international one. Although we now live in a more highly interconnected world, economic disparity, unequal access to communication technology and efficient transportation systems, political control (e.g. censorship of websites) and lack of proficiency in an international language (e.g. English) are still serving as barriers to participation for many.

Changing demographics

Human migration entails physical movement by people from one place to another, sometimes over long distances. While only a few groups have retained a nomadic lifestyle in modern times, various forms of migration have persisted and even increased in the last few decades. This movement of individuals, families or large groups is bringing about more diversity and, nowadays, all contemporary, urban societies are culturally plural. This is creating more opportunities for daily interaction with people from diverse linguistic and cultural backgrounds and another reason why intercultural communication knowledge and skills have become vital. (See Chapter 8 for more discussion on migration and intercultural transitions.)

Migration can take many forms. It may involve voluntary movement within one's region, country or beyond, and be motivated by a range of aspirations (e.g. higher education opportunities, better job prospects, residence in a more peaceful environment, intercultural marriage, life in a warmer climate). Sometimes, however, migration is involuntary, such as in the case of **ethnic cleansing** (e.g. the violent removal of an ethnic or religious group by another) and **human trafficking**/the modern slave trade (the illegal trade of human beings for sexual exploitation or forced labour).

Individuals may be displaced by war, economic crises, religious persecution, natural disasters or other calamities. The United Nations 1951 Convention Relating to the Status of Refugees, as amended by the 1966 Protocol, defines a **refugee** as an individual who:

> owing to well-founded fear of being persecuted for reasons of race, religion, nationality, membership of a particular social group or political opinion, is outside the country of his nationality and is unable or, owing to such fear, is unwilling to avail himself of the protection of that country; or who, not having a nationality and being outside the country of his former habitual residence, is unable or, owing to such fear, is unwilling to return to it.
>
> (United Nations High Commissioner for Refugees (UNHCR) 1992/1979: 5)

Immigration, that is, moving from one's home country to reside in another, is providing more possibilities for intercultural interaction in many parts of the world. As a consequence of economic instability and armed conflicts, more and more people are on the move. In their November 2010 report, the International Organization for Migration (IOM) noted that the number of international migrants rose from 150 million in 2000 to 214 million in 2010, with 57 per cent moving to high-income countries. If this trend continues, there could be 405 million international migrants in 2050. The report also states that there are now 20 cities with more than a million foreign-born residents, including nine in North America.

Several special migrant populations are also contributing to growing **multicultural diversity** in many parts of the world, such as the 26 million internally displaced persons (e.g. almost 20 per cent in Sudan), the nine million refugees (which rises to 15 million with people in 'refugee-like' situations) and health care migrants (almost 30 per cent of doctors and 10 per cent of nurses born in sub-Saharan Africa are abroad) (International Organization for Migration 2010). Because of poor economic conditions in some Asian countries (e.g. Indonesia, the Philippines), workers in many occupations (e.g. domestic helpers, nurses) are compelled to seek better wages in more affluent places (e.g. the Arabian Gulf countries, Germany, Hong Kong, Singapore). Due to the financial crisis in Europe, university graduates and other workers in Greece, Spain and Italy are also on the move to more economically stable countries.

In 2010, most of the 57 million migrants in the Americas settled in the United States (43 million) and Canada (7.2 million); Argentina had 1.4 million migrants and Venezuela a million. Asia has about 60 per cent of the world's population but only 30 per cent of the world's migrants. The Asian countries with the most migrants and the highest share of migrants in their populations are the Arabian Gulf states (e.g. Bahrain, United Arab Emirates). Australia had almost five million migrants in 2010, and New Zealand almost a million (International Organization for Migration 2010).

In 2010, Europe's 73 million migrants was a third of the global total, with 60 per cent in five countries: Russia, 12 million; Germany 11 million; and France, the UK and Spain about 6.5 million each. New policies in some countries (e.g. Russia, the UK) have been put in place to reduce the influx of migrant workers, but return bonus programmes in the Czech Republic and Spain attracted few jobless migrants who agreed to leave and not return. 'In today's economic and war-torn climate, we can expect to see an increase in migrating populations as new markets are sought and as people leave their current home countries in search of work and/or safety' (Moon 2010: 39).

As well as a long-term change in residence (e.g. immigrants, refugees), people flows may be transitory (e.g. tourist vacations, pilgrimages, education abroad sojourns). In 2009, for example, there were 3.4 million international students in the world, an increase of more than 75 per cent since 2000; a quarter were from China, India and South Korea, and a third were studying in the United States and the United Kingdom (UNESCO 2012). In some countries, international students are regarded as probationary immigrants and are allowed to stay and work after graduation if they get a job offer. This policy is also contributing to long-term linguistic and cultural diversity within receiving nations.

Current demographic trends are providing more opportunities for intercultural interaction in educational institutions, in the workplace, and in one's personal life. With this growing migration comes an increased need for intercultural understanding and changes in the ways that people see themselves. For example, individuals who move to different cultural environments for long-term residence may develop hybrid identities, with ties to more than one cultural group. Others may feel more like citizens of the world.

'With the world becoming more and more linked by immigration, communication, media, economy, and transportation,' Kim (2010: 170) speculates that 'cultural mixing is likely to further increase multiculturalism and within-culture variance in the future'. In some parts of the world, there is now greater social acceptance of romantic intercultural/interracial/interethnic relationships and, consequently, more children of mixed heritage, who may speak (or, at least, are exposed to) more than one language at home. These developments have implications for the development of multilingual, multicultural, hybrid identities, a subject that is explored in Chapter 6. Intercultural friendship, romance and marriage are discussed in Chapter 9.

Conflict and peace

> The fault lines that divide us as peoples and nations have become deeper, more raw, and more lethal in our nuclear age. It is essential that we enhance our understanding of conflict and its terrain so that we can navigate the physical, psychological, and spiritual chasms that threaten to swallow us, creative potential and all.
>
> (LeBaron & Pillay 2006: 12)

In some contexts, increasing diversity has been accompanied by rising intercultural and interracial tension and threats to stability and peace. As the world becomes more and more interdependent, the mutual understanding of people from diverse linguistic and cultural backgrounds becomes even more vital to peace, cooperation and stability. For Peck (1978), the key to community and world peace is 'the acceptance, in fact, the celebration of our individual and cultural differences'.

Conflict is an unavoidable feature of human interaction. Whether in a family setting, among friends or colleagues, in educational or health institutions, the workforce (e.g. businesses), government bodies, international organizations or in regional/national/international negotiations, disagreements and disputes between individuals and groups may develop. As Scollon *et al.* (2012: xiii) explain,

Dramatic advances in information technology, especially the growth of the World Wide Web, and the rapid globalization of the world's economy have in many ways brought people closer together, while at the same time, wars, terrorism, environmental devastation, and massive changes in the world economic order have resulted in greater political and social fragmentation.

Global warming (the rising of the temperature in the earth's atmosphere and oceans), the dramatic increase in the earth's population (already exceeding seven billion), globalizing forces, the global economic crisis, migration and fierce competition for limited natural resources are all contributing to increased contact, stress and conflict between culturally diverse people. Nowadays, it is imperative that all of us acquire the knowledge, respect and skills necessary to mediate intercultural disagreements in an effective, appropriate and peaceful manner.

Intercultural conflict is defined by Ting-Toomey (2012: 279) as 'the perceived or actual incompatibility of cultural values, situational norms, goals, face orientations, scarce resources, styles/processes, and/or outcomes in a face-to-face (or mediated) context'. Divergent behaviours (e.g. unfamiliar communication styles, different expressions of politeness) can make intercultural negotiations more stressful and even more complicated when a second language is involved. In situations like this, van Meurs and Spencer-Oatey (2010: 59) warn that 'conflict cannot be managed effectively without simultaneously considering both culture and communication'. Neuleip (2012: 41) further argues that

> while the dream of a global village holds promise, the reality is that diverse people have diverse opinions, values, and beliefs that clash and too often result in violence. Only through intercultural communication can such conflict be managed and reduced.

Intercultural conflict frustrations may boil over if we do not know how to deal with culture- or language-based conflict communication issues in a competent manner: 'The need to summon creativity and exercise the choice to cooperate has never been more urgent' (LeBaron & Pillay 2006: 12).

If inappropriate or ineffective **conflict negotiation strategies** are continuously employed, misunderstandings can quickly evolve into a complicated and protracted intercultural conflict situation. Unfortunately, it is not difficult to identify long-standing domestic or international disputes that necessitate effective intercultural communication knowledge and skills to bring about a just, ethical resolution (e.g. the Palestinian-Israeli conflict). Consequently, Kim and Ebesu Hubbard (2007) argue that **intergroup relations** is arguably the most serious of all the problems confronting 'humankind, and is the single most vital domain in which intercultural communication has important ideas, theories, and facts to contribute' (p. 233).

In today's globalized world, learning to manage intercultural conflicts appropriately and effectively is not just an imperative for world leaders. In our personal, academic and professional lives, it is becoming increasingly important for all of us to develop **intercultural conflict competence**, which entails 'the mindful management of emotional frustrations and conflict interaction struggles due primarily to cultural, linguistic, or ethnic group membership differences' (Ting-Toomey 2012: 279–80). To accomplish this, LeBaron and Pillay (2006) argue that we need both '**conflict fluency**' and '**cultural fluency**'. The former means 'recognizing conflict as a difference that offers us choices and growth', while the latter entails recognizing that culture is 'a series of underground rivers that profoundly shape not only who we are, but how we cooperate and engage conflict' (LeBaron & Pillay 2006: 12). (See Chapter 10 for more discussion on intercultural conflict mediation and resolution.)

Ethics

> Significant global and regional problems of climate change and environmental degrada-tion, poverty, disease, and war point to the necessity of meaningful communication across cultural boundaries. Addressing problems like these require decision makers to com-municate ethically their concerns about what is right, good, or virtuous across cultural boundaries and to understand others who communicate their concerns in return.
>
> (Tompkins 2011: 211)

The world we live in is increasingly interconnected and this means that individuals of different ages, genders, languages, socioeconomic status, races, religions and ethnicities must coexist on our planet. As well as opening up exciting possibilities for collaboration and enrichment, this contact can present challenging ethical issues and concerns in all areas of life (personal, legal, medical, political, professional, recreational, religious, business, etc.).

The word 'ethics' stems from the Greek 'ethos', which refers to the character and sentiment of the community. **Ethics** may be defined as principles of conduct that help govern the behav-iour of individuals and groups, that is, they provide direction for how we live our life (Blackburn 2009; Johannesen *et al.* 2008). In essence, the moral or ethical environment in which we live

> determines what we find acceptable or unacceptable, admirable or contemptible. It deter-mines our conception of when things are going well and when they are going badly. It determines our conception of what is due to us, and what is due from us, as we relate to others. It shapes our emotional responses, determining what is a cause of pride or shame or anger or gratitude, or what can be forgiven and what cannot. It gives us our standards – our standards of behavior.
>
> (Blackburn 2009: 1)

A **code of ethics** consists of guidelines that spell out what is 'right' or 'wrong' behaviour in everyday life as well as in professional contexts (e.g. educational, business, health care, legal). These fundamental principles stem from core beliefs and the ancient wisdom of religion, as well as its teachers and traditions. We also continuously receive messages from our families, friends and co-workers about what constitutes ethical behaviour.

Throughout the world, religious codes of ethics serve as life guides for believers (Fasching *et al.* 2011). In Christianity, for example, the 'Ten Commandments' is a set of biblical principles. As well as instructions to worship only God, keep the Sabbath (the holy day) and honour one's parents, the Commandments include prohibitions against idolatry (the worship of a physical object as a god), blasphemy (irreverence towards religious or holy persons or things), murder, theft, envy and adultery (sexual infidelity to one's spouse). Jews are guided by ten Commandments that are similar to those adapted by Christians. The 'Five Precepts of Buddhism' (do not kill, steal, lie, misuse sex, consume alcohol or drugs) are somewhat similar to the second half of the Ten Commandments in Christianity, although they are considered recommendations not commandments.

Muslims are guided by the 'Five Pillars of Islam', which the Qur'an (holy book) presents as a framework for worship and a sign of commitment to the faith. They include (1) the shahada (creed), the declaration of faith linked to the belief that the only purpose of life is to serve and obey God, which is achieved through the teachings and practices of the Last Prophet, Muhammad; (2) prayers five times a day (salat); (3) fasting during the holy month of Ramadan (sawm); (4) almsgiving to the poor (zakāt) and (5) the pilgrimage to Mecca, a holy place in

Plate 1.4 Buddhist monks are guided by a code of ethics or precepts linked to their religious beliefs © Jane Jackson

Saudi Arabia, at least once in a lifetime (hajj). Believers recite prayers in Arabic, the language of the Qur'an. Although only 15 per cent of Muslims speak Arabic as a first language, all believers are expected to learn the basics to be able to say prayers and read the holy book (Begley 2009; Nurmila 2009).

Hinduism also has a strict code of conduct that followers are expected to abide by in their daily lives. It consists of ten restrictions (yamas) (non-violence, truthfulness, no stealing, sexual moderation, patience, perseverance, compassion, honesty, moderation of the appetite, cleanliness) and ten observations (niyamas) (e.g. show remorse, be content, give wisely, worship) (Smith 2009).

In Sikhism, 'Rahit' refers to the precepts for pious moral, spiritual and ethical life. As well as prohibitions against the cutting of body hair, eating meat, using intoxicants and committing adultery, believers are required to meditate upon only one Waheguru (Naam Simran). Sikhs also must perform daily prayers (Namm Japna); earn an honest and truthful living (Kirat karni); share money, food, affection and time with the needy (Wand Chhakna); maintain special articles of clothing (the five Ks or Karars); respect all people including those from all religions and races; control their lust, anger, greed, ego and attachment to worldly goods (Singh 2011).

Followers of other religions or sects also have their own rules or codes to live by. For some devotees, 'ethics is not only tied up with religion, but is completely settled by it. Such people

Plate 1.5 Muslims perform salat, that is, they pray five times a day facing Mecca © Jane Jackson

Plate 1.6 The Hajj (Arabic ﺞﺣ) is one of the largest annually occurring pilgrimages in the world. One of the five pillars of Islam, it is a religious duty that must be carried out by every able-bodied Muslim who can afford to do so at least once in his or her lifetime © Jane Jackson

do not need to think too much about ethics, because there is an authoritative code of instructions, a handbook of how to live' (Blackburn 2009: 9). By contrast, other 'believers' may only observe some of the commandments or recommendations, and this may vary throughout their lifetime. Individuals who do not belong to any official religion or sect may consider themselves spiritual beings and follow their own code of ethics.

In truth, all of us are guided by ethical principles, whether religious in orientation or not. Atheists (non-believers in the existence of deities), for example, have beliefs that guide their daily life. While some ethical principles may be below our level of awareness, they are still giving us messages about what is appropriate or inappropriate. As noted by philosopher Carl Wellman,

> An ethical system does not solve all one's practical problems, but one cannot choose and act rationally without some explicit or implicit ethical system. An ethical theory does not tell a person what to do in any given situation, but neither is it completely silent; it tells one what to consider in making up one's mind what to do. The practical function of an ethical system is primarily to direct our attention to the relevant considerations, the reasons that determine the rightness or wrongness of any act.
>
> (Wellman 1988: 305)

Fundamental notions about what is right and wrong not only affect our behaviour in our personal and professional life (e.g. business/educational/legal/medical practices), they impact our attitudes towards those who have divergent beliefs and traditions. Uncomfortable with difference and feeling under threat, people may disrespect the preferred identities of others and resort to using unethical, harmful language that is racist or sexist. Fear of difference can lead to **Otherization** or **Othering**, that is, the labelling and degrading of people who are different from oneself (Dervin 2012; Holliday 2012). As noted by Jandt (2007: 42), the 'collective pronouns *us* and *them* become powerful influences on perceptions' and can lead to the use of oppressive language and racist, exclusionary behaviour. (See Chapter 7 for more discussion on racism and racist discourse.)

Personal growth and responsibility

> Through the course of our lives, we have many opportunities to learn about others — their cultures, their ways of being in the world, and their diverse stories and meanings. We can choose to go toward these opportunities or move away from them. We can live amidst differences and ignore them, or notice the differences that divide us and plumb them for their richness.
>
> (LeBaron and Pillay 2006: 11)

When we encounter individuals who have different ideas about what is right or wrong, we may be compelled to question our own beliefs, values and patterns of behaviour. While this can be very uncomfortable and even seem threatening at times, it can also be an opportunity for learning. As we become more aware of different codes of ethics and ways of being, we may think more deeply about our own beliefs, identities and position in society. Learning more about oneself is an important, necessary part of becoming an ethical intercultural communicator.

The study of language and intercultural communication offers significant possibilities for personal growth and expansion. As we encounter linguistic and cultural difference in our personal, educational or professional life, whether on home soil or abroad, we are afforded opportunities to discover more about ourselves and people who have been socialized in a different environment. Exposure to different beliefs and practices coupled with critical reflection on our own intercultural attitudes and behaviours can gradually propel us to higher levels of intercultural competence *if* we are truly open to this possibility.

Enhancing our intercultural communication understanding and skills necessarily means building awareness of ourselves as well as learning more about individuals who speak a different first language and have different values and habits. As Rothman (2008: 15–16) states:

> A commitment to intercultural competence is not only a commitment to learning more about other cultures and to the development of culturally appropriate communication skills. It also involves the commitment to personal awareness, to personal growth, to understanding, and to unlearning (as possible) any biases, stereotypes, or prejudices ... the complete elimination of *all* biases within ourselves will remain an elusive, though always worthwhile, goal to pursue.

The acquisition of (inter)cultural knowledge and skills, accompanied by critical reflection on 'real world' intercultural interaction (e.g. face-to-face and online) can, ultimately, lead to a broadened sense of self and more satisfying intercultural relations. In the chapters that follow, we explore ways to cultivate an open mindset and more effective language and intercultural communication skills.

THE CHARACTERISTICS OF AN ETHICAL INTERCULTURAL COMMUNICATOR

A number of interculturalists (e.g. Chen & Starosta 1998; Hall 2005; Kale 1991) have proposed guidelines or principles for universal ethical intercultural communication. That is, they have suggested behaviour we can adopt in intercultural interactions to make the world a better, more equitable place.

An individual who is an ethical intercultural communicator:

1   regards people as equal, even when their beliefs or values differ;
2   actively seeks out and interacts with persons of diverse backgrounds (e.g. ethnic, religious, gender, linguistic, physically disabled, etc.);
3   listens attentively and refrains from making snap, negative judgments about the behaviours of people from a different cultural or linguistic background;
4   patiently asks questions to confirm the intended meaning;
5   recognizes that misunderstandings may arise due to linguistic and/or cultural differences;
6   seeks and provides (verbal and nonverbal) feedback to ensure that messages were received as intended;
7   makes a genuine effort to learn about the language and cultural practices of people who have been socialized in different cultural backgrounds;
8   works from the perspective that the behaviour of people from other cultural backgrounds is apt to be rational when understood in its situational and cultural context;
9   values intercultural cooperation and peaceful conflict mediation/resolution;
10 recognizes diversity within cultural groups and acknowledges that no individual can serve as a representative of an entire community or culture;

11 seeks to include all voices in intercultural interactions;
12 treats people of other cultures with respect and dignity.

(adapted from Chen & Starosta 1998)

With enhanced self-awareness and more profound understanding and acceptance of other worldviews and practices (e.g. cultural, linguistic), we have the potential to enrich ourselves, our families and the world around us. All of us can and should make a difference. Throughout the text, we explore ways to communicate in productive and ethically responsible ways across cultural differences of ethics, values and ways of being.

SUMMARY

In this chapter we reviewed definitions of intercultural communication, interpersonal communication and cross-cultural communication. We then examined seven reasons why it is important to study language and intercultural communication today: globalization, internationalization, transportation and technological advances, changing demographics, conflict and peace, ethics and personal growth/responsibility. Finally we discussed ways to become more open, ethical intercultural communicators, a necessity in today's increasingly interconnected and multicultural world. In the chapters that follow we explore many of these issues in more depth.

discussion questions

1   What are some reasons why people might be reluctant to communicate with people who have a different linguistic and cultural background?
2   In what ways is the region where you live changing demographically? What do you think the population will be like in 20 years? In 50 years? Do you think the need for bi(multi)lingualism and intercultural competence is growing?
3   Besides the reasons mentioned in this chapter, identify and discuss three other imperatives for studying language and intercultural communication today.
4   Why are you interested in learning more about language and intercultural communication? What do you hope to gain by exploring the issues and themes in this text?
5   Review the propositions for ethical intercultural communication. Are there any that you disagree with? Which ones do you think would be the most difficult to follow? Why? Are there any propositions that should be added to the list?

further reading

Brannigan, M. (2004) *Ethics and Culture*, New York: McGraw-Hill.

This text explores the rich ethical traditions of the West and the East.

Hall, B.J. (2005) *Among Cultures: The Challenge of Communication,* 2nd edn, Belmont, CA: Thomson Wadsworth.

This undergraduate text includes a chapter devoted to ethics. The author also discusses the importance and benefits of studying intercultural communication.

Martin, J.N., Nakayama, T.K. and Flores, L.A. (eds) (2002) *Readings in Intercultural Communication: Experiences and Contexts,* 2nd edn, Boston: McGraw-Hill.

This undergraduate reader includes four chapters on ethics and intercultural communication.

Smith, H. (2009) *The World's Religions*, New York: HarperOne.

This book explores the essential elements and teachings of the world's predominant faiths, including Hinduism, Buddhism, Confucianism, Taoism, Judaism, Christianity, Islam and the native traditions of Australia, Africa, Oceania and the Americas.

Sorrells, K. (2013) *Intercultural Communication: Globalization and Social Justice*, Thousand Oaks, CA: Sage.

Following a social justice approach, this text examines intercultural communication within the geopolitical, economic and cultural context of globalization, and offers a dynamic and complex understanding of culture to help address challenges in modern life (e.g. discrimination, racial profiling, ethnic conflict, wealth disparities).

CHAPTER 2

The history of the study of language and intercultural communication

Multiple strands of research have influenced what we [interculturalists] study today and how we study it . . . Modern scholars can benefit from studying the past because it will help to reveal why we study what we do, and why we use the methods that we do.

(Leeds-Hurwitz 2011: 30)

learning objectives

By the end of this chapter, you should be able to:

1   identify and describe the early roots of the study of language and intercultural communication
2   explain how this field of study is both multidisciplinary and interdisciplinary
3   identify the primary disciplines and subdisciplines involved in language and intercultural communication research and practice
4   describe historical approaches in the study of language and intercultural communication in different parts of the world
5   describe how different conceptualizations of culture have influenced research and practice in this field of inquiry
6   explain the principles of linguistic relativity and linguistic determinism
7   identify and describe three of the most common approaches in intercultural communication research
8   explain the strengths and weaknesses of the various approaches to the study of language and intercultural communication
9   identify key professional organizations and journals devoted to the study of language and intercultural communication.

INTRODUCTION

To better understand current approaches and issues in the study of language and intercultural communication, as advocated by Leeds-Hurwitz (2011) and other scholars, it is useful to have some knowledge of the historical roots and key developments that have taken place in a particular time and context. Conceptualizations of culture have shifted over time and this has impacted on research traditions, methodologies and theories, as well as modes of intercultural education and training.

Introductory intercultural communication texts typically include only a cursory review of the history of the field and focus almost exclusively on the work of American scholars. Most of the more lengthy historical reviews have been written by communication specialists and are largely limited to the contributions of American scholars (e.g. Leeds-Hurwitz 1990, 2011; Rogers & Hart 2002). This chapter assumes a more general, global perspective. It provides a brief overview of key developments in this relatively new field of study and draws attention to geographic locations and issues that have largely been overlooked in contemporary literature on language and intercultural communication. As well as highlighting the multidisciplinary and interdisciplinary nature of the field, it draws attention to the many disciplines and subdisciplines that have contributed to our understanding of language and intercultural communication. While not exhaustive, this review helps to understand the evolution of the field, including the development, foci and valuable contributions of researchers and practitioners in different parts of the globe.

THE MULTIDISCIPLINARY AND INTERDISCIPLINARY NATURE OF THIS FIELD OF STUDY

First, it is important to recognize that at different stages in history, in different parts of the world, the study of language and intercultural communication has been both a multidisciplinary and interdisciplinary field of inquiry. In a **multidisciplinary** approach, scholars from different disciplines investigate an issue separately, with each discipline retaining its own methodologies and assumptions. As van den Besselaar and Heimeriks (2001: 2) explain, 'in multidisciplinary research, the subject under study is approached from different angles, using different disciplinary perspectives ... neither the theoretical perspectives nor the findings of the various disciplines are integrated in the end'. For example, an applied linguist and a speech communication specialist in Berlin may separately explore a related issue or topic using different methodologies and theoretical frameworks. The applied linguist may analyse the intercultural discourse of American exchange students interacting with local German friends, while the speech communication specialist administers a questionnaire survey to local and international students to determine their perceptions of intercultural friendships. These scholars are apt to be unaware of each other's work, especially if they tend to limit their professional reading to publications in their discipline or **subdiscipline** (a field of specialized study within a broader discipline). While a multidisciplinary approach can certainly enrich one's discipline or subdiscipline, there is usually not a significant impact on other areas of study.

In an **interdisciplinary** approach, scholars from multiple disciplines work together to examine an issue or topic of concern. For example, in New Zealand, a sociolinguist, social psychologist and speech communication specialist may collaborate on an intercultural communication project (e.g. an investigation of the language and (inter)cultural learning and adjustment of international exchange students in a **mixed-method study** that incorporates both quantitative and qualitative data). As a collaborative approach 'creates its own theoretical, conceptual and methodological identity', van den Besselaar and Heimeriks (2001: 2) claim that 'the results of an interdisciplinary study of a certain problem are more coherent and integrated'. Of course, this approach is challenging as there may be fundamental differences in understandings of various concepts (e.g. notions of culture), theories and methodologies since each discipline and subdiscipline has its own traditions and philosophy. Proponents of interdisciplinary research, however, emphasize that the potential benefits of dialogue, collaboration and complementary theories and methodological approaches make it worth the effort.

Although intercultural communication as a field of study has a relatively short history, it is very complicated as there are multiple disciplines (and subdisciplines) involved with different trajectories in different parts of the world. Some scholars have worked outside their main field of study (e.g. collaborating with colleagues in different disciplines or subdisciplines), while many others have not and are much less familiar with developments in other areas. One's understanding of the field is therefore shaped by one's disciplinary roots *and* the breadth of one's knowledge and experiences in intercultural communication research and practice. This review is based on the belief that it is most helpful to have a broad, inclusive overview of the field.

In language and intercultural communication studies, the primary academic disciplines are anthropology, linguistics, psychology, sociology and communication. M.J. Bennett (1998a) identified some of the dimensions that have been explored by intercultural communication scholars in various disciplines:

- perception, interpretation, attribution (psychology, linguistics, communication)
- verbal communication (linguistics, communication)
- nonverbal communication (communication)
- communication styles (linguistics, communication)
- values and assumptions (psychology, anthropology, sociology)
- cultural adaptation (communication, linguistics, psychology)
- identity (linguistics, psychology).

As Table 2.1 illustrates, scholars in many subfields (e.g. anthropological linguistics, intercultural pragmatics, intercultural rhetoric, psycholinguistics, sociolinguistics, etc.) are now exploring language and intercultural communication issues so the scope of the field has widened considerably since its inception. Over time, it has become highly diverse in terms of disciplinary perspectives, methods, theories and objects of study.

As the world has become increasingly interconnected, intercultural communication has also become a concern in other subject areas, including management, marketing, health education, tourism, translation and law, to name a few. In many parts of the world, intercultural communication courses are now offered in multiple departments and faculties, including General Education programmes.

The wide scope and multidisciplinary nature of this field of inquiry make this review daunting. Although many scholars from diverse backgrounds in different parts of the world have made and continue to make valuable contributions, what follows is a selective account of classic and contemporary works and worldviews that have impacted on language and intercultural communication research and practice. Much of the review focuses on the United States, Europe and Asia (primarily East Asia) as most of the research has been conducted in these regions. In the review, we look at efforts to cross traditional boundaries between academic disciplines (interdisciplinary approaches) as this field of study has evolved and matured. Finally, we turn our attention to regions that are underrepresented in the literature, and the promise for the emergence of new localized or indigenized perspectives in this exciting, critical area of study.

Table 2.1 Intercultural communication: contributing disciplines/subdisciplines

Anthropology
    Cultural anthropology
    Linguistic anthropology
    Psychological anthropology
    Social anthropology
Communication
    Intercultural communication
    International communication
    Interpersonal communication
    Speech communication
Cultural studies
Education
    Cross-cultural training
    Intercultural education
    International education
    Second language education
    Second language teacher education
Ethnology
Linguistics
    Applied linguistics
    Psycholinguistics
    Sociolinguistics
    Pragmatics
        Cross-cultural pragmatics
        Intercultural pragmatics
        Interlanguage pragmatics
    Rhetoric
        Contrastive rhetoric
        Intercultural rhetoric
Psychology
    Cross-cultural psychology
    Social psychology (language and social psychology)
Sociology

THE STUDY OF LANGUAGE AND INTERCULTURAL COMMUNICATION

U.S. American contributions

The early work of anthropologists and linguists

We begin by looking at the influence of anthropology and linguistics in the United States. In the late 1880s, Franz Boas, a German immigrant who became one of the founders of American anthropology, raised awareness of the diversity of human cultures. Although he did not research intercultural interactions, in his descriptions of North American Indian languages and discussions of the 'cultural unconscious', Boas (1940) drew attention to the close connection between language and culture (Hart 2005; La Brack & Bathurst 2012).

Boas' interest in nurturing the relationship between linguistics and anthropology inspired his students, including Edward Sapir, who along with Dell Hymes helped found **linguistic anthropology,** the interdisciplinary study of how language influences social life. More specifically, linguistic anthropology entails 'the study of language as a cultural resource and speaking as a cultural practice'; basically, it 'examines language through the lenses of anthropological concerns' (Duranti 1997: 2, 4). Linguistic anthropologists (e.g. A. Duranti, Dell Hymes, Elinor Ochs, Bambi B. Schieffelin) have contributed to the field of language and intercultural communication by exploring topics such as language and cultural socialization; the role language plays in shaping communication; the relationship between language, social identity and group membership; and language as a cultural representation of our social world.

The Sapir-Whorf hypothesis

Drawing on his observations of Hopi and Apache Indians, as well as ideas put forward by Boas and other German philosophers (e.g. Humboldt 1836/1907), Sapir (1921) and his student Benjamin Whorf (1939, 1956) hypothesized that differences in the way languages encode cultural and cognitive categories significantly affect the way the users of a particular language view the world around them. The **Sapir-Whorf hypothesis** became an important foundational concept in the study of language and intercultural communication.

Linguistic determinism, the strong form of this theory, argues that our language *determines* our ability to perceive and think about objects: 'If we don't have a word for something in our language, this theory predicts that we won't think about it or notice it' (West and Turner 2011a: G-6). For example, if your first language does not have words for certain colours, it would be difficult to recognize or identify them.

In recent decades, scholars have widely rebuked the strong version of the Sapir-Whorf hypothesis, including Scollon *et al.* (2012: 17) who wrote: 'We do not take the extreme deterministic position that a language solely determines the thought patterns of its speakers . . . reality is far too complex to allow for such a simple statement'. Yule (1996) also criticizes linguistic determinism, noting that it 'fails to take into account the fact that users of a language do not inherit a fixed set of patterns to use. They inherit the ability to manipulate and create with a language, in order to express their perceptions' (p. 248). Experiments have also not supported the strong version. For example, 'although the Dani, a New Guinea tribe, use only two colour terms . . . it was found that they could recognize and distinguish between subtle shades of colours that their language had no names for (e.g. pale blue vs. turquoise)' (Holmes 2001: 324).

Linguistic relativity, the weaker version of the Sapir-Whorf hypothesis, is more accepted today. It posits that language *influences* our thinking but does not determine it. Scollon *et al.* (2012: 17) explain that 'languages, like all cultural tools, have various built-in affordances and constraints which limit and focus the kinds of meanings that can be expressed with them'. What this means is that 'if we don't have a word for something in our language, this theory predicts it will be difficult, but not impossible, to think about it or notice it' (West & Turner 2011a: G-6). The implications of this theory for language and intercultural communication are explored further in Chapter 4.

Insights from ethnography

While linguistic anthropologists were theorizing about the connection between language, thought and culture, other scholars were exploring various cultural dimensions through ethnography, the primary research methodology in sociocultural anthropology, sociology and other disciplines. **Ethnography** refers to

> the study of people in naturally occurring settings or "fields" by methods of data collection which capture their ordinary activities, involving the researcher participating directly in the setting, if not also the activities, in order to collect data in a systematic manner but without meaning being imposed on them externally.
>
> (Brewer 2000: 189)

Ethnographic fieldwork involves first-hand, naturalistic, sustained observation and participation in a particular cultural setting with the aim of developing a deeper understanding of how individuals ('members of a cultural group') perceive their social and cultural worlds and interact with each other (Denzin 1996; Hammersley & Atkinson 1995). For many early ethnographers, this meant learning a new language while conducting 'participant observation' in the **field** (cultural setting), sometimes over many years. **Participant observation** is 'a method in which observers participate in the daily life of the people under study' (Brewer 2000: 190). Over time, ethnographers 'develop an understanding of what meanings are associated with the ways of talking and behaving that they both observe and are involved in' (Roberts et al. 2001: 10). Early on, this mode of primary research raised further awareness of the language-culture connection.

In their ethnographic fieldwork in the mid-1930s and 1940s, like Boas and Sapir, American anthropologists (e.g. Margaret Mead, Ruth Benedict, Gregory Bateson, Clyde Kluckhohn) recognized language as a vital element of culture. Echoing Sapir's views, Kluckhohn (1949) observes that every language has a unique way of viewing the world and interpreting experience. As well as linguistic elements, anthropologists in this era examined differences in values and behaviour among cultural groups. Their understandings of national character, culture and personality led to the **'culture as nation' perspective**, that is, 'a view of peoples within national boundaries as essentially homogeneous, possessing certain core characteristics' (Martin et al. 2012: 18).

The influential work of E.T. Hall and the FSI (Foreign Service Institute)

While many scholars were interested in culture and intercultural relations, it was not until after World War II that the formal, academic study of intercultural communication emerged (Leeds-Hurwitz 1990; Martin & Nakayama 2007). In the aftermath of the war, the United States was preoccupied with broadening its foreign relations and influence. Large numbers of American diplomats, government officers and business personnel were sent abroad to establish socioeconomic, military and political ties; however, complications soon arose due to the limited linguistic and intercultural communication skills of the envoys (Kitao 1989; Rogers & Hart 2002). In response, in 1946 the Federal Government established the Foreign Service Institute (FSI) to prepare government officers, diplomats, and other professionals (e.g. business experts) to advance U.S. national foreign affairs interests in Washington and overseas (Leeds-Hurwitz 1990; Rogers et al. 2002).

In 1955, one of the educators employed by the FSI was Edward T. Hall, an anthropologist who is often referred to as the 'founding father' of the formal study of intercultural communication (Leeds-Hurwitz 1990; Martin *et al.* 2012; Neuliep 2012). His interdisciplinary work was influenced by cultural anthropology, linguistics, ethnology (the study of animal behaviour) and Sigmund Freud's psychoanalytic theory, which focused on the dynamics of personality development. Hall was especially interested in nonverbal behaviours, that is, 'all the behaviors that occur during communication that do *not* involve verbal language, and include facial expressions, nonverbal vocal cues, gestures, body postures, interpersonal distance, touching, and gaze' (Matsumoto & Hwang 2012: 130). In his work, Hall focused on the unconscious aspects of cultural behaviour (e.g. nonverbal cues or what he termed '**microculture**') and their implications for intercultural interactions (Hall 1959; Rogers *et al.* 2002). In his view, 'culture is communication and communication is culture' (Hall 1959: 186), a notion that is explored further in Chapters 3 and 4. (Also, see Chapter 5 for a discussion of nonverbal communication.)

Drawing on his observations and understanding of cultural groups, Hall published *The Silent Language* in 1959, in which he outlined a broad theory of culture and described how its rules influence people's worldview and behaviour. This seminal work helped establish intercultural communication both as a term and a field of study. Several other influential books followed, including *The Hidden Dimension* in 1966, *Beyond Culture* in 1976 and *The Dance of Life* in 1983. All of these publications, which drew on cultural observations in natural settings, stressed the importance of recognizing, respecting and valuing cultural difference.

Along with Raymond Birdwhistel, George Trager and other linguists, Hall set about designing training programmes for FSI clients. Realizing that learning the language of the target country (e.g. grammar, vocabulary) would be insufficient, they aimed to draw attention to the influence of culture on communication. The demands of the FSI clients also shaped their interdisciplinary approach to teaching, as Leeds-Hurwitz (1990: 263) explains:

> the students in the FSI classes had no interest in generalizations or specific examples that applied to countries other than the ones to which they were assigned; they wanted concrete, immediately useful, details provided to them before they left the U.S.

Accordingly, language and culture-specific materials were designed to help them learn how to communicate 'appropriately' in the target culture in both their professional and daily life. The FSI staff also devised activities to enhance their clients' ability to analyse their intercultural experiences and make adjustments in their nonverbal and verbal communication while in the host environment.

Preoccupied with intercultural training, E.T. Hall was not concerned with establishing a new academic discipline, and in the 1960s there were still no particular theories or **paradigms** (philosophical frameworks) driving intercultural communication research (Leeds-Hurwitz 1990; Rogers & Hart 2002). As Pusch (2004) explains, early work in intercultural communication in the United States 'did not grow from abstract intellectual inquiry'; it 'emerged from experience and was built on practical application' (p. 15), such as the training of American diplomats and other government personnel at the FSI. Much of this early work was interdisciplinary as scholars from different disciplines (e.g. anthropology, linguistics) worked together for common aims.

The establishment of intercultural communication as an academic subdiscipline

In 1960, President John F. Kennedy initiated the **Peace Corps**, a volunteer programme run by the U.S. government to promote world peace and friendship. The opportunity to volunteer in developing countries increased interest in knowing more about how to communicate effectively with people of diverse cultural backgrounds, and by the late 1960s and early 1970s several American universities had started to offer courses in intercultural communication (e.g. the University of Pittsburgh, Michigan State University, the University of Rhode Island) (Asante *et al.* 1979; Kitao 1989) and numerous intercultural communication texts were published. By the late 1960s, intercultural communication in the United States was becoming recognized as an academic subdiscipline; at most universities, it was a designated area of study and research within communication departments (Martin *et al.* 2012; Monaghan 2012).

The formation of professional bodies devoted to intercultural communication

Around this time, professional organizations began to form to promote and enhance language and intercultural communication research and teaching. Some preexisting organizations also began to support special interest groups in this area. In 1970, the International Communication Association established a separate Division of Intercultural Communication; five years later, the Speech Communication Association (now the National Communication Association) created a similar division, reflecting mounting interest in this area of study.

In 1974, the Society for International Education, Training and Research (SIETAR) (originally SITAR) was established in the United States to bring together educators from different disciplines who share an interest in intercultural relations. This interdisciplinary, professional service organization aims to implement and promote cooperative interaction and communication among people of diverse languages, cultures and ethnic groups. Along with the establishment of several key professional organizations, by the mid-1970s the number of publications that centred on intercultural communication had increased significantly. In 1977, for example, the *International Journal of Intercultural Relations* began publication.

More widespread offering of intercultural communication courses

By the 1980s, more than 200 U.S. American institutions of higher education were offering undergraduate-level courses in intercultural communication, and there were around 60 graduate-level courses (Kitao 1989). The majority were taught by professors in Communication Departments, and most of the courses and texts included only minimal discussion of linguistic elements (e.g. a lecture or chapter on the structure of human language; the relationship between language, culture and thought). Topics such as the bilingual and multilingual dimensions of intercultural interaction, the role of language in intercultural adjustment/competence and the language, culture and identity connection received scant attention. Further, as noted by Yep (1997), most of the first texts in intercultural communication did not examine 'intercultural interactions within the larger social, historical, and political contexts' (p. 82). The impact of power, language, discourse and positioning in intercultural/second language relationships was generally overlooked.

The influence of Social Science traditions

By the mid-1980s, much of the intercultural communication research by U.S. communication specialists had become aligned with behavioural social psychological approaches (**structuralism/functionalism**) (Bormann 1980; Martin *et al.* 2012). In this Social Science tradition, culture is generally viewed as a stable, fixed variable defined by group members (usually on a national level). Structuralists/Functionalists aim to determine causal relationships between culture and communication behaviours (e.g. German conflict negotiation styles, Japanese self-disclosure) in order to predict potential 'problems' in intercultural communication (e.g. Gudykunst & Nishida 1989). Reflecting the 'culture as nation' perspective, a proliferation of intercultural guides appeared on the market; many focused on cultural 'Do's and Don'ts' for specific countries (e.g. How to do business with the Japanese, Understanding the French).

Leeds-Hurwitz (1990) and Moon (2008), among others, speculate that this shift to structuralism/functionalism by many intercultural communication researchers (e.g. especially speech communication specialists) was partially driven by pressure to gain credibility and acceptance from colleagues in Communication Departments and other more established subject areas (e.g. psychology), who were trained in quantitative research methodologies and the functionalist (Social Science) tradition, and sceptical of the merits of qualitative research (e.g. ethnographic, anthropological studies, qualitative case studies).

Theory-building

In the 1980s and early 1990s, intercultural communication research extended interpersonal communication theories to intercultural contexts. Many U.S. American scholars focused on increasing our understanding of how relationships are initiated and maintained between people who have been socialized in different linguistic and cultural contexts. Social scientists also developed theories to explain how members of a culture respond when 'strangers' (outsiders) behave in ways that are unexpected and unfamiliar. These researchers primarily theorized about cross-cultural differences in interpersonal communication from an '**etic**' **perspective** (outsider's stance) (Headland *et al.* 1990).

For example, building on Simmel's (1950) notion of the 'stranger', Bill Gudykunst and his colleagues extended the **uncertainty reduction theory (URT)** ('anxiety uncertainty management' theory) to intercultural contexts. They hypothesized that when individuals are anxious when communicating with people who are not affiliated with their own groups (e.g. individuals who differ from them in terms of 'culture, ethnicity, gender, age, disability, social class or other group memberships'), this anxiety negatively impacts on intercultural relations (Gudykunst 2004: 3). In another example, Howard Giles (a British-born applied linguist) and his colleagues developed the **communication accommodation theory (CAT)** (Gallois *et al.* 2005; Giles & Ogay 2006; Giles *et al.* 2012), which basically says that people in intercultural interactions 'adjust their language toward or away from their conversational partner' (Brown & Eisterhold 2004: 100). (The CAT is explored further in Chapters 6 and 9.)

The contributions of specialists in various subdisciplines

By this stage, much of the work on language and intercultural communication had become multidisciplinary and there was little interaction or sharing between scholars from different disciplines. Also, more subdisciplines, fields of specialized study within a broader discipline, began to emerge. For example, specialists in intercultural rhetoric and intercultural pragmatics began to investigate topics of interest to the broader field of language and intercultural communication (e.g. politeness norms, degree of directness in different languages and cultural settings).

Contrastive and intercultural rhetoric

The roots of the subfield of intercultural rhetoric can be traced back to the work of Robert Kaplan, an American applied linguist. Influenced by Boas' views of culture and the Sapir-Whorf hypothesis, Kaplan initiated contrastive rhetoric as a field of study in the 1960s. Richards and Schmidt (2010: 119) define **contrastive rhetoric** as 'the study of similarities and differences between writing in a first and second language or between two languages, in order to understand how writing conventions in one language influence how a person writes in another'. Contrastive rhetoric research is based on the view that 'rhetorical features differ across languages and this difference causes written communication problems' (Kubota 2012: 100).

The number of international students in U.S. universities grew significantly in the 1950s and 1960s, and Kaplan observed that many newcomers had difficulty with written academic discourse in English. He attributed this, in part, to interference from linguistic and cultural conventions in their first language. More specifically, he speculated that the cultural thought patterns of second language writers and the ways they organize their ideas (discourse structure) in English are influenced by their first language. In their writing, their sense of audience and choice of topic and vocabulary were also assumed to be affected in the same way to some degree. Consequently, he hypothesized that 'each language and each culture has a paragraph order unique to itself, and that part of the learning of a particular language is the mastery of its logical system' (Kaplan 1966: 14).

Drawing on his analysis of ESL (English as a Second Language) student essays, Kaplan (1966) identified five types of paragraph development, each reflecting distinctive rhetorical tendencies. He claimed that Anglo-European expository essays are developed linearly, whereas Semitic languages use parallel coordinate clauses; Oriental languages prefer an indirect approach, coming to the point in the end; while in Romance languages and in Russian, essays include material that, from a linear point of view, is irrelevant. He then presented diagrams purporting to represent the rhetorics of the five cultural traditions: Oriental, English, Semitic, Russian and Romance (*see* Kaplan 1966).

Based on these understandings, Kaplan (1966) advised second language writing teachers to pay attention to cultural difference as first-language habits may interfere with their students' academic writing in English. While well intentioned, critics maintain that 'the focus on cultural difference has produced essentialized images of English and non-English languages as well as users of the languages' (Kubota 2012: 100) and in the process privileged the writing of native English speakers (Connor 2008; Pennycook 1998). This approach is rebuked for ignoring individual differences and reinforcing the notion that writers from a particular language background are bound to use rhetoric that is characteristic of the cultural group they are affiliated with. (Stereotyping is discussed further in Chapter 7.)

In 2004 contrastive rhetoric as a field of study was reformulated as **intercultural rhetoric**, partly as a consequence of changed views about culture (Atkinson 2012; Connor 2004, 2008, 2011). Writing specialists then began to focus more attention on 'the interactive situations in which writers with a variety of linguistic and social/cultural backgrounds negotiate

L2 writing in a great variety of situations for a variety of purposes' (Connor 2008: 312). While much of the early work in contrastive rhetoric centred on student essays written in a second language, contemporary intercultural rhetoricians conduct investigations of intercultural writing in multiple genres (e.g. L2 academic journal articles, business reports, emails, student essays), and explore how different 'rhetorical practices across languages and cultures' influence each other.

The 'ethnography of communication'

While Kaplan and his colleagues were preoccupied with written discourse in the 1960s, other applied linguists in the United States focused their attention on oral discourse and inter-cultural communication in context. Drawing on the anthropological tradition of ethnography, Dell Hymes, John Gumperz and other sociolinguists developed the **'Ethnography of Communication'** (also known as **'Ethnography of Speaking'**) to study the communication patterns of speech communities (Gumperz & Hymes 1964, 1972). For Hymes (1986: 54), a **speech community** is 'a community sharing rules for the conduct and interpretation of speech, and rules for the interpretation of at least one linguistic variety'.

Researchers who follow the Ethnography of Communication approach investigate 'the ways in which native speakers understand interaction within their cultures' (Kiesling 2012: 77). As well as developing an **'emic' perspective** or insider's description, their work includes an **'etic' perspective** (researcher's description of language use in context). These ethnographers analyse and compare 'the ways of speaking used by different cultures for the same or similar speech events' (Kiesling 2012: 7). A **'speech event'** is 'a set of circumstances in which people interact in some conventional way to arrive at some outcome' (Yule 1996: 135). Examples include conversations, prayers and lectures. (Speech events are discussed further in Chapters 3 and 4.)

Ethnography of Communication scholars (e.g. Gumperz & Hymes 1964, 1972; Hymes 1974) argue that the analyses of communication variability should focus on specific situations of speaking as 'interactively constituted, culturally framed encounters', and 'not attempt to explain talk as directly reflecting the norms, beliefs and values of communities seen as a disembodied, hypothetically uniform wholes' (Gumperz & Cook-Gumperz 2012: 66). In other words, it is imperative that researchers study language and intercultural communication in context, and recognize the creative, individual aspects of language use in order to avoid stereotyping.

Interactional sociolinguistics

Building on Ethnography of Communication research, John Gumperz (1999) developed **inter-actional sociolinguistics**, 'a form of micro-sociolinguistics which studies the use of language in face-to-face interaction and which assumes that language as it is used in social interaction is constitutive of social relationships' (Trudgill 2003: 64–5). Interculturalists who employ this approach have primarily focused on how communicators in particular contexts 'use language to maintain, develop, alter, refine, and define social relationships' (Trudgill 2003: 65).

Gumperz (1982a), for example, drew attention to unequal power relations in interracial and interethnic communication through publications and a training video. *Crosstalk: An Introduction to Cross-Cultural Communication* examined multiracial, second-language interaction in various settings and situations (e.g. a job interview, a banking transaction) in the UK (Gumperz, first edition 1979; second edition 1990). These early ethnographic studies of language and intercultural communication, especially those that incorporated a critical perspective, began to raise awareness of power, injustice and inequities in intercultural relations (e.g. Gumperz 1982a, 1982b).

Pragmatics and intercultural communication

While sociolinguists and rhetoricians were making useful contributions to our understanding of language and intercultural communication, in the late 1970s another subfield of linguistics emerged that has also enhanced the field. **Pragmatics** is 'the study of the relationships between linguistic forms and the users of those forms' (Yule 1996: 4). More simply, it is 'the study of language use in context' (Zhu Hua 2011: 423). Pragmatics is concerned with 'people's intended meanings, their assumptions, their purposes or goals, and the kinds of actions (for example, requests) that they are performing when they speak' (Yule 1996: 4).

Of particular interest are politeness phenomena and speech acts that are studied with the context in mind. **Politeness** refers to 'showing awareness of another person's public self-image' (Yule 1996: 132), whereas a **speech act** is 'a term used in discourse analysis, ethnography of speaking, and pragmatics for the minimal unit of analysis of conversational interaction' (Trudgill 2003: 125). **Discourse analysis** is 'a broad term to refer to the investigations of spoken or written language' (Llamas *et al.* 2007: 202). Examples of speech acts are greetings, introductions, requests, apologies, jokes, refusals, warnings, questions and summonses. The ability to comprehend and produce communicative acts in a culturally appropriate and effective manner is referred to as **pragmatic competence** (Kasper 1997). This notion encompasses one's knowledge about social distance, the social status between the speakers involved, cultural knowledge such as politeness and linguistic knowledge. **Social distance** refers to 'the degree of closeness' or 'solidarity' between people (Swann *et al.* 2004: 288); **social status** denotes the honour or prestige attached to an individual's position in society.

Interlanguage pragmatics is a sub-branch of pragmatics, which focuses on the acquisition and use of pragmatic norms in a second language, e.g. how second language learners produce and understand speech acts, how their pragmatic competence emerges over time (e.g. Kasper 1998; Kecskes 2012). **Cross-cultural pragmatics** primarily focuses on speech acts in different cultures, politeness norms in different languages and cultural/communication breakdowns or **pragmatic failures**, that is, 'the inability to produce and to understand situationally appropriate language behavior' (LoCastro 2003: 229). Most studies use a comparative approach to examine different cultural norms in different language use (e.g. politeness norms in Japanese business meetings vs. those in German business meetings) (e.g. Blum-Kulka *et al.* 1989; Thomas 1983).

While both of these branches have made useful contributions to our understandings of language and intercultural communication, another related sub-branch of pragmatics has emerged that is devoted to language use in intercultural interactions. **Intercultural pragmatics** is concerned with 'how the language system is put to use in social encounters between human beings who have different first languages, communicate in a common language, and, usually, represent different cultures' (Kecskes 2012: 67). Research in intercultural pragmatics has four principal areas of concern: (1) interaction between native speakers and non-native speakers of a language, (2) lingua franca communication in which none of the interlocutors has the same first language, (3) multilingual discourse and (4) language use and development of individuals who speak more than one language (Kecskes 2012: 67). This approach recognizes that meaning construction and comprehension in communicative events are influenced by both prior experience and actual situational circumstances. Politeness (and perceptions of impoliteness) in intercultural interactions is a primary area of interest in intercultural pragmatics and more broadly in the field of language and intercultural communication.

Interpretive approaches to intercultural communication research and practice

Along with the development of several key subfields, there has also been a shift in approaches to research. By the 1990s, more scholars in North America had become interested in **interpretive approaches** to studying language and intercultural communication in context. For example, building on Dell Hymes and John Gumperz's work on the 'ethnography of speaking' (Gumperz & Hymes 1972), Ron Scollon and Suzanne Wong Scollon (1995, 2001) devised a discourse-based form of interpretive research for their investigations of social interactions in Alaska, Hawaii, Hong Kong and elsewhere. In particular, they examined intercultural discourse in face-to-face conversations within speech events such as meetings, conversations and interviews. Through discourse analysis, these applied linguists analysed 'the way sentences are put together to form texts' (Scollon *et al.* 2012: 7). **Discourse** includes not just language but 'thinking, valuing, acting, and interacting, in the "right" places and at the "right" times with the "right" objects' (Gee 2010: 34). The examination of discourse in intercultural interactions involving a second language raised awareness that communication difficulties that are often attributed to cultural difference may actually be due to a language barrier (Scollon *et al.* 2012).

Multidisciplinary and interdisciplinary orientations to research and practices

By the 1990s, intercultural research was well underway in a number of disciplines (e.g. anthropology, communication, education, linguistics, psychology, management) and subdisciplines (e.g. intercultural pragmatics, intercultural rhetoric, sociolinguistics, social psychology) in the U.S. Although the majority of intercultural communication courses were still taught by communication specialists, more departments in other disciplines (e.g. Linguistics, Curriculum and instruction, Cultural studies, Management, General Education, etc.) were offering their own courses. Despite these developments, few researchers and practitioners crossed academic lines, even though the early roots of the field were interdisciplinary. Applied linguists criticized speech communication specialists for not paying enough attention to the language dimension in intercultural communication, while second language scholars were rebuked for ignoring the cultural dimension in second language education, an issue that we revisit in Chapter 12.

To promote a return to more interdisciplinary research, theory and practice, in 1997 a group of researchers from multiple disciplines formed the International Academy for Intercultural Research (IAIR). By way of a biennial conference and the *International Journal of Intercultural Relations*, the organization is still encouraging the exchange of ideas between scholars from diverse academic backgrounds in different parts of the world.

Critical approaches to intercultural communication research and practice

In the last decade, in particular, the cross-fertilization of ideas has helped to raise awareness of the theoretical and methodological shortcomings of the traditional functionalist paradigm (and some interpretive research). As noted by Martin *et al.* (2012: 27),

> some versions of these paradigms overlooked questions about the relationship between and among culture, communication, and politics, in terms of situated power interests, historical contextualization, global shifts and economic conditions, different politicized identities in terms of race, ethnicity, gender, sexuality, region, socioeconomic class, generation, and diasporic positions.

This realization has led many contemporary scholars in the United States (e.g. Claire Kramsch) to adopt a **critical approach to intercultural communication** research and practice. Firmly rejecting the conceptualization of 'culture as nation', critical theorists argue that the functionalist approach reinforces stereotypes and homogenizes cultures (ignores diversity within cultural groups). They urge scholars to consider the sociopolitical/historical dimensions of language and intercultural communication research and practice (Kramsch 1993, 1998; Kramsch & Uryu 2012). The growing importance of the critical dimension is reflected in the publication of Nakayama and Halualani's *Handbook of Critical Intercultural Communication* in 2010.

Although less dominant today, the structuralist/functionalist research paradigm is still followed by a number of contemporary communication and culture researchers in North America and elsewhere, and is still evident in many intercultural communication textbooks and other publications. 'Value frameworks' (e.g. individualism/collectivism) are still used to predict communication behaviours (e.g. conversational barriers, conflict styles, 'face' concerns, anxiety/uncertainty management strategies), and variations *within* cultures are sometimes overlooked. Throughout this text, **reductionism** (the tendency to ignore variations within cultures) is problematized in line with critical understandings of language and intercultural communication.

While the roots of intercultural communication as a field of inquiry are typically attributed to the United States, work in this domain has also been underway in Europe for many decades.

European contributions

The development of language and intercultural communication research and practice in Europe shares some similarities with that of the United States, as well as differences. On the European continent, historical events and individual scholars have influenced the emergence of particular strands of research and methodological approaches at different points in time.

The 'culture as nation' perspective

Similar to North America, in the 1970s and 1980s, European intercultural communication scholarship in disciplines such as psychology and sociology, or applied fields such as business and management, tended to follow a functionalist paradigm, adhering to a 'culture as nation' perspective. One of the most influential scholars who has followed this tradition is Geert Hofstede, a cross-cultural psychologist from the Netherlands. Between 1967 and 1973, in more than 70 countries, he surveyed employee values in the workplace. In his empirical research, **values** are defined as 'broad preferences for one state over another' (Hofstede 1980, 1991). In this and other large-scale, cross-national studies, he identified four dimensions that appeared to distinguish national groups: power distance, uncertainty avoidance, individualism vs. collectivism and masculinity vs. femininity (Hofstede 1997). Later, he added a fifth dimension to his model: long term orientation (LTO), which was initially called Confucian dynamism (Hofstede 2001).

While widely criticized today for **essentialism** (ignoring diversity within cultures) (e.g. Holliday 2012), Hofstede's work still influences the research and teaching of intercultural communication in Europe, North America, and other parts of the world, especially in relation to business, education, management and health care settings. (See Chapter 11 for a more critical discussion of Hofstede's work within the context of the global workplace.)

The intercultural dimension of intercultural teaching and learning

This is certainly not a complete picture of research and practice in intercultural communication in Europe. After World War II, industrialized European countries experienced significant social and political upheaval due to an influx of immigrants from Asia and other parts of the world. A large number of non-native speakers were in need of language training as well as assistance with intercultural adjustment and long-term adaptation; consequently, in the 1970s and 1980s, many European second language educators and scholars directed their attention toward the (inter)cultural dimension in language education (Byram 1997; Corbett 2003; Kelly 2012).

In the U.S., intercultural communication is often viewed as a subdiscipline of communication even though scholars from other disciplines have made valuable contributions to the field. In Europe, many prominent intercultural communication scholars are from language-oriented disciplines including applied linguistics, linguistics and language education rather than speech communication (e.g. Byram 2006, 2008; Dervin 2012; Guilherme 2012). By the early 1990s, many European universities had established programmes and courses in intercultural communication and were embedding a cultural dimension in language courses to better prepare students and professionals (e.g. language teachers, business managers) for diverse, multicultural environments (Kelly 2012).

Michael Byram, Professor Emeritus at Durham University (UK) has played a leading role in raising awareness of the importance of the intercultural dimension in second language teaching and learning in Europe and beyond. Noting that many interculturalists ignore the linguistic dimension in their work, he makes a clear distinction between **intercultural competence** and **intercultural communicative competence.** The former refers to the ability to interact appropriately in one's own language with people who have a different cultural background, whereas the latter denotes 'the ability of second language speakers to mediate/interpret the values, beliefs and behaviours (the "cultures") of themselves and of others and to "stand on the bridge" or indeed "be the bridge" between people of different languages and cultures' (Bryam 2006: 12). The dimensions of intercultural (communicative) competence are discussed throughout the book and are the primary focus of Chapter 12.

Since his groundbreaking book, *Teaching and Assessing Intercultural Communicative Competence* appeared in 1997, Byram has authored or co-authored many other volumes that have focused on foreign language teaching and intercultural competence, such as

Developing Intercultural Competence in Practice (Byram *et al.* 2001), *Intercultural Experience and Education* (Alred *et al.* 2003) and *Becoming Interculturally Competent through Education and Training* (Feng *et al.* 2009), to name a few. He has been influential in setting foreign language education policies in Europe; for example, he worked with the Council of Europe to develop *The Common European Framework of Reference for Languages: Learning, Teaching, Assessment*, which set intercultural competence as an important goal for language learners (Byram & Parmenter 2012). Byram and his colleagues have also raised awareness of language and intercultural learning in study abroad contexts (Alred & Byram 2002; Byram & Feng 2006; Roberts *et al.* 2001). Most recently, Byram (2008, 2011a, 2011b, 2012) has argued that foreign language education has a vital role to play in fostering 'intercultural citizenship', a complex notion that is explored in Chapter 12.

Interpretive and critical approaches to intercultural communication research and practice

As well as theorizing about intercultural communication competence, applied linguists and other European scholars have been investigating a wide range of issues inherent in intercultural interaction and learning in diverse contexts (e.g. attitudes toward cultural others; language and inter/bicultural identities; the relationship between language, identity, and cross-cultural adjustment; cultural variations in communication styles, communication breakdowns in intercultural encounters, etc.) (Piller 2007, 2011, 2012; Kotthoff & Spencer-Oatey 2009).

In their investigations of language and culture learning and teaching at home and abroad, many researchers have adopted an interpretive research paradigm, often utilizing ethnographic methods (Byram & Feng 2004, 2006; Roberts *et al.* 2001) or the perspective of interactional sociolinguistics, building on the work of Gumperz and others (e.g. House 2003; Rampton 1995). The work of European interculturalists has not been confined to educational contexts. In the last few decades, intercultural interactions in businesses and organizations (e.g. Spencer-Oatey 2010), health care (e.g. Sarangi 2012), tourism (e.g. Jack & Phipps 2005, 2012), and many other 'real world' settings have been subjected to systematic interpretive or critical discourse and ethnographic investigations. Most of these studies have aimed to enhance intercultural relations.

Professional organizations devoted to language and intercultural communication

In Europe, several professional organizations were formed in the 1990s to facilitate interaction among scholars and practitioners interested in language and intercultural communication. Seventeen years after the founding of SIETAR USA, SIETAR Europa was born and, since 1991, it has been serving as an umbrella organization for a number of national SIETAR groups in Europe (e.g. SIETAR Austria, SIETAR France, SIETAR Germany, SIETAR Netherlands, SIETAR United Kingdom). Young SIETAR, a global branch formed in Europe in 1994, provides a forum for students and young professionals to share ideas and discuss issues of interest (e.g. language and intercultural communication in the workplace) either in face-to-face meetings or online (www.youngsietar.org/).

Each regional group of SIETAR and Young SIETAR hold an annual conference and, less frequently, there is a GLOBAL SIETAR conference, bringing together interculturalists from many parts of the world. With more than 3,000 members, SIETAR has become the world's largest interdisciplinary network for students and professionals working in the field of intercultural communication. Intercultural business education and workplace communication are primary concerns of SIETAR and the influence of Hofstede is evident in meetings. Interpretivist and critical approaches to language and intercultural communication are also becoming more commonplace in the work presented at SIETAR conferences.

In the 1990s, the Nordic Network of Intercultural Communication (NIC) was formed to promote cooperation between intercultural communication researchers and practitioners in the Nordic countries (including the Baltic region). Since 1994, the main activity is an annual conference on intercultural communication, which is open to scholars and practitioners in other parts of the world. Many of the sessions are devoted to the linguistic dimension of intercultural interactions and innovative ways to integrate language and culture education.

The International Association for Languages and Intercultural Communication (IALIC), which was established in the United Kingdom in 1999, provides a specialist forum for academics, practitioners, researchers and students interested in language and intercultural communication issues. According to the IALIC website, '[w]orking within an interdisciplinary and critical framework, members share a unique concern for the theoretical and practical interplay of living languages and intercultural understanding' (IALIC n.d.). Linked to the organization is the journal *Language and Intercultural Communication,* which includes many publications that draw attention to the importance of critical perspectives. The organization also host conferences that deal with language and intercultural communication issues (e.g. in the UK, Hong Kong, Malaysia).

Asian contributions

The influence of American-European perspectives and traditions

After World War II, collaboration and exchange between American, European and Asian scholars grew and this impacted on the development of language and intercultural communication research and practice in Asia. Students from Japan, China, and other parts of Asia travelled to Western countries for undergraduate and postgraduate studies in this new field of inquiry. While some returned to their home countries to teach related courses and direct research programmes, others remained abroad, where they have made and continue to make valuable contributions. Scholars of non-Asian origins have also conducted research on language and intercultural communication involving Asians and this, too, has enriched the field.

Japanese contributions

Japan was the first Asian country to establish a professional organization in intercultural communication. In 1953, shortly after the country regained its independence from post-World War II occupation, the Japan Center for Intercultural Communications (JCIC) was established to promote peace and increase mutual international understanding (http://home.jcic.or.jp/en/enkaku_02.html). In light of developments in the global media, JCIC was re-inaugurated in 1980 under a new structure; the organization currently focuses on intercultural communication activities that utilize information technology and international telecasts.

Similar to their FSI counterparts in the United States, Japanese scholars recognized that effective intercultural communication requires more than mastery of foreign languages (Kawakami 2009; Kitao & Kitao 1989). As U.S.–Japan ties strengthened, much of the work of Japanese scholars focused on East–West cultural differences in values (e.g. 'Asian collectivism' versus 'Western individualism') and verbal and/or nonverbal patterns of communication, building on the work of Hofstede (1980) and Hall (1959, 1966). A number of contrastive studies identified and compared specific individualistic and collectivistic influences on communication behaviours (e.g. face negotiation, conflict resolution styles) (e.g. Kincaid 1987). Some Japanese researchers employed Hall's (1976) notions of 'high'- and 'low'-context communication to compare and contrast Eastern and Western styles of communication (See Chapters 4 and 12). At this early stage, work generally followed research paradigms (e.g. functionalism/structuralism) and methodologies (e.g. large-scale surveys) that had been developed in the United States, which is not surprising since this is where most of the Japanese interculturalists had received their postgraduate education.

In 1985, more than 30 years after JCIC was established, an affiliate group of SIETAR was formed in Japan to enhance intercultural and global relations. Reflecting the strength of the economy and the international status of the country, interest in the English language and related cultures (e.g. business English and American culture) intensified. At the same time, the number of expatriates (e.g. American business professionals, Japanese English language teachers from English-speaking countries) increased significantly and the demand for Japanese language and culture courses grew, accordingly. An active member of the Global SIETAR network, SIETAR JAPAN has responded to these developments by holding annual meetings and workshops (e.g. in 2011 a workshop was entitled 'The language and culture gap: Adding cultural content to English language teaching in Japan').

Chinese contributions

Japan is certainly not the only Asian country with scholars devoted to language and intercultural communication research and practice. Since Mainland China began opening up to the world in the late 1970s, interest in this area of study has grown tremendously in this vast, populous country. In the 1980s and 1990s, similar to Japan, Chinese researchers primarily applied the ideas and techniques developed in Western contexts in their investigations of local intercultural communication interaction and education. Much of their work followed the functionalist paradigm and consisted of comparative or experimental design studies similar to those underway in Japan, the United States and Europe (e.g. Hofstede's work). Early on, Mainland Chinese scholars were also concerned with the language–culture connection and the role that culture plays in intercultural, linguistic misunderstandings (e.g. 'pragmatic failures'). (Dai n.d.).

Min-Sum Kim (2010) and Xiaodong Dai (n.d.) maintain that it was not until the 1990s that intercultural communication became a recognized sub-area of communication studies in Asia, and this was primarily in Japan and Greater China. This development led to the establishment of more professional organizations in the region. In 1995, for example, the China Association for Intercultural Communication (CAFIC) was founded in Mainland China to promote research and development in this emergent field of study. Around this time, several universities in the country began to offer intercultural communication courses (e.g. Harbin Institute of Technology, Beijing Foreign Studies University, Helongjiang University, Fujian Normal University) (Xiaodong Dai n.d.).

In the 1990s, several Mainland Chinese scholars began to exert a major influence on intercultural communication research and practice in the country. For example, Wenzhong Hu, the first president of CAFIC and co-founder of intercultural communication as a discipline in China, conducted empirical studies of language and U.S.–Chinese intercultural relations (Hu 1994; Hu & Grove 1999). Daokuan He, another co-founder, drew attention to diverse problems in intercultural communication (e.g. communication breakdowns due to 'pragmatic failure'), nonverbal forms of communication and intercultural communication theory. Yihong Gao focused on sociocultural and sociolinguistic issues (e.g. the impact of identity and culture in language teaching and learning in China, while Yuxin Jia stressed the importance of theoretical research. Until very recently, most scholars largely relied on Western concepts and theories, or adaptations of these constructs.

In the last decade, more Chinese interculturalists have been conducting systematic research to address intercultural topics and issues such as nonverbal behaviour, cultural values, linguistic/pragmatic failure and the influence of globalization on language, identity and intercultural interaction (Xiaodong Dai n.d.). There are now several regional research centres devoted to intercultural communication studies, including the Intercultural Studies Center at Beijing Foreign Studies University (BFSU) and the Intercultural Institute at the Shanghai International Studies University (SISU). Several universities offer PhD programmes in this field of study (e.g. BFSU, SISU, Zhejiang University) and intercultural communication conferences are now held in China (e.g. CAFIC) on a regular basis.

Asian professional organizations devoted to intercultural communication

While some professional intercultural communication organizations in Asia are national, the International Association for Intercultural Communication Studies (IAICS) is international. It originated from a series of Asian–American conferences in the U.S. in the 1980s. In 1985, its first international conference, 'Cross-Cultural Communication: East and West', was held in Seoul, Korea. Since then, biennial conferences alternate between North America and Asia; to date, meetings have been held in mainland China, Hong Kong, Japan, South Korea and Taiwan. These events are facilitating interdisciplinary exchanges between Asian scholars and researchers in other parts of the world who are concerned with issues related to language and intercultural communication. This cross-fertilization is also enhancing the multidisciplinary and evolving interdisciplinary nature of this field of study.

As interest in intercultural communication has intensified, other Asian countries have also established professional intercultural communication organizations. In the Middle East, for example, the Arabian Society for Intercultural Education, Training and Research (SIETAR Arabia) was formed in 2005 and a year later, SIETAR India was launched with the Inaugural Conference 'More Masala for the Melting Pot: Sharing Cultures and Competence for Collaboration'. A member of Global SIETAR, this national organization facilitates interaction among intercultural educators and scholars in India and beyond, with the aim of advancing 'the body of knowledge and practice in the field' (Sietar India n.d.).

An increase in Asian-oriented language and intercultural communication research

With the rise of Asia on the world stage, in the last 20 years there has been a distinctive trend of growth in language and intercultural communication research on Asia and, increasingly, by Asian scholars. More educators and researchers from this continent are joining professional organizations dedicated to this discipline. Many are participating in international or regional conferences and presenting or publishing papers on language and intercultural communication. Scholars from Asia or Asian diasporas (e.g. overseas communities of Asians) have made major contributions to the field of language and intercultural communication.

On this continent, most studies on language and intercultural communication in Asia have centred on East Asia (e.g. China, South Korea Japan, Hong Kong, Taiwan and Singapore). Since fewer scholars from South Asia, Southeast Asia and the Middle East are conducting research and publishing in this area of study, Kuo (2010) cautions that we must be mindful of this when digesting publications about intercultural issues in Asia (e.g. discussions of 'Asian styles of communication'). It is inappropriate to generalize findings in one Asian setting to all of Asia, just as it is inappropriate to generalize findings in the U.S. to all 'Westerners'. Such categories are far too broad to be meaningful as they ignore the immense diversity within. (Chapter 7 discusses generalizations and stereotypes.)

A call for more indigenous research and practice

Just as interpretive and critical perspectives are becoming more prevalent in North America and Europe, Asian scholars are increasingly drawing attention to short-comings in intercultural communication research and practice that homogenize cultures (e.g. the 'culture as nation' orientation). Recent writings have also raised awareness of Eurocentric biases in Western intercultural communication theory. In response, many scholars are now calling for more indigenous perspectives (Ishii 1984; Kuo 2010; Miike 2007, 2009). Kuo (2010), for example, points to 'the dominance of Western-oriented paradigm in Asian communication research . . . and a growing concern and appeal for a reflective Asian culture-based approach for communication research and theory construction' (p. 151).

In her book *Non-Western Perspectives on Human Communication,* Min-Sum Kim (2002) draws attention to limitations in structuralist (positivistic) research on communication/conflict styles and builds a strong case for a shift away from Anglo-centred perceptions of intercultural communication. In particular, she criticizes the pervasive European–American belief in the autonomous individual and the individualism–collectivism dichotomy: 'we need to recognize one major stumbling block in knowledge production in Western contexts: a cultural view that the individual, *a priori*, is separate and self-contained, and must resist the collective' (Kim 2007: 283). Gordon (1998/99) also critiques Western bias in communication theorizing, and calls for multicultural communication perspectives to be generated and shared internationally. More recently, Min-Sum Kim implores intercultural communication researchers in Asia to:

1   recognize the complexity and increasing hetereogeneity of Asian communication styles;
2   acknowledge the traditions of Asia as sources of concepts in intercultural communication;
3   reconsider the 'Western research paradigm' in their own studies (adapted from M.S. Kim 2010: 166).

In language and intercultural communication studies, Shi-xu, the Director of the Institute of Discourse and Cultural Studies at Zhejiang University in China, also appeals for a critical review of concepts, theories and methods that have originated in the West. He argues that much current research and pedagogy in the field 'obscures the power-saturated nature of intercultural contact and communication. That is, it presumes that different cultures are in equal relation to one another' (Shi-xu 2005: 201). Further, in his view,

> through the entire modern world history, the West has never seen, spoke of, or dealt with, the non-Western Other as equal, or as merely or simply 'different'. Rather, it has often treated the Other as deviant, inferior and so to be controlled and controllable.
>
> (p. 201)

Similar to Min-Sum Kim (2002, 2007, 2010) and other critical theorists, Shi-xu advocates the construction of indigenous intercultural communication theories that recognize the power dimension in intercultural relations.

Scholars in Asia are now stimulating deeper, critical reflection on a range of core issues in language and intercultural communication (e.g. identity, belonging and language choice; Western bias in theories and research paradigms). Wang and Kuo (2010: 152) maintain that in Asia, '[s]ignificant progress has been made in the pursuit of theory construction, especially in areas that closely deal with culture and communication issues, e.g. intercultural communication, postcolonial or cultural studies'. As Kuo (2010) observes, distinctive Asian perspectives promise to enrich this field of study.

Contributions from other world regions

While this historical review so far has focused on the contributions of scholars in the United States, Europe and Asia (primarily East Asia), interest in language and intercultural communication research and practice has been on the rise in other corners of the globe, including Australia, which now has a vibrant, multiethnic community of intercultural practitioners and researchers. Many geographic regions, however, are still not adequately represented in the research and literature in this field of study. For example, as noted by Miller (2005), relatively few interculturalists have conducted research in the vast continent of Africa:

> Africa is apparently so far from the center of intercultural communication literature as to be beyond the margins. The currents of research occasionally stray briefly near the continent's northern and southern edges, but the remainder of that vast and rich cultures and people remains virtually uncontemplated. That this indicates undervaluing of African people and cultures is perhaps obvious. That it represents a weakness in the understanding of communication across the globe is less obvious but equally true. It is time for the field of intercultural communication to emulate the example of cartography and discard its distorted representations of the planet. It is time we studied Africa.
>
> (p. 227)

Despite compelling imperatives for intercultural competency worldwide, some populations, issues, languages and geographic locations remain on the margins, while others continue to receive considerable research attention. Western theories and practices still dominate, although this is gradually changing as more scholars from other regions (including underrepresented areas) begin to develop indigenous theories and practices. The voices of interculturalists from diverse linguistic, cultural and disciplinary backgrounds (e.g. Africa, the Arab world, Latin America) are needed to further enhance and broaden this field of study. In particular, Kubota (2012), Miike (2008) and Miller (2005), among others, call for more Afrocentric and Asiacentric research that challenges Eurocentric perspectives and privileges indigenous worldviews.

FUTURE DIRECTIONS

To effectively and appropriately address language and intercultural communication issues involving people in underrepresented areas of the world, it is vital for students from diverse backgrounds to undertake undergraduate and postgraduate studies in this important field. By conducting systematic, indigenous research, newly qualified scholars and experts in these regions may contribute to the wider academic community through fresh perspectives, context-specific studies and meaningful findings that will lead to advances in both theory and practice (e.g. the teaching of intercultural communication, the role of culture in second language teaching, cross-cultural adjustment).

More collaboration between language and intercultural communication scholars in different parts of the world should spur the development of new concepts, theories and methodologies that will help us to better understand complex intercultural communication issues in a wide range of contexts and situations. As China and India are transforming the geopolitical framework and becoming key players on the world stage, we are likely to see the development of more Asia-oriented language and intercultural communication theories and practices in the near future. With the advent of the 'Arab Spring', more attention is also being paid to language and intercultural communication in the Middle East. Further, instead of simply replicating Western research, more Asian scholars are already conducting local studies that reflect 'Asian cultural characteristics and style' (So 2010: 245). Indigenous research in non-Western countries is contributing to local understandings and enhancing the global, international field of language and intercultural communication.

SUMMARY

This chapter provided a brief overview of the history of the multidisciplinary and interdisciplinary nature of the field of language and intercultural communication, largely focusing on the contributions of scholars in the United States, Europe and Asia (mostly East Asia) as much of the work has been conducted in these regions. While not exhaustive by any means, this review identified major trends and developments in research perspectives and methods. We learned how the disciplinary roots (e.g. education, linguistics, psychology, sociology, speech communication), understandings of culture and the context (e.g. historical, geographic, linguistic, political, sociopolitical) have shaped the work of scholars, including their research foci, theories, methodologies and practical applications (e.g. language and intercultural education in schools, universities, the workplace).

We discovered that researchers today are increasingly crossing disciplinary boundaries and adopting a critical approach in their work; many are shying away from 'culture as nation' orientations that ignore diversity and power imbalances in intercultural interactions. A greater variety of approaches is also being employed in both research and practice (e.g. more mixed-method, interpretive studies that make use of both quantitative and qualitative measures, critical ethnography) to study language and (inter)cultural communication in context. Further, more researchers in non-Western contexts are undertaking indigenous research. All of these developments are expanding the knowledge base, and contributing to the theoretical and practical growth in this vital, exciting field of study.

discussion questions

1   Why is it useful to have some understanding of the historical development of the study of language and intercultural communication?
2   Why might the study of language and intercultural communication be considered both *interdisciplinary* and *multidisciplinary*? Define these terms in your own words and provide examples of each orientation.
3   Identify the primary academic disciplines and subdisciplines that have contributed to our current understandings of language and intercultural communication. With a partner, discuss the contributions that each has made to the broader field of language and intercultural communication.
4   In the United States, how did sociopolitical and business interests influence the work of early researchers in this field of study? Do you think that this also applies to the U.S. and other contexts today? How do researchers decide what to study and how?
5   Identify three research paradigms that have influenced investigations of the study of language and intercultural communication. What methodologies are associated with each? Describe the strengths and weaknesses of each paradigm.
6   With a partner, review the websites of two intercultural communication organizations (e.g. IALIC, SIETAR USA, SIETAR Europa, SIETAR Japan). What are their mission statements? Who is their target population? What activities do they support? What publications, if any, are associated with them? What issues are discussed at events they support? Which topics or issues are particularly relevant for your context?
7   Scan several issues of two journals that are devoted to language and intercultural communication issues (e.g. *International Journal of Intercultural Relations*, *Language and Intercultural Communication*, *Journal of Intercultural Communication*). What issues and topics does each focus on? Who is their target population? What topics interest you the most?
8   When reading a publication about language and intercultural communication (in print or online) why is it important to consider the context and the author's perception of culture?
9   Why has much of the language and intercultural communication research in Asia followed research paradigms, methodologies and theories developed in the United States? What are the advantages and limitations of this?
10 Why are language and intercultural communication scholars increasingly calling for more indigenous research in non-Western contexts?
11 Think about a context that is very familiar to you. What language and intercultural communication issues do you think are most important to explore? What approach do you think would be most effective? Why?

further reading

Leeds-Hurwitz, W. (2011) 'Writing the intellectual history of intercultural communication', in T.K. Nakayama and R.T. Halualani (eds) *Handbook of Critical Intercultural Communication*, Malden, MA: Blackwell, pp. 262–81.

In this historical review, the author interrogates core assumptions that have guided intercultural research.

Martin, J. N., Nakayama, T. K. and Carbaugh, D. (2012) 'The history and development of the study of intercultural communication and applied linguistics', in J. Jackson (ed.) *The Routledge Handbook of Language and Intercultural Communication*, Abingdon: Routledge, pp. 17–34.

Drawing on their training in different research paradigms (functionalist/post-positivist, interpretive, critical), the authors survey the major strands of research that have influenced contemporary language and intercultural communication studies.

Monaghan, L. (2012) 'Perspectives on intercultural discourse and communication', in C.B. Paulston, S.F. Kiesling and E.S. Rangel (eds) *The Handbook of Intercultural Discourse and Communication*, Oxford: Wiley-Blackwell, pp. 19–36.

This historical review examines the impact of anthropology, linguistics, intercultural communication, and discourse analysis on research and practice in intercultural discourse and communication.

Piller, I. (2007) 'Linguistics and intercultural communication', *Language and Linguistic Compass*, 1(3): 208–26.

This article highlights several key contributions of linguistics to the study of intercultural communication.

Zhu Hua (2011) 'Introduction: Themes and issues in the study of language and intercultural communication', in Zhu Hua (ed.) *The Language and Intercultural Communication Reader*, Abingdon: Routlege, pp. 1–14.

This reading provides an overview of areas of concern in the study of language and intercultural communication.

CHAPTER 3

Culture and the primary socialization process

> Culture is one of the two or three most complicated words in the English language.
>
> (Raymond Williams 1981: 3)

> There are no simple answers or easy items to memorize about any culture. Cultures are dynamic – as you are – and this ever-changing nature makes any attempt at static pieces of knowledge problematic.
>
> (Martin *et al.* 2002: 3)

learning objectives

By the end of this chapter, you should be able to:

1 identify functions and characteristics of culture
2 explain the language and cultural socialization process
3 define and give examples of subcultures/co-cultures
4 describe at least seven facets of culture
5 define and provide an example of cultural beliefs, values and worldviews
6 define what is meant by a 'cultural script' and provide an example
7 explain why culture is a difficult construct to pin down.

INTRODUCTION

This chapter explores ideas or assumptions about the fundamental nature of culture and linguistic and cultural socialization. It does not aim to provide the definitive interpretation of culture, rather it draws attention to various elements that merit our attention. Drawing on literature from a broad range of disciplines, we explore the following facets of the culture concept: culture as learned; culture as shared (group membership); culture as relative; culture as dynamic and mediated; culture as individual, fragmentary and imaginary, culture as contested; and culture as communication. Each perspective provides a focus for thinking about culture, language and intercultural communication.

CONCEPTIONS OF CULTURE

The word 'culture' stems from the Latin word *cultura*, which literally means to till or cultivate the ground. When the concept of culture first emerged in eighteenth-century Europe, it was associated with the process of cultivation or improvement, as in agriculture or horticulture. By the mid-nineteenth century, however, some scholars were using the word 'culture' to denote a 'universal human capacity' (Levine 1971). Over time, the term began to refer to the fulfilment of national ideals and the enhancement of the individual, especially through education. In 1869, Matthew Arnold, an English poet and cultural critic, wrote that 'having culture' meant to 'know the best that has been said and thought in the world'. This notion of 'high culture' was linked to the arts (e.g. fine paintings, classical music, literature) and individuals who are refined, well educated and/or wealthy (the elite). In contrast, 'low culture' ('popular culture' or 'folk culture') was associated with elements in society that have mass appeal, that is, the sports, food, dress, manners and other habits of the 'common people' (the masses) who have less education, money and sophistication.

In his book *Primitive Culture* (1871), English anthropologist Edward Burnett Tylor defines culture as 'that complex whole which includes knowledge, belief, art, morals, law, custom, and any other capabilities and habits acquired by man as a member of society' (p. 1). This broad conception, which encompasses elements of both 'high' and 'low' cultures, served anthropologists well for 50 years. Since then, numerous definitions and interpretations have been formulated by scholars in diverse disciplines. In 1952, Kroeber and Kluckhohn published a critical review of more than 162 notions of culture, ranging from 'learned behaviour' to 'ideas in the mind', and so on. They then put forward the following definition, which is still widely quoted today:

> Culture consists of patterns, explicit and implicit, of and for behavior acquired and trans-mitted by symbols, constituting the distinctive achievements of human groups, including their embodiments in artifacts; the essential core of culture consists of traditional (i.e. historically derived and selected) ideas and especially their attached values; culture systems may, on the one hand, be considered as products of action, and on the other as conditioning elements of further action.
>
> (Kroeber & Kluckhohn 1952: 181)

Characterizing culture as a 'system', Kroeber and Kluckhohn's (1952) definition emphasizes the transmission of elements (e.g. beliefs, values) that help group members interpret their social worlds and function in their daily life. For these cultural anthropologists, culture is displayed through patterns of behaviour, symbols, products and **artifacts** (things created by humans, usually for a practical purpose) (Merriam-Webster online n.d., a). A **symbol** is 'a sign, artifact, word(s), gesture, or nonverbal behavior that stands for or reflects something mean-ingful' to individuals in a particular context (Ting-Toomey & Chung 2012: 309). (Chapter 4 discusses symbols that are employed in the communication process.)

Scholars have continued to reflect on and debate the qualities and dimensions of culture and, in a more recent publication, Baldwin *et al.* (2006) examined more than 300 definitions from a wide array of disciplines (e.g. anthropology, cultural and social psychology, cultural studies, education, international business, linguistics, political science). Their review demon-strated how our understandings of culture have changed considerably over time.

Today, the concept of culture remains complex, variable and difficult to define. In fact, Williams (1981: 3) goes so far as to refer to culture as 'one of the two or three most complicated words in the English language'. To help you make sense of this elusive construct, the following section examines some basic ideas or assumptions about the qualities and fundamental nature of culture. Discussion centres on seven perspectives: culture as learned; culture as shared (group membership); culture as relative; culture as dynamic and mediated; culture as individual, fragmentary and imaginary; culture as contested; and culture as communication.

FACETS OF CULTURE

Culture as learned

Our cultural orientation begins at birth. As we grow and learn our first language (or multiple languages simultaneously), we become accustomed to particular **ways of being** (e.g. modes of verbal and nonverbal behaviour, philosophy of life). The process of learning one's culture is referred to as **enculturation**; it entails 'observation, interaction, and imitation and is both conscious and unconscious' (Fortman & Giles 2006: 94). A life-long process, adults, as well as children, learn to act in certain ways in local settings they encounter later in life (e.g. business professionals become accustomed to a particular workplace culture).

Socialization, a concept from sociology, refers to 'the process by which we all come to believe that there is a "right" way to think, express ourselves, and act' (Cushner & Brislin 1996: 5). Put another way, socialization is 'the process by which a person internalizes the conventions of behavior imposed by a society or social group' (Kramsch 1998: 131). Brown and Eisterhold (2004) explain the process in this way: 'Through interaction, members of a given culture socialize and are socialized by others. Culture emerges through action while it is simultaneously organizing action, offering its members a perspective on the meaning of that action' (p. 25).

Language, of course, plays a vital role in enculturation. As Clyne (1994:1), an applied linguist, explains:

> Language represents the deepest manifestation of a culture, and people's value systems, including those taken over from the group of which they are part, play a substantial role in the way they use not only their first language(s) but also subsequently acquired ones.

Children acquire language and culture together in what is basically an integrated process; at an early age they learn sociocultural content by way of language-mediated interactions (Ochs & Schieffelin 1984). It is through **language and cultural socialization** that our primary cultural beliefs, values, norms and worldviews are internalized, to varying degrees.

Beliefs

Beliefs are 'a set of learned interpretations that form the basis for cultural members to decide what is and what is not logical and correct' (Lustig & Koester 2010: 86). In essence, beliefs are the basic assumptions we make about ourselves, about others in the world and about how we expect life to be. Many core beliefs are religious in nature and central to a person's sense of self. In Islam, for example, Muslims believe that there is no God but Allah and Muhammad is His messenger. Devotees are guided by messages in the Qur'an (holy book). Christians believe that Jesus is the Son of God and the saviour of humanity. A fundamental belief of

Buddhism is reincarnation, that is, the concept that people are reborn after dying. Atheists do not believe in a divine being, whereas followers of some religions worship multiple deities.

Other core beliefs may relate to notions of health and wellness (e.g. ideas about the source and appropriate treatment of illnesses). One of the central ideas in traditional Chinese medicine, for example, is the belief that certain foods have a 'hot' (heat-inducing) quality, while others have a 'cold' or chilling effect on one's organs and 'energy' level. An imbalance of natural 'heat' and 'cold' in one's body is thought to cause disease or make one more susceptible to illness. In this belief system, the eating of too many 'hot' (Yang) foods (e.g. garlic, chili peppers, chocolate, french fries) could cause a rash or fever, while the consumption of too many 'cold' (Yin) foods (e.g. watermelon, lemon, seaweed) could bring about stomach pains or diarrhoea. Thus, believers strive to maintain a balance of Yin and Yang forces in their diet. Health care providers who are unfamiliar with this system may understand the individual words used to explain an illness, but fail to grasp the concept. In today's multicultural world, familiarity with diverse cultural beliefs (and communication styles) is necessary to facilitate optimal health care interactions and outcomes.

Beliefs may also be **peripheral**, that is, they may simply relate to personal perceptions and tastes (e.g. ideas about the best way to learn a foreign language or prepare for the TOEFL, an English language proficiency test). Peripheral beliefs may also be superstitious in nature. A **superstition** is 'a belief, half-belief, or practice for which there appears to be no rational

Plate 3.1 In traditional Chinese culture, red is considered an auspicious or lucky colour. At this temple in Beijing, red cards are decorated with images or symbols that are designed to bestow luck, health and prosperity © Jane Jackson

Plate 3.2 In Turkey, nazars or charms are used to protect oneself from the curse of the evil eye. Wearing or hanging up the charm is thought to ward off the negative energy that is being directed towards you (e.g. envy, jealousy)
© Jane Jackson

substance' (Encyclopedia Britannica n.d.). Believing a 'lucky' coin will help you perform well on the TOEFL would be an example.

Many people have non-scientific beliefs about ways to ward off misfortune, foretell the future or prevent/cure minor ailments. Throughout history, folk traditions (e.g. belief in curses or the 'evil eye' in Turkey and Egypt) have been found in most parts of the world. Some superstitions and folk traditions are limited to a particular country, region or village, or to a specific social group. For example, the number '4' is considered unlucky by many Hong Kongers as it can be read as *shi* in Chinese, which is a homophone for death. Consequently, some high-rise residential buildings in Hong Kong omit all floor numbers with '4' (e.g. no 4th, 14th, 24th floors, etc.). Compared with core beliefs, peripheral beliefs may be more easily reflected upon and changed through education and life experience.

Values

Values are shared ideas about what is right or wrong, fair or unfair, just or unjust, kind or cruel or important and unimportant (Lustig & Koester 2010; Ting-Toomey & Chung 2012). During the period of primary socialization, we learn to think things ought to be or people ought to behave in a particular way; during this process, we form views about the nature and significance of human qualities such as honesty, integrity and openness. **Valence** refers to the positive or negative nature of a particular value, while **intensity** points to its importance or strength for the individual. As discussed in Chapter 1, values impact on one's sense of ethics and, to varying degrees, serve as guiding principles in one's daily life.

Worldviews

Cultural values and beliefs cover many aspects of society (e.g. freedom, equality, the right to pursue happiness); together they form an individual's perception of the world. **Worldview** is defined by Jandt (2007: 436) as 'philosophical ideas of being, a culture's beliefs about its place in the cosmos, and beliefs about the nature of humanity'. For McDaniel *et al.* (2009: 14), worldview is 'what forms people's orientation toward such philosophical concepts as God, the universe, nature, and the like'. More simply, it is our overall way of looking at the world. It is a bit like viewing life through an invisible pair of glasses or contact lenses, which serve as a filter to help us make sense of humanity.

As noted by Samovar *et al.* (2010), worldviews cover a broad range of weighty concerns and issues, e.g. 'What is the purpose of life? Is the world ruled by law, chance or "God"? What is the right way to live? How did the world begin? What happens when we die?' (p. 98). Our worldviews, which form a complex framework of ideas and beliefs, influence the way we perceive and communicate with others: 'Normally, worldview is deeply embedded in one's psyche and usually operates on a subconscious level' (McDaniel *et al.* 2009: 14). When we interact with individuals who have been socialized in other contexts, we may be surprised, or even shocked, to discover conflicting views about fundamental life questions. (Chapter 10 explores intercultural conflict situations that stem, in part, from the collision of divergent worldviews, values and beliefs.)

Infants are not born with a worldview. Our understandings of life form during the socialization process and continue to evolve as we mature. Religion often plays a fundamental role in shaping worldviews, including one's ideas about nature, deity (divine or supreme being) and the origin of life on earth. For example, while Muslims, Jews and Christians believe that the universe is created and originated by God, Buddhists and Taoists worship multiple gods or god-like beings. According to the Taoist creation theory, the beginning of the universe consisted of Yin and Yang forces that consolidated to form the earth in the centre. Hindus believe there is one Divine Power with multiple forms, whereas atheists (non-religious people) do not recognize a divine power as the creator of nature.

Religion can also shape one's ideas about sin (violations of the accepted moral code) and the consequences for what happens after death. Notions of judgment and punishment (and forgiveness) for violations committed during one's lifetime are core elements in many religions. Religious (and non-religious) worldviews related to sin, mortality and the afterlife can impact on how people lead their lives.

Buddhists, for example, believe that each life continues after death in some other form (human, divine or animal) depending on one's behaviour. Hindus also believe in the afterlife. Depending upon one's karma, the consequences of actions in one's present life, the soul may be reborn in either a higher or lower physical form after death. Through devotion or correct behaviour, devotees believe it is possible to ascend through the orders of reincarnation, achieve liberation from the cycle of rebirth, and be reunited with the Divine Power.

Christians, Jews and Muslims believe there is only one life. There are different views about what happens after death. Some believe the soul may ascend to heaven and be judged by God; or, the soul and the body may be raised on the Day of Judgment at the end of time

Plate 3.3 Prayer wheels play an important role in Tibetan Buddhist tradition and have been used for over a thousand years © Jane Jackson

and will then be judged. Muslims, for example, maintain that paradise awaits those who have lived by the will of Allah and those who have not done so cannot enter.

Religious beliefs can also influence one's perception of time. For example, in Islam, Christianity and Judaism, time is viewed as linear (e.g. life has a beginning, middle and end) whereas in Buddhism, Hinduism and Sikhism cyclical dimensions of time are emphasized (e.g. the process of creation moves in cycles and is never ending). Notions of life, death and time together influence one's worldview, and shape how one sees and interprets life.

Followers of a particular religion or sect may accept some religious beliefs and reject others. This means that an individual's worldview is not necessarily aligned with the fundamentals of a single religion, if any. In today's multicultural world, we are exposed to diverse beliefs, practices and worldviews. As we mature, we carry with us a tapestry of different notions about life, which draw on our unique, varied experiences and evolving understandings of the world.

Traditions

Throughout our life, we are also exposed to both religious and non-religious traditions. Culturally-shared **traditions** are customs or rituals that have been passed down from one generation to another. Each tradition has its own rituals and practices, some of which are linguistic in nature (e.g. the use of a specific language, dialect or expressions on certain occasions such as prayers and funerals). Influenced by the culture's core beliefs and values, traditions may take the form of festivals or other celebrations. In Taoism, for example, there are hundreds of local festivals such as *Ching Ming*, the veneration of the dead, the *Hungry Ghosts' festival* for the release of the restless dead and the *moon festival* to celebrate the autumn harvest. In Christianity, the main festivals celebrate the life of Jesus Christ: his birth at *Christmas* and his death and resurrection at *Easter*. In Islam, *Ramadan* is the holy month of fasting, while *Eid al-fitr* marks the end of Ramadan and the giving of the Qur'an (the holy book) to Muhammad, the messenger of Allah (God). Other religions have special days and observances that are meaningful to devotees.

Cultural traditions also include healing rituals, folk art, handicrafts, myths and legends, the singing of folk songs in a certain dialect, funeral rites and celebrations of birthdays/weddings/anniversaries/the coming of age/the birth of a child, etc.

When a baby is born into a Sikh family, the Mool mantra, the core teaching of Sikhism, is whispered into the baby's ear. The baby is then named at the gurdwara, or place of worship. The Guru Granth Sahib is opened and the first letter of the first word on the page gives the first letter of the baby's name. At death, the body is cremated and the ashes thrown into running water (OABITAR n.d.; Smith 2009).

Plate 3.4 Christmas is an annual commemoration of the birth of Jesus Christ and a holiday that is celebrated by millions of Christians on December 25th (or in early January by Orthodox Christians). Popular modern customs associated with this holiday include Christmas Eve services in church, large family meals with special food and decorations (e.g. turkey and cranberry sauce), carol singing, gift-giving, Christmas pageants, nativity scenes, a decorated Christmas tree, street lights, etc. © Jane Jackson

Before birth and in the first months of life, Hindus organize many ceremonies, including the reciting of scriptures to the baby while still in the womb, the casting of the child's horoscope shortly after birth and a gathering to mark the cutting of the baby's hair for the first time. At death, bodies are cremated and the ashes thrown onto a sacred river. The River Ganges, a trans-boundary river in India and Bangladesh named after a Hindu goddess called Ganga, is the most sacred river of all (OABITAR n.d.; Smith 2009).

In Taoism, horoscopes are cast at birth. After a month a naming ceremony is held. At death, the body is buried and paper models of money, houses and cars are burnt to help the soul in the afterlife. After about ten years, the body is dug up and the bones buried again in an auspicious site. In Theravada Buddhism, funerals are occasions for teaching about the impermanence of human life and for chanting paritta (protection) for the deceased.

Many Christians are baptized into the Church while they are babies although this can be done at any time in life. At death, Christians are laid to rest in the hope of the resurrection of the dead. Cremation and burial are both considered acceptable.

In Judaism, baby boys are circumcised eight days after birth. The names of girls are announced in the synagogue on the first Sabbath after birth. As for death, burial takes place within 24 hours of death and cremation is quite rare. The family is in full mourning for seven days and, for 11 months, the special prayer Kadish is recited every day.

In Islam, the call to prayer is whispered into the baby's ear at birth. After seven days, the baby is given a name, shaved and baby boys are circumcised. At a person's death, the body is washed as if ready for prayer and then buried as soon as possible. Cremation is not permitted.

With the passage of time, the significance of cultural traditions may change, along with the ways they are enacted. Within the same context, some individuals may have a strong attachment to a certain tradition or custom, whereas others (e.g. family members from a different generation) may be more ambivalent. People may gradually have little or no understanding of the origins of certain customs but still have an emotional attachment to them and a desire to share them with their own children when they become parents.

Cultural norms

During the process of **primary socialization**, elders (e.g. parents, religious figures, teachers) and the media (e.g. television) convey messages about what is expected (e.g. forms of address, communication styles, nonverbal behaviour) in various situations and contexts (e.g. familial, religious, social, academic, professional). At an early age, we learn what is considered polite (and impolite) behaviour (e.g. 'good manners'), that is, we discover what we can and cannot say (or do) in certain situations. Implicit or explicit messages are also relayed about social hierarchies and one's positioning (and possibilities) in specific settings, such as interactions with grandparents/elders/authority figures or people of a different gender/cultural background/socioeconomic status. These 'shared expectations of appropriate behaviors' (including language usage and communication styles) are referred to as **cultural norms** (Lustig & Koester 2010: 89). Accordingly, Wardaugh (2006), a sociolinguist, refers to culture as 'the "know-how" that a person must possess to get through the task of daily living' (p. 221). We are not born with this knowledge; it is learned in particular sociocultural and linguistic contexts.

Cultural schema

Through enculturation, we become habituated to expect certain arrangements (e.g. procedures) and behaviours (e.g. discourse, social norms of politeness) in specific settings. Gradually, by way of experience, we form mental pictures of various scenes. Thus, related to this notion of 'cultural norms' is the concept of **cultural schema**, that is, 'a mental structure in which our knowledge of the world is organized so that it can be efficiently used in thinking, communication, etc.' (Spencer-Oatey 2008a: 336). In Mumbai, India, for example, a lecture schema has a lecturer standing behind a podium delivering a formal speech on an academic topic using powerpoint; students sit in rows facing the front and raise their hands when they wish to ask a question. In other cultural settings, this schema may vary a little or considerably (e.g. in Sydney, Australia, the organization of the room may differ, including the type and placement of the furniture and the positioning of the lecturer; the dress and behaviour (degree of formality) of the lecturer and students may also be different).

Cultural scripts and language socialization

Through the primary socialization process, we learn 'norms of interaction, which are basically "rules" of how interactants are supposed to behave, for example, who should talk and when, how turns might change' (Kiesling 2012: 81). Through exposure to our social worlds, we learn **'cultural scripts'** and the style of communication that is appropriate in specific contexts (Goddard 2004; Wierzbicka 2006). A cultural script, which is a type of schema, refers to 'a pre-existing knowledge structure for interpreting event sequences' (Yule 2008: 134). Basically, it is a sequence of actions that is associated with a particular event or situation. One learns these scripts through observation and experience, that is, through enculturation.

In Tokyo, for example, a visit to a public bath house (sentō) might start with the payment of an entrance fee to the attendant, followed by disrobing in a change room that is reserved for members of one's sex. Then, one may sit on a stool near faucets where one washes oneself. It is only after one is thoroughly clean that one steps into the communal bath (same sex), which is usually quite hot. One may chat with other bathers or simply relax in silence. After soaking, one gets out of the water, rinses, dries off, gets dressed and heads home. Embedded in this schema are notions of what is proper in this context. For individuals who are new to the sentō and not used to public nudity, this may be a shocking event! A trip to a public bath house in other parts of the world (e.g. Finland, Germany, Hungary, South Korea, Turkey) would not be the same experience due, in part, to different 'event sequences' or procedures that stem from variations in etiquette (norms of politeness) and attitudes towards such aspects as sex, nudity, cleanliness and communication. When one is unfamiliar with the prevailing 'cultural script', one may feel like a fish out of water.

Very often, a cultural script entails 'cultural rules of speaking'; that is, one learns to expect and use certain expressions (e.g. verbal/nonverbal forms of politeness) and other forms of discourse in particular situations. This 'acquisition of linguistic, pragmatic, and other cultural knowledge through social experience' is referred to as **language socialization** (Duff 2010: 427). As we are socialized by and through language into the practices of our own community (and others), we gradually develop cultural and communicative competence in these settings.

As the following examples illustrate, the scripts that we learn may vary from one cultural context to another:

A Russian cultural script
[*Many* people think like this]
when I feel (think) something
I can say to other people what I feel (think)
it will be good if someone else knows what I feel (think)

A Malay cultural script
[*Many* people think like this]
when I feel (think) something
I can't always say to other people what I feel (think)
it will be good if I think about it before I say it
(Wierzbicka 2006: 308).

A high-level Anglo cultural script connected with 'personal autonomy'
[*Many* people think like this]
When a person does something, it is good if this person can think about it like this:

'I am doing this because I want to do it'
(Goddard 2006: 6).

(N.B. The qualifier 'many' was added to draw attention to the fact that these understandings may be shared by many people in a particular context but not by everyone.)

Cultural scripts offer insight into localized assumptions and expectations about social interaction but they are not definitive, prescriptions for real-life events, as Goddard (2004: 7–8) explains:

> A cultural script is not intended as a description of actual behaviour, but as a depiction of shared assumptions about how people think about social interaction. Individuals may or may not follow the cultural guidelines; they may follow them in some situations but not in others; they may defy, subvert or play with them in various ways; but even those who reject or defy culturally endorsed modes of thinking and modes of action are nonetheless aware of them. It is in this sense that cultural scripts can be regarded as part of the interpretive backdrop of actual social interaction.

While cultural scripts influence how particular encounters unfold in a specific setting, there will naturally be variations in the behaviour (e.g. speech, nonverbal communication) of participants as a consequence of differing levels of **sociopragmatic competence**. 'Sociopragmatic competence in a language comprises more than linguistic and lexical knowledge. It implies that the speaker knows how to vary speech-act strategies according to the situational or social variables present in the act of communication' (Harlow 1990: 328). The sociocultural context will largely determine the appropriate form of a particular **speech act** (apology, request, refusal, etc.).

When an individual behaves in ways that deviate from accepted norms of behaviour, social sanctions may be imposed. **Social sanctions** are 'the measures used by a society to enforce its rules of acceptable behavior' (Mosby 2009). For example, if children use profanity in class or when talking with their grandparents, they would likely be considered rude; for punishment, they might be verbally reprimanded or excluded from activities. Similar to values and beliefs, unwritten rules about what is acceptable behaviour (actions and responses) can differ among cultures as well as *within* cultural groups. Among individuals and groups, both the intensity and significance of cultural norms are variable. This means that there are apt to be differences in the use of cultural scripts and expressions of politeness, including **honourifics** (titles or expressions in some languages that convey respect towards a social superior).

In the environment where we are born and raised, we may be largely unaware of our cultural orientation, especially its deeper aspects, such as our belief systems, values, worldviews, traditions and norms of behaviour (e.g. cultural scripts). For this reason, many scholars describe our primary culture as 'invisible' or 'silent' (Furstenberg *et al.* 2001; Hall 1959, 1966; Kramsch 1993). Further, as today's world becomes increasingly interconnected and diverse, the number of children who are in contact with multiple languages and cultures, both at home and in the wider community, is becoming more common. Hence, the primary socialization process is increasingly multicultural and, in many cases, bi- or multilingual. (The process of second language/cultural socialization is discussed in Chapter 8 when we explore intercultural transitions.)

Culture as shared

All of us live out our lives as members of groups. Initially, the groups to which we belong are decided by others (e.g. our parents and other elders). In our formative years, our family, community, religion (if any), school and home country serve as sources for our primary cultural orientation, promoting certain beliefs, values, traditions, languages and norms either directly or indirectly. As we mature and experience life, we gradually make more choices for ourselves.

This notion of culture as 'shared' among group members is conveyed in many definitions, including the one formulated by Lindsay *et al.* (1999: 26-7):

> Culture is everything you believe and everything you do that enables you to identify with people who are like you and that distinguishes you from people who differ from you. Culture is about groupness. A culture is a group of people identified by the shared history, values, and patterns of behavior.

This perspective draws attention to the idea of membership and community. It raises questions such as how people identify with particular groups/communities, how outsiders identify individuals with these groups/communities and how different groups view and interact with others (Baldwin *et al.* 2006; Hecht *et al.* 2005).

Race

Cultures may be distinguished from one another by a wide variety of means such as geographical location, language, race, ethnicity, sexual orientation, religious or political affiliation, clothing, food and so on. Definitions of **race** have varied over time and across cultures. Today, race is a very politically charged, controversial term. As Samovar *et al.* (2010) explain, race is basically 'a social construct arising from efforts to categorize people into different groups' (p. 156). Anthropologists originally divided people into groups (e.g. Mongoloid, Caucasoid, Negroid) based on physical appearance (e.g. skin colour, facial features). Modern science, however, has found little genetic variations between members of 'different races' and with more interracial marriages, this classification system is regarded by many as obsolete.

> Most people think of 'race' as a biological category – as a way to divide and label different groups according to a set of common inborn biological traits (e.g. skin color, or shape of eyes, nose, and face). No consistent racial groupings emerge when people are sorted by physical and biological characteristics. For example, the epicanthic eye fold that produces the so-called "Asian" eye shape is shared by the Kung San Bushmen, members of an African nomadic tribe. Race is not a biological category, but it does have meaning as a social category. Different cultures classify people into racial groups according to a set of characteristics that are *socially* significant. The concept of race is especially potent when certain social groups are separated, treated as inferior or superior, and given differential access to power and other valued resources.
>
> (U.S. Department of Health and Human Services, Office of the Surgeon General 2001: 9)

While the term 'race' is 'frequently used in everyday discourse and social perception', it has 'no defensible biological basis' (Smith *et al.* 2006: 278).

Ethnicity

Ethnicity is also a social construct; however, it is 'a broader and more flexible cultural description than the biologically based or inflected categorization by race' (Brooker 2003: 92). Zenner (1996: 393–94) defines an **ethnic group** as 'a group of people of the same descent and heritage who share a common and distinctive culture passed on through generations'. **Heritage** refers to aspects that are inherited or linked to the past (e.g. language, rituals, preferences for music, certain foods, dress). Ethnic groups may be distinguished by a wide range of characteristics, such as ancestry, language or accent, customs or traditions, physical features, a common sense of history, family names, diet, forms of dress and religion. Perceptions of ethnic differences are not inherited; they are learned. Examples of ethnic groups are Indigenous Australians, Italian Americans, Malays and Chinese. (Notions of racial and ethnic identities are discussed in Chapter 6.)

Subcultures

As well as dominant cultures, numerous smaller cultures coexist in the same context. Identifiable groups within the larger cultural environment are referred to as subcultures, subgroups or co-cultures. Liu *et al.* (2011: 293) define a **subculture** as '[t]he smaller, coherent collective groups that exist within a larger dominant culture and which are often distinctive because of race, social class, gender, etc.' Subcultures may also be delimited by age (e.g. youth culture, Generation Z), appearance (e.g. dress, body piercings), behaviour (e.g. geeks, nerds), language (e.g. use of slang, terminology, code-mixing), nonverbal actions (e.g. use of certain gestures), physical disability (e.g. deaf culture), profession (e.g. legal culture, business culture), sports (e.g. football culture), technology (e.g. online/digital culture) and many other attributes. Some scholars prefer to use the term **co-culture** to make it clear that no one culture is inherently superior to others.

Speech communities

A **speech community** refers to 'a group of people who use the same variety of a language and who share specific rules for speaking and for interpreting speech' (Salzmann *et al.* 2012: 226). Speech communities typically share vocabulary and grammatical conventions, speech styles and genres and norms for how and when to speak in certain contexts. For Senft (2009: 6), 'Language is a mirror of the culture of its speech community'. Membership in a speech community is acquired through 'local knowledge of the way language choice, variation, and discourse represents generation, occupation, politics, social relationships, identity, etc.' (Morgan 2006). It is through living and interacting together that people in a speech community come to share a specific set of norms for language use. Put another way, they develop sociopragmatic awareness and learn how to function in ways that are deemed appropriate in that particular context. Thus, speech communities may emerge among any groups that interact frequently and share certain norms and belief systems.

Ingroups and outgroups

'Individuals are keenly aware of the critical attributes of the group with which they identify' (Fortman & Giles 2006: 96). We usually know rather quickly whether we are 'insiders' or 'outsiders' in relation to a particular group or community. We may feel welcomed and have a strong sense of belonging when in contact with certain people, whereas we may feel no personal connection or even experience resistance or rejection in the company of others. **Ingroups** refer to 'groups with whom one feels emotionally close and with whom one shares an interdependent fate, such as family or extended family, a sorority or fraternity, or people from one's own cultural or ethnic group' (Ting-Toomey & Chung 2005: 380–81). In contrast, **outgroups** are 'groups with whom one feels no emotional ties and, at times, from whom one may experience great psychological distance as a result of perceived scarce resources and intergroup competition' (Ting-Toomey & Chung 2005: 383).

Individuals are not entirely free to move in and out of groups/subgroups at will. One's religious or political affiliation, gender, age, socioeconomic status, ethnicity, physical appearance (e.g. dress, adornments such as tattoos and body piercings, skin colour, disability) and other attributes/aspects may exclude one from becoming a member of a particular cultural group or community. Language may also play a leading role in enabling or negotiating entry. For instance, one's **accent** (the way one pronounces words when one speaks) or **dialect** (variety of language used in a specific region) can signify and reinforce membership in a particular group. These same linguistic features may also serve as a barrier in other situations and prevent individuals from being accepted by other groups or communities.

In Hong Kong, speaking Cantonese can serve as glue to bond local Chinese youth and distinguish them from Mainland Chinese who speak Putonghua (Mandarin) and expatriates (e.g. American-born Chinese) who speak English. In some informal contexts the use of English by local Cantonese speakers is frowned upon; those who insist on conversing in this second (or third) language risk being labelled as 'weird' or branded as 'show-offs' by their Chinese peers (Jackson 2010). Fear of being 'outgrouped', that is, being rejected or rebuked by members of one's cultural group (one's 'ingroup'), can compel people to conform (e.g. adhere to familiar cultural scripts; use a certain language, accent or dialect). The desire to fit in and nurture one's sense of belonging in a group can be powerful motivating factors in many contexts, whereas in other settings, individuals may be less concerned about standing out.

As noted in the previous section, cultures as groups adopt particular practices and behaviour (e.g. linguistic codes, cultural scripts, etiquette), which involve explicit or implicit rules and codes of conduct that are generally understood and shared by members. Even if one adopts these practices, however, one may not be welcomed or accepted by other members either formally or informally. Membership is not solely in the hands of the potential participant; it is subject to the varied and subtle ways in which the group chooses to accept or reject members. Receptivity to new group members can vary significantly from one cultural context to another.

Discourse communities

As we grow, learn another language, travel or study abroad, join the workforce and interact with people from other cultures, subcultures and/or speech communities, we become members of diverse groups. For example, we may join multiple **discourse communities**, which Hewings and Hewings (2005) define as 'groups of people who share particular registers and use the kinds of text (both spoken and written) in which these registers occur' (p. 37). **Registers** are 'linguistically distinct varieties in which the language is systematically determined by the context' (Davies 2005: 114). For example, environmental engineers, business executives, English for Specific Purposes (ESP) teachers, golf enthusiasts and writing specialists tend to use a particular register when interacting with peers. Naturally, within each of these communities, there will also be individual variations in cultural practices (e.g. discourse, communication styles), an element that is discussed further in Chapter 4.

Whereas 'speech communities' are 'sociolinguistic groupings with communicative needs such as socialisation and group solidarity', 'discourse communities' are 'groupings based on common interests' (Swann *et al.* 2004: 84–5). Applied linguists from Australia, Taiwan, Spain and Egypt could belong to the same discourse community (e.g. be affiliated with the same professional group), though they may individually be members of four distinct speech communities (e.g. Australian English, Taiwanese Hokkien, Spanish, Egyptian Arabic).

As we join more groups and become exposed to diverse ways of being, further layers or levels may be added to the complex cultural mix that forms our evolving sense of self. The complex relationship between language, identity (e.g. cultural, ethnic, hybrid, linguistic, personal, racial, social) and belongingness (e.g. group membership) is explored in more detail in Chapter 6.

Culture as relative

> The reason man does not experience his true cultural self is that until he experiences another self as valid, he has little basis for validating his own self. A way to experience another group is to understand and accept the way their minds work. This is not easy. In fact, it is extraordinarily difficult, but it is of the essence of cultural understanding.
>
> (Hall 1976: 213)

The notion of 'culture as relative' refers to the belief that a culture can really only be understood or appreciated when reference is made to another. As mentioned earlier, one's primary culture is sometimes described as 'invisible', as much of what we have learned from our parents (and other members of our community) is below our level of awareness and simply accepted as 'normal' (e.g. beliefs, cultural scripts, values).

Agar (2006: 8) maintains that 'culture becomes visible only when differences appear with reference to a newcomer, an outsider who came into contact with it'. This means that our cultural frameworks may remain largely unexamined until we encounter other ways of being. This exposure can raise our awareness of unique aspects of our cultural group(s). Initially, we may only notice visible differences (e.g. dress, food, language). Gradually, with more inter-cultural contact *and* critical reflection, we are apt to become more aware of less obvious aspects that differ from what we have grown accustomed to (e.g. different beliefs, practices, values, worldviews, linguistic norms of politeness). Through this process of discovery, we begin to understand that culture is not an absolute concept; rather, it is relative, as culture may only be truly understood in relation to another.

Ethnocentricism

The natural process of contrasting and comparing cultures can be helpful in raising awareness of ourselves as cultural beings, while simultaneously learning about other perspectives and ways of life. It can also be highly problematic, however, as there is a natural tendency to resort to an 'us' vs. 'them' perspective, whereby 'us' is viewed very favourably (e.g. the home culture, familiar ways of being) and the unfamiliar is continuously cast in a negative light (or vice versa). In this state, ethnocentric discourse, like the following, usually prevails: '*We're* always so polite but *those people* are just plain rude . . . Why are they doing it that way?! Those guys are really weird!'. **Ethnocentricism** is defined by Berry *et al.* (2011: 469) as '[a] point of view that accepts one's group's standards as the best, and judges all other groups in relation to theirs'. An **ethnocentric mindset** does not foster the respect that is essential for cordial intercultural relations.

When encountering cultural difference, individuals may make snap judgments about unfamiliar behaviours and resort to a 'culture as nation' perspective (e.g. view all members of a particular nation, region or ethnic group as possessing similar traits and behaviours, overlooking individual differences).

Early in a semester-long sojourn in Madrid, Singaporean exchange students may observe the boisterous behaviour of a few local teenagers who are drinking alcohol and conclude that all Spanish youth are loud, jovial alcoholics. In case discussions at a Swedish university, local business students may note the reticence of a few Chinese exchange students and decide that all Asian students are shy and lacking in confidence. In both scenarios, the observers are making assumptions about the behaviours of others, which may be quite inaccurate. Not all Spanish teenagers drink alcohol to excess; many are very quiet. The Chinese business students may have different notions of participation and may be actively engaged in the discussion by listening attentively. They may also be very outgoing, self-assured and expressive in their first language when hanging out with their friends outside of class.

In these examples, the observers are using very broad categories (e.g. Spanish youth, 'Asian' students) and making sweeping generalizations, ignoring individual variations. They are overlooking the very real possibility that they have misinterpreted the behaviour they have witnessed. The Singaporean and Swedish students are also assuming that the way they behave and the way people from 'the other cultural group' act are common to all members of their respective cultural groups.

In both scenarios, the observers are using a contrastive approach to try to make sense of unfamiliar behaviours. Without critical awareness, however, this approach may reduce culture to monolithic, static categories, ignoring the diversity within. **Essentialism** and **reductionism** occur 'when one treats a heterogenous collection as homogenous', e.g. 'as if, all those of a single nation or even subgroup have the same cultural characteristics. This obscures the differences within culture. Second, these definitions can obscure the dynamic nature of culture' (Baldwin *et al.* 2006: 56). With limited intercultural awareness and sensitivity, individuals may resort to using even broader categories (e.g. regional, ethnic) to label people (e.g. Asians are . . . Arabs are . . . Africans are . . .). (See Chapter 7 for more discussion about the negative consequences of stereotyping.)

Ethnorelativism

As we live in an increasingly diverse world, it is important for all of us to negotiate intercultural encounters with an open mind. For this reason, many interculturalists advocate the development of an ethnorelative perspective.

> Fundamental to **ethnorelativism** is the assumption that cultures can only be understood relative to one another and that particular behavior can only be understood within a cultural

context. There is no absolute standard of rightness or "goodness" that can be applied to cultural behavior. Cultural difference is neither good nor bad, it is just different . . . One's own culture is not any more central to reality than any other culture, although it may be preferable to a particular individual or group.

(M.J. Bennett 1993: 46)

An **ethnorelative mindset** is basically the opposite of an ethnocentric stance. In the former, the experience of one's own beliefs and behaviours is recognized as just one version of reality among many other possibilities. An ethnorelative orientation does not mean that one must accept all cultural differences or no longer prefer a particular worldview. In contrast with an ethnocentric perspective, however, it implies that 'ethical choices will be made on grounds other than the ethnocentric protection of one's own worldview or in the name of absolute principles' (M.J. Bennett 1993: 46). As discussed in Chapter 1, ethical reasoning and choice should begin with an open mindset and be informed by knowledge of diverse cultural norms, practices and worldviews, including our own. (Chapter 7 delves further into the dangers of essentializing cultures and identities by looking at the world through an ethnocentric lens.)

Culture as dynamic and mediated

As noted by Baldwin *et al.* (2006), an essentialist perspective largely overlooks 'the dynamic nature of culture' (p. 56). With more recognition of the complexity and sociopolitical nature of life, there has been a shift away from a product-oriented view of culture as static and unitary. Most scholars now regard culture as dynamic and mediated through discourse. Berger (1969), for example, argues that '[c]ulture must be continually produced and reproduced . . . Its structures are, therefore, inherently precarious and predestined to change' (p. 6). Markus *et al.* (1996) reinforce this notion of culture as fluid and emergent through interaction in particular contexts:

> Cultural influence does not just involve a straightforward transmission of the 'way to be.' If entering a conversation, it matters what the conversant brings to the conversation, and whether and how the cultural messages and imperatives are accepted, or rather resisted and contested.

(p. 863)

For this reason, Street (1993) and Scollon *et al.* (2012) prefer to depict culture as a verb. For these applied linguists, 'culture is not something that you think or possess or live inside of. It is something that you *do*. And the way that you do it might be different at different times and in different circumstances' (Scollon *et al.* 2012: 5). Culture is created and challenged through discourse. Thus, in their intercultural work, instead of focusing on cultural facts, products, artifacts or patterns of thinking, these scholars examine 'people doing things' using systems of culture. For example, they conduct critical analyses of the discourse in intercultural business meetings in English with Chinese and American managers.

Scollon *et al.*'s (2012) view of culture contrasts sharply with Matthew Arnold's (1869) notion of individuals 'having culture' and Geert Hofstede's (1991) depiction of culture as 'software of the mind', that is, 'mental programming' or 'patterns of thinking, feeling, and potential acting which were learned throughout [one's] lifetime' (Hofstede 1991: 4). Hofstede (1991) maintains that the 'collective programming of the mind' distinguishes the members of one group of people from another. Nowadays, however, there is more recognition of the limitations of intercultural and cross-cultural research that 'categorizes people and characteristics as set, unchanging, and unconnected to issues of gender, class, and history' (Martin & Nakayama 2000: 61). Simply put, we can no longer ignore the dynamic, mediated nature of culture. Over time, all cultures shift and change.

Our own cultural profile is not fixed or static; it continues to evolve as we mature and experience life (e.g. engage in intercultural discourse). As Skelton and Allen (1999: 4) explain, 'any one individual's experience of culture will be affected by the multiple aspects of their identity—race, gender, sex, age, sexuality, class, caste position, religion, geography, and so forth—and it is likely to alter in various circumstances'. Noting that cultures and identities are dynamic, Martin et al. (2002: 3) warn that 'this ever-changing nature makes any attempt at static pieces of knowledge problematic'. (See Chapter 6 for a discussion of identity in relation to intercultural communication.)

When we encounter people who have been socialized in other linguistic and cultural environments, we are naturally exposed to new, unfamiliar ways of being (e.g. different discourse, cultural scripts, worldviews). This contact need not be face-to-face; in today's interconnected world, we may also participate in online cultures (e.g. chat rooms, Facebook). All of these experiences will be filtered by our frame of reference, which draws on our cultural knowledge and life experiences. **Intercultural interaction** (e.g. communication with individuals from other subcultures, speech communities, discourse communities) offers the potential for further self-expansion, *if* we are genuinely open to this possibility.

Culture as individual, fragmentary and imaginary

Culture is a variable concept. Within cultural groups, perceptions of cultural elements vary from individual to individual. Even the ways we choose to display our cultural membership may differ. A particular language/dialect or our choice of dress may be used to mark our affiliation with a group. For example, the use of Welsh in Wales or Gaelic in Ireland can serve as powerful markers of one's cultural identity.

Referring to culture 'as a process not a thing', Freadman (2004) maintains that 'what we call our "own" culture is incomplete and fragmentary', explaining that it is 'traversed by ignorance' and 'imperfectly owned' (p. 16). An individual's interpretation of his or her own culture (or subgroup) will necessarily be subjective, personal and partial. New cultural insights and understandings that arise as we learn and grow will always be subject to filtering by each individual. Further, we can never fully grasp all of the knowledge and practices associated with any cultural group that we belong to. Our understandings of 'our culture' (or any cultural group that we belong to) are incomplete and dependent on our experience, level of cultural knowledge and awareness and our individual point-of-view. Moreover, just as understandings of the same culture differ from one person to the next, how that culture is represented and understood by others also differs.

Culture is variable and continuously produced through discourse. Thus, language interaction is central to how culture evolves within and between groups at every level (Scollon et al. 2012). As Geertz (1973) explains, social reality is constantly being constructed and mediated by individuals through the exchange of messages in particular sociocultural contexts.

Benedict Anderson, an international studies scholar, coined the term **imagined community**, which helps us to understand how notions of culture are socially constructed and subject to individual interpretation. Anderson (1983, 1991) maintains that the idea of a nation and a national identity are 'imagined' by people. As none of us will ever meet the vast majority of members of the nation in which we live, he questions how we can regard ourselves and others as belonging to a particular 'national culture'. What does 'national culture' actually mean? Anderson (1983, 1991) suggests that we belong to an 'imagined community' in which we *assume* that other members follow norms, practices and beliefs similar to our own. People who belong to the same religion or gender, or share a common language, descent and/or history (e.g. an ethnic group) may also feel or *imagine* this sense of community or nationhood.

Along similar lines, Moon (2008) challenges conceptions of 'culture as nation', in which 'differences within national boundaries, ethnic groups, genders, and races are obscured, and hegemonic notions of "culture" are presented as "shared" by all cultural members' (p. 17). **Hegemony** refers to 'domination through consent where the goals, ideas, and interests of the ruling group or class are so thoroughly institutionalized, and accepted people consent to their own domination, subordination, and exploitation' (Sorrells 2013: 251). Within the contexts of nations, there may be strong political agendas and forces (overt or covert), which push nationals to perceive of themselves as possessing common traits and agendas (e.g. a 'national culture').

In reality, culture is multiple, complex, variable and layered. It is also imagined and subject to individual interpretation and enactment. Therefore, a nuanced understanding of culture is needed. As Baldwin *et al.* (2006: 56) warn, 'structural definitions of culture, especially those that frame culture merely as a list of aspects, run the risk of essentializing cultures'. In intercultural communication research, critical scholars (e.g. Dervin 2012; Holliday 2012; Kramsch & Uryu 2012) argue that the unit of analysis should not be limited to a single national culture, largely ignoring diversity within sub-groups or co-cultures as well as among individuals. In today's increasingly interconnected, relativistic world, cultural boundaries are becoming blurred and intermingled, which make the homogenizing notion of 'national cultures' obsolete. In many intercultural communication texts, however, as noted in Chapter 2, national groups (or even people who live on the same continent) are still treated as homogeneous, as if all members have the same cultural characteristics. For example, Asians are often portrayed as passive collectivists, while Americans and Australians are depicted as proactive individualists with little concern for family. (See Chapter 7 for more on stereotypes.)

Culture as contested

Notions of culture as contested or subject to different, sometimes conflicting, interpretations have emerged from such scholarly areas as critical pedagogy, critical theory and cultural studies, as well as postmodernist thought in relation to culture (Baldwin *et al.* 2006; Moon 2002, 2008). From this perspective, culture is viewed as 'an apparatus of power within a larger system of domination where meanings are constantly negotiated' (Sorrells 2013: 251). Giroux (1988: 171), an American cultural critic, refers to culture as

> the representation of lived experiences, material artefacts, and practices forged within the unequal and dialectical relations that different groups establish in a given society at a particular historical point. In this case, culture is closely related to the dynamics of power and produces asymmetries in the ability of individuals and groups to define and achieve their goals. Furthermore, culture is also an arena of struggle and contradiction, and there is no one culture in the homogeneous sense. On the contrary, there are dominant and subordinate cultures that express different interests and operate from different and unequal terrains of power.

Moving away from a product-oriented, static and unitary perspective of culture, there is growing recognition among scholars that culture is multiple and contested at many levels, both externally and from within. It may be contested at the level of the nation state (e.g. protests against long-established cultural practices and beliefs, differing imaginings of what constitutes 'national culture') or within sub-groups (e.g. rejection of particular forms of verbal or nonverbal behaviour, differing understandings of what membership means). Culture may also be contested at the discourse level (e.g. differing conceptions and use of terms, expressions, communication styles). At the individual level, one may also question one's values and practices when encountering cultural difference. For these reasons, Giroux (1988: 97) depicts culture 'as a terrain of struggle'.

Critical scholars, such as Giroux (1988), Moon (2002, 2008) and Sorrells (2012, 2013), among others, recognize that human behaviour (e.g. communication) is always constrained by societal structures (e.g. political hierarchies, the legal system, the economic system, the educational system, religious hierarchies, family structures, the health care system, language policies, etc.), which may privilege some individuals and disadvantage others. 'Culture is not a benignly socially constructed variable, but a site of struggle where various communication meanings are contested within social hierarchies' (Martin *et al.* 2012: 28). Cultural systems may categorize people according to language, race, social or economic status, etc., resulting in an unequal distribution of power, privilege and resources.

Critical discourse analysts such as Scollon *et al.* (2012) investigate the ways in which discourse practices reproduce and/or transform power relations within cultural groups. **Discourse** here refers to 'particular uses of language in context' as well as 'the world views and ideologies which are implicit or explicit in such uses' (Swann *et al.* 2004: 83). **Critical discourse analysis** is a form of discourse analysis that has 'the clear political aim of attempting to reveal connections of hidden relationships encoded in language that may not be immediately evident, in order to bring about social change' (Llamas *et al.* 2007: 210). Critical discourse analysts often explore the social practices and interactions of disadvantaged groups such as minorities, e.g. the discourse of second-language immigrant children and teachers from the majority culture in an inner city school in New York.

Power (unequal relations between individuals and groups) (Schirato & Yell 2000: 191) is an element that cannot be overlooked when discussing culture. '**Power relations** (an imbalance of power between individuals or groups) are arguably part of every communicative event or practice, and every social relation, whether or not they are explicitly or overtly at stake' (Schiarto & Yell 2000: 191). Consequently, Moon (2002, 2008) views culture as 'a site of struggle' between the discourses and ideologies of the interactants. **Ideology** is 'a system of ideas which promote the interests of a particular group of people' (Holliday 2011: 198). (In relation to communication, power is discussed further in Chapter 4.)

Culture is not simply passed from one generation to the next; rather it is 'a contested zone' in which different groups struggle to define issues with their own interests in mind (Martin & Nakayama 2010a; Moon 2002). Consequently, Hannerz (1996) describes cultural processes as dynamic 'organizations of diversity' that intersect national and regional boundaries. This conception of culture 'simultaneously acknowledges the overlapping nature (i.e., sharedness) of various cultural realities within the same geographical space, while recognizing that cultural realities always have some degree of difference' (Moon 2002: 15–16).

When you learn another language, interact with people who have been socialized in a different environment or move to another country to live, your understandings of culture may be contested or challenged as you encounter differing belief systems, ideas and values. As the unfamiliar is compared and contrasted with the familiar, both consciously and subconsciously, you may initially feel insecure about your place in the world. As Chapter 8 explains, you may experience disequilibrium while adjusting to a new environment. In this process of personal discovery and expansion, your beliefs, values, worldviews and self-identities may be challenged, reoriented, and modified.

Culture as communication

> Culture is a code we learn and share, and learning and sharing require communication. And communication requires coding and symbols, which must be learned and shared. Communication and culture are inseparable.
>
> (Smith 1966: 7)

Culture is developed, shaped, transmitted and learned through both verbal and nonverbal forms of communication. It is through the act of communication that cultural characteristics (e.g. customs, norms, roles, rituals, laws) are created and shared by humans. Individuals may not set out to create a culture when they interact in relationships, groups, organizations or societies, but cultures naturally take shape and evolve through social discourse and interaction. Communication and communication media make it possible to preserve and pass along cultural elements from one place and time to another (e.g. from one generation to the next).

The reverse is also true; that is, communication practices are largely created, shaped and transmitted by culture. Over time, through communication and interaction, members of a culture develop history, patterns, customs and rituals that distinguish them from other groups and influence how they interact with each other as well as outsiders. While creating this set of shared experiences, group members develop specific ways of communicating verbally and nonverbally (e.g. discourse norms, cultural scripts). Consequently, for E.T. Hall (1959: 186), 'Culture is communication and communication is culture'. The communication–culture relationship, which is very complex and personal, is explored in more detail in the next chapter.

THE TEXT'S CONCEPTION OF CULTURE

The conception of culture that is used in the remainder of this text draws on the many facets described above. Culture, in part, involves membership in a community or group that shares a common history, traditions, norms and imaginings in a particular **cultural space** (e.g. a neighbourhood, region, virtual space). Much of this is below our level of awareness and may not become apparent until we encounter cultural difference. In other words, culture is relative.

Culture is not just about the group. Recognizing the perspective of the individual in relation to the group is also an important dimension of the culture concept. As well as being a manifestation of a group or community, culture is subject to an individual's unique experience within it, or apart from it. Culture is dynamic, multiple and contested. It is a very complex construct that is difficult to pin down.

SUMMARY

The purpose of this chapter was to introduce the concept of culture and the process of language and cultural socialization, and lay the foundation for the remainder of the text.

We examined many definitions and conceptions of culture, and considered some important qualities or dimensions associated with it (culture as learned; culture as shared, as in group membership; culture as relative; culture as dynamic and mediated; culture as individual, fragmentary and imaginary; culture as contested; and culture as communication). The chapter concluded with a summary of core dimensions of culture.

discussion questions

1   What are some possible ways to define culture? Provide your own definition.
2   Compare and contrast the following conceptions of culture. Which of the definitions or elements in the definitions do you feel are the most useful and why? Are there aspects that you disagree with?

   a.   'Culture is the fabric of meaning in terms of which human beings interpret their experience and guide their action' (Geertz 1973: 24).
   b.   'Culture is a verb' (Scollon *et al.* 2012: 5).
   c.   Culture is 'the totality of communication practices and systems of meaning' (Schirato and Yell 2000: 1).
   d.   'Culture is the collective programming of the human mind that distinguishes the members of one human group from those of another. Culture in this sense is a system of collectively held values' (Hofstede 1981: 24).
   e.   Culture is 'the shared patterns of behaviors and interactions, cognitive constructs, and affective understanding that are learned through a process of socialization. These shared patterns identify the members of a culture group while also distinguishing those of another group' (Center for Advanced Research on Language Acquisition (CARLA), University of Minnesota, n.d.).
   f.   Culture is 'the membership in a discourse community that shares a common social space and history, and a common system of standards for perceiving, believing, evaluating, and acting' (Kramsch 1998: 127).
   g.   Culture is 'the process by which people make sense of their lives, a process always involved in struggles over meaning and representation' (Pennycook 1995: 47).
   h.   Culture is 'the unwritten rules of the social game' (Hofstede n.d.).
   i.   Culture is 'the social cement of all human relationships; it is the medium in which we move and breathe and have our being' (Scovel 1994: 205).

3   What are the limitations of the 'culture as nation' perspective? What are the implications for intercultural communication research and practice?
4   If you think of a tree as a metaphor for culture, what elements can you see (e.g. the branches)? What elements are invisible?
5   Define subculture and co-culture. Discuss examples of subcultures/co-cultures that you are familiar with in your context. What are some ways in which membership is enacted?

6 How is culture a contested site? Give examples in contexts that you are familiar with.

7 What does Senft (2009) mean when he says that '[l]anguage is a mirror of the culture of its speech community' (p. 6)? Can you think of examples to support this view?

8 Identify a situation you are familiar with and give an example of a cultural script that is associated with it. Have you ever been in another cultural context, where a different cultural script was more widely followed?

9 How are culture and communication related?

further reading

Baldwin, J.R., Faulkner, S.L., Hecht, M.L. and Lindsley, S.L. (eds) (2006) *Redefining Culture: Perspectives across the Disciplines*, Mahwah, NJ: Lawrence Erlbaum.

This volume provides a listing of over 300 definitions of culture from a wide array of disciplines. The authors examine how the definition of culture has changed historically.

Gezon, L. and Kottak, C. (2011) *Culture*, Boston: McGraw-Hill.

This magazine style text introduces students to notions of culture, largely drawing on understandings from cultural anthropology.

Hall, E.T. (1976) *Beyond Culture*, New York: Anchor Books.

This book is written by the scholar who is regarded by many as the founding father of the field of intercultural communication. In this volume, he describes the many influences of culture on the way people live and interact, with a special emphasis on nonverbal codes.

Kroeber, A.L. and Kluckholn, C. (1952) *Culture: A Critical Review of Concepts and Definitions*, Cambridge, MA: The Museum.

This classic reviews more than 162 definitions of culture by scholars from diverse disciplines.

CHAPTER 4

Language, communication, culture and power in context

The way people communicate is the way they live. It is their culture. Who talks with whom? How? And about what? These are questions of communication and culture.

(Smith 1966: 1)

Language is the most fully articulated of all media of human communication.

(Kress 1988: 183)

To be mindful intercultural communicators, we need the knowledge of both verbal and nonverbal communication in order to communicate sensitively across cultural and ethnic boundaries.

(Ting-Toomey 1999: 113)

learning objectives

By the end of this chapter, you should be able to:

1 define communication
2 describe the process of human communication
3 identify nine properties of communication
4 describe the nature of language and communication
5 explain the relationship between language, communication, culture, power and context
6 identify and describe multiple verbal communication styles
7 identify the traits associated with high-context and low-context cultures
8 explain the communication accommodation theory (CAT) and the difference between 'convergence' and 'divergence'
9 identify the elements in the audience design framework and explain its relationship to the CAT
10 explain the merits and limitations of communication style typologies
11 identify the traits and behaviours of an effective intercultural communicator.

INTRODUCTION

As we learned from Chapter 3, the relationship between culture and communication is not straightforward, rather it is multifaceted, personal and intertwined. Accordingly, E.T. Hall (1959: 186) famously states that 'Culture is communication and communication is culture'. To be an effective intercultural communicator, it is essential to understand the process of human communication and the impact of cultural dimensions and power in communicative events that take place within a particular environment.

To better understand the role of communication in intercultural interactions, this chapter examines the nature, properties and components of communication. After reviewing the process of human communication, we discuss individual and cultural variations in communication styles (e.g. direct, indirect, formal, informal). We primarily focus on verbal communication as the next chapter centres on nonverbal codes. Finally, we review the characteristics of an effective intercultural communicator in second language situations.

DEFINITIONS OF HUMAN COMMUNICATION

Similar to culture, human **communication** is difficult to define and, over time, scholars have put forward a wide array of definitions. Table 4.1 presents some of the most common elements associated with communication, along with definitions that illustrate the dimension that is emphasized. As one might expect, there is some overlapping, with elements from one definition appearing in another.

Table 4.1 Properties and definitions of communication

1	Process	Communication is 'a symbolic process whereby reality is produced, maintained, repaired, and transformed' (Carey 1989: 23).
		'Communication can be defined as the symbolic process by which we create meaning with others' (Moon 2002: 16).
2	Dynamic	'Because we view communication as a process, we also perceive it to be dynamic, ever-changing, and unending' (Barker & Barker 1993: 3).
		'Communication is the process by which we understand others and in turn endeavor to be understood by them. It is dynamic, constantly changing and shifting in response to the total situation' (Anderson 1959: 5).
		'Communication is dynamic. This means that communication is not a single event but is ongoing, so that communicators are at once both senders and receivers' (Martin & Nakayama 2008: 36).
3	Interactive/ transactive	Communication is 'message exchange between two or more people' (Guirdham 2011: 381).
		Communication is 'the process by which individuals try to exchange ideas, feelings, symbols, meanings to create commonality' (Schmidt *et al.* 2007: 59).
		'Communication in face-to-face encounters can be seen as constituted by interactive exchanges of moves and countermoves involving speakers and listeners who actively co-operate in the joint production of meaningful interaction' (Gumperz & Cook-Gumperz 2012: 66).

4	Symbolic	Communication is 'the transmission of information, ideas, emotion, skills, etc., by the use of symbols—words, pictures, figures, graphs, etc. It is the act or process of transmission that is usually called communication' (Berelson & Steiner 1964. 527).
		'The words we speak or the gestures we make have no inherent meaning. Rather, they gain their significance from an agreed-upon meaning. When we use symbols to communicate, we assume that the other person shares our symbol system . . . these symbolic meanings are conveyed both verbally and nonverbally' (Martin & Nakayama 2010b: 94).
5	Intentional and unintentional	'In the main, communication has as its central interest those behavioral situations in which a source transmits a message to a receiver(s) with conscious intent to affect the latter's behaviors' (Miller 1966: 92).
		'Unintentional messages are not purposeful, but may be transmitted by action as well as by words' (Tubbs 2009).
		'Communication does not have to be intentional. Some of the most important (and sometimes disastrous) communication occurs without the sender knowing a particular message has been sent' (Martin & Nakayama 2008: 36).
6	Situated and contextual	'Communication involves the creation, constitution, and intertwining of situated meanings, social practices, structures, discourses, and the nondiscursive' (Halualani & Nakayama 2010: 7).
		'Communication is dependent on the context in which it occurs' (Neuliep 2012: 14).
7	Pervasive	Communication is 'the process through which participants create and share information with one another as they move toward reaching mutual understanding. Communication is involved in every aspect of daily life, from birth to death. It is universal. Because communication is so pervasive, it is easy to take it for granted and even not to notice it' (Rogers & Steinfatt 1999: 113).
		'We cannot not communicate' (Watzlawick *et al.* 1967: 49).
		'If two humans come together it is virtually inevitable that they will communicate something to each other . . . even if they do not speak, messages will pass between them. By their looks, expressions and body movement each will tell the other something, even if it is only, "I don't wish to know you: keep your distance"; "I assure you the feeling is mutual. I'll keep clear if you do"' (Argyle & Trower 1979).
8	Power-infused	'Communication is the mechanism by which power is exerted' (Schacter 1951: 191).
		'Power is always present when we communicate with each other although it is not always evident or obvious' (Martin & Nakayama 2008: 48).
9	Cultural	'Culture is communication and communication is culture' (Hall 1959: 186).
		'Communication is a process of utilizing cultural resources' (Sorrells 2013: 10).
		'Every cultural practice is a communicative event' (Kress 1988: 10).

THE COMPONENTS OF HUMAN COMMUNICATION

Before we examine the properties of communication and their implications for intercultural interactions, it is helpful to identify the key components in the communication process. As illustrated in Figure 4.1, the basic elements are: sender, encoding, message, channel, noise (interference), receiver, decoding, receiver response, feedback and context.

In this process model, the components may be defined as follows:

Sender: The person who is sending a message (verbally or nonverbally), which may be intentional or unintentional. 'A sender is someone with a need or desire, be it social, work, or information driven to communicate with others' (McDaniel *et al.* 2009: 8).

Encoding: The process of putting an idea or message into a set of symbols (e.g. words, gestures).

Message: What is conveyed verbally (e.g. in speech, writing) or nonverbally from one person (the sender) to one or more persons (the receiver(s)). The form and content of the message may differ. In a spoken apology, for example, the *message form* is how the apology is made (e.g. type of sentence structure, use or non-use of politeness discourse markers, type of intonation) and the *message content* is the substance of the apology (e.g. regret about an overdue assignment).

Channel: The way in which a message is conveyed from one person to another. The most common channels or paths of communication are speech, writing and nonverbal signals.

Noise (Interference): Any disturbance or defect that interferes with or distorts the transmission of the message from one person to another (e.g. background sounds, fatigue, lack of concentration on the message, feeling unwell, unfamiliar jargon, use of specialized professional terminology, a hearing impairment, an unfamiliar accent, etc.).

Receiver: The person (or persons) who is receiving the message that is being sent, whether intentional or not.

Decoding: The process by which the receiver tries to understand the meaning of a message that is being sent, that is, the receiver translates or interprets the meanings of the symbols.

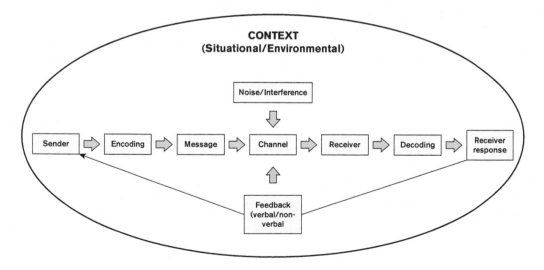

Figure 4.1 A process model of communication

Receiver response: The verbal or nonverbal reaction, if any, of the receiver after decoding the message.

Feedback: Verbal or nonverbal signals that receivers give to a speaker to indicate they have processed what the speaker has said (e.g. smiles, nods, grunts, comments). These may be intentional or unintentional (below the level of awareness of the sender).

Context: The overall environment in which the communication occurs (e.g. physical, psychological, sociocultural, political, sociorelational, etc.).

COMMUNICATION PROPERTIES

To better understand human communication and its implications for intercultural interactions, we now take a closer look at the key properties of communication that are identified in Table 4.1. When appropriate, reference is also made to Figure 4.1.

Property 1: Communication as a process

Most scholars view communication as a process, that is, it involves 'an interrelated, interdependent group of elements working together to achieve a desired outcome or goal' (Barker & Barker 1993: 10). As Figure 4.1 shows, the communication process entails multiple components and steps (e.g. people who are sending and receiving a message, the ideas and emotions that are being communicated, the channel through which the communication takes place, the context).

Although individual (verbal/nonverbal) messages and interactions have definite beginnings and endings (e.g. greetings and words of farewell), the overall process of communication does not. How two individuals interact with each other on a particular day is very much influenced by how they interacted previously. As a Russian proverb says, 'Once a word goes out of your mouth, you can never swallow it again'.

Think about the last time you had a disagreement with one of your friends. You may have said some things that you now regret. Communication, however, is irreversible. You cannot take back what you have said or done. An apology may soothe hurt feelings and help repair the relationship; however, expressions of regret cannot erase past interactions (e.g. previous verbal and nonverbal behaviour). This also means that the messages you communicate now can affect your interpersonal relationships and future interactions.

This communication process also applies to intercultural interactions. When you are interacting with someone who has been socialized in a different linguistic and cultural environment, the history you are developing together impacts on any communication that you have today and in the future. When the communication process goes well and both speaker and receiver feel respected and understood, relationships are enhanced. Conversely, when the communication process is unsuccessful (e.g. 'noise' interferes with the message), misunderstandings may occur; this can then negatively impact on the interpersonal relationship and limit the desire for further interaction. Hence, the communication process influences interpersonal relations (e.g. relationship building), an element that is discussed in more detail in Chapter 9.

Property 2: Communication as dynamic

Communication, like culture, is characterized by energy or action; it is always developing and never passive or static. A model, like the one depicted in Figure 4.1, can provide an indication of the elements involved in communication; however, because communication is a flexible, dynamic and adaptive process, it is not possible to fully capture its essence in a written definition or graphic model. At best, models are representations that raise our awareness of the complexity of the steps and elements involved. 'To fully appreciate the process, one must be a part of it or witness it in motion' (Neuliep 2012: 12).

In intercultural interactions, the various elements in the communication process are also interdependent, variable and dynamic. As well as being irreversible, intercultural communication is time-bound and flexible. No two interactions will be exactly alike. Factors such as time, location, topic and circumstances (e.g. attitudes towards the other communicator, the tenor and quality of the previous communication) influence the dynamic communication process, rendering it complex and impossible to replicate.

Property 3: Communication as interactive and transactive

Although people may engage in **intrapersonal communication**, that is, they may talk to themselves (e.g. work through ideas in their head or out loud), most scholars maintain that interaction between two or more people is a fundamental dimension of communication. Active participation means that people are consciously directing their messages to someone else. Thus, the communication is **transactive**. Because individuals both send and receive (and interpret) messages, communication is a two-way process; this makes it **interactive**, as the multi-directional arrows in Figure 4.1 illustrate. Therefore, 'communication in face-to-face encounters can be seen as constituted by interactive exchanges of moves and countermoves involving speakers and listeners who actively co-operate in the joint production of meaningful interaction' (Gumperz & Cook-Gumperz 2012: 66).

In a communicative event, you may send verbal and nonverbal messages to another person, who is likewise communicating thoughts, ideas and emotions to you. The receiver's body language, facial expression, eye contact and tone in her voice give you an indication of how your message is being received and interpreted. Thus, as the model shows, each person in an interactional setting simultaneously sends (encodes) and receives (decodes) messages.

Consider the following scenario. Your friends have just seen 'the Avengers'; they give the movie a glowing review and encourage you to go and see it. When they are speaking, it is clear to you that they are sending you messages (e.g. recommending that you see the movie). Even if you do not utter a single word, you are also sending messages to them, although you may not be aware you are doing so. For example, your eye contact, smiles (or frowns), raised eyebrows and other nonverbal reactions are communicating your interest (or disinterest) in what they are saying. Both you and your friends are sending and receiving messages simultaneously. If you have a shared history and have been socialized in a similar linguistic and cultural environment, you may understand one another quite easily. When you interact, you may not even need to finish each other's sentences. What happens, however, when the communicators do not share these common understandings?

If you are interacting with someone who is not fluent in the language that you are using, the verbal messages you are sending may be misunderstood. As Gumperz and Cook-

Gumperz (2012) explain, in many intercultural communicative events, 'inferences necessary to understand it [the message] rest on familiarity with a complex body of social relational assumptions that reveal culturally specific knowledge acquired through participation' (p. 66). What this means is that the possibility of miscommunication may arise if the receiver has been socialized in a different cultural context and does not share the same background knowledge as you. Your communication partner may understand the words but not the intended meaning. Nonverbal signals may also be misinterpreted or ignored. (See Chapter 5.)

If you are using a second language in unfamiliar situations, you may become quite frustrated at times and feel misunderstood. As you become more proficient in the language and more knowledgeable about the cultural context and prevailing **sociopragmatic norms** (rules governing the appropriate use of discourse in social situations), the transmission and decoding of messages should become much easier and more efficient. Familiarity with the prevalent **cultural scripts** (local conventions of discourse), politeness markers, nonverbal behaviour used in particular settings may ease your anxiety and help you to make communication choices that are more appropriate. This knowledge and awareness can facilitate both interactive and transactive dimensions of communication.

Property 4: Communication is symbolic

Communication is also symbolic. Ting-Toomey and Chung (2005) define a symbol as 'a sign, artifact, word(s), gesture, or nonverbal behavior that stands for or reflects something meaningful' (p. 31). Basically, it is 'an arbitrarily selected and learned stimulus that represents something else' (Neuliep 2012: 12). An individual's emotions and ideas can be conveyed to another person by means of language, gestures or other forms of nonverbal communication. Put another way, meanings are transmitted by way of verbal and nonverbal symbols. During the primary socialization process, these symbols are learned. (See Chapter 3 for a lengthier discussion of enculturation.)

Typically, the words, nonverbal codes, or other symbols that are used by a particular cultural group have no natural relationship with what they signify, that is, the symbols are **arbitrary**. They are selected and learned within a particular linguistic and cultural context. Outside of this environment, they may mean something different or nothing at all and, consequently, may be easily misunderstood or simply overlooked.

Kress (1988:183) observes that language is 'the most fully articulated of all media of human communication'. It is a key element that distinguishes humans from other animals. **Language** is 'a system comprised of vocabulary and rules of grammar that allows us to engage in verbal communication' (West & Turner 2011a: G-6). A verbal language (e.g. Arabic, Chinese, English, Russian) is a code made up of symbols. For example, the letters of the English alphabet (e.g. 'a, b, c') are a set of symbols that represent sounds. When we combine individual symbols into words (e.g. 'h+o+u+s+e'), they become meaningful to English speakers. By using symbols, people can represent their thoughts and ideas orally or through writing. Once an idea has been encoded with symbols, it becomes a message, following the process displayed in Figure 4.1. When verbal communication is employed, people ('senders') encode their thoughts and send them to someone else (the receiver) in the form of words, which may be accompanied by nonverbal behaviours. The individual then listens to the verbal message and translates, or decodes it along with nonverbal information. **Interaction**, then, is the process of encoding and decoding messages. While people who speak different languages may use different codes, the process is the same.

Plate 4.1 The image and words in these signs may be comprehensible to someone from Spain but not be well understood by a newcomer who is unfamiliar with Spanish language and culture © Jane Jackson

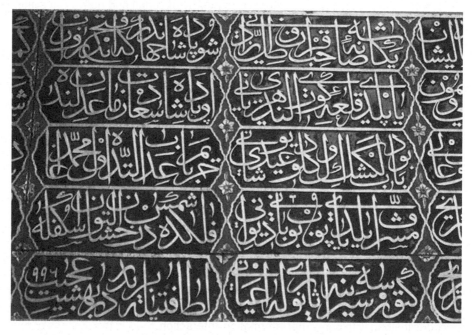

Plate 4.2 The Arabic language is a code made up of symbols (script). It is written from right to left, in a cursive style, and includes 28 letters © Jane Jackson

Plate 4.3 Japanese calligraphy is a form of artistic writing of the Japanese language © Chan Sin Yu

Some languages are 'phonetic', that is, there is a direct relationship between the spelling (symbol) and the sound, as in Slavic languages, for example. That means you can look at a written word and know how to pronounce it, or you can hear a word and know how to spell it. Other languages (e.g. Chinese, Japanese) are not phonetic; there is no relationship between the written symbols and the way you say the words.

To facilitate the second language learning of phonetic languages, the International Phonetic Association devised the **International Phonetic Alphabet (IPA)**, an alphabetic system of phonetic notation based primarily on the Latin alphabet (International Phonetic Association n.d.). The IPA represents the qualities of speech that are distinctive in spoken language: phonemes, intonation and the separation of words and syllables. It serves as a standardized representation of the sounds of spoken language, and is widely used today by linguists, translators and foreign language speakers. This system aids intercultural communication by helping second language speakers express themselves in ways that are comprehensible to others.

Human languages also use different linguistic codes or symbols for writing. In English, for example, the verbal symbols (letters) that form the word 'h+o+u+s+e' have no natural connection with 'a building that serves as living quarters for one or a few families' (Merriam-Webster Online n.d., b). In other languages, as Figure 4.2 illustrates, different symbols (e.g. letters, characters) have been arbitrarily chosen to signify the meaning of 'house'. Moreover, what this actually means in different cultural settings varies, depending, in part, on the experiences of the people in that particular context. For example, when Filipinos say the Tagalog word for 'house' ('bahay'), they may visualize something quite different from first language speakers of English in Scotland, or Arabic speakers in the Sudan who say the word for 'house' in their first language. In other words, conceptions may vary along with the words (symbols) used.

Similar to language, nonverbal symbols (e.g. gestures) are arbitrary. Raising your fist in the air with knuckles pointed outward is an expression of victory in Argentina. In Britain, however, the sign for victory is an erect forefinger and middle finger in the shape of the letter V. This same movement symbolizes the number '2' in the United States and, in Australia, it may be seen as an insult! Nonverbal symbols may have a particular meaning in one context but mean something entirely different in another part of the world, or they may not communicate anything at all.

On the field, football players use different symbols (e.g. gestures) to communicate with each other. To be effective, one's communication system should only have meaning for members of one's own team and especially not one's opponents! People smugglers and drug dealers also have an elaborate linguistic and nonverbal code that allows them to share information about their illegal activities, without disclosing information to law enforcement.

Language	Original form/script	Transliteration (if the Roman alphabet is not used)	Illustrations of a 'house' (many possibilities in different cultural contexts)
Arabic	بَيْت	beyt	
Chinese	家	jiā	
French	maison		
German	haus		
Hebrew	בַּיִת	beit	
Hindi	घर	ghar	
Italian	casa		
Japanese	宅	taku	
Korean	집	jip	
Norwegian	hus		
Polish	dom		
Portuguese	casa		
Russian	дом	dohm	
Slovenia	hiša		
Swahili		nyumba	
Swedish	hus		
Tagalog	bahay		
Urdu	مکان	makaan	

Figure 4.2 Linguistic codes/symbols for the word 'house'

Twins and other siblings may develop their own communication codes that are incomprehensible to their parents. (Chapter 5 explores forms and functions of nonverbal communication, including gestures and other symbols that may be culture-specific.)

In these examples, the verbal and nonverbal symbols are only meaningful to people who have learned to associate them with particular ideas. In our everyday life, all of us are surrounded by specialized symbols that carry meaning for 'ingroup members' who have been socialized in a particular cultural group. Consequently, 'outgroup members' may easily misinterpret or fail to notice messages that are being transmitted. As one might expect, the interpretation of verbal and nonverbal communication is an aspect that can pose challenges when the communicators have been socialized in different linguistic and cultural contexts.

Property 5: Communication is both intentional and unintentional

It is also important to recognize that communication may be both intentional and unintentional. An example of **intentional communication** is a situation in which two or more people consciously engage in interaction with a specific purpose in mind. For example, if Jessica says to Heejun, 'Would you like to go to the basketball game tonight?' and he replies, 'Sure. What time should we leave?' intentional communication has occurred and they'll soon head off to the event together. **Unintentional communication** may also be taking place, however. For example, Heejun may believe that Jessica is asking him to go to the game because she is romantically interested in him, when, in fact, she just wants to go with him as a friend.

Communication is not always straightforward. When we hear a message, we also interpret, and possibly misinterpret, the intention and meanings that lie behind the verbal and nonverbal communication. When interactants do not share the same background and experiences, there are more possibilities of miscommunication, especially when a second language is involved.

If you go abroad to work or study, or you engage in intercultural interactions in your home environment, you may find yourself in situations in which you either misinterpret or are unsure of your communication partner's intentions. When a second language is involved, you may understand each word that is spoken (or written) but still find it challenging to figure out what the speaker's motives or intentions are (e.g. what lies behind the words). This is also the case for nonverbal behaviour, the focus of Chapter 5.

In intercultural situations, the communication process may be complicated by a range of factors: different understandings of when and how to convey messages (e.g. variations in communication styles, including the degree of directness), differing views about gender relations and differing expectations about what constitutes 'appropriate' verbal and nonverbal behaviour in a particular situation and context. **Cultural schema** (mental representations of a context or situation) and **cultural scripts** (cultural rules of speaking and interpretation) are apt to vary somewhat in different linguistic and cultural settings and, initially, newcomers may find the communication process confounding. They may find it difficult to 'read' the intentions of their communication partner. (See Chapter 3 for examples of cultural scripts and schema.)

Our behaviour, whether intentional or not, communicates ideas and attitudes to others. This means that we need to be mindful of the messages that we are sending and the possibility that our verbal and nonverbal actions are not being understood in the ways that we have intended or would like them to be. As Ting-Toomey (1999: 113) observes, mindful intercultural communicators need 'the knowledge of both verbal and nonverbal communication in order to communicate sensitively across cultural and ethnic boundaries'. Even if you are trying your best to be pleasant and polite, you may, inadvertently, be giving a very different impression to people who have been socialized to regard your behaviour as unacceptable or rude. When we lack awareness of prevailing norms (e.g. cultural scripts), we may commit **faux-pas**, that is, we may unintentionally violate accepted social rules of behaviour and misinterpret the behaviours of our intercultural communication partners.

In intercultural encounters, especially those that take place in a second language, it is essential to recognize that all of us have been socialized in particular environments, which have given us ideas about what is acceptable (and unacceptable) behaviour in certain contexts. The socialization process guides us to react and interpret behaviours in specific ways. In intercultural interactions, it can be helpful to bear in mind that individuals with a different language and cultural background are usually not behaving in a particular way to deliberately annoy you! With more intercultural awareness and understanding, you can suspend your judgment and allow more time to figure out why someone is communicating in this way. You can also reflect more on how your own behaviour is being interpreted by others.

Property 6: Communication is situated and contextual

As Figure 4.1 illustrates, all communication takes place within a particular context or environment. In many ways, the context defines the meaning of any message as it impacts on the form and interpretation of both verbal and nonverbal communication. For Hall and Hall (2002: 166), **context** is 'the information that surrounds an event; it is inextricably bound up with the meaning of that event'.

In interactions, Cruse (2006: 35) regards the following contextual elements as essential to interpret utterances and expressions:

1   preceding and following utterances and/or expressions ('co-text')
2   the immediate physical situation
3   the wider situation
4   knowledge presumed shared between speaker and hearer.

Communication may be complicated, in part, due to different perceptions about what constitutes appropriate or polite behaviour in a particular context. Differing understandings of who should speak and what may be said can complicate intercultural interactions.

At the health clinic at my university in Hong Kong, for example, the context of the doctor's office dictates where the patient will sit (e.g. in a chair alongside the physician's desk) as well as the kind of communication that will occur (e.g. disclosure of medical problem following questions by the physician). In other words, a particular schema and cultural script are expected. When I lived in Egypt, I discovered that the cultural schema and script differed somewhat so I learned to adjust my expectations and behaviour accordingly.

In secondary schools in rural Malaysia, as in other parts of the world, students learn to expect certain roles and responsibilities of teachers and students. If the Malaysian students go on exchange to Australia, they may be quite surprised when they encounter differences (e.g. variations in classroom interaction patterns, a different teacher–student relationship and perhaps a more interactive, informal style of communication). In their home environment, they may have become accustomed to teachers asking nearly all of the questions in their English language lessons; in Australia, they may, initially, find it strange to be in a situation in which students ask many questions in class and also respond to the comments of other students in discussions. In effect, they are exposed to different cultural scripts and schema or 'cultures of learning', a notion that is discussed further in Chapter 8.

These examples illustrate the potential effect of the environment on communication. As Table 4.2 shows, there are many types of context and contextual elements that can influence the communication process (e.g. cultural/microcultural, environmental/physical, perceptual, psychological, (socio)relational, situational, temporal, etc.). The chart provides descriptors and examples of multiple contextual elements that can influence communication.

Table 4.2 Contexts that influence the communication process

Type of context	Descriptor	Examples
Cultural	All of the factors and influences that make up one's culture, that is, all the learned behaviours and social norms that affect interaction and hierarchy (e.g. status and positioning of the communicators)	If you have been socialized to believe it is rude to make direct eye contact with authority figures, out of politeness you likely avoid this. If your communication partner has been socialized to believe that direct eye contact signals trustworthiness and respect, there is the potential for misunderstanding
Environmental	The physical environs where you are communicating, including the location, distance between interactants, noise level, temperature, seating arrangement, technology, furniture, temperature, season, etc.	Communicating in a hot, noisy construction site differs from interaction that takes place in a quiet, air-conditioned office
Perceptual	The individual characteristics of the interactants: the motivations, intentions, and personality traits people bring to the communication event	When you are asking your professor for an extension for an overdue paper, you are apt to have a very different demeanour and intentions from when you are asking a close friend to go out for a bite to eat.
Physiological	The health, well-being, illness, and disabilities (e.g. hearing loss) of you and the other interactant(s)	Communicating with someone who is hearing impaired and feeling unwell differs from communicating with a healthy person who has excellent hearing
Psychological	Who you are and what you bring to the interaction, e.g., your needs, desires, values, personality, attitudes, feelings, emotion, perceptions, pressure, stress level, trauma, self-concept, views, bias, stereotypes, prejudice and prior experience	If you have an ethnocentric mindset, the way you communicate with someone from another culture may be disrespectful (intentionally or unintentionally)
Relational	The personal relationship between you and the other person (e.g. your history together, the feelings you and the other person have about each other and the relationship)	You are apt to be more guarded and less open when interacting with someone you do not trust. Past disagreements may affect current interactions

Table 4.2 continued

Type of context	Descriptor	Examples
Situational	The psycho-social environs, that is, the location where you are communicating	An interaction that takes place in the lecture theatre is very different from one that takes place in a karaoke lounge
Social	Power, hierarchy, the social relationship between you and the other person, social distance, cultural rules of behaviour, politeness norms, formality, history, relationship and gender	The power distance and social relationship between you and your professor differs from that of the power distance and social relationship between you and a close friend or family member
Sociorelational	Social roles and group memberships (e.g. demographics), age, gender, religious affiliation, education level, and socioeconomic status	The way you communicate with a monk or priest differs from the way you interact with a close friend of the same age, ethnicity and gender
Temporal	Time and timing of the interaction	The way you interact may differ depending on whether the interaction is at 5 am, noon, or midnight

N.B. 'You' refers to both participants (sender and receiver) in the communicative event

Property 7: Communication as pervasive

'We cannot not communicate' (Watzlawick *et al.* 1967: 49). This means that anytime you are perceived by another person, you are communicating messages about yourself and your emotions, even though they may be below your level of awareness. For example, the clothes you wear, your hairstyle, your tattoos or body piercings, your jewellery, your facial expressions, your body type (e.g. athletic), your body movements, your posture and your tone of voice are just some of the many ways in which you are conveying messages about yourself to others. (More elements are explored in Chapter 5 when we focus on nonverbal communication.)

Communication is a human endeavour. As communication is symbolic and continuous, it is impossible for us not to communicate, as Argyle and Trower (1979: 4) explain:

> If two humans come together it is virtually inevitable that they will communicate something to each other [. . .] even if they do not speak, messages will pass between them. By their looks, expressions and body movement each will tell the other something, even if it is only, "I don't wish to know you: keep your distance"; "I assure you the feeling is mutual. I'll keep clear if you do".

Because communication is a normal feature of everyday life, 'it is easy to take it for granted and even not to notice it' (Rogers & Steinfatt 1999: 113).

Property 8: Communication as power-infused

Although not always obvious, power influences the communication process. Communication is rarely between individuals with the same amount of power and prestige. In most interactions, it is the person (or persons) with more power and status who determines how the communication process unfolds (e.g. which language or dialect is used, the communication style that is accorded more respect, who speaks for longer). As Martin and Nakayama (2008) explain, individuals in power 'consciously or unconsciously, create and maintain communication systems that reflect, reinforce, and promote their own ways of thinking and communicating' (p. 48).

When people from different linguistic and cultural backgrounds interact they do not share an equal **power status**. As Kubota (2012: 97) explains, 'actual intercultural interactions are largely influenced by where one is positioned in the power hierarchy in terms of race, ethnicity, gender, age, language, physical ableness, sexual identity, and other social categories'. One's accent, adaptive ability, communication style, nationality and other characteristics (e.g. personal, social, cultural) may also impact on one's degree of power or positioning in a communicative event. Therefore, in intercultural interactions it is incumbent on us to be mindful of 'whose communication styles, both verbal and nonverbal communication, and whose behaviors are seen as "normal" as well as how communication is used to marginalize and exclude' (Sorrells 2013: 232).

In many contexts around the world, women struggle for respect when communicating in a male-dominated environment, as their language use and speech style may differ from those of men in power. In the United States, sociolinguist Deborah Tannen (2001) claims that girls are socialized to believe that 'talk is the glue that holds relationships together' (p. 85); consequently, women tend to engage in '**rapport-talk**', that is, in conversations they 'try to seek and give confirmation and support, and to reach consensus' (p. 25). In contrast, boys learn to view conversations as '**report-talk**' (e.g. the transmission of information) and, as men, they negotiate to maintain the upper hand in verbal interactions in order to protect their status or authority (Tannen 2001: 24). As women try to advance in society (e.g. move up the corporate ladder), they may feel pressured to conform to the dominant, male-oriented styles of communication and, even if they do, they may be regarded as 'bitchy' or overly aggressive (Tannen 2001). While this is certainly changing as women gain more equality, these barriers are still an issue in many contexts.

Minority group members may also face similar obstacles in communicative events involving people from the majority culture. As they struggle to have their voices heard, they may feel disrespected and disempowered by those who have a more prestigious accent and style of communication, and other characteristics that are valued in that context. Individuals and groups can resist (e.g. withdraw, avoid interacting with 'outgroup' members except when absolutely necessary, use their first language) but, in the process, they may be sidelined and have fewer opportunities to advance.

In intercultural encounters, the use of a particular language or language variety is often power-laden. For example, if you speak English as a first language and are conversing with someone who is not fluent in the language, you clearly have an advantage. You can speak more quickly, make jokes and employ a much wider range of vocabulary and verb tenses without much effort. Your communication partner, however, may not fully understand your accent or the vocabulary that you use and, in particular, may have trouble making sense of idioms, slang, sarcasm and humour. Your rapid rate of speech and communication style may also pose a challenge. All of these factors make the communication process more challenging and exhausting for a second language speaker who is not proficient in the language. In situations like this, your higher level of confidence and facility in the language accord you more power and prestige, although you may be unaware of this.

Learning another language can enable you to appreciate what it is like to struggle to express one's ideas and emotions in a second language. It can help you to become a more empathetic communicator, who is sensitive to the needs of the receiver. Becoming bilingual or multilingual can also open up more possibilities to communicate with people from diverse linguistic and cultural backgrounds.

Property 9: Communication as cultural

As noted in Chapter 3, culture shapes communication (and vice versa). 'Communication and culture are so closely bound together that virtually all communication engaged in by humans is culturally linked' (Prosser 1976: 417). Through **enculturation**, the process of primary language and cultural socialization, we learn how to communicate in ways that are deemed appropriate in our culture. Even if we do not always follow prevailing norms of communication in our home environment, we are familiar with them as we are continuously exposed to them in daily life. The verbal and nonverbal symbols we use to communicate with our 'ingroup' members (e.g. close friends and family members, people who share the same language, ethnicity and religion) are strongly influenced by our linguistic and cultural socialization. 'The way people communicate is the way they live. It is their culture. Who talks with whom? How? And about what? These are questions of communication and culture' (Smith 1966:1). For these reasons, Hall (1976) refers to communication as 'internalized culture' (p. 69).

People from different linguistic and cultural backgrounds have been socialized to communicate in different ways (e.g. use specific styles of communication). Through the process of enculturation, we learn to view and communicate in ways that follow conventions or norms that are prevalent in specific contexts in our culture (e.g. expressions of politeness, cultural scripts).

In intercultural communication, one of the most obvious communication differences may be language, as one or both of the speakers in an intercultural event is likely using a second language (or different dialect) to communicate. According to the weaker version of the **Sapir-Whorf hypothesis**, which was discussed in Chapter 2, the use of language is affected by culture. '**Linguistic relativity**', the weaker version of the hypothesis, posits that the language one speaks influences our thinking patterns and, at least potentially, our communicative behaviour (Holmes 2001). In other words, how we view or see the world is influenced by the grammar or structure of our language (e.g. lack of the future tense will affect how we understand and express this dimension).

LoCastro (2003) explains the connection between worldview, language, thought, culture and communication:

> the linguistic social action of speakers of a particular language mirror the underlying worldview of the speakers; manifestations of the cultural models of thought are embedded in talk both in the micro features and at the macro level. The list of micro behaviors includes prosodic features, listener behavior, turn-taking, conversational routines, constituents of an activity type, conventional indirectness, nonverbal cues, and speech act realizations.
> (p. 227)

Even members of different cultural groups who speak the same language may have different worldviews and values. They may associate different meanings with the same verbal and nonverbal symbols and this of course affects the communication process. For example, although English is the dominant language spoken in the United States and Britain, many words and phrases have different meanings in American and British English; there are also differences between the languages with regard to pronunciation, punctuation and spelling. The British have a variety of colloquialisms or slang not well understood by Americans and vice versa. English has been acquired and shaped in different cultural environments and this has led to variations in the language.

Today, English is an international language with many varieties around the world (e.g. Indian English, Nigerian English, Singaporean English) and, as one might expect, among World Englishes, there are many differences in pronunciation, punctuation, spelling and idiomatic expressions. Local cultural elements, including other languages in use, influence the way each variety has developed over time. In addition, culture influences the style of communication that is used in different contexts (e.g. degree of directness).

Culture also impacts on nonverbal communication. Nonverbal symbols, gestures and perceptions of personal space and time vary significantly from culture to culture. In Canada, for example, adults of the same sex who are not romantically involved with each other generally stand about two-and-a-half feet, or an arm's length, away from each other when communicating. In many Middle Eastern cultures, people from the same sex stand closer to one another when interacting. In the Sultanate of Oman, two male friends walking together may hold hands

Plate 4.4 These Chinese women demonstrate their friendship by walking arm in arm © Jane Jackson

as a sign of trust and solidarity. In China, two female friends may do the same. If one is unfamiliar with this behaviour, it is easy to jump to the wrong conclusions and misinterpret what you are seeing (e.g. assume that the individuals are gay). As Schmidt *et al.* (2007: 61) explain, 'even it were possible to send a message without any cultural influences, the receiver will automatically interpret it through the filter of their own cultural conditioning'. (See Chapter 5 for a more in-depth discussion of nonverbal communication and its implications for intercultural relations.)

In sum, much of communication is influenced by the linguistic and cultural socialization process in one's home environment. Through enculturation, we become habituated to expect certain verbal and nonverbal behaviour in specific situations and contexts. To complicate matters, while many of our messages are sent intentionally, many others (e.g. nonverbal messages) are unintentionally influencing how others view us.

LANGUAGE, CULTURE AND VERBAL COMMUNICATION STYLES

So far, we have examined several properties of communication and core elements in the communication process. Many interculturalists maintain that our preferred ways of communicating are influenced by our cultural background and the language(s) we speak, that is, each of us is affected by enculturation. Let's take a look at variations in speech and communication styles and their potential implications for intercultural interactions.

Styles of speech

Linguistic style refers to an individual's 'characteristic speaking pattern', which includes such features as degree of directness or indirectness, pacing and pausing, word choice and the use of such elements as jokes, sarcasm, figures of speech (e.g. metaphors, irony, hyperbole), stories, questions, silence and apologies (Tannen 1995). For Deborah Tannen (1995), a sociolinguist who has written widely on gender, language, culture, power and communication, linguistic style is 'a set of culturally learned signals by which we not only communicate what we mean but also interpret others' meaning and evaluate one another as people' (Tannen 1995: 139). Hence, one's **speech style** is made up of choices regarding a wide range of linguistic elements (e.g. vocabulary, syntactic patterns, volume, pace, pitch, register, intonation).

While studying speech styles in the U.S., Tannen (1995, 1996, 2001) concluded that gender differences are built into language: 'because boys and girls grow up in what are essentially different cultures ... talk between women and men is cross-cultural communication' (Tannen 2001: 18). In her work, she attributed linguistic variations to the primary socialization process and culturally-embedded notions of gender. 'Each person's life is a series of conversations, and simply by understanding and using the words of our language, we all absorb and pass on different, asymmetrical assumptions about men and women' (Tannen 2001: 243).

Tannen's publications drew attention to gender variations in linguistic styles in interpersonal communication and their potential impact on gender relations, power relations and intercultural relationships. Shi and Langman (2012: 169), however, caution that

> all research that examines "women" and "men" as members of groups will invariably lead to stereotyping of behavior and essentializing of the categories of "men" and "women" in

ways that assume that there are no differences among women as a whole, and men as a whole, and, in contrast, vast differences between women and men.

(Notions of gender, identity, and stereotyping are discussed further in Chapters 6 and 7.)

Communication accommodation theory (CAT)

Language and social psychologists are also interested in the relationship between language, speech behaviours and culture. Howard Giles and his associates have developed the **communication accommodation theory (CAT)** to describe and explain why individuals modify their speech communication practices depending on who they are talking to. More specifically, this framework explores the reasons for, and consequences arising from, speakers *converging* toward and *diverging* away from each other (Giles & Ogay 2006; Giles *et al.* 2012). CAT has received empirical support when examined in diverse languages and cultures, as well as in applied intercultural settings and electronic interaction (see Gallois *et al.* 2005).

To win approval, speakers often accommodate their speech to that of their addressee through the act of **convergence**. More specifically, individuals sometimes shift their style of speech (e.g. adjust their speech rate, accent, content) to become more similar to that of their addressees in order to emphasize solidarity and reduce **social distance** (the degree of closeness or separation between groups) (Giles & Ogay 2006). Convergent moves are generally received favourably by recipients and this satisfaction may then generalize to more positive feelings about the entire culture or group to which the converger belongs (Gallois & Callan 1997).

Conversely, speakers may choose to maintain their style of speech to emphasize their affiliation with their ingroup and differentiate themselves from the addressee (or a particular group). By accentuating language (and cultural) differences, this strategy of **divergence** (e.g. switching to an ethnic dialect or language when speaking to a host national) leads to an increase in social distance (Giles *et al.* 2012). Such moves are often viewed negatively by communication partners and taken rather personally.

In sum, this social psychological theory of language and social interaction posits that style shifts in intercultural discourse may have consequences for interpersonal relations, with the act of convergence bringing interactants closer together, and divergence having the opposite effect. (CAT is discussed further in Chapter 6 in relation to identity and language use.)

Speech style as audience design

A related theory of speech style has been developed by Allan Bell, a sociolinguist in New Zealand. For this scholar, **speech style** is 'the dimension of language where individual speakers have a choice' (Bell 2007: 95). He explains:

> We do not always speak in consistently the same way. In fact we are shifting the way we speak constantly as we move from one situation to another. On different occasions we talk in different ways. These different ways of speaking carry different social meanings. They represent our ability to take up different social positions, and they affect how we are perceived by others.
>
> (Bell 2007: 95)

Relevant to this discussion is the sociolinguistic term **style shifting**, which refers to the process of adjusting or changing from one style of speech to another (Eckert & Rickford 2001). Most typically, style shifts are automatic or unconscious reactions to a situation, an audience, or a topic, although they may also be deliberate. For example, a speaker may intentionally switch to another dialect or style of speech to enhance social relations (e.g. lessen the distance between herself and her listener). **Code-switching** involves changing between different languages, whereas style shifting occurs within the same language.

In an effort to explain observed variations in speech styles, Bell (1984, 2002, 2007) developed the '**audience design framework**'. The main elements are summarized as follows.

1 Style is what an individual speaker does with a language in relation to other people.
2 Style derives its meaning from the association of linguistic features with particular social groups. The social evaluation of a group is transferred to the linguistic features associated with that group.
3 Speakers design their style primarily for and in response to their audience. (This aspect relates to the notions of 'convergence' and 'divergence' in the communication accommodation theory.)
4 Audience design applies to all codes and levels of a language repertoire, monolingual and multilingual.
5 Style variations in speech between different social groups are normally greater than differences within individual speakers of a particular group.
6 Speakers are able to design or adjust their style of speech for a range of different addresses.
7 Style shifts according to topic or setting derive their meaning and direction of shift from the underlying association of topics or settings with typical audience members.
8 A style shift in language initiates a change in the situation, that is, language helps shape the situation.
9 The linguistic features associated with a group can be used to express affiliation with that group. An individual may employ a particular style or language variety to demonstrate a sense of belonging to another group.

(adapted from Bell 2007: 97–8)

The CAT and the 'audience design framework' both indicate that speakers may make choices about their speech styles that can influence interpersonal, intercultural relations (e.g. bring individuals closer together or pull them further apart). It is also necessary to bear in mind that power relations, positioning and situational/contextual constraints can limit one's choices.

Communication style

While linguistic style focuses on patterns of language use, the term 'communication style' is more broad. Saphiere *et al.* (2005) define **communication style** as 'the way in which we communicate, a pattern of verbal and nonverbal behaviors that comprises our *preferred ways* of giving and receiving information in a specific situation' (p. 5) (emphasis added). More specifically, for Barnlund (1975: 14–15), communication style refers to

the topics people prefer to discuss, their favorite forms of interaction – ritual, repartee, argument, self-disclosure – and the depth of involvement they demand of each other. It includes the extent to which communicants rely upon the same channels – vocal, verbal, physical – for conveying information, and the extent to which they are tuned to the same level of meaning, that is, to the factual or emotional content of messages.

For Zhu Hua (2011: 419), communication style is simply 'the way individuals or a group of individuals communicate with others'. In other words, 'if the message content is the *what* and the communicators the *who*, then communication style is the *how*' (Saphiere *et al.* 2005: 5).

Our preferred ways of communicating include **speech style preferences**, that is, the speech we are most comfortable using in interactions. One's communication style and speech style preferences impact on how we behave in communicative events, including intercultural encounters. In particular, our communication style may influence:

1   how we organize and present information (e.g. how we structure an argument to persuade others of our viewpoint or position)
2   how we give praise and how we react to receiving praise (e.g. how often we give compliments, the ways in which we compliment others, how we respond when someone compliments us)
3   the timing and manner of **self-disclosure** (the sharing of personal details that our listeners would not normally know about us) and how we respond to the personal information that others reveal to us
4   how we express agreement or disagreement and how we respond to the way our interactant communicates agreement or disagreement to us
5   how we build interpersonal relationships (e.g. develop a close connection with others, establish intimacy with a romantic partner, build trust with someone from another linguistic and cultural background)
6   how we convey politeness (and impoliteness) (e.g. our use of discourse markers or expressions of politeness) and how we perceive politeness (impoliteness) in the communicative actions of others
7   how we negotiate (e.g. mediate conflict situations) and respond to the negotiation or conflict management style of our interactant, e.g. our willingness to adjust the way we communicate, that is, our willingness to converge in negotiations to reach an amicable settlement (conflict negotiation strategies are discussed in Chapter 10)
8   how we make decisions and solve problems or disputes, and how we respond to the problem-solving approach of others
9   how and when we interrupt and prefer to be interrupted (and how often) as well as how we respond to being interrupted
10 how we apologize and make requests or refusals (and other speech acts) and how we respond to the speech acts of others in various contexts and situations.

(adapted from Saphiere *et al.* 2005: 5)

Communication styles differ, in varying degrees, in diverse linguistic and cultural settings as each of us becomes accustomed to expressing ourselves in particular ways during the socialization process. Over time, we learn to expect certain patterns of communication (e.g. cultural scripts, cultural schema) in particular settings (e.g. in the doctor's office, in the classroom, in a restaurant). Through enculturation, we learn norms of social discourse and preferred ways of interacting with others, taking into account such aspects as social status, age, gender, power and positioning.

High-context vs. low-context communication

The anthropologist E.T. Hall (1976, 1983) drew attention to the influence of culture on communication styles and categorized cultures into two broad types: 'high-context' and 'low-context'. For Hall (1983), context features and communication styles among cultures are closely correlated with the cultural dimensions of **individualism** and **collectivism**. On the individualism–collectivism continuum, collectivist cultures, to varying degrees, emphasize the following traits: 'community, collaboration, shared interest, harmony, tradition, the public good, and maintaining face' (Anderson *et al.* 2003: 77). In contrast, individualistic cultures place more emphasis on 'personal rights and responsibilities, privacy, voicing one's opinion, freedom, innovation, and self-expression' (Anderson *et al.* 2003: 77).

High-context culture is characterized by 'pre-programmed information that is in the receiver and in the setting, with only minimal information in the transmitted message' (Hall 1976: 101). In other words, most of the information is communicated through indirect and nonverbal means with a reliance on mutually shared knowledge. In this form of communication, the context, 'the information that surrounds an event', is 'inextricably bound up with the meaning of that event' (Hall & Hall 2002: 166). In **indirect communication**, implicit verbal messages, subtle nonverbal behaviours (e.g. pauses, silences, the use of space, gestures, and avoidance of eye contact) are frequently employed to convey ideas.

High-context communication occurs in cultures that stress communication through 'the context of the social interaction' (e.g. the speakers' social roles, gender, age, status, and other cultural elements) and 'the physical environment in which the interaction is taking place' (DeCapua & Wintergerst 2004: 71). Attention is paid to the relationship between individuals and the need to maintain harmony. Hall (1981) found this style of communication common in 'collectivist-oriented' nations such as China, Japan, Kuwait, Mexico, Nigeria, Saudi Arabia, South Korea and Vietnam.

By contrast, in **low-context cultures**, explicit verbal messages are the norm: 'Most of the information must be in the transmitted message in order to make up for what is missing in the context' (Hall 1976: 101). Therefore, 'a large amount of information is explicitly communicated through direct, specific, and literal expressions' (Sorrells 2013: 262). In **direct communication**, the speaker's intentions and views are made clear by the use of clear, direct speech and a forthright tone of voice. Opinions and desires are stated directly and clarity in speech is admired. Individuals who have been socialized in a low-context culture are more accustomed to people 'speaking their mind' or 'telling it like it is'.

Although the context (e.g. sociocultural, physical) also influences the communication process in low-context cultures, 'the primary responsibility for ensuring that listeners correctly receive and interpret verbal messages rests on speakers' (DeCapua & Wintergerst 2004: 71). To try to ensure that sent messages are interpreted as intended, speakers employ elaborate, direct verbal modes of communication. Hall (1976) claims that low-context communication styles are most common in more 'individualistic-oriented' nations, e.g. Australia, Canada, Denmark, Germany, the U.K., the U.S., Switzerland and Sweden.

What are the implications for intercultural communication? In a low-context culture, much of the information in interactions is expressed verbally, as directness, precision, clarity and lack of ambiguity are valued. To someone from a high-context culture, receiving very detailed information may make the individual feel as if she is being treated as a child. Conversely, when interacting with someone from a high-context culture, individuals who have been socialized in a low-context culture may fail to understand subtle messages that are being transmitted (e.g. through the tone of voice, silence). Initially, interactions between low-context and high-context communicators may be frustrating and lead to mistrust and anxiety until the individuals develop more understanding of variations in communication styles.

Limitations of communication style typologies

Many interculturalists (e.g. Bill Gudykunst, Y.Y. Kim, Stella Ting-Toomey) have been greatly influenced by E.T. Hall's continuum of high- and low-context styles of communication and it is still widely referred to in intercultural communication texts and other publications. While this framework provides a general, broad indication of communication styles and patterns that are common in particular contexts, we must be cautious and not assume that everyone in a particular part of the world behaves in certain ways. For example, not all Japanese favour indirect styles of communication, just as not all Germans have a very direct style of communication. Not all Chinese business executives prefer a formal style of communication in meetings, just as not all American executives adopt an informal style in their meetings. The degree of directness and formality may vary among individuals.

People may also favour one communication style over another in particular situations (e.g. use more indirect communication with family members and more direct communication in the workplace). For these reasons, Saphiere *et al.* (2005) also have misgivings about 'an oversimplified relationship portrayed between high context and indirect communication and between low context and direct communication' (p. 263). While communication typologies may help us to make sense of the ways people interact in our own and other environments, they are limiting.

Our communication style preferences reflect not only our linguistic and cultural socialization, but our individual, personal preferences and unique experiences. While much of our language use and nonverbal behaviours are learned through enculturation, each of us makes creative use of language and speech/communication styles. Consequently, there is tension between scholars who classify cultural groups into categories, especially large groups such as nations or ethnic groups, and critical scholars (e.g. Dervin 2012; Holliday 2012; Moon 2008, 2010) who argue that it is too easy to essentialize cultural groups and overlook individual variations. (Reductionism and stereotyping are discussed further in Chapter 7, while the use and limitations of 'cultural difference' frameworks are explored in Chapter 11.)

CHARACTERISTICS OF AN EFFECTIVE INTERCULTURAL COMMUNICATOR IN SECOND LANGUAGE SITUATIONS

In intercultural interactions, you may find yourself in situations where you are using your first language to communicate with someone from a different linguistic and cultural background. The following are some suggestions to become an effective intercultural communicator in such situations:

1 Be patient. Allow more time for the interaction.
2 Try to avoid the use of idioms that may be easily misunderstood; bear in mind that jokes and sarcasm often do not translate well across cultures.
3 Pay attention to the content meaning of the messages you are sending and receiving.
4 Be aware of your rate of speech and speak more slowly *if* this appears to help your listener.

5 To gauge how your message is being received, be attentive to the other person's verbal and nonverbal behaviour (feedback). Remember, that you are also sending messages nonverbally, which may not be interpreted in the way you expect.

6 Whenever feasible, use culture-sensitive probing questions to check to see if your message has been understood in the way that you intended.

7 Listen attentively and pay attention to both verbal and nonverbal messages of your communication partner before responding.

8 Be mindful of the power dynamics and their potential impact on intercultural relations and the communication process (e.g. the advantages you may have as a first language speaker).

9 Be sensitive to the benefits of convergence and the potential negative consequences of divergence in terms of your speech/communication style and language choice.

10 Be sensitive to the cultural beliefs, values, gender differences and politeness norms that may underlie different styles of communication. Remember that all of us have been socialized to expect certain speech/communication styles and cultural scripts in particular situations although we may not always adhere to these norms.

11 Recognize your personal style of communicating and make an effort to determine how your communication partners are perceiving you. Effective intercultural communication requires a high level of self-awareness and listener sensitivity.

12 To further enhance interpersonal, intercultural relations, build up your repertoire of communication styles (e.g. familiarity with direct-indirect, formal-informal communication strategies). Adapting your communication style to put your interactant at ease may help you to create a positive impression and facilitate your communication.

13 Bear in mind that miscommunication may be due to language barriers rather than cultural difference (and vice versa).

While these strategies have been suggested with second language situations in mind, many may also enhance your interaction with people who share your first language but differ from you in terms of age, gender, religion, etc. As a sensitive and respectful intercultural communicator, you can take steps to reduce the power gap and cultivate more equitable, satisfying relationships. (Throughout the text, more suggestions are offered to enhance intercultural relations; Chapter 12 examines core elements in intercultural (communicative) competence.)

SUMMARY

Communication is a complex, dynamic process, which entails the encoding and decoding of verbal and nonverbal messages within a particular cultural, physiological, sociorelational and perceptual environment. As well as multiple dimensions of context, the relationship between culture and communication is complex and influenced by many factors (historical relations, gender, language, power, etc.). An understanding of the elements in the communication process and the potential impact of variations in speech/communication styles can help you to become a more effective, listener-sensitive, intercultural communicator. It can enhance your interpersonal, intercultural relationships and communication in second language situations.

discussion questions

1   Offer a definition of human communication. Identify and explain the basic elements of communication to a classmate.
2   Describe the relationship between language, culture and power.
3   Why is context important in any discussion of language, culture and power?
4   Do you agree with Frederico Fellini (1920–93), an Italian film director and writer, that 'a different language is a different vision of life'? Why or why not?
5   How can knowledge of the communication process help you become a more effective intercultural communicator?
6   With regard to intercultural interactions, why does Ingrid Piller (2012) caution us 'not to mistake language problems for cultural problems' (p. 11)?
7   With a partner, identify five strategies to employ to become a more effective intercultural communicator, especially in situations where one of the communicators is not fluent in the language being used.
8   Describe your style of communication. Does it vary depending on the context? If yes, how? How might this knowledge enhance your intercultural interactions?
9   Why do Saphiere *et al.* (2005) say that typologies of communication styles are 'useful, yet limiting'? Do you agree? Why or why not?
10 Think about an intercultural interaction in a second language that did not go well. After reading this chapter, what might you do differently if you found yourself in a similar situation?

further reading

Bonvillain, N. (2011) *Language, Culture and Communication,* 6th edn, Upper Saddle River, NJ: Prentice Hall.

Using data from cultures and languages throughout the world, this book explores the connections between language, culture and communicative meaning.

Brown, S. and Eisterhold, J. (2004) *Topics in Language and Culture for Teachers,* Ann Arbor, MI: University of Michigan Press.

This introductory language and culture text is designed for future teachers, anthropologists and applied linguists. From a variety of perspectives, the book explores the interrelationships between language and culture that have the most significant implications for the classroom and wider, global community.

Kramsch, C. (1998) *Language and Culture,* Oxford: Blackwell.

This compact book offers an accessible survey of key language concepts such as social context and cultural authenticity, using insights from such fields as linguistics, sociology, and anthropology.

Saphiere, D.H., Mikk, B.K. and Devries, B.I. (2005) *Communication Highwire: Leveraging the Power of Diverse Communication Styles*, Yarmouth, ME: Intercultural Press.

The authors introduce the notion of communication styles and explain how communication style preferences reflect our personal and cultural upbringing, and also vary depending on the context and cultural setting.

CHAPTER 5

Language and nonverbal communication

Fie, fie upon her!
There's language in her eye, her cheek, her lip,
Nay, her foot speaks; her wanton spirits look out
At every joint and motive of her body.

William Shakespeare

When the eyes say one thing, and the tongue another, a practiced man relies on the language of the first.

(Ralph Waldo Emerson 1930: 118)

learning objectives

By the end of this chapter, you should be able to:

1 define nonverbal communication
2 describe the relationship between verbal and nonverbal communication
3 identify the characteristics and functions of nonverbal communication
4 identify different types of nonverbal codes
5 provide examples of cultural universals in nonverbal behaviours
6 explain the influence of culture on nonverbal communication
7 discuss the relationship between nonverbal communication and power
8 explain the importance of nonverbal elements in intercultural communication
9 describe the relationship between nonverbal communication and gender
10 explain how nonverbal communication can be a barrier in intercultural interactions.

INTRODUCTION

Learning to communicate effectively and appropriately in intercultural interactions requires knowledge of both verbal and nonverbal code systems. Just as our verbal behaviours (e.g. language use, linguistic norms of politeness) are influenced by the cultural socialization process that was described in Chapter 3, many of our nonverbal actions (e.g. use of space, gestures, volume of speech) are affected by our linguistic and cultural background.

In this chapter, we begin by delving into the nature and importance of nonverbal communication, and then examine the relationship between verbal and nonverbal communication and consider how they differ. Discussion then centres on the characteristics and functions of nonverbal communication. Next, we review various types of nonverbal codes and discuss the influence of culture on nonverbal behaviour, drawing attention to universal nonverbal cues as well as cultural variability. We then discuss the implications of the nonverbal expectancy violation theory for intercultural communication. The chapter concludes with a discussion of practical ways to enhance the nonverbal dimension of intercultural interactions.

THE NATURE AND IMPORTANCE OF NONVERBAL COMMUNICATION

As noted by Matsumoto and Hwang (2012: 130), 'no discussion of communication is complete without the inclusion of nonverbal behaviors'. First, it is helpful to review definitions of nonverbal communication and nonverbal behaviour. While many scholars use these terms interchangeably, there are differences between them that are useful to note. We begin by looking at how nonverbal communication is conceptualized.

Definitions of nonverbal communication and nonverbal behaviour

Similar to verbal communication, there are multiple definitions of **nonverbal communication**. Liu *et al.* (2011: 139) refer to it simply as 'communication without using words' or 'the use of non-spoken symbols to communicate a message'. For Hickson *et al.* (2004), the nonverbal dimension of communication is

> that aspect of the communication process that deals with the transmission and reception of messages that are not a part of the natural language systems . . . Any aspect of communication that does *not* include words is considered part of the nonverbal code.
>
> (pp. 8–9)

For Samovar *et al.* (2010), nonverbal communication involves 'all those nonverbal stimuli in a communication setting that are generated by both the source and his or her use of the environment and that have potential message value for the source or receiver' (p. 246). This definition draws attention to the boundaries of nonverbal communication and points to the process involved, which may include both intentional and unintentional messages.

Nonverbal communication often occurs through the interaction of the speaker (dress, voice, distance maintained), the receiver (posture, facial expression, distance kept from the speaker) and the situation as perceived by the interactants (the social context, the environment, the time of the interaction). With this in view, Hickson *et al.* (2004: 482) depict nonverbal communication as 'a process whereby people, through the intentional or unintentional manipulation of normative actions and expectations, express experiences, feelings and attitudes in order to relate to and control themselves, others, and their environments'.

What all of these definitions of nonverbal communication have in common is the notion that nonverbal acts are communicating a message, whether on purpose or not. The perception of some form of intent is sufficient for a nonverbal act to be deemed communication. 'Nonverbal communication occurs when a message is decoded (or interpreted) as having some meaning, *regardless of the sender's intent* (Hickson *et al.* 2004: 11–12) (emphasis in original). Since 'people who are behaving are not necessarily communicating', Hickson *et al.* (2004) distinguish between the terms nonverbal behaviour and nonverbal communication. For these nonverbal specialists, the former may consist of body movements or other nonverbal acts that are not intended to send a message and where no message is interpreted by others. For example, you may scratch your arm, bend over or squint and not aim to communicate any thoughts or ideas to others, and no particular message is interpreted by those around you. This chapter is concerned with acts of nonverbal communication, whether intentional or not.

Importance of nonverbal communication

Why study nonverbal communication? Some scholars believe that it is the single most powerful form of communication. Psychologist Albert Mehrabian (1982), for example, estimated that 93 per cent of meaning is conveyed through nonverbal communication channels (e.g. body movements, facial expressions, vocal qualities). More recently, researchers have suggested that this figure is an overestimation (Matsumoto & Hwang 2012; Moore *et al.* 2010). Even so, most agree that a significant amount of our communication is nonverbal, noting that nonverbal acts are a better indicator of the true meaning than the actual words.

Many nonverbal acts are **innate** (existing in one from birth) and **universal**, that is, people in different cultures share a similar understanding of particular cues. Other elements and dimensions of nonverbal communication vary depending on the cultural context. Considering the significance of **nonverbal codes** (all symbols that are not words, e.g. bodily movements, use of space and time, clothing and adornments and sounds other than words), intercultural communication studies are needed in a variety of contexts that consider nonverbal acts, both alone and in connection with verbal communication.

THE RELATIONSHIP BETWEEN VERBAL AND NONVERBAL COMMUNICATION

When individuals interact face-to-face, their communication may consist of verbal and/or nonverbal components. Verbal communication typically includes sound, words, speaking and language. In the transmission of messages, nonverbal codes often interact with verbal codes. For example, gestures and **facial expressions** (facial motions that convey one's emotional state) may accompany words, and language use may vary with regard to such aspects as accent, rate, tone and volume of speech, all of which are considered nonverbal features. Both verbal and nonverbal codes may communicate meaning together or separately, as Hickson *et al.* (2004: 9) explain:

> Nonverbal communication is complex because it creates communication by use of non-verbal behaviors, either by themselves or combined with words. It may be shared *between* people (interpersonally) or *within* a person (intrapersonally). It may be intentional or unintentional. It may also be used without words, or it may take on meaning only when it is used in combination with words. (emphasis in the original)

Both verbal and nonverbal channels of communication consist of symbols and patterns that are learned over time. Just as different societies and cultures may have different languages or dialects, some of their nonverbal codes and norms of behaviour (e.g. accepted patterns or rules) may vary across cultures and differ depending on the context and situation.

During the **primary socialization** process, children develop the ability to appropriately use and interpret verbal and nonverbal cues in a particular cultural context. As they mature, they acquire their first language (and perhaps others), that is, they learn the meanings of words and expressions along with rules of verbal communication (e.g. the politeness norms of speech, cultural scripts for greetings/requests/refusals, grammar rules). Over time, children also become more aware of multiple forms of nonverbal cues and learn the norms for nonverbal behaviour (e.g. emotional display, use of space) that are prevalent in various situations in their environment. In contrast with language learning, however, most of the learning of nonverbal cues is implicit. While children may learn some grammar rules and vocabulary through formal language education, they learn how to use and interpret nearly all nonverbal cues by observing and imitating the actions of others rather than through direct instruction.

Many communication specialists maintain that nonverbal communication is more important than verbal communication in face-to-face situations. Why might this be the case? Even if adults are not aware they are doing so, they continuously use and observe nonverbal cues (e.g. eye movements, posture, facial expressions) and form judgments about speakers and their messages (verbal and nonverbal), drawing on what they have learned during the socialization process. (This aspect is discussed further when we turn our attention to the nonverbal expectancy violation theory.)

Nonverbal communication specialists Mark Hickson, Don Sacks and Nina-jo Moore explain that 'most verbal communication carries with it a greater amount of intent, but nonverbal communication tends to be more primitive and less controllable than its verbal counterpart' (Hickson *et al.* 2004: 11–12). As people are thought to have less control over their nonverbal actions, adults generally consider the nonverbal message to be more truthful and accurate when contradictory messages are sent through verbal and nonverbal channels. Children, however, typically rely on verbal expressions for meaning as they have not yet developed the ability to interpret nonverbal acts and read between the lines. With less awareness of nonverbal cues, young children tend to depend on the literal meaning of words and are generally more trusting of the verbal message.

FUNCTIONS OF NONVERBAL COMMUNICATION

Nonverbal communication can serve a number of functions. While many messages are conveyed nonverbally without the awareness of the senders, in other situations, nonverbal messages are intentional and purposeful. Individuals can choose to send nonverbal messages in many different forms in order to convey specific meanings in a range of situations. Some nonverbal functions are associated with verbal forms of communication (oral or written), while others do not involve words. To communicate effectively, whether in **intracultural interactions** (the exchange of messages between people who share the same cultural background) or intercultural situations, it is helpful to be aware of the various functions of nonverbal communication.

Self-presentation

We routinely use nonverbal signals to let other people know who we are, that is, we convey aspects of our identities and personality through nonverbal means. We disclose information about ourselves through our physical appearance, our tone of voice, our posture, our mode of dress and our adornments (e.g. body piercings, tattoos, makeup). We also reveal personal dimensions of ourselves (e.g. our personality, degree of openness, values) through our use of time, body odour, use of space, the ways we decorate our homes (or dorm rooms) and many other nonverbal means.

At times, our nonverbal behaviour is intentionally designed to manage the impressions that others have of us. For example, the outfit you wear to a job interview may be carefully selected to send a message to the interviewer about your maturity, sense of responsibility and seriousness. When you go out on a date, your clothes and accessories may be chosen to showcase your personality, emphasize your best features and convey your interest in your romantic partner. Whether intentional or not, every day we continuously convey information about ourselves through nonverbal channels. This means we can also learn a great deal about others by paying close attention to the way they present themselves nonverbally.

Conveying relationship messages

Through nonverbal means we indicate our relationship with others, whether we realize it or not. We demonstrate how well we know or feel about someone through our facial expressions (e.g. smile, frown, raised eyebrows), speech qualities (e.g. loud voice, aggressive tone), how closely we stand or sit by him or her and so on. For example, in some cultural settings we may walk arm in arm with a romantic partner and when sitting, we may lean forward and frequently touch each other as we chat. We may also convey intimacy by using a soft tone of voice and whispering into each other's ears. Conversely, we may reveal our distrust, dislike or lack of interest in another person through other nonverbal actions, such as avoiding **eye contact** (not looking at his or her eyes), folding our arms, leaning away from him or her when talking and keeping a large physical distance between us when standing.

Nonverbal communication can also indicate and reinforce the power dimension in relationships. For example, in a work situation, an employer may stand further away from her employees than she would her close friends; to emphasize her authority, she may also talk in a louder, more assertive voice with subordinates. In a formal dinner, seating/serving arrangements may also nonverbally communicate status and **power** (authority or strength). At a formal banquet in Mainland China, for example, the attendees may gather at a round table and sit in assigned places according to their status; the guest with the highest rank is usually positioned to the right of the host and is the first person to be offered a serving from the communal dishes. In a similar event in Canada, the attendees may sit at an oblong table and be served individual dishes. The guest with the highest position is usually seated next to the host at the head of the table and is the first to be served; the other attendees may sit anywhere they like regardless of rank or status. When guests are expecting certain formalities and conventions, it can be confusing when different procedures are followed in other cultural settings. Unintentionally, hosts may not display the degree of respect and formality that guests have become accustomed to in their home environment and if individuals are not flexible, relationships can be put in jeopardy.

Replacing verbal messages

Nonverbal messages can also be used as a substitute for verbal messages. For example, instead of verbally telling students to be quiet, a primary teacher may simply hold a finger to her lips and as long as the students understand this gesture (and are willing to comply), this simple action may be quite effective.

In some situations, using words to communicate may simply not be a viable option. When conducting an orchestra in a concert hall, for example, a conductor uses gestures (e.g. hand movements) to convey messages to a large number of musicians. If there is a major event at your university, the campus police may use hand signals to direct traffic as talking to each motorist individually would be impractical.

In electronic communication (e.g. emails, Facebook, instant messages, web forums) it is now common to insert **emoticons**, pictorial representations of facial expressions (e.g. punctuation marks and letters, images), in order to convey the tenor of a text. For example, instead of words, people often use the emoticons for a smiley face :-) and sad face :-(to alert others to their mood.

Throughout the world, a range of signs and symbols are used to regulate behaviour and draw attention to hazardous situations (e.g. steep slope ahead, kangaroo crossing, slippery road when wet). While many symbols and illustrations may clearly be associated with what they represent (e.g. pictures of related objects, lines in the shape of a particular object, a smile indicating a happy person), all symbols are basically arbitrary and may not be interpreted in the same way by people who have been socialized in a different cultural environment.

Repeating verbal messages

Nonverbal messages may also be used to repeat what we say verbally. For example, emoticons may accompany speech in emails (e.g. a statement about feeling sad may be accompanied by the image of a person with a sad face). If a visitor asks you where the cafeteria is, you may say that it is next to the campus bookstore while using your finger or arm to point in that direction. In this scenario, your nonverbal cue is repeating your words.

When using a second language that you are not fluent in, you may frequently use gestures to accompany your words, especially if you lack confidence in your oral skills and are concerned that your verbal message will not be clear. Of course, your gestures might also be misinterpreted.

Emphasizing verbal messages

Nonverbal messages may be used to emphasize the emotions or depth of feelings that lie behind the words we are speaking. For example, a furrowed brow can convey concern as you verbally tell a friend that you are sorry that her pet has died. A look of surprise (e.g. wide eyes, raised eyebrows) can emphasize your shock when you exclaim that you cannot believe that one of your friends is getting married to someone she has dated for only three weeks. In both examples, the verbal and nonverbal codes are in sync and are apt to convey a clear meaning to a close friend, who is familiar with the way you communicate nonverbally.

Relaying awkward messages

Ideas or messages that are difficult or awkward to express verbally may sometimes be communicated more easily and effectively through nonverbal means. For example, when someone has passed away, it is not easy to find exactly the right words to say to loved ones. In lieu of

www.jti.co.jp

煙の行方。
本人だけが、
他人事だった。

Where does the smoke go?
Only the person producing
it is unconcerned.

ROUTE
OF
SMOKE

SMOKER ── NEGLECT

が
た は
け は
づ ナ
な ー
気 る
マ 。
あ わ
変

Plate 5.1 In many parts of the world, attitudes towards smoking have changed significantly in recent decades. This bilingual anti-smoking message appears all over Japan. Would you understand the nonverbal message without the words? What signs, if any, are posted in your neighbourhood? How is the anti-smoking idea conveyed in your context, if at all? © Chan Sin Yu

words, sympathy and solidarity may be conveyed through a facial expression or a gentle touch on the arm, or by simply being present in a room.

In another scenario, nonverbal channels may be used to avoid an awkward verbal encounter. For example, when you come across someone you don't wish to talk to, instead of giving a lengthy verbal excuse that does not ring true, you can keep on walking slowly and indicate that you are in a rush to get somewhere. You could tap your watch, shrug your shoulders or raise your hands in the air to indicate that the situation is not in your control, smile and keep on moving without exchanging a single word.

In contexts where direct discourse (saying what's on your mind) is considered too aggressive, individuals who are asked if they agree with a suggestion may remain silent and keep their eyes downcast to avoid an unpleasant, awkward confrontation. People who have been socialized to understand this indirect form of communication are apt to quickly realize that their suggestion has been rejected, whereas individuals who are used to direct discourse may miss these nonverbal cues and press for a verbal response. When it does not come, they may be quite perplexed and irritated!

Regulating interactions

Nonverbal codes are frequently used to regulate conversations and other communicative events. Ekman and Friesen (1969: 82) coined the term **'regulators'** to refer to

> actions which maintain and regulate the back-and-forth nature of speaking and listening between two or more interactants. They tell the speaker to continue, repeat, elaborate, hurry up, become more interesting, less salacious, give the other a chance to talk, etc. They tell the listener to pay special attention, to wait just a minute more, to talk, etc.

Through nonverbal actions (e.g. hand gestures, head nods, forward leans, gaze, other body movements) we can tell others to do or not to do something while we talk. We can give young children a stern look when we wish them to stop poking each other while we are talking with them.

Directing **turn-taking** is another common form of nonverbal communication in interactions. In a small group discussion, you may use a hand gesture to signal that you are giving the floor to someone else. Alternatively, you can nonverbally indicate you wish to speak by leaning forward or touching the arm of the person who is talking. The rules of nonverbal politeness will vary depending on the cultural setting, the situation (e.g. formal event, informal chat) and the characteristics of the interactants (e.g. age, gender, cultural background, status) and the relationship between them.

Displaying emotions

Nonverbal communication may also reveal our emotions, attitudes and mental state. The term **emotional display** refers to the expression of our emotions. For example, if we are bored in a lecture we may yawn frequently and our shoulders may slump. If we are happy, we may smile broadly. When we are very familiar with people and their habits, we may ascertain their state of mind simply by observing their nonverbal behaviour. Words are often not needed to know when a friend is depressed, sad or worried. Even if she says she is fine, we may rely more on nonverbal messages to gauge her mood. The better we know someone and the cultural context, the more likely we are to accurately interpret his or her affective state. This awareness then helps us to respond appropriately.

As noted by Keltner and Ekman (2003: 412), 'emotions are expressed in multiple channels, including the face and voice, and through words, prosody, and grammatical devices'; touch and body language (e.g. posture) may also disclose our affective state. The display of emotions (e.g. disgust, fear, guilt, pride, shame) can vary in different cultural settings (Ekman 2004; Matsumoto 2009) and this can be confusing for newcomers as we naturally look for clues about how people feel about us and our relationships. Keltner and Ekman (2003: 413) also observe that '[i]ndividuals vary, according to their personality, in how they express emotion in the face and voice'. Some aspects of emotional display are universal, while others are culturally variable and also subject to individual differences.

Plate 5.2 Look carefully at the statue of this Chinese peasant woman. Can you read her mood?
© Jane Jackson

Rituals

All cultures have **rituals** (a set of actions or rites performed for symbolic meaning) that include nonverbal actions. It is common for nonverbal acts to feature in demonstrations of patriotism (e.g. saluting the flag), national holidays, public ceremonies, religious activities (e.g. praying, worship, baptism), weddings, etc. Over time, specific actions become routinized and passed from one generation to another through enculturation, as explained in Chapter 3.

Even the ways people greet each other often involve nonverbal codes and these may vary from one cultural setting to another. In Thailand, for example, the traditional greeting referred to as the *wai* in Thai (ไหว้, pronounced [wâːj]) consists of a slight bow, with the palms pressed together in a prayer-like fashion. The higher the hands are held in relation to the face and the lower the bow, the more respect or reverence the giver of the *wai* is showing. This salutation is traditionally used when formally entering and leaving a house; the *wai* may also be used to convey gratitude or to apologize.

In Argentina, people usually give each other a peck on the check when they greet friends and family and even acquaintances. Men may also hug and kiss their friends, both male and female, and in a more formal situation they may shake hands, at least when meeting for the first time. In other parts of the world, different nonverbal actions or rituals may be performed to greet people.

Plate 5.3 Acts of patriotism often include nonverbal acts such as the display of national or regional flags, especially at special events such as national holidays © Jane Jackson

CULTURE AND TYPES OF NONVERBAL COMMUNICATION

There are numerous types or forms of nonverbal communication. In this chapter, we review the following:

1   Paralanguage (vocalics)
2   Kinesics (body language)
3   Oculesics (eye contact or movement)
4   Proxemics (social distance)
5   Haptics (touch)
6   Olfactics (smell)
7   Physical appearance and artifacts
8   Chronemics (time).

Paralanguage

Paralanguage (also called **vocalics**) is concerned with the study of **vocal cues**, that is, the nonphonemic qualities of language that convey meaning in verbal communication (Moore *et al.* 2010). These include such aspects as accent, cadence (melodic feature), emphasis, loudness, pause (including silence, a form of vocalic behaviour), pitch, nasality and tone, rate of speech and tempo. **Vocal qualities** may consist of a harsh voice, a tense voice, a whispery voice, a breathy voice, a raspy voice, etc. **Vocal characterizers** include belching, crying, gasping, grunting, laughing, sighing, yawning and so on, as long as these sounds transmit messages. Thus, paralanguage or vocalics is concerned with 'the nonverbal messages of the voice that add to the meaning of verbal communication, or that stand alone as a meaning-making entity' (Hickson *et al.* 2004: 258). These nonlinguistic dimensions of communication are important as they are 'often what give verbal messages their full meaning' (p. 258).

Nonverbal communication specialists Hickson *et al.* (2004) cite eight attributes of sound that contribute to the vocalic meaning associated with speech: loudness, pitch, duration, quality, regularity, articulation, pronunciation and silence. More than just volume, **loudness** refers to the degree of intensity of the voice. For example, in a meeting a speaker may lower her voice and have a loud presence. **Pitch** is the range of one's voice during conversation and is linked to the frequency of a sound. **Duration** refers to how long a particular sound is made. **Voice quality**, as noted above, refers to the specific **vocal characteristics** (e.g. degree of raspiness, harshness) of the speaker's voice. **Articulation** refers to the clarity and control of the sounds being produced, whereas **pronunciation** is concerned with the clarity and control of the sound being produced, the rhythm and the rate of speech. **Silence** refers to the absence of sound. Both positive and negative attitudes can be expressed through silence. In a face-to-face discussion, silence can communicate a lack of understanding or even disapproval in some contexts.

Paralanguage varies across cultures. **Vocal qualifiers** such as volume, pitch, rhythm and tempo may differ among people who have been socialized in different cultural settings. In some cultures, for example, speaking loudly indicates sincerity, whereas in others it is interpreted as aggressive. The practice of belching during or after a good meal is common and accepted in some cultural settings (e.g. parts of Mainland China), yet considered vulgar in others. Vocal segregates (sounds such as mmmm, uh-huh, oooo) and vocal rate (the speed at which people talk) may also differ among cultures and be interpreted differently. Even the use and perception of the meaning of silence are influenced by culture. For example, among indigenous people in Northern Canada, it is not unusual for friends to enjoy each other's company by sitting together without talking for long periods. Visitors who are not used to this practice may feel uncomfortable and compelled to talk. Not surprisingly, variations in paralanguage can lead to miscommunication and negative valuations of people who are communicating in ways that are unfamiliar. What is deemed polite behaviour in one context, may be considered rude or weird in another.

Kinesics

Kinesics is a broad category of nonverbal actions. It encompasses the study of body movement (**body language**), e.g. body posture, gestures, facial expressions and eye movements. Basically, kinesics is concerned with the messages that are conveyed through physical movement, either by the body as a whole or by specific parts (e.g. the face, hands, arms). It also deals with **posture** (the ways people stand and sit) and **eye-related movements** (e.g. the rolling of the eyes, the arching of eyebrows), which convey meaning to others, whether intentional or not. Kinesics includes the study of **affect (affective) displays**, that is, the use of physical movement (e.g. facial expressions, posture) to convey the intensity of an emotion (Matsumoto 2009).

Plate 5.4 Emotions are expressed through many channels. The Filipina seller is making a gesture to the photographer. Can you read this nonverbal emblem and his affective state? © David Jackson

Plate 5.5 This Chinese man is riding his bicycle through an alley in Beijing. Without saying a single word, he is communicating his emotions. How would you interpret his mood? Do you think a smile is a universal marker of happiness? © Jane Jackson

Body language communication varies from one cultural setting to another. In Egyptian culture, for example, vigorous hand movements and body gestures are often used to express anger. In a Japanese context, locals may be just as furious but as their nonverbal behaviours are more contained or less expressive they may appear to be less agitated.

Kinesics also includes communication through the use of smiling, frowning, giggling and so on; these nonverbal cues may differ among and within cultures. Around the world, a smile usually signals happiness; however, in some cultural contexts it can also mask sadness or be used to conceal embarrassment. For example, in Japan and South Korea, people may smile or even laugh or giggle in situations they find awkward or overly personal (e.g. when they are embarrassed about a mistake they have made at work, when someone reveals that a close friend has just passed away). Communication partners from other cultural backgrounds who are unfamiliar with this nonverbal behaviour may mistakenly interpret the smile or laugh as uncaring, rude and a bit strange. Misunderstandings like this can negatively impact intercultural relations.

Gestures

Gestures are typically hand or facial movements that are used to illustrate speech and convey verbal meaning. Ekman and Friesen (1969) identified five types of gestures:

> **Illustrators**: Shape/illustrate what is being said (e.g. pointing, outlining a picture of a referant).
> **Emblems**: Direct replacements for words (e.g. OK signal in the U.S.).
> **Affect displays**: Convey the intensity of an emotion (e.g. frown, dropping one's shoulders to signify sadness/empathy).
> **Regulators**: For controlling the flow of conversation (e.g. hand gestures, head nods).
> **Adaptors**: Used unintentionally to relieve tension (e.g. scratching, smoking).

Speech illustrators are gestures or movements that are directly linked to speech, that is, they illustrate or emphasize the verbal message, even though the user may not be conscious of their use (Ekman & Friesen 1969; Matsumoto & Hwang 2012). Drawing on the work of Efron (1968), Ekman (2004: 41) classified illustrators into the following categories:

> Batons (movements that emphasize a particular word or phrase);
> Ideographs (movements that draw a thought or outline a path);
> Deictic movements (e.g. pointing to draw attention to someone or something);
> Kinetographs (e.g. to illustrate bodily action);
> Spatial movements (e.g. to illustrate spatial relationships);
> Pictographs (e.g. to draw a picture of their referent);
> Rythmic movements (e.g. to illustrate the pacing of an activity or event).

Most of these illustrative gestures are performed with the hands and all of them may be linked to verbal behaviour (e.g. volume of speech, speech context, verbal meaning) as it occurs in real time. Except for the first two types, batons and ideographs, illustrators have meaning even without language (Matsumoto & Hwang 2012).

Cultural differences are evident in the amount, type and frequency of illustrative gestures that are used in different parts of the world. In Latin and North African cultures, for example, large, illustrative gestures often accompany speech, that is, individuals in these cultural settings tend to be highly expressive in their gesticulation. In contrast, from an early age, children in East Asian cultures are discouraged from using such gestures in public so they tend to be relatively less expressive in their use of gestures (Matsumoto & Hwang 2012). Of course, there are variations within cultures and differences depending on the context and situation.

Emblems or **emblematic gestures** are used to convey messages without speech. Every culture has emblematic gestures, which are associated with particular words or phrases. Ekman (2004) maintains that '[e]mblems are the only true "body language", in that these movements have a set of precise meanings, which are understood by all members of a culture or subculture' (p. 39). Within cultures, some of these gestures are gender-specific (e.g. in traditional cultures, obscene gestures may primarily be used by males in the company of other men and if used by females they are considered very shocking). Examples of emblems are the peace sign (two fingers up, palm facing outward), and the OK sign (thumb up, hand in fist), which are generally understood by people who have been socialized in the U.S and Canada. Emblems such as these permit communication across distances when verbal messages cannot be easily heard, or when speech is not permitted or safe.

Had too much to drink (France)

Anger (Japan)

Come here (Japan)

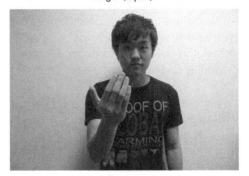

Come here (U.S.)

No! (U.S.)

Don't do that! (France)

Money (U.S.)

Money (Japan)

Figure 5.1 Examples of culture-specific emblems

Since emblems are culture-specific, their meanings often vary in different cultural settings, and a gesture that is positive in one context may be deemed offensive in another. For example, the American A-OK sign has sexual implications in many parts of Europe and is regarded as an obscene gesture. Placing both hands at the side of one's head and pointing upwards with the forefingers signals that one is angry in Japan; in other contexts it refers to the devil; and in others it means that one wants sex. In other cultural settings, it may have no meaning at all. The inverted peace sign – two fingers up in a fist pointed inward toward oneself – is interpreted as an insult in England and Australia. (See Figure 5.1 for examples of emblems that are culture-specific.)

While emblems tend to be culture-specific, David Matsumoto and other nonverbal researchers are discovering that recent advances in technology and social media (e.g. Facebook, films, YouTube) are making it easier for people to view gestures that are common in other cultural settings, especially those that are used in the U.S. Some gestures are becoming universally recognized due to globalization and the influence of mass media (e.g. television, the Internet, the press). For example, American emblems for 'hello', 'good-bye', 'yes' and 'no' are now widely understood on all continents (Hwang *et al.* 2010; Matsumoto & Hwang 2012).

Posture

While vocal cues (e.g. tone, volume of voice) and facial expressions (e.g. frowns, smiles) can convey specific emotions (e.g. anger, fear, happiness), one's body **posture** is more apt to reveal one's general state of mind and attitude (e.g. mood, emotion, feeling). For example, the way we stand can reveal whether we are interested or disinterested in someone and whether we are being attentive or not. Our posture can indicate if we are open or closed to what our communication partner is saying. The way we stand can also signal our status in relation to another speaker (Matsumoto & Hwang 2012; Mehrabian 1969). For instance, we are apt to be more erect when communicating with someone of a higher status. Studies suggest that people from diverse cultural backgrounds interpret postures according to similar dimensions (i.e., degree of acceptance or status being conveyed) but differ in terms of the degree of importance placed on specific aspects of these dimensions (Kudoh & Matsumoto 1985; Matsumoto & Kudoh 1987).

Facial expressions and emotional display

The English naturalist Charles Darwin (1872) argued that all humans possess the ability to express emotions in exactly the same ways, primarily through their faces. Anthropologist Margaret Mead (1930), however, later argued that facial expressions of emotion are culture-specific and learned in each culture like verbal language. This issue has been debated for decades. In a series of studies conducted in the 1960s by Paul Ekman and his colleagues, participants from different parts of the world were shown images of facial expressions. Interestingly, all of them agreed on the following emotions that were conveyed in the faces they viewed: anger, disgust, fear, happiness, sadness and surprise, lending support for the notion of universal facial expressions (Ekman 1972, 1973; Ekman & Friesen 1971; Izard 1971). A seventh facial expression – contempt – was later found to be universally recognized (Ekman & Heider 1988; Matsumoto 1992). These findings led Ekman (2009:1) to the following conclusion:

In business and in life, it doesn't matter what language you speak, where you live, what you do for a living—the facial expressions you show for anger, fear, sadness, disgust, surprise, contempt and happiness will be the same. You share these expressions with all human beings, and many of them with the great apes.

Over the past four decades, there have been well over 100 judgment studies that have demonstrated the pancultural recognition of these seven expressions (Elfenbein & Ambady 2002; Matsumoto 2001). More than 75 studies have found that these facial expressions are spontaneously produced by individuals all over the world to convey similar emotions (Matsumoto *et al.* 2008). These findings provide strong evidence for the universal facial expressions of emotions that are depicted in Figure 5.2. The implication is that these expressions are biologically innate.

Despite the existence of universal facial expressions of emotion, people around the world express certain emotions differently. Nonverbal communication specialists Ekman and Friesen (1969) coined the term **cultural display rules** to account for cultural differences in facial expressions of emotion. At a young age, we learn to manage and modify our emotional expressions in particular situations and social contexts. Ekman and Friesen (1969) identified six ways in which expressions may be managed when emotion is aroused:

1   Individuals can express emotions as they feel them with no modification.
2   They can amplify (exaggerate) their expressions, e.g. feelings of sadness may be intensified (amplification) at funerals.

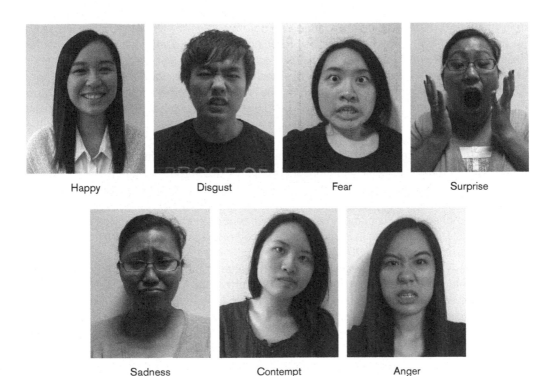

| Happy | Disgust | Fear | Surprise |

| Sadness | Contempt | Anger |

Figure 5.2 The seven universal facial expressions of emotion

3   They can minimize their expressions, e.g. minimize feelings of sadness at weddings to avoid upsetting others.
4   People can mask or conceal their emotions by expressing something other than what they feel, as when physicians hide their emotions when communicating with patients with terminal illness.
5   Individuals may also learn to neutralize their expressions, expressing nothing, e.g. when playing poker.
6   They can qualify their feelings by expressing emotions in combination, e.g. when feelings of sadness are intermingled with a smile, with the smile commenting on the sadness, saying 'I'll be OK.'

When spontaneous expressive behaviours have been studied, all of the behavioural responses described have been identified (Cole 1986; Ekman & Rosenberg 1998). Based on their own work and that of other nonverbal communication specialists, Matsumoto and Hwang (2012) conclude that when emotions are aroused, displays may be *either* universal *or* culture-specific, depending, in part, on the context.

Oculesics

Oculesics is concerned with eye behaviour as an element of communication (e.g. eye contact, dynamic eye movement, pupil dilation, static/fixed gaze, gaze direction and intensity). The term **gaze** refers to a person's behaviour while looking at someone or something. It can be a powerful form of nonverbal communication and, to complicate matters, its use and interpretation may vary in different cultural settings and contexts, as well as among genders. Research on humans and non-human primates has revealed that gaze serves multiple functions; for example, it can express emotions, intentions or attitudes. Gaze can also convey group membership and empathy (Argyle & Cook 1976) as well as dominance, power, or aggression (Fehr & Exline 1987). In North America, Matsumoto and Hwang (2012) note that the power of gaze is evident in 'the staring game,' in which two people stare at each other to see who can outlast the other; the one who smiles or looks away first is the loser, whereas the one who stares the longer is declared the winner.

To foster group membership, unity and stability, cultures create unwritten rules or norms for gazing behaviour in specific situations and contexts. Not surprisingly, there are numerous cultural differences in gazing rules and visual behaviour, which can lead to misunderstandings in intercultural interactions. In North America, for example, **direct eye contact** (looking into the eyes of the other person) is common about 40 per cent of the time while talking and 70 per cent while listening, whereas in Japan, it is more common to look at the throat of the other person (Matsumoto & Hwang 2012).

In North America, from an early age, children are taught to look directly into the eyes of their older interlocutor to demonstrate respect. In North Asia, however, this same behaviour is deemed disrespectful and children are expected to look away (e.g. downward) to show deference to their elders. Intercultural misunderstandings inevitably arise due to differing norms. Individuals who are expecting direct eye contact may find it difficult to 'read' the situation when their communication partner does not make eye contact with them; they may view gaze avoidance as disrespectful, insincere or even deceitful. Conversely, individuals who are not expecting direct eye contact may judge people who gaze directly at them as aggressive or arrogant; feeling under threat, they may be unwilling to engage further.

In Arab cultures, it is common for both speakers and listeners to look directly into each other's eyes for long periods of time, indicating keen interest in the conversation. In Mediterranean society, men often look at women for long periods of time and this may be interpreted as impolite staring by women from other cultures. As norms for gazing vary among cultures, one's nonverbal behaviour may not be interpreted as intended and the consequences may be unexpected, quite bewildering and even disturbing.

Proxemics

Proxemics is concerned with the social use of space in a communication situation. As well as the effective use of space in businesses, homes and other social settings (public or private), it encompasses the arrangement of space (e.g. furniture, architecture) to encourage or inhibit communication. **Interpersonal distance** is thought to help regulate intimacy by controlling exposure to the senses (sight, smell, touch). The closer people are to each other when they interact, the greater the sensory stimulation (smells, sights, touch) (Hall 1963, 1968).

Plate 5.6 This is a hutong (narrow street or alley) in Beijing where houses are very close together. What does this use of space indicate about social relations? © Jane Jackson

In *The Hidden Dimension* (1966), Hall proposed a theory of proxemics based on the notion that human perceptions of space are shaped and patterned by culture. He analysed both the personal spaces that people form around their bodies as well as their culturally-shaped expectations about how streets, neighbourhoods, housing estates and cities should be organized spatially. Hall (1966) concluded that the ways people in various cultures define and organize space are internalized at an unconscious level.

Hall's (1959, 1966) classic work on proxemics identified four levels of interpersonal space use in the United States, which vary depending on the type of social relationship involved: intimate, personal, social and public. He then placed these spatial zones on a continuum, ranging from **intimate space** (reserved for private situations with people who are emotionally close to us such as family members, lovers and very close friends, 0–18 inches) to **personal space** (informal distance reserved for close friends, colleagues and some acquaintances, 18 inches to 4 feet) to **social space** (formal distance between acquaintances at a social function such as a party, 4–12 feet), and **public space**/distance (less personal contact in public situations, beyond 12 feet). Violations of these zones can cause discomfort and anxiety.

Culture plays a significant role in determining what distance is deemed appropriate in certain social situations. While people from all cultural backgrounds appear to use space according to the four major distinctions proposed by Hall (1959, 1966), they differ in the amount of space or distance linked to each category. In Latin America, for example, people who are complete strangers may greet one another by kissing on the cheeks and then sit very close to each other. In contrast, North Americans may shake hands with a stranger but stand several feet apart from each other when interacting for the first time.

There are also cultural variations in interpersonal space related to gender. For example, it is acceptable in Western countries for men and women to sit or stand close to each other when talking, whereas in some Muslim countries it is taboo for there to be interaction between males and females in certain social situations. These nonverbal 'rules' vary within nations and regions and depend on the context, gender, and relationship between the interactants.

As a consequence of the primary socialization process, people from different cultural backgrounds have different expectations of what is socially acceptable in terms of interpersonal distance. Hall (1968: 88) observed that 'physical contact between two people [. . .] can be perfectly correct in one culture, and absolutely taboo in another'. Not surprisingly, then, problems can arise when people of different cultures come into contact with one another. As noted by Hall (1968), conflicting expectations of spatial behaviour can lead to 'significant misunderstandings and intensified cultural shock' (p. 87). For example, if a Northern European woman is greeted by a Latin American male she barely knows, she may feel as if her space is being invaded if he kisses her on both cheeks and stands close to her. She may feel a bit threatened and consciously or subconsciously step back to regain her physical space and sense of security. Although unintentional, her actions may be considered rude by the Latin American. If the woman does not accept the kiss and extends her hand, he might view her actions as standoffish or impolite.

As this example illustrates, individuals from different cultural backgrounds may have divergent beliefs regarding which spatial zones are appropriate in a given situation. While North Americans tend to prefer more personal distance in social interactions, Latin Americans may be more at ease with more intimate contact when interacting with others. Being sensitive to such differences is critical to successful intercultural communication. It is also important to recognize and be sensitive to individual variations.

Plate 5.7 In our home environment we become used to having a certain amount of personal space. In a small island in the Philippines, these locals are used to sharing very tight quarters in public transport. Imagine you are on board this jeepney. How might you react? © David Jackson

Haptics

Haptics refers to the use of touch in communication, including the type of contact as well as its frequency and intensity. Touch can send multiple messages, many of which are affective or emotional in nature. In a communicative event, for example, touch can disclose one's attitude towards one's communication partners, including distinct emotions such as anger, fear, disgust, love, gratitude and sympathy. Touch can also be used to provide support and encouragement, display intimacy, signal approval or, alternatively, convey dislike, distrust and rejection. As well as attachment, bonding or protection, touch can indicate compliance, and visibly mark differences in power, status and prestige.

Like many other elements of nonverbal communication, haptics is very much a function of culture. From a young age, through the process of primary socialization, we learn rules for touching in various situations (e.g. the type and amount of touching considered appropriate when interacting with parents, siblings, teachers, acquaintances of the opposite sex, romantic partners). When, how, where and whom we feel comfortable touching varies considerably in diverse cultural contexts.

Edward T. Hall (1966) drew attention to cultural differences in the use of touch and made a distinction between what he termed **high-contact** and **low-contact cultures**. In the former, people display considerable interpersonal closeness or immediacy, e.g. they encourage touching and touch more often than those in low-contact cultures. High-contact cultures are generally located in warmer countries near the equator (e.g. Columbia, Egypt, Indonesia, Western Africa), while low-contact cultures are found in cooler climates farther from the equator (e.g. Britain, South Korea, Sweden).

In Latin American, Mediterranean and Middle Eastern contexts (high-contact or high-touch cultures), people tend to employ a lot of social touching in greetings and conversation (e.g. hugs, hand-holding, kisses) with members of the same gender. In moderate-touch cultures such as North America and Northern Europe, touching (e.g. handshakes, back slapping, sporadic shoulder or arm touching) is used less frequently. In low-contact cultures such as those in North Asia, social touching among acquaintances is more rare than in high-contact cultures.

It is important to note, however, that the cultural and social rules governing touch are situational and vary *within* cultures. Touching behaviours may also change over time due to exposure to other norms of touching (e.g. observation and firsthand experience with other cultural norms in the multicultural workplace, the mass media). The amount, type, frequency and meaning of touch may differ depending on the gender, age and situation, as well as the relationship between the people involved. For example, while people in Mainland China may be reserved when interacting with acquaintances, they may use a significant amount of social touching in conversations and interactions with family members and close friends of the same gender. This means that while classification systems can provide a general picture of nonverbal behaviours, we must be aware of and sensitive to possible variations in different situations and contexts.

Recent research in diverse cultural settings has demonstrated that the way touch is used and interpreted may differ depending on one's socialization and degree of intercultural aware-ness and sensitivity (Hertenstein *et al.* 2006, 2009). Violations of the cultural rules regarding touch are likely to be interpreted in the same way as those of personal space, with negative consequences. In business situations in various cultural contexts, for example, handshakes may vary in terms of the strength of the grip and arm movements. In some Asian countries, handshakes tend to be less firm than in North America and Northern Europe. Consequently, a tight grip and vigorous handshake may be considered rude and overly aggressive. Conversely, business people in Belgium or Germany who are expecting a firm handshake are apt to be surprised when they receive a weak handshake from a Japanese businessman and they may regard him as insecure or standoffish.

Olfactics

Olfactics (also known as **olfaction**) is the study of how we use and perceive odours (e.g. perfumes, spices, body scent, deodorant). Some studies indicate that there is a universal preference for some scents, which is likely due to biological make-up and evolution (Liu *et al.* 2011). For example, the fragrances jasmine, lavender and roses tend to communicate a soothing and relaxing feeling to individuals no matter the cultural background.

There are also cultural differences related to olfactics. Smell can be used to communicate position, social class and power, and this varies according to the cultural context. Synnott (1993) claims that odour is used to categorize people into social groups of different status, power and social class because of the meanings or status attributed to a specific scent. In Switzerland, for example, wearing an expensive perfume, cologne or after-shave can signal status and wealth. The strong odour of sweat, on the other hand, can indicate manual labour and a lower status. Synnott (1993) argues that perceived foul odours are one of the criteria by which negative identities are attributed to some social or ethnic groups. For example, the smell of curry is linked to South Asians and this can sometimes be used as basis for discrimination (e.g. refusing to rent apartments to people from India and Pakistan).

People's smell preferences are not universal but vary across cultures. For example, the Dogon people of Mali find the scent of onions very attractive, and young men and women rub fried onions all over their bodies (Neuliep 2006); in stark contrast, the smell of onion from a person's mouth is considered bad breath in many other cultures and people use breath mints to conceal it (Liu *et al.* 2011: 150-51). Hence, similar to other nonverbal codes, olfactics can impact on intercultural communication and one's willingness to engage.

Physical appearance and artifacts

Physical appearance is also considered a form of nonverbal communication among human beings. As well as **physical features** (e.g. body type, deformities, eye shape, gender, height, skin colour, weight), this type of nonverbal code includes **artifacts** (objects affiliated with a particular culture), such as various forms of decorative ornamentation (e.g. accessories, body piercings, brand names and logos, choice of colour, clothes, grooming, hairstyle, jewellery, makeup, tattoos). What we choose to wear (e.g. designer watches, eyeglasses, clothes, purses) or surround ourselves with (e.g. cars) communicates something about our preferred identities. These artifacts may project gender, role or position, class or status, personality and group membership or affiliation. Our physical appearance and artifacts may send messages about us that are below our level of awareness.

Appearance messages are generally the first nonverbal codes we process and, as such, they can have a profound impact on any verbal communication that follows. When we first meet people, we often form judgments about their personality, abilities and other attributes based on the way they look and what they wear, among other things. We quickly form an impression about their degree of similarity to us (e.g. age, dress, adornments, skin colour) and assess such aspects as their social standing, credibility, financial status and general attractiveness (Hickson & Stacks 1993; Moore *et al.* 2010). These first impressions can affect our desire to interact and form personal relationships. More specifically, they can influence our comfort level and our subsequent willingness to disclose our ideas and feelings. For example, we may be less inclined to develop friendships with people we perceive as very different from ourselves. Of course, just as we are judging others, our observers are forming opinions about us (e.g. our identities, manners, positioning or status, sense of style).

Our perceptions of what is attractive, beautiful or appropriate (e.g. adornments, dress) are influenced by our culture and the media (e.g. television, magazines, social media) as well as our intercultural experience and degree of openness. Through the primary socialization process, we build up expectations of what physical appearance and attire are acceptable in certain situations and contexts. We may not be consciously aware of how we are reading visual cues (e.g. dress, body shape, weight) but the messages and our reactions can be quite powerful. For example, police and military uniforms subliminally communicate the authority of those wearing them. In some contexts, they can instill fear rather than respect. Well-groomed executives wearing tailored suits project success and credibility, whereas adults wearing wrinkled, soiled sportswear in a business setting may transmit messages of failure (e.g. limited education, a poor work ethic, low status) and a lack of credibility. People who are obese may be perceived as lazy and unproductive, while blondes may be viewed as sexually permissive

Plate 5.8
Uniforms can
convey a range
of emotions in
people (e.g.
respect, fear).
When you look at
this policeman
what is your
reaction? © Jane
Jackson

and lacking in intelligence. In some quarters, Muslim women who wear the veil may be perceived as subservient, religious fanatics, whereas in others they may be accorded more respect than women who are uncovered.

Culture clashes may erupt in intercultural situations due to differing ideas about what is appropriate attire in certain social situations. In the United Arab Emirates, for example, local women launched a Twitter campaign to object to 'scantily clad' women from other countries who visit the shopping malls and other public places (e.g. foreigners wearing short shorts and halter tops). In another example, in 2004, the French law on secularity and conspicuous religious symbols in schools came into effect. It bans the wearing of conspicuous religious symbols in public (including government-operated schools in France), including the niqab, a veil that covers a woman's face so that only her eyes are exposed through a slit. Mismatches between traditional and modern values about what is appropriate attire may lead to intercultural misunderstandings and conflict.

Although subliminal messages about physical appearance are below our level of awareness, they are often more powerful than conscious, overt messages. Advertisers take advantage of this to persuade us to buy certain products to become more attractive, slimmer, whiter, etc. Young, beautiful people usually appear in advertisements to communicate the subconscious message that the advertised product is associated with youth and beauty (according to prevailing views about what this actually is). Due to globalization, many beauty brands and products are now sold around the world with implicit or explicit notions about what it means to be beautiful (usually a Western image). Influenced by these messages, some people are taking drastic steps to alter their appearance. Young models may become anorexic (develop an eating disorder) as they strive to obtain a weight well below what is normal for them. In an effort to conform to prevailing standards of beauty, in many cultural settings, strict diets and exercise programmes abound. Some Asian women are seeking plastic surgeons to add a crease to their upper eyelid so that their eyes will look larger and, in some cases, more Westernized.

The colours we wear can also send messages to others, whether intentional or not. Some colours may have a particular meaning in certain cultural contexts, while in others they may mean something completely different or signify nothing at all. If someone is dressed in black from head to toe, for example, it might indicate the person is in mourning, while in another context it might signify an individual's membership in a gang, or it might simply serve as an indicator of the person's degree of sophistication and style. The colour one chooses to wear may simply be linked to personality traits and preferences rather than cultural norms.

Chronemics

Chronemics is the study of how people use and structure time. The way that we perceive and value time, organize our time and respond to time impacts on the communication process. To complicate matters, all of these elements may vary depending on the cultural environment and what individuals have become accustomed to during the socialization process.

Time perception, which includes punctuality and willingness to wait, may play a significant role in the nonverbal communication process. The use of time can affect one's lifestyle, daily routine, rate of speech, movements and how long one is willing to listen or wait for others. Time can also be used to reinforce one's status. For example, in most companies the boss can interrupt progress to hold an impromptu meeting in the middle of the work day, yet the average worker would have to make an appointment to see the boss. The way different cultures perceive time can influence communication as well.

Monochronic and polychronic time orientations

Cultures are usually categorized into two time system categories: **monochronic** and **polychronic** (Hall & Hall 1990). The characteristics associated with each are presented in Table 5.1.

In a monochronic time orientation, tasks are done one at a time and time is segmented into precise, small units so that one's day is scheduled, arranged and managed. Time is basically like a commodity; hence, the common saying, 'Time is money'. Monochronic cultures include Canada, East Asia, England, Japan, Germany, Northern Europe and the United States. Individuals who have been socialized in these contexts typically value schedules, tasks and 'getting the job done.' In workplace situations, individuals are committed to regimented

Table 5.1 Characteristics of monochronic and polychronic time systems

In a monochronic time system, people tend to:	In a polychronic time system, people tend to:
do one thing at a time	do many things at once
concentrate on the job	be highly distractible and subject to interruptions
take time commitments (deadlines, schedules) seriously	consider an objective to be achieved, if possible
be low-context and need information	be high-context and already have information
be committed to the job	be committed to people and human relationships
stick to plans	change plans often and easily
be concerned about not disturbing others; follow rules of privacy and consideration	be more concerned with those who are closely related than with privacy
show great respect for private property; seldom borrow or lend	borrow and lend things often and easily
emphasize promptness	base promptness on the relationship
be accustomed to short-term relationships	have strong tendency to build lifetime relationships

schedules and may view those who do not subscribe to the same perception of time as disrespectful and disorganized.

In a polychronic time orientation, multiple tasks can be performed simultaneously, and schedules follow a more fluid approach. Latin American, African, Asian and Arabic cultures generally follow the polychronic system of time. Unlike Americans and most Northern and Western European cultures, individuals from these cultures are much less focused on the preciseness of accounting for each and every moment. In contrast with monochronic cultures, polychronic cultures prioritize tradition and relationships over tasks. Consequently, individuals are not ruled by schedules and have a more informal, elastic perception of time. They may arrive late for events with family or close friends and, as they may schedule multiple appointments simultaneously, it is difficult to keep to a tight schedule. Polychronic cultures include Egypt, India, Mexico, Pakistan, the Philippines and Saudi Arabia. As one might expect, intercultural conflict may arise when people familiar with different time systems interact.

THE NONVERBAL EXPECTANCY VIOLATION THEORY

The **nonverbal expectancy violation theory**, which was developed by Judee Burgoon (1978), suggests that during the socialization process we build up expectations (mostly subconscious) about how others should behave nonverbally in particular situations and contexts. In other words, we learn social norms of nonverbal behaviour and become comfortable with **nonverbal cues** (all potentially informative behaviours that are not purely linguistic in content) that are familiar to us, just as we become used to particular verbal expressions of politeness (e.g. greetings, cultural scripts).

When our nonverbal expectations are violated, we are apt to react in specific ways. For example, when someone stands too close to us or stares at us longer than we are used to, we likely feel uneasy and even threatened; we may view this person and the relationship nega-tively. We may then extend this perception to all perceived members of this individual's culture. As nonverbal communication often takes place at a subconscious level, we likely have little awareness that we are making positive or negative judgments about others based on their vio-lation of our expectations of certain nonverbal behaviours (Burgoon 1995; Floyd *et al.* 2008).

The expectancy violation theory, which has been applied to a wide range of nonverbal behaviour such as body movement, facial expression, eye contact, posture, touch and time management, helps explain common reactions to unexpected nonverbal behaviour in inter-cultural interactions (Burgoon 1978). When expectations are not met, the violation can exert a significant impact on people's impressions of one another and this in turn can influence the outcomes of their interactions. Therefore, this theory has significant implications for ways to enhance intercultural relations. In particular, it raises awareness of the importance of becoming more attuned to one's expectations for specific nonverbal behaviours and the need to recog-nize that differing norms may prevail in different cultural settings. Additional ways to enhance one's nonverbal interactions in intercultural interactions are explored in the next section.

NONVERBAL INTERCULTURAL COMMUNICATIVE COMPETENCE

Although studying nonverbal communication cannot ensure competence in interpersonal communication, more awareness of the dimensions of nonverbal behaviour and the potential variations across and within cultures can help to enhance one's interaction with people who have been socialized in a different cultural environment. The following are some practical suggestions to optimize the nonverbal dimension in intercultural interactions.

1   Become more attuned to your own nonverbal behaviour and expectations in diverse settings, as well as your attitudes towards nonverbal behaviour that differs from your own.
2   Recognize that people communicate on many levels (e.g. multiple nonverbal channels). Be attentive to voice qualities (e.g. volume, tone), eye contact, facial expressions, hand and feet movements, body movement and placement, gestures, posture, gait and appearance. In a new environment carefully observe nonverbal communication in specific settings. Becoming more aware of the nonverbal communication of your hosts can help you determine what messages they are sending.
3   In intercultural interactions, note the nonverbal behaviours of your communication partners, and check to see if their nonverbal communication is telling you that they understand or misunderstand you. Your ability to read nonverbal communication can improve with practice.
4   If individuals say something verbally and their nonverbal communication conveys another message, seek verbal clarification.
5   Be aware that you are often being evaluated by your nonverbal communication. When people meet you for the first time they are observing your nonverbal behaviour (e.g. your appearance, gestures, voice qualities) and forming an impression of you. For example, in an interview (e.g. for scholarships, study abroad, a job), the interviewers are apt to assess your nonverbal behaviours as well as your verbal comments. Through nonverbal channels you are sending signals about your degree of self-confidence, level of interest and motivation, attitude towards the interview, emotional state and many other personal attributes and characteristics. Think about what messages your posture, eye contact and other nonverbal behaviours are sending.

6   Check your perceptions of others' nonverbal behaviour to see if you are accurate or if you are misreading nonverbal cues.

7   Seek verbal clarification for unexpected nonverbal behaviour instead of rushing to judgment.

8   Expand your nonverbal communication repertoire. In new cultural settings, for example, observe and practice new nonverbal behaviours and see what you are comfortable with.

9   Become more aware of your prejudicial assumptions that are linked to nonverbal behaviour. When you have an adverse reaction to someone from another cultural background, reflect on the basis for it. Is unfamiliar nonverbal behaviour the source of your discomfort? For example, is the person standing very close to you and making you feel uneasy? Has he or she been socialized to be more familiar with less personal distance between people?

10 Never assume that individuals who have a different linguistic and cultural background understand your nonverbal messages. When in doubt, use verbal checks to ensure that your meaning has been interpreted as intended.

11 Be flexible and adaptable in your nonverbal communication in intercultural encounters. Try synchronizing your behaviour to that of your communication partners as this may communicate respect and the desire to cultivate the relationship.

12 When working in a diverse group or leading a meeting with people from different cultural backgrounds, be attentive to nonverbal cues as they can tell you:

- when you've talked long enough or too long
- whether it is appropriate to interrupt a speaker as well as the accepted ways to do so
- when someone else wishes to speak or take the floor
- the mood of the group
- their feelings about your comments and suggestions.

Listen attentively and observe the nonverbal behaviour of group members and you'll be a more effective group member and communicator.

13 Whenever possible, try to accompany your nonverbal messages with some type of verbal follow up that reiterates or emphasizes your nonverbal message.

14 Be aware that your physical appearance and attire are continuously sending out messages about who you are and how you feel about the people around you.

15 Finally, remember that your cultural background plays a significant role in the nonverbal messages you send and how you interpret nonverbal messages.

Similar to verbal codes, nonverbal acts vary among people from different cultural backgrounds, and these differences can sometimes lead to misunderstandings and conflict. Making an effort to enhance one's nonverbal communication repertoire is vital for effective intercultural interactions. To become a competent intercultural communicator, it is imperative to recognize the power and multiple dimensions of nonverbal communication in interpersonal relations. One's nonverbal communication skills can improve with practice and, ultimately, strengthen relationships with individuals who have been socialized in a different cultural setting.

SUMMARY

While our language system is undeniably a vital component of communication, nonverbal actions that occur on their own or accompany spoken messages can be even more significant and powerful. Nonverbal cues account for most of the communication we have with others in face-to-face interactions and when there is a discrepancy between verbal and nonverbal messages, adults tend to believe the latter. Although nonverbal communication and verbal communication differ in many ways, the two systems often function together. It is important to recognize that we both send and receive nonverbal information through multiple sensory channels (e.g. visual, auditory, smell, touch) with or without speech.

This chapter introduced many different functions and types of nonverbal codes (e.g. haptics, kinesics, oculesics, olfactics, physical appearance and attire, proxemics, paralanguage). While some elements appear to be universal, the use of nonverbal codes can vary among individuals from different cultural backgrounds (e.g. differing gestures as well as norms and interpretations of nonverbal actions). The nonverbal expectancy violation theory suggests that when we encounter unfamiliar nonverbal behaviours we may instinctively react in a negative way and not even realize why. To become a competent intercultural communicator in today's globalized world, it is imperative that we enhance our knowledge of nonverbal communication and expand our repertoire of nonverbal behaviours and strategies so that our communication is more appropriate and effective in diverse contexts and situations.

discussion questions

1 Why is it important to study nonverbal communication?
2 What are the major differences between verbal and nonverbal communication?
3 Identify five ways in which we communicate nonverbally and provide examples of each.
4 Explain how culture, language and nonverbal communication are connected.
5 In your home environment, how much difference is there in the ways males and females use nonverbal communication? Have you observed any gender differences in other cultural contexts? Please provide examples.
6 Through the process of primary socialization, we learn to speak at a preferred volume in certain contexts. Can you think of any situations in which you have negatively judged others who speak much louder or more softly than you are used to?
7 This chapter has identified many forms of nonverbal communication. Which ones do you think are the most problematic for you in intercultural interactions?
8 Drawing on your own experience, give examples of cultural variations in gestures and facial expressions. How do you feel when someone behaves in ways that you do not expect?
9 Consider one of the spaces where you hang out (e.g. a cafeteria, a karaoke lounge, a sports bar, a library). Note the furnishings, the décor, the architecture and the nonverbal actions of the staff. What values are conveyed by the furnishing and the décor (e.g. the ways in which tables are arranged)? What do you observe about the use of space?
10 After reading this chapter, do you think you will respond differently when someone from another linguistic and cultural background violates your expectations for nonverbal behaviour? Please explain.

further reading

Andersen, P.A. (2008) *Nonverbal Communication: Forms and Functions,* 2nd edn, Long Grove, IL: Waveland Press.

Drawing on theory and research, the author discusses the major forms, functions and uses of nonverbal communication.

Burgoon, J.K., Gurrero, L.K. and Floyd, K. (2009) *Nonverbal Communication*, Boston: Allyn and Bacon.

Referring to both classic and contemporary research on nonverbal communication, this volume uses current examples to illustrate nonverbal communication.

Guerrero, L.K. and Hecht, M. (2008) *The Nonverbal Communication Reader,* 3rd edn, Long Grove, IL: Waveland Press.

This volume introduces multiple dimensions of nonverbal communication, drawing on classic and contemporary research.

Hall. E.T. (1984) *The Dance of Life: The Other Dimension of Time*, New York: Anchor Books.

This book explores the cultural nature of time.

Hall, E.T. (1990) *The Hidden Dimension*, New York: Anchor Books.

This classic explores variations in the use of space across cultures and discusses how that use reflects cultural values and norms of behaviour.

Knapp, M.L. and Hall, J.A. (2009) *Nonverbal Communication in Human Interaction,* 7th edn, Belmont, CA: Wadsworth Publishing Co.

This introductory text is designed for courses on nonverbal communication.

Matsumoto, D. and Hwang, H.S. (2012) 'Nonverbal communication: The messages of emotion, action, space, and silence', in J. Jackson (ed.) *The Routledge Handbook of Language and Intercultural Communication,* Abingdon: Routledge, pp. 130–47.

In this chapter, the authors review the key findings of research that has examined the influence of culture on various nonverbal behaviours (e.g. facial expressions, gestures, gaze, voice, interpersonal space, touch, posture, gait).

Moore, N-J, Hickson, M. and Stacks, D.W. (2010) *Nonverbal Communication: Studies and Applications,* 5th edn, Oxford: Oxford University Press.

Balancing theory and practice, this volume is designed to help students understand how nonverbal communication impacts 'real world' interactions.

CHAPTER 6

Language and identity in intercultural communication

Through others we become ourselves.

(Vygotsky 1997: 105)

'Where are you from?'
'What is your nationality?'
'You have an accent.'
'But, I never think of you as . . .'
'I didn't know you were . . .'

(James 2001: 1)

Identity is not something one has, but something that develops during one's whole life.

(Beijaard *et al.* 2004: 107)

learning objectives

By the end of this chapter, you should be able to:

1 define identity
2 identify and discuss multiple characteristics of identity
3 explain how identities are shaped and formed
4 identify, define and provide examples of different types of identity
5 describe ways in which people communicate their identities to others
6 explain how individuals negotiate their identity in intercultural interactions
7 explain what is meant by 'encapsulated marginality' and 'constructive marginality'
8 explain how and why identities may be contested or challenged
9 describe the relationship between language, culture and identity
10 explain the role of identity in intercultural communication.

INTRODUCTION

Identity is a principal topic in the study of language and intercultural communication. Our sense of self and positioning in the world impact on our relationships with other human beings and affect the quality of our life and interpersonal relationships. The language we use and our cultural socialization profoundly influence how we see ourselves and communicate with people who have a different background (e.g. linguistic, cultural, religious). Without a doubt, the connection between language, culture and identity is a core element in intercultural experience.

After defining what is meant by identity, this chapter explores the impact of the socialization process on identity development in various cultural contexts. We then turn our attention to other characteristics and facets of identity that can influence intercultural relations. The focus then shifts to a discussion of some of the major types of identities (e.g. personal, social, cultural, racial, ethnic, language, multicultural/multilingual, gendered, sexual, age, religious, physical ability, national, regional, global, organizational, virtual) that can impact on our language use and intercultural communication. Throughout, attention is drawn to the complex connection between identities, language and culture.

CHARACTERISTICS OF IDENTITY

Identity is basically our self-concept or sense of self. It defines how we see ourselves and our place in the world. Before we examine various types of identities, it is helpful to have an understanding of current views about the characteristics of identity. The way we view this construct today is quite different from past conceptions. Recent scholars who have researched the formation and dimensions of identity have generally concluded that identities are: (1) developed through primary socialization, (2) formed in different ways in different parts of the world, (3) multiple and complex, (4) both dynamic and stable, (5) both chosen and ascribed, (6) variable in strength and salience, and (7) conveyed through verbal and nonverbal means. Now, let's examine each of these characteristics in more detail.

Identities are formed during the socialization process

When we are very young we begin to form our sense of self through the **primary socialization** process that was discussed in Chapter 3. Social institutions such as the family, the education system, religious organizations and the mass media (e.g. television) all play a role in determining how we develop as social beings. Thus, our sense of self is socially constructed. As young children, we continuously receive messages about who we are and how others see us. Over time, through observation and social interaction, we acquire the means to identify with or relate to our peers, our neighbours, the communities in which we live and the people we come across in our everyday life: 'Through others we become ourselves' (Vygotsky 1997: 105). We also form ideas about individuals and groups who differ from us.

As we establish our own identities, we learn what makes us similar to some people and different from others (e.g. gender and age affiliations, ethnic and religious bonds). In the process, we develop the knowledge and skills necessary to form and nurture social connections with members of the groups we belong to. How we see ourselves affects who we feel close to and what communities and groups we spend most of our time with. Messages from those who are closest to us can influence our choice of friends, who we develop a romantic relationship with and who we may eventually choose as a life partner. Dominant values and beliefs can impact on our views about intercultural marriage, homosexuality and a range of other sensitive social dimensions of identity. Cultural and social identities help people fit into particular societies and cultures. Although our identities can provide us with a sense of belonging in an increasingly complex world, they can also serve as barriers to successful intercultural interactions, an aspect that is explored in the next chapter.

Identities are shaped in diverse ways in different cultural contexts

The primary socialization process differs among and within cultures. The ways in which young children are socialized in different social and cultural settings influences how they view and position themselves in the world. Enculturation can impact on how they interact with others, including people from different linguistic and cultural backgrounds.

In some contexts, **individualism** ('the dimension of culture that refers to the rights and independent action of the individual'; Jandt 2007: 430) is stressed and young children are encouraged to develop a strong sense of self (e.g. to figure out and verbally express their personal preferences, to assume responsibility for their own actions). In the U.S., for example, an **independent self-construal** tends to be promoted, that is, 'a self-perception that emphasizes one's autonomy and separateness from others' (Smith *et al.* 2006: 277). While family is still very important in U.S. societies, parents strive to foster self-reliance and a strong, independent identity in children so that they will develop into mature, responsible adults who can fend for themselves and make a worthwhile contribution to society. Parents may offer advice and guidance; however, young adult children generally choose their post-secondary education path, life partners and careers. There is an emphasis on 'finding yourself' and being 'true to yourself'.

In cultures that tend to be more **collectivist** ('the dimension of culture that refers to interdependence, groupness, and social cohesion'; Jandt 2007: 426), 'we' rather than 'I' is emphasized. In many Asian, African and Latino societies, for example, an **interdependent self-construal** is fostered, that is, 'a self-perception that emphasizes one's relatedness to others' (Smith *et al.* 2006: 277). Throughout one's life, family tends to dominate, and children are generally encouraged to view themselves in relation to others. The involvement of parents and grandparents in their children's life decisions (e.g. choice of major/university, selection of spouse, the timing of one's marriage, career path, place of residence) may continue well into adulthood. Family duties and responsibilities (e.g. looking after one's elderly parents) are emphasized and several generations of a family may live together.

Although the process of identity formation may differ among and within cultures, all of us develop a sense of who we are and how we fit in society (e.g. independent self-construal, interdependent self-construal) through messages we receive from the world around us. In varying degrees, we are all influenced by the primary socialization that is prevalent in our environment.

Identities are multiple and complex

Individuals have multiple identities, asserting different aspects of themselves in diverse social and cultural contexts and circumstances. As Mort (1989: 169) explains,

> We carry a bewildering range of different, and at times conflicting, identities around with us in our heads at the same time. There is a continual smudging of personae and lifestyles, depending where we are (at work, on the high street) and the spaces we are moving between.

Identities are multifaceted, complex and sometimes contradictory. Rather than a single, fixed identity, people have many dimensions to their sense of self. Oetzel (2009: 369) argues that it is this 'constellation of identities that makes us who we are'.

A 21-year-old male, for example, may define himself primarily as a caring son and elder brother in his family in New York, as a devoted Jew in his religious community, as a hard-working bilingual (English–Hebrew) English major on his home campus at NYU (New York University), as a fun-loving American exchange student while taking part in a semester-abroad programme at a university in Edinburgh, as a faithful gay partner in his sexual life and as a clever comedian when in the company of his closest friends. This example illustrates the complexity of identities, reminding us that it is possible for people to assert different facets of themselves in different social situations. Whether we are aware of it or not, each of us has multiple dimensions to our identities that become evident at different times and in particular social situations and contexts.

Identities are dynamic

Early identity scholars tended to portray identity as singular and fixed by the time children reach adolescence, with one's social and cultural group membership clearly defined through the process of socialization (Erikson 1968). While some aspects of our identity may remain stable after we reach maturity, most identity researchers now stress the dynamic or fluid nature of identities. They recognize that many dimensions may change or evolve over time. As noted by Beijaard *et al.* (2004: 107), 'identity is not something one has, but something that develops during one's whole life'. For example, the meanings that young adults or middle-aged people attribute to certain aspects of their identity (e.g. age, ethnicity, gender, language, nationality) may be quite different from when they were young children or adolescents.

Recognizing the dynamic nature of identity, cultural theorist and sociologist Stuart Hall (1990: 222) writes,

> Identity is not as transparent or unproblematic as we think. Perhaps instead of thinking of identity as an already accomplished fact, which the new cultural practices then repre-sent, we should think instead of identity as a 'production,' which is never complete, always in process and always constituted within, not outside representation.

People may give little thought to their ethnicity and other facets of their identities until they travel or study abroad and/or experience life as a minority for the first time. Being different from the majority may serve as a stimulus for deeper reflection on multiple dimensions of one's identities (e.g. cultural, ethnic, linguistic, religious, national). When Hong Kong Chinese students venture outside Asia they are often misidentified as Japanese, Koreans or Mainland Chinese. This unsettling experience tends to raise their awareness about the personal meaning of their regional, ethnic and linguistic identities. In this situation, some decide to present themselves as Chinese instead of insisting on recognition of their Hong Kong identity. Much to their surprise, they may become more nationalistic, that is, for the first time in their life, they may feel some attachment to the 'Motherland' (Mainland China). Feeling disrespected, some become more regionalistic and cling more tightly to their Cantonese selves and unique Hong Konger identity (Jackson 2008, 2010).

As we mature and gain life experience whether in our home environment or abroad, we may express our evolved sense of self in a variety of ways. For example, we may strive to convey a more cosmopolitan, global identity through the use of an international language we have mastered in adulthood (e.g. English). We may also alter our nonverbal behaviours to reflect changes in our socioeconomic status and social identities. Youth may live in casual clothing but when they become professionals they may wear formal business suits and hold themselves in a more sophisticated way to emphasize their professional identity. Their communication style and language choice may also change as they strive to project a certain image to people they wish to impress (e.g. supervisors, colleagues).

Other aspects of one's identity (e.g. gender, ethnicity, religion) may also have different meanings and significance at different stages in one's life. As an adult, a Nepalese male may feel a strong emotional attachment to his Buddhist self and yet have given it little thought as a child. A Burmese refugee in Thailand may become more strongly connected to his first language and ethnic identity in a foreign land.

The identities that people claim and the significance they attach to them may change as a consequence of personal, economic and social circumstances (e.g. study abroad, more intimate intercultural interactions, a higher level of education and wealth, deeper reflection on one's place in the world, more exposure to other groups and societies, interethnic marriage, travel, encounters with racists, etc.). A dramatic increase in the prevalence of electronic social media and the frequency of intercultural contact can also influence how individuals view their identities. People are also impacted by external developments in the world around them (e.g. changes in societal views about gay marriage, mental and physical disabilities, homosexuality, interracial marriage, political freedom).

A shift in attitudes and perceptions may also bring about the use of different **identity labels**. For example, in the U.S., the terms 'African American' or 'black' are now used instead of 'coloured' or 'Negro'. In the 1950s and 1960s, American Civil Rights leaders objected to the word Negro, which was associated with a long, painful history of slavery, segregation and discrimination and this brought about a shift in terms. In Canada and Greenland, many natives now consider the label 'Eskimos' to be pejorative and prefer to be referred to as 'the Inuit'. In other parts of the world, group identity labels are changing as people who were oppressed fight for more recognition and respect.

Identities are both avowed and ascribed

Identity is concerned with the way individuals or groups see, define and express themselves, as well as how other individuals or groups define or label them. Our **avowed identity** is the one that we wish to present or claim in an interaction, whereas an **ascribed identity** is the one that others give to us (or we give to someone else).

Avowal refers to 'the process of telling others what identity(ies) you wish to present or how you see yourself' (Oetzel 2009: 62). Individuals and groups can freely select some dimensions of their identities that they wish to present to others. We may choose to convey a particular image through our dress, adornments, speech and mannerisms. For example, in Britain, Jameela, an immigrant from Pakistan, may proudly wear shalwar kameez (a long tunic and pants with embroidery that is distinctive of her home village).

Through language, we may also directly state parts of our identity that are especially meaningful or important to us (e.g. 'I am a British Pakistani', 'I'm a vegan', 'I am lesbian' or 'I am a dentist'). Within the same environment, there are also variations in the ways individuals from the same groups view aspects of their identities. For example, being Japanese may be a source of great pride for Tomoko but of little importance to Katsumi, even though they have been socialized in the same city and are affiliated with the same ethnic group.

We are not entirely free to adopt any identities we want, however. The perception of others also impacts on how we are viewed and positioned in a specific situation and context. **Ascription** refers to 'the process of assigning in another person what you think his or her identity should be' (Oetzel 2009: 62). Factors such as age, language, accent, ethnicity, skin colour, social class, dress, communication styles and sex (etc.) can influence how others see and categorize us. Thus, our preferred identities may not be the ones that are recognized and respected by others.

Let's look at some examples. After many months abroad, an international exchange student may feel at home in her new world and wish to be seen as a member of the host community; yet, her physical appearance, second language accent, temporary status and lack of familiarity with local social norms may distinguish her from locals who persist in treating her like an outsider. A Latino woman may wish to be identified primarily as a department head rather than as a Latino or a woman. Her colleagues and students, however, may persist in viewing her in terms of her ethnicity and gender characteristics. Consequently, she may find it a struggle to assert her preferred identity and authority. Similarly, a fresh graduate in a new job may aspire to be seen as a capable adult but in the eyes of his older, more experienced supervisor, he is still a mere child. Conversely, a physically-active and mentally-sharp retiree in her late sixties may consider herself a vibrant being; much to her dismay, however, she is regarded as 'over the hill' by younger members of the community and talked to in a patronizing way. Failing to acknowledge and respect the preferred identities of individuals and groups can have negative consequences for intercultural interactions and relationships, an aspect that is explored in the next chapter.

Identities are variable in salience and intensity

While each of us has multiple identities, this does not mean that each dimension is of equal importance to us at all times. Depending on the context and situation, there will naturally be aspects or dimensions that we wish to emphasize more than others or that other people will consider more important. For example, our perception of our cultural identity may vary for multiple reasons, as Fong and McEwen (2004: 166) observe:

> Some members will identify with particular communicative cultural practices, while other members may choose not to partake and identify themselves as enacting the same expressions, rituals, and so forth because of differing preferences, values, attitudes, beliefs, and so.

Identity salience is 'the degree to which an identity is prominent or stands out to us in a given situation' (Oetzel 2009: 59). The salience of a particular identity can influence one's emotional state and behaviour since each identity carries with it certain understandings (e.g. knowledge), beliefs and expectations (Forehand et al. 2002).

When we are in an environment where the majority of people speak a different language and are visibly different from us, our ethnic, language or national identity may become more salient. A devout Muslim exchange student in New Zealand during Ramadan (the holy month of fasting) may find that her religious affiliation has become even more meaningful to her, especially if none of her classmates are fasting. In a similar situation, feeling under pressure to conform to the behaviour of the majority, another Muslim student may distance himself from his religious affiliation and choose not to fast in order to fit in with his new peers.

Elements of our identity may become more evident and significant to us when they are contested or challenged. The term **contested identity** refers to facets or elements of one's identity that are not accepted by the people we are in contact with.

> 'Where are you from?'
> 'What is your nationality?'
> 'You have an accent.'
> 'But, I never think of you as . . .'
> 'I didn't know you were . . .'
>
> (James 2001:1)

These are just some of the many questions that Carl James and other minority members or newcomers experience. It can be very unsettling to discover that you are not viewed as you see yourself or wish to be identified.

Identity intensity refers to the degree of significance of a particular identity (Collier 1994). The strength of one's attachment to a facet of one's identity can vary depending on the circumstances. For example, people with a weak ethnic identity may demonstrate little interest in being affiliated with other individuals from their ethnic group and may shun organized cultural events. They may insist on using a different language, wear jeans instead of ethnic dress and live a different lifestyle from the majority of people who have the same ethnicity. In contrast, individuals with a strong ethnic identity may wear clothing and eat certain foods that visibly link them to their ethnic group; they may actively participate in functions linked to their ethnic group (e.g. religious services, community celebrations, weekly social gatherings). They may also primarily use the language(s) associated with their ethnicity (e.g. a Sri Lankan international exchange student in London may use Tamil instead of English as much as possible when not in classroom situations).

Identities are expressed verbally and nonverbally

On a daily basis, we intentionally express and negotiate our identities through a range of verbal and nonverbal means, depending, in part, on what messages we wish to send about ourselves to others. We continuously convey information that is below our level of awareness, especially through nonverbal channels. In face-to-face interactions, our communication partners are interpreting our actions and processing our appearance, while making assessments about who we are and what groups we belong to. Their views about our identities may differ from our own perceptions.

Our language and communication styles can express multiple dimensions of our identity. For example, the use of one's mother tongue can serve as a marker of one's cultural or regional affiliation. When far away from home in an alien environment, familiar accents and expressions can provide a sense of comfort and belonging. Regional accents and dialects can bind people together and foster harmony among community members; they can also intentionally or unintentionally separate individuals and groups who speak in a different way or use a different language.

Bilingual or multilingual individuals may feel they are conveying different dimensions of their identities depending on the language they are using. For example, a young woman who speaks French at home, German with her boyfriend and English in the workplace may project different self-images in different situations and, occasionally, some elements may conflict with each other.

We also express ourselves through a variety of nonverbal messages. For example, our appearance (e.g. clothing, jewellery, tattoos, hairstyle) communicates aspects about our identities that we wish to convey to others. For Sikhs, five items of dress and physical appearance (the 'Five Ks') represent discipline and spirituality: kesh (uncut hair and the wearing of a turban), kirpan (a ceremonial sword), kangha (a small wooden comb), kara (a steel bracelet) and kachera (cotton boxer shorts). Together, these five items signify a unique Sikh identity.

Following the cultural tradition of their family and community, some Muslim girls may wear the hijab (head covering) to school. While this mode of dress is common in some Islamic countries, it has been banned in some secular nations (e.g. France) as it is interpreted as a religious marker of identity that can separate people from each other. In Chapter 7 we explore identity barriers and discriminatory practices that can hinder intercultural relations.

TYPES OF IDENTITIES

As we develop and mature, we identify with many different groups based on such aspects as age, language, gender, religion, ethnicity, social class and so on. Some aspects of our identity are linked to our personal interests and preferences, while others are influenced by our geographic location and the messages we receive from those around us (e.g. political campaigns that promote a particular national, ethnic or regional identity). In this digital, global age, new forms of identity (e.g. virtual or cyber identities, e-identity) are also emerging. All of these dimensions reveal who we are and can influence how we present ourselves and interact in different contexts and situations. Let's take a look at some of the many types of identities that can impact on our intercultural interactions and influence the quality of the relationships that develop.

Personal identity

Martin and Nakayama (2008) define **personal identity** simply as 'a person's notions of self' (p. G-5). In conceptions of this type of identity, most scholars emphasize aspects or dimensions of ourselves that distinguish us from other people (e.g. our age, personal interests and pursuits, personality). Oetzel (2009), for example, observes that personal identities consist of the 'unique qualities of ourselves such as personality and relationships' (p. 369). Along similar lines, Liu *et al.* (2011: 290–91) maintain that personal identity 'defines an individual in terms of his or her difference to others. Aspects of personal identity include age, gender, nationality, and religion'.

Social identity

According to **social identity theory (SIT), social identity** consists in part of our social group membership affiliations (Tajfel 1981, 1982), as well as the 'emotional significance' of that membership. For Wintergerst and McVeigh (2011: 233), social identity simply refers to 'the portion of one's identity defined by associates, group memberships, and roles'. In their definition, Liu *et al.* (2011) draw attention to the affective dimension of social identification. For these scholars, social identity denotes 'those parts of an individual's self-concept which derive from his or her knowledge of membership in a social group together with the value and emotional significance attached to that membership' (p. 292).

In their conceptualizations of social identity, other interculturalists have drawn attention to certain dimensions and sub-categories. Oetzel (2009) notes that social identities encompass 'aspects we share with other individuals who belong to the same perceived group such as age, class, gender, national culture, religion, and ethnicity' (p. 371). More recently, Ting-Toomey and Chung (2012: 309) state that social identities 'include cultural or ethnic membership, gender, sexual orientation, social class, political or religious affiliation, age, disability, professional, and also family and relational role identities'. Most discussions of social identity focus on the formation of the attachments we forge with others through the socialization process.

Basically, social identity relates to how we identify ourselves in relation to others based on what we have in common. For example, we can identify ourselves according to our religion (Taoist, Jain, Christian), place of origin, (Gibraltar, Macau, North Korea), political affiliation (Green party, Independent, Muslim Brotherhood), profession or educational status (university student, English language teacher, civil engineer), language and accent (Yorkshire accent, Singlish, Tagalog) or relationship (step-mother, great-aunt, first cousin, friend, lover). Some of our social identities are stigmatized (drug addict, homeless person, unemployed, high school dropout). Most social identities are multiple (e.g. a multilingual, gay British Indian male student who is a devout Hindu and belongs to Green Peace). Together, all of our diverse roles and attributes help us to realize our overall social identity, which continues to evolve throughout our life as our preferences, interests, financial situation, job status, marital situation and other social dimensions change.

Our social identity can provide us with a sense of self-esteem and a framework for socializing as it influences how we chose to behave in social contexts (e.g. respond to other people). In experiments carried out by social psychologists Henri Tajfel and John Turner, people were found to favour members of their own social group, regardless of whether they were assigned to a particular group based on having only a simple element in common or even if the formation of their group was purely arbitrary. As well as affecting how you view yourself and your ingroup, aspects of your social identity can have negative consequences (e.g., people may treat you with disrespect when they have little regard for your language and social status). (Ingroups and outgroups are discussed in Chapter 3 and the 'ingroup-favouritism principle' is examined in Chapter 7.)

Cultural identity

Social scientists and intercultural communication scholars have put forward many definitions of **cultural identity**. For Jandt (2013: 62), it is simply 'identification with and perceived acceptance into a culture', while Wintergerst and McVeigh (2011: 230) refer to it as 'that part of identity determined by one's cultural background or way of life'. Most recently, Sorrells (2013: 15) depicts cultural identity as 'our situated sense of self that is shaped by our cultural experiences and social locations'. Bradford *et al.* (2004) observe that cultural identities are **relational**, that is, our emotional attachment to a particular group is impacted by how we believe others perceive our group:

> Cultural identities are more than just collections of cultural values, attitudes, beliefs, and norms. Cultural identities also include emotional evaluations of others' perceptions of our cultural groups. During communicative interactions, individuals may apply various communicative strategies to negotiate cultural identities that are positive and fulfill social needs.
>
> (Bradford *et al.* 2004: 315)

The notion of '**cultural membership**' is also conveyed in the following definition offered by Liu *et al.* (2011: 283): cultural identity refers to 'our social identities based on our cultural membership, they are our identification with and perceived acceptance into a larger culture group into which we are socialized and with which we share a system of symbols, values, norms, and traditions'. Similar to Bradford *et al.* (2004), Ting-Toomey and Chung (2012) stress the emotional connection that this affiliation can inspire in members of a particular culture. For these speech communication specialists, cultural identity refers to 'the emotional significance that we attach to our sense of belonging or affiliation with the larger culture' (Ting-Toomey and Chung 2012: 74). Through the process of primary socialization, individuals internalize, to varying degrees, the sociocultural value patterns of their community. It is through shared experiences and teachings that members of a cultural group develop a sense of belonging in a process that is referred to as **cultural identity formation.**

Multiple elements and conditions may impact on the development of one's cultural identity. For example, language, physical appearance, race, history, gender, sexuality, religious beliefs, ethnicity and other shared attributes may bind people together. In diverse multicultural nations where there is considerable ethnic and linguistic diversity such as Australia and Canada, cultural identity may be based primarily on social values and beliefs that are perceived to be shared (e.g. multicultural values).

While some individuals may feel a strong attachment to the larger cultural group (e.g. an Australian cultural identity), others may feel a weak bond to it; other elements of their identity may be more important (e.g. an Aboriginal cultural identity). They may identify themselves as Aussies in some circumstances and as part of a particular minority group (e.g. Aborigines, speakers of the Warlpiri language) in other circumstances.

Cultural identity may contribute to one's well-being as the affiliation with a group can provide a sense of security and comfort. It facilitates access to social networks, in which individuals feel that they share similar values, ethics and aspirations. While these attachments can be beneficial, strong cultural identities also have the potential to serve as barriers between groups. Minorities may feel excluded from the majority culture and individuals may become less accepting and tolerant of cultural practices and beliefs that differ from their own.

Racial and ethnic identity

Before we define what is meant by racial and ethnic identities, it is important to have an understanding of what is meant by '**race**' and '**ethnicity**'. As noted in Chapter 3, although some people use these terms interchangeably, there are differences in their meaning:

> Race and ethnicity both involve drawing boundaries between people. A conceptual distinction can, however, be made between race and ethnicity. While racial boundaries are drawn on the bases of physical markers, ethnic boundaries are drawn on the basis of cultural markers.
>
> (Pilkington 2003: 27)

Further, cross-cultural psychologists Smith *et al.* (2006: 278) note that race is 'a term frequently used in everyday discourse and social perception, but which has no defensible biological basis . . . We prefer to use ethnicity'. Parker and Mease (2009: 315) concur, pointing out that '[t]he classifications that constitute references to "race" – Asian, black, white, etc. – are social and historical constructions that have economic and political functions, but no biological determinant'. Accordingly, they define race as 'a product of human social and historical processes that have arbitrarily (but purposefully) created categories of people that are positioned differently in society' (Parker & Mease 2009: 315). Socially constructed racial hierarchies elevate some racial groups (e.g. whites) at the expense of others (e.g. blacks). **Racial identity**, which is also a contested notion, refers to one's 'biological/genetic make-up, i.e. racial phenotype' (Block 2007: 43) (e.g. black, white, biracial).

Ethnicity denotes groups of people who share common geographical origins, values and beliefs and customs and traditions. In contrast with the notion of 'race', ethnicity is not based on supposed innate biological differences; rather, it implies similarities derived from belonging to, or being brought up as part of a specific group. Puri (2004: 174) explains:

> Ethnicity is . . . a form of collective identity based on shared cultural beliefs and practices, such as language, history, descent, and religion. Even though ethnicities often allude to enduring kin-based and blood ties, it is widely recognized that they are cultural, not biological ties.

Ethnic identity is linked to one's perceptions and emotions regarding one's affiliation with one's own ethnic group(s) (Fong 2004). Martin and Nakayama (2010b: 185) recognize the following dimensions of ethnic identity: '(1) self-identification, (2) knowledge about the ethnic culture (traditions, customs, values, and behaviors), and (3) feelings about belonging to a particular ethnic group'. For immigrants, an ethnic identity may involve a shared sense of origin and history with ancestors and ethnic groups in distant cultures in Asia, Europe, South America or other parts of the world. A **minority identity** basically refers to one's sense of belong to a minority group, whereas a **majority identity** is one's identification with the dominant or majority group.

While ethnicity may be very important to some, for others, it is of little concern. Individuals who are affiliated with the majority ethnic group (e.g. Han Chinese in Mainland China, white Anglo-Saxons in Britain) may not think much about their ethnic identity, whereas ethnicity may be a core part of the identity of minority members (e.g. Miao, Utsuls, Uyghurs, Tibetans in China; South Asians in Britain). Minority members may speak a different home language, practice a different religion, wear clothing that is particular to their group and maintain customs and traditions that distinguish them from the majority. These differences may be a source of great pride, and minorities may resist policies and practices that conflict with or diminish the status of their first language, religious beliefs and customs. Other minorities may choose to blend in with the majority and downplay their ethnicity. Over time, their offspring may have little emotional connection, if any, to their ethnic group and scant knowledge of the first language of their parents or grandparents. (Chapter 8 further discusses the identities and adaptation strategies of immigrants.)

The notion of ethnic membership or affiliation has also become much more complex due to increasing intercultural contact. With more romantic relationships between people from different ethnic backgrounds, many offspring do not fit neatly into a specific ethnic (or racial) group. For example, U.S. President Barak Obama is of mixed heritage. His mother was a white American, secular humanist (non-religious) with predominantly English roots as well as some

Plate 6.1 This young Chinese woman is dressed in a traditional costume in a venue frequented by tourists and wealthy Chinese in Beijing. What identity is projected through her dress and demeanour? If she was wearing jeans and a t-shirt would your impression differ? Why is it important to consider the situation and context when forming ideas about identities?
© Jane Jackson

German, Scottish, Welsh and Irish ancestry, while his father, a black man, was a Muslim Luo Kenyan from Africa. Mariah Carey, an American singer, has both Irish roots (mother's side) and Hispanic-African heritage from her Venezuelan father. With more intermarriage among individuals from different ethnic backgrounds, the number of people of dual or mixed heritage is becoming increasingly common, especially in parts of the world where there are many immigrants.

Similar to 'race', the terms 'ethnic' and 'ethnicity' are contested as they can be used to categorize and marginalize people (e.g. differentiate them from the majority). In Britain, for example, 'ethnic dress', 'ethnic languages', 'ethnic food' and 'ethnic music' may be used to single out people who are different from the perceived white British norm. Ironically, this majority is actually ethnically diverse (e.g. a mix of people with English, French, Irish, Italian, Scottish heritage). This notion of 'Otherization' is explored further in Chapter 7.

Class identity

One's socioeconomic status may also play a role in one's identity make-up and, subsequently, impact on intercultural relationships. Martin and Nakayama (2008: G-1) define **class identity** as 'a sense of belonging to a group that shares similar economic, occupational, or social status'. A core element in ingroup identification, it may influence who we identify with and associate with. Social class identity can also shape our perceptions and reactions to language use (e.g. accents, dialects) and communication styles in particular settings and contexts.

While often below our level of awareness, we are continuously communicating our economic, social and occupational status through our verbal and nonverbal behaviours. For example, our class identity is indicated through our dress and adornments (e.g. tattoos, jewellery, business suits, designer bags), as well as our posture/stance. Some schools require children to wear uniforms to downplay class differences and build up a shared sense of belonging to the institution. In the military, where hierarchy is very important, personnel often wear different uniforms and other **emblems of identity** (e.g. badges) that indicate their rank. They may also be addressed by different titles and speech (e.g. more formal greetings for senior ranking officers). In some business contexts, more senior staff may wear formal business suits, while entry-level workers wear more casual, informal clothing.

A person's prestige, social honour or popularity in a cultural group may be linked to his or her level of education, intellect or talent rather than economic status or material possessions. In some contexts, for example, individuals who are well educated may be admired for their clever use of words and expressions in poetry and novels although they may have very limited financial resources. Gifted musicians, painters, and other artists who have little money may also be accorded a high status in some contexts and people may use honourifics or terms of respect when addressing them.

Our class status or economic position in society is often reflected in our language use and the ways in which we communicate (both verbally and nonverbally). In particular, the vocabulary and dialect that we use may be linked to our level of education and status. In professional work situations, senior managers may use more direct forms of discourse and less slang than entry-level workers. People with a higher level of education may employ a wider range of vocabulary and, in some cases, may be multilingual as they have had more opportunities to study other languages and travel to other countries.

Individuals who are similar to the majority in terms of economic, education or social status may give little thought to their class identity until they are in the company of people who have a much higher or lower status. Differences in dress, accent, dialect or behaviour can affect communication in diverse cultural settings and may create a barrier between people. In the company of individuals or groups who possess a higher class status, for example, people may feel compelled to adjust their communication style, accent or mode of dress in an effort to fit in and gain more power and respect. While they may initially feel like they are wearing a mask, over time, they may become more comfortable and proficient in another style of communication. Individuals may use an informal, colloquial style when hanging out with friends and family, and switch to a more formal code at work. They may also interact in one language in a work situation and switch to a different language or dialect during their free time.

In the presence of people with a higher social status, individuals from a lower social class may also follow a different path. Strongly resenting those in power, they may retain their usual ways of being (e.g. communication style) and refrain from adopting behaviours that make them feel like imposters. They may even employ creative strategies to avoid personal contact with people with a higher status. (These communication behaviours are linked to the communication accommodation theory that was discussed in Chapter 4.) In the next chapter, we discuss social categorization and the hazards of stereotyping, prejudice and racism.

Language identity

Block (2007: 40) defines **language identity** as 'the assumed and/or attributed relationship between one's sense of self and a means of communication which might be known as a language (e.g. English), a dialect (e.g. Geordie) or a sociolect (e.g. football-speak)'. Language identity is linked to **language expertise** (one's degree of proficiency in a particular language), **language affiliation** (one's attitudes towards and feelings about the language) and **language inheritance** (being born into a family or community where the language is spoken) (Block 2007; Leung *et al.* 1997; Rampton 1990). Language identity is also associated with the notions of avowal and ascription that were explained earlier in this chapter. For example, individuals may wish to be affiliated with a particular social or cultural group through the use of their second language (**avowed identity**), but first language speakers may persist in viewing them as outsiders no matter how well they master the language (**ascribed identity**).

Many dimensions of our social and cultural identities (e.g. gender, class, nationality, ethnicity) are shaped by the language(s) we speak. During the socialization process, language becomes strongly intertwined with culture and identity. Within a particular environment, at a certain period of history, language develops according to the needs and interests of the inhabitants. Over time, social and cultural groups develop certain ways of being, including communication styles and linguistic norms (e.g. cultural scripts, use of particular discourse markers of politeness) (see Chapter 3). In essence, identities emerge from linguistic practice and linguistic performance. Knowing the language of one's group and ancestors can provide a sense of grounding and belonging for many people. It can be a powerful marker of identity, especially when individuals find themselves in situations where the majority use a different language, dialect or sociolect.

Drawing on their extensive fieldwork in the Creole-speaking Caribbean and among West Indian communities in London, sociolinguists Le Page and Tabouret-Keller (1985) observed that people's utterances may serve as 'acts of identity', that is, dimensions of one's identities (e.g. gender, class, nationality, ethnicity, personal) may be conveyed through language choice and use (e.g. accent, code-mixing, jargon) in particular sociocultural settings and situations. With each speech act (e.g. request, apology, refusal), individuals perform 'acts of identity' to varying degrees; in the process, they disclose their solidarity with (or separation from) the people they are communicating with.

Related to this notion of 'acts of identity' is the **Communication accommodation theory (CAT)**, which posits that language may be used as an identity marker to either draw us closer to or further apart from individuals with a different linguistic and cultural background (e.g. those who possess different social and cultural identities from ourselves) (Giles *et al.* 2012). **Convergence** occurs when individuals (e.g. second language speakers) adjust their speech patterns to match those of people belonging to another group (e.g. first language speakers who may possess different social and cultural identities from themselves). **Divergence** happens when individuals (e.g. second language speakers) adjust their speech patterns to be distinct from those of people belonging to another group (e.g. first language speakers who possess different social and cultural identities from themselves).

Similar to other types of social and cultural identities, language identities can change during the course of one's lifetime. For example, you might learn Tagalog as a child in the Philippines and then immigrate to Australia in your twenties, where you live and function in English in your social and professional life. You may marry a native English-speaking Australian and have children who speak only English. Over time, your proficiency in your second language grows to the extent that you feel very confident and at ease when using it in a variety of contexts in your daily life. As you form strong ties with English speakers, you develop a sense of belonging in that linguistic community. In some circles, however, the identity you wish to project (e.g. your English language self) may not be fully recognized and accepted by locals. In other words, it may be contested or challenged. No matter how fluent you are in English, you may still be positioned as a second language speaker since your accent and other linguistic (and non-linguistic) features differ from that of locals. As well as raising further awareness of the notions of avowal and ascription, this scenario draws attention to the potential loss of one's first language and attachment to one's cultural roots. A certain richness of communication and connection is lost when individuals are no longer able to speak the first language of their parents or ancestors. This also has implications for how people (e.g. immigrants, refugees) view their sense of self.

Learning a second language (or more) need not lead to the loss of one's first language and cultural identity, however. Cummins (1994), for example, distinguishes between **subtractive bilingualism**, in which a second language is added at the expense of the first language and culture and **additive bilingualism**, in which the first language and culture continue to be nurtured as a second language develops. In the latter, the individual is enriched by learning two or more languages and cultures and, over time, develops a more broadened sense of self.

Multicultural and multilingual identities

What does it mean to 'be multicultural' or to possess a multicultural identity? Nowadays, in many parts of the world, individuals have more interaction with people from diverse linguistic and cultural backgrounds whether through immigration (e.g. refugees, legal and illegal immigrants), higher education (e.g. more diverse campuses due to internationalization policies), travel, sojourning (e.g. study and residence abroad), marriage (e.g. interethnic, interreligious unions), employment (e.g. expatriates), long-term volunteer work (e.g. missionaries), adoption or birth (e.g. parents with diverse multicultural backgrounds). Individuals who have sustained contact with people from diverse cultures may develop a sense of attachment to multiple ethnic groups and linguistic communities, or they may feel as if they have no ties or affiliation with any group in particular.

Martin and Nakayama (2008: G-4) define a **multicultural identity** as '[a] sense of in-betweeness that develops as a result of frequent or multiple cultural border crossings'. These interculturalists point out that people with many intercultural experiences may develop 'an identity that transcends one particular culture', that is, border crossers may 'feel equally at home in several cultures' (p. 112) as well in multiple languages. They may develop **hybrid (mixed) identities** that integrate diverse cultural elements (e.g. multiple languages, local values, global perspectives) (Kraidy 2005; Kramsch 1993, 2009) that help them to function in today's multicultural world.

Janet Bennett, an American interculturalist, observes that individuals with intense exposure to diverse cultures may internalize multiple 'cultural frames of reference' and respond to this development in different ways; in her words, they may experience **encapsulated marginality** or **constructive marginality**:

> The encapsulated marginal is a person who is buffeted by conflicting cultural loyalties and unable to construct a unified identity. In contrast, by maintaining control of choice and the construction of boundaries, a person may become a 'constructive' marginal. A constructive marginal is a person who is able to construct context intentionally and consciously for the purpose of creating his or her own identity.
>
> (J.M. Bennett 1993: 113)

Janet Bennett (1993) stresses that the use of the term 'marginality' is not intended to be negative, rather it is meant to indicate 'a cultural lifestyle at the edges where two or more cultures meet, which can be either encapsulating or constructive' (p. 113).

Marginality or a state of inbetweenness may develop through intense exposure to other cultures in one's family or community, whether at home or abroad. This is especially the case for **global nomads**, that is, individuals who have an international lifestyle (e.g. living and working in more than one country for a long period of time), including those who have grown up in many different cultural contexts because their parents have frequently relocated (e.g. diplomats and other foreign service staff, the military, expatriate professionals, etc.). Other interculturalists refer to the latter as **third culture kids (TCKs)**, as in the following definition by David Pollock:

> A Third Culture Kid (TCK) is a person who had spent a significant part of his or her developmental years outside the parent's culture. The TCK frequently builds relationships to all of the cultures, while not having full ownership in any. Although elements from each culture may be assimilated into the TCK's life experience, the sense of belonging is in relationship to others of similar background.
>
> (cited in Pollock & Van Reken 2009: 13)

Children who are raised in many different cultural environments (or in multicultural households) may experience a more complex form of primary socialization than those who are raised in a setting where they are part of the majority in terms of ethnicity, first language, religion, etc. At a young age, TCKs are apt to receive mixed messages from those around them (e.g. ideas about what is 'right' and 'wrong', 'fair' and 'unfair') and have more contact with differing social norms of behaviour (e.g. linguistic).

When individuals are exposed to cultural values, practices and identities that sometimes conflict with each other, it can be very disquieting and, in some, it can lead to **identity confusion**. For example, the following was written by a young Chinese woman who grew up in Mainland China, moved to Hong Kong as an adolescent and then attended university in Hong Kong, England and Ireland before becoming an ESL teacher in Hong Kong:

> A person's sense of identity is often greatly influenced by the cultural background he/she grows up with. In my case, traditional Chinese culture plays an important role during my early years. Later, Hong Kong culture and Western culture also greatly influenced me . . . as a result of growing up and having different experiences my perception about who I am changes over time. I am now still a little bit confused about myself.

As noted by Nguyen and Benet-Martínez (2010: 96), '[t]he process of negotiating multiple cultural identities is complex and multi-faceted' and, in some, intense feelings of loss and inbetweenness may emerge. Individuals with encapsulated marginality may feel torn between different cultural worlds, identities and languages. Some may experience difficulty making life choices and feel on the margin of all of the languages and cultures they are in contact with.

While some border crossers may suffer from identity confusion and fragmentation, others may take full advantage of the opportunities that their mobility and multicultural, multilingual experiences afford them. With a positive, open mindset, they may recognize and embrace their ability to comfortably and appropriately interact in different cultural settings in multiple languages. Sparrow (2000), for example, explains her adaptable **multicultural identity** in this way:

> I think of myself not as a unified cultural being but as a communion of different cultural beings. Due to the fact that I have spent time in different cultural environments, I have

developed several cultural identities that diverge and converge according to the need of the moment.

(Sparrow 2000: 190)

Individuals who possess a multicultural identity may develop a 'psychological state of not owning or being owned by a single culture' (Ryan 2012: 428). This can be disconcerting for some and liberating for others. (Later in the chapter, we discuss the development of both local and global identities.)

Gender/gendered identities

When asked to describe our identity, it is natural to mention one's gender. It is also one of the ways that others often categorize us, drawing on their own ideas, experiences and expectations. **Gender**, which comes from the Latin word *genus*, meaning kind or race, refers to one's identification as male, female or, less commonly, both male and female or neither. Gender may be based on such aspects as one's legal status, personal preferences, physical appearance, public persona, activities and interests and social interactions, among others.

Because gender is such a basic category, it is inevitable that there are numerous meanings associated with it. For example, developmental psychologists have linked the following dimensions to gender categories: 'personality traits (e.g. being competitive or being aware of the feelings of others), role behaviors (e.g. taking care of children or assuming leadership roles), physical characteristics (e.g. having broad shoulders or a soft voice), and a host of other associations' (Deaux 2001: 1060).

Language use has also been tied to gender. Differences in vocabulary and communication styles may serve as markers of one's gender in a particular cultural context (Samovar *et al.* 2010). In some settings, for example, females may use more hedging devices (e.g. expressions such as 'maybe', 'sort of', 'what I mean is') and rising intonation than males. Certain words may be used exclusively by males, with females using other expressions to convey similar emotions and meanings. If females express themselves in ways similar to the men they may, in some contexts, be regarded in a very negative way (e.g. as overly aggressive, vulgar) (Cameron 2009; Coates 2004; Tannen 1996, 2001).

To better understand the notion of gender, it is helpful to consider how the World Health Organization (WHO) defines it. For the WHO (n.d.), gender refers to 'the socially constructed roles, behaviours, activities, and attributes that a given society considers appropriate for men and women'.

A number of definitions of **gender identity** have also been put forward by international organizations and scholars in different disciplines. For example, Liu *et al.* (2011: 285) define it as 'a part of a personal identity that entails the social roles, assumptions, and expectations established for each sex'. For Wintergerst and McVeigh (2011: 230), gender identity refers to 'identification based on one's gender, and society's conceptualization of the role of that gender'. Noting that gender identity differs from biological sex or sexual identity, Ting-Toomey and Chung (2012: 69) define gender identity as 'the meanings and interpretations we hold concerning our self-images and expected other-images of femaleness and maleness'. All of these scholars note that one's understanding of gender develops as children during the socialization process. As this takes place in particular sociocultural, historical contexts, it is not surprising that different gender-related behaviours are promoted.

Instead of viewing gender as a single social category, some scholars prefer to use the term **gendered identities**. The plural form acknowledges that 'multiple identities are shaped by one's gender, and that social identities can intersect and overlap with one another' (Deaux 2001: 1061). Rather than being singular and fixed, gender identities are multi-dimensional and constructed in particular social contexts through the process of **gender socialization**. For example, relationships (e.g. wife, husband) and professions (e.g. nursing, engineering) frequently have multiple gender implications within particular cultures. To complicate matters, expectations of roles and responsibilities evolve over time and vary in different cultural settings, even among people who are categorized as belonging to the same gender. An individual's identity as a female, for example, may differ depending on whether she sees herself as a traditional woman or a feminist. Due to globalizing forces and the increasing interconnectedness of the world, the roles of women, in particular, are changing, along with communication styles, language use and values. Nowadays, women in many cultures are in professions that were once reserved for males, and vice versa.

Just as gender-related behaviours vary among individuals and within cultures, notions of what it means to be male or female or masculine or feminine also differ. As Sorrells (2013: 53) explains,

> Differences between masculinity and femininity are symbolically embodied, performed, and communicated within our specific cultural contexts through the way we walk; through our gestures, speech, touch, and eye contact patterns; through the way we use physical space and the gendered activities we participate in; through our hairstyles, clothing, the use of makeup or not; and through colors, smells, and adornments.
>
> (Butler 1990; Wood 2005)

In all cultures, variations in gender roles may also exist that differ from majority practices. For example, **gender-crossing** (e.g. beginning life as a male and assuming female behaviours and characteristics) has existed in societies for generations (e.g. Hijaras in Pakistan, Fafafinis in Samoa). People who are categorized as neither male nor female (either by themselves or by social consensus) may sometimes be labelled as a **third gender**. The Fafafinis, for example, were born male and raised to assume female gender roles. **Transgender** refers to 'people whose gender identities differ from the social norms and expectations associated with their biological sex' (Sorrells 2013: 53). When societies develop fixed expectations of gender roles and behaviour, those who do not fit the norm may be subjected to gendered inequality and oppression (Abbott 2000), an aspect that is explored further in the next chapter.

Sexual identity

To understand the relationship between sex and identity, it is essential to first distinguish between what is meant by 'sex' and 'gender'. As discussed in the previous sub-section, gender is associated with culturally-influenced perceptions of masculine and feminine attributes, roles and behaviours. In contrast, **sex** refers to the biological and physiological characteristics that define men and women. Whereas 'male and female' are sex categories, 'masculine' and 'feminine' are gender classifications. Gender characteristics and functions (e.g. roles and responsibilities) may differ considerably among and within cultures; however, sexual characteristics and functions are much less variable. For example, no matter the culture, most women menstruate and can give birth whereas men cannot, women have developed breasts that can provide milk for babies while men do not, men have testicles while women do not and so on.

Accordingly, scholars distinguish **sexual identity** from notions of gendered identities that were defined in the previous sub-section. The former refers to how one thinks of oneself in terms of who one is sexually and romantically attracted to. While related to sexual identity and sexual behaviour (e.g. actual sexual acts), one's **sexual orientation** refers to desires, fantasies and attachments to sexual partners. Sexual identity may or may not relate to one's actual sexual orientation, e.g. individuals may be attracted to members of the same sex but project a sexual identity that differs from this orientation.

Sexual orientation implies an enduring pattern of attraction (e.g. emotional, romantic, sexual) to members of the opposite sex, the same sex or both sexes, and the genders associated with them. In North America, these attractions are usually referred to as **heterosexuality** (sexual attraction to members of the opposite sex), **homosexuality** (sexual attraction to members of the same sex) and **bisexuality** (sexual attraction to both males and females). Cultures may use diverse terms and definitions of sexualities and the attitudes towards those who differ from the majority vary considerably. Accordingly, the ways that people view themselves and their sexual orientation may also differ. For example, in parts of the world where gays and lesbians have gained more rights and respect, more are willing to claim a sexual identity that embraces their homosexuality. In homophobic environments, people may try to conceal their homosexual or bisexual identities for security reasons, e.g. fear of being outgrouped (rejected by ingroup members), discriminated against or worse (e.g. physically abuse, imprisonment, murder).

The way you view and categorize sexualities may differ from those of individuals who have been socialized in a different cultural environment. The language used to identify people according to their sexual preference (e.g. identity labels) can also vary. These terms or labels offer insight into an individual's or society's value judgments and degree of openness to people who are different.

Age identity

In most cultures, age is an important element for individuals, groups and societies. Age can influence one's self-image, personality, language use, attitudes and communication with others. It can also determine one's positioning and status in family, work, leisure and social settings (e.g. religious, political and secular community organizations).

Age identity refers to how people feel and think about themselves and others based on age. It is concerned with the inner experience of a person's age and the aging process. Westerhof (2008) defines age identity as 'the outcome of the processes through which one identifies with or distances oneself from different aspects of the aging process' (p. 10). In scientific research, a person's age identity is typically measured by responses to such questions as 'How old do you feel?', 'To which age group do you belong?', 'How do you perceive and understand your own aging process?' and 'In what ways do you communicate your age to others?'

Several dimensions of age identity have been scrutinized, including how people feel, act, look, behave (e.g. functional capacities, interests, hobbies, social roles and activities), think (e.g. cognitive and linguistic functioning, attitudes, values) and express themselves (e.g. language use, colloquialisms) at different stages of their life. In diverse settings, research on aging has examined how individuals from different cultural backgrounds: (1) identify with or classify themselves into larger age groups, (2) compare themselves to peers of the same age (e.g. ingroup identification), (3) perceive and distinguish themselves from other age groups (e.g. outgroups) and (4) communicate verbally and nonverbally with individuals from their own and other age groups.

The relationship between language, age and culture is of particular interest to intercultural communication specialists who are concerned with the adjustment of immigrants and sojourners (temporary residents) in new linguistic and cultural environments. As noted by many cross-cultural psychologists, it is not unusual for different generations to have disparate values, worldviews, philosophies and ways of speaking. In immigrant families, people from older generations (e.g. from the 'old country') may use a dialect, expressions or colloquialisms that are foreign to younger members of their families who have grown up in the receiving country. While children may learn the primary language of the 'new country' at school and informally in the wider community, parents or grandparents may have little or no command of the language and, not surprisingly, intergenerational problems may arise.

Older immigrants who had senior professional positions in their home country may find themselves in occupations with less status. Without a good command of the new country's language they may feel devalued and depressed. Their young children, who have more proficiency in the local language and more informal exposure to cultural practices, may serve as interpreters or cultural brokers for their elders, which further challenges traditional notions of age and status.

Views about age and the process of growing older also vary among cultures and shape one's expectations of roles, status and responsibilities as well as everyday social interactions. Our perceptions of age and the aging process are conveyed by our family members, religious organizations, schools and peers, as well as through advertisements, the television, the Internet and other forms of mass media and social networks. In traditional, less industrialized contexts, the wisdom and life experiences of older people are prized. In tribal areas in Northern Thailand, for example, as a marker of respect, younger people may use relationship titles or honourifics when addressing their elders.

In industrialized nations, people with the most experience are typically in senior posts in most fields and industries (e.g. higher education, business, health care, politics), although the technological revolution is now propelling younger people into very lucrative, powerful positions. For example, Mark Zuckerberg, an American computer programmer, co-founded the social networking site Facebook when he was only 19. In 2010, at the age of 26, he was identified by *Time Magazine* as one of the most influential men in the world. As the chairman and chief executive officer (CEO) of Facebook, Inc. he is now worth billions. While his wealth is extreme, there are many other young entrepreneurs who have played a role in the digital revolution and become very successful at a young age.

Undeniably, youth is highly valued in Western cultures. This is evident in the marketing campaigns that bombard people with messages about the significance of looking young and staying fit. Annually, millions of dollars are spent on cosmetic products and surgical procedures in an effort to fight against the natural aging process. Due to technological advances (e.g. social media) and globalizing forces these notions are spreading across the globe and challenging traditional perceptions of age and the aging process. As people are living and working longer in modern societies, views about what it means to be old are changing.

Religious identity

In many parts of the world, one's affiliation with a religion is a core dimension of one's identity, and it can have a profound impact on one's daily life. **Religious identity** basically refers to one's sense of belonging to a particular religious group. Similar to other aspects of identity, a religious identity may mean different things to individuals, and the importance of one's religious affiliation may also change over time with exposure to other beliefs and practices. In some cultural settings, one's religious affiliation is considered a private affair and there is a clear separation of religion and government; in other contexts, religion permeates all dimensions of life.

Religious identity formation is concerned with the process by which individuals decide what their relationship to religion will be. In many contexts, messages from family and religious figures begin at a very early age and are reinforced through various rituals (e.g. prayers, weekly sermons that have messages about moral behaviours) and ceremonies (e.g. baptism and confirmation for Christians, the bar mitzvah to mark a Jew's coming of age). One's affiliation with a particular religion may also be conveyed and reinforced through one's dress (e.g. the wearing of a skull cap or robes of a particular colour), adornments/jewellery (e.g. wearing a necklace with a cross), personal grooming (e.g. the growing of a beard by male devotees) and the eating of special foods (e.g. kosher foods by Jews, halal food by Muslims). The use of a particular language or dialect may also be linked to one's religion (e.g. Arabic in Islam as the holy book, the Qur'an, was written in this language).

Membership in a religious group can offer believers a sense of community and provide inner fulfilment. While one's religious identity can be a great source of strength and provide a purpose or direction for one's life, in some situations it can serve as a barrier to intercultural communication. For example, people may refuse to socialize or interact with atheists or followers of a different faith. When individuals who are in positions of power have little respect for the religious views and ideals of members of another religious group (including atheists or non-believers), disputes and even wars may result. This aspect is discussed further in Chapter 7 when we examine the impact of stereotyping, prejudice and racism and reflect further on ways to develop a more respectful mindset.

Physical and mental ability identity

All people have a **physical ability identity** as each of us has both physical capabilities and limitations. No human is perfect. We may be limited in some ways by our height, weight, body shape, chronic illness or other physical features. Throughout our life, we may strive to overcome multiple dimensions of our physical ability, especially as we age. Some people are temporarily disabled (e.g. broken leg or jaw), while others are born with disabilities (e.g. cerebral palsy, blindness, deafness, inability to speak). Individuals may become permanently disabled through illness or accidents, or they may develop chronic conditions (e.g. multiple sclerosis, Parkinson's disease) that impact on their quality of life and impede their communication with others.

We also have a **mental ability identity** that is linked to our cognitive abilities (e.g. degree of intelligence), mental health (e.g. stable, depressed) and ability to function in everyday life. Some people may be of above average intelligence (e.g. intellectually gifted), while others may be below average (e.g. intellectually challenged, developmentally delayed). Some individuals have been born with less cognitive ability, whereas others have suffered a diminished mental capacity as a consequence of illness, drug use, an accident or the aging process. Individuals may also suffer from a mental illness or disorder (e.g. autism, bipolarism, schizophrenia).

How people view their mental state, cognitive ability and physical capabilities impacts on their sense of self and positioning in society. Individuals with disabilities, whether mental or physical, may regard themselves as members of a special cultural group with their own values, practices, language and communication patterns (e.g. deaf culture, blind culture). As noted by Braithwaite and Braithwaite (2003), group members who share similar perceptions, concerns and aspirations may work together to fight for more respect and recognition in the wider society. Chapter 7 discusses prejudicial attitudes and discriminatory practices related to the treatment of people with physical and mental disabilities.

National identity

Most people have a **national identity**, which is related to their affiliation with and sense of belonging to a particular state or nation. While some scholars limit this type of identity to official citizenship, others refer to it as the feeling one shares with a group of people in a nation, regardless of one's citizenship status. For example, illegal immigrants who have spent much of their life in a particular country may possess a sense of belonging to their adopted home even if they have no legal papers to formalize this sentiment. Accordingly, Liu *et al.* (2011: 289) prefer to describe national identity as 'a type of identity that is characterized by one's individual perception of him- or herself as a member of a nation'.

One's national identity may be associated with specific symbols (e.g. flags, flowers, colours), language(s) (e.g. dialects, code-mixing, bilingualism policy), ethnicity, music (e.g. national anthem in a particular language or languages, folk songs), cuisine (e.g. local dishes, a special type of cooking), political system (e.g. democracy, communism), religion(s), TV stations (and other forms of media), heroes (Olympians, war heroes), special feats (e.g. inventions), a shared history and so on. Verbal and nonverbal symbols may serve as a bond for many nationals; however, it is important to recognize that people within a nation may have very different understandings and emotions in relation to each symbol (e.g. use of 'official' language, oath of allegiance, national anthem).

The strength of one's national identity may vary over time. When under threat, whether real or imagined, one's national identity tends to strengthen and draw individuals closer to other people from the same nation. National identity can be a great source of pride and provide individuals with a sense of belonging; however, it can also lead to negative perceptions and mistreatment of people who are affiliated with other nations. These identity markers may serve as the basis for people from other countries to treat nationals in a particular way (e.g. display admiration, convey disrespect and hostility).

Regional identity

Linked to national identity is the notion of **regional identity**, which conveys the idea that part of an individual's identity is rooted in his or her region of residence. Basically, it involves a sense of belonging similar to that of national identity but on a smaller scale or level. In many nations, people from particular regions have distinct identities, which may vary in importance among the inhabitants. For some, regional identities may be even more meaningful and significant than their national affiliation. Other individuals, of course, may distance themselves from a regional label, preferring to be linked to a broader, more national or even international persona.

Regional identities may be inspired by cultural, ethnic, religious, linguistic or political ties as well as geography. For example, people who live on an island or in an isolated, mountainous region may develop bonds and habits (e.g. linguistic, cultural, religious) that distinguish them from people in other parts of the country. If the inhabitants do not feel understood or respected at the national level, regional ties can sometimes be a powerful motivating force that drives independence movements. In some cases, this has led to the creation of autonomous regions or states (e.g. Bosnia, Herzegovina, Slovenia, Namibia).

In many regions, people are distinguished from the rest of their nation by their own unique linguistic and cultural identities, which are accompanied by special forms of dress, artwork, food and social norms such as unwritten rules of politeness (e.g. verbal and nonverbal greetings). Because of ethnic or religious ties, inhabitants in a particular region may feel a stronger connection with each other than people in other parts of their nation. Regional accents and dialects may identify people as being from a particular region. For example, in Britain someone from Yorkshire typically has a very different accent compared with a lifelong resident of London. In Canada, French is the primary language of the province of Québec, and for many French-speaking Québécois, their regional identity is much stronger than their national identity. This is also the case in many other regions of the world (e.g. the Basque region of Spain, the Kurdish region of Iraq).

As well as by geography, regions may be emotionally separated from the rest of a nation due to political and historical reasons. For example, after being a colony of Britain since the 1800s, in 1997 Hong Kong reunited with Mainland China and is now a Special Administrative Region (SAR) in this populous nation. Although China is governed by the Communist Party, Hong Kong has aspirations of democracy. In addition to politics, language is also closely intertwined with the regional identity of Hong Kongers. The use of Cantonese distinguishes Hong Kong Chinese from Mainlanders who speak Putonghua (Mandarin), the official language of the 'Motherland' or another Chinese dialect. Similar to other types of social identity, the meaning and significance of regional identities may change over time (e.g. as a consequence of policies to instill national sentiment).

Global identity

Chapter 1 discussed how globalization has made our world increasingly interconnected, facilitating mobility and interaction between people from diverse backgrounds. As well as national, regional or local identities, more and more individuals are developing a **global identity** that affords them 'a sense of belonging in a worldwide culture' (Arnett 2002: 777).

A global identity is often associated with the use of an international language. For example, as mentioned earlier in the chapter, individuals who speak English as an additional language may feel connected to speakers of the language in distant lands and, over time, develop a global persona. Third culture kids (TCKs) and other multicultural individuals who are open to what the world has to offer welcome diverse intercultural and linguistic experiences. As they acquire a more cosmopolitan outlook, they may nurture both local and global selves.

Through a global identity (and global language), we can recognize and appreciate our connection with people in other parts of the world. Our broadened mindset can help us to solve the pressing issues facing us today (e.g. food shortages, global warming, territorial disputes). As noted by Gerzon (2010: xvii), 'we human beings are now being challenged to realize that we are something more than citizens of separate nations, members of different races, and followers of different religions. We are also global citizens'. In Chapter 12 we discuss global citizenship and ways to nurture a more intercultural, global mindset, whether in one's home environment or in an international setting.

Organizational identity

People may also develop an **organizational identity**, that is, a sense of attachment to organizations, whether in their social, educational, religious or professional life. For example, my university follows a college system and all undergraduates and professors are linked to a particular college. In a large institution like this, it is easier for people to get to know one another in smaller groups and the colleges arrange activities designed to build up a sense of belonging among members. For many students, their college identity becomes so strong that it persists well after graduation. Graduates may maintain Facebook contact with each other and regularly attend functions organized by their alumni associations for many years after leaving our campus.

When people enter the workforce, they are often employed by a company or organization and, through a variety of activities, they become inducted into the culture of that organization. Over time, they may build up a degree of loyalty and pride in the organization, and acquire a company identity. In some contexts, individuals spend their entire career with a single company and their primary identity is work-related. In many parts of the world, however, people are changing jobs and relocating much more frequently for a variety of reasons (e.g. economic recessions, more opportunities for advancement). As one might expect, this is impacting on organizational identities and bringing about more diversity in the workplace, an aspect that is discussed further in Chapter 11.

Within an organization or workplace, language can serve as a powerful marker of one's membership or affiliation. For example, the use of specialized terms and informal discourse that is only fully understood by members of one's organization (or work team) can reinforce the distinctiveness of one's group and bolster one's organizational identity or sense of belonging.

Organizational identity can also be linked to the notion of 'communities of practice' (Lave & Wenger 1991). Eckert and McConnell-Ginet (1992: 464) define a **community of practice** as 'an aggregate of people who come together around mutual engagement in an endeavor'. Through social and professional interaction with more experienced members, newcomers form an understanding of their roles and responsibilities, that is, they learn about particular '[w]ays of doing things, ways of thinking, ways of talking, beliefs, values, power relations—in short practices' (Eckert & McConnell-Ginet 1992: 464). While engaging in the practices of their organization (or other type of group), members gradually move from 'apprentices' to 'experts'; in the process, they construct identities in relation to the group or community.

Identities are partly shaped and conditioned by social interaction and social structure (Block 2007, 2013). Similar to many other types of identity, the salience and strength of one's organizational identity may vary and change over time depending on many factors (e.g. perceived benefits of the affiliation, desire and need to/pressure to fit in, current attitude towards the organization, views of outsiders about the organization). As economies come under pressure, people in many parts of the world are less likely to be affiliated with one employer for their entire working career. Consequently, in the employment domain, loyalty to a particular organizational identity may weaken.

Professional identity

Related to the notion of organizational identity is the formation of a **professional identity**, which refers to an individual's sense of belonging in a particular profession (e.g. teaching, nursing, business, etc.). This form of identity encompasses beliefs, attitudes and understanding about one's roles within the context of work (Adams *et al.* 2006; Lingard *et al.* 2002) and is characterized by the use of specialized terms (e.g. jargon) and communication styles.

Professional identity formation refers to how individuals develop a sense of what it means to be a member of a particular profession, and how this identity distinguishes them from other professional groups. This developmental process is closely linked to the notion of 'communities of practice' that was described above (Lave & Wenger 1991). For example, if you decide to become an English as a second language teacher you will attend teacher education and applied linguistics courses and likely participate in a practicum (e.g. practice teaching in a school) as an 'apprentice'. By observing and interacting with experienced professionals ('experts'), you develop an understanding of the worldview (e.g. beliefs and attitudes) that is emphasized in your chosen profession, as well as the theories and methodologies that one is expected to master (Alsup 2006; Granello & Young 2012). As your professional identity takes shape, you discover the boundaries of the teaching profession and the ways to behave or interact with other teachers and students. In particular, you learn the language and communication styles that are appropriate in different situations.

Virtual (cyber and fantasy) identities

In this era of advanced information technology, **cyberculture** has emerged from the use of computer networks for communication, business and entertainment. The Internet, gaming and multi-user domains (MUDs) are spawning new types of identity. In online virtual communities (e.g. online chat rooms, online multi-player games, social gaming, social media and texting), a user may create a **virtual (cyber) identity** or **e-identity**, which serves as an interface between the physical person and the virtual person that other users view on their computer screen. As noted by J. Suler (2002: 455), 'multiple aspects of one's identity may be dissociated, enhanced, or integrated online'. Users may create a persona that is far different from who they are in real life and the language they use and the way they express themselves may differ considerably from their communication style in face-to-face interactions.

When you become a member of an online community, you usually have some control over how much personal information, if any, you wish to reveal about yourself. You can choose to let other users see how you actually look or you can post the photo of someone else. You can also decide if others can hear your voice. Suler (2002: 455) explains that 'the desire to remain anonymous reflects the need to eliminate those critical features of your identity that you do NOT want to display in that particular environment or group'. Advocates of cyber communication maintain that this allows people to engage in intercultural communication with individuals they might never meet in real life. As people may not see your physical characteristics, they are reliant on the personal details you provide about yourself in texts (e.g. your age, ethnicity, first language), the images (e.g. photos, artwork) you post, as well as your use of emoticons (pictorial representations of facial expressions and other symbols that are meant to convey particular emotions).

Cyberculture and the possibility of anonymity have significantly altered the ways many people communicate on a day-to-day basis. Spending too much time immersed in virtual reality with one's cyber identity(ies) can cause some to lose touch with the real world. In South Korea, for example, psychologists are counselling a growing number of young people who are addicted to online gaming. Lost in a fantasy world, some find it difficult to communicate with people in direct physical interactions and feel like outsiders in their home environment.

In all cultures, there are also forms of **fantasy identities**, which centre on 'characters from science fiction movies, comic books (manga), and anime' (Samovar *et al.* 2012: 224). Each July, Hong Kong hosts one of the world's largest animation and comic book fairs, attracting thousands of fans who bring super heroes (e.g. Thor, Spiderman, Captain America, Optimus Prime) to life through colourful costumes. These events bring together young people and adults from different backgrounds, who share a passion for particular fantasy characters. Annually, Star Wars conventions in the U.S. also attract people who dress up like their favourite characters.

SUMMARY

Identity is a core element in intercultural interactions. We all have multiple identities (e.g. age, ethnic, gender, religious, national, cyber) that impact on how we see ourselves and others. Identities are dynamic and influenced by the language and cultural socialization process, our sociocultural environment and our desire to fit in with particular groups. While we may wish to project a certain identity, others may view us in a different way, which can be very disconcerting. Identities are complex and subject to negotiation and may be contested in diverse contexts. While our affiliations with particular groups can provide us with a sense of belonging, our identities and attitudes can also serve as barriers to intercultural communication, an aspect that is explored in Chapter 7.

discussion questions

1 How have perceptions and definitions of identity changed over the years?
2 Who are you? Make a list of ten statements about your identity (I am . . .). Write as many statements about yourself as you can possibly think of in ten minutes. What do these statements reveal about your cultural identity? Personal identity? Ethnic identity? What other facets of your identity have you disclosed? How has your linguistic and cultural background influenced who you are today and who you hope to be in the future?
3 What does it mean to say that the process of identity construction is 'complex, multifaceted, dynamic, and dialogic' (Schecter & Bayley 2002: 49)?
4 In a small group, discuss how language use and gender identity/roles may differ in different cultural contexts.
5 According to Mary Fong and Rueyling Chuang (2004), each and every speech community is layered with the multiple identities of its individual members. What do they mean by this? Do you agree?
6 How do you define yourself in your home environment? Does this change when you are outside your home country or region?

7 Why do bi and multilingual speakers sometimes feel like they have different identities when speaking different languages? Reflecting on your own experiences,
   describe your sense of self when using different languages in different contexts.
8 Identify features of your language or language usage that may signal your ethnic
   identity or other facets of your identity.
9 Have you ever been in a situation in which your preferred identities were not
   recognized or respected? Describe your emotions and response.
10 Why is it important to recognize and respect the preferred self-identities of the
    people we are communicating with?
11 Reflect on what you have learned about identity in this chapter. What are the impli-
    cations for intercultural relations? How might this knowledge impact on the way
    you communicate with people with a different linguistic and cultural background?

further reading

Block, D. (2009) *Second Language Identities*, London: Continuum.

Drawing on social science theory, the author discusses identity formation and change
in foreign language learners, adult migrants and study abroad students.

Edwards, J. (2009) *Language and Identity: An Introduction*, Cambridge: Cambridge
University Press.

The language we use forms an important part of our identity. This book discusses the
relationship between our identity as members of groups (e.g. ethnic, national, religious,
gender) and the language varieties associated with each group.

Kim, M.S. (2002) *Non-Western Perspectives on Human Communication: Implications
for Theory and Practice*, Thousand Oaks, CA: Sage.

The author proposes a non-Western way of conceptualizing identity, or the self, and
challenges readers to re-examine their approach to intercultural study.

Kim, Y.Y. (2009) 'The identity factor in intercultural competence', in D. Deardorff (ed.)
The SAGE Handbook of Intercultural Competence, Thousand Oaks, CA: Sage, pp.
53–65.

In this chapter, the author discusses the role that identities can play in intercultural relations.

Noels, K.A., Yashima, T. and Zhang, R. (2012) 'Language, identity and intercultural
communication', in J. Jackson (ed.) *Routledge Handbook of Language and Intercultural
Communication*, Abingdon: Routledge, pp. 52–66.

In this chapter, the authors critically examine how scholars in social psychology, communication and applied linguistics define identity; their review highlights the complex
relation between language and identity in intercultural communication.

Pollock, D.C. and Van Reken, R.E. (2009) *Third Culture Kids: Growing Up Among Worlds*, Boston: Nicholas Brealey Publishing.

Drawing on interviews and personal writings, this book explores the challenges and benefits of being Third Culture Kids (TCKs), young people who have spent a significant part of their developmental years abroad.

Riley, P. (2008) *Language, Culture, and Identity*, London: Continuum.

This book examines the complex and dynamic relation between language, culture and identity. It discusses how language shapes and is shaped by identity in particular social, linguistic, cultural and ethnic contexts.

Shi, X. and Langman, J. (2012) 'Gender, language, identity, and intercultural communication', in J. Jackson (ed.) *Routledge Handbook of Language and Intercultural Communication*, Abingdon: Routledge, pp. 167–80.

In this chapter, the authors discuss the major topics and theoretical approaches that have shaped language, gender and identity studies.

CHAPTER 7

Ethnocentricism and Othering

Barriers to intercultural communication

'I'm not racist, but . . .'
'It's just a joke.'
'Some of my best friends are . . .'

(James 2001:1)

It is not our differences that divide us. It is our inability to recognize, accept, and celebrate those differences.

(Lorde 1986: 197)

Change your thoughts and you change your world.

(Peale 2007: 233)

learning objectives

By the end of this chapter, you should be able to:

1 explain the process of social categorization
2 describe the relationship between perception and social categorization
3 discuss the implications of social categorization and Othering for intercultural relations
4 define and discuss the nature of ethnocentrism
5 distinguish between a generalization and a stereotype
6 describe the process of stereotyping and provide examples of stereotypes (e.g. racial and ethnic, language, gender, religious)
7 identify at least four reasons why people stereotype
8 provide examples of sexist and ageist language
9 explain how stereotypes can serve as barriers to intercultural communication
10 define and provide examples of bias and prejudice
11 describe the causes of prejudice
12 define and provide examples of discrimination and discriminatory language
13 define and discuss the nature of racism
14 identify three types of racism and provide an example of each
15 describe the potential impact of racism and xenophobia on intercultural relations
16 identify ways to combat ethnocentric tendencies and biases.

INTRODUCTION

In the previous chapter, we examined the nature, characteristics and multiple types of identities that exist in today's complex world. While identity can provide us with a sense of belonging, it can also serve as the basis for negative views and reactions to people who are different from us. We are naturally drawn to people who share a similar language, culture and way of being and we may unconsciously or consciously shy away from those who do not belong to our ingroup. As Samovar *et al.* (2012: 169) explain, '[o]ur preference for things we understand and are familiar with can adversely influence our perception of and attitude toward new and different people and things. This can lead to stereotyping, prejudice, racism, and ethnocentricism'.

Social categorization and ethnocentricism lie at the heart of identity biases and discrimination. Consequently, this chapter begins by examining these processes, which all too often create barriers to successful, equitable intercultural interactions. We then examine what lies behind racist and xenophobic behaviour (e.g. racist discourse, exclusion). Finally, we discuss ways to overcome ethnocentricism and identity biases.

SOCIAL CATEGORIZATION AND OTHERING

Social categorization refers to the way we group people into conceptual categories in order to make sense of our increasingly complex social environment. This entails the act of **perception**, that is, 'becoming aware of, knowing, or identifying by means of the senses' through a three-step process involving selection, organization and interpretation (Jandt 2007: 433). Throughout each day we are continuously exposed to a variety of perceptual stimuli (e.g. sights, sounds, smells) that can be overwhelming. To cope, we try to reduce information to manageable forms. In the process, we typically place people into different groups and categories based on our current understandings, perceptions and experience (Allport 1954). In other words, we make inferences about individual behaviour based on group patterns. Unfortunately, this can easily lead to essentialism.

> Essentialism is the position that the attributes and behavior of socially defined groups can be determined and explained by reference to cultural and/or biological characteristics believed to be inherent to the group. As an ideology, essentialism rests on two assumptions: (1) that groups can be clearly delimited; and (2) that group members are more or less alike.
>
> (Bucholtz 2003: 400)

Essentialism and other negative consequences of Othering can be very harmful to intercultural relations as noted by many interculturalists, including Prue Holmes (2012: 468):

> the cognitive activities of categorization and generalization that occur normally in the human brain are an important way of making sense of the world around us. Although such categorizations are useful as sense-making strategies for human behavior, if unchecked, they can lead to more extreme understandings of cultural difference, such as ethnocentrism, stereotyping, and prejudice—the roots of racism.

Otherization or **Othering**, a form of social representation, involves 'the objectification of another person or group' (Abdallah-Pretceille 2003). In this process, culture is used to account for all of the views and behaviours of 'the other', largely ignoring the complexity and diversity of individual characteristics (e.g. thoughts, emotions, actions) (Holliday 2006, 2012; Dervin 2012; Virkama 2010). This leads to reductionism or essentialism, that is, 'pretending that knowing the other takes place through knowing her culture as a static object' (Abdallah-Pretceille 2003: 13). Instead of seeing people from different cultural and linguistic backgrounds as individuals, in the eyes of an ethnocentric person, they are merely representatives of a particular culture, and tied to a rigid set of characteristics and behaviours.

Social categorization and Othering are linked to the **social identity theory** that was developed by Henri Tajfel and John Turner in the 1970s and 1980s to explain intergroup behaviour (Tajfel 1982; Tajfel & Turner 1979, 1986). A basic tenant of this theory is the notion that individuals tend to categorize people in their social environment into ingroups and outgroups (e.g. 'us' and 'them') (Wodak 2008).

Ting-Toomey and Chung (2012: 303) define **ingroup members** as 'people with whom you feel connected to or owe a sense of loyalty and allegiance, such as family members, close friends, or familiar others within the community'. For Jandt (2007: 430), an ingroup is a '[c]ohesive group that offers protection in exchange for loyalty and provides its members with a sense of identity'. Ingroups ('us') typically consist of people from the same perceived ethnic or religious group, or peers of the same age, gender, class, political affiliation or occupation, etc. This also means that we usually belong to multiple ingroups at the same time and one's ingroups may change at different stages of one's life.

In contrast, **outgroup members** are 'those with whom one feels emotionally and psychologically detached, such as strangers, unfamiliar others, or members who belong to a competitive or opposing group' (Ting-Toomey & Chung 2012: 306). Who we perceive as outsiders ('them') may also change as we gain more life experience (e.g. engage in more intercultural interactions).

One of my students wrote the following in a journal, disclosing how she defined one of her most important ingroups. Her comments reveal ways in which negative perceptions can serve as barriers to interactions with outgroup members.

> I strongly recognize myself as belonging to a religious group, and I find my particular religion a concrete and absolute thing in culture that conspicuously differentiates me from nonbelievers . . . The way I choose friends and socialize with other people is very much based on my religion, too. I see nonbelievers as human beings belonging to their flesh. Thus, I share no common points with them in their spiritual aspects, and I should not adopt their thoughts and behaviors.

The social identity theory posits that it is natural for people to seek ways to 'strengthen their self-esteem' and to 'strive to achieve or to maintain a positive social identity' (Tajfel & Turner 1979). Positive ingroup membership can help to accomplish these aspirations by providing a sense of belonging and camaraderie among those who are thought to share similar beliefs, values and traditions or ways of being (e.g. communication styles). People tend to view their ingroup more positively than other groups as they gain positive self-esteem from their group memberships.

Group characteristics are developed over time within specific social, historical, linguistic, religious, political and geographic contexts. By observing how other group members behave and act (e.g. use language and nonverbal means of communication), we discover what values and attributes are associated with and prized by our ingroup(s). The typical characteristics of the group gradually become norms for one's own behaviour, reinforcing one's group membership. This learning is part of the socialization and identity formation processes that were discussed in Chapters 3 and 6. The emotional and cognitive significance of our ingroup membership becomes salient and is often strengthened when in the presence of outgroup members, especially when there is discord or rivalry between groups. In times of heightened tension and conflict, emotive 'us' vs. 'them' discourse may prevail.

Individuals with a strong ingroup identification tend to more fully adopt the values, behaviours and practices that are associated with their particular ingroup(s). As well as guiding thoughts and actions, the group's norms serve as a basis for Othering, that is judging outsiders (outgroup members) by one's own standards. People who have a more intense connection with their ingroup identity see themselves as more typical group members and are more apt to evaluate the performance of ingroup members more favourably than outsiders (Tajfel & Turner 1979).

Ingroup-favouritism (sometimes called **ingroup bias)** refers to situations in which people give preferential treatment to those who are perceived to be in the same ingroup. Ting-Toomey and Chung (2012: 303) define the **ingroup-favouritism principle** as 'a positive attachment to and predisposition for norms that are related to one's ingroup'. If ingroup members feel under threat from outsiders, ingroup favouritism may be accompanied by outgroup derogation (e.g. 'us' vs. 'them' discourse whereby us is positioned more favourably). Insufficient knowledge about outsiders and negative expectations can heighten one's anxiety level and reduce the desire to interact with people outside one's ingroup (Gudykunst 2005). Not surprisingly, then, favouring one's ingroup can lead to the negative consequences of Othering, e.g. prejudice, discrimination, sexism, ageism and racism.

ETHNOCENTRICISM

Through the process of primary socialization, people in all cultures develop expectations and shared understandings about the most appropriate ways to behave in different situations and contexts. Basically, from our parents, teachers and religious leaders we learn the social rules and ways of being (e.g. linguistics norms of politeness) that are preferred by members of our particular ingroup (e.g. ethnic group, religious group). We are exposed to worldviews endorsed by those who are closest to us and over time we develop common ideas about what is 'right' and 'wrong', 'fair' and 'unfair', etc. If we have limited contact with other cultural groups, we may also assume that everyone does things as we do.

The ingroup-favouritism principle is closely linked to the notion of **ethnocentricism**, which derives from the Greek words *ethnos*, meaning 'nation' or 'people,' and *kentron*, meaning *centre*. The term ethnocentrism was coined by William G. Sumner, an American sociologist, who observed the tendency of people to differentiate between their ingroup (e.g. ethnic group) and outsiders in a way that privileges their own group members. He defines ethnocentricism as '[t]he sentiment of cohesion, internal comradeship, and devotion to the ingroup, which carries with it a sense of superiority to any out-group and readiness to defend the interests of the ingroup against the out-group' (Sumner 1911: 11). Individuals with an ethnocentric mindset see people from other cultural backgrounds as inferior or insignificant compared with their own ingroup members. Ethnocentric behaviour may be characterized by arrogance, vanity and even contempt for people who do not belong to one's ingroup.

Ethnocentric thinking may cause us to make false assumptions and premature judgments about people who have been socialized in a different cultural environment. When we only draw on our own cultural (and linguistic) norms to evaluate unfamiliar practices (e.g. cultural scripts, sociopragmatic norms, customs, ethics, religious traditions), we are engaging in Othering and behaving in an ethnocentric way. We are 'assuming that the worldview of one's own culture is central to all reality' (M.J. Bennett 1993: 30) and that our ways are the *only* proper ways to think and behave. As noted by Lustig and Koester (2010: 150), '[w]hen combined with the natural human tendency to prefer what is typically experienced, ethnocentricism produces emotional reactions to cultural differences that reduce people's willingness to understand disparate cultural messages'. An ethnocentric mindset can hold one back from initiating and maintaining healthy intercultural relationships.

Ethnocentric tendencies can impact on the way we communicate with people who are different from ourselves. For example, ethnocentric individuals who are using their first language when conversing with minority members who are not fluent may speak in ways that convey indifference or a lack of respect. They may use complex grammatical structures, jargon or idioms, speak very rapidly and switch topics frequently, knowing full well that their speech is incomprehensible to their audience. Through their verbal and nonverbal behaviours (e.g. patronizing tone of speech), they may also communicate with adult second language learners in ways that position their interlocutors as young children or less than intelligent adults.

Ethnocentric people may also make comments that disparage their interlocutors and other individuals who they perceive to be from a lesser group or category. For example, they may display disrespect for members of the opposite sex or denigrate people from a different region who speak with a different accent or communication style. To create social distance from outsiders who they dislike, fear, distrust or simply disrespect, ethnocentric individuals may also limit future intercultural interactions.

In stark contrast with ethnocentricism, **cultural relativism** refers to the view that beliefs, value systems and social practices are culturally relative, that is, no culture is inherently superior to another. Ethnorelativism means 'to understand a communication practice from the other person's cultural frame of reference' (Ting-Toomey & Chung 2012: 301). From an ethnorelative perspective, 'different cultures are perceived as variable and viable constructions of reality' (M.J. Bennett 1993: 66). This position acknowledges that there is no absolute standard to compare and contrast different ways of being. As noted in the first chapter, however, this does not mean that we accept practices that harm others. Later in this chapter we discuss how to minimize the ethnocentric tendencies that exist in all of us.

STEREOTYPING

Ethnocentrism often results in **stereotyping**, a strong tendency to characterize people from other cultural backgrounds unfairly, collectively and usually negatively. A **stereotype** is a preconceived idea that attributes certain characteristics (e.g. personality traits, intelligence), intentions and behaviours to all the members of a particular social class or group of people (Allport 1954; Bar-Tal 1996; Holliday 2010).

Before we go further, it is important to distinguish between stereotypes and generalizations. A **generalization** is 'a statement about common trends within a group, but with the recognition that further information is needed to ascertain whether the generalization applies to a particular person' (Galanti 2000: 335). Although stereotypes and generalizations may seem similar, they function in different ways. For example, if you meet an Egyptian man and assume that he has many children, you are stereotyping him. If, on the other hand, you say to yourself, 'A lot of Egyptians have many children, I wonder if Sami does,' then you are generalizing. Whereas a stereotype imposes one's assumptions on others based on commonly held beliefs, a generalization is a starting point and you understand that much more information is needed to determine if your ideas or perceptions apply to a particular individual (or group) or situation.

We are not born with stereotypes, we learn them during the process of socialization by way of messages about outgroup members from parents, grandparents, teachers, the clergy, etc. As we mature, we are influenced by portrayals of different groups in the media (e.g. television dramas, sitcoms, movies, comedy shows, newspapers, the Internet) as well as our own life experiences (e.g. intercultural encounters, travel). Stereotypes may also emerge out of fear, ignorance or distrust of people who are different from ourselves (e.g. physical attributes, intelligence, colour of skin, etc.).

There are many reasons why people resort to stereotyping: to quickly process new information about a person or situation, to organize previous experiences, to stress differences between themselves and other individuals or groups (e.g. to convey that 'us' is superior to 'them'), to make predictions about other people's behaviour, to simplify their life and so on.

The process of stereotyping typically involves the following steps:

1   Often individuals are categorized, usually on the basis of easily identifiable characteristics such as sex or ethnicity.
2   A set of attributes is ascribed to all (or most) members of that category. Individuals belonging to the stereotyped group are assumed to be similar to each other, and different from other groups, on this set of attributes.
3   The set of attributes is ascribed to any individual member of that category.

(Hewstone & Brown 1986: 29)

Stereotyping about groups of people can be based on a wide range of characteristics (e.g. language/accent, ethnicity, physical appearance, nationality, religion, geographic location, class, age, sex, gender, etc.). The following list provides a few examples of people or groups that are often stereotyped (e.g. in the mass media, films):

- cities (Beijingers, Bostonians, Parisians, Singaporeans, Berliners)
- regions within countries (Newfies in Canada, Northerners, Yorkshire folk)
- dialects (Ebonics in the U.S., Yakuzas in Japan)
- race (African Americans, Caucasians, Hispanics, Native Hawaiians)
- religion (Atheists, Buddhists, Christians, Jews, Muslims, Hindus, Sikhs)
- ethnic groups (Chinese, black Africans, Arabs, Hispanics)
- national groups (U.S. Americans, Iranians, Irish, Italians, North Koreans)
- age (youngsters, adolescents, teenagers, middle-aged, senior citizens)
- vocations (teachers, garbage collectors, clergy, newscasters, football players)
- social class (poor, white collar, blue collar, upper middle class, the corporate rich)
- physical attributes (obese, anorexic, dwarfs, tall, jocks)
- disabilities (deafness, blindness, mentally disabled)
- gender (masculinity, femininity)

When people stereotype, they typically apply a commonly held generalization of a group to every single person in the cultural group. For example, in many parts of the world, U.S. Americans are stereotyped (e.g. in the media, movies) as friendly but arrogant and ignorant about world affairs, while the British are perceived as reserved and uptight, etc. In Hong Kong, Mainland Chinese are often stereotyped as loud, aggressive and lacking in manners, whereas in Mainland China, Hong Kongers are sometimes branded as materialistic and devoid of culture. In the following excerpt, for instance, a Hong Kong student discloses the stereotype she harbours of Mainland Chinese:

> From my own experience of the Mainland, I have a bad impression that people there are less civilized than Hong Kong people. They are untrustworthy, unfair, and unjust. Bribery and corruption are all around in court, in schools, in companies, and even in streets . . . They are less educated in the concepts of hygiene: they squat in toilets, spit around the streets, and throw rubbish all around . . . It is not surprising there are a lot of contagious diseases. The Mainland Chinese are just inferior to us Hong Kong people. Hence, it is a torture for me to visit my relatives in the Mainland.

Individuals who have only encountered a few people from a particular group may overgeneralize what they have observed and this can lead to stereotyping. For example, if you interact with a Frenchman for the first time in your life and you perceive him to be very rude and arrogant, you may erroneously conclude that all French are lacking in manners. Similarly, if you chat with an Indonesian girl who is very shy and reticent, you may draw the incorrect conclusion that all Indonesians (or even Asians) are poor conversationalists.

Stereotypes are often infused with emotion, and usually portray individuals or groups in a negative light (e.g. 'Don't employ Mexicans as they're all lazy', 'Women are not as intelligent as men', 'Males are not good at learning foreign languages'). Some overgeneralizations may stress positive characteristics or behaviours. For example, Asians are often assumed to excel in mathematics and the learning of musical instruments (e.g. the violin, piano). In reality, not all Asian students are good at maths and many have no musical talent – as in other ethnic groups. When a stereotype overgeneralizes the positive characteristics attributed to a particular group, individuals who do not fit the mould are disadvantaged.

Stereotyping related to gender is common in many parts of the world. The behaviour, conditions or attitudes that promote stereotypes of social roles based on gender is referred to as **sexism**. As men are most often in positions of power, this typically entails sexist behaviours that foster prejudice and discriminate against females. **Gender stereotyping** refers to simplistic overgeneralizations about the gender characteristics, differences and roles of males and females. For example, believing that a woman is incapable of holding public office because 'females are too emotional' is a gender stereotype. Denying men the opportunity to teach in a primary school because 'males are not good with young children' is another example. Stereotypes such as these are typically expressed through **sexist language**, that is, the use of words or phrases that unnecessarily emphasize gender, or ignore, belittle or stereotype members of either sex.

Sexist language is linked to power and oppression. As males tend to be in positions of power, not surprisingly, sexist discourse often portrays females in a negative light. For instance, when two professors are formally introduced in a conference meeting as Dr. Martin Shore and Mrs. Nakano, the male lecturer is accorded more respect. His academic title is verbally acknowledged, whereas her status is ignored, even though she also has a PhD and, actually, a much higher academic rank. In this scenario, the language used privileges the male professor and diminishes the professional status of Professor Nakano; the introduction also discloses her marital status, which is a personal detail that is not relevant to the meeting.

Ageism refers to the stereotyping or discrimination of a person or group of people due to their age. As Hopkins (2010: 8) observes, ageism 'works to create and sustain assumptions about aged individuals and their behaviours, attitudes, and values'. **Ageist stereotyping** involves categorizing individuals into groups according to their age and then ascribing certain characteristics and behaviours to all people of that age group (e.g. teenagers, Generation X, senior citizens). In many cases, these overgeneralizations can be harmful to people. For example, not all teenagers are irresponsible, immature and selfish; in fact, many are quite the opposite! Not all people who are over 65 are too old and feeble to work! **Ageist language** can also be used to convey stereotypes of people based on their age. For example, older people are portrayed as mentally and physically challenged when labels such as old-timers, old folks and golden agers are used. Stereotypical language and images such as these can diminish people and lead to exclusion and other discriminatory practices.

Dervin (2012), Samovar *et al.* (2010), Sorrells (2012) and other interculturalists have identified a number of ways in which stereotypes can become engrained and serve as barriers to intercultural communication:

1   Stereotypes can lead us to believe that a commonly-held belief is actually true, when in fact it is not.
2   Stereotypes may compel us to only accept information that is in accord with our previous perceptions of a particular outgroup. Even if we meet an individual who does not fit our preconceived ideas, we may choose to ignore this new information.
3   Stereotypes are difficult to change, in part, because many were formed in childhood through messages from people we love and respect, as well as through portrayals in the media (e.g. TV, movies). Therefore, we may fail to modify the stereotype even when it no longer fits with our actual observations and experience.
4   When we stereotype we assume that all members of a group possess the same characteristics and we fail to recognize or acknowledge individual variations.
5   Stereotypes generally reduce people to a single aspect of their identities (e.g. trait, characteristic or dimension), overlooking the dynamic and multifaceted nature of identities.
6   When we stereotype, we send and interpret messages in ways that do not convey recognition of the unique, individual characteristics of others; instead, we rely on oversimplified, overgeneralized perceptions, which is not fair to the people we are communicating with as it reduces them to mere 'cultural representatives'.
7   Stereotyping can lead to the use of language that diminishes the worth of individuals, perpetuates overgeneralizations, and leads to inequality (e.g. sexist language, ageist discourse).
8   Stereotyping devalues individuals and groups, and can result in or perpetuate inequality (e.g. gender inequality, age inequality, religious inequality and so on), which is very damaging to intercultural relations.

Intergroup communication is impacted in negative ways by the common practice of stereotyping and Othering. Later in this chapter, we discuss ways to avoid stereotyping and cultivate more respectful intercultural relations.

BIAS AND PREJUDICE

To become a more respectful intercultural communicator, it is imperative to have an understanding of what is meant by bias and prejudice; like stereotyping, these are common phenomena that can negatively impact on intercultural relations worldwide. As Omaggio Hadley (1993: 368) observes, '[f]or good or for bad, we all have biases. We see things in terms of what we know'. A **bias** is a personal preference, like or dislike, which can interfere with our ability to be objective, impartial and without prejudice. For example, some people have a bias against blondes and do not regard them as intelligent; hence, the pejorative term 'blonde bimbo'. Others are biased towards people with body art and fail to recognize the positive, unique qualities in individuals with tattoos and piercings.

Prejudice refers to 'dislike or hatred of a person or group formed without reason. It is culturally conditioned since it is rooted in a person's early socialization' (Maude 2011: 112). In other words, we learn to dislike or distrust people who are not like ourselves as we are influenced by negative messages or images that we receive from those who are closest to us (e.g. parents, religious figures) and the media. Thus, prejudicial thoughts are closely linked to rigid and faulty stereotypes that form during the primary socialization process.

Noting that prejudice is 'a universal psychological process', Lustig and Koester (2010: 156) observe that

> [p]rejudiced attitudes include irrational feelings of dislike and even hatred for certain groups, biased perceptions and beliefs about the group members that are not based on direct experiences and firsthand knowledge, and a readiness to behave in negative and unjust ways toward members of the group.

Unfortunately, prejudice is common all over the world as it serves many economic, psychological and social functions (Allport 1954; Samovar *et al.* 2010).

People may experience prejudicial thoughts and emotions for a variety of reasons:

- *to 'fit in' and feel more secure.* For example, Ali was born in Australia to immigrant parents from Yemen, who have become successful merchants in Melbourne. To fit in with the majority culture, he might display disdain for Arab immigrants (e.g. make derogatory comments about newcomers) and refuse to learn Arabic or use the language in public, fearing he would be treated as an outsider (immigrant) if he did so.
- *to provide a scapegoat for difficulties in times of trouble (e.g. economic, social, interpersonal).* In Manchester, England, for example, Sven, a 28-year-old skinhead (an unemployed white supremacist who dropped out of secondary school) blames his unemployment status on immigrant workers; at the same time, he denigrates their work ethic, skills and output.
- *to boost their self-image and self-esteem.* For example, a well-to-do homemaker without higher education may give orders to her amah (live-in nanny) and frequently criticize and disrespect the young woman (e.g. her second language accent, ethnicity, work ethic, appearance, etc.) to feel more powerful and in control. Her Filipino helper may, in fact, have a university degree but be forced to work abroad due to poor economic conditions in her home country.
- *to strengthen ingroup bonds and gain social distance from outgroups.* To feel closer to other believers, a devout Catholic may only socialize with other Catholics and harbour prejudice against other branches of Christianity (as well as other religions) and stress how Catholic doctrine is different and superior.
- *to justify a group's domination over another.* In some countries, beliefs about the lack of mental toughness and 'emotional nature' of women allows men to exclude women from certain occupations and positions, e.g. senior administrative posts, posts within the military.

Many forms of prejudice negatively impact on intercultural relations. For example, individuals may be prejudiced towards people who have a different accent, second-language speakers, individuals with a different sexual orientation/preference, believers of another religion (or individuals who are atheists, non-believers), minority group members, foreigners and people who have a different skin or hair colour, etc.

Ignorance and fear are often at the root of prejudice. For example, people who have limited intercultural experience may fear interactions that could lead them to unchartered waters. It is also easier to blame others than acknowledge limitations in oneself or other ingroup members.

As noted by Samovar *et al.* (2010), prejudice may be expressed overtly or in indirect ways. For example, while individuals may be prejudiced towards a particular person or group (e.g. those who differ from them in terms of age, class, language, skin colour, sex, gender, ethnicity, level of education, physical abilities, etc.), they may not act on their beliefs or negative **attitudes** (a learned tendency to evaluate a person, behaviour, or activity in a particular way). Instead of actively discriminating against outgroup members, they may try to keep their prejudicial thoughts and biases hidden, recognizing that it is not politically correct to openly disparage others based on religion, gender, sexual orientation, etc.

Convinced of the superiority of their ingroup, ethnocentric individuals may also display overt prejudice towards people who are not outgroup members. They may express prejudice by employing ethnocentric speech to denigrate outgroup members, that is, they may talk in a way that is demeaning or disrespectful of others or their ingroup(s) (e.g. use sexist/ageist language, derogatory terms). People who are prejudiced may adhere to stereotypes even when confronted with evidence that conflicts with their negative perceptions. Therefore, prejudice is destructive and very harmful to intercultural relations.

DISCRIMINATION

Discrimination can be thought of as 'the expression of prejudice' (Samovar *et al.* 2006: 175) or 'prejudice "in action"' (Lustig & Koester 2012: 158). Basically, it is the prejudicial or unequal treatment of certain individuals based on their membership, or *perceived* membership, of a particular group or category. The United Nations International Convention on the Elimination of all forms of Racial Discrimination (ICERD) (1989) defines **racial discrimination** as

> any distinction, exclusion, restriction, or preference based on race, colour, descent, or national or ethnic origin, which has the purpose or effect of nullifying or impairing the recognition, enjoyment, or exercise, on an equal footing, of human rights and fundamental freedoms in the political, economic, social, cultural, or any other field of public life.

Discrimination can take place in multiple forms and encompass many issues. For example, individuals or groups may be discriminated against (e.g. receive fewer benefits or be denied opportunities) based on their age, language, accent, sex, gender, pregnancy, race/colour of skin, religion, national origin, medical condition (e.g. AIDS, cerebral palsy, bipolarism), mental or physical ability and so on. Individuals or groups (e.g. ethnic minorities) who are discriminated against do not enjoy the same privileges and respect as the rest of society. The term **human rights** refers to the basic rights and freedoms to which all humans are entitled, including the right to life and liberty, freedom of thought and expression and equality before the law.

Discrimination may occur in all domains of life (e.g. in the workplace, at social functions, in public transportation, housing, education, etc.).

The following scenarios illustrate discriminatory practices:

Plate 7.1 New immigrants sometimes face discrimination and harsh living conditions as they struggle to find their way in a new environment © Jane Jackson

- A second language speaker with a high proficiency in English is denied a job as a clerk because she is not a native speaker of the language. She is more than capable of doing the required tasks and is more competent than the native speaker who was offered the post.
- A security guard refuses to allow a blind woman to enter the library with her seeing-eye dog.
- A Muslim woman applies for a job as a secretary. Even though she is the best applicant she is not offered the job due to her religion.
- An HIV-positive student is not accepted by a private school as the administrators fear that he will eventually get AIDS and this will endanger others and harm the reputation of the school.
- A junior high school teacher only encourages boys to major in physics and chemistry as he believes that hard sciences are too difficult for girls.
- After discovering that a tenant is gay, a homophobic landlord accuses him of making too much noise and evicts him even though the heterosexual tenants are much noisier.
- Young girls wish to attend school like their brothers but the village men refuse to allow females to be educated.
- An Indian couple wishes to rent an apartment that was advertised in the local newspaper but the landlord tells them that he no longer has any vacancies. This was not true and later the same day he rents the apartment to a white applicant.

- A high school graduate with an impressive academic record is invited to a selection interview for a prestigious college; when the Chinese interviewers discover she has a Filipina mother and her parents are divorced, they choose a Chinese candidate instead, even though that person's qualifications are not as impressive.
- A very energetic, physically fit 55-year-old man applies for a job that he is well qualified for; however, he is rejected as he is considered too old by the potential employer.
- A university graduate who has cerebral palsy applies for a job with a company and even though she is physically and intellectually able to perform the required tasks, the interviewer cannot see past her disability and refuses to offer her the post.
- Only males are allowed to participate in study abroad programmes even though female students are also keen to go abroad to further their education.

These examples highlight the diverse ways in which people in positions of power may discriminate against others.

Individuals may also believe that they are the victims of discrimination when this may not actually be the case. When members of a minority group are visibly different from the majority, they may understandably feel insecure and when intercultural encounters do not go well they may attribute it to discrimination. For example, a Chinese student who was having difficulty adjusting to England wrote the following in her sojourn diary:

> The British don't accept us to be in their country. Discrimination is still there, though there may be laws to protect you . . . Now, I feel more about my Chinese identity. It will never equal to western people. We are too different. We don't understand, or refuse to understand each other fully. They are too far ahead of us. (I notice the use of 'we', 'I' versus 'they' here; there is really a distinction).

Perceptions of discrimination, whether real or imagined, need to be acknowledged and processed as they will, inevitably, impact on intercultural relations and the willingness for further intercultural encounters. This aspect is discussed further at the end of this chapter.

Discriminatory language

Discrimination may also manifest itself through language use. **Discriminatory language** may take many forms (e.g. derogatory labels, offensive terms, stereotypes, trivializing language). People who are different from ourselves may be labelled in a pejorative way, largely ignored or verbally referred to in a demeaning way, which can be very hurtful to the group or individuals that are targeted. In Australia, for example, the term 'abos' is sometimes used for Indigenous Australians, 'pooftas' for gay men, 'queue jumpers' for refugees or asylum seekers, 'welfare cheats' for the unemployed, 'wogs' for European immigrants and their children, 'spazzes' for people living with cerebral palsy and 'geriatrics' for older people (Equal Opportunity Unit 2005; Pauwels 1991). Referring to a woman as 'just a housewife' or 'just a girl' is also dismissive; expressions of this nature foster unequal treatment and respect.

In many cultural settings, individuals with mental illnesses are ostracized and stigmatized. The pejorative terms used to depict people with mental illness or cognitive impairment reflect the level of ignorance and lack of tolerance that are prevalent in the community. Undeniably, language plays a powerful role in perpetuating discrimination.

Discriminatory practices

What lies behind discriminatory practices? Why do people use discriminatory language and engage in other acts that deny individuals and groups the rights and privileges that they themselves enjoy? Discrimination can be motivated by many factors. People may feel compelled to promote and protect their ingroup and also be motivated by the rather unattractive desire to denigrate or put down others.

Discriminatory beliefs and practices are often driven by fear and ignorance, and the craving of power over others. In contexts where people are very superstitious, mental illness and physical abnormalities may be considered a curse (e.g. a consequence of the sins of parents) and marginalized or hidden from mainstream society. Able-bodied individuals may not make eye contact with people who are disabled and refrain from interacting with those who have mental or physical disabilities.

Discrimination has also been linked to the potential dark side of identities (Samovar et al. 2010). Lustig and Koester (2012: 159), for example, warn that 'the formation of one's cultural identity . . . can sometimes lead to hostility, hate, and discrimination directed against nonmembers of that culture'. Strong ingroup affiliations can foster ethnocentric practices, including discrimination and exclusion.

Combating discrimination

Perceptions and attitudes towards differences and disabilities can and do change over time. For example, with more education, superstitions diminish and there is more awareness and recognition of the valuable contributions that disabled people can make in society (e.g. in their home environment, in the workplace). The pejorative labels used to identify people who are physically and mentally different from the majority are then considered unacceptable. To eradicate barriers to equality, people in many parts of the world are fighting discriminatory language and other practices.

In some regions, individuals and groups are still pushing for equal education benefits. In 2012, Malala Yousafzai, a 15-year-old Pakistani schoolgirl, survived a murder attempt by the Taliban (Islamic fundamentalists) as she fought for the right of girls to attend school in the Swat Valley of Pakistan. In 2013, she became the youngest nominee for the Nobel Peace Prize. As she recovers, Malala continues to press for women's rights and education for all children. Inspired by her courage, young people and adults all over the globe are joining her crusade to combat gender discrimination.

People are also combating other forms of discrimination. For example, some strive to protect language rights (e.g. mother tongue teaching, bilingual policies in governments, more opportunities for lower income children to learn an international language), equal pay/compensation (e.g. equal pay for women and minorities), and protection from sexual harassment (bullying or coercion of a sexual nature), etc. Some also fight for disabled individuals to have more opportunities to actively contribute to society (e.g. in the workplace). Medical professionals (e.g. mental health experts, rehabilitation specialists, physicians) and, in some cases, caregivers may play a role in advocating for the rights of those who are affected by mental and physical disabilities. Groups may lobby against the use of degrading labels (e.g. mentally retarded) and other forms of language that undermine the dignity of individuals with mental or physical limitations.

In a growing number of nations, **anti-discrimination legislation** now exists to protect the rights of individuals and promote equality among people regardless of their differences (e.g.

sex, gender, religion, ethnicity, social class, physical ability). In the U.S., **affirmative action** (known as **positive discrimination** in the U.K.), refers to education, business or employment policies that aim to redress the negative, historical impact of discrimination by taking factors such as race, sex, religion, gender or national origin into consideration in hiring/promotion/ selection situations. In some educational and employment settings, **racial quotas** have been set, that is, there are numerical requirements for the selection and promotion of people from a group that is deemed disadvantaged (e.g. African American students, females). Individuals from disadvantaged groups may be admitted to college with a lower entrance standard than the norm. This policy is controversial and opponents refer to it as **reverse discrimination**, that is, unfair treatment of the majority (or group that is generally considered to have more power and privilege).

RACISM

As discussed in the previous chapter, '**race**' is a contested term that 'has no defensible biological basis' (Smith *et al.* 2006: 278). It is a social construction that historically has privileged people in positions of power (e.g. whites in Britain, Australia, and the United States, etc.). Based on the notion that superiority is biologically determined, 'race has always been established as relationships of domination, oppression, and privilege that position people differently in society' (Parker & Mease 2009: 316). The social category of race has long been associated with colonialism and the abuse of power (e.g. the dominance of white rulers in British colonies).

While scholars and human rights advocates now rally against the use of race in social categorization, in many parts of the world, perceived racial differences continue to be used to classify groups and explain or predict people's behaviour. Census takers (e.g. those who are officially counting the population in a nation) usually ask survey respondents to declare their race from a pre-determined list of categories (e.g. black, Caucasian, Chinese, Hispanic, Japanese and so on). While this information may be used in a positive way (e.g. to determine areas of need for particular health care services), racial categories, which are largely arbitrary, and census data can also be used by ethnocentric individuals and institutions as a basis for treating people less favourably.

Sociologist Gail Lewis explains that racial categorization usually entails a three-step process (**racialization**), which she describes as follows:

1 human populations are divided into discrete categories based on variations in physical features;
2 meaning is then linked to this physical variation, with the view that it is possible to know 'the potentialities, behaviours, needs, and abilities of an individual based on her or her "racial" belonging';
3 this 'social process of categorization and classification' is regarded as 'a product of nature' – that is, 'racial division is said to be natural'.

(Lewis 1998: 99–100)

The placing of racial groups in a hierarchy in society stems from ethnocentric perspectives, ignorance and prejudice. When power, hatred and oppression accompany prejudicial attitudes and discrimination, **racism** may prevail.

Racism is the belief in the inherent superiority of a particular race. It denies the basic equality of humankind and correlates ability with physical composition. Thus, it assumes that success or failure in any societal endeavor will depend upon genetic endowment rather than environment and access to opportunity.

(Leone 1978: 1)

Liu *et al.* (2011: 291) define racism as '[t]he belief that one racial group is superior and that other racial groups are necessarily inferior'. Along similar lines, Ting-Toomey and Chung (2012: 307) explain that racism relates to 'a personal/institutional belief in the cultural superiority of one race and the perceived inferiority of other races'. Ethnocentric attitudes and feelings of superiority that lead to racist behaviours can have dire consequences for oppressed people in all areas of life (e.g. educational, social, employment, religious) and, in extreme cases, can lead to persecution and even death.

Types of racism

Racism can exist on different levels, e.g. individual, institutional, systemic. **Individual racism** refers to a person's attitudes, beliefs and actions, which can support or perpetuate racism; these racist thoughts and behaviours may be below the person's level of awareness. Individuals may demonstrate their racist beliefs through the telling of racist jokes or by using racial slurs. They may also express their belief in the inherent superiority of their racial group in less direct ways (e.g. by only interacting with members of their racial or ethnic ingroup or by not objecting when others use racial slurs). All the while, they may deny they are racists and become very upset when their behaviours are labelled as such. Accordingly, they may make routine state-ments of denial such as "'I have nothing against [. . .], but", "my best friends are [. . .], but", "we are tolerant, but . . ."' (Wodak 2008: 65). "'I'm not a racist, but . . ."' "It's just a joke." "Some of my best friends are . . ."' (James 2001:1).

Racism may also exist on an institutional level and even be pervasive in public organi-zations and corporations (e.g. schools, businesses, governments bodies). Economic, social, and political structures, and institutional systemic policies and practices may privilege a particular racial or ethnic group and place others (e.g. minorities) at a disadvantage. For example, racism in schools can lead to unequal treatment for second language, minority children (e.g. lack of access to linguistic, cultural, and material resources, premature streaming into vocational certificate programmes instead of university-bound academic tracks even if the students are very bright). In hospital settings, patients from a minority racial or ethnic group may not receive the same care and attention as members of the majority group (or whatever group is most privileged). **Institutional racism** can result in differential access to the goods, services and opportunities of society.

Systemic racism can lead to the mistreatment of people on a wide scale (e.g. minorities in a particular nation may suffer injustices in all aspects of life due to racist policies). For example, in the United States, from the 1400s to 1865, African Americans (previously labelled as 'negros') were subjected to slavery and some were even murdered (e.g. the victims of mob lynchings or hangings) due to racist beliefs and practices, which are still an issue in con-temporary U.S. American society and other parts of the world. In South Africa, from 1948 to 1994, apartheid, a system of **racial segregation** (the separation of people into racial groups in daily life), was enforced through legislation until multi-racial democratic elections eventually brought it to an end. The legacy (e.g. poverty, unequal job opportunities) persists.

Plate 7.2 While apartheid may be over, many South African blacks still live in poverty and have not yet realized the dream of economic independence and stability. The effects of decades of racism linger © Jane Jackson

In other extreme cases, racial hatred and bigotry can culminate in **genocide**, 'the deliberate and systematic destruction, in whole or in part, of an ethnic, racial, religious, or national group' (Funk 2010: 1). In the **holocaust**, for example, millions of people who were deemed racially (or otherwise) inferior (e.g. Jews, the Roma, the mentally or physically disabled, Slavic groups) were massacred in the 1930s and 1940s by Adolf Hitler and the German military. More recently, in 1994, in Rwanda, a sovereign state in Central and Eastern Africa, nearly 100,000 Hutus were murdered by the ruling Tutsis, who professed themselves to be racially superior.

Worldwide, strong ingroup preferences, feelings of superiority based on perceived 'racial' or biological differences and the abuse of power can lead to racist discourse and other acts (e.g. vandalism, physical attacks, ridicule, name-calling, arson, spray painting symbols of hate on buildings linked to minority group members). When there is a power imbalance, individuals or groups with racist attitudes may deny the rights of those they consider 'inferior'. Often these racist thoughts and actions are driven by fear and ignorance, feelings of superiority (or inferiority) and entitlement, and a desire to control others.

Racist discourse and behaviours

Racists, individuals who believe that people who have a different skin colour (or ethnicity) are inferior, may convey their hatred and bigotry in their speech (both oral and written) as well as their nonverbal behaviours. Through their actions they may express, confirm, legitimize and reinforce oppressive power relations and racist ideologies (beliefs) related to the dominant group. Wetherell and Porter (1992: 70) define **racist discourse** as 'discourse which has the effect of categorizing, allocating and discriminating between certain groups . . . it is discourse which justifies, sustains and legitimates . . . (racist) practices'. Racist discourse may be directed at individuals or groups who are racially or ethnically different or it may include derogatory comments about ethnically different others by those in positions of power. It may take the form of insults, disrespectful forms of address, slurs, taunts and other expressions that convey the speaker's feelings of superiority.

Although there are now more regulations protecting human rights in many sectors of society, in many parts of the world (e.g. **anti-racist legislation** governing schools, the workplace), racism is still widespread and people may convey racist beliefs in a more subtle way. For example, those in positions of power may frequently interrupt ethnic minority speakers, give them little time to speak and/or insist on discussing topics that embarrass or belittle them. Their intonation, facial expressions and posture may also convey a lack of respect of outgroup members (e.g. people who are perceived to be members of a different 'race' or ethnic group with lower social standing).

Whether overt or covert, racism can be extremely detrimental to intercultural relations and world peace. It can threaten the fabric of social harmony and be harmful to society.

XENOPHOBIA

Xenophobia is a severe aversion to or irrational fear (phobia) of 'foreigners' or 'strangers', that is, basically anyone who is different from oneself or one's ingroup, especially in terms of culture (ways of being), language and politics. While racism is linked to prejudice based on ethnicity, ancestry or race, xenophobia is broader; it encompasses any kind of fear related to an individual or group perceived as being different. The target of this hostility may be a group that is not accepted by mainstream society (e.g. minorities, immigrants, members of other ethnic groups).

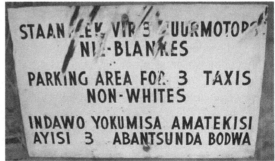

Plate 7.3 This racist sign was posted in South Africa during the apartheid era © Jane Jackson

Plate 7.4 During apartheid, taxi drivers who were not white were required to park in a special area. Inequality during this time period was pervasive © Jane Jackson

Xenophobic individuals do not recognize that their views are rooted in deep insecurities, e.g. the perceived threat of losing one's own identity, culture and positioning. Gripped with anxiety, individuals in this state may fear the loss of their imagined superiority or racial purity (e.g. interracial marriages involving their children). On a regional or national level, this may lead to discriminatory policies and anti-immigration legislation. Xenophobia is dangerous as it has the potential to spawn hostile and violent reactions, e.g. mass expulsion, brutal killings of immigrants or particular ethnic groups, such as the atrocities that have taken place in Bosnia, Nazi Germany and Darfur.

OVERCOMING ETHNOCENTRICISM AND IDENTITY BIASES

In this chapter, we have discussed the negative consequences of social categorization and Othering, especially in situations where individuals cling to a rigid sense of self, resist other ways of being and do not respect the preferred identities of others. Ethnocentricism, prejudice, discrimination, racism and xenophobia can destroy opportunities for dialogue and friendship with people who have been socialized in a different environment. In today's interconnected world, it is imperative that we develop more awareness of the multiple dimensions of our identities and the ways in which our cultural perceptions and attitudes can influence our interactions with people from outside our ingroups. After all, 'intercultural communication involves people from dissimilar cultures, and this makes difference a normative condition. Thus, our reaction to, and ability to manage, those differences is key to successful interactions' (Samovar *et al.* 2010: 169).

To be a competent intercultural communicator, it is vital to acknowledge the impact of the socialization process on our identities and actions (verbal, nonverbal), as well as how we view the behaviours of people who are different from ourselves. For example, what messages about your identities and cultural membership did you receive from your parents, grandparents, religious figures, teachers, the media, etc.? What messages did you receive about the appropriate ways to use language and various nonverbal codes in particular contexts?

It is natural for us to make generalizations to cope with the complex environment in which we live but this common practice can lead to stereotyping if we are not vigilant. What stereotypes have you been exposed to throughout your life? What messages did you receive about people from other linguistic and cultural backgrounds (outgroups) that you now recognize as stereotypes? Also, consider your language usage. Do you or any of your friends use terms or make jokes that might be offensive to people from other cultures? In what situations have you used the categories of your own culture to judge and interpret the behaviours of people who are culturally (and linguistically) different from you?

To be mindful intercultural communicators, we must recognize the harmful effects of ethnocentricism and stereotyping, and take steps to 'recognize, accept, and celebrate' cultural difference (Lorde 1986: 197). It takes time and conscious effort to nurture an ethnorelative mindset, as noted by one of my students:

I think the most challenging aspect of communicating with someone from another cultural background is the cultural differences. People need to move away from their own culture's perspectives to see things from the partner's point of view . . . To gain new perspectives, one may have to reduce one's self-centeredness and pay more effort to build up the relationship. One needs to remove one's prejudices and stereotypes of people from other cultural backgrounds. It takes time and energy to remove the cultural barrier and build up intercultural relationships.

To enhance intercultural interactions, we need to recognize the dimensions of our identities that are meaningful to us (e.g. ethnicity, gender, religion, nationality). Are there any aspects that you are particularly sensitive about (e.g. age, sexual orientation, gender, cultural)? How do you define yourself and how would you like others to define you? How do you communicate this to others? How do you feel when others do not recognize your preferred identities? Do you think you clearly indicate how you wish to be viewed or identified?

It is also important to address the following questions and respond in an honest way: Do you respect the identities of others? Are you attentive to messages that individuals from other linguistic or cultural backgrounds send about their preferred identities? Do you avoid the use of sexist or ageist language? If an intercultural encounter does not go well, do you automatically assume that someone from another culture is discriminating against you? Do you quickly label the individual as a racist or do you take time to reflect on other possible explanations for the miscommunication? After unsatisfactory intercultural interactions do you reevaluate your own actions and responses or do you tend to always blame the negative outcome on your communication partners?

While discrimination, prejudice, racism and xenophobia exist everywhere in the world, it is unhelpful to attribute every negative encounter to these phenomena. In intercultural incidents, it is more constructive to begin by considering a range of possibilities (e.g. an emotional reaction to the omission of discourse markers of politeness, lack of recognition or respect for one's preferred identities). Differing linguistic/cultural norms and ignorance (e.g. lack of knowledge of cultural beliefs, values, practices) may lie at the heart of the miscommunication rather than malice or ill-will.

Understanding what intercultural differences annoy you is crucial so that you can work on ways to reduce your negative feelings and become more sensitive to your own actions that may annoy others. Also, identify stereotypes that have become entrenched in your mind so that you can take steps to eradicate them. Be mindful of the language you use (e.g. avoid the use of terms and jokes that belittle people from other linguistic and cultural backgrounds). Knowing how you see yourself and wish to be positioned in various contexts (e.g. at home, in a foreign land) are key elements in intercultural communication. Heightened self-awareness can help you to become a more successful communicator. It can enable you to be more sensitive to the preferred self-identities of people you interact with and more accepting of different ways of being.

All of us experience emotional, visceral reactions to the world around us. It is natural. As we respond to perceptual stimuli (sights, sounds, smells, touch), we often reveal our attitudes and prejudices towards 'outgroup members'. If we are sensitive to our own emotions and behaviours when interacting with people from a different culture we are better positioned to recognize the messages that we are sending.

In an intercultural situation, if you react negatively to something or someone, reflect on what may be the source of your displeasure or discomfort. For example, were you socialized to expect a larger personal distance between speakers than your communication partner? Did the person stand very close to you and invade your personal space? Were you expecting the person to speak more quietly? Were you expecting to hear 'excuse me' or 'I'm sorry' when he or she brushed up against you? Recognizing that someone from another cultural (and perhaps linguistic) background may have learned different social norms can diminish some of the negative feelings that arise. Realizing that the person is not deliberately trying to annoy you is a good start! You can then make an effort to be more accommodating and less hasty in making negative evaluations. One of my students offers the following helpful advice:

Opening our eyes to see cultural differences is one thing. Opening our heart to accept and respect the differences is another thing. To be open-minded and competent in intercultural contacts, we have to set aside our cultural biases, perceptions about beliefs, values and norms and our expectations on others. This process often involves a lot of internal struggles and anxieties. A way to cope with these internal struggles is to lighten up a bit and be able to laugh about ourselves. The key to deal with cross-cultural communication is to have a sense of humor.

If you are reacting strongly to some aspect of another culture, seek out an explanation in the ethnocentric preferences that you have developed during the process of primary socialization. To avoid ethnocentrism and stereotyping, remember that people who have been socialized in other cultural contexts will not necessarily behave in the same way that you do. Their beliefs, values and practices may differ. Therefore, instead of interpreting anything new based on your own social and cultural norms and values, try to understand how a concept, product or practice fits into the other culture. When people act differently from what you expect, try to avoid making snap judgments, e.g. labelling anything different as 'strange', 'weird' or 'wrong'. Acknowledge differences and try to understand what lies behind these differences.

When interacting with people from a different culture, we may need to adjust our behaviors. I'm still learning to put myself into others' shoes and interpret others; behaviors from their cultural perspectives instead of mine. When I come across people of other cultures violating the rules of our culture, I step back and see the causes of problems in miscommunication before I make negative comments on others. How can we judge anyway if the standard is not the same?

(University student)

Making a genuine effort to develop friendships with people from a different linguistic and cultural background can be one of the best ways to enhance one's intercultural understanding. One of my students who had very strong negative views about Mainland Chinese was assigned a roommate from Beijing. While very unhappy at first, the stereotypical image she had built up in her mind gradually faded away as she got to know the young woman as a person.

When I knew I had to stay with a Beijing girl for the whole semester, I was quite nervous and disappointed because of my prejudice towards Mainlanders. Nonetheless, after nearly a month of getting along together, I found that there were many things valuable in her mind that we don't have. For instance, she is hard-working and just sleeps very little. She is polite and sweet to everyone. She is not so uncivilized or dirty as I had imagined. She baths every day, though not usually at night like me. Still, she keeps personal hygiene and her things are clean and packed tidily . . . I realized how unfairly my prejudice made me look down upon our Mainland fellows.

After this positive experience, my student resolved to overcome her tendency to stereotype: 'I'm trying to move from a critical perspective to a sympathetic view, to understand more from the perspectives of Mainlanders and to appreciate their valuable, genuine and sincere characters rather than to criticize their place.' She also recognized that this would not be easy as prejudicial thoughts about Mainland Chinese had been built up in her mind since childhood.

Recognizing one's prejudicial thoughts (that exist in all of us) is a very important first step. A shift in attitude, a willingness to learn about other ways of being and a strong desire to develop meaningful, equitable intercultural ties can also propel individuals to higher levels of intercultural compctcnce. While it is difficult to avoid social categorization and stereotyping, these are steps that all of us can take to ensure more mutually beneficial and respecttul intercultural relations. With more self-awareness and self-monitoring, you can avoid an 'us' vs. 'them' mentality and become a more mindful intercultural communicator.

SUMMARY

While ingroup affiliations provide us with a sense of belonging, our identities, attitudes and mindset can also serve as significant barriers to intercultural communication. Ethnocentrism, the belief that one's own culture is superior to all others, leads us to categorize and judge the world around us using our own cultural frame (e.g. beliefs; values; social, cultural and linguistic norms or rules of behaviour) as a guide or yardstick. Ethnocentrism can result in even more serious reactions to cultural difference, such as stereotyping, discrimination and prejudice, which lie at the heart of racism, whether overt or covert. It can also lead to xenophobia, an intense, irrational dislike or fear of people who are different from us (e.g. foreigners).

This chapter discussed the potentially harmful consequences of ignoring our ethnocentric tendencies. Even if we are well intentioned, our verbal and nonverbal behaviours can convey a lack of respect for people who differ from us in some way (e.g. age, gender, language, ethnicity, skin colour, sexual orientation). This can then impede the development of positive intercultural relations and we will miss out on many of the opportunities that our diverse world offers us. This chapter suggests a different path: 'Change your thoughts and you change your world' (Peale 2007: 233). All of us can take steps towards a more ethnorelative perspective and reap the benefits with more positive intercultural interactions.

discussion questions

1   How might our perceptions of our cultural identity influence our communication with people who have a different linguistic and cultural background?

2   Identify a linguistic and cultural group in your community that you do *not* belong to. What are your attitudes towards individuals who are linked to this group? How have these attitudes been formed? Do you think your views might change in the future? If yes, how and why?

3   What factors influence one's attitudes towards people who speak a different language or have a different accent?

4   Define ethnocentrism and explain how it can lead to stereotyping and prejudice.

5   In a small group, discuss your reaction to the following comment by Gordon Allport (1954) in his book *The Nature of Prejudice*: 'Most of the business of life can go on with less effort if we stick together with our own kind. Foreigners are a strain.' Do you agree or disagree with this statement?

6   In a small group, discuss the causes of prejudice. Cite examples from your personal experience and discuss ways to combat prejudiced behaviour.

7   In some parts of the world, xenophobia and violence are sometimes linked to football

(soccer) or other sports. Why do you think this is the case? Do you think sports officials have a responsibility to address this? If yes, what steps should be taken?

8 Why are immigrants and minority groups often the targets of prejudice and discrimination? What is the impact of this and how might it be combated?

9 How can one's accent serve as an identity marker? Provide examples of situations in which it may serve as a barrier.

10 Identify three types of racism and provide an example of each. What steps can be taken to combat racism and xenophobia?

11 In this chapter we examined numerous ways to combat ethnocentric tendencies and biases. What other suggestions do you have to foster a more ethnorelative perspective in intercultural interactions? Share your views in small groups.

further reading

Bakanic, V. (2008) *Prejudice: Attitudes about Race, Class, and Gender*, Englewood Cliffs, NJ: Prentice Hall.

The author examines the role of structural inequality and the cognitive dimension of prejudice.

Brown, R. (2010) *Prejudice: Its Social Justice,* 2nd edn, West Sussex: Wiley-Blackwell.

From a social psychological perspective, the author analyzes the prejudices and stereotypes of individuals as part of a pattern of intergroup processes. Numerous examples of prejudice in everyday life are provided.

Hill, J.H. (2008) *The Everyday Language of White Racism*, West Sussex: Wiley-Blackwell.

The author examines everyday language in the U.S. to reveal the underlying racist stereotypes that persist in American culture.

Lippi-Green, R. (2012) *English with an Accent: Language, Ideology, and Discrimination in the United States*, London: Routledge.

The author discusses the ways in which discrimination based on accent functions to both support and perpetuate social structures and unequal power relations.

Lustig, M.W. and Koester, J. (2006) *Among Us: Essays on Identity, Belonging, and Intercultural Competence*, Boston: Pearson, Allyn and Bacon.

This collection of essays addresses four main themes: identity, negotiating intercultural competence, racism and prejudice and belonging to multiple cultures.

Valentine, T. (2003) *Language and Prejudice*, New York: Longman.

This book focuses on the way language influences and prejudices perceptions of race, gender, age, disabilities and sexual preferences.

CHAPTER 8

Intercultural transitions

From language and culture shock to adaptation

I met a lot of people in Europe. I even encountered myself.
(James Baldwin 1924–87, quoted in Rains 2011)

Perhaps travel cannot prevent bigotry, but by demonstrating that all peoples cry, laugh, eat, worry, and die, it can introduce the idea that if we try and understand each other, we may even become friends.
(Maya Angelou, quote on Maya Angelou Quotes, online, n.d.)

If you reject the food, ignore the customs, fear the religion and avoid the people, you might better stay home.
(James A. Michener 1907–97, quoted in Safir and Safire 1982)

learning objectives

By the end of this chapter, you should be able to:

1 identify and describe types and dimensions of boundary crossers
2 define and describe the process of acculturation and second language socialization
3 describe four patterns of acculturation in immigrants
4 identify factors that facilitate or hinder acculturation and second language socialization
5 define transition shock and identify five types
6 describe the causes and symptoms of language and culture shock
7 describe the positive and negative effects of language and culture shock
8 identify and describe the stages in the U-curve and W-curve adjustment models
9 describe the causes and symptoms of reverse (reentry) culture shock
10 identify weaknesses in the curve models of adjustment
11 describe the core elements in the integrative communication theory of cross-cultural adaptation
12 discuss the role of language in cross-cultural adjustment and adaptation
13 identify and discuss strategies to enhance intercultural transitions (e.g. cope with language and culture shock).

INTRODUCTION

Each year, millions of people cross borders to study, work, perform military duties, represent their government, conduct business, do volunteer work, take part in peace missions or engage in tourism. Some choose to make another territory or country their new home; others are forced to seek temporary or permanent refuge in a foreign land. When people leave all that is familiar and enter a region that is new to them, they naturally come into contact with groups and individuals who have different linguistic and cultural backgrounds. In the process, newcomers may be exposed to unfamiliar languages or dialects, values, norms, beliefs and behaviours (e.g. verbal, nonverbal), which may be both exhilarating and confounding. A myriad of internal and external factors can impact on the transition to a new environment.

This chapter begins by describing and contrasting several types and dimensions of boundary crossers. The next section focuses on the long-term acculturation and adaptation of immigrants and other settlers before our attention shifts to the short-term adjustment and adaptation of sojourners. After describing several types of transition shock, discussion centres on language and culture shock (causes, symptoms, degree of difficulty and potential benefits). Several of the most well-known models of sojourner adjustment (e.g. the U- and W-curve adjustment models) are then reviewed and critiqued. Next, Kim's (2001, 2005, 2012) integrative communication theory of cross-cultural adaptation, which relates to both long-term and short-term boundary crossers, is explained. The chapter concludes with practical, research-inspired suggestions to optimize intercultural transitions.

TYPES AND DIMENSIONS OF BOUNDARY CROSSERS

All over the world, more and more people are on the move, leaving behind the familiarity and security of their home environment for new, unchartered terrain. Among these boundary crossers we may find tourists, student sojourners (e.g. international exchange students), business people, expatriate workers and their families, military personnel, diplomats, immigrants, asylum seekers, refugees, indigenous peoples, third culture kids (TCKs) and many other individuals or groups. Before we examine the psychological, cultural, linguistic, physiological and social impact of crossing cultures, it is helpful to be familiar with the following basic dimensions that differentiate boundary crossers: 'voluntary-involuntary' and 'permanent-temporary' (Berry 1990; Sam & Berry 2006; Ward et al. 2001).

Voluntary–involuntary

Nowadays, people venture abroad with diverse motives, e.g. for adventure, pleasure, work, economic necessity/benefits, family unification, a better quality of life, a safer environment, etc. As noted in Chapter 1, some individuals or groups opt to travel or move abroad of their own free will, whereas others are compelled to do so, often because of circumstances that are well beyond their control. Whether the move is voluntary or involuntary can have a profound impact on the nature and quality of the transition to the new environment.

Voluntary transitions

Voluntary migrants are those who willingly chose to travel abroad: 'In voluntary cases, one makes contact with another (others), driven by one's interest in a cultural Other (e.g. travel) or the needs of social life and survival (e.g. trade)' (Kramsch & Uryu 2012: 212). Typically, this category includes tourists, travellers or other temporary visitors, student sojourners, business people, expatriates, missionaries and immigrants. Among these groups, tourists are the most numerous.

The United Nations World Tourism Organization (UNWTO) defines **tourism** as 'a social, cultural and economic phenomenon which entails the movement of people to countries or places outside their usual environment for personal or business/professional purposes' (http://media.unwto.org/en/content/understanding-tourism-basic-glossary). In 2011, there were 983 million international tourist arrivals worldwide, with a growth of 4.6 per cent as compared to 940 million in 2010 (UNWTO n.d.).

The number of secondary school pupils and university students who opt to undertake part of their studies in another country is also on the rise. The United Nations Educational, Scientific and Cultural Organization (UNESCO) estimated that there were more than 3.6 million students being educated at the tertiary level outside their home country in 2010, up from an estimated

Plate 8.1 In many regions, tourism has become a major industry boosting the local economy and bringing people from diverse linguistic and cultural backgrounds into contact with one another
© Jane Jackson

1.7 million in 2000. By 2025, nearly eight million students are expected to be educated trans-nationally (Atlas of Student Mobility, n.d.).

Some students voluntarily travel abroad to improve their second language skills and cultural understanding; others seek to enhance their subject matter knowledge and job prospects. **International education** refers to 'the knowledge and skills resulting from conducting a portion of one's education in another country' or, more generally, 'international activity that occurs at any level of education (K-12, undergraduate, graduate, or postgraduate)' (Forum on Education Abroad 2011: 11). **Education abroad** denotes 'education that occurs outside the participant's home country. Besides study abroad, this term ecompasses such international experiences as work, volunteering, non-credit internships, and directed travel, as long as these programmes are driven to a significant degree by learning goals' (Forum on Education Abroad 2011: 11). In North America, **study abroad** is considered 'a subtype of education abroad that results in progress toward an academic degree at a student's home institution' (Forum on Education Abroad 2011: 11). This typically includes such activities as classroom study, research, internships and **service learning**. A service-learning programme is 'a subtype of field study program in which the pedagogical focus is a placement in an activity that serves the needs of a community' (Forum on Education Abroad 2011: 15). For example, a group of American university students may participate in a semester-long service-learning project in Guatemala, in which they work with the homeless, tutor EFL students, volunteer in an orphanage or assist human rights workers under the supervision of a faculty member.

Individuals may also choose to work abroad temporarily. Others migrate to another country to seek a better life (e.g. earn more money, procure more educational, professional and social opportunities for themselves and their families, join family members who have immigrated earlier). Immigrants are a very diverse group (e.g. differing aspirations and expectations for their new life, disparate levels of education and linguistic competence). The majority voluntarily move to a country where host nationals speak a different language and have customs, worldviews and habits that differ from what they are accustomed to in their country of origin.

Involuntary transitions

Not all migration is voluntary. For a variety of reasons, individuals or groups may become **involuntary migrants**, that is, they may be compelled to move to a different region or country.

> in involuntary cases, intercultural contacts are often driven by rather negative elements such as power struggles between different ethnic or cultural groups (e.g. war) or a powerful group's political, economic, ideological, and cultural imposition and domination of the less powerful Other (e.g. colonization).
>
> (Kramsch & Uryu 2012: 212)

As noted in Chapter 1, migration is sometimes forced on individuals or groups such as refugees. At the beginning of 2011, there were approximately 10.5 million refugees under the auspices of the UNHCR (United Nations High Commissioner for Refugees); more than half were in Asia and around 20 per cent in Africa (UNHCR n.d.). 4.8 million Palestinian refugees were also in camps overseen by the United Nations Relief and Works Agency for Palestine Refugees in the Near East (UNRWA), an organization that was established in 1949 to care for displaced Palestinians (UNHCR n.d.). Due to humanitarian crises and unstable political situations, the number of refugees is escalating and many are not included in the UNHCR statistics.

Refugees and asylum seekers involuntarily, and often quite suddenly, find themselves in an alien environment in order to escape wars, abuse, political/sexual/religious/ethnic persecution, famine, earthquakes and other natural disasters and oppression in their homeland. Whereas the term **refugee** refers to a person who has been granted protection in a country outside his or her homeland, an **asylum seeker** is seeking protection as a refugee and is waiting for his or her claim to be assessed by a country that has signed the Geneva Convention on Refugees (UNESCO). If successful, permission may be granted to settle in the new country. Those who are denied the right of abode, even after multiple appeals, are usually repatriated or sent to another country. The review process can be very protracted and the outcome uncertain.

Not surprisingly, unlike voluntary migrants, refugees may have more conflicted emotions about being in a foreign land, and face more stress and uncertainty about what lies ahead. As noted by Berry *et al.* (2011: 311), 'most of them live with the knowledge that "push factors" (rather than "pull factors") led them to flee their homeland and settle in their new society; and, of course, most have experienced traumatic events, and most have lost their material possessions'. Instead of carefully planning their new life abroad, some have fled their home country in great haste without a clear vision of their future. They may have entered a refugee camp without knowing if, when or where they will be relocated. Reluctant to leave their homeland, some refugees spend much of the remainder of their life in their new country dreaming of a return home, which may never be possible. While some migrants voluntarily cross borders and come into contact with people from the host culture, this is not the case for refugees. All of these elements play a role in the transition to a new way of life (e.g. the quality of one's adjustment).

Temporary–permanent

Boundary crossers may also be distinguished by the length of their stay in the new environment as well as the nature and purpose of their visit. For example, tourists and travellers typically visit for only a few days or weeks and have little interaction with host nationals, whereas international students and expatriates may stay for a longer period of time (e.g. many months or years) before returning to their home country, going on to another destination, or deciding to apply for permanent residency in the host country. Immigrants or refugees may remain in the receiving country for the rest of their life.

Temporary

A **sojourn** refers to 'a period of time spent living in a cultural setting different from one's own' (Forum on Education Abroad 2011: 15). **Sojourners** are individuals who are in the new environment temporarily for a specific purpose (e.g. study, work, business) and often for a specific length of time (e.g. several days, months, or years). When they arrive in the new environment, they already plan to return to their home country or go on to another destination at some point. The term 'sojourner' includes many sub-categories, such as tourists, international students, 'third culture kids' (TCKs) or global nomads, business executives and other expatriate workers, international civil servants or diplomats, aid workers, missionaries, military personnel and guest workers.

Plate 8.2 Tourists usually stay abroad for a short time to sight-see and have varying degrees of exposure to the local language and culture © Jane Jackson

Tourists are the most numerous group of sojourners. They usually stay abroad for only a short time (e.g. a few days to several weeks or months) to sight-see, enjoy themselves and get a taste of a different linguistic and cultural environment. Several sub-groups of tourists have focused aims, such as eco-tourists (those who travel to explore nature) and travellers (e.g. backpackers who travel for an extended period and seek out interactions with locals). Thus, while tourists are temporary visitors, they may differ in terms of their motivation, expectations, activities and degree of contact with host nationals.

Expatriates are individuals who are engaged in employment abroad (e.g. EFL teachers from Australia in Malaysia, American bankers who work for a multinational firm in Tokyo, British surveyors employed in Libya). Expatriate workers may or may not be accompanied by family members and the amount of contact they have with host nationals varies considerably. Some expatriates reside and work in a compound that is segregated from the local population (e.g. American engineers in Saudi Arabia), whereas others live, work and spend most of their free time with host nationals.

As noted in Chapter 1, with the advent of globalization, more and more institutions of higher education (and secondary schools) have officially or informally adopted an internationalization policy that has created more opportunities for young people (and teachers) to travel abroad (Kälvermark & van der Wende 1997; Knight 2004, 2008). Some students join 'year abroad' or semester-long exchange programmes; an even greater number are taking part in short-term sojourns, ranging from four to seven weeks, or micro-sojourns lasting three weeks

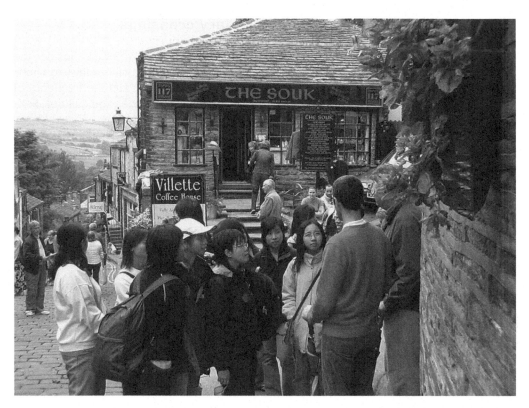

Plate 8.3 The majority of students who study abroad do so in a second language and in many cases that language is English, the de facto language of internationalization and globalization © Jane Jackson

or less (Forum on Education Abroad 2011; Spencer & Tuma 2008). Students may also decide to do their full undergraduate or graduate degrees at institutions outside their home country. The majority of international students study in a second language, and as the de facto language of internationalization is English many non-English speaking countries now offer full-degree programmes in this language (Jenkins 2013; Knight 2008; Knight & Lee 2012).

Permanent

Whereas sojourners are only temporarily in the host environment, immigrants and refugees may settle in a country that is not their place of birth. Immigration is not a new phenomenon but the number of people who are leaving their home country to permanently reside in another has never been greater (van Oudenhoven 2006). Whether due to 'push' or 'pull' factors, these boundary crossers end up calling another nation their home. Some become permanent residents and eventually gain citizenship in their adopted country. While some immigrants are able to hold dual or multiple citizenship, others are required to renounce their original citizenship if they officially change their nationality.

The multidimensional nature of boundary crossings

To understand the process and impact of intercultural transitions, we must consider the motivation for boundary crossings (e.g. forced or voluntary), the duration of the stay (e.g. short-term or long-term), the nature of the move (e.g. tourism, study, work) and the frequency of crossings (e.g. habitual crossings, degree of exposure to other languages and cultures, first-timers). Differences in status, power, size of the group, rights and resources (e.g. economic, political, social) influence how newcomers perceive and interact in the new environment. Individual characteristics or attributes such as attitudes, motives, values, personality and abilities (e.g. proficiency in the host language) also play a role in determining how newcomers respond to their new environment and host nationals.

Individuals (e.g. student sojourners, expatriates) may also change their status from temporary sojourners to permanent residents or immigrants. For example, international exchange students may remain abroad to work after their studies are finished. This life-changing decision would impact on their perceptions of their adopted land (and home country), as well as their intercultural relationships and self-identities. Nonetheless, in this chapter, we keep the distinction between these groups to better understand the nature of transitions.

TRANSITIONING TO A NEW CULTURE: LONG-TERM AND SHORT-TERM ADAPTATION

Exposure to an unfamiliar linguistic and cultural environment can have a profound, long-lasting impact on both temporary and permanent boundary crossers. In the last few decades, educators and researchers from a variety of fields have devoted considerable attention to the linguistic, sociocultural, psychological and physical challenges that newcomers face in a foreign land. Early theories and explorations tended to focus on long-term settlers (e.g. immigrants and refugees); however, with an increase in temporary stays in another culture there is now considerable interest in the intercultural contact and transitions of sojourners.

Long-term adaptation: immigrants and other settlers

For many decades, social psychologists, communication specialists, applied linguists and other scholars have studied the adaptation of immigrants and refugees who settle in a new cultural environment more or less permanently, either voluntarily or due to circumstances beyond their control. Their work has drawn attention to variations in attitudes towards linguistic and cultural difference, the quality and degree of contact with people in the host environment, second language and culture-learning strategies, differences in the desire or ability of settlers to 'fit into' the new environment and variations in the attitudes of host nationals towards newcomers.

Acculturation and second language socialization

In Chapter 3, we explored **enculturation**, the process by which individuals acquire the knowledge, skills (e.g. language, communication), attitudes and values necessary to become functioning members of their culture. In contrast, **acculturation** is the term used to refer to the changes that take place after contact between individuals or groups with different cultural

Plate 8.4 This street painting offers insight into the daily life of early Chinese immigrants in North America © Jane Jackson

backgrounds. One of the most widely quoted definitions was put forward by Redfield *et al.* (1936: 149–52):

> those phenomena which result when groups of individuals having different cultures come into continuous first-hand contact, with subsequent changes in the original culture patterns of either or both groups . . . under this definition acculturation is to be distinguished from cultural change, of which it is be one aspect, and assimilation, which is at times a phase of acculturation.

More recently, acculturation is defined by Berry *et al.* (2011: 464) as 'changes in a cultural group or individuals as a result of contact with another cultural group'. This contact may bring about cultural changes in both parties (e.g. immigrants as well as host nationals).

Closely tied to acculturation, **second language socialization** refers to the process by which novices in an unfamiliar linguistic and cultural context gain intercultural communicative competence by acquiring linguistic conventions, sociopragmatic norms, cultural scripts and other behaviours that are associated with the new culture (Duff 2010; Ochs & Schieffelin 1984). This transformation entails knowledge gains in social, cultural and linguistic domains and is closely tied to the notion of identity reconstruction or expansion that was described in Chapter 6. For example, in a new environment one can gain a deeper understanding of one's strengths and weaknesses, as noted by James Baldwin, an American civil rights activist who travelled abroad: 'I met a lot of people in Europe. I even encountered myself'. Ultimately, this knowledge can eventually lead to personal transformation, an aspect that is explored further in this chapter when we examine Kim's (2001) integrative communication theory of cross-cultural adaptation.

Acculturation patterns

Researchers have discovered that the ways in which individuals and groups respond to intercultural contact and the process of acculturation can differ significantly. This is partly attributed to the tension between the desire to develop a sense of belonging in the new culture (acquire a local identity, master the host language, make friends with host nationals) and the desire to maintain one's own culture and language (e.g. cultural identity, traditions, values, practices). **Cultural maintenance** refers to the effort to sustain elements of one's culture or heritage by preserving core values, traditions, ways of being, etc. especially when faced with pressure to adopt a more dominant culture (e.g. the majority culture) (Berry 2006); **language maintenance** refers to 'the preservation of a language or language variety in a context where there is considerable pressure for speakers to shift towards the more prestigious or politically dominant language' (Swann *et al.* (2004: 172). The ways that individuals and ethnocultural groups respond to the process of acculturation are referred to as **acculturation strategies**.

John Berry (1974, 1997, 2003), a cross-cultural psychologist, developed an acculturation theory to illustrate the cultural and psychological dimensions of acculturation and variations in the retention or reshaping of cultural identities. In his framework, he identifies four different strategies or modes of acculturation that long-term settlers may adopt in the new environment: assimilation, integration, separation and marginalization.

Assimilation occurs when individuals do not retain their original cultural identity and link to their heritage/culture; instead, they seek close interaction with the host culture, and adopt the cultural values, norms and traditions of the new society. People who assimilate into the new culture are apt to focus on mastering the host language and rarely use their first language. When they have children, they may use their second language at home and their children may grow up knowing very little about their heritage and the first language of their parents and grandparents.

Integration occurs when people take steps to maintain their cultural heritage and original cultural identity while developing harmonious relationships with other cultures (e.g. host nationals). In countries that have a large multilingual and multicultural population, immigrants may continue to use their first language at home and among members of their ethnic community but also master the primary language of their new country and interact with host nationals and people from other cultures. People who adopt this strategy aim to integrate into the new society. Although they take on some characteristics of the host culture, they retain elements of their original culture that they value.

Separation (segregation) refers to the acculturation strategy in which individuals strive to maintain their cultural heritage and avoid participation in the larger society of their new

Plate 8.5 The lives of early Chinese immigrants in Canada are captured in this street painting in Chinatown in Victoria, B.C. © Jane Jackson

country. They do not wish to be closely linked to the host culture (e.g. be associated with values and traditions they do not accept) and may resist or, at least, not invest in learning the dominant language of the community. Much of their time is spent interacting in their first language with people from their ethnic group.

Marginalization refers to the acculturation strategy in which people do not nurture their cultural heritage (and first language) and resist interacting with people in the larger society. Marginalized and isolated individuals reject both the new and old culture. They display little or no interest in maintaining the identity of their own cultural group and make no effort to develop a cultural identity linked to the dominant culture. This form of acculturation tends to be characterized by isolation and confusion.

Within the context of acculturation, Berry *et al.* (2011) define **adaptation** as the process of coping with the experiences and strains of acculturation. Many cross-cultural psychologists distinguish between **psychological adaptation** (feelings of personal well-being and self-esteem) and **sociocultural adaptation** (competence in dealing with life in the larger society) (Ward *et al.* 2001). **Acculturative stress** refers to 'a negative psychological reaction to the experiences of acculturation, often characterized by anxiety, depression, and a variety of psychosomatic problems' (Berry *et al.* 2011: 465).

Short-term adaptation: sojourners

Most investigations of short-term sojourners (e.g. international exchange students, expatriates) have focused on the need to quickly adjust to their new environment. Research has largely centred on practical ways to help people adjust and optimize their temporary stay abroad (e.g. learn the host language, communicate in culturally appropriate ways with host nationals, cope with culture difference). The next section focuses on the challenges that they may face before, during and after their stay abroad.

TYPES OF TRANSITION SHOCK

Transition shock is a broad construct, which refers to the state of loss, disorientation and identity confusion that can occur when we enter a new situation, job, relationship or physical location and find ourselves confronted with the strain of adjusting to the unfamiliar (e.g. novel perspectives, different roles) (J.M. Bennett 1998). Moving from secondary school to university or from one's family home to a dormitory are examples. Starting a new job or becoming single after a long-term romance has ended are other life transitions that people may experience. Events such as these can have an emotional, psychological, behavioural, cognitive and physiological impact. Several sub-categories of transition shock are especially relevant to our discussion of boundary crossings: culture shock, role shock, language shock and identity or self shock.

Culture shock

When sojourners cross borders, they travel with the language, values, beliefs and habits that they developed in their home culture through the process of enculturation that was described in Chapter 3. In an unfamiliar linguistic, physical and social environment, it is quite common to experience stress and confusion when confronted with new ideas and behaviours. This experience can be very unsettling for sojourners (and long-term settlers) and how they respond can have a profound impact on the quality and lasting impact of their stay abroad.

In 1950, anthropologist Cora DuBois used the term **culture shock** to refer to the disorientation that many anthropologists often experience when entering a new culture to do fieldwork (La Brack & Berardo 2007). A decade later, another anthropologist, Kalvero Oberg (1960), extended the term to encompass the transition of any individuals who travel outside their home environment and face challenges adjusting to a new culture. Since then, many definitions have been put forward. For Peter Adler (1975: 13), culture shock is 'a set of emotional reactions to the loss of perceptual reinforcements from one's own culture, to new cultural stimuli which have little or no meaning, and to the misunderstanding of new and diverse experiences'.

Role shock

Role shock is characterized by lack of knowledge and confusion about the norms of behaviour in a new culture (e.g. the social 'rules' of politeness, business etiquette) (Byrnes 1966). When you enter a new, unfamiliar situation you are apt to be exposed to roles and responsibilities that diverge from what you are used to in your home environment. For example, you may encounter different expectations for the behaviour of males and females in particular contexts. In an unfamiliar country, students may be surprised to discover that the roles of teachers and learners differ from what they have become accustomed to. In a new job in an unfamiliar country, it can be stressful to discover that the relationship between employer and employee is much more formal (or less formal) than expected.

Language shock

Boundary crossings frequently involve exposure to a language that is not one's mother tongue. **Language shock** refers to the challenge of understanding and communicating in a second language in an unfamiliar environment (Smalley 1963). Hile (1979) describes it as 'the frustration and mental anguish that results in being reduced to the level of a two-year-old in one's ability to communicate'. Not having enough language skills to perform simple daily tasks can be very frustrating and humbling. Even if you speak the same first language as host nationals, differences in accent, cultural scripts, norms of politeness, dialects, humour, vocabulary, slang and communication styles can impede communication. In the host environment, nonverbal behaviours (e.g. body language, paralanguage) can be confounding for newcomers. Language and culture shock can lead to temporary disorientation and discomfort in unfamiliar surroundings.

Identity or self shock

Crossing borders can also raise awareness of one's sense of self and even challenge self-identities that have long been taken for granted. **Identity** or **self shock** refers to 'the intrusion of inconsistent, conflicting self-images', which can involve 'loss of communication competence', 'distorted self-reflections in the responses of others' and 'the challenge of changing identity-bound behaviors' (Zaharna 1989: 501). As newcomers try to make sense of their new environment and communicate who they are, they are sometimes dismayed to discover that they are not perceived as they would like. Communicating one's preferred identities through a second language can be frustrating and easily misunderstood. With exposure to new ways of being, newcomers may also experience some confusion about who they are and how they fit into the world around them, as Zaharna (1989: 518) explains:

> For the sojourner, self-shock is the intrusion of inconsistent, conflicting self-images. At a time when we are searching for meaning "out there," our own internal axis for creating meaning is thrown off balance. Our frustration becomes not so much trying to make sense of the Other (i.e. culture shock) but rather the Self (i.e. self-shock).

This form of transition shock emerges from 'a double-bind of increased need to confirm self-identities, with diminished ability to do so' (Zaharna 1989: 516). When we realize that our usual ways of conveying our identities are misunderstood by others, we may lack the knowledge and skills to change the situation. In an alien environment, it can be very unsettling when our preferred self-labels are not understood or accepted. For example, Korean or Japanese students may be identified as Chinese when abroad and vice versa. Second language speakers who are very fluent in the host language may be dismayed to be constantly reminded that they are foreigners because of their accent or vocabulary choice.

When individuals or groups cross borders and experience culture shock, they may confront all of the dimensions mentioned: role shock, self shock and language shock as culture is intertwined with each of these elements.

LANGUAGE AND CULTURE SHOCK

Causes of language and culture shock

Moving from one linguistic and cultural environment to another can cause stress, anxiety and confusion. What are the main sources of language and culture shock? Furnham and Bochner (1986), Klopf and McCroskey (2007), Nolan (1999), Oberg (1960), Ward *et al.* (2001) and many other scholars have offered a range of explanations:

Unrealistic, romantic expectations. If you have decided to move to a new environment expecting it to be perfect (e.g. an idyllic, stress-free oasis), it can be quite a shock to discover that it is not like in your dreams. Similar to home, there are bound to be elements of the new culture that are not pleasing to you. Idealistic, romantic notions of host nationals that have been formed by reading novels or watching movies are unlikely to match reality. For example, Elsa, a student sojourner, made the following comments in her diary as she travelled from Asia to England:

> During the flight, the images, or, I should say, my imagination about what England is like and how British people look like, kept lingering in my mind. In my opinion, Britain is quite a traditional, old-fashioned country. People there are all with perfect propriety. Gentlemen and ladies in nice suits and gowns are the most outstanding images that first come to my mind whenever I think of England.

A few weeks later she was much less enthusiastic when she wrote:

> I used to think that all English were polite and gentle. Some are gentlemen but a lot are not . . . From reading books, I thought that all the British people are very cultured, going to the theatre and reading literature but I was too naïve. That makes me a little bit disappointed as I expected that the whole country was very cultured . . .

Ward *et al.* (2001) observe that sojourners who hold unrealistic expectations about the host country may become disillusioned and withdraw when confronted with reality.

Inadequate preparation. If you experience language and culture shock soon after your arrival in a new country, it may come as a surprise if you have given little thought to what life will be like in the host culture. You may not have considered language- and culture-learning strategies that could help you adjust and make connections with host nationals. Without adequate preparation and limited understanding of culture shock, you may be ill-equipped psychologically to deal with the natural ups and downs of adjustment.

Abrupt change. Nowadays, with advances in transportation we can easily travel from our home environment to distant lands in a matter of hours. In our journey we may cross several time zones and arrive in a place with a very different climate as well as many unfamiliar practices (e.g. cultural, dietary, linguistic, religious, political, social, etc.). This can be a shock to one's system, as noted by Wood and Landry (2010: 48):

> Change feels too fast. Contact with difference, the unfamiliar, the strange and the 'Other' . . . can be and usually is unsettling in spite of the occasional speck of delight and surprise. The abrupt loss of the familiar and moving from one environment where one has learnt to function easily and successfully to one where one cannot is dramatic for both [short-term and long-term sojourners].

Lack of familiarity with signs and symbols. In our home environment, we are surrounded by physical and social signs that help us to make sense of our world and enable us to function in everyday life. When we enter an unfamiliar milieu we are suddenly exposed to verbal and nonverbal codes and social behaviours (e.g. words, communication styles, gestures, customs, cultural scripts) that are foreign to us. Our inability to comprehend these signs and symbols can induce acculturative stress, as Oberg (1960: 177) explains:

> Culture shock is precipitated by the anxiety that results from losing all our familiar signs and symbols of social intercourse. These signs or cues include the thousand and one ways in which we orient ourselves to the situations of daily life: when to shake hands and what to say when we meet people, when and how to give tips, how to give orders to servants,

Plate 8.6 We may experience culture shock in a new environment due to the loss of the familiar and uncertainty about local social norms and practices © Jane Jackson

how to make purchases, when to accept and when to refuse invitations, when to take statements seriously and when not. Now these cues which may be words, gestures, facial expressions, customs, or norms, are acquired by all of us in the course of growing up and are as much a part of our culture as the language we speak or the beliefs we accept. All of us depend for our peace of mind and our efficiency on hundreds of these cues, most of which we do not carry on the level of conscious awareness.

Loss. When you move to a new environment, you leave behind much of what is familiar to you. As Swallow (2010) observes, 'everything is unfamiliar, weather, landscape, language, food, dress, social roles, values, customs, and communication – basically, everything you're used to is no longer there'. Some sojourners experience intense feelings of grief and loss as they miss their first language, people, places, possessions, and other aspects (e.g. food, expressions of courtesy, sounds, smells) that are dear to them in their home environment.

Sensory overload. In unfamiliar surroundings and situations it is not unusual to feel over-whelmed and overstimulated by the multitude of new sights, sounds and smells that you

Plate 8.7
Newcomers can easily be overwhelmed by the wide variety of unfamiliar sights, scents, sounds and choices © Jane Jackson

Plate 8.8 Imagine you are to travel to a beautiful beach in the Philippines. Would you be prepared to get on board this jeepney? © David Jackson

experience. Pulled in many different directions, you may feel pressured to deal with too many things at once. According to Nancy Arthur (2004: 27–8), a cross-cultural psychologist and counsellor, '[i]n familiar cultural environments, cognitive and sensory processes normally operate through automatic and unconscious processing of information. However, in unfamiliar cultural environments, a conscious and deliberate effort must be made to process and understand the meaning of new information'. Not surprisingly, newcomers may experience sensory and cognitive overload and fatigue as they expend a considerable amount of energy continuously processing new information.

Unfamiliar 'ways of being'. In a new cultural environment, you are bound to encounter unfamiliar worldviews and ways of doing things. You may be confronted with different ideas about what is appropriate behaviour for males and females. Religious practices (e.g. interrupting work for daily prayers) may be new to you. Modes of transportation may also be very different from what you are used to.

If you opt to study abroad, you may also encounter new **'cultures of learning'**, as Cortazzi and Jin (1997: 83) explain:

> a culture of learning depends on the norms, values and expectations of teachers and learners relative to classroom activity . . . It is not simply that overseas students encounter different ways of teaching and different expectations about learning; rather such encounters are juxtaposed with the cultures of learning they bring with them.

For example, you may find that you are expected to speak up in class much more than you are used to and teachers may provide less support (e.g. no powerpoint slides, lecture notes or other handouts) or vice versa (Jackson 2013). These new behaviours can be very confusing and difficult to accept at first.

Feeling trapped. People who stay abroad for less than three weeks (**micro-term sojourners**) and even tourists who are abroad for longer know that if they are really uncomfortable in the new environment they can seek refuge in their hotel room or hostel and will soon escape to the safety and security of home. **Short-term sojourners** (e.g. those who will stay several months) and certainly **long-term sojourners** (e.g. expatriates who live abroad for many years) face a different situation. Newcomers who study, live or work alongside host nationals need to be able to function in the host culture. As Nolan (1999: 78) explains, 'you can't turn off your new country, not even for a second. It's always there, pushing in on you in a thousand ways, all at once'. Sojourners who are unable to cope may take flight and head for home earlier than planned.

Ambiguity and uncertainty. It can be very frustrating to discover that your usual ways of accomplishing daily tasks and interacting with people do not work well in the new culture. Initially, you may be quite unsure about when and what will happen (e.g. who speaks first, what responses are deemed appropriate in a particular situation). **Cultural scripts** (e.g. local conventions for apologies, requests, refusals) may be mystifying. Displays of emotion, gender relations and the rules for social interactions may be quite different from what you are used to and in many situations you may not know how to respond. You may also be surprised at the ways in which people react to what you say and do. **Tolerance of ambiguity** refers to one's ability to cope with situations that are not clear. Individuals who have a low tolerance of ambiguity may find adjustment more difficult than those who are less stressed in situations where they do not fully understand the context. (Chapter 9 discusses the uncertainty reduction theory and the uncertainty/anxiety management theory.)

Lack of socio-emotional support. Crossing linguistic and cultural boundaries can be very stressful. If this is your first foray abroad and you are on your own, there are bound to be times when you find life difficult. When you feel blue, you are apt to miss the support of your family members and confidants who are far away. Until you make new friends and develop a support system (e.g. ties with locals and other international students), you are surrounded by strangers in a foreign environment.

No matter where you are in the world, you can suffer personal disappointments, worries and hardship (e.g. relationship breakups, the serious illness of family members or friends, financial difficulties, academic failure). Events that would be unsettling in your home environment can seem even more overwhelming in the host culture, especially if you are not physically close to your loved ones. Even minor difficulties that would easily be dealt with at home can seem insurmountable if you are more emotional and plagued with self-doubts.

Standing out. In your home environment, you can easily blend in if you are visibly similar to other members of the majority culture. If you display similar identity markers (e.g. religious clothing, tattoos), speak the same first language or dialect as the majority and use nonverbal behaviours familiar to home nationals, you can go about your business without attracting attention. If you cross borders and become a visible minority for the first time in your life, it can be quite a shock as this novice sojourner from Hong Kong discovered:

The scene in Heathrow Airport, when I was suddenly surrounded only by foreigners (mostly 'giant' Westerners whose skin, eye and hair colours were different from mine; speaking English or other foreign languages) struck me a great deal. And due to these intrinsic differences between them and me, psychologically I felt distanced from them though all of us were now under the same roof . . . my mind was occupied by uncertainty, curiosity and my effort to force out the courage to face the new . . .

Even if you can physically blend into a new environment, you may discover that eyebrows are raised as soon as you utter a few words. Your accent, nonverbal behaviour and communication style can signal that you are a stranger. The adornments and clothing you wear (e.g. body piercings, jewellery, short skirts, head scarf) may be commonplace in your home environment but set you apart in another cultural context. Being stared at (and perhaps ridiculed) can be unnerving.

Discrimination or perceptions of discrimination. If you have grown up in an environment where you are a member of the group that has the most influence and prestige, it can be a shock to enter a world in which you are a minority member with less status and power. When intercultural interactions do not go well, you may feel that people in the host culture are treating you unfairly because of your accent, ethnicity, race, gender, religion, nationality, etc. In some situations, your instincts may be valid, whereas in others, your perception of discrimination or racism may be due to an elevated stress level and misunderstandings about linguistic and cultural norms in the host culture. For example, the annoyed look of a host national may be due to your unintentional breaking of social norms (e.g. omitting the word 'thank you') rather than prejudice. Whether real or imagined, negative encounters like this can lead to withdrawal from the host culture: 'being discriminated against can turn people inwards and cause a sense of isolation or diminished self-importance' (Wood & Landry 2010: 48).

Language shock. If you have entered a new linguistic environment and do not speak the local language or your proficiency is at the beginner's level, you can feel helpless and dependent. You may have a basic grasp of the local language but lack familiarity with **sociopragmatic norms** (e.g. cultural scripts for social situations, routinized expressions of politeness) and this can be a significant barrier to communication and hamper your adjustment. Even if you have studied the language in an academic setting for many years and attained a high score on a language proficiency test, it can be unsettling to discover that your speech (e.g. accent, style of communication) is not easily understood by locals. Your formal language lessons at school may not have equipped you for informal, social situations. Initially, you may find idiomatic expressions, humour, satire, social discourse and communication styles impenetrable. Body language and other nonverbal codes may also be difficult to decipher. Second language socialization can be challenging.

Language fatigue. Interacting with people in a second language can be very exhausting, especially if you are not used to functioning in the language on a daily basis. If your proficiency is not advanced you may find that you need to translate oral speech in your head and then respond. As the comments of this second language sojourner reveal, this can be very taxing until your profiency improves.

I really think that my English is not okay. I need time to translate what I want to say: grammar and articles and tenses are all wrong . . . And it's so tiring to use English all day.

I find that my English vocabulary is not enough . . . And the translation is really killing me! . . . It is getting harder and harder for me to translate and I feel tired. I just speak Cantonese by instinct . . . I think my mind will burst . . . It's really killing me. My mood is on the drop. Maybe there is a maximum capacity of learning a foreign language that is preventing my further improvement.

Miscommunication. If you enter a new environment with little or no proficiency in the host language it can be very challenging to express your needs, ideas and emotions in verbal and nonverbal ways that are meaningful to your hosts. If you arrive with an advanced level of proficiency in the host language, your hosts are apt to expect you to speak and interact in ways that are appropriate in that context. In other words, they may expect you to have much more sociopragmatic knowledge and awareness than you actually possess. A language barrier can lead to frustration and misunderstandings for both newcomers and host nationals.

Conflict in values. When you travel to a new environment you bring with you the values and worldviews that have been nurtured in your home country during the process of enculturation. In your new surroundings, you are bound to encounter people who do not necessarily share your perspective. Unless managed with skill, conflicting values and expectations can serve as a barrier to intercultural relations. (Conflicts in interpersonal relations are examined further in Chapters 9 and 10.)

Change in status or positioning. As a stranger or newcomer, you may discover that you have lost your status and positioning in the host culture. Back home, you may have been accorded respect as a top undergraduate with a high GPA but in the new environment you may find yourself in classes with many students who are more proficient in the language of instruction and have more background knowledge about the local culture. Until you find your feet, this loss in status can shake your self-confidence.

Symptoms of language and culture shock

Cross-cultural psychologists, counsellors, educators, and other scholars (e.g. Arthur 2004; Bochner 2006; Gebhard 2010; Ward *et al.* 2001; Winkelman 1994) have identified a number of cognitive, psychological (emotional) and physiological symptoms linked to language and culture shock. Their research suggests that when you enter another culture to live, work, or study, you *may* experience some of the following symptoms:

- a change in sleep patterns (e.g. experience trouble falling asleep (insomnia) or sleep much more than usual)
- frequent mood swings and heightened irritability (e.g. be easily bothered by things that would normally not trouble you)
- feeling vulnerable, powerless, lost and insecure (e.g. preoccupation with your safety, constant fears about being robbed, cheated, or exploited)
- excessive worrying about one's state of physical or mental health
- continuous concern about the purity of the water and food (e.g. you develop an obsession about cleanliness manifesting in excessive washing of hands)
- unfamiliar body aches and pains (e.g. skin rashes, hives, headaches, stomach aches, allergies) and frequent illnesses (e.g. colds, general malaise)

- loss of appetite or overeating (e.g. significant weight loss or gains)
- feeling sad and lonely even when in the company of other people
- homesickness (e.g. constant, deep longing for your family and friends back home)
- utopian, unrealistic views about your home culture and language
- fear of trying new things, meeting local people or going to unfamiliar places (e.g. continually declining invitations to go out, staying inside more than usual)
- feelings of inadequacy (e.g. loss of self-confidence due to the inability to express yourself clearly in the host language and perform basic tasks)
- increased consumption of alcohol or drugs
- frequent perceptions of being singled out, overlooked or discriminated against (e.g. not treated with the same respect as locals)
- pressing desire to interact with people just like yourself (e.g. individuals from the same linguistic and cultural background who 'really make sense' and 'understand you')
- cognitive impairment (e.g. difficulty concentrating and making decisions, inability to solve simple problems)
- frequently questioning your decision to go abroad and counting the days until you return home
- constantly comparing the new environment with your home culture, with the former cast in a negative light (e.g. constant complaints about the local weather, food, people, customs, etc.)
- hostility towards members of the host culture and frequent 'us' vs. 'them' discourse (e.g. negative stereotyping of host nationals)
- resentment and lack of desire to interact with people from the host culture
- loss of identity or confusion about who you are and how you fit into the world
- refusal to learn/use the host language and interact with host nationals.

Degree of language and culture shock

Not all boundary crossers suffer from transition shock in the same way or to the same degree. Adler (1975), Furnham and Bochner (1986), Ward *et al.* (2001) and other researchers have identified a range of factors that may account for disparate experiences.

Quality of information (degree of fact-finding, amount and calibre of information about new environment, knowledge about the process of intercultural adjustment). Individuals who enter a new environment armed with current information about the host country (e.g. language, history, climate, 'cultures of learning', politics, religious practices, customs, etc.) and the process of adjustment are better equipped to deal with culture shock than those who arrive without having done any groundwork.

Cultural similarity (the degree of similarity between one's home culture and the host culture in terms of values, beliefs, nonverbal behaviours, customs, 'cultures of learning', etc.). **Cultural distance** refers to 'the major differences concerning cultural values, language, and verbal and nonverbal styles between one's home country and the host society' (Ting-Toomey & Chung 2012: 299). When the cultural distance is greater, the culture shock may be more severe. For example, students from Wuhan, China may find it more challenging to adjust to Berlin than Singapore. A Brazilian may find it easier to adjust to Lisbon than Nairobi.

Linguistic similarity (the degree of similarity between one's first language and the host language). Sojourners who speak a romance language such as French may find it easier to cope in a Spanish-speaking environment than in an environment where a Semitic language (e.g. Arabic) is the dominant medium of communication. When the language or dialect is from the same family (e.g. romance languages), it is easier to pick up the rhythm of the language as well as the script (written form).

Communication style similarity (the degree of similarity between one's communication style and the common communication styles in the host culture). For example, Japanese nationals who are most familiar with an indirect style of communication are apt to find it less challenging to move to an environment where a similar style is widely used. If they transfer to Germany or another country where more direct styles of communication are favoured they may find adjustment more difficult.

Interpersonal dimensions (e.g. age, fortitude, independence, previous travel, proficiency in the host language, resourcefulness, tolerance of ambiguity). All of these traits or personal characteristics can impact on one's ability to deal with difficulties that arise. Individuals who are more resilient and tolerant of ambiguity are better positioned to cope with the strains of adjustment.

Physiological factors (mental and physical condition, medical or dietary issues, ability to tolerate changes in temperature/time zones, resilience). Individuals who are less physically robust (e.g. become ill easily, are susceptible to changes in the weather/diet) and not emotionally stable may be more affected by the adjustment process. **Resilience** refers to an individual's ability to cope with stress and adversity.

Socio-emotional support (friendship circles, intracultural and intercultural relationships, family support). The strength of one's bonds with other people (e.g. friends in the host culture) and the amount of **socio-emotional support** (warmth and nurturance) they provide can have a significant impact on how one's sojourn unfolds. Those who avoid host nationals and spend all of their time with people from their home country may benefit from the camaraderie and suffer less culture shock; however, this **avoidance strategy** can limit their personal development (e.g. second language/culture learning). Conversely, those who make more of an effort to develop friendships with host nationals may suffer more from culture shock due to more exposure to the host culture but, ultimately, they may benefit much more from the sojourn (e.g. become more proficient in the host language, develop a deeper understanding of the host environment, experience more personal growth) (Gareis 2012; Hendrickson *et al.* 2010; Kinginger 2009).

Degree of control (amount of control over such aspects as one's move abroad, living conditions in the new environment, sojourn duration, free time, selection of courses, etc.). Individuals who have chosen to go abroad are apt to be more motivated than those who venture abroad for the sole purpose of fulfilling a programme or job requirement. One's degree of autonomy in other aspects (e.g. housing, selection of courses/host institution/destination) can result in differences in the ways individuals view and respond to acculturative stress).

Geopolitical factors (relationship between the home country and the host nation; international, national, regional, or local tensions). If sojourning in a region that has strong, favourable ties with one's home country, one may view the host country positively and feel secure and well received by host nationals. Conversely, if the host country has tense or hostile relations with one's home country, the sojourner may be apprehensive about entering and not be welcomed in the same way.

Agency (the capacity to make choices). Two sojourners with a similar background can be in the host environment at the same time. One may take advantage of every opportunity possible to interact with locals and practice the host language, whereas the other person may constantly pine for home and spend all of his free time on Skype complaining to friends and family back home about the weather, food, local people, etc. in his first language. While one sojourner is overwhelmed with feelings of homesickness, the other is willing to try new things, makes friends with host nationals and begins to 'fit into' the new environment. This disparate outcome evokes a well-known quote from the American author James A. Michener: 'If you reject the food, ignore the customs, fear the religion and avoid the people, you might better stay home'.

Duration and spatial factors (length of stay, location of residence, geographical locale). Sojourners who reside in an apartment with home nationals and only stay a short time in the host culture likely have less opportunity to develop interpersonal relationships with host nationals than those who stay longer and live in a homestay or dormitory with locals. The amount and quality of exposure to the host culture can impact on the degree of language and culture shock that one experiences.

Positive and negative effects of language and culture shock

Early conceptions of culture shock were largely negative. In fact, Oberg (1960: 177) referred to it as 'an occupational disease of people who have been transplanted abroad'. For many decades, 'disease'-oriented perceptions persisted and pre-sojourn orientations usually emphasized practical ways to avoid culture shock. Nowadays, however, there is growing recognition of the positive dimensions of this phenomenon and the focus has shifted to productive ways to manage the stress that naturally occurs as one enters and adjusts to a new environment. Further, more scholars are drawing attention to the potential for language and culture stress to lead to deeper levels of '**whole person development**' (e.g. emotional intelligence and resourcefulness, interpersonal communication skills, intercultural competence, independence, maturity) and **identity expansion** (e.g. a broadened, more inclusive sense of self, the development of a global outlook) (Jackson 2012; Kinginger 2009). Dealing with the challenges of transitions can result in new, deeper understandings of oneself and more motivation to persevere in the host culture.

> In the encounter with another culture the individual gains new experiential knowledge by coming to understand the roots of his or her own ethnocentricism and by gaining new perspectives and outlooks on the nature of culture . . . Paradoxically, the more one is capable of experiencing new and different dimensions of human diversity, the more one learns of oneself.
>
> (Adler 1975: 22)

While language and culture shock can be debilitating for some, it can also lead to significant learning and personal growth, as noted more recently by Lantis and DuPlaga (2010: 60–61):

By getting "culture shocked," you are challenging yourself, surpassing your comfort zone, and becoming much more aware of your identity and of the world around you. You are building skills, gaining confidence, and forging relationships that surpass your former boundaries. Ultimately, you are learning what it means to be a global citizen.

When newcomers immerse themselves in the host culture, they gain more access to host nationals and local practices or ways of doing things. As noted in Chapter 6, **communities of practice (CoP)** are 'groups of people who share a concern or a passion for something they do and learn how to do it better as they interact regularly' (Wenger 2006). Significant contact with the local language and cultural practices can certainly be exhausting and stressful at times; however, the discomfort can also lead to more awareness and understanding of both Self and Other. For example, first-hand exposure to new communities of practice can compel individuals to reflect on and even question their behaviours, self-identities, values and beliefs. It can motivate newcomers to master the host language and enhance their intercultural competence to better 'fit into' the new environment. As sojourners become more tolerant of ambiguity and develop better intercultural communication skills, they are apt to experience more success in overcoming difficulties. Successfully dealing with language and culture shock can be a source of pride and can help sojourners become more self-confident and independent.

STAGES OF CULTURE SHOCK AND ADJUSTMENT

The U-curve adjustment model

Since the term culture shock was introduced, scholars have created various models to try and depict the stages of culture shock and adjustment that sojourners may experience in a new culture. One of the earliest and most well-known models is the **U-curve adjustment model** (Lysgaard 1955), which is illustrated in Figure 8.1.

The U-shaped model includes four stages, which have been given various names by different scholars (e.g. Lysgaard 1955; Oberg 1960):

1   the honeymoon stage (initial euphoria): fascination and excitement about the new culture, curiosity about linguistic and cultural differences and an emphasis on cultural similarities;
2   culture stress and shock (crisis and frustration): confrontation with different values and behaviours, confusion and anxiety and criticism/rejection of the new language and culture;
3   adjustment (integration or recovery): the learning of new linguistic, social and cultural norms, an increase in one's level of comfort and well-being and respect for the new culture (e.g. different ways of being) and language;
4   mastery (adaptation and acceptance, biculturalism): awareness and understanding of cultural differences, an increase in autonomy and satisfaction, a dual cultural/linguistic identity.

Reentry and the W-curve adjustment model

Gullahorn and Gullahorn (1963) maintain that returnees often experience a similar period of adjustment when they return home, so they extended the U-curve model by adding two stages:

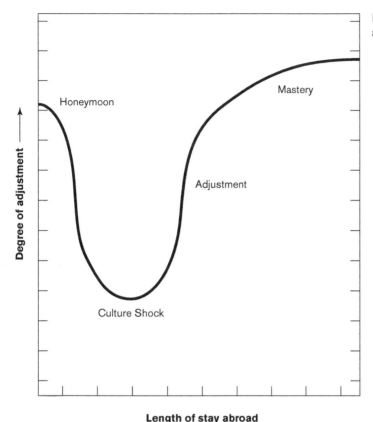

Figure 8.1 The U-curve adjustment model

reentry or reverse culture shock and resocialization, the process of readjusting one's attitudes and behaviours to feel at ease in one's 'home environment' after a period away (see Figure 8.2). Since then, many versions of their W-shape adjustment model have been proposed by interculturalists (e.g. Kohls 2001; Ting-Toomey & Chung 2012).

As variations of this model are still widely used today, the proposed stages are explained along with relevant 'real world' examples from student sojourners.[1]

The honeymoon phase (initial euphoria). When sojourners first arrive in the host culture, the curve model suggests that most are excited and looking forward to what lies ahead. Similar to the early stage of a romance, newcomers may initially overlook negative aspects of the host culture and take delight in discovering new sights, sounds and smells. This buoyant mood is captured in a diary entry written by a second language sojourner soon after her arrival in the host culture:

> Waking up this morning, I could hardly believe I was in England. It was all like a dream, a dream that came true finally . . . I looked around my bedroom and then viewed through the window: the air was still and quiet amidst birds' chatter, everything was clear like a framed picture, with no sign of impurities or pollution which very often surround my living place back home. The colours of my room, the neighbouring houses, the trees and the sky, were plain, fresh and lively. A sense of satisfaction ran through my heart.

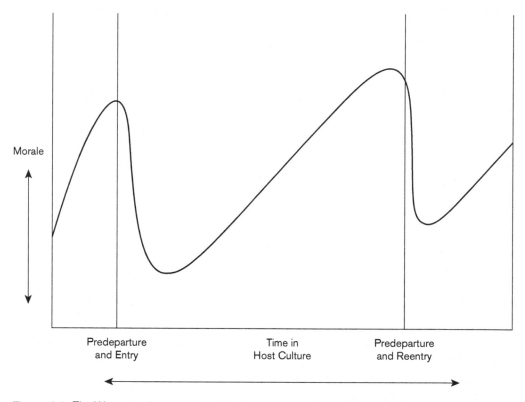

Figure 8.2 The W-curve adjustment model

Hostility phase. In the model, the second phase is sometimes referred to as 'culture shock', 'crisis stage' or 'disintegration'. After the initial euphoria fades away, sojourners may feel uncomfortable in the new environment, especially if they are a visible minority or they stand out in some way (e.g. speak with a different accent, wear different clothing, eat different food, have different values). For example, in a post-sojourn interview, an international exchange student disclosed the following:

> You feel that you are different from the people there – your skin color, your language, and your thoughts. Everyone likes to be with people who are like them. I felt isolated and a bit depressed because they were all familiar with each other and I knew nobody . . . I had difficulties with communication and felt unwelcome by locals. That was far from my expectation before going on exchange. I was desperate to go home at that time.

Newcomers may also be overwhelmed and frustrated by the psychological, cognitive, and physical demands of the new culture and the disintegration of almost everything familiar. Bombarded by stimuli that are difficult to process, excitement may be replaced by frustration and disappointment. In an irritable state, differences between the home culture and host environment are viewed as problems. For example, student sojourners may discover that their roommates have values and practices that they find difficult to accept. In this hostile phase, much of their discourse may be replete with 'us' vs. 'them' comments, with host nationals portrayed unfavourably, as in the following stereotypical comments by a disgruntled exchange student:

I think people in North America lead a really dissolute life. They tend to treat sex casually. They also don't have any goals. They just drink, take drugs and have sex all the time. All the students have the characteristics of a typical North American. They don't know what they are doing in their life. People said foreigners are polite but I don't think so. I think they're rather rebellious and impolite.

Sojourners may also discover that their second language skills are not as well developed as they had assumed. Unexpectedly, they may experience difficulty communicating with people from the host culture, especially in informal situations where colloquialisms are frequently used: 'Although my English isn't good enough to express myself fully, it wasn't a big problem in my coursework. The language problem was more apparent when I chatted with my class-mates as I didn't understand their jokes or know how to respond.' As well as being mentally and physically exhausting at times, using a second language can make it more challenging to cultivate intercultural relationships, an issue that is explored further in Chapter 9.

When classes get underway, student sojourners may come face to face with differing expectations and learning and teaching styles and long for familiar 'cultures of learning'. For example, a Chinese exchange student in the U.S. said:

Sometimes the professor might look at you to force you to answer her questions, but when I had no idea what she was talking about I had to avoid having any eye contact with her. It was so embarrassing. Also, it was so hard for me to fit in. Students kept raising their hands! The most general arguments had been said and then I could not follow their flow so I had no choice but to stay quiet. Once the professor came to me and told me that I was too passive in class. She suggested that I ask more questions instead of answering them but it wasn't easy as I am a passive person and I just wasn't used to this fast pace.

In this stage, homesickness may set in and sojourners may question their decision to go abroad. A small number who suffer severe symptoms of language and culture shock may head home.

Humorous stage. This third phase is sometimes termed the 'reorientation and re-integration phase' or 'adjustment and recovery'. The curve model suggests that sojourners in this phase have regained their sense of humour. They have begun to realize that many of the problems that they have experienced in the new environment are due to cultural difference (including their response to it) or language problems rather than deliberate attempts by locals to annoy them. While comparisons are still made between their home and host cultures, this model suggests that the sojourners are more balanced in their views by this stage. They are more aware of linguistic or cultural differences that may have led to misunderstandings.

With a more positive mindset, they are better able to interpret subtle linguistic and cultural cues, and those who are using a second language find it easier to express themselves in the language. A female sojourner in the Netherlands remarked:

I had difficulty communicating with locals in the beginning but after many weeks had passed, I found that they were nice people. It's just that they dared not to speak in English. Also, by then I knew more about their culture and began to like this country. True, I did experience culture shock at the beginning but I learned to overcome it.

At the host university, student sojourners may have started to form friendships with other international students and perhaps some local students as well. These interpersonal connections help them to feel a bit more connected to the local scene. Although better able to function in the host culture, they may still experience difficult days (e.g. occasional bouts of homesickness).

The 'At home' stage. This phase is sometimes referred to as 'adaptation' or 'resolution'. The curve model suggests that sojourners in this stage feel more at home and happy in the host environment. In a more relaxed frame of mind, they demonstrate more understanding and appreciation of the host language and culture and their new way of life. A sojourner in London wrote:

> Midway through the semester, my life took a turn. By then, I'd made more friends, including some English mates, and had even begun to dream in English! I realized I'd developed a sense of belonging to Bloomsbury, my neighborhood. From the Indian restaurant to the corner shop to my residence hall, social bonds began to form. Overcoming adversities with positivity allowed me to see more and discover more, and with the positive energy this generates, others could feel this . . . Studying abroad is not easy. It is a test of the strength of your character but if you champion it and open yourself up, it can change your life completely.

When using the host language in daily life, sojourners are better able to communicate their ideas and feelings in ways that are context-appropriate as their sociopragmatic awareness has increased. They may actively participate in activities and have a circle of friends they can confide in, which boosts their self-confidence and sense of belonging.

By this time, student sojourners may have become more receptive to new 'cultures of learning' as they better understand what lies behind different practices. For example, a Chinese exchange student who spent a semester in the U.S. revealed the following in a post-sojourn interview:

> In the Human Resources Management course, I didn't like the professor in the beginning. He didn't teach much. Instead, he assigned the teaching job to groups with each group responsible for teaching one chapter. I thought, "You are the professor, why don't you teach?" Gradually, I noticed that he made additional comments to what the students taught. This helped the students to think and learn more . . . The interaction between the teacher and the students took up almost the whole class and you had to think independently. Soon everybody was in a heated discussion and the students would come up with all kinds of answers, including ones you cannot think of, and those you feel too shy to voice out. But they just did! In the beginning, you might not be willing to participate but gradually in such an environment, I became better in communication. One of the benefits is that I no longer get nervous in these situations. I became accustomed to thinking, discussing, and speaking up in a group environment. This is the greatest thing I gained. This helped me to develop one of the most important skills in the business field. In this field, you always need to communicate with others. My communication and cooperative skills are much better after this experience. In the past, I wouldn't dare to challenge others whenever I had a different point of view. I've become bolder to speak out my views and add to the points of others, although my attitude is still not very aggressive.

With enhanced self-confidence, sojourners in this stage may employ more culturally appropriate problem-solving and conflict mediation techniques. They are more adept at coping with challenges that come their way.

This model also suggests that some sojourners may feel that they have developed a bilingual and bicultural identity by this stage. **Biculturalism** is characterized by proficiency and comfort with both one's original culture and the culture of the new country or region (Berry 1997; Fantini 2012a). As noted by Kanno (2003: 3), bilingual individuals may 'incorporate these languages and cultures into their sense of who they are'. Like the following student, sojourners who develop a broadened sense of self may believe that they have been 'transformed' into a more open-minded person while abroad.

When you go to a multicultural, multilingual country to study, you have the chance to get to know people with different nationalities who speak many languages . . . You can learn to think from different angles. After spending a year abroad, I've become much more open-minded. I embrace other cultures and languages, and no longer see the world from a single angle.

(A year-long sojourner)

Reentry or Reverse culture shock. **Reentry** refers to the process of returning home after spending time abroad (Martin & Harrell 2004; Niesen 2010; Smith 2002). The **W-curve model** suggests that many returnees experience ups and downs that are similar to what they experienced abroad. **Reentry** or **reverse culture shock** may be defined as 'the process of readjusting, reacculturating, and reassimilating into one's own home culture after living in a different culture for a significant period of time' (Gaw 2000: 83–4).

Returnees may experience disorientation, surprise and confusion when they do not easily fit back into their home environment. This malaise may be due to a variety of reasons (e.g. a shift in perspectives, boredom with the familiar, appreciation of the host country's customs or values, idealized images of the home country formed while abroad). The shock of reentry can sometimes be more severe and painful than the initial culture shock in the host country, in part because it is not expected (LaBrack 2003; Martin & Harrell 2004; Smith 2002; Szkudlarek 2010). After all, the sojourner is returning 'home'.

In the beginning, those who more fully integrated into the host culture (e.g. made close friends with host nationals or other international students) and functioned well in the host language in their daily life may find it more difficult to readjust to their home culture and first language use in daily life. They may miss their more independent lifestyle and friends made abroad, and find it difficult to fit back into the rhythm of local life. One returnee said:

My adjustment on reentry has been more difficult than what I experienced abroad. I'm still not fully readjusted now. The whole living schedule and sleeping times have changed. Before going on exchange I was able to sleep very little and do a lot of things during the day but now I find this living style is very tiring. I wish I was living the comfortable Norwegian lifestyle but if I do, I won't have enough time to get everything done! I don't know how to cope with that. I'm still working on this . . . still adjusting to being back.

(Year-long exchange student)

While excited to share their experiences, returnees may find that their friends and family quickly tire of their international stories. Disillusioned, returnees may consider host nationals boring and provincial; they may long for the life they had during the sojourn and view it through rose-tinted glasses. They may miss not being able to converse as much in their second language as they did while abroad. Their discourse may be full of complaints about their home culture. This time, 'them' vs. 'us' discourse may elevate all aspects in the host culture and denigrate local ways of being.

Returnees may realize they have changed but find it difficult to put into words. They may feel torn between the values and behaviours of the host country and their home environment. Some may suffer from **identity confusion**, that is, they may feel as if they are caught between two distinct worlds, the one they left behind and the one they have returned to. They may not feel that they fit into either. Like the following returnee, many feel unsettled in this stage:

> While abroad, I missed home quite a lot in the beginning but now that I'm back, I feel estranged. I feel my existence here is meaningless. In the U.S., I had a great time with my boyfriend, my roommates, and my newly met friends. Here, I feel alone. Although I'm physically back, my memories remain in L.A.

(See Chapter 6 for more discussion about identity misalignments and the state of cultural marginality or inbetweenness).

Resocialization stage. The final phase in the model is sometimes referred to as 're-integration', 'the independence stage' or 'acceptance and understanding'. In this stage, returnees are beginning to feel more at home and are better able to communicate effectively and appropriately with their family members, friends and colleagues. Similar to recovery and adjustment phases in the host country, the returnees start to readjust to the home country and reintegrate into the local way of life. The initial reentry shock has subsided and they are better able to find a sense of balance between their 'new old' home and the culture they have just left. A returnee recounted this process in an interview:

> It took me some effort to get used to the local lifestyle again as I'd become accustomed to the way of living in Korea. When I came back home I had to readjust to many things. I had such a wonderful and splendid life in Korea but when I came back, I felt . . . umm . . . It was just . . . so different! I have had to accept it and adapt. You have to try your best to adjust since there's no choice for you! And gradually you feel like you fit in. Now, I am in a better place in my head. I'm doing more things with my friends and I'm happy. I'm also keeping in touch with my friends in Seoul through Facebook.

Returnees may take pride in having developed a hybrid, multicultural identity and display more interest in both international and local happenings. The W-curve model suggests that returnees in this stage are able to identify and appreciate multiple ways in which they have changed for the better due to their international and intercultural experiences. They may make an effort to diversify their social networks to include both local and international friends, and maintain contact with friends made abroad. Feeling more stable and self-confident, they may make plans for more stays abroad, like the following year-abroad returnee:

> Before this sojourn, I never considered working overseas but after experiencing the lifestyle in the U.S., I've started to consider a career abroad. My worldview broadened and I have a more global mindset now. I can view things from a global perspective instead of just looking at them from my home city's perspective.

Criticisms of the U-and W-curve adjustment models

While the U-curve and W-curve adjustment models (or variations of them) are widely used in the preparation of sojourners, a growing number of researchers are discovering that many people experience developmental trajectories that differ from what is portrayed in these models. Berardo (2006, 2012), La Brack (2010, 2011), La Brack and Berardo (2007) and Ward *et al.* (1998, 2001) argue that the curves of adjustment models are not backed up by empirical research and cannot accurately predict 'the depth, length, or even occurrence of culture shock' (La Brack 2010: 2). Questions are also being raised about the applicability of the curved models of adjustment for all types of sojourners. La Brack (2011), for example, points out that the W-curve model 'does not fit the global nomads and third culture kids (TCKs) very well, nor does it fit "heritage-seeking" students or education abroad populations from refugee/immigrant backgrounds' (p. 2). A **heritage student** is 'a student who studies abroad in a location that is linked in some way (for example, linguistically, culturally, historically) to his/her family or cultural background' (Forum on Education Abroad 2011: 34).

In mixed-method investigations of student sojourners (summer immersion, semester- and year-long sojourners), Jackson (2008, 2010, 2012, 2013) found that some sojourners endure significant ups and downs while abroad whereas others do not. Some experience many symptoms of language and culture shock during their sojourn, while others claim their transition to the new culture was smooth and symptom free. Some suffer from identity confusion while abroad, whereas others do not. The amount and quality of contact with the host language and culture varies considerably among sojourners and this naturally impacts on their learning. Some sojourners develop close bonds with host nationals and become more fluent in the host language whereas many others cling to friends from their home country and do not enhance their linguistic or interpersonal skills. (Variations in social networks are discussed further in Chapter 9.)

The degree of reentry culture shock also varies. Some return home with higher levels of intercultural sensitivity, broadened self-identities and a strong desire to use their second language in intercultural interactions. Along with a more open mindset, these returnees may feel that they have developed more cosmopolitan, multicultural identities. With heightened interest in international affairs, they may have taken steps towards a more global identity. In contrast, others are very negative about their sojourn experiences and have become even more ethnocentric and nationalistic after their stay abroad. Overwhelmed by culture difference and ill-equipped to manage language and culture shock, some return home with reinforced stereotypes of host nationals, heightened xenophobia and little interest in further developing the social dimension of their second language proficiency (Jackson 2008, 2010, 2012).

A complicated mix of individual elements (e.g. sojourn aims, adaptive stress, personality, resilience, mindset, awareness of language and culture learning strategies), level of intercultural competence and external factors (e.g. degree of host receptivity, housing arrangement, exposure to host culture) account for differences in the developmental trajectories of sojourners and significant variations in sojourn outcomes. As noted by Coleman (2009), Jackson (2012), Kinginger (2009) and other language and education abroad researchers, the experience of sojourners is much more complex and variable than what is suggested by the curves of adjustment models. More longitudinal, mixed-method research or ethnographic studies are needed that capture the 'whole person development' of sojourners before, during and after stays abroad.

Despite the limitations detailed above, variations of the U- and W-curve adjustment models remain popular in pre-sojourn orientations, sojourn support programmes and reentry debriefings as they are simple to grasp and seem plausible. In light of recent research, more educators view these models as 'useful heuristic devices to raise issues related to cultural adjustment but no longer present them as phases that everyone will automatically experience' (Forum on Education Abroad 2009: 41). Although the curves models cannot accurately predict the developmental trajectories of sojourners, they raise awareness of the *potential* ups and downs that one might experience during acculturation and reentry.

AN INTEGRATIVE COMMUNICATION THEORY OF CROSS-CULTURAL ADAPTATION

In an effort to overcome the limitations of the curve models and incorporate common elements in long-term and short-term adaptation, Kim (2001, 2005, 2012) proposed the **integrative communication theory of cross-cultural adaptation** to depict an individual's gradual adaptation to a new environment. Her model raises awareness of multiple individual and contextual elements that can influence the developmental trajectories.

To understand Kim's theory, it is essential to have a basic understanding of key terms. For Kim (2012: 233), **cross-cultural adaptation** refers to 'the phenomenon in which individuals who, upon relocating to an unfamiliar cultural environment, strive to establish and maintain a relatively stable, reciprocal and functional relationship with the environment'. This process includes the individual and the environment as well as the process and outcomes of communication activities (e.g. intercultural interactions in the host culture). In the new environment, re-socialization activities drive acculturation, that is, 'the change in individuals whose primary learning has been in one culture and who take over traits from another culture' (Marden & Meyer 1968: 36). New cultural understandings and behaviours are not just added to one's internal framework. When new learning takes place, '**deculturation** (or unlearning) of some of the old cultural habits has to occur, at least in the sense that new responses are adopted in situations that previously would have evoked old, habitual ones' (Kim 2012: 233).

In her theory, Kim (2012: 233–34) addresses the following questions: (1) 'what is the essential nature of the adaptation process individual settlers undergo over time?' and (2) 'why are some settlers more successful than others in attaining a level of psychosocial fitness in the host environment?' At the heart of her framework is the **stress-adaption-growth dynamic**, which is based on the notion that acculturative stress (e.g. language and culture shock) can gradually lead to adaptation. As newcomers grapple with challenges in the host environment, they become more aware of culture difference and more adept at coping with the strain of living in the new culture. Over time, stress-adaptation experiences bring about new understandings and behavioural changes, which enable the individual to more effectively manage challenges. Life in the new environment gradually becomes less stressful.

In Kim's model, **host communication competence** refers to 'the overall internal capacity of a stranger to decode and encode information in accordance with the host cultural communication practices' (ibid: 236). This includes **cognitive competence** ('knowledge of the host language and culture, history, social institutions, and rules of interpersonal conduct'), **affective competence** ('the emotional and motivational capacity to deal with the various challenges of living in the host environment') and **operational competence** ('the capacity to express outwardly by choosing a "right" combination of verbal and nonverbal acts in specific social transactions of the host environment') (ibid: 236).

Environmental factors also play a role in the adaptation of newcomers. Kim's theory cites three elements in particular that can impact on how a newcomer's adaptation proceeds: **host receptivity** ('the degree to which the receiving environment welcomes and accepts strangers into its interpersonal networks and offers them various forms of informational, technical, material and emotional support'), **host conformity pressure** ('the extent to which the host environment challenges them, implicitly or explicitly, to act in accordance with the normative patterns of the host culture') and **ethnic group strength** ('the relative status or standing of a particular ethnic group in the context of the surrounding host society') (ibid: 237).

Individual differences among newcomers can also influence the adaption process, including: (1) **preparedness** ('the level of readiness to undertake the process of cross-cultural adaptation by developing host communication competence and participating in host social communication activities'), (2) **ethnic proximity/distance** ('the extent to which the ethnicity of an individual immigrant or sojourner plays a role in the cross-cultural adaptation process by serving either as a certain level of advantage or handicap', that is, whether it motivates or demotivates host nationals to welcome them into their social networks) and (3) **personality predisposition** ('three interrelated personality resources') (ibid: 237–38). With reference to the latter, Kim maintains that the following personality resources or traits facilitate adaptation: (1) **openness** ('an internal posture that is receptive to new information'), (2) **strength** ('the quality of resilience, patience, hardiness and persistence') and (3) **positivity** ('an affirmative and optimistic outlook that enables the individual to better endure stressful events with a belief in the possibilities of life in general') (ibid: 238).

Kim's theory also identifies several potential benefits of adaptive change: 'increased **functional fitness** in carrying out daily transactions' (e.g. knowing one's way around in the new environment), 'improved **psychological health** in dealing with the environment' (a high level of host communication competence to be able to overcome culture shock and engage in social communication activities that reduce one's level of stress) and the 'emergence of an **intercultural identity orientation**' ('an orientation towards self and others that is no longer rigidly defined by either the identity linked to the "home" culture or the identity of the host culture') (ibid: 238). Individuals who are genuinely open to this process of change may undergo **intercultural transformation**, that is, they may develop 'a new, alternative identity that is broader, more inclusive, more intercultural' (Kim 2001: 232–33). Thus, this model views culture shock as a potentially positive catalyst for personal growth and learning, including identity expansion.

OPTIMIZING INTERCULTURAL TRANSITIONS

If you decide to study, live or work in an unfamiliar linguistic and cultural environment, there are steps you can take to ease your transition. Drawing primarily on research that has focused on short-term sojourners, this section offers suggestions to optimize your sojourn and reentry experience.

Prior to the sojourn

Research your destination.
Set realistic goals and expectations.
Take a course in intercultural communication. (Make good use of the knowledge and skills you are developing in this course!)
Practice your second language.
Attend pre-sojourn orientations, when available.
Take advantage of online materials. (Consult the list at the end of this chapter.)

In the new environment

Familiarize yourself with the local context.
Be patient! Language and culture shock are natural and adjustment takes time.
Keep in touch with family and friends back home.
Develop a routine and take care of your health.
Take part in any orientation activities arranged by the host university.
Join extracurricular activities and have fun.
Be open to new experiences. Be adventurous!
Take the initiative to develop diverse social networks (e.g. form friendships with host nationals, international students, co-nationals).
Recognize hot button issues (e.g. culture differences that annoy you).
Find a cultural mentor and seek help when needed.
Revisit and revise the goals you set prior to the sojourn.
Enhance your second language skills (e.g. take the initiative to practice the language in informal situations, pay attention to sociopragmatic dimensions).
Recognize the limitations of your linguistic and cultural knowledge.
Limit negative thoughts and refrain from making snap judgments about cultural difference.
Anticipate setbacks and persevere when you experience setbacks.
Develop the habit of self-analysis and critical reflection.
Consult recommended online resources.

Prior to returning home

Begin your reentry preparations while abroad.
Say meaningful good-byes.
Take advantage of online materials that provide advice on reentry.
Set goals for your return home.

Back on home soil

Share your international stories in small doses and demonstrate interest in others (e.g. local happenings, the experiences of your friends and family members).
Participate in reentry debriefings or courses, when available.
Be patient. Refrain from making snap judgments about your home culture (or the host culture).
Avoid 'shoeboxing' your international experience (e.g. join international/second language organizations and study abroad alumni groups, share your experiences with a wider audience, e.g. local school children).
Serve as a buddy for newcomers or volunteer to orientate students who will venture abroad.
Talk with people who understand your transition (e.g. other returning exchange students).
Stay in touch with friends abroad and continue to expand and diversify your social networks (e.g. make friends with incoming international exchange students).
Continue to practice your second language.
Critically reflect on your international/reentry experience.
Consult online resources on reentry.
Make concrete plans for further intercultural/international experience.

SUMMARY

In this chapter, we reviewed several types of boundary crossers and discussed variations in long-term and short-term adaptation. The phenomenon of transition shock (e.g. culture shock, language shock, role shock, self shock) was examined and the U- and W-curve adjustment models were described and critiqued. Kim's (2001, 2005, 2012) integrative communication theory of cross-cultural adaptation, which is intended to account for both short-term and long-term adaptation, was also discussed. This model raises awareness of the multifarious internal and external elements that can impact on an individual's acculturation and self-identities.

The chapter drew attention to the natural ups and downs of the process of adapting to an unfamiliar linguistic and cultural environment. While we cannot fully eliminate transition stress when we cross borders, there are steps we can take to reduce our stress level and optimize our stay in a new environment. Returning home also requires preparation and readjustment. Crossing borders can lead to significant personal growth and the emergence of a more intercultural self *if* one is open to change. As noted by Maya Angelo, a celebrated author and civil rights activist in the U.S., 'Perhaps travel cannot prevent bigotry, but by demonstrating that all peoples cry, laugh, eat, worry, and die, it can introduce the idea that if we try and understand each other, we may even become friends.' International experience, coupled with critical reflection, can lead to more linguistic and (inter)cultural awareness, identity expansion, the acquisition of new skills and understandings and even suggest new possibilities for one's life.

discussion questions

1 Define the term acculturation and identify factors that can facilitate or hinder this process.
2 Explain what is meant by the following terms: sojourner, long-term expatriate, immigrant, refugee and asylum seeker. How might their adaptation differ? Why?
3 Define 'transition shock'. Identify three types that are especially relevant for sojourners and provide examples to illustrate each.
4 Have you ever experienced language and culture shock in a foreign land? Describe your symptoms and coping strategies. Share your experiences with your classmates.
5 Explain how anxiety and a low tolerance of ambiguity can negatively impact one's adjustment in a new environment.
6 Discuss the role that second language skills (e.g. fluency in the host language, sociopragmatic awareness) can play in the intercultural adjustment/adaptation process.
7 How have views about culture shock changed since Oberg's (1960) publication?
8 Describe the 'stress-adaptation-growth' dynamic. What factors can influence this process?
9 What factors in the host environment may impact on one's second language development, culture learning, and intercultural adjustment?
10 In small groups, discuss the following situation. Two Taiwanese sojourners of a similar age and background (e.g. same ethnic group, gender, education level, first

language, grade point average, proficiency level in French) join a six-week French immersion programme in the South of France. Neither has previous travel experience. At the end of their sojourn, one is delighted with her progress in French and feels at home in the host environment, whereas her classmate laments the fact that she did not have enough opportunity to use the language and believes that she gained little from her stay abroad. What might account for these very different outcomes?

11 Why do some sojourners develop a multicultural identity while others become more ethnocentric and nationalistic (e.g. develop stronger ties to their home country)?

12 Define what is meant by reentry or reverse culture shock. In small groups, discuss strategies to ease the transition back home. How can returnees extend their sojourn learning?

13 Imagine that you will soon join a semester-long international exchange programme in a second language context that you have never visited. What would you do to prepare? What ideas did you learn from this chapter that you think would be most helpful to you? (If you have already participated in an education abroad programme, share your insights and advice.)

further reading

Dowell, M-M. and Mirsky, K.P. (2003) *Study Abroad: How to Get the Most Out of Your Experience*, Upper Saddle River, NJ: Prentice Hall.

This text is designed to foster reflection on study abroad sojourns so that participants will enhance their intercultural awareness and make the most of their stay in a new culture.

Gebhard, J.G. (2010) *What Do International Students Think and Feel?: Adapting to U.S. College Life and Culture*, Ann Arbor, MI: University of Michigan Press.

This book presents personal narratives of international students who recount their adjustment to life in the U.S. and their return to their homeland.

Hansel, B. (2007) *The Exchange Student Survival Kit*, 2nd edn, Boston: Intercultural Press, Inc., Nicholas Brealey Publishing.

This practical guide aims to help student sojourners adjust to life abroad and make the most of international exchange programmes.

Kauffmann, N.L., Martin, J.N. and Weaver, H.D. with Weaver, J. (1992) *Students Abroad: Strangers at Home, Education for a Global Society*, Yarmouth, ME: Intercultural Press.

This book examines study abroad sojourns from the perspective of students, focusing on their intellectual development, growth in international/intercultural understanding and personal change.

Kohls, L.R. (2001) *Survival Kit for Overseas Living: For Americans Planning to Live and Work Abroad*, 4th edn, Boston: Intercultural Press, Inc., Nicholas Brealey Publishing.

The author offers practical strategies to facilitate respectful intercultural explorations, while adjusting to a new environment.

Lantis, J.S. and DuPlaga, J. (2010) *The Global Classroom: An Essential Guide to Study Abroad*, Boulder, CO: Paradigm Press.

The authors offer practical suggestions for student sojourners to help optimize their stays abroad. This book encompasses three phases: pre-sojourn preparation, sojourn and reentry.

Paige, R.M., Cohen, A.D., Kappler, B., Chi, J.C. and Lassegard, J.P. (2006) *Maximizing Study Abroad: A Student's Guide to Strategies for Language and Culture Learning and Use*, Minneapolis, MN: Center for Advanced Research on Language Acquisition, University of Minnesota.

This guide provides students with tools, creative activities and advice to prepare for and enhance their culture and language learning while studying abroad. It can also help returnees adjust to life when they return home.

Slimbach, R. (2010) *Becoming World Wise: A Guide to Global Learning*, Sterling VA: Stylus.

This book is designed to help sojourners optimize their stays abroad by cultivating mindfulness and a global perspective.

Storti, C. (2001) *The Art of Crossing Cultures*, 2nd edn, Boston: Intercultural Press, Inc., Nicholas Brealey Publishing.

This guidebook offers suggestions to facilitate adjustment to a new culture, whether for work or study. A model of culture shock is explained and examples of cross-cultural misunderstandings are provided with the aim of raising awareness of ways to enhance intercultural relations.

Storti, C. (2003) *The Art of Coming Home*, Boston: Intercultural Press, Inc., Nicholas Brealey Publishing.

This guide explores the challenges people often face when returning home after a sojourn (e.g. study abroad, work): reentry culture shock and readjustment.

VIDEO AND ONLINE RESOURCES

Culture Shock: International Students in the United States (2006) CustomFlix.

This DVD addresses cross-cultural adaptation and culture shock issues. Focusing on the arrival and initial adjustment period, international students share their views about their experiences adjusting to life in the United States.

The Global Scholar. (http://globalscholar.us/)

The 'Global Scholar Online Courses' website provides online curriculum to orient, train, and support students before, during and after they study abroad.

What's up with culture? (http://www2.pacific.edu/sis/culture/)

In a project funded by FIPSE, the U.S. Department of Education, this online material is designed to enhance the ability of students to make successful cultural adjustments both before going overseas and upon returning home from studying abroad.

NOTE

1   This chapter draws on investigations of the international exchange experiences of university students from Hong Kong and Mainland China who took part in either a semester or year abroad international exchange programme in one of 40 countries. This research was generously supported by the Research Grants Council of the Hong Kong SAR (Project No. 2110167; RGC Ref No. CUHK444709).

CHAPTER 9

Intercultural interpersonal relationships

Because we live in a world in which there is increasing contact with diverse others, understanding how differences are bridged – regardless of which socially constructed boundary we happen to be speaking – is an important pursuit.

(Vela-McConnell 2011: 3)

Communication between and among individuals is forever changed because of technology. People are now able to initiate, maintain, and terminate relationships through technological means ... The effects of technology on our interpersonal relationships are unprecedented, unpredictable, and unstoppable.

(West & Turner 2011b: 379)

... a key to maintaining an intercultural friendship lies in effective communication between members.

(Lee 2008: 52)

learning objectives

By the end of this chapter, you should be able to:

1 define what is meant by an intercultural interpersonal relationship
2 identify and describe ten categories of intercultural interpersonal relationships
3 discuss how society influences intercultural interpersonal relationships
4 identify the benefits of intercultural interpersonal relationships
5 define the terms 'social networks' and 'friendship networks'
6 identify and describe three types of social networks
7 describe cultural differences in the notion of friendship
8 discuss the role that language and humour can play in intercultural relations
9 describe the contact hypothesis and its implications for intercultural interpersonal relationships
10 describe the role and challenges of computer-mediated communication in intercultural friendships and romance
11 identify internal and external factors that facilitate or hinder intercultural interpersonal relationships (friendship, romance, marriage)
12 identify constructive ways to nurture intercultural interpersonal relationships.

INTRODUCTION

Meaningful communication with other human beings is essential for our physical and mental health. No matter what part of the world we live in, forming intimate relationships is a vital element in life. This chapter begins by examining the connection between interpersonal communication and intercultural relationships. We then look at several categories of intercultural interpersonal relationships (interethnic, interracial, international, interreligious) as well as ties between people who differ in terms of social class, language, age, ability (e.g. physical, mental), gender and/or sexual orientation. Next, we discuss the numerous benefits of initiating and sustaining intercultural interpersonal relationships in today's interconnected world.

We then turn our attention to issues related to intercultural friendships and social networks (e.g. differing cultural perceptions, cyber connections, the formation of intercultural friendships/networks, barriers to the development of friendships between people from different backgrounds). Next, we shift our focus to romantic intercultural relationships and briefly look at factors that facilitate or hinder successful intercultural romance and marriage. Throughout, the impact of language, culture and context in intercultural interpersonal relationships is emphasized. Finally, drawing on recent research findings, this chapter concludes with suggestions for ways to enhance intercultural interpersonal relationships.

INTERPERSONAL COMMUNICATION AND INTERCULTURAL RELATIONSHIPS

As well as satisfying emotional and practical needs, interpersonal communication plays a major role in facilitating our social relationships. **Interpersonal communication** can be defined as 'a special form of human communication that occurs when two people interact simultaneously and attempt to mutually influence each other, usually for the purpose of managing relationships' (Beebe *et al.* 2010: 174). This interaction, which may take place face-to-face, on the phone or, increasingly, online, helps us to initiate and sustain personal bonds with other human beings.

While most of our encounters with people are fleeting and impersonal, for a variety of reasons we crave a closer, unique connection with certain individuals (e.g. 'significant others', close friends). Forging personal, intimate ties with fellow human beings is central to our socioemotional, mental and physical well-being. These bonds help us to define our personal and social identities. Interpersonal relationships, in turn, enable us to develop a sense of belonging in the complex, dynamic world in which we live.

To foster interdependence and camaraderie, we need to have well developed **interpersonal communication skills**, that is, communication strategies and techniques that can be improved through knowledge, practice, feedback and reflection (Trenholm & Jensen 2011; Wood 2013). Successful interpersonal communication requires that we have confidence in ourselves as well as the ability to listen and understand. Language, culture and context play a central role in determining how our social relationships are formed and maintained.

An **interpersonal relationship** refers to the connection or affiliation between two or more people, which fulfils physical, social or emotional needs. This association may vary in many ways, including duration and intensity. **Short-term relationships** consist of interpersonal connections that are very brief (e.g. lasting a few weeks or months), whereas **long-term relationships** are characterized by an intimate interpersonal affiliation that lasts many years and perhaps throughout one's lifetime. Interpersonal relationships may be intense or rather distant. The connection between individuals may be based on common interests or concerns, love, physical or sexual attraction ('chemistry'), religious beliefs, work, politics, social commitment or other factors. The specific situations in which interpersonal relationships are shaped can range from educational or family settings, work, clubs or organizations, neighbourhoods and places of worship. All of our interpersonal relationships are developed within the context of particular social, cultural, linguistic, political and environmental influences.

Relational bonds, that is, the interpersonal connection between individuals, serve as the basis of social groups and society as a whole. These ties may be guided by law, tradition or mutual agreement between individuals. As we grow and mature, and possibly move to other parts of the world either temporarily or permanently, some of our affiliations fluctuate from time to time; that is, they differ in intensity and degree of intimacy. Some relationships endure while others come to an end for a variety of reasons (e.g. faded chemistry, conflict, infidelity, different life paths, etc.).

Compared with previous decades, **intercultural interpersonal relationships** (e.g. friendships, dating, co-habitation, marriages involving people with different cultural or religious backgrounds) have become much more commonplace and accepted in many parts of the world. Despite this, communication difficulties and other threats to these relationships still exist. Developing satisfactory intercultural bonds is believed by many to be more challenging than **intracultural relationships** (interpersonal bonds that form between individuals who share the same linguistic and cultural background) or **intraracial relationships** (interpersonal relationships between individuals from the same socially-constructed racial group). Not all societies are receptive to intercultural relationships, especially when they are of an intimate or romantic nature. Negative reactions can certainly hamper or even lead to the failure of intercultural unions. Along with individual characteristics and skills, societal norms and attitudes can play a significant role in determining whether intercultural connections flourish or falter.

CROSSING BOUNDARIES IN INTERCUTURAL INTERPERSONAL RELATIONSHIPS

Intercultural interpersonal relationships can take many forms and cross one or more socially- and historically-constructed boundaries (e.g. class, race, language, religion). People may develop affiliations with individuals from different ethnic, linguistic, national, racial and religious backgrounds or form bonds with those who differ in terms of such dimensions as age, ability, gender, social class and sexual orientation (Sorrells 2013; Vela-McConnell 2011). The following section briefly describes various types of intercultural relationships and provides examples of each.

Interracial intercultural relationships

As noted in previous chapters, **'race'** is a culturally and historically-transmitted concept. Orbe and Harris (2008: 8) define it as 'a largely social – yet powerful – construction of human difference that has been used to classify human beings into separate value-based categories'; however, as Goodman *et al.* (2012: 251) point out, '[a]mong humans there are no races except the human race'. Notions of race form the basis of racism and many interculturalists prefer not to use the term. Nonetheless, perceptions and attitudes towards 'race' *can* still impact intercultural communication, and the formation of interracial relationships remains a sensitive issue in many parts of the world (Babbitt & Sommers 2011; Goodman *et al.* 2012; Orbe & Harris 2008; Smith & Hattery 2009).

Interracial communication refers to 'interactions between two individuals in a situational context where racial difference is a salient issue' (Orbe & Harris 2008: 268). Bonds between people from different racial groups are referred to as **interracial intercultural relationships**. An example would be a romance between a woman who is racially identified as Vietnamese and a man who is **biracial**, that is, he has both Hispanic and African roots. A friendship between a black man and a white South African male would be another example. If an Australian Aborigine forms a romantic attachment with a white Australian, this, too, would be considered an interracial intercultural relationship.

Attitudes towards the crossing of racial boundaries have changed significantly in much of the world, due in large part to anti-racist/social justice education and legislation (Fella & Ruzza 2013; Kailin 2002; Sensoy & Diangelo 2012). Despite this, as discussed in Chapter 7, racism persists and there are members of society who still view interracial relationships with suspicion, fear and disdain. In some situations, people may tolerate **interracial friendships** (relationships between friends who are affiliated with a different race) but object to more intimate, romantic ties (e.g. dating, marriage) (Goodman *et al.* 2012; Orbe & Harris 2008; Smith & Hattery 2009; Vela-McConnell 2011).

Interethnic intercultural relationships

In Chapter 6 we learned that one's ethnicity can also impact on intercultural relations. Different from race, **ethnicity** is defined by Orbe and Harris (2008: 8) as 'a cultural marker that indicates shared traditions, heritage, and ancestral origins'. An individual may be considered racially Asian but Japanese in terms of ethnicity. An African American from Puerto Rico may be categorized as black in terms of race but be ethnically Hispanic.

Relationships between individuals affiliated with different ethnic groups are referred to as **interethnic relationships** (Gaines *et al.* 2006). Friendship between a French Canadian and a Canadian with Irish–Scottish heritage or a romance between a Malaysian Singaporean and a Chinese Singaporean would be deemed interethnic. In both examples, the interethnic relationships are between individuals from the same racial group. Interethnic relationships may also develop between people who are categorized as belonging to differing races and ethnicities. For example, a friendship between an Indian Singaporean and a Chinese Singaporean, or a romance between a Latino American woman and an African American man cross both ethnic and racial boundaries.

International intercultural relationships

Relationships that develop between people that bridge 'national cultural and citizenship lines' are referred to as **international relationships** (Sorrells 2013: 152). On a university campus in Denmark, friendship between a Kenyan international exchange student and a Danish business major would be considered an international intercultural relationship. A romance that develops between a Syrian refugee and a Turkish citizen would also be categorized as an international union. Many international, intercultural relationships are interethnic, interracial and, possibly, interreligious. In other words, international relationships often cross more than one social boundary.

Interreligious intercultural relationships

Increasingly, intercultural relationships involve multiple religions. **Interreligious intercultural relationships** refer to interpersonal connections between people with different religious orientations such as ties between Buddhists, Christians, Hindus, Muslims, Jews or other faiths (or non-believers). **Interfaith** or **interreligious friendship** is characterized as an interpersonal relationship or friendship bond between individuals who are affiliated with a different religion.

The attitudes towards interreligious unions are viewed differently in different parts of the world, depending, in part, on the nature of the relationship (e.g. friendship, romance), the particular gender and religions involved and the sociocultural, historical context (Jones *et al.* 2009; Mackenzie *et al.* 2009; Reuben 2002). In the same environment, views about interfaith friendships and marriage may vary among people from different generations as well as among individuals of all ages as there are bound to be different degrees of openness.

A **pluralistic society** is made up of people from numerous cultural and ethnic backgrounds, whereby cultural diversity among citizens is acknowledged and encouraged. In a **religious pluralistic society**, many different religious beliefs, concepts and ideologies coexist. In such environments, individuals from different religious backgrounds may become friends or marry and live together in harmony, whereas in less open contexts strong social or religious sanctions (or even laws) may discourage or even prevent interfaith marriage.

Social class differences in intercultural relationships

Multiculturalism, globalization, immigration, the spread of democracy, ease of travel and the Internet are creating more possibilities for relationships to form between individuals who have a different social background and status. **Social class** refers to 'a social grouping of people based on common economic and other characteristics determined by society and reflecting a social hierarchy' (Goodman *et al.* 2012: 252). In different geographical locations at specific times in human history, individuals or groups have been divided into social classes that have been accorded different degrees of power, prestige and influence. In industrial Britain, for example, people were recognized as belonging to one of the following classes: the upper class, middle class, working class or under class (impoverished). In India, the Hindu caste system, a hereditary division of labour and status, ascribed at birth, long dictated the kind of life people could lead. Those who were classified as 'untouchables' or 'Dalits' were at the bottom of the caste system and not allowed to freely associate with people from other castes.

The caste system is officially banned in modern, democratic India and the rigid class system that dictated everyday life in industrial Britain is no longer in force. Nonetheless, differences in social classes and discrimination persist. All over the world, groups of people are still distinguished by inequalities in such areas as authority, economic resources, power, education, working and living conditions, life-span, religion and culture. **Social markers** or indicators of class are still present and evolving. These context-dependent markers may include one's cultural background, accent, proficiency in another language (bilingualism, fluency in an international, prestigious language), wealth and income (e.g. 'new' versus 'old' money), material possessions (e.g. a fancy car, a large house), level and source of education, the prestige of one's occupation, racial or ethnic origin, the reputation of one's neighbourhood and so on (Block 2013; Meyerhoff 2010; Wardaugh 2010).

Although it has become much more feasible for bonds to form between individuals from different social classes, negative views about these unions persist and can certainly hamper their development. **Classism**, prejudice or discrimination on the basis of social class, encompasses individual attitudes and behaviours as well as policies and practices that privilege one class over another. Unfortunately, in many regions, **social class prejudice** still exists, that is, people harbour negative personal attitudes towards individuals of another class. As noted in Chapter 7, prejudice remains a powerful barrier to the formation of interpersonal relationships between individuals who display different social markers (e.g. accent, speech style) and have a different class culture and status.

Language differences in intercultural relationships

Language plays a significant role in the formation and maintenance of our intercultural relationships, whether our communication is primarily face-to-face, on the phone or online (e.g. email, Skype, text messaging). (Language in computer-mediated relationships is discussed later in this chapter.) In interpersonal situations, whether we realize it or not, our speech and nonverbal behaviours can convey information about our social status, personality, temperament, group affiliations and so on. Our communication partners continuously form impressions of us based, in part, on our language use. As we speak, they are considering how to respond or proceed (e.g. whether to share personal information, get to know us better or discontinue the interaction, etc.). Our language and communication skills (both verbal and nonverbal) influence the quality and longevity of our interpersonal relationships, whether intracultural or intercultural.

In conversations, our speech can build and demonstrate solidarity with our communication partners or it can lead to miscommunication, conflict and separation. As discussed in Chapters 4 and 6, the **communication accommodation theory (CAT)** posits that individuals may adjust their language use or patterns (e.g. choice of accents or dialects, style of communication) to bring them closer to or further apart from their interlocutors (Gallois *et al.* 2005; Giles *et al.* 2012). **Convergence** refers to the ways in which individuals adapt their communicative behaviours in order to reduce social differences between themselves and their conversation partners. These actions are believed to facilitate relationship building. People who become very close friends may even develop their own way of talking with each other that is unique to them. In contrast, **divergence** refers to the distancing of oneself from one's interlocutors by accentuating differences in one's speech (e.g. accent, communication style) or nonverbal behaviours (e.g. gestures, personal distance). Whether deliberate or not, as one might expect, acts of divergence can hamper the development of interpersonal relationships.

Nowadays, alliances frequently form between people who speak a different first language or dialect. In many parts of the world, English is the **lingua franca**, that is, the medium of communication between people who do not have the same first language. As English is the most dominant language of international communication in both face-to-face interactions and online, in many intercultural encounters, one or more of the communication partners are apt to be using this language (Jenkins 2007, 2013; Mackenzie 2013; McKay & Bokhorst-Hong 2008).

When people from different linguistic and cultural backgrounds interact, the language that is used can be a powerful advantage for the most proficient speaker. For example, a native speaker of English who is communicating in the language with a less proficient speaker is privileged in this situation. The use of a second language in intercultural interpersonal relationships also increases the likelihood of miscommunication, an issue that resurfaces when we discuss barriers to intercultural friendships and romance.

Age differences in intercultural relationships

Outside one's family circle, children tend to form close interpersonal bonds with peers, that is, those who are near in age, education and social class as they naturally spend much of their time together during their schooling. When people enter the workforce and gain more exposure to other social circles, either in face-to-face situations or online, friendships or romances may form with individuals who are from a different generation. Attitudes towards age gaps in interpersonal relationships vary in different sociocultural contexts. The degree of acceptance or non-acceptance of the age difference may depend on the nature of the bond (e.g. friendship, romance) and the gender(s) involved, as well as other dimensions (e.g. social, cultural, economic, political, historical) (Cupach & Spitzberg 2011; Lehmiller & Agnew 2011).

In North America, for example, wealthy older men have long formed intimate relationships (including marital unions) with considerably younger women. These 'May–December' unions are generally accepted as normal; however, when older women form romantic attachments with younger men, they are sometimes referred to as 'cougars', with their male partners dismissed as mere 'toy boys'. Among some elements of society, a double standard still exists. In Asia, as well as in Western nations, it is not unusual for older, white males to marry considerably younger Asian women; it is rare, however, for young white males to marry older Asian women (Constable 2005; Nemoto 2009; Waters 2005; Yancey & Lewis 2009). Societal norms and attitudes towards these age gaps are influenced by prevalent values and beliefs, which are conveyed by society, the mass media (e.g. television, films, the press) and social media (e.g. Facebook, twitter).

Ability differences in intercultural relationships

The way society views people with disabilities (e.g. physical handicaps, cognitive impairment, mental illness) influences the interpersonal relationships that disabled individuals form with members of the community who are not disabled. Although the United Nations Convention on the Rights of Persons with Disabilities (United Nations Enable n.d.) is bringing about positive changes in many countries, disability rights movements are at different stages in different parts of the world. In some contexts, formal education emphasizes the acceptance of people who are disabled and laws have been adopted to safeguard their rights, whereas in other cultures, the disabled are shunned by the majority. This is resulting in differing opportunities for relationships to form between able-bodied individuals and those who are disabled.

Inclusiveness is defined by Orbe and Harris (2008: 267) as 'general acceptance and appreciation of differences' within a community or society. **Social inclusion** refers to the act of giving all people in society an opportunity to participate irrespective of their background or characteristics (e.g. mental or physical disability, race, language, culture, gender, age, social status, etc.). **Social exclusion** refers to the opposite behaviour (e.g. barring individuals or groups from participating in one's activities, strongly discouraging or preventing ingroup members from forming relationships with people who are disabled or from a different social class, etc.).

Although the situation is improving in much of the world, segregation is still limiting interactions between disabled and able-bodied individuals. In some environments, people who are physically different or intellectually challenged are viewed with great suspicion. Considered a curse on the family or community, disabled individuals may be abandoned or kept hidden from the rest of society (Barron & Amerena 2007). In many countries, children with disabilities have no access to education or have limited opportunity to pursue higher education for multifarious reasons (e.g. inadequate access and resources for the disabled, prejudice). Cultural stigmas can significantly curtail opportunities for the development of interpersonal bonds between disabled people and other members of society (World Health Organization 2011).

In much of the world, attitudes towards physical disabilities differ from those towards intellectual impairment or mental illness. Negative societal attitudes can make it particularly difficult for those with known mental illness (e.g. bipolarism, schizophrenia) or disability (e.g. autism, developmentally delayed) to form and sustain relationships with other people. This also makes it more difficult for individuals with mental illness to seek professional help (Watson *et al.* 2012). In some societies, pejorative terms are still used to label individuals with mental or physical abilities and they may be ostracized or excluded from mainstream society. (Chapter 7 discusses discrimination against people with disabilities.)

Gender differences in intercultural relationships

Gender can also impact on intercultural interpersonal relationships. Communication between boys and girls and men and women has been the subject of research for many decades (e.g. Shi & Langman 2012; Tannen 1996, 2001; Wood 2009). As noted in Chapters 4 and 6, differences in language patterns and use (e.g. word choice, communication style), self-identities, expectations, roles and responsibilities, privileges and constraints, status, power and positioning can influence interpersonal alliances that form between men and women in a particular cultural context. Relationships between males and females in intracultural relationships are complicated and in intercultural or interracial unions even more so as the partners have been socialized in different linguistic and cultural environments (Renalds 2011; Smith & Hattery 2009; Vela-McConnell 2011).

Sexual orientation and intercultural relationships

Intercultural interpersonal relationships may also form between individuals who have a different sexual orientation. According to the American Psychiatric Association (n.d.),

> '**Sexual orientation**' is a term frequently used to describe a person's romantic, emotional or sexual attraction to another person. A person attracted to another person of the same sex is said to have a **homosexual orientation** and may be called **gay** (both men and women) or **lesbian**. Individuals attracted to persons of the other sex are said to have a **heterosexual orientation**. Sexual orientation falls along a continuum and individuals who are attracted to both men and women are said to be **bisexual**. (Bolding added to the original.)

Understandings of sexual orientation are shaped within particular cultural contexts and are sometimes influenced by religious doctrine. While some groups maintain that sexual orientation is a matter of choice and can be changed, it is more widely accepted in academia that it is innate and develops as one matures: 'Individuals may become aware at different points in their lives that they are heterosexual, gay, lesbian, or bisexual' (www.psychiatry.org/mental-health/people/lgbt-sexual-orientation).

Attitudes towards sexuality and sexual orientation are influenced by one's culture. Prevailing norms and perceptions can significantly impact one's willingness to develop an interpersonal relationship with individuals who have a sexual orientation that differs from the majority. For example, if homosexuality is deemed socially unacceptable or even legally banned, gays are forced to hide their sexual orientation or risk harm. In hostile situations like this, it is very difficult or even impossible for individuals who are openly gay to form relationships with heterosexuals. Conversely, in inclusive societies where there are no social sanctions against such relationships, heterosexual–homosexual friendships are more commonplace and widely accepted.

Multiplex intercultural interpersonal relationships

Intercultural interpersonal relationships often involve multiple cultural differences and the crossing of more than one socially- and historically-constructed boundary (e.g. age, class, language, ethnic, national, racial, regional, religious, sexual orientation, etc.). In England, for example, a wealthy, middle-aged Muslim businessman from Pakistan may meet and develop a **romantic relationship** with an ethnic Chinese immigrant, a 30-year old Christian woman from a lower middle-class family in Malaysia. As their relationship evolves through English, their lingua franca, at times, they may need to negotiate a language barrier as well as cultural differences in gender roles and expectations, communication styles, values, religious beliefs and practices. If their romance becomes serious (e.g. they contemplate co-habitation or marriage), they would also likely need to deal with external pressures including the attitudes of their family members, friends, religious leaders (imam or minister) and the larger society towards such a union.

BENEFITS OF INTERCULTURAL INTERPERSONAL RELATIONSHIPS

Although crossing boundaries to establish intercultural interpersonal relationships can be challenging, it can also be highly rewarding. Developing connections with individuals who are different from oneself in terms of age, language, gender, ethnicity, race, ability, sexual orientation, religion, social class and nationality can enrich one's life in multiple and often unexpected ways. Potential benefits include, but are not limited to: heightened self-awareness, more understanding of other 'ways of being', the breaking-down of stereotypes, more sensitivity towards identity issues, the acquisition of new skills and pursuits, the refinement of one's intercultural interpersonal communication skills and more appreciation of diversity.

Heightened self-awareness

When you develop a relationship with someone from another cultural, linguistic, or religious background, you are apt to be exposed to different values, communication styles, cultural scripts, traditions, languages or dialects and other ways of being. This can spur critical thinking about the messages you received from your ingroup (members of your culture) about outgroups (e.g. people who have a different religion, sexual orientation from your ingroup). Intercultural relationships can raise awareness of the many ways in which the socialization process has shaped your life (e.g. attitudes, values, beliefs) and self-identities. It can also enhance your awareness of your language use and communication style (verbal and nonverbal).

Sustained intercultural contact can prompt you to think more deeply about many aspects of your life (e.g. cultural heritage, language use, beliefs, daily rituals, etc.). While linguistic and cultural differences can be a source of irritation, they can also lead to heightened awareness of your attitudes, identities and habits *if* you cultivate a **reflective mindset**, that is, the ability to revisit and make meaning from your experience. Reflecting on your intercultural interactions can prompt you to consider how your habitual ways of interacting may be impacting others.

Intercultural relationships can help you to recognize unique elements of your own culture and language. When questions are raised about your habitual ways of doing and saying things, you may find it difficult to explain communication styles, traditions, beliefs and daily actions that you have long assumed were commonplace. You may not be able to answer queries about the history of your culture (or religion). You may be stumped by questions about the grammar, vocabulary, idiomatic expressions and other features of the language you learned as a child. This can motivate you to actively seek more knowledge about your own culture, language, religion and heritage, which can be a very positive outcome of intercultural relationships.

More understanding of different ways of being

When you develop a personal connection with someone from another linguistic and cultural background you are apt to gain exposure to new ways of thinking, acting and communicating (e.g. unfamiliar worldviews, daily practices, linguistic expressions, communication styles). Over time, you may develop a deeper understanding of what it really means to speak another language and be affiliated with another group (e.g. linguistic, religious, ethnic, etc.).

The breaking-down of stereotypes

Positive first-hand experience with individuals from another cultural, religious or language background can challenge preconceived notions or stereotypes about the group(s) they are associated with. Unfortunately, some people who develop intercultural relationships retain entrenched stereotypes and simply view their new friends or romantic partners as exceptions; however, if you cultivate an open mindset, negative images and misperceptions are likely to dissipate as you gain a deeper understanding of differing practices and beliefs. Even if you disagree with certain cultural elements, honing the ability to see another perspective can enhance future relationships.

Intercultural interpersonal relationships may compel you to critically reflect on how your home environment and personal experiences have influenced your perceptions and attitudes towards people who are different. Before personal contact, your stereotypical views may have been below your level of awareness and simply taken for granted.

More sensitivity towards identity issues

Through sustained intercultural interactions, you may discover which facets of your identities become salient in different contexts. If you are observant and have well-developed listening skills, you may also uncover clues about the preferred self-identities of your communication partners. This awareness can help you to understand how your intercultural friends or romantic partners view themselves and their place in the world. These discoveries can enhance your interpersonal connections.

The acquisition of new skills and pursuits

Interpersonal intercultural relationships can introduce you to clubs, organizations and a range of activities that might otherwise be unknown to you. Exposure to novel situations and practices offers the opportunity to learn a new hobby or skills (e.g. Cajun cooking, cricket, sitar playing, mahjong). Without your intercultural friends and/or romantic partners opening the door for you, you may miss out on these delights.

Hiroko, a Japanese international exchange student in Vienna, learned how to make mouth-watering apple strudel from her Austrian housemates. While working in Tokyo, Leo, an Australian English language teacher, discovered the art of karaoke singing when he became friends with some Japanese colleagues. Vincent, a university student in New Zealand, took great pride in learning how to play the ruan, a traditional Chinese guitar, from Chen Peiyan, an immigrant from Xian, China who had become a trusted friend.

Developing a relationship with someone from a different linguistic background also opens up the possibility of learning an additional language or dialect. The desire to deepen one's intercultural friendship or romance can be a powerful source of motivation to master a second language. For example, Elena, a Russian, met and fell in love with Ahmed, a Jordanian law student, while doing an internship in the U.S. As their friendship blossomed into a romance, she became inspired to study Arabic, something she had never contemplated before. When she visited his family in Amman she was able to converse with his relatives. In some situations, like Elena's, new intercultural, international alliances can lead to the opportunity to get to know, and even visit or live in, another part of the world. Intercultural interpersonal relationships can open your eyes to new worlds and vistas.

The refinement of intercultural interpersonal communication skills

Interpersonal communication is the primary way in which humans build, nurture and transform relationships. To develop effective and meaningful interpersonal relationships, we need to develop **communication competence**, that is, 'the ability to achieve one's goals in a manner that is personally acceptable and, ideally, acceptable to others' (Adler *et al.* 2013: G-2). **Appropriate communication** refers to communication that enhances the relationship while **effective communication** is associated with communication that achieves the desired results (Wiemann *et al.* 1997). Both dimensions can be improved through practice.

Developing interpersonal affiliations with people who have a different cultural background can also facilitate the enhancement of one's intercultural communication skills, which is vital in today's globalized world. Successful, meaningful relationships require effective interpersonal skills and when cultural differences are involved, it is imperative that we develop **intercultural communication competence**. This entails

impression management that allows members of different cultural systems to be aware of their cultural identity and cultural differences, and to interact effectively and appropriately with each other in diverse contexts by agreeing on the meaning of diverse symbol systems with the result of mutually satisfying relationships.

(Kupka 2008: 16)

Through sustained intercultural interactions, you can learn to be sensitive to the preferred identities of others, and discover how to deal with misunderstandings that naturally arise. Over time, you can hone your intercultural competence and become more 'Other-centred' ('partner-centred'), which, in turn, nurtures your relationship.

If you are communicating in a second language with someone from another cultural background, it is important to develop **intercultural communicative competence**, 'the complex of abilities needed to perform effectively and appropriately with others who are linguistically and culturally different from oneself' (Fantini 2007: 12). (Chapter 12 explores this construct in more detail.) Being able to communicate effectively and appropriately in multiple languages affords more possibilities for intercultural dialogue and friendship.

Enhanced appreciation of diversity

Finally, as you gain more exposure to people from different linguistic and cultural backgrounds and develop meaningful intercultural relationships, it is possible to gain more understanding and genuine appreciation of diversity, which is very significant as our world is becoming more interconnected. Accepting and embracing someone who is culturally and ethnically different from yourself sets a positive example for others in our increasingly multicultural world.

As you build intercultural relationships, develop more intercultural knowledge and break down stereotypes, you can share your new understandings and attitudes with those around you. In this way, your more open mindset can have a positive impact on your friends, family and colleagues who have not yet forged any intercultural ties, perhaps due to negative images of people who have a different cultural, linguistic or religious background.

Intercultural relationships that differ from the norm (e.g. intracultural bonds) threaten 'the established and taken-for-granted order of our larger society' and have 'the potential to move our society in the direction of increased egalitarianism' (Vela-McConnell 2011: 183). Individuals who dare to cross boundaries, whether in terms of language, race, sexual orientation, class or other variable can inspire others to form similar relationships. Gradually, relationships that were once seen as taboo may become accepted as normal.

INTERCULTURAL FRIENDSHIP AND SOCIAL NETWORKS

Increased migration, ease of travel, ethnically diverse communities and enhanced opportunities computer-mediated communication (CMC) (e.g. Facebook, email, blogs, MySpace, twitter, Internet relay chats, etc.) have made it more possible for intercultural friendships to form and this is leading to more diverse social networks.

Intercultural friendship is a personal connection or affiliation forged between people who have a different cultural background. Increasingly, these interpersonal relationships entail the use of a second language (e.g. an international language or lingua franca) by one or more of the friendship partners. Rooted in anthropology, a **social network** refers to 'the multiple web of relationships an individual contracts in a society with other people who he or she is bound to directly or indirectly by ties of friendship, kinship or other social relationships' (Trudgill 2003:

121–22). Sociolinguist Miriam Meyerhoff (2010: 295) notes that in a social network 'not all members may know each other . . . and some members may know each other in a different capacity from others'. For example, a woman may form interpersonal relationships at work, have a different set of friends in her social life and yet another group of acquaintances in the sports club where she works out. Many of these individuals may never meet but they are still linked to each other by having a common friend. Their friends are also part of this woman's wider social network even if she does not interact with them. A **friendship network**, a type of social network, includes individuals who are very close personal friends, acquaintances (e.g. those who are more distant) and 'friends of friends'.

As more and more people are coming into contact with individuals who have a different background (e.g. cultural, linguistic, religious) or orientation (e.g. sexual), researchers are beginning to take a closer look at the formation and quality of intercultural interpersonal relationships. Questions such as the following are driving their studies: what factors facilitate or hinder the development of intercultural friendships and multicultural/multilingual social networks? How are the Internet, social media and mass media affecting the development of intercultural alliances? What steps can be taken to nurture friendships that cross linguistic and social boundaries? In what ways are diverse friendship alliances and networks impacting society?

As noted in the previous chapter, the number of students who travel to another country for part of their education has grown exponentially in recent years; accordingly, more attention is being paid to the friendship patterns and social networks of local and international students (e.g. Gareis 1995, 2000, 2012; Green 2013; Hendrickson *et al.* 2010; Lee 2006; Li 2010). Many of these studies have revealed that during their stay abroad, students tend to maintain or develop friendship networks with individuals from their own country (**co-nationals** who speak the same first language) or individuals from other foreign countries (**multi-nationals**) (e.g. other international exchange students). While most express the desire to develop friendships with people from the host country (**host nationals**) prior to their sojourn, for a variety of reasons (e.g. culture shock, ethnocentrism, a language barrier, limited host receptivity, lack of intercultural competence, different understandings of friendship), many return home disappointed (Gareis 2012; Hendrickson *et al.* 2010; Kinginger 2009).

In both domestic and international settings, researchers have also carried out investigations of intercultural and interracial friendships in the workplace (e.g. multinational firms) or community (e.g. expatriate or immigrant families and host nationals) (e.g. Chen & Nakazawa 2012; Diggs & Clark 2002). Their work is informing us of potential barriers to successful intercultural interpersonal relationships and the diversification of social networks. Those who advocate the crossing of social boundaries voice concerns about the numerous internal and external challenges individuals may face in forming and sustaining intercultural friendships in educational, work or leisure settings, as well as in cyberspace (e.g. Li 2010; Marcoccia 2012; O'Dowd 2001, 2012). Their research is raising awareness of the most effective ways to nurture meaningful intercultural interpersonal bonds.

Cultural perceptions of friendship

A life without a friend is a life without a sun. (German proverb)

It is better to be in chains with friends than to be in a garden with strangers. (Persian proverb)

Life without a friend is like death without a witness. (Spanish proverb)

It is better in times of need to have a friend rather than money. (Greek proverb)

Life without friends is not worth living. (Turkish proverb)

What do these proverbs from different lands have in common? All of them point to the pivotal role friends play in our lives irrespective of the language(s) we speak or our cultural background. No matter where we reside in the world, friendship matters. It is through friendship that we gain much-needed practical and socio-emotional support and a sense of how we fit into society. Along with family relationships, friendship bonds help us to navigate the increasingly complex world in which we live. In situations where families are fragmented, close friendships can become even more crucial.

> Through friendship we gain practical and emotional support, and an important contribution to our personal identities. Friendship also helps to integrate us into the public realm and "act as a resource for managing some of the mundane and exceptional events" that confront us in our lives.
>
> (Allan 1989: 114)

Unlike relationships with family members or kinship bonds, friendship is more voluntary, although it is important to recognize that it is subject to the constraints of economic, political, linguistic, social, and cultural circumstances and other factors (e.g. proximity or nearness). Within a particular cultural context, linguistic sanctions as well as social norms and expectations play a role in determining who we form friendships with and how.

To complicate matters, the meaning attached to the word 'friend' varies in different regions of the world. As noted by Badhwar (1993: 36), 'no account of friendship enjoys universal acceptance'. One's conception of what it means to be a 'friend' is culturally constructed and situated, and varies to some degree in different cultural contexts (Chen & Nakazawa 2012; Collier 1996, 2002). In some cultures, specific linguistic terms or expressions are used to identify and distinguish between sub-categories of friends.

> across all cultures and languages there is a word for a close relationship established outside the narrow family context . . . We find indications that some languages, during some periods of their development, gave more emphasis to an objective or material reality, such as the importance of mutual help, in close relationships, whereas other languages stressed the affective union of friendship, referring to a subjective reality . . . The scope of the connotations related to the words used for friendship seems to reflect the socio-historical circumstances under which the friendship was important. The horizon of these meanings includes family issues, ritual functions, mutual assistance, kindness, war comradeship, conflict solution, intimacy, and affection.
>
> (Krappman 1998: 24)

Since we live in a diverse, dynamic world, it is not surprising that differing understandings of friendship have formed in different regions. Even within the same sociocultural context, notions of friendship can differ among individuals due to such factors as age, class, religion, gender and intercultural experience, among others (Adams *et al.* 2000, Chen & Nakazawa 2012; Lee 2008).

In the United States, the term 'friend' can encompass casual acquaintances as well as lifelong, intimate companions (Gareis 1995, 2012). In this context, a **casual friend** or

acquaintance refers to someone you have been introduced to but do not know very well. You might say hello when you meet and engage in small talk (e.g. chat about the weather or an assignment) but not reveal many personal details about yourself. The connection with acquaintances tends to be friendly but rather superficial. In contrast, a **close friend** refers to someone you can rely on to provide emotional support and perhaps lend a hand when needed. This relationship is more intimate and you are apt to share more personal details about yourself (e.g. your family problems, love life) and engage in a much deeper level of conversation on a wider range of topics. Within this sub-category, U.S. Americans may also designate one or more individuals as their **best friends** to indicate that they are especially close to them.

In general, European Americans tend to have a large collection of 'friends', which changes over time and, in most cases, involves only very limited mutual obligations, if any. Although most are casual relationships, these individuals are often referred to as friends, which can confuse people who have divergent understandings of what friendship means. Collier (1996, 2002), for example, discovered that conceptions of friendship differed among ethnic groups in the U.S.: African Americans emphasize the importance of respect and acceptance, Latinos tend to value relational support, Asian Americans stress the positive sharing of ideas, and for European Americans, recognition of individual needs is paramount. Not surprisingly, these different notions of friendships (e.g. expectations regarding obligations and trust) can cause misunderstandings and result in negative impressions.

In many cultural contexts, a clear distinction is made between friends and acquaintances. In China, the following proverb conveys the message that it is best to have a few close, lifelong friends rather than a large number of acquaintances who come and go: '*One's acquaintances may fill the world, but one's true friends can be but few*'. Another Chinese saying, '*Cooked at one stirring makes friends too easily*' underscores the need for adequate time and commitment to build up a genuine, long-lasting friendship. Researchers have found that friendship patterns among Chinese nationals are characterized by strong social bonds and obligations that develop over a long period of time. Li (2010: 15–16), for example, asserts that 'Chinese people make friends that tend to last longer and each party expects full support of resources, time, and loyalty from the other instead of casual, short-term friendships'. In traditional Chinese culture, lifelong friends may be considered like family members.

Cooper *et al.* (2007) reviewed cross-cultural studies of friendship and identified a number of cultural variations in intercultural friendships, including: 'selection (who can be a friend), duration (how long the friendship lasts), the number of friends, the responsibilities and prerogatives of a friend, and how long a relationship exists before it can be considered a friendship' (p. 169). While most research of this nature has focused on face-to-face interactions, the Internet and social media are also influencing intracultural and intercultural friendships.

Language and intercultural cyber friendship

Technology and English, the primary lingua franca of the Internet, are changing the nature of interpersonal communication in much of the world. As noted by West and Turner (2011b: 379), 'communication between and among individuals is forvever changed because of technology . . . The effects of technology on our interpersonal relationships are unprecedented, unpredictable, and unstoppable'. New communication technologies (e.g. the Internet, email, Ipads) and social media (e.g. Facebook, Twitter) are being introduced at a rapid pace. These innovations are expanding possibilities for the development and maintenance of both intracultural and intercultural relationships, especially among individuals who are able to converse in English or another international language.

Communication that is facilitated by computer technologies (e.g. the use of two or more networked computers) is referred to as **computer-mediated communication (CMC)**. Walther (1992: 52) defines it as 'synchronous or asynchronous electronic mail and computer conferencing, by which senders encode in text messages that are relayed from senders' computers as receivers'. In **synchronous communication** (e.g. Skype, chat rooms, Internet relay chat) all participants are online at the same time, whereas **asynchronous communication** (e.g. email) occurs with time constraints, that is, the receiver of an email message may not read it until several hours or days after it has been sent.

The rise of the Internet has led to the development of a virtual community of **netizens**, that is, individuals who actively engage in online interactions. While English is the primary lingua franca in cyberspace, the speed and format of CMC is bringing about new language forms (e.g. abbreviations), symbols and communication styles, which impact interpersonal relationships. To save time, netizens tend to communicate through **netspeak** (chatspeak or cyber-slang), 'an informal, concise and expressive style' (Marcoccia 2012). As CMC (email, chat rooms) is primarily text-based and dependent on verbal language, it has fewer nonverbal cues than in face-to-face interactions. To compensate for the lack of nonverbal information in text messages, graphic accents and symbols have become a regular feature in CMC (West & Turner 2011b). For example, emoticons (e.g. sad faces) and articons (e.g. pictures of objects) are frequently used to replace or enhance a verbal message.

In addition to email, the emergence of **social networking sites (SNSs)**, such as Facebook, twitter, MySpace, and LinkedIn, is making it possible to initiate and maintain interpersonal relationships online, instead of relying solely on face-to-face communication or phone calls, as in years gone by. As long as they have access to the Internet, people can now share personal information with friends and their wider social networks through Facebook, blogs, video chats, instant messaging, text messaging and other media. Photos and video clips can be uploaded to one's Facebook account or circulated via email within a matter of minutes. Facebook allows us to 'friend' people we barely know. Although not a social network, Skype, online video software, is also a widely used social tool that is connecting people around the world.

Intrigued by these innovations, researchers have been asking a number of key questions about the impact of the digital revolution on interpersonal communication and intercultural relations, such as, are the Internet and the proliferation of SNSs facilitating or hindering the formation of meaningful friendships and romantic connections between individuals from disparate linguistic and cultural backgrounds? How is the dominance of English on the Internet impacting on intercultural relations? What is the impact of netspeak on the interpersonal intercultural connections of netizens? What is the relationship between online interactions and face-to-face meetings within the context of intercultural friendship formation? Do they complement one another?

While researchers acknowledge that text-based CMC differs from face-to-face interaction, they disagree about its impact on interpersonal and intercultural relationships. Proponents maintain that the Internet increases the possibility for contact between people from diverse backgrounds:

> The ability to reach so many different people from so many different places so quickly gives communication a new sense of power. Wherever we live, we can use the Internet to help bring diversity and new cultures into our lives, changing our social, political, and business lives.

> (Gamble & Gamble 2013: 37)

Individuals can now become acquainted with each other online without revealing many personal details (e.g. their ethnicity, first language, race, religion, nationality, etc.). As noted by Marcoccia (2012: 358), 'some aspects of people's identity such as their ethnic group, gender, social class and accent are hidden in the text-based environment of Internet-mediated communication'. Netizens can freely express their views without revealing their real names and embarrassing themselves or their families. Advocates of Internet-mediated communication maintain that this is a positive feature as it enhances free speech and reduces the negative impact of stereotypes and personal biases. They argue that people who might never have the opportunity to meet face-to-face can cross social and cultural boundaries (e.g. age, language, race, religion, sexual orientation) and form relationships online, which in turn can break down barriers and lead to enhanced intercultural understanding (Ritchie 2009; Simons 1998).

Critics, however, maintain that the use of technology does not necessarily lead to effective communication or the development of meaningful interpersonal intercultural relationships. People may misrepresent themselves (e.g. lie about who they are) and, even if they are fully honest about their identities and what they stand for, the absence of personal information can limit the formation of meaningful intercultural friendships (Zimbler & Feldman 2011).

Compared with face-to-face interactions, emails, online discussion forums and Internet relay chats (and many other Internet tools) are characterized by fewer social cues (e.g. nonverbal signals, sociopragmatic information) and this can make it challenging to clearly convey one's ideas and emotions. Messages may not be interpreted as intended, especially when individuals from diverse linguistic and cultural backgrounds are interacting online in a second language.

While 'the informal and friendly style which characterizes much of the interaction on the Internet' is familiar to people who have been socialized in the U.S. and other 'individualistic nations', O'Dowd (2001) contends that it can be confusing and unsettling for netizens who are used to a greater power distance and more formal discourse between people who do not know each other well. Even if non-native speakers of English have studied English in school for many years, informal discourse and colloquialisms may be baffling at times and lead to miscommunication.

> Internet-mediated global English is the lingua franca of the Internet. It is an opportunity for intercultural dialogue but also an obstacle in the sense that this 'cyberlingua franca' is not necessarily suited to any specific culture. CMC has a reduced social dimension. This characteristic aids intercultural communication because it reduces cultural differences, but, at the same time, it is an obstacle to intercultural communication because it increases misunderstandings or aggressiveness.
>
> (Marcoccia 2012: 366)

Much more research is needed to determine the potential of CMC and SNSs for the formation and maintenance of intercultural friendships, especially as new communication tools become available. While the Internet, in theory, can reduce the perceived distance between individuals from different linguistic and cultural backgrounds, intercultural interactions can also be rife with misunderstandings. The dominance of English and American values may be barriers to the formation of equitable intercultural friendships in cyberspace.

Building intercultural friendships and social networks

Recent studies of intercultural friendship and social networks have identified a number of internal and external factors that facilitate the formation and maintenance of friendship bonds between individuals who are culturally different, including those who do not speak the same first language. While most investigations have focused on face-to-face interactions, in the past decade more attention is being paid to **cyber friendships** (e.g. email relationships) and ties formed through online social networking sites (SNS) (e.g. Facebook, MySpace, Skype). This is enriching our understanding of the nature, complexity and variability of intercultural friendships.

A review of recent research on intercultural friendship reveals that a wide range of elements play a role in determining the potential for these interpersonal relationships, including: proximity, social networks, similarity-attraction, personality, willingness to communicate (WTC), empathy, identity recognition and validation, uncertainty reduction/anxiety management, disclosure and relational intimacy, shared identity and relational maintenance, intercultural communication competence and social acceptance. Let's take a look at each of these variables.

Proximity. All intercultural interpersonal relationships are affected by the affordances and constraints in one's environment. To develop intercultural friendships we first need to have the opportunity to come into close contact with people from different linguistic and cultural backgrounds. If you study, live or work in a multicultural, multilingual environment, you are better positioned to initiate and develop intercultural friendships than if you are a member of the majority culture and live in a society that is much less diverse. In an environment where many people from different linguistic and cultural backgrounds intermingle in all aspects of life, it is easier to form intercultural relationships in both formal settings (e.g. at school, at work, in a place of worship) and informal situations (e.g. at a health club or social organization). Hence, proximity or nearness plays a role in the formation of intercultural alliances.

With an increase in CMC and SNSs (e.g. Facebook) it is becoming more possible to make connections with people who come from a different background (e.g. language, social class, race, culture). Marcoccia (2012: 353) asserts that the Internet offers its users 'an unprecedented level of contact with people from other cultural and social groups'. As the Internet reaches across national borders, proponents argue that it affords us more possibilities to develop intercultural ties, especially if we can communicate in an international language. 'By enabling us to join a wide range of online communities and interact with people who hold different worldviews, the Internet enhances our ability to communicate within and across cultural boundaries' (Gamble & Gamble 2013: 40). For this to happen, at minimum, one needs to have access to this technology and proficiency in an international language. As discussed in Chapter 1, the disparity between rich and poor nations means that there is unequal access to the Internet, SNSs and international language education. Not everyone has the opportunity to develop intercultural interpersonal relationships online.

Social networks. The degree of diversity in one's social networks also influences one's opportunity to meet and interact with diverse individuals. If some of our family members, friends (acquaintances, close friends) or 'friends of friends' already have intercultural or interracial friendships, we are more apt to develop interpersonal relationships with people who are linguistically, racially and culturally different (Chen 2002; Vela-McConnell 2011). We are more likely to view these relationships as 'normal'.

Similarity–Attraction. The **Similarity–Attraction Hypothesis** posits that we are drawn to people we perceive to be similar to us (e.g. those who share our first language, race, ethnicity, beliefs, values, religion, worldview, group affiliations, etc.) (Adler *et al.* 2013; Byrne 1969). While there are naturally multiple differences in individuals who form intercultural friendships, there are also similarities. In intercultural interactions, research suggests that we are attracted to what we have in common (e.g. similar personal characteristics, interests, values, experiences, etc.) (Osbeck *et al.* 1997; Vela-McConnell 2011).

In intercultural relationships, Chen (2002: 244) observes that '[g]reater perceived similarity facilitates a communicative relationship; interactions, once started, may lead to perception of greater similarity or convergence of partners' behavior, or both'. In a study of Japanese and U.S. American students, Kito (2005) also found that individuals in both groups were attracted to their intercultural friends due to perceived similarity (e.g. shared interests, values, etc.). Let's look at some other examples that illustrate this theory.

While in Vancouver for a year-long exchange programme, Irena, an avid tennis player from Moscow, was attracted to Parnchand, a Thai student who shared her love of the game. By the end of their sojourn, they had become close friends. Juanita, a Brazilian exchange student, discovered that she and Amena, a Bahrani medical student, shared a common interest in nature photography and this led to a meaningful friendship. Linguistic and cultural differences became less important as their connection deepened.

Personality. Intercultural friendship formation has also been linked to certain personality traits (e.g. extroversion, desire to help others, open-mindedness) (Gareis 2000, 2012; Peng 2011). In some studies, an extroverted personality has been found to enhance the likelihood of an individual to reach across social boundaries to initiate relationships with individuals from different backgrounds (Ying 2002).

While similarities in personality have been found to be the basis of friendship formation (Mehra *et al.* 2001), differing personality traits may also work well if they complement one another, as in the following example. Nuran, an Egyptian American physiotherapist did not come from the same cultural or linguistic background as Meedy, an Indonesian doctor, but their religious affiliation brought them together. As their relationship grew they discovered that their temperaments made them very compatible. Nuran was outgoing and talkative, whereas her Indonesian friend was quiet and reserved. Meedy was happy to let Nuran take the lead. In this intercultural friendship, shared interests and beliefs drew them together and their different personalities complimented each other.

Willingness to communicate (WTC). Another personality trait that is linked to interpersonal communication and intercultural friendship is **willingness to communicate (WTC)**. In first-language contexts, McCroskey and Richmond (1987) characterize WTC as an individual's general personality orientation towards talking. Associated with a fairly stable personality trait, WTC is believed to develop as we mature, bringing about a 'global, personality-based orientation toward talking' (MacIntyre *et al.* 2003: 591). In second language interactions, level of proficiency and confidence in one's second language ability both influence one's willingness to speak. MacIntyre and his colleagues (1998: 547) define WTC as an individual's 'readiness to enter into discourse at a particular time with a specific person or persons, using a L2'. One's **language anxiety** (degree of nervousness when using the L2) and WTC impact on one's desire to initiate and sustain intercultural friendships in a second language (L2).

Empathy.   Several studies of intercultural friendships have revealed that **empathy**, the ability to understand another person's feelings and point of view (Cornes 2004; Krajewski 2011), plays a vital role in determining the quality and longevity of both intracultural and intercultural friendships. Empathy has both cognitive and affective (emotional) dimensions:

> The cognitive aspect of empathy entails an ability to effectively comprehend a distressing situation and to recognize another's emotions and assume that person's perspective . . . The affective aspect of empathy requires an individual to experience a vicarious emotional response to others' expressed emotions.
>
> (Knafo *et al.* 2008: 737)

The ability to empathize with the perspective of someone from another cultural background is a key ingredient in successful intercultural relationships.

Identity recognition and validation.   Understanding the personal meaning of one's self-identities and recognizing the preferred identities of one's communication partners are crucial elements in the formation of mutually satisfying intercultural friendships. Respecting the preferred self-identities of one's communication partners plays an important role in the development of trust in intercultural friendships. This, in turn, influences one's willingness to share personal information and spend time together.

Uncertainty reduction/anxiety management.   One's ability to predict and explain behaviour, especially in initial interactions, can influence the formation and quality of intercultural friendships. The **uncertainty reduction theory (URT)** posits that the greater our ability to predict and explain our communication partners' behaviour, the greater the chance that our relationships will become more intimate (e.g. progress from stranger or acquaintance to close friend) (Berger & Calabrese 1975). As we become more familiar with our communication partners, we develop more understanding of their communication style, values and beliefs and our ability to predict their behaviour increases.

The URT is linked to the **uncertainty/anxiety management theory (AUM)**, which suggests that our enhanced knowledge and understanding of our communication partner reduces our level of stress or anxiety. As our sense of apprehension or fear diminishes, we can become more open to forming relationships with people who are different from us (Gudykunst 2004).

Disclosure and relational intimacy.   Researchers have also identified a linkage between self-disclosure and friendship development. **Self-disclosure** refers to 'the process of deliberately revealing information about oneself that is significant and that would not normally be known by others' (Adler *et al.* 2013: G-11). Altman and Taylor's (1973) **social penetration theory (SPT)** suggests that as self-disclosure increases in depth (degree of intimacy on a particular topic), amount and breadth (the number of topics about which one self-discloses to one's communication partner), our relationships become more intimate. While this theory assumes that self-disclosure leads to the development of positive impressions, this is not necessarily the case in all cultures. Cross-cultural studies have identified cultural variations in the topics, timing, amount of self-disclosure and degree of relational intimacy in interpersonal relationships (e.g. Cahn 1984; Chen 2010, 2012). In a study of intercultural friendships, Chen and Nakazawa (2012: 146) found there is 'a complex interplay among cultural backgrounds, friendship types, and degrees of friendship in influencing patterns of self-disclosure'.

Linked to disclosure is the notion of **relational intimacy**, which refers to 'the closeness one feels and/or enacts towards one's friend' (Chen & Nakazawa 2009: 83). In a survey of 252 ethnically diverse university students, Chen and Nakazawa (2012) discovered that cultural dissimilarities in disclosure had the most impact in the early stages of the relationship. As relational intimacy increased, the depth and frequency of self-disclosure also tended to increase, lending partial support for the applicability of social penetration theory to intercultural and interracial friendships. In general, as the relationships grew, 'self-disclosure exchanges progressed from public-outer areas of the selves to all public, immediate, and private areas of the selves' (Chen & Nakazawa 2009: 93); however, there was less negative self-disclosure. The researchers concluded that 'communication in close intercultural friendship may not be as personalistic as that in close intracultural friendship and may be more complex' (Chen & Nakazawa 2012: 147).

Shared identity and relational maintenance. Successful intercultural bonds depend on one's interpersonal communication skills and ability to relate to one's communication partner. **Relational identity** is defined as 'a privately transacted system of understandings that coordinate attitudes, actions, and identities of participants in a relationship' (Lee 2006: 6). **Mutual facework** refers to the process of developing a shared sense of identity in a relationship (Ting-Toomey & Kurogi 1998; Tracy 2002). Domenici and Littlejohn (2006: 94) explain that '[w]orking together to build, maintain, or threaten the status of the relationship constitutes the work of mutual face'. **Relational maintenance**, 'communication aimed at keeping relationships operating smoothly and satisfactorily' (Adler *et al.* 2013: 287), requires the ability to read one's partner and recognize when he or she needs more personal space and privacy, or more support and closeness. Individuals who are more skilled at reading their intercultural partners are better positioned to respond appropriately. (See Chapter 10 for more discussion on Facework.)

Intercultural communication competence. People have varying degrees of intercultural competence. Those who are interculturally sensitive and possess well-developed intercultural communication skills are apt to be less fearful of interacting across social boundaries and more strongly motivated to establish friendships with people who differ from them in terms of first language, gender, ethnicity, religion, etc. Individuals who possess a high level of intercultural sensitivity and intercultural competence are also better positioned to nurture intercultural relationships and deal with misunderstandings that arise. As noted by Chen (1992), an individual's degree of 'other-orientation, sensitivity, and the ability to provide positive feelings predict success in initiating and managing intercultural friendships'.

Lee (2008: 52) suggests that 'a key to maintaining an intercultural friendship lies in effective communication between members'. When interacting in a second language, fluency in the language *and* intercultural competence can greatly facilitate the formation of intercultural bonds. Individuals who are confident, fluent speakers of a second language are better positioned to use their second language to initiate interactions with potential intercultural friends than those who are excessively worried about making grammatical mistakes or saying the wrong word. This is linked to the notion of willingness to communicate (WTC) that was discussed above.

Social acceptance. As noted by Sorrells (2013: 156), 'intercultural relationships do not occur in a vacuum'. Our perceptions of intercultural interpersonal unions are shaped within our particular socio-historical, political and linguistic context. When we cross boundaries, we are impacted to varying degrees by the beliefs and attitudes that are prevalent in our environment (e.g. the perceptions of our family members, community, religious figures, the mass media) and the degree of openness towards friendships and romance between people from different backgrounds. The attitudes towards intercultural interpersonal relationships in one's social networks and community can impact our willingness to initiate interactions with people who are culturally different. In environments where anti-racist, multicultural education is a regular feature in classrooms and diverse social networks are commonplace, the atmosphere is apt to be much more conducive to the formation of intercultural friendships.

Barriers to intercultural friendships

Many interculturalists contend that intercultural friendships are more difficult to initiate and maintain than relationships between individuals who share the same linguistic and cultural background. Chen and Nakazawa (2009: 77), for example, state that '[i]ntercultural and interracial relationships face barriers, tensions, and challenges that are absent from intracultural and intraracial relationships'. Researchers have identified a number of internal and external factors that can hamper the development of satisfying intercultural friendships (limited contact opportunities; differing motives; unmet expectations; anxiety and uncertainty; differences in communication styles; differing values, worldviews and perceptions; stereotyping, prejudice and discrimination; language barrier; miscommunication). Let's examine each in turn.

Limited contact opportunities. As noted in the previous section, demographic variables play an important role in the formation of intercultural friendships. For example, individuals from the majority culture who live in an area where there are few people with a different linguistic or cultural background (e.g. ethnic minorities, international students) have less opportunity to form intercultural friendships than those who reside in a multicultural, multilingual neighbourhood.

While it is now possible to make intercultural connections online, in a review of recent research on social networking sites, Neuliep (2012: 338) observes that 'SNSs are used primarily for social interaction with friends with whom users have a preestablished relationship offline', adding that 'they serve mostly to support preexisting social relations within geographically bound communities'. He concludes that 'SNSs such as Facebook are not the primary means by which people meet and initiate relationships with others from different cultures' (p. 338). More studies are needed that explore the connection between CMC, SNSs and intercultural friendships.

Contact frequency, duration, and quality. As well as having sufficient opportunities for intercultural interactions, there must be adequate, quality time together to grow the relationship. For example, while third culture kids (TCKs) or global nomads have exposure to different language and cultures, if they move from place to place very frequently, there may not be sufficient time or they may be less motivated to develop deep interpersonal relationships, as noted by Heidi Sand-Hart, a TCK:

> I have often been surrounded by people who don't fully understand me. In order for people to understand the many facets and undercurrents of my TCK traits, it takes time, and usually time is not on my side. Therefore I have often been misunderstood, and felt alone

in a crowd and isolated. Just as you're allowing some of the walls to fall and getting closer to someone, it's time to move on. You begin to hold onto people and circumstances less and harden yourself a little in relationships.

(Sand-Hart 2010: 137–38)

Unmet expectations. When people from different cultural backgrounds interact, they may have different understandings of friendship as ideas about what friends should and should not do are formed in our home environment during enculturation. Conflicting cultural expectations of roles and obligations can lead to misunderstandings. DeCapua and Wintergerst (2004) and Gareis (2000), for example, note that differing conceptions of friendship can result in confusion and hurt feelings between international students and their U.S. American hosts. In particular, the newcomers may feel let down by American students who are very friendly but less forthcoming with offers of help.

Disparate motives and degree of investment. If an intercultural interpersonal relationship is to flourish, both parties must have a sufficient level of interest, motivation, time, energy and commitment to interact and nurture the connection. Without this degree of investment, intercultural friendships may not move beyond the category of 'acquaintance' ('hi-bye' friend), as noted by the following TCK:

The most important aspect in life is relationships, and my friends have been ripped away from me at every turn. It takes so much energy and effort to maintain hope in new friendships, when you keep losing them all the time . . . Sometimes I don't see the potential of making a new friend; I see the work involved in getting to know them and quickly analyse whether it's worth it or not. This has been ingrained into my mentality from the routine of making and breaking friends so frequently. I am aware that it is a gamble, since you can miss out on a lot of friendships . . .

(Sand-Hart 2010: 136)

Anxiety and uncertainty. Another challenge is the management of anxiety and uncertainty that naturally arises when one interacts with individuals who have a different linguistic and cultural background (e.g. different values, ways of being). This is linked to the AUM theory that was mentioned previously. If you have a high level of anxiety and lack confidence in your ability to come up with interesting talking points, or you worry excessively about making mistakes when communicating in a second language, inhibitions and lack of WTC can hold you back from initiating and developing intercultural friendships. For example, Mandy, a bright Taiwanese university student, wished to join an international exchange programme in Dublin. Her application was successful; however, as the departure date approached she grew increasingly nervous about what lay ahead.

Because I'll be in a foreign country for such a long time, there'll be lots of problems. I really want to make friends with people from other cultures but I'm worried that I won't be able to get along well with the local students. I don't know what we can talk about and I've never used English much outside of class.

Lacking confidence in her interpersonal skills and informal English language skills, she withdrew. Her fears and lack of self-esteem also held her back from initiating conversations with international students on her home campus.

Cultural differences in communication styles. Differences in communication styles can also impede the development of intercultural friendships and lead to misunderstandings. In the U.S., for example, students are encouraged to express their opinions in class and to challenge the views of others, in ways that are deemed polite in their context. If they go to Japan, South Korea or another East Asian country on exchange and continue to pose questions and openly disagree with the comments of their professor or another student, they may be considered loud and aggressive, and 'too proud' (arrogant). Local students who have been socialized to value the comments of their professors much more than their fellow students may resent the newcomers for speaking up and 'wasting valuable class time' (Jackson 2013; Ryan 2013).

In East Asian contexts, incoming international exchange students from the U.S. and other countries that encourage direct discourse may attribute the reticence of local students to shyness, weak second language skills, insufficient knowledge or lack of preparedness for class. While some of their assumptions may be valid at times, the behaviour may also be due to cultural differences in communication styles, learning and teaching philosophies, 'cultures of learning' and social norms of discourse and demeanour in classroom settings (Cortazzi & Jin 2013; Jackson 2003, 2013; Ryan 2013). (See Chapter 8 for more discussion on 'cultures of learning'.)

Differing values, perceptions, and worldviews. When individuals cross cultural boundaries, they are exposed to differing values, perceptions and worldviews. If one or more of the communicators has very limited intercultural experience, assumptions may be made that their ingroup's values, perceptions and worldviews are shared by everyone. It can be quite a surprise to discover that this is not the case. When Larona, a university student from rural Botswana, travelled to San Francisco for a semester abroad, she found it difficult to accept some of the habits and values of her American roommate. She was especially shocked to discover that the young woman often spent the night with her boyfriend in his dorm room.

Stereotypes, prejudice, and discrimination. As noted in Chapter 7, ethnocentrism can lead to negative perceptions and attitudes towards individuals and groups who are different. When individuals first meet someone from another linguistic or cultural background, they may have already formed an impression of that person based on stereotypes or previous interactions with people they associate with the same group.

Within the context of race relations in the U.S., Gordon Allport (1954) proposed the **'contact hypothesis'**, which suggests that increased contact between different cultural or ethnic groups can lead to mutual acceptance and reduced levels of tension/prejudice. Multiple studies have found that if intercultural relations are to be successful, certain conditions need to be met, such as social and institutional support, equal status between groups, intergroup cooperation and the likelihood of meaningful interpersonal relationships (Pettigrew & Tropp 2011). When these conditions are not in place, stereotypes may persist and intercultural friendships do not materialize or progress.

Contested identities/identity misalignments. In order for intercultural friendships to work well, the individuals involved must recognize and demonstrate respect for each other's preferred self-identities. As noted in Chapter 6, in intercultural interactions one's preferred identity may be misunderstood and contested or challenged. For example, it can be very upsetting for people who speak English as an additional language to be constantly reminded of this, especially when they see themselves as fluent speakers of this global language.

When sojourners or immigrants cross cultural and linguistic boundaries they may experience identity confusion and this can negatively impact on the development of intercultural friendship. If one feels insecure and confused about one's identities and positioning, it can be difficult to forge meaningful ties with people from other cultures. Feeling under threat, individuals may become defensive and cling more tightly to a national identity (Block 2007, 2013; Jackson 2010). Ethnocentricism is not conducive to the formation of intercultural interpersonal relationships.

Language and culture barrier. It is generally easier to explain your thoughts and feelings to individuals who share the same linguistic and cultural background. Intercultural friendships, however, often involve the use of a second language. In many relationships, for example, one or more of the friends may interact in English or another language or dialect that is not a first language. If not fully proficient in the language, it may be difficult to communicate ideas and feelings, especially in informal situations. It can also be challenging to accurately interpret messages (verbal and nonverbal) that are being transmitted. Many international students, for example, have learned formal English in classrooms in their home country; outside of academic situations, they are confused by idiomatic expressions and other forms of informal, social discourse that require background knowledge they do not possess (Gebhard 2010). In some intercultural relationships, people may attribute misunderstandings to cultural difference when a language barrier is to blame, and vice versa.

Expectancy violations. Through the process of primary socialization in one's home environment (**enculturation**), we learn to expect certain behaviours (verbal, nonverbal) in certain situations and when social norms are broken (e.g. cultural scripts for such speech acts as greetings, refusals, apologies, requests are not followed) we may be quite shocked. Individuals who break social norms of behaviour (e.g. omit expressions of politeness) may be perceived as rude or ungrateful. A visibly negative reaction (e.g. puzzled look, frown, raised eyebrow, scowl) may then be taken personally, and, in some cases, wrongly interpreted as prejudice.

Not surprisingly, as suggested by the **expectancy violation theory** (Burgoon 1978), negative perceptions can curtail the cultivation of intercultural friendships. Insufficient cultural knowledge (e.g. lack of familiarity with linguistic and cultural norms in other cultures) can hamper intercultural relationships. (See Chapter 5 for more discussion of the expectancy violation theory in relation to nonverbal behaviour.)

Humour and emotional display. Cross-cultural differences in **humour styles** (the ways people use humour in everyday life) can also lead to interactional difficulties and negative reactions (e.g. Miller 1995; Yamada 1997). The ability to recognize and create humour is vital in the development and maintenance of meaningful intercultural interpersonal relationships. As noted by Bell (2006), Matsumoto (2009) and others, shared laughter binds people together.

While humour is a universal phenomenon, how, when and why it is used can vary considerably among cultures. Very often, humour relies on common understandings of culturally specific topics. People who share a common history and language are apt to use the same forms and styles of language or, at minimum, be familiar with them. This facilitates relationship development as they can understand each other's jokes and sense camaraderie between them. Individuals who have been socialized in a different environment, however, may fail to grasp what lies behind jokes. The stories and sarcastic remarks that send their intercultural friends into fits of laughter may be a complete mystery to them.

Cast on the outside, those who do not share the same humour may become quite irritated, especially if no attempt is made to help them understand the jokes. In some situations, this can be a significant barrier to the enhancement of cordial intercultural relationships. Lana, for example, found it challenging to build a warm relationship with her host family during her sojourn in England. Unable to grasp their humour, she felt like an outsider: 'I was so frustrated that I couldn't get their jokes. Everyone was laughing so happily at something which I could not understand!'

In some situations, offensive humour (e.g. jokes about ethnic groups) may also serve as a barrier to the development of intercultural friendships. If one's communication partner remains silent when one's ethnic group (or other ingroup) is maligned, this can lead to the demise of the relationship.

Emotional display. Cultural variations in the display of feelings and emotions can also be a barrier to the development of satisfying intercultural friendships (Matsumoto & Hwang 2012; Safdar *et al.* 2009). **Emotion regulation** refers to the process of modifying one's emotions and expressions in particular situations (Gross 1998) and as noted by Safdar *et al.* (2009: 1), '[c]ulturally shared norms dictate how, when, and to whom people should express their emotional experiences'. As people from different cultural backgrounds may have learned to express (or suppress) their emotions differently (verbally and nonverbally) in certain contexts, this can result in misunderstandings.

Limited emotional intelligence and sensitivity. Adler *et al.* (2013: 246) define **emotional intelligence** as 'the ability to understand and manage one's own emotions and to be sensitive to others' feelings'. Individuals who have limited 'emotional intelligence' and intercultural sensitivity are apt to have a more difficult time building respectful, mutually satisfying intercultural friendships. They may be perceived as lacking empathy or viewed as too emotional and unstable. In some Asian countries, for example, people may smile when embarrassed or unsure how to respond and this can easily be misinterpreted as uncaring and insensitive by newcomers to the region.

Facework and conflict management. When people from different cultural or linguistic backgrounds interact, misunderstandings and conflicts are bound to occur from time to time. Without mutual facework and effective conflict management skills and techniques, small problems may spiral into major disputes that can lead to permanent break-ups. (See Chapter 10 for a more in-depth discussion of intercultural conflict, facework, and conflict mediation techniques.)

Social sanctions. Even if individuals who cross social boundaries (e.g. class, language, race, sexual orientation, religion) do not harbour negative sentiments about others, they may encounter a negative reaction from family members, ingroup friends and the community in which they live. Hostile, racist contexts where segregation is the norm can certainly inhibit the formation and maintenance of intercultural friendships.

Despite these potential barriers, there is reason for optimism. With an open mindset and commitment, people can and do overcome obstacles and develop long-lasting friendships that cross linguistic and cultural boundaries. For example, in her investigation of intercultural friendships between Chinese and American students on a U.S. campus, Li (2010: 64) drew the following conclusion:

Although intercultural friendships might seem challenging in the beginning stages, if the dyad is able to understand cultural influences on perceptions of self and others in the process of friendship and identify the factors that influence the formation and maintenance of intercultural friendships, intercultural friendships can be as strong and last as long as intracultural friendships.

INTERCULTURAL ROMANCE AND MARRIAGE

Where there is love there is no darkness. (Burundi proverb)

The heart that loves is always young. (Chinese proverb)

A life without love is like a year without summer. (Lithuanian proverb)

It's better to have loved and lost, than to have never loved at all. (Alfred Lord Tennyson, Britain)

Love is a flower which turns into fruit at marriage. (Finnish proverb)

All of these international sayings clearly convey the notion that love and romance are important. While humans in all corners of the globe crave affection, there are differences in our perceptions of love and marriage. Just as views about intercultural friendship have evolved over time, attitudes towards intercultural and interracial romance are shifting in many parts of the world. These days, more people are dating and even marrying individuals who have a different cultural and linguistic background. The Internet (e.g. dating, matchmaking sites) and SNSs are playing a role in bringing people from different cultures together for romance and marriage, with English or another international language often serving as the lingua franca. According to a study conducted by the PEW Research Center, in 2010 one in 12 married couples in the U.S. involved an interracial union (Wang 2012). Further, in more regions and nations around the globe, it is now possible for people of the same sex to marry legally (Corvino & Gallagher 2012; Phy-Olsen 2006).

Terms associated with intercultural romantic relationships

Before we examine factors that facilitate or hinder intercultural romance, it is helpful to understand some of the many terms and issues that are associated with this complex topic. Many of the terms relate to the nature and quality of the relationship.

A **platonic intercultural relationship** refers to an affectionate friendship between individuals of the opposite sex who have different cultural backgrounds; the connection does not involve sexual relations. A **casual intercultural relationship**, or **casual intercultural dating** are the terms used to describe a physical and emotional relationship between two people from different cultural backgrounds who may have a sexual relationship without necessarily expecting the commitments of a more formal romantic relationship. **'Friends with benefits'** refers to a casual sexual relationship among friends who are not romantically or emotionally involved.

Intercultural romance is characterized as a close interpersonal relationship between individuals from diverse cultural backgrounds who share a romantic love for each other. An **intimate intercultural couple** refers to a romantic union between 'partners from different countries, nationalities, ethnicities, and religions who may possess quite divergent beliefs, assumptions, and values as a result of their socialization in different sociocultural spaces' (Killian 2009: xviii). **Intercultural gay (lesbian) romance** refers to a romantic relationship between two males or two females. **Intercultural cyber or online romance** is a romantic relationship that is primarily mediated through online or Internet contact. In net discourse, this contrasts with conventional intercultural offline romantic relationships, which are initiated and largely maintained through face-to-face interactions (Döring 2002).

   Intercultural marriage entails a social union or legal contract between individuals from different cultural backgrounds who may possess differing values, worldviews and personal philosophies (Renalds 2011; Romano 2008). This definition encompasses bonds between individuals who cross social and culturally-constructed boundaries (e.g. linguistic, ethnic, racial, religious, social class, etc.). **Interfaith marriage** refers to marriage (a religious or civil union) between partners professing different religions (Jones *et al.* 2009). **Racial endogamy** denotes marriage within one's own racial group (Goodman *et al.* 2012), whereas **interracial marriage** refers to a union between individuals who are regarded as members of different races (Smith & Hattery 2009; Yancey & Lewis 2009). A marriage between a Filipino Catholic woman and a black Muslim man is an example of an interfaith, interracial marriage. **Interethnic marriage** refers to marriage between people with different ethnic backgrounds (e.g. bonds between a Welsh woman and a Scottish man). **Monogamy** refers to the practice of being married to only one individual at a time, whereas **polygamy** denotes the practice of having more than one spouse at a time (Jacobson & Burton 2011; Numila 2009). **Same-sex marriage** or **gay marriage** refers to a union between members of the same sex (e.g. a marriage between two women or between two men) (Corvino & Gallagher 2012; Phy-Olsen 2006). **Co-habitation** refers to living together in a sexual relationship without being legally married. Among individuals and cultural groups, reactions to co-habitation, same-sex marriage and multiple marital partners differ. Conventions and attitudes towards the dissolution of marriage (e.g. divorce) are also impacted by social and religious mores and laws, which vary significantly among cultures.

Factors that facilitate or hinder intercultural romantic relationships

Similar to intracultural unions, some intercultural romances and marriages are more successful than others. Even with an increase in global interconnectedness, significant cultural variations still exist in mating rituals and practices (courtship or dating behaviours) such as the age of sexual consent for males and females, parental involvement in match-making and the degree of male–female contact permissible prior to marriage, etc. (Hamon & Ingoldsby 2003; Jankowiak & Paladino 2008). Differences in attitudes towards premarital sex may cause intergenerational and interethnic conflict especially among immigrants in Western countries (Lamanna & Reidmann 2011); practices that differ from those of the majority culture (e.g. homosexual romance, arranged marriages) may be met with hostility in some quarters (Phy-Olsen 2006).

   Based on interviews with intercultural couples, Romano (2008) compiled a list of factors or characteristics that contribute to successful marriages between people who have different cultural backgrounds: commitment to the relationship, ability to communicate, sensitivity to each other's needs, a liking for the other's culture, flexibility, positive self-image, love as the main marital motive, common goals, spirit of adventure and sense of humour.

   Relational intimacy and the development of a relational identity also help determine the fate of these unions. Within the context of intercultural romance and marriage, **third-culture**

building refers to the melding of different cultural identities and practices to form an identity that is unique to the romantic partners or family unit (Rosenblatt 2009). **Relational interdependence** (mutual dependence or reliance on each other) not only helps couples embrace and reconcile differences, it can help to cushion them from negative forces (e.g. hostile reactions from family members and religious figures who disapprove of the relationship). While intercultural couples may develop 'their own intricate, multilayered systems', they are impacted by 'the many other systems in which they are embedded, including their families and cultures of origin and an assortment of other economic, legal, political, and social systems' (Rosenblatt 2009: 3).

As well as prejudice and racism, intercultural couples may face a number of other obstacles, including: a language barrier, conflicting ideas about premarital sex, differing expectations and perceptions of roles and responsibilities (e.g. disparate views about appropriate duties for wives and husbands), differing ideas about acceptable displays of affection in public and private domains, conflict management differences, a power imbalance, family pressures and social constraints, differing perceptions of child rearing and unfamiliar beliefs and traditions (e.g. religious ceremonies and customs).

ENHANCING INTERCULTURAL INTERPERSONAL RELATIONSHIPS

> There are those individuals from diverse backgrounds who have created a world, at least within their own private lives, that is not broken by the socially constructed boundaries of race, class, gender, sexual orientation, religion, ability, and age; people who have established deep, lasting relationships with others from very different backgrounds.
>
> (Vela-McConnell 2011: 3)

How have these individuals been able to develop successful intercultural interpersonal relationships? How can you bridge linguistic and cultural barriers to initiate and maintain rewarding and mutually-satisfying relationships? Drawing on recent research on intercultural interpersonal relationships (friendships, romance, marriage), the following section offers practical suggestions to initiate and optimize relationships with individuals who are linguistically and culturally different.

- If you do not have any intercultural interpersonal relationships, reflect on the reasons why this is the case. Are your fears or attitudes (or those of your family/social networks) keeping you from making intercultural connections? If yes, challenge yourself to leave your comfort zone and initiate a relationship with someone from a different linguistic and cultural background, whether face-to-face or online. Bear in mind that intercultural connections must be genuine and respectful if they are to be meaningful.
- Perceptions of relationships differ across cultures. Consider your own views and expectations and how these ideas formed. How might these understandings differ from those of your intercultural partners?
- Do not assume that you or your intercultural friend or partner is an ambassador for a particular linguistic or cultural group. When you get to know someone from another linguistic or cultural background, you are developing an interpersonal relationship with an individual.
- Cultivate an open mindset. Refrain from forming expectations of behaviour based solely on your own language and culture. For example, be attentive to differences in

communication styles and recognize the validity of differing social norms (e.g. cultural scripts) and worldviews. Avoid making snap judgments about behaviours that puzzle or annoy you and make an effort to view the world from your partner's perspective.

■ Be attentive to differences in disclosure norms, values, verbal and nonverbal behaviours, and make an effort to develop relational intimacy.

■ Work to eliminate any personal biases and prejudices that you may have that could negatively impact on your intercultural interpersonal relationships.

■ Recognize the importance of respect and genuine concern in intercultural friendships and romances. Are you attentive to the needs of your communication partners or overly focused on your own interests?

■ Assess your level of intercultural sensitivity and intercultural communication apprehension. Based on what you have learned in this book and elsewhere consider constructive ways to overcome impediments to the development of healthy intercultural interpersonal relationships.

■ Make a personal commitment to devote the time necessary to enhance your interpersonal intercultural communication skills to develop meaningful relationships (face-to-face and online).

As our world is becoming increasingly diverse and interdependent, it is vital for us to acquire the knowledge, skills and mindset that can nurture meaningful connections with people who have a different cultural or linguistic background. While intercultural interpersonal relationships (e.g. friendships, dating, marriage) can be more challenging than intracultural connections, they are well worth the extra time and effort involved. 'Because we live in a world in which there is increasing contact with diverse others, understanding how differences are bridged – regardless of which socially constructed boundary we happen to be speaking – is an important pursuit' (Vela-McConnell 2011: 3).

SUMMARY

In this chapter, we reviewed various categories of intercultural interpersonal relationships and discussed the many potential benefits of face-to-face or online connections with people who have a different linguistic or cultural background. We examined differing cultural perceptions of friendship and identified a number of internal and external factors that can either facilitate or hinder intercultural or interracial friendships and diverse social networks. Then, we turned our attention to romantic relationships (e.g. dating, co-habitation, marriage) between people from different cultural backgrounds. After reviewing key terms associated with this topic, we examined multiple variables that can lead to success or failure in intercultural romance and marriage. Finally, we discussed ways to optimize intercultural interpersonal relationships.

discussion questions

1   Why do people tend to form friendships with people who have a similar background?
2   Define what friendship means to you. What do you expect of your friends?
3   Identify different types of friendship that are common in your context. In your first language, what words are used for each type? Provide examples of different categories of friends.
4   Identify challenges people may experience in initiating and maintaining intercultural relationships.
5   How can language impact intimate intercultural relationships?
6   Define social networks. Draw diagrams to illustrate your social networks. Do you have friends from other linguistic and cultural backgrounds? If not, why not?
7   What role can self-disclosure and relational maintenance play in intercultural interpersonal relationships (e.g. platonic, romantic)?
8   Define the concept of 'face' and explain how facework can influence the quality of intercultural relationships.
9   In today's globalized world, how has technology changed the way intercultural friendships and romances are formed and maintained?
10 Intercultural marriages are on the rise in many parts of the world. Discuss the benefits and challenges of these unions.
11 In small groups, discuss the challenges bilingual intercultural couples might face, especially if they decide to make their relationships permanent.
12 Based on your own intercultural experiences and what you have read in this chapter and elsewhere, identify five strategies that might enhance intercultural interpersonal relationships (e.g. friendship, platonic friendship, romance, marriage). Share your ideas with your classmates.

further reading

Bystydzienski, J.M. (2011) *Intercultural Couples: Crossing Boundaries, Negotiating Diffference*, New York: New York University Press.

The author examines the multidimensional experiences of intercultural couples who negotiate their identities, gender expectations, language use, family relations, child-rearing, financial matters and lifestyle.

Hruschka, D.J. (2010) *Friendship: Development, Ecology, and Evolution of a Relationship (Origins of Human Behavior and Culture)*, Berkeley, CA: University of California Press.

In this multidisciplinary book, the author synthesizes cross-cultural, experimental and ethnographic data to better understand the broad meaning of friendship, how it develops, how it interfaces with kinship and romantic relationships and how it differs from place to place.

Karis, T.A. and Killian, K.D. (ed.) (2009) *Intercultural Couples: Exploring Diversity in Intimate Relationships*, New York: Taylor and Francis.

This edited collection covers a broad range of topics and issues related to intercultural couples, including bilingualism, interfaith relationships and Internet-mediated relationships.

Rabotin, M. (2011) *Culture Savvy: Working and Collaborating Across the Globe*, Alexandria, VA: ASTD Press.

The author draws attention to how fear, stereotypes and misunderstandings negatively impact intercultural relations. Suggestions are offered to develop respectful, rewarding friendships with individuals who have been socialized in a different cultural and linguistic background.

Romano, D. (2008) *Intercultural Marriage: Promises and Pitfalls*, 2nd edn, Boston: Intercultural Press, Inc., Nicholas Brealey Publishing.

Written by an intercultural counsellor, this book explores the benefits and challenges of intercultural marriage (e.g. linguistic, religious, cultural difference).

Shelling, G. (2008) *In Love but Worlds Apart: Insights, Questions, and Tips for the Intercultural Couple*, Bloomington, IN: AuthorHouse.

The author discusses ways to develop and nurture intercultural intimate relationships (e.g. romances, marriages).

Vela-McConnell, J.A. (2011) *Unlikely Friends: Bridging Ties and Diverse Friendships*, Lanham, MD: Lexington Books.

This accessible book focuses on successful friendships that cross one or more social and cultural boundaries (e.g. age, race, gender, class, sexual orientation, religious affiliation). The author raises awareness of interpersonal techniques that can enhance intercultural interpersonal friendship.

CHAPTER 10

Managing language and intercultural conflict

Intercultural conflict frustrations often arise because of our lack of necessary and sufficient knowledge to deal with culture-based conflict communication issues competently. When a second language is involved, the situation may be exacerbated. Our cultural ignorance or ineptness oftentimes clutters our ability to communicate appropriately, effectively, and adaptively across cultural and linguistic lines.

(Ting-Toomey 2012: 279)

Peace is not the absence of conflict but the presence of creative alternatives for responding to conflict. Dorothy Thompson (1893–1961), American freelance journalist.

(J.J. Lewis n.d.)

In a few decades, the relationship between the environment, resources and conflict may seem almost as obvious as the connection we see today between human rights, democracy and peace.

(Wangari Maathai 1940–2011, 2004 Nobel Peace Prize
Laureate. Nobel Women's Initiative n.d.)

learning objectives

By the end of this chapter, you should be able to:

1 identify and describe the nature and characteristics of conflict
2 define intercultural conflict and describe its characteristics
3 describe the role of language in intercultural conflicts
4 identify five types of conflict
5 explain the potential impact of culture in conflict situations
6 explain why it is important to consider the impact of social, political and historical elements in intercultural conflicts
7 explain the role of face and face saving in conflict situations
8 identify preventative strategies that you can use to avoid threatening the other person's face in a conflict situation
9 offer suggestions and strategies for dealing effectively and appropriately with intercultural conflicts.

INTRODUCTION

Today's globalized world is characterized by increasing contact between people with diverse backgrounds in all spheres of life (e.g. education, family, work, recreation, social, domestic and international politics, worship, etc.). Linguistic and cultural differences among individuals or group members, whether in a multicultural classroom, in linguistically and culturally diverse families, in multinational business teams, in international peace negotiations or other domains, can be a source of misunderstanding and conflict. 'Conflict breeds conflict, unless it is managed successfully' (Gudykunst 2004: 276). It is therefore imperative that we develop the knowledge and skills that can help us to resolve conflicts in a respectful, peaceful manner. It is not just world leaders who require intercultural conflict competence. All of us need to hone the ability to deal appropriately and effectively with misunderstandings and conflict situations on an interpersonal level.

This chapter begins by describing the nature and characteristics of conflict. Next, we explore the domains and types of conflict, and the role(s) of language and culture in conflict situations, especially intercultural interactions. We then turn our attention to intercultural conflict communication styles and the impact of face and facework in conflict situations. Finally, we discuss intercultural conflict competence and constructive ways to resolve language and intercultural misunderstandings and conflict situations.

THE NATURE AND CHARACTERISTICS OF CONFLICT

There are many definitions of **conflict**. One of the most widely quoted is by Mortensen (1974: 93), who defines it simply as 'an expressed struggle over incompatible interests in the distribution of limited resources'. More recent definitions tend to be variations of this. Folger *et al.* (2013: 4), for example, refer to conflict as 'the interaction of interdependent people who perceive incompatability and the possibility of interference from others as a result of this incompatability'. For Adler *et al.* (2013: 351), conflict denotes 'an expressed struggle between at least two interdependent parties who perceive incompatible goals, scarce resources, and interference from the other party in achieving their goals'. Conflict is also viewed as 'an inevitable part of the human experience' (Roloff 1987), which 'permeates all social relationships' (Liu *et al.* 2011: 197).

As the above conceptions illustrate, scholars generally agree on the nature and characteristics of conflict and the relationship among those involved. Basically, conflict centres on 'incompatabilities, an expressed struggle, and interdependence among two or more parties' (Putnam 2006: 5). To gain a better understanding of how conflict impacts on everyday life, we now take a closer look at the common elements in these definitions.

Incompatabilities.   In a conflict situation, it appears as if an individual or group's gain means another's loss. The parties involved may have incompatible goals or aspirations or they may favour incompatible means to the same ends (e.g. differing decision-making techniques, conflicting communication styles). For example, an individual may employ aggressive tactics to dominate a situation, whereas the other party wishes to negotiate a settlement through lengthy, informal conversations.

An expressed struggle.   For conflict to develop, the parties involved must recognize that they disagree about something. You may be annoyed that someone keeps arriving late to meetings but unless you convey your displeasure either verbally or nonverbally in such a way that this person is aware of your displeasure, there is no conflict.

Scarce resources.   Interpersonal conflicts arise when people believe that there are insufficient resources (e.g. materials, food, time, wealth, quality education) for everyone. Many students may wish to join a second language immersion programme but there are a limited number of places; conflict may develop if the selection criteria are not transparent or perceived as fair. In families, sibling rivalry may intensify if children feel that their parents are not distributing their time evenly. Conflict may also erupt if one child is given more allowance or privileges than another.

Scare resources can also lead to conflicts on a larger scale. In some parts of the world, limited resources (e.g. water, arable land) are leading to violent disputes as people struggle to survive. Wangari Maathai, the 2004 Nobel Peace Prize Laureate, warns that '[i]n a few decades, the relationship between the environment, resources and conflict may seem almost as obvious as the connection we see today between human rights, democracy and peace' (Nobel Women's Initiative n.d.). As the effects of global warming intensify (e.g. flooding, droughts) crops will fail in areas that used to be bountiful; the availability of food will drop and prices will rise, spawning more conflicts as people struggle to feed their families.

Interdependence.   Individuals or groups that are involved in a conflict are interdependent in some ways, even if they are not willing to acknowledge this. In interpersonal relationships, for example, parties depend on each other for psychological, emotional, and material resources (Folger *et al.* 2013; Roloff 1981). The well-being of one is affected by the behaviour of the other party and vice versa. Resentment and hostility may cloud their judgment. A negative mindset may prevent people from recognizing that they need to accept their interdependence and work together in order to resolve their conflict.

Inevitability.   As conflict is an inevitable fact of life, people routinely find themselves in conflict situations, whether in their personal life, social life, or at work. Siblings may routinely come into conflict with each other and their parents about daily activities. At universities, students who work on projects together may differ about how they should proceed. Romantic partners may find themselves in conflict about whether they should have sex or live together before marriage. When intercultural couples have children, they may find themselves in a conflict situation when they discover they have very different views about child-rearing practices and the role of religion and extended family members in their daily life. In the workplace, conflict about tasks and responsibilities may develop within work teams.

On the world stage, conflicts are bound to develop within regions and between nation-states as groups compete for limited resources (e.g. land, water). This does not mean that violence is also inevitable. Later in this chapter, we discuss peaceful ways to resolve conflict situations.

DOMAINS AND TYPES OF CONFLICT

An inevitable part of life, conflict can occur in any context where humans interact, e.g. one's home environment, social or educational settings, the workplace, within organizations. In all arenas within one's community, conflict may arise between individuals or groups (e.g. families, work or project teams, juries, clubs, political parties, etc.). Conflict can also erupt on the regional, national or international stage (e.g. intergroup ethnic disputes, regional wars). Contentious, divisive issues can surface at any time in any arena of life.

Conflict can take many forms and cross one or more socially- and historically-constructed boundaries (e.g. age, gender, ethnicity, race, language, religion, etc.). As well as perceiving incompatibility with individuals who share similar roots (e.g. the same first language and cultural histories), people may come into conflict with individuals or groups with different cultural, ethnic, linguistic, national, racial, political and religious backgrounds (Chen & Starosta 1998; Folger *et al.* 2013; Orbe & Harris 2008). Gender and age gaps may also trigger or complicate conflict situations. Let's take a look at several types of conflict and examples of each.

Intracultural conflict

A clash of opposing assumptions, beliefs, opinions, needs and goals may occur whenever human beings come together, even if they share much in common (e.g. the same language, ethnicity). **Intracultural conflict** refers to a struggle between individuals with a similar linguistic and cultural background. For example, two Australian EFL teachers in Seoul may become embroiled in a conflict situation when they vehemently disagree about the pedagogy that should be used in their language programme. Malaysian parents who share the same first language and cultural background may find themselves in a highly emotional conflict situation when they have opposing views about what medium of instruction is best for primary children (e.g. a local dialect or English).

Interpersonal conflict

Interpersonal conflict basically refers to conflict or a struggle between two or more people who may or may not have a similar linguistic and cultural background. Describing interpersonal conflict as 'a problematic situation', Abigail and Cahn (2011: 4) associate it with the following characteristics:

1   the conflicting parties are interdependent
2   they have the perception that they seek incompatible goals or outcomes or they favour incompatible means to the same ends
3   the perceived incompatibility has the potential to adversely affect the relationship leaving emotional residues if not addressed
4   there is a sense of urgency about the need to resolve the difference.

In an interpersonal conflict, a struggle may occur when the communication partners cannot come to an agreement on a way to meet their needs or goals. In this situation, individuals may feel pulled in different directions. For example, you may wish to go to Switzerland to take part in a German language immersion programme but your parents insist that you work during the summer. Your partner wants to go to see a French movie with you but you want to stay home and finish writing an essay that is due. Different aims, expectations and experiences can lead to interpersonal conflict.

Intergroup conflict

Intergroup conflict refers to disputes that arise between two or more groups of people (e.g. different ethnic groups, work groups, study groups, sports teams, debate teams, choirs, etc.). Group conflict situations may develop 'when two work, cultural, or social groups seek to maximize their own goals without locating perceptual congruities' (Chen & Starosta 1998: 143). Disparate objectives, values, communication styles and a wide range of cultural differences may cause friction between groups. For example, business majors may come into conflict with English majors about the use of the same meeting space or other resources (e.g. funds, computers).

Organizational conflict

Organizational conflict refers to disputes that can arise within an organization (e.g. a business, educational institution, a department, political party, social club, etc.) as a result of competing needs, values, beliefs and interests. Within organizations, conflict can assume many forms. There can be a clash among or between formal authority figures (e.g. senior administrators, executives, professors) and individuals or groups with less power and status (e.g. office workers, junior staff, students). Discord about a range of organizational or work-related issues may erupt between individuals, departments, unions and management. Even among those of the same rank (e.g. students, clerks, managers), disputes may occur about aspects such as the division of labour, the choice of language in meetings, the way duties or revenue should be divided, how tasks should be carried out, the hours of work, etc. Subtler forms of conflict (e.g. jealousies, rivalries, a clash of personalities) may also prevail as individuals and groups struggle to enhance their positioning and gain more power and privileges. Competing needs and demands may lead to protests and labour disputes (e.g. the refusal to use a particular language in meetings).

Within organizations, as well as in other contexts, conflicts may be either affective or cognitive in nature. **Affective conflict** refers to a type of conflict that centres on an emotional conflict between parties. Affective conflicts can be very destructive to companies (and interpersonal relationships) if unresolved. A **cognitive conflict** refers to a type of conflict that centres on the completion of a task. Cognitive conflicts often highlight important problems a company or organization needs to fix. (Also, see Chapter 11.)

Intercultural conflict

Intercultural conflict refers to 'the experience of emotional frustration in conjunction with perceived incompatibility of values, norms, face orientations, goals, scarce resources, processes, and/or outcomes between a minimum of two parties from two different cultural communities in an interactive situation' (Ting-Toomey & Oetzel 2001: 17). More recently, Oetzel and Ting-Toomey (2006) explain that this state of discord can arise due to 'the diverse cultural approaches people bring with them in expressing their different cultural or ethnic values, identity issues, interaction norms, face-saving orientations, power resource transactions, divergent goal emphasis, and contrastive conflict styles' (p. 545). **Conflict style** refers to a preferred way of behaving in conflict situations.

Intercultural conflict may materialize as '[o]ur cultural ignorance or ineptness oftentimes clutters our ability to communicate appropriately, effectively, and adaptively across cultural and linguistic lines' (Ting-Toomey 2012: 279). Limited second language proficiency may exacerbate conflict situations. In a multicultural classroom, disparate views about what constitutes appropriate communication behaviours may lead to conflict between local and international students who have been socialized in a different linguistic and cultural environment. In discussions, an international exchange student may frequently speak up and interrupt other speakers. While this may be quite normal (and expected) in her home environment, her discourse may be perceived as overly direct and aggressive in this context. Tension and discord may prevail when students in the host culture are not accustomed to this style of communication. In another intercultural situation, an Algerian exchange student may find herself embroiled in a tense conflict with her Belgian professor who disapproves of her attending class wearing the hijab (headscarf worn by some Muslim women).

Intercultural conflicts may also arise in meetings or teams that involve students, workers or professionals from diverse backgrounds. For example, disputes may surface due to differing ideas about how a task should be divided and accomplished based on their experiences in their home culture. If group members do not share the same linguistic and cultural norms of politeness, tempers may flare. Lack of familiarity with **cultural scripts** (e.g. routines for requests, refusals, apologies) may result in miscommunication and **misattributions** (inaccurate assumptions), which may spiral into conflict situations.

Interracial conflict

Under the broad category of intercultural conflict, there are many sub-categories including interracial, interethnic and interreligious conflict. **Interracial conflict** refers to a conflict situation whereby race or racial difference is an issue (Orbe & Harris 2008). For example, a dispute between an African American customer and an Asian American shopkeeper may escalate when claims of overcharging and racism are voiced. When black drivers are stopped by white policemen in California, the drivers may claim that they are victims of racial profiling. Convinced that they have been singled out by law enforcement personnel because of their skin colour, a verbal disagreement may quickly escalate into a heated exchange.

Interethnic conflict

Interethnic conflict refers to a conflict situation between individuals or groups affiliated with different ethnic groups, whereby ethnicity is salient. A strong ethnic identity accompanied by ethnic hatred/distrust and inequalities (e.g. unequal financial resources) can lead to conflict situations that may escalate into violence. Conflict between Mexican Americans and European Americans may develop when different views are expressed about proposed changes to U.S. immigration laws. In Cyprus, conflict between Greek and Turkish Cypriots may surface when changes are proposed in educational language policies.

An extreme form of ethnic conflict may result in **ethnic cleansing** (the systematic and violent removal of an ethnic or religious group from a particular territory) and **genocide** (the widespread killing of a national, ethnic, racial or religious group). In the 1990s, for example, in the former Yugoslavia, Bosnian Muslims and Bosnian Croats were forced to flee their homes by Serbs; many were also raped and murdered. In Rwanda, in 1994 the Hutus slaughtered thousands of members of the minority Tutsi population. In 1991, The United Nations Security Council established the **International Criminal Court (ICC)** in the Hague, the

Netherlands to try **'crimes against humanity'**, that is, the systemic practice of serious offences against people that are either carried out or condoned by a government (e.g. widespread murder, religious persecution, rapes as a weapon of war, etc.). Many of these crimes involve atrocities that stem from ethnic conflicts, such as in Rwanda and Yugoslavia.

International conflict

International conflict has traditionally referred to disputes between different countries (e.g. the Iran–Iraq war) as well as conflict between people and organizations from different nation-states (e.g. trade disputes between Mexico and the United States, disagreements between the governments of different nations). Nowadays, the term encompasses inter-group conflicts within a nation such as when one group is fighting for independence or for more political, social or economic power (e.g. the conflict in Syria or Mali). Some international conflicts (e.g. the Israeli-Palestinian conflict) are protracted and not easily solved.

While international conflicts often involve different national governments, disputes may also erupt between business professionals and/or private businesses or organizations from two different countries. **Private-sector international conflict** is similar to private domestic interpersonal or business conflicts except that it is apt to be more complicated by factors such as linguistic and cultural differences (e.g. variations in communication practices, socio-pragmatic norms), distance and ambiguity about which laws prevail. Jurisdictional disputes and other intercultural complications may arise.

Interreligious conflict

Interreligious or **interfaith conflict (religious conflict)** refers to disputes or conflict situations between individuals or groups affiliated with different faiths, whereby religion is a salient issue. For example, with both Muslim and Christian populations in sub-Saharan Africa growing rapidly, issues of interfaith conflicts are increasing in this part of the world. Interfaith conflict has led to sectarian violence and even murder in Egypt, India, Nigeria and many other nations. Religious disputes may also arise between individuals or groups affiliated with different sects or branches within the same religion. In Ireland, among Christians, there are long-running tensions between Catholics and Protestants and in Iraq there are conflicts between Sunni and Shia Muslims. Intense passions and beliefs make interreligious conflicts difficult to resolve.

Intergenerational conflict

Intergenerational conflict refers to disputes between individuals or groups from different generations, whereby age and divergent life experiences are salient issue. For example, conflict between middle-aged immigrant parents and their children may arise due to differences in language practices, values, beliefs and behaviours. A young female Muslim who was born and raised in Manchester, England may insist on using English at all times and refuse to communicate with her immigrant parents in Urdu, their first language, especially in public. Her parents may forbid her from dating in secondary school and start the process of arranging a marriage for her with a cousin from their home village in Pakistan. In extreme cases, conflict can escalate and lead to an **honour killing**, whereby the young woman is murdered by relatives who believe that her actions (e.g. premarital sex, refusal to accept an arranged marriage) have brought dishonour on the family. Intergenerational conflict has been the subject of many compelling films, e.g. *Bend it like Beckham*, *The Joy Luck Club*.

Gender conflict

Disputes may also occur between males and females in domestic, social or work environments. **Gender conflict** refers to conflict situations in which gender is a key factor. In a work situation, for example, interpersonal conflict may arise between male and female co-workers due to differences in communication styles and role expectations, as well as a power imbalance. Globally, more women are entering the workforce and joining professions once reserved for males. In many regions, women are gaining more access to positions of power in all sectors of society (e.g. education, government, work, the military, etc.). As they compete for jobs and better salaries and benefits, conflicts can arise when men (and some women) feel threatened by these changes. Accordingly, females may experience discrimination and possible retribution (e.g. intimidation, violence). As they fight for their rights, they may come into direct conflict with males who are resistant to change and unwilling to share power and resources.

Multiplex conflict

A **multiplex conflict situation** refers to disputes between individuals or groups that cross multiple social and historical boundaries (e.g. ethnic, linguistic, international, racial, social, gender, religion, political). For example, imagine an interpersonal conflict situation that involves a white Catholic male from Ireland who speaks English as a first language and a black Muslim female from the Sudan who speaks English as a second language. A language barrier and multiple cultural differences (e.g. religious, social class, cultural) could complicate the communication process and pose challenges for the resolutions of conflicts that arise.

While most conflict situations involve two or more people, individuals can sometimes experience conflict with themselves. **Intrapersonal conflict** or **self-conflict** refers to the internal struggle that can occur within one's own mind. This conflicted state can develop 'when we find ourselves having to choose between two or more mutually exclusive options' (Gamble & Gamble 2013: 218). Within the same individual, conflicting ideas about what is the right course of action may lead to confusion and feelings of inbetweenness. Trying to decide whether to follow their heart and major in Spanish or heed their parent's advice and study business can lead to self-conflict in students. A sojourner who has just returned from a lengthy stay abroad may also experience intrapersonal conflict. For example, the returnee may feel torn between certain values and practices (e.g. communication styles) in the host culture and those in her home environment. Pulled in multiple directions, she may experience marginality and other symptoms of reverse culture shock. Caught between the desire to make a better life for his family in a new country and fond memories of peaceful times in his homeland, a refugee may experience intrapersonal conflict and self-doubts while adjusting to life in a new country.

On a daily basis, the news media draws our attention to conflicts at the international, national or regional level; however, as noted above, disagreements and disputes may also arise between individuals in everyday life. The remainder of the chapter largely focuses on conflict that arises between two (or more) persons or groups with different backgrounds (e.g. cultural, linguistic, religious, ethnic, etc.).

CULTURAL DIMENSIONS OF CONFLICT SITUATIONS

Culture plays a role in all conflict situations, whether intracultural or intercultural in nature. It can be a dominant factor or it may influence the conflict in more subtle ways. Both personal characteristics and cultural dimensions may fuel disagreements and conflicts between individuals and groups. In particular, intercultural conflict situations may be exacerbated by a range of cultural elements, including mismatched expectations, higher levels of ambiguity and uncertainty, language and nonverbal barriers, face and identity needs and differing perceptions and understandings of conflict. Let's take a closer look at each of these factors.

Mismatched expectations. The **expectancy violation theory** posits that individuals have culturally-based expectations about how people should behave in a communicative event (e.g. conversations, arguments) and when individuals or groups do not perform as expected, miscommunication and negative perceptions are apt to develop (Burgoon 1995). Expectations in conflict situations are influenced by the underlying values and norms (e.g. sociopragmatic rules of discourse) that are prevalent in a particular culture. Ideas about what is appropriate verbal and nonverbal behaviour in conflicts are learned during the process of socialization and vary among cultures. Not surprisingly, as noted by Ting-Toomey and Oetzel (2001: 17), intercultural conflict involves 'emotional frustrations or mismatched expectations that stem, in part, from cultural group membership differences'. In intercultural disputes, negative emotional reactions to unexpected behaviours can lead to an escalation in the conflict.

During **enculturation**, the socialization process, we develop ideas about what is appropriate or inappropriate behaviour by observing those around us. **Cultural norms** or rules serve as a guide for what we should or should not do in a conflict situation. A **conflict script** refers to 'the interaction placement and appropriate sequence of verbal and nonverbal message exchanges' (Ting-Toomey & Oetzel 2001: 11). Basically, this cognitive structure describes appropriate actions and sequences of events in a dispute (Folger *et al.* 2013: 56). For example, a conflict script can signal who should speak first during the process of negotiation. It can also indicate how and when one should apologize and in what language, depending on the nature of the conflict.

Recent studies suggest that people have implicit culturally-based scripts that shape their expectations about how a conflict should unfold and be resolved (Folger *et al.* 2013). Some researchers have also found variations in the conflict scripts of men and women in the same cultural context (Fehr *et al.* 1999). When people from different cultural backgrounds interact, there are bound to be difficulties when they expect different conflict scripts to prevail.

Ambiguity and uncertainty. When people interact with individuals who have a different linguistic and cultural background, there is bound to be more ambiguity and uncertainty than in intracultural interactions. The parties involved may not know whether the conflict is seen in the same way and they may be unsure how to handle the dispute in a manner that is mutually acceptable. Sensitive intercultural communicators may be nervous about the possibility of offending others. There may also be uncertainty in the meaning of verbal expressions when a second language is involved. Individuals with a low tolerance of ambiguity are apt to find intercultural conflict situations more stressful than intracultural events. Their heightened emotions may make it more difficult to resolve the conflict.

The **uncertainty reduction theory (URT)** (Berger & Calabrese 1975), which was introduced in Chapter 9, suggests that people are uncomfortable with ambiguity and strive to reduce uncertainty in communicative events (e.g. intercultural conflict situations). **Cognitive uncertainty** refers to uncertainty about the ways in which an individual's culturally-influenced attitudes and beliefs impact on his or her way of thinking. Linked to the expectancy violation theory, **behavioural uncertainty** has to do with one's uncertainty about how the other person will behave in an intercultural conflict situation. The **uncertainty/anxiety management theory (AUM)** suggests that as we gain more knowledge and understanding of our communication partner, our level of stress or anxiety subsides. As our apprehension diminishes, we can become more effective at resolving conflicts with people who have been socialized in a different linguistic and cultural context (Gudykunst 2004).

Language and nonverbal barriers. Language is a key factor in all conflict situations, whether the parties involved share the same cultural background or not. As well as word choice and verbal communication style (e.g. direct or indirect, emotionally expressive or restrained, formal or informal), our nonverbal behaviours (e.g. tone of voice, body language, gestures, posture, facial expressions, use of space) impact on the outcomes of both intracultural and intercultural interactions.

Whether intentional or not, intercultural conflict may escalate when a person directs inappropriate verbal or nonverbal behaviour towards another. For example, standing very close to someone to emphasize a point may be quite acceptable in one's home environment but may backfire if one's communication partner is used to more personal distance. Feeling under threat, the person may respond in unexpected ways and the conflict may escalate.

In intercultural interactions, it is common for one or more interactants to use a second language and if not fluent, the possibility of miscommunication and misunderstandings is greater. Even if the intercultural communicators speak the same first language, there may be differences in their preferred communication style, which can complicate the conflict situation. If a speaker insists on using a direct style of communication with someone who is much more at ease with subtle ways of communicating, a negative reaction may worsen the conflict situation. Direct communicators may be viewed as abrasive, rude and confrontational, while those who favour an indirect style may be regarded as weak and indecisive. Misattributions and hurt feelings may make it more difficult to resolve conflicts. (Chapter 4 provides examples of various communication styles.)

Although language can sometimes result in intercultural conflict or exacerbate conflict situations, it is also the primary vehicle for solving intercultural conflict, as explained later in the chapter. In addition, context-appropriate nonverbal behaviours can also facilitate conflict resolutions.

Face and identity needs. In all cultures, people are concerned about how they are viewed by others and this also applies to conflict situations. Drawing on Goffman's (1969) notion of face as a social phenomenon that is created through communication, Brown and Levinson (1978: 66) define **face** as 'the public self-image that every member wants to claim for himself, [. . .] something that is emotionally invested, and that can be lost, maintained, or enhanced, and must be constantly attended to in interaction'. As well as our public image, face encompasses our identity, self-esteem and honour. In intercultural conflict situations, our face is particularly vulnerable as we are often less certain about what will happen (e.g. how our partners will react to what we say and do). The concept of face is especially problematic in ambiguous situations when the identities of the parties are called into question. In intercultural interactions, conflict situations may arise when difficult, awkward and unexpected requests are made. Individuals may be embarrassed and unsure how to respond.

Dimensions of face include positive and negative elements. **Positive face** refers to a person's desire to gain the approval of other people, whereas **negative face** is the desire to have autonomy and not be controlled by others. **Positive facework** emphasizes the need for acceptance, respect and inclusion, while **negative facework** refers to the degree to which the disputants protect themselves from interference (Ting-Toomey 1990). In conflict situations, individuals strive to protect and manage their self-image.

Facework refers to the 'specific verbal and nonverbal behaviors that we engage in to maintain or restore face loss and to uphold and honor face gain' (Ting-Toomey 2005: 73). How people manage their self-image in conflict situations varies among cultures. 'While face and facework are universal phenomena, how we "frame" or interpret the situated meaning of face and how we enact facework differ from one cultural community to the next' (Ting-Toomey 2005: 73). Naturally, this can lead to misunderstandings and an escalation of disputes. The importance of facework is explored further in the chapter when we examine the conflict face negotiation theory.

Differing perceptions and understandings of conflict. The way conflict is viewed and approached is influenced by our gender and cultural background. Through enculturation, we acquire the attitudes, knowledge structures, behaviours and strategies that are most commonly used to define and respond to disagreements and conflict situations. From an early age, we learn how to deal with conflict by observing our parents and other members of our culture both in the community and through the mass media (e.g. television). We receive messages about what is appropriate for males and females in conflict situations. As our attitudes and perceptions of conflict are shaped within particular environments, it is not surprising that researchers have discovered individual and cultural differences in this domain.

In cultural contexts where **collectivism** is prevalent, the needs and wants of groups are given priority over individuals and conflict tends to be viewed as destructive and harmful for relationships (e.g. China, Japan) (Ting-Toomey & Takai 2006; van Meurs & Spencer-Oatey 2010). To preserve relational harmony and one's public face, **pacifism** is generally favoured, that is, individuals strive to avoid conflict situations. If conflicts arise, people tend to restrain their emotions and try to manage disputes indirectly. Those who use this approach think that relationships are made stronger and conflicts are lessened when emotions are kept in check. This perspective is clearly conveyed in the following Chinese proverb: 'The first person to raise his voice loses the argument'. It is also important to note, however, that some researchers in East Asia have recently identified generational differences in people's perceptions of conflict. Zhang *et al.* (2005), for example, found that young men and women in modern China increasingly prefer collaborative problem solving to resolve disputes, whereas their elders still favour avoiding conflict situations.

In contexts that are more **individualistic** (self-reliance and personal independence are stressed) (e.g. Germany, the United States), people tend to perceive conflict (e.g. the open discussion of conflicting views) as potentially positive. Instead of shying away from conflict situations, individualists maintain that it is best to approach conflict directly (e.g. analyse the situation and take steps to find a solution). Persons who employ this style believe that it is better to show emotion during disagreement than to hide or suppress feelings. For these individuals, this outward display signals one's concern and commitment to resolving the conflict. Through enculturation, people in individualistic cultures have developed the belief that working through conflicts constructively can defuse more serious conflict situations and bring about stronger, healthier and more mutually satisfying relationships (Orbe & Everett 2006; Ting-Toomey 2012; Ting-Toomey & Takai 2006).

Gender also impacts on how conflict is defined and resolved. Although a direct approach to conflict resolution may be prevalent in some contexts, the type of conflict, the relationship of the disputants and individual preferences may lead to subtle differences in the way conflict situations unfold.

When individuals or groups from different cultural backgrounds engage in conflict, they may have differing ideas about how disputes should be handled. As noted by Ting-Toomey and Oetzel (2001: 1), 'How we define the conflict problem, how we "punctuate" the differing triggering event that leads to the conflict problem, and how we view the goals for satisfactory conflict resolution are all likely to vary across cultures, situations, and individuals'. It is not difficult to imagine how misunderstandings and conflict situations can escalate when people have conflicting ideas about how their differences should be handled.

INTERCULTURAL CONFLICT STYLES

During the process of socialization within one's cultural or ethnic group, we learn particular ways to handle conflict situations. From our elders, we learn when it is appropriate to display emotions and when it is not. We also learn subtle nuances that lead to variations in how we act and respond in a variety of conflict situations in different domains (e.g. family, workplace, etc.). Some researchers (e.g. Filley 1975; Moberg 2001) maintain that we gradually develop a particular orientation toward conflict. **Conflict interaction style** refers to 'patterned responses to conflict in a variety of dissenting conflict situations' (Ting-Toomey & Oetzel 2001: 45).

A number of taxonomies have been developed to conceptualize conflict styles. For example, Blake and Mouton (1964) and Hall (1969) identified five types of conflict behaviour: a competing style (strategies are used to reach one's own goals at the cost of the other party's goals or feelings), an accommodating style (one's own goals are sacrificed for the sake of the other person/the relationship), an avoiding style (behaviours that either ignore or refuse to engage in the conflict), a collaborating style (parties work together cooperatively until a mutually agreeable solution is found) and a compromising style (there is a give and take of resources with no one achieving his or her original goal).

Rahim (1983) categorized and measured the following conflict styles based on the individual's concern for self or other: dominating style (high self/low other concern), obliging style (low self/high other concern), avoiding style (low self/other concern), integrating style (high self/other concern) and compromising style (moderate self/other concern). Rubin et al. (1994) view conflict styles in terms of withdrawing, yielding, problem solving or inaction. More recently, Wilmot and Hocker (2010) identified the following five conflict styles: avoidance (lose-lose), accommodation (lose-win), competition (win-lose), passive aggression (indirect aggression or opposition), direct aggression (confrontation), compromise (negotiated lose-lose) and collaboration (win-win).

In Western contexts, these typologies (or variations of them) are widely used by interpersonal and organizational communication specialists to help them make sense of differences in **conflict management** (the process by which individuals or groups try to find a satisfying outcome in conflict situations). To measure the conflict styles that feature in these taxonomies, a number of survey instruments have been developed (e.g. Hall's (1969) conflict management survey, Rahim's (1983) organizational communication conflict instrument).

Most conceptualizations of conflict styles have been shaped within Western, individualistic cultural contexts and questions have been raised about their applicability in other settings, especially in collectivist cultural contexts such as those in Asia (Kozan 1997; Hammer 2004, 2005; Kim & Leung 2000; Ting-Toomey et al. 2000). Since the underlying conceptual frameworks of most of these taxonomies are not grounded in culturally-based patterns of difference,

Hammer (2004, 2005) argues that they are not useful to identify and compare intercultural conflict styles.

With the limitations of previous taxonomies in view, Hammer (2004, 2005) devised the **intercultural conflict style model** that is presented in Figure 10.1. This model is based on two core dimensions that he maintains are influenced by cultural values and beliefs: (1) the degree of directness when dealing with conflicts (**direct conflict styles** vs. **indirect conflict styles)** and (2) divergent ways of coping with the affective dimension of conflict interaction (**emotional expressive styles** vs. **emotionally restrained styles**). These responses are linked to individualism–collectivism and high-/low-context communication patterns, which were discussed in Chapter 4.

As Figure 10.1 illustrates, Hammer's (2004, 2005) model identifies four basic, conflict resolution styles that can be found in different cultural groups: discussion (direct and emotionally restrained), engagement (direct and emotionally expressive), accommodation (indirect and emotionally restrained) and dynamic (indirect and emotionally expressive). Let's take a brief look at each.

The **discussion style** emphasizes a verbally direct approach to conflict situations that is tempered by an emotionally restrained response. People who adopt this style generally follow the maxim, 'say what you mean and mean what you say'. They pay careful attention to their word choice so that their views are clearly conveyed. Intense expressions of emotion are avoided; instead, people prefer to calmly discuss disagreements in a conversational, informal style, drawing on facts whenever possible rather than personal feelings. The discussion style is widely used by European-Americans, Australians and other people from individualistic nations.

The **engagement style** is characterized by a more verbally direct and confrontational or direct approach to dealing with conflict. The display of intense verbal and nonverbal expressions of emotion is considered an acceptable way to demonstrate one's sincerity, concern and willingness to work hard to resolve conflict. Some studies have linked this style to African Americans, Southern Europeans and some Russians (Martin & Nakayama 2011).

The **accommodation style** emphasizes a more indirect and emotionally restrained approach to dealing with conflict. To prevent a dispute from escalating, people who use this style employ ambiguous language, silence and avoidance. **Emotional restraint** (controlling the expression of one's emotions) is regarded as essential to maintain interpersonal harmony among the parties. Intermediaries (e.g. mutual friends, colleagues) or mediators may also be

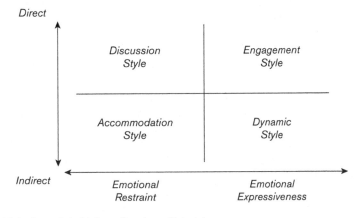

Figure 10.1 A model of intercultural conflict style

used to manage conflict. **Mediation** refers to the settlement or negotiation of a conflict or dispute by an independent person. **Negotiation** is a process by which the parties or group resolve a dispute by holding discussions and coming to an agreement that is mutually acceptable. **Mediators** or **intermediaries** are third parties that may facilitate negotiations and dialogue between the disputants. The accommodating style is often used by Latinos, American Indians and Asians.

The **dynamic style** involves the use of indirect strategies and emotionally intense expression to deal with substantive disagreements. **Emotional expression** refers to observable verbal and nonverbal actions that convey emotions. People who adopt the dynamic style may use linguistic devices such as hyperbole and metaphors. They may also repeat their message, use ambiguous language, tell stories or use third party intermediaries to try to resolve conflicts. Thus, this style is characterized by emotionally confrontational discourse and expression. Hammer (2005) asserts that the credibility of each party is linked to the degree of emotional expressiveness. The dynamic style may be used by Arabs in conflict situations.

For Hammer, 'the ability to recognize and respond appropriately to cultural differences in conflict style is critically important in effectively managing and resolving disagreements and conflict' (Intercultural Conflict Style, ICS n.d.). To facilitate this, he devised the Intercultural Conflict Style Inventory, a tool that is now widely used to measure preference for the cross-cultural conflict styles that feature in his model. As well as learning about their own conflict style, respondents are provided with information about the strengths and weaknesses of the other cross-cultural approaches to dealing with conflict. Hammer (2004, 2005) maintains that heightened awareness of culturally-based styles can help resolve intercultural conflict.

While some cross-cultural studies indicate that people in different cultures tend to display consistent styles across a variety of conflict situations, it is important to recognize that individual-level factors also influence actions and behaviours. Cai and Fink (2002), Gudykunst and Kim (2003), Oetzel (1998) and many other interculturalists caution us to be wary about making generalizations about cultures and conflict styles. Cultures are complex and dynamic. As conditions change, individuals and speech communities adapt their language use, nonverbal behaviours, communication strategies and conflict styles. People may vary their responses to disagreements and conflicts depending on the setting and situation (e.g. the language being used, the status and power of the disputant, the degree of familiarity with the parties involved, the level of formality, etc.). We must keep in mind that taxonomies can lead to errors and stereotyping if not verified by experience (LeBaron 2003). Folger *et al.* (2013: 133) conclude that 'while culture is likely to affect the choice of conflict style, there is no simplistic, cut-and-dried formula, It is just one of many factors that should be taken into account'.

FACEWORK AND INTERCULTURAL CONFLICT RESOLUTION

Concerned about an overreliance on Western notions of conflict and conflict interaction styles, Ting-Toomey (2005, 2012) developed the **conflict face negotiation theory**, which addresses the ways face-losing and face-saving behaviours influence intercultural conflict situations. In particular, her theory helps explain why individuals from high-context cultures (e.g. collectivist, Asian settings) tend to manage conflict differently from people who have been socialized in low-context cultures (e.g. individualistic, Western contexts). As you will see, in this framework, identity is positioned as a major factor in intercultural conflict episodes.

As noted earlier in this chapter, face is present in every culture on our planet although the ways individuals or groups interpret the meaning of face and enact facework varies. Within the context of the conflict face negotiation theory, **face** refers to a 'claimed sense of desired social self-image in a relational or international setting' (Ting-Toomey 2012: 285).

> Face is tied to the emotional significance and estimated calculations that we attach to our own social self-worth and the social self-worth of others. It is therefore a precious identity resource in communication because it can be threatened, enhanced, and undermined, and bargained over.
>
> (Ting-Toomey 2005: 73)

Ting-Toomey's theory identifies several types of face. **Self-face** refers to the 'protective concern for one's own image when one's own face is threatened in the conflict situation' (Ting-Toomey & Takai 2006: 701). **Other-face** is 'the concern or consideration for the other conflict party's image in the conflict situation' (ibid, p. 701). **Mutual-face** refers to 'the concern for both parties' images and/or the "image" of the relationship (ibid, p. 701). **Mutual facework** is the process of constructing a shared sense of identity (Ting-Toomey & Kurogi 1998). Communicating respect and a positive regard for self and others is referred to as **face management**, while facework refers to 'the specific verbal and nonverbal behaviors that we engage in to maintain or restore face loss and to uphold and honor face gain' (Ting-Toomey & Takai 2006: 701). Cultural, relational and situational factors impact on the facework strategies that are used in conflict situations.

The conflict face negotiation theory is based on the following assumptions: (a) people in all cultures try to maintain and negotiate face in communicative events; (b) the concept of face is especially problematic in emotionally threatening or identity-vulnerable situations when the situated identities of the communicators are challenged; (c) the cultural value scales of individualism–collectivism (Ting-Toomey 2010a; Triandis 2002) and small-large power distance (Hofstede 2001; House *et al.* 2004) shape facework concerns and styles; (d) the value patterns inherent in individualism and collectivism shape members' preferences for self-oriented facework or other-oriented facework; (e) small and large power distance value patterns shape members' preferences for **horizontal-based facework** (informal–symmetrical strategies/equal treatment) versus **vertical-based facework** (formal–asymmetrical strategies/deferential treatment); (f) the value dimensions coupled with individual, relational and situational factors, influence the use of specific facework behaviours in particular cultural scenes; and (g) **intercultural facework competence** is 'the optimal integration of knowledge, mindfulness, and communication skills in managing vulnerable identity-based conflict situations appropriately, effectively, and adaptively' (Ting-Toomey & Takai 2006: 702).

Intercultural conflict involves behaviours that can be both **face-threatening** (actions that cause someone to be humiliated) and **face-saving** or **face-giving** (actions that protect or support an individual's self-image or reputation). **Face maintenance** refers to 'the desire to project an image of strength and capability, or conversely, to avoid projecting an image of incapability, weakness, or foolishness' (Ting-Toomey 1990: 80). In an antagonistic conflict situation, individuals or groups may experience **face loss** when they are not treated in a way that respects their preferred self-identities (e.g. position, status, self-image). A face-threatening act involves a stressful episode in which one's identity is challenged or ignored. The conflict face negotiation theory posits that repeated face loss and face threat frequently result in an escalation in the conflict situation or a breakdown in negotiations.

In an intercultural conflict situation, individuals may have very different ideas about what language and communication styles are appropriate. **Face threats** (challenges to an individual's self-image) may intentionally or unintentionally occur due to **sociopragmatic expectancy**

violations (e.g. nonverbal acts or language usage that is perceived to be inappropriate in relation to one's self-ascribed status or role identity) (Spencer-Oatey 2008b; Thomas 1995). People from different linguistic and cultural backgrounds may not share the same understandings about what discourse and nonverbal behaviours are appropriate in a particular setting or situation, and misunderstandings can easily become conflict situations (Arundale 2006; Culpeper *et al.* 2003; Ting-Toomey 2009, 2012). In a discourse community, individuals become familiar with specific face-related conflict behaviours and may be unsure how to respond when second language speakers do not speak or behave in the ways they expect (Arundale 2006; Spencer-Oatey 2005, 2008b). In intercultural interactions, individuals or groups may be surprised and even shocked when they are exposed to unfamiliar facework and **conflict management styles** (preferred ways of dealing with conflict situations) (e.g. animated displays of emotion, swearing).

Spencer-Oatey (2000, 2008b) observes that people from different linguistic and cultural backgrounds may adopt different strategies to manage face and maintain **rapport** (mutual empathy and understanding) in interpersonal interactions and conflict situations: a **rapport-enhancement orientation** (a desire to strengthen or enhance harmonious relations between interlocutors), a **rapport maintenance orientation** (a desire to maintain or protect harmonious relations), a **rapport-neglect orientation** (a lack of concern for the quality of interpersonal relations perhaps because of a focus on the self) and a **rapport-challenge orientation** (a desire to challenge or impair harmonious relations between the interlocutors).

When a second language is involved in the conflict situation, various linguistic elements and paralanguage (e.g. the tone of voice, word choice) can result in a mismatch between **facework styles** (pattern of behaviours designed to manage face). Disparate conflict goals, assumptions and **facework strategies** (steps taken to manage face) can further complicate the situation. Whether intended or not, both linguistic and non-linguistic elements can hamper rapport between the interlocutors, derail the conflict management process and lead to an escalation in the intercultural conflict.

INTERCULTURAL CONFLICT COMPETENCE

To prevent miscommunication and misattributions from continuously spiralling into major intercultural conflicts, it is essential to have an understanding of the components of intercultural conflict competence. While Chapter 12 explores the construct of intercultural (communicative) competence more broadly, this section focuses on attributes and characteristics of individuals who skilfully manage intercultural conflict situations.

First, it is important to define what is meant by intercultural conflict competence. As noted in Chapter 1, Ting-Toomey (2012: 279–80) refers to it as 'the mindful management of emotional frustrations and conflict interaction struggles due primarily to cultural, linguistic, or ethnic group membership differences'. This term encompasses the use of effective and appropriate facework strategies in intercultural conflict situations (e.g. conflict facework competence as defined in the conflict face negotiation theory). **Conflict facework competence** entails

> the development of a deep knowledge structure of the cultural-framed social setting, the key conflict parties' socio-cultural and personal identities, the conflict speech event, and the activation of culturally/linguistically appropriate and effective facework negotiation skills in respect to all the situational and multi-layered features.
>
> (Ting-Toomey 2012: 286)

Interculturalists (e.g. LeBaron 2003, LeBaron & Pillay 2006, Ting-Toomey 2004, 2009, 2012) have identified a number of core elements in intercultural conflict competence: culture-sensitive knowledge, mindfulness (mindful awareness, mindful fluency), constructive conflict communication skills (e.g. second language proficiency, sociopragmatic awareness, intercultural and interpersonal conflict management skills) and communication adaptability. Let's look at each in turn.

Culture-sensitive knowledge. Ting-Toomey (2004, 2009, 2012) maintains that culturally-based knowledge is the most vital ingredient in intercultural conflict competence. Without it, individuals may adhere to an ethnocentric stance and judge all unfamiliar conflict behaviours as weird or unsophisticated in comparison with their own (or their ingroup's) ways of dealing with disputes. With more knowledge of diverse ways of handling conflicts (e.g. awareness of the conflict scripts and styles that are prevalent in other cultural settings), individuals can suspend negative valuations and reflect on what may lie behind unfamiliar or unexpected behaviours in misunderstandings and conflict episodes.

With more cultural knowledge, one can learn to reframe one's interpretation of a conflict situation and take into account the other person's cultural frame of reference. At the same time, it is essential to bear in mind that not all individuals from a particular linguistic, cultural or ethnic background behave in the same way. Not all individuals who share a similar linguistic, cultural or ethnic background adopt the same conflict style. As well as recognizing individual factors, it is vital to develop knowledge about the potential impact of a variety of elements that can influence how the conflict situation unfolds (e.g. quality and type of relationship between the disputants, setting) in a particular social, political and historical context.

Mindfulness. To effectively manage intercultural conflicts, one must recognize the potential impact of one's personal and cultural communication expectations, conflict communication style, cognitions and emotional display on the conflict situation. At the same time, it is essential to become attuned to the other conflict party's communication assumptions, cognitions, language use and emotions (LeBaron 2003; LeBaron & Pillay 2006; Ting-Toomey 1999, 2012). **Mindful awareness** requires us to 'reflect on our own cultural ways of knowing and being, noticing how they are continually shaped by memories, experiences, and interpretations' (LeBaron 2003: 12). This process can draw our attention to the ways we frame conflict situations and make choices that ultimately either heighten tension or resolve intercultural conflicts. Recognition of face and identity needs (our own and those of the other person) is essential to resolve tense situations in a sensitive manner. **Mindful fluency** requires us to 'tune into our own cultural, linguistic, and personal habitual assumptions in scanning a problematic interaction scene' (Ting-Toomey 2012: 288). In other words, it is necessary to develop awareness of both self and other in conflict episodes.

We must also be open to learning other **conflict management practices** (ways to resolve disputes) from our communication partners. In order to accommodate intercultural differences, we must learn to see the unfamiliar behaviour from multiple cultural perspectives (Langer 1989, 1997). In other words, it is useful to view intercultural conflict episodes from an ethnorelative orientation rather than a narrow, ethnocentric lens. For example, if a second language speaker is using indirect responses or silence in a conflict situation, instead of rushing to a negative valuation, a **mindful communicator** may consider her emotional and cognitive reaction and reflect on why the individual may be responding in this way. The sensitive intercultural communicator may then consider modifying her approach to enact facework-sensitive behaviours.

Constructive conflict communication skills. Language is a core element in intercultural conflict situations and if disagreements and disputes are to be resolved in a manner that is mutually satisfactory, interactants need well developed interpersonal communication skills and, in many cases, proficiency in a second language. **Constructive communication skills** refer to 'our operational abilities to manage a conflict situation appropriately and effectively via skillful language, verbal, and nonverbal behaviors, whether in a first or second language' (Ting-Toomey 2012: 288). In particular, skills such as deep listening, de-centring, face-sensitive respectful dialogue skills, mindful reframing, comprehension checks and collaborative conflict negotiation skills are essential for intercultural mediators, especially when a second language is involved (Barge 2006; Coleman & Raider 2006; Ting-Toomey 2004, 2012).

Communication adaptability. Finally, in intercultural conflict episodes we must be flexible and willing to modify our interaction behaviours and goals to meet the specific needs of the situation. Our cognitive, affective and behavioural adjustments should help facilitate the resolution of intercultural conflict situations (Rogan & Hammer 2006; Ting-Toomey 2009, 2012). For example, **dynamic conflict code-switching** (e.g. adapting our conflict style to meet the other conflict party's communication approach, using their first language) can signal our respect and desire to preserve the relationship and resolve the conflict in an amicable way. (This notion is similar to the act of convergence that is associated with the CAT, the communication accommodation theory that was introduced in Chapter 4.)

Individuals who develop the skills and attributes of intercultural conflict competence are in a much stronger and healthier position to deal with difficulties that arise when communicating with people who have been socialized in a different linguistic and cultural environment.

MANAGING LANGUAGE AND INTERCULTURAL CONFLICT SITUATIONS

> The ability to thrive in a multicultural world is now central to our survival; it is a basic life-skill on our shrinking planet. In every land, people from around the world pass through, communicating, coupling, trading, and sometimes fighting. They make things together, share strategies and resources, draw on commonalities to build bridges, and come into conflict over differences . . . The need to summon creativity and exercise the choice to cooperate has never been more urgent.
>
> (LeBaron & Pillay 2006: 12)

While conflict is part of every culture and is unavoidable in human life, there are steps we can take to enhance our intercultural conflict competence and prevent intercultural disagreements from escalating into destructive conflicts.

- In a conflict situation, be aware of your own goals and those of others. Look for common grounds or overlapping between your aims and those of the other person.
- Bear in mind that the way conflict is expressed, perceived, and dealt with varies among cultures. In intercultural interactions, your communication partner may not view the situation as you do and may try to manage the conflict in ways that are unfamiliar or uncomfortable for you. Make an effort to understand the situation from the other person's perspective and refrain from dismissing a different conflict style as simplistic and unworkable.
- Stay centred and push yourself to go beyond traditional stereotypes and dualistic ('us' vs.

'them') thinking, whereby 'us' is superior. While approaches to conflict vary across cultures, remember that not everyone who is affiliated with a particular cultural or ethnic group follows the styles identified in the taxonomies that have been discussed in this chapter. For example, don't automatically assume that your Japanese groupmate will be non-expressive and accommodating, or that your German friends will adopt an expressive, confrontational style in conflict situations. Observe and learn from experience.

- Listen attentively before responding. Conflicts can escalate when we do not listen to each other. Even if you feel that you are becoming emotional, try to be patient and attend to what others are saying. In second language situations be sensitive to the possibility that you are misunderstanding what is being said. It is also conceivable that you are not conveying your ideas or feelings in a way that is being understood as you would like. Lack of fluency in the language being used may serve as a barrier in conflict situations. Patience, careful listening and explicit comprehension checks (e.g. asking questions to be sure one's message is clear) are essential in intercultural interactions, especially when a second language is involved. In a conflict situation, plan your message with care, especially when either you or your communication partner is using a second language.

- When misunderstandings and conflict arise, try to understand both sides of an issue and be open to differing perspectives. Together, you and the other communicators may synthesize your ideas and come up with a creative third perspective or resolution that is mutually acceptable.

- If you are accustomed to verbally and nonverbally conveying your emotions, recognize that this may have negative consequences when the other person is used to a more indirect style of communication. Be careful of your word choice and monitor your nonverbal behaviours. Avoid actions that may appear threatening such as standing very close to the other person. While it is normal to become angry in some conflict situations, it is essential to move past the hostility and refrain from seeking retribution. Carefully observe the nonverbal behaviours of other people involved in your disagreement. Monitor and adapt your nonverbal behaviours in conflict situations.

- Be sensitive to face and identity needs (your own and those of the other party). In particular, make use of positive facework strategies and demonstrate respect for the other person's identities and position within a particular sociocultural context.

- Avoid personal attacks, offensive or abusive language, profanity, name calling and emotional overstatements in conflict situations. Disagreements may escalate if degrading or disrespectful comments are made about an individual's culture, language (e.g. accent, dialect), ethnicity, religion or background. Also, remember that ignoring the discriminatory or racist behaviour of others gives permission for these offences to continue.

- Even in difficult situations, try to retain your sense of humour and be willing to let go of your hostility and feelings of revenge. Lessen your defensiveness in conflict situations. Be willing to admit mistakes, learn from them, and apply what you have learned in future intercultural interactions.

- Be sensitive to the power dimension in all conflict situations. **Interpersonal power** refers to 'the ability to influence another in the direction we desire—to get another person to do what we want' (Beebe *et al.* 2010: 218). In conflict situations, some individuals may have more power or control. For example, if you are using your first language with a non-native speaker who is not fully proficient in the language, remember that you are apt to be in a stronger position to convey your ideas in a persuasive manner.

- Check your perceptions of an intercultural conflict with trusted friends or colleagues who are familiar with the linguistic and cultural background of the other party in the dispute.

Intermediaries may be able to suggest more effective and appropriate ways to diffuse the situation. In particular, their feedback may help you to understand what lies behind unfamiliar actions. They may also suggest ways to adapt your verbal and nonverbal communication style to resolve the conflict in mutually acceptable ways.

■ Recognize that people have different conflict styles, which often have cultural origins as well as personal characteristics. Failure to recognize and respect individual and cultural differences can lead to negative evaluations of persons and an escalation of the dispute.

■ Generate possible solutions to the conflict instead of focusing on the difficulties. Be proactive. Work with your communication partner to try to negotiate a solution that is mutually acceptable.

■ Identify your preferred conflict management style, especially if it differs from that of the other disputants. (You could use one of the taxonomies discussed in this chapter.) What language and communication style do you use in conflict situations? What nonverbal behaviours do you use to complement or substitute your verbal message? Even though we may modify our conflict strategies depending on the situation and the type of conflict, we are apt to rely on a similar style in most situations. When we interact with others, we may find that some conflict situations are more challenging than others since our preferred conflict style may not be compatible with the other person. As well as becoming more self-aware, be attentive to the behaviours and reactions of your communication partners. How do people respond to your verbal and nonverbal actions in a conflict situation?

■ Be creative and expand your repertoire of conflict management strategies. If a particular way of dealing with conflict is not working, be willing to experiment with a different style. For example, if you are used to using very direct discourse to get your point across, and this is negatively impacting on your interactions with a Taiwanese friend, try to use more indirect expressions and a less expressive approach. Adaptability and flexibility are central in the enhancement of intercultural relations including conflict situations.

■ Recognize the importance of context in conflict situations. Conflict styles within a multicultural family context are apt to have different dimensions and consequences in workplace environments or public settings.

■ Finally, recognize that disputes do not need to end a relationship. Instead of isolating yourself from or fighting with the other party, try to start a dialogue to resolve your differences. If necessary, wait until tempers have cooled. Dialogue should be sincere, respectful and not rushed. Be attentive and open to different ways of seeing the conflict. Dialogue can help you to reach a deeper understanding of diversity conflict experiences.

SUMMARY

It is essential that we enhance our understanding of conflict and its terrain so that we can navigate the physical, psychological, and spiritual chasms that threaten to swallow us, creative potential and all. Enhancing our understanding of conflict necessarily means building awareness of ourselves—the common sense we share in cultural groups—and coming to know something of those who are different from us by culture and worldview.

(LeBaron & Pillay 2006: 12)

Conflict between individuals and groups is a natural feature of the human condition. When we interact and form bonds with other individuals, groups or entities (e.g. organizations, nations), disagreements inevitably arise from time to time. Doreen Thompson, a freelance journalist, observes that 'Peace is not the absence of conflict but the presence of creative alternatives for responding to conflict'. How we perceive and manage conflict defines the quality of our interpersonal, intercultural and international relationships. Our ability (or inability) to resolve conflicts can lead to either their enhancement or demise. Whether the conflict is at the individual level, or on the national or world stage, all of us must heed LeBaron and Pillay's advice and develop the knowledge, skills and mindset that facilitate the resolution of disputes. As our world is becoming more interdependent, intercultural conflict competence is essential for all members of the human race.

This chapter began by defining conflict and describing characteristics of conflict situations. After identifying particular domains of conflict, we reviewed numerous types as well as sub-categories of intercultural conflict (e.g. interethnic, interreligious, intergenerational). We also looked at variations in the way conflict is viewed and managed. After reviewing dimensions of intercultural conflict styles and various conflict taxonomies, we turned our attention to the role of face and facework in conflict resolution. The remainder of the chapter focused on intercultural conflict competence and constructive, practical ways to manage language and intercultural conflict situations.

discussion questions

1 As the world becomes more interconnected and each nation more multicultural, why do we continue to witness intercultural conflicts across the world? Is conflict innate to human nature? Are conflicts a natural consequence of the process of globalization?
2 What are the main sources of intercultural conflicts at the individual level? At the regional or national level? At the international level?
3 Why is it important to understand the context in which intercultural conflict occurs?
4 Identify four types of intercultural conflict and provide examples of each.
5 How might power differentials come into play in intercultural conflicts that involve a second language? Provide examples to illustrate your points.
6 Describe the following intercultural conflict styles: discussion, engagement, accommodation and dynamic. Provide examples of each.
7 In small groups discuss your personal conflict style. What style do you use most often? Did your family, friends, educational, religious and political institutions influence this style? How does it affect your relationships with others? Discuss whether a different approach might lead to different outcomes.
8 Explain how face-concerns can influence the ways we manage conflict in intercultural situations. Provide examples.
9 Recall a conflict that you have experienced. Did your linguistic and cultural background affect how you handled the situation? If yes, how?
10 What types of intercultural conflicts occur on your campus or in your community? What groups have frequent disputes? How do groups manage and address these conflicts?
11 In this chapter a number of suggestions have been offered to help manage language and intercultural conflict situations. Which ideas do you think are the most useful? In small groups discuss other constructive ways to resolve intercultural conflicts, especially those that involve a second language.

further reading

Abigail, R.A. and Cahn, D.D. (2011) *Managing Conflict through Communication,* 4th edn, Boston: Allyn and Bacon.

This text introduces the study of conflict and covers such topics as anger management and facework in relation to interpersonal conflict, group conflict, organizational conflict and social conflict.

Cupach, W.R., Canary, D.J. and Spitzberg, B.H. (2009) *Competence in Interpersonal Conflict,* 2nd edn, Long Grove, IL: Waveland Press, Inc.

This text presents a conceptual framework to explain why communication competence is central to conflict management. The authors offer constructive guidelines that provide a basis for dealing with conflicts in five settings: intercultural, organizational, familial, mediation and violence in intimate relationships.

Domenici, K. and Littlejohn, S.W. (2006) *Facework: Bridging Theory and Practice,* Thousand Oaks, CA: Sage.

In this book, identities facework is presented as central to intercultural communication, including the management of conflict situations.

Folger, J.P., Poole, M.S. and Stutman, R.K. (2013) *Working through Conflict: Strategies for Relationships, Groups and Organizations,* 7th edn, Boston: Pearson.

This accessible text provides an introduction to conflict and conflict management that is grounded in theory, research and practice. It includes a chapter on face-saving.

LeBaron, M. (2003) *Bridging Cultural Conflicts: A New Approach for a Changing World,* San Francisco, CA: Jossey-Bass.

Mindful awareness, cultural fluency and conflict fluency are introduced as tools for grappling with intercultural conflict in a wide range of interpersonal, community, organizational and political contexts. LeBaron draws on Western and Eastern approaches to conflict resolution.

LeBaron, M. and Pillay, V. (2006) *Conflict Across Cultures: A Unique Experience of Bridging Differences,* Boston: Nicholas Brealey Publishing.

Drawing on examples from a variety of cultures, this text illustrates techniques to resolve conflicts that stem from cultural difference. The authors describe and identify the processes, tools and skills that facilitate successful conflict resolution.

Oetzel, J.G. and Ting-Toomey, S. (eds) (2006) *The SAGE Handbook of Conflict Communication: Integrating Theory, Research, and Practice,* Thousand Oaks, CA: Sage.

This comprehensive handbook synthesizes key theories, research and practice in conflict communication in a variety of contexts (e.g. conflicts in relationships and families, conflict at work, conflict in communities, conflict in international and intercultural situations).

Ting-Toomey, S. and Oetzel, J.G. (2001) *Managing Intercultural Conflict Effectively*, Thousand Oaks, CA: Sage.

Integrating intercultural research and theory, the authors present a practical framework for understanding intercultural conflict in various settings (e.g. within the family, within business organizations, within small groups). Suggestions are offered to deal with conflict more effectively.

CHAPTER 11

Language and intercultural communication in the global workplace

... the increasing expansion of business activities into the international market and international recruitment have made linguistic and cultural diversity common attributes of a majority of workplaces in the world today, where most of the daily interaction among people inevitably involves intercultural communication.

(Sharifian & Jamarani 2013: 13)

The extensive use of English as the primary business language is fortunate for English-speaking citizens; however, recognize that for most people in the world English is a second language.

(Krizan *et al.* 2011: 50)

As commerce continues to become more globalized and many countries become more linguistically diverse, the demand for multilingual communicators continues to grow as well. The ability to communicate in more than one language can make you a more competitive job candidate and open up a wider variety of career opportunities.

(Thill & Bovée 2013: 79)

learning objectives

By the end of this chapter, you should be able to:

1 discuss the impact of globalization on today's workforce
2 describe the role of English in the global workforce
3 define diversity and identify the benefits of diversity for the global workplace
4 discuss the role of language, culture and power in the global workplace
5 identify challenges to diversity in the global workplace
6 explain the key elements in five cultural difference frameworks employed by social scientists to explain intercultural communication in the workplace
7 discuss the impact of the cultural difference frameworks on intercultural business education and diversity training
8 identify the limitations and dangers of the cultural difference frameworks
9 explain interpretive, experiential and critical approaches to understanding language and intercultural interactions in the global workplace
10 identify constructive ways to enhance language and intercultural communication in the global workplace.

INTRODUCTION

Today's interconnected world economy has had a profound impact on the global workplace. Large corporations and even small businesses have become increasingly multicultural and multilingual. Migration and global workforce mobility are resulting in more intercultural contact as temporary workers and long-term expatriates intermingle with locals, including immigrants from many parts of the world. In organizations, it is now common for people to work together in teams or on projects with individuals who have a different linguistic, religious and cultural background or disability.

This chapter begins by exploring the impact of globalization on the workplace and the role of international English as the de facto language or lingua franca of global business. Next, we discuss the benefits of diversity in the global workforce and identify potential barriers to successful intercultural communication and integration in global organizations and work environments. We then review and critique five cultural difference frameworks that have been widely applied to business and management contexts. Attention then shifts to alternative, less essentialist approaches to understanding intercultural interactions in the global workplace. These new understandings have implications for the preparation and support of current and future global workers (leaders and employees) in diverse organizations. Finally, the chapter concludes with some practical suggestions to enhance intercultural communication in the diverse, multilingual workplace.

GLOBALIZATION AND DIVERSITY IN THE WORKPLACE

> In a global environment characterised by complexity and ambiguity, one certainty about the future of organisations is that they are becoming increasingly multicultural and people will need to know more about culture and cultural differences to be effective in their everyday working lives ... The social context in which we live makes the understanding of intercultural interaction a prerequisite for those who aspire to successful careers.
>
> (Mughan & O'Shea 2010: 109)

Globalization is not new; the exchange of ideas, goods and people has long been a part of human history. As noted in Chapter 1, what is different today is the significant increase in the speed and volume of this contact due, in part, to advances in information and communication technologies as well as modes of transportation. The modern world is experiencing much greater cultural, economic, political and social interconnectedness (Eitzen & Zenn 2011; Held *et al.* 1999; Sharifian & Jamarani 2013). Nowadays, communication and organizational operations increasingly cross national boundaries and involve global business operations. The term **multinational business** signifies 'operations targeted toward and conducted in two or more countries', whereas **global business** is 'a broader term meaning operations and strategies to serve a world market' (Krizan *et al.* 2011: 37).

One of the consequences of globalization is increasing diversity in the workplace, which is profoundly changing the nature of organizations (Barak 2010; Goodall *et al.* 2010; Guirdham 2011; Varner & Beamer 2011). **Diversity** encompasses differences among humans in terms of culture, language, race, ethnicity, gender, socioeconomic status, age, physical abilities, religious beliefs, political beliefs or other ideologies. Diversity can also apply to national origin, physical attributes, sexual orientation and regional differences. **Surface-level diversity** refers to 'differences that are easily seen and generally verifiable via a quick assessment of physical characteristics, including gender, age, race, and national origin/ethnicity' (Baldwin *et al.* 2013: 471), whereas **deep-level diversity** relates to differences that lie below the surface and are not so easily observable such as attitudes, beliefs, knowledge, skills and values or worldviews. Later in the chapter, we take a closer look at the benefits and challenges posed by increasing diversity in the global workplace. Before we do, let's turn our attention to the linguistic dimension of intercultural business interactions and consider the impact of the dominance of English in the global workplace.

ENGLISHIZATION, IDENTITY AND THE GLOBAL WORKFORCE

Partly as a consequence of globalization, the dominance of **global English** in business and other sectors has strengthened significantly in recent decades: 'English is not only a language of wider communication in the modern world, it is far more than that – it is, in a singularly powerful sense, *the* "global language" of commerce, trade, culture, and research in the contemporary world' (Reagan & Schreffler, 2005: 116). With the emergence of the 'knowledge society' or 'knowledge economy', English has become the lingua franca for business negotiations, multinational organizations, scientific communication, diplomacy, academic conferences and international education in many nations on all continents (Jenkins 2013; Mackenzie 2013). In many transnational corporations and outsourcing jobs, English is now a requirement for employment (McKay & Bokhorst-Heng 2008; Seargeant 2013). In transforming English language learning and use into commodities for a global marketplace, the linguistic and cultural capital or value of English (Bourdieu, 1986, 1991) has increased markedly in the last 20 years.

The response to the spread of English in the global workforce varies. In some regions, the language is considered a homogenizing, Western vehicle of **power** (authority or strength), domination and privilege and is met with resistance and suspicion. The rise of English as the primary language of global business can have negative consequences for individuals and groups who do not have access to quality education in the language. As noted by Krizan *et al.* (2011: 50), '[t]he extensive use of English as the primary business language is fortunate for English-speaking citizens; however, recognize that for most people in the world English is a second language'. Accordingly, critics of globalization warn that lack of proficiency in English and the skills prized by today's knowledge industries (e.g. advanced technological skills) can disadvantage individuals and organizations by denying them access to resources and global markets (e.g. lucrative contracts, intercultural/international contracts). This can lead to a **power imbalance**, that is, an unequal distribution of influence and control with certain individuals, groups or nations dominating others. This imbalance perpetuates economic disparity, privileging Western citizens, nations, and corporations (McKay & Bokhorst-Heng 2008; Sorrells 2012, 2013).

In today's global marketplace, business professionals who speak English as an additional language routinely communicate in the language with professionals who have another first language. In these situations, they may speak a localized variety of English rather than a 'native-speaker, standard' form of the language (e.g. Received Pronunciation). This phenomenon is prevalent in business interactions in a growing number of postcolonial contexts (e.g. Singapore, Ghana, Hong Kong, Indonesia, Liberia).

The spread of English or **Englishization** in organizations and businesses in many parts of the world has also brought about an increase in both code-switching and code-mixing among bilingual or emerging bilingual employees (Coulmas 2005; Myers-Scotton 2006). Globally,

English has become the most widely-used language in both code-mixing and code-switching styles of communication.

Kachru (2005), for example, observes that many South Asian professionals routinely mix English with their mother tongue in oral and written discourse in both business and social contexts. This practice has been attributed to a number of motives (e.g. sociolinguistic, psycholinguistic, situational, instrumental, identity):

> It is not necessarily for lack of competency that speakers switch from one language to another, and the choices they make are not fortuitous. Rather, just like socially motivated choices of varieties of one language, choices across language boundaries are imbued with social meaning.
>
> (Coulmas 2005: 109)

Kachru (2005: 114) agrees, adding that, 'the social value attached to the knowledge of English' in many situations, including intercultural business interactions, may be even more important than instrumental motives.

When English serves as 'an indicator of status, modernization, mobility and "outward-looking" attitude', South Asians and business professionals in many other parts of the world may seek to enhance their social positioning and work status by incorporating it into their discourse (Kachru 2005: 114). Code-mixing then functions as 'an index of social identity' (Myers-Scotton 2006: 406) and workplace prestige (McKay & Bokhorst-Heng 2008). In Nigeria and Sri Lanka, for example, the desire for an elevated social status can motivate educated elites (e.g. business executives, team leaders) to use a mixture of English and the vernacular in social and workplace contexts. Trudgill (2003: 23) explains that code-mixing may serve as a strategy to project a **dual identity**: 'that of a modern, sophisticated, educated person *and* that of a loyal, local patriot'. Language usage in the bilingual or multilingual workplace can be more complicated than it first appears.

As noted in Chapter 6, it is important to remember that there is a close connection between language, culture and identity. The choice of the language and variety one uses (e.g. regional dialect, accent, code-mixing) can impact on one's status and positioning within organizations. Both linguistic and social restrictions influence code choices and attitudes in the bilingual or multilingual workplace (Coulmas 2005; Myers-Scotton 2006; Seargeant 2013). In some contexts or situations, for instance, employees who are non-native speakers of English may switch less frequently to English or even shun code-mixing completely to maintain ingroup ties (e.g. fit in with their work team). Cliques may also form among speakers who use a particular variety of the language. (This issue is explored further when we discuss challenges in the diverse workplace.) Second language speakers may also use particular codes to 'renegotiate and perhaps resist the established identities, group loyalties, and power relations' (Canagarajah 1999: 73). The relationship between code choice, identity and culture in the global workplace as well as in the wider society is dynamic, complex and context-dependent and power-laden.

THE BENEFITS OF DIVERSITY IN THE WORKPLACE

> Differences in everything from age and gender to religion and ethnic heritage to geography and military experience enrich the workplace. Both immigration and workplace diversity create advantages — and challenges — for business communicators throughout the world.
>
> (Thill & Bovée 2013: 69)

In today's globalized world, an organization's success increasingly depends on its ability to embrace and manage diversity. A multicultural and multilingual workforce can be beneficial in a number of ways. It can add value to businesses and organizations by helping them to become more adaptable, flexible and productive. Synergy and enhanced creativity can lead to innovations, more effective problem solving and better relations with diverse customers or clients both in their home environment and abroad. Diversity in the workplace can help organizations and businesses to extend into the global marketplace and, ultimately, enhance their reputation and competitive advantage. As well as bolstering organizations, diversity can strengthen the personal growth and intercultural sensitivity of staff, which can then lead to positive intercultural interactions in other life domains. Let's take a look at each potential benefit in more detail.

Increased adaptability and productivity

When managed well, diversity can help organizations become more adaptable to the increasingly complex, dynamic and interconnected world in which we live and work. As well as unique individual characteristics, each employee possesses strengths derived from his or her linguistic, gender and cultural socialization. Co-workers with diverse backgrounds, ages, religions and attributes bring unique experiences, ideas and perceptions to groups and work teams. Pooling their varied skills and knowledge can strengthen the team's productivity and responsiveness to the changes being brought about by globalization. Diverse employees can help companies adapt to demographic changes in their physical location as well as fluctuating markets and customer demands. When handled properly, diversity in the workplace can leverage the strengths and talents of each worker to enhance the adaptability, flexibility, productivity and overall performance of organizations. It can provide them with a competitive advantage.

Companies that embrace diversity in the workplace can inspire all of their employees to perform to their highest ability. Company-wide strategies can be devised and put in place to optimize the potential of all members. Their contributions can also be recognized and rewarded (e.g. individual or group recognition, depending on what is appropriate in that context). When employees from diverse backgrounds feel valued and included in decision making, they are apt to be more invested in the success of the organization. All of these steps can lead to higher levels of satisfaction and, ultimately, more productivity, profit and return on investment.

Synergy and enhanced creativity

Businesses and organizations that employ a diverse workforce can generate a greater variety of solutions to a wide range of issues (e.g. problems in service, sourcing, allocation of resources, labour disputes, expansion in the global marketplace). The sharing of diverse experiences can inspire idea creation and increase innovation. For this to materialize, leaders (e.g. administrators, team leaders, unit managers) must cultivate an open, responsive atmosphere in teams and other workplace domains or activities.

Fluency in more than one language, exposure to different cultures (e.g. international internships or work placements, service learning, study abroad sojourns), experience with physical limitations, previous work situations (e.g. diverse group or teamwork) and intercultural competence must be valued in the modern workplace. With support and encouragement, the sharing of diverse perspectives can generate novel ideas for such aspects as products, customer interaction strategies and advertising methods. In a receptive atmosphere, a variety of perspectives can provide sparks for creativity to flourish and increase the breadth of idea generation.

When employees from different backgrounds are encouraged to express their views in ways that are comfortable for them, they are more likely to contribute. A diverse workforce that is at ease expressing viewpoints that differ from the majority can generate a much larger and more varied pool of innovative proposals. **Cultural synergy** refers to the combined power of different cultural elements (e.g. people from diverse backgrounds) working together to create a greater, stronger effect than if they were separate. In the global workplace, this **collaboration** can be a positive force for creativity and change. Clever, forward-thinking organizations that draw on the ideas of diverse employees to develop business plans and strategies can more effectively meet the needs of diverse customers and clients.

Enhanced relations with diverse customers/clients

With increasing global mobility, a company's current and potential customers or clients are more likely to come from a variety of linguistic and cultural backgrounds. A diverse workforce can strengthen the organization's relations with multicultural and multilingual populations and better meet the needs of specific customer groups (e.g. minorities who are not fluent in the primary language of the community, members of a particular religion). Ideally, the cultural and linguistic diversity of the staff base reflects the community that the organization serves.

Employing staff from diverse backgrounds can increase the overall responsiveness of service and enhance worker–customer relations. Employees that resemble the natural diversity in society can help a company to increase and improve customer relationship connections. Shared visions and understandings can allow employees to reach out to customers in more appropriate and effective ways. When customers feel that their needs and concerns have been properly addressed, they are likely to be more satisfied. Customers who feel heard and understood are more likely to become repeat customers.

If customers or clients can use their first language when interacting with customer service representatives, they are apt to feel more at ease with both the representative and the company. In Brussels, for example, multilingual customer service representatives may interact with French-speaking, Dutch-speaking, German-speaking or English-speaking customers in their first language. As noted by Thill and Bovée (2013) and other business communication specialists, fluency in more than one language can be a great asset in organizations. With the intensification of globalization and migration, one can expect the demand for bilingual or multilingual communicators to grow.

International reach

Diversity in terms of language competency and ethnic affiliations can also benefit a company that has global aspirations or ties. As well as interacting with local minorities, bilingual or multilingual employees can help a business to explore and enter new global markets and cope with the challenges of international partnerships. Administrators and other employees with international experience and well-developed intercultural communication skills can assist a company to provide customers with culturally- and linguistically-appropriate products to customers both locally and abroad.

Globally-minded individuals with intercultural competence, second language skills and business acumen can help an organization to expand its reach and offer culturally- and linguistically-appropriate services to foreign clients. **Business acumen** refers to one's ability to understand business situations and make appropriate decisions in a short amount of time. Skilled, globally-minded employees can help small businesses to better understand the needs of diverse customers, broaden their range or services or products and widen the international scope of their operation.

Enhanced reputation and competitive advantage

Organizations that promote diversity and inclusion are much more likely to be viewed favourably by multicultural customers, local and global business partners and the media. When a business develops a reputation as an open, inclusive workplace, it also has a greater chance of recruiting and retaining talented individuals from diverse backgrounds. Positive, multicultural environments can attract the best and brightest from all backgrounds. With a capable, diverse workforce, companies are then better positioned for success in the competitive marketplace.

Personal growth and intercultural development

As well as enhancing the competitiveness of organizations, workplace diversity has the potential to stimulate personal growth in employees and their leaders. Exposure to new cultures, languages, perspectives (e.g. different worldviews), values and behaviours (e.g. communication styles) can help individuals develop intellectually, psychologically and socially. Through sustained intercultural contact and interactions, employees may begin to see their work and surroundings in a new light. If observant and open to novel ideas and ways of being, over time they can enhance their intercultural awareness and sensitivity. They may also become motivated to learn another language and venture abroad. Their horizons may be broadened as friendships develop with people from diverse backgrounds.

As they become more receptive to diversity, individuals can acquire the habit of considering issues and situations from multiple perspectives instead of relying on a monocultural lens and familiar ways of doing things. Gradually, they may shift from an ethnocentric to an ethnorelative orientation and acquire more effective and appropriate ways to communicate with people (e.g. colleagues, customers) who have a different linguistic and cultural background. They may become more at ease when interacting with people who have disabilities. Interacting with culturally diverse co-workers and customers/clients has the potential to gradually break down the subconscious barriers of ethnocentrism and xenophobia that were discussed in Chapter 7. This can have benefits that extend well beyond the workplace. As well as adding value to organizations, it can help employees to become more responsible citizens and mindful members of society.

THE CHALLENGES OF DIVERSITY IN THE WORKPLACE

no one can be exempted from dealing with issues related to cultural diversity ... Establishing common ground with others and developing the necessary empathy and degree of intercultural awareness, while constantly challenging one's own perspectives, has therefore become almost a daily obligation for all those involved in the work process.

(Guilherme *et al.* 2010: 243)

Although there are many rewards to be gained from workplace diversity, it can also pose challenges for both front-line employees (e.g. blue collar workers) and administrators (e.g. managers, team leaders, supervisors). To reap the benefits of diversity, it is essential for organizations to recognize potential difficulties and know how to deal with them in an effective, ethical manner. Some of the most common challenges of workplace diversity are: a language barrier (power imbalance), translating/interpreting limitations, conflicting communication styles (both verbal and nonverbal), variations in emotional display, a clash in values, conflict (interpersonal, intercultural and organizational), opposition to change, resistance to integration, gender differences, religious differences, sociocultural differences, ethnocentrism and assumptions of similarities, prejudicial attitudes, discrimination and racism. Let's examine each in more detail.

A language barrier

In a diverse workplace, individuals who are not fluent in the primary language of communication are disadvantaged. It can also be very challenging for proficient speakers to explain ideas and procedures to second language workers or colleagues who are not fluent in the primary language. Communication difficulties are compounded when jargon, slang and special codes are used in business contexts. Ineffective communication can result in confusion, frustration, misunderstandings, lack of teamwork, conflict, anger and low morale. In worst case scenarios, it can also result in accidents and injuries in the workplace.

When workers find directions confusing and do not understand what is expected of them, naturally, it is difficult to perform. This can lead to a decrease in productivity and frustration for all involved. For example, if a manager gives instructions about completing a report and the employee cannot fully comprehend what has been said, errors may ensue. Tasks may not be carried out in a satisfactory manner, especially if managers do not use explicit comprehension checks to ensure that the directions have been processed as intended.

Communication problems may also arise among individuals who speak different varieties of the same language. For example, using the same terms and expressions in Britain and Australia may lead to misunderstandings when the meanings differ. In the workplace, it is also essential to bear in mind that language barriers may be misinterpreted as cultural misunderstandings, and vice versa.

When many employees are not fully proficient in the primary language of the workplace, companies may organize language for specific purposes courses that are tailor-made for them. For example, in a second language context, a branch of a global company may arrange English language courses for employees that are directly related to the language needs of their specific jobs (e.g. separate classes for secretarial staff, managers, phone operators, etc.).

Outsourcing, the contracting out of an internal business process to a third party organization, often requires workers to perform tasks in a second language. At call centres in Egypt, India and the Philippines, for example, employees learn English expressions (e.g. colloquialisms) and master accents that can be understood by the international customers they serve (e.g. the North American market).

For diversity to benefit a workplace, language barriers must be overcome in ways that are constructive and culturally sensitive. As well as targeted language lessons for second language speakers, it is helpful for those who speak the primary language of the workplace to learn at least basic expressions in the languages of their minority colleagues. For example, in a workplace situation in Vancouver where many of the employees are from Mainland China, it can be conducive to positive working relations if local English-speaking employees learn to say at least some phrases in Mandarin. For diversity to succeed in the workplace, language barriers need to be overcome in creative and sensitive ways.

Translation/interpreting limitations

To deal with a language barrier in intercultural interactions, companies often seek help from bilingual speakers (e.g. their employees) who do not have special training in translating/interpreting. Recognizing the difficult nature of this work, corporations may hire professional translators and interpreters. **Translation** refers to the written form of mediation (e.g. translation of written business documents and texts), while **interpreting** the oral form (e.g. the interpreter translates spoken communication). **Simultaneous interpreting** refers to the act of interpreting while the speaker is talking (e.g. at an international business conference or meeting); **consecutive interpreting** takes place after the speaker has finished. As different skills are required, translators and interpreters usually receive different, specialized training.

In the global workplace, both translation and interpreting are challenging endeavours and hiring bilingual speakers who are not professionally trained can easily lead to miscommunication. At minimum, professional **interpreters** need to possess the following knowledge and skills: adequate understanding of the subject to be interpreted, familiarity with both cultures, extensive vocabulary in both languages and the ability to express thoughts clearly in both languages. Expressions in one language do not necessarily have an equivalent meaning in other languages, and concepts may be difficult to describe or explain in another language, especially for non-professionals (House 2012). Complications may then arise when the meaning in the translation is inaccurate.

Culture brokers or intermediaries may also be employed to bridge cultural differences in the workplace (e.g. facilitate the negotiation of international contracts, mediate intercultural conflicts, help immigrant workers adjust to the workplace). **Culture brokering** refers to the act of bridging or mediating between groups or people who have different cultural backgrounds in order to reduce conflict or effect change (Jezewski & Sotnik 2001). A cultural broker or 'go-between' may advocate on behalf of individuals or groups (e.g. second language workers in a factory) to enhance working conditions and benefits.

Conflicting communication styles

Workplace settings typically involve both individual and group tasks. When people differ in terms of age, gender, language, culture, ethnicity and many other aspects, it can be difficult for them to work together in a productive way, especially if they have divergent communication styles and are unwilling to adapt. Instead of synergy, negative attitudes and lack of acceptance of differing verbal and nonverbal communication styles and degrees of formality can impede intercultural interactions, productivity and camaraderie in the workplace. For example, in some contexts business executives are accustomed to a formal style of communication and can feel quite uncomfortable when their communication partners have a more relaxed, informal style. The use of first names may be considered too personal by some and this may negatively impact business relationships. A mismatch of communication styles may also lead to poor outcomes in intercultural job interviews as illustrated in *Cross-Talk,* a video produced by Gumperz (1979/1990) to draw attention to sources of miscommunication in intercultural organizational settings.

An employee who is used to **direct language** and a more direct style of communication (e.g. giving explicit directions, clearly expressing likes and dislikes), for example, may become easily frustrated, irritated and confused when interacting with a co-worker or supervisor who has a more indirect style (e.g. infers, suggests, implies views or changes the subject rather than stating opinions directly). Examples of **indirect language** include: 'I have one small suggestion', 'I'm not sure if this is relevant but . . .'. In both written communication (e.g. emails, letters) and oral discourse (e.g. conversations, meetings), **hedging**, the use of cautious or vague language, may be used by indirect communicators (e.g. 'It may be that . . .', 'Perhaps, that might work . . .', 'It appears that . . .') .

The direct communicator, who is more used to 'telling it like it is', may mistakenly assume that the less direct speaker does not have a strong opinion about an issue and is rather indecisive or weak. If an employee does not verbally respond, the direct communicator may also incorrectly believe that the individual has understood, agreed, approved or accepted what has been proposed. When suggestions are made in an indirect way, they are apt to be overlooked by employees or managers who are more used to people explicitly stating what is on their minds. Conversely, individuals who are more at ease with a less direct style of communication may perceive direct communicators as rude, aggressive or overly concerned.

Intercultural communication differences may also arise with regard to what is considered important to share or communicate in a meeting or other business event. Views about how and when ideas should be introduced and expressed may differ. Expectations about when and how feedback (including reprimands) should be given or received also vary among individuals from different cultural backgrounds. Communication style differences between male and female employees may also complicate workplace interactions.

Variations in emotional display/nonverbal codes

Workers may find some of the affective verbal and nonverbal behaviour (e.g. emotional displays) of their colleagues baffling and annoying. In particular, the ways individuals from different cultural backgrounds respond to reprimands and requests may differ and this can lead to misattributions and misunderstandings. When a boss publicly reprimands an employee for failing to carry out a task in a satisfactory manner, the response may not be as expected and this can easily lead to more anger and mistrust. In some Asian contexts, for example, individuals who are reprimanded in the workplace may smile and look away. Rather than amusement, this nonverbal behaviour is a sign of embarrassment as the person is losing face in front of others. Individuals who are not familiar with the local culture, however, can misinterpret this response as uncaring or defiant. Not surprisingly, negative perceptions and reactions can hinder intercultural communication and trust in the workplace.

A clash in values

Cultural values are judgments about what is considered good and bad, important and unimportant in a particular culture. During enculturation, as children we learn what is acceptable and unacceptable behaviour in particular contexts and situations. As we develop **socio-pragmatic competence**, we learn to consider the status of our communication partners when we speak and express ourselves nonverbally. For example, we use a different style of speech when interacting with our grandparents and peers. This learning continues when we enter the workforce.

Even if we are working in our home environment and are members of the majority culture, we still need to learn new cultural rules within an organization or corporation (e.g. **corporate culture**, that is, the culture of the particular business). For example, we learn appropriate ways to represent our employer and interact with supervisors, co-workers and clients. We learn what level of formality is appropriate in particular situations (e.g. dress, linguistic expressions, verbal and nonverbal communication styles).These organizational behaviours are guided by the prevalent values of the company and the wider community. Therefore, individuals who come from a different cultural background may face more value conflicts than those from the majority culture. Cross-cultural psychologists have raised awareness of the challenges and consequences of conflicting values and expectations in the workplace. (Later in this chapter, we examine and critique Hofstede's (2001, 2003) influential international study of cultural values in the workplace as well as other cultural difference frameworks.)

Conflict (interpersonal, intercultural, organizational, gender, etc.)

Just as in other domains of life, conflicts and disputes may occur in workplace situations. When employees from diverse backgrounds interact they bring with them ideas, values and expectations that have been influenced by their upbringing and life experiences. As discussed in the previous chapter, men and women learn strategies to avoid or cope with confrontations within particular cultural contexts. Some approaches work well in some business settings but are less than optimal in others. Well-intended conflict management techniques may backfire and disputes may escalate.

Intercultural conflicts in organizations may stem from a range of factors, including differences in communication or work styles among team members, different views about the best ways to achieve company goals, disparate values, disagreements about policies and procedures, perceptions of discrimination (e.g. ethnic, gender, religious) and miscommunication due to a language barrier, etc. When individuals have a different **work ethic** (set of values based on hard work and discipline) this can cause friction.

Conflicts that are repressed or denied may fester and build resentment and frustration, creating additional problems for the organization. If managers and employees are not skilful in managing disagreements in the workplace, they may spiral into conflicts that are more difficult to resolve. (See Chapter 10 for more discussion on intercultural conflict and conflict resolution.)

Opposition to change

In any work situation, employees may refuse to accept that the social, linguistic and cultural makeup of their workplace has become or is becoming more diverse. Some may be uncomfortable working alongside people with disabilities or individuals who speak a different language, have a different skin colour or belong to another religion. Individuals may reject the notion that change is inevitable. The 'we've always done it this way' mentality can curtail new ideas and inhibit growth in a company. Those who vehemently oppose workforce diversity may reject diversity initiatives and make the work environment unpleasant and less productive. Negative attitudes and a lack of willingness 'to bend' can destroy creativity, synergy and harmony in the workplace. Intentionally or unintentionally, local or long-serving staff may make newcomers (and their ideas) feel unwanted. If opposition is not handled well, diversity may not provide the intended benefits to the company and highly qualified individuals (e.g. second language speakers from minority backgrounds) who do not feel valued or respected may seek posts in more welcoming, multicultural environments.

To deal with resistant employees, companies need to clearly explain the reasons for diversity and identify the many benefits that diversity brings to both management and employees. Alleviating fears about workplace diversity (e.g. anxiety about the loss of jobs) may reduce some of the opposition.

Resistance to integration

In workplace settings, it is not unusual for exclusive social groups or cliques to form. Newcomers who differ from the majority in terms of language, ethnicity, age, physical ability, gender, etc. may find social integration at work to be very challenging. Informal divisions may already exist among staff that are difficult to penetrate. For example, people from different ethnic or linguistic groups may cluster together and avoid social interactions with 'outsiders' during breaks and lunches. Some employees may socialize outside of work and avoid interactions with those who are not part of their clique. Lack of social integration among diverse employees can hinder interpersonal relations and limit the sharing of knowledge, ideas, skills and experience. This, in turn, can curb productivity growth and limit the effectiveness of teams.

Gender differences

Attitudes towards men and women in the workplace vary among cultures and these differences influence intercultural communication in businesses. In some cultural contexts, males hold all or nearly all of the positions of power and women, if employed at all, are assigned subservient or supportive roles. Even in organizations that have long been open to females, the number of female executives tends to be smaller in comparison with males. Gender inequality in the global workplace remains a contentious issue in much of the world.

Females who have risen to senior posts in companies that are open to gender diversity may find it challenging to communicate with officials or representatives from male-dominated environments. Males (and some women) who find themselves in situations where they need to report to a female supervisor for the first time in their life may initially react in negative, hostile ways. As more females assume leadership roles and participate in all levels of an organization or company, males and females need to learn how to work together and demonstrate respect for each other.

Religious differences

In many cultures, religion plays a dominant role in daily life, including the workplace. When employees from different faiths interact at work, conflict may arise. Immigrants from nations where breaks are routinely given for prayers, for example, may find it difficult to adjust to a secular work environment where employees are discouraged from openly expressing religious differences. Some international companies permit employees to form faith-based support groups and arrange religious activities, while others do not. Some allow employees to observe certain religious holidays, whereas others limit days off to national holidays. Attitudes towards religion in the workforce vary significantly and can impact on workforce relations.

Sociocultural differences

Enculturation influences understandings of what social behaviours are considered appropriate in particular contexts and situations, including business contexts. **Business protocol** is a general term that encompasses the discourse, nonverbal behaviour, dress, procedures and social conventions that are expected within a particular company or organization. **Business etiquette** refers to rules that guide social behaviour in workplace situations (e.g. greetings in business meetings, the exchanging of business cards, seating arrangements in business meetings/dinners, table manners in business lunches and formal dinners). **Business netiquette** refers to guidelines for courtesy in the use of email and the Internet for communication purposes.

Among individuals from different linguistic and cultural backgrounds, sociocultural norms and values in business situations can vary in a number of key areas (e.g. roles and responsibilities, attitudes towards work and definitions of success, manners, concepts of time, degree of openness to people from outgroups, gift giving, level of formality in emails/face-to-face meetings, etc.). Contrasting work ethics among team members can be a major source of friction in the workplace.

Gift giving refers to the ritual of providing gifts to business clients. In international business, gift giving etiquette varies from one culture to another (when to present a gift, how to present it, what to present). The type of gift is often linked to rank and seniority. When individuals do not follow the expected rules (e.g. consider the status of individuals when giving gifts, offer name cards in expected ways), misunderstandings and controversy may ensue.

Ethnocentricism and assumptions of similarities

As noted in Chapter 7, ethnocentricism is the tendency to judge people from other cultures according to the standards, behaviours and customs of one's own culture. Typically, ethnocentric individuals elevate their own culture or group to a status or position above all other cultures or groups. Problems can occur between employees from different cultural backgrounds when individuals assume that their own cultural norms are the right way and only way to accomplish tasks. Ethnocentric individuals may also wrongly believe that the patterns of behaviour that they are accustomed to in their own cultural environment are universal (e.g. what they say or do, think or believe is shared by everyone). People in the workplace who have an ethnocentric mindset are not likely to communicate successfully with individuals or groups from other cultural backgrounds. Not surprisingly, their sense of superiority and entitlement can lead to resentment, hostility and anger.

Distorted images and perceptions of people who are different from us in some ways (e.g. age, gender, race, accent, dialect, physical ability, religion, etc.) can also have a negative impact on the work environment. Assigning a broad range of characteristics or attributes to an individual on the basis of perceived membership in a particular cultural or social group is referred to as stereotyping. Stereotypes are often based on false assumptions and anecdotes. Characteristics thought to be common to a group are then applied to every person perceived to be affiliated with that group. Whether the values or attributes that are assigned are positive or negative, stereotyping can be harmful. Assuming that an immigrant worker from Bangladesh will be computer illiterate and speak little English, that a Chinese manager will be a whiz in math or that an older employee will not be able to master new technology are all examples of stereotyping in the workplace. (See Chapter 7 for more on stereotyping.)

Prejudicial attitudes, discrimination, harassment and racism

In the workplace, employees may harbour negative attitudes toward people who differ from them in terms of religion, age, language, gender or other variables. This can lead to a lack of tolerance, bias and unfairness. Prejudice and acts of discrimination and racism can extend beyond individuals. **Workplace discrimination** (or **employment discrimination)** refers to unfair practices in hiring, promotion, job assignment, termination and compensation. It also includes various types of **harassment**, that is, behaviours of an offensive or threatening nature. **Sexual harassment** in the workplace refers to repetitive and unwanted sexual advances, where the consequences of refusing could be very disadvantageous to the victim. For example, a female secretary who is propositioned by her manager may be directly or indirectly threatened with the loss of her job if she does not comply.

Organizational policies, social attitudes and individual beliefs can all be imbued with prejudice. Women and minorities may be passed over for promotion; second language speakers or people from a particular religion or race may be excluded from positions of power. Due to prejudice, they may find it difficult to break through the **glass ceiling**, 'the unseen, yet unbreachable barrier that keeps minorities and women from rising to the upper rungs of the corporate ladder, regardless of their qualifications or achievements' (Federal Glass Ceiling Commission 1995).

CULTURAL DIFFERENCE FRAMEWORKS AND THE GLOBAL WORKPLACE

In the last few decades, a number of scholars from diverse disciplinary backgrounds (e.g. anthropology, cross-cultural communication, psychology, international business/management) have tried to account for differences between people from different cultures. Their work primarily draws on notions of culture as learned patterns of behaviour that are developed within groups through interaction in a shared social space. It is through enculturation that values (attitudes and beliefs), work ethics and worldviews are thought to be transmitted from one generation to another. Thus, at the heart of most cultural difference studies is the conviction that we need to identify core values or 'shared value orientations' within cultural groups in order to understand why people from different cultural backgrounds behave differently in similar situations (e.g. display a different work ethic). Most cultural difference frameworks aim to identify culture-specific rules, goals and values that influence the ways people communicate and behave in particular societies and cultures.

This section reviews five models that have influenced the way intercultural communication is viewed in the global workplace: Hall's (1959, 1966, 1968, 1976) dimensions of culture difference (monochronic vs. polychronic communication, high/low-context communication, use of personal space), Kluckhohn and Strodtbeck's (1961) five value orientations, Hampden-Turner and Trompenaars' (1998) seven value dimensions, Hofstede's (1984) value-orientations framework and the GLOBE cultural framework (House *et al.* 2004).

Hall's dimensions of cultural difference

Anthropologist Edward T. Hall (1959, 1966, 1968, 1976, 1983, 1998) wrote many books and articles that centre on dimensions of cultural difference, including the monochronic–polychronic time system (See Chapter 5), use of personal space (Chapter 5), and low-context vs. high-context communication (Chapter 4). Based on his observations, he classified cultures according to differences in these dimensions. As elements of his cultural difference framework have been discussed in previous chapters, this section briefly explains how his understandings of culture shaped his views about cultural difference and intercultural interactions.

Hall (1998) distinguishes between 'conscious' and 'unconscious' culture, that is, elements that are visible, explicit and *sensible* (i.e., able to be sensed) and those that are invisible, nonverbal and unconsciously learned over time. For this scholar, **'unconscious' culture** includes all dimensions of nonverbal communication (e.g. gestures, eye contact, facial expressions, differences in time orientation, use of personal space, silence). In a low-context culture, for example, business professionals provide many details in their conversations and do not make assumptions about their communication partner's knowledge. The aim is to be explicit so that one's message is clear. **Conscious cultures** fall into the low-context communication framework, whereby most of the meaning is conveyed in the verbal code. According to Hall (1976), examples of low-context cultures are Germany, the United States and the United Kingdom.

In a high-context culture, business professionals use language and behaviour (e.g. nonverbal actions) that assume that others know much of what they know. By contrast, unconscious cultures have high-context communication, where the information tends to be located in the physical context or internalized within an individual and little information is in the coded, explicit part of the message. Examples of high-context cultures include Japan and China.

Hall (1976) also maintained that there was a strong correlation between high-context and low-context cultures and collectivism–individualism, a dimension that features in Hofstede's (2001, 2003) framework. Membership in a collectivist or individualistic culture influences how individuals relate to co-nationals and also impacts on how much information they believe should be provided in interactions with non-group members.

Kluckhohn and Strodtbeck's cultural orientation framework

Based on a review of hundreds of ethnographic investigations of ethnic groups in different parts of the world, anthropologists Kluckhohn and Strodtbeck (1961) developed the *Cultural Orientation Framework,* which identifies five problems or challenges that all cultures face.

1   What is the character of innate human nature? (the human nature orientation)
2   What is the relationship of people to nature? (the human–nature orientation)
3   What is the temporal focus of human life? (the time orientation, e.g. future, present, or past oriented ways of thinking and acting)
4   What is the modality of human activity? (the activity orientation, e.g. 'doing' or action oriented as opposed to 'being', which is person oriented)

5   What is the modality of an individual's relationship to other people? (the relational orientation)

Kluckhohn and Strodtbeck (1961) also identified three possible ways in which cultures typically respond to each of these universal problems (e.g. a view of the character of human nature as evil, a mixture of good and evil, and good; a past, present or future time orientation). Their framework has been used by business professionals and other border crossers to develop an understanding of broad differences in values among various cultural groups.

Hampden-Turner and Trompenaars' value dimensions

Another value-orientation framework that is used in business and management research and practice was developed by Hampden-Turner and Trompenaars (1998). Drawing on the work of anthropologists and sociologists, these management philosophers identified seven dimensions of cultural variability:

1   Universalism vs. particularism (What is most important, rules or relationships?) (**Universalism** refers to the application of the same rules for everyone regardless of their status or relationship. Universalists try to treat people fairly based on certain standards or rules, whereas in **particularism**, individuals may be treated differently depending on interpersonal relationships and obligations. For particularists, relationships come before rules. Cultures will have elements of both universalism and particularism but tend to be more one than the other.)
2   Individualism vs. collectivism (Do we function in a group or as individuals?)
3   Neutral vs. emotional (Do we display our emotions, or do we hide them?)
4   Specific vs. diffuse (Do we handle our relationships in specific and predetermined ways, or do we see our relationships as changing and related to contextual settings?)
5   Achievement vs. ascription (Do we have to prove ourselves to receive status, or is status given to us?)
6   Sequential vs. synchronic (Do we do things one at a time or several things at once?)
7   Internal vs. external control (Do we believe that we can control our environment, or do we believe that the environment controls us?)

To determine the impact of culture on people's behavioural choices, Hampden-Turner and Trompenaars (1998) devised scenarios of everyday dilemmas with a limited number of possible resolutions. Each option was linked to one of the seven dimensions they had identified. Approximately 15,000 respondents in 50 countries took part in their study. The researchers then calculated the percentage of individuals per country who selected a particular response. These statistics were then used to formulate generalizations about how people in a particular culture are most apt to respond to everyday dilemmas and interactions with people. Hampden-Turner and Trompenaars (1998) maintain that participants' responses revealed the values that are deeply entrenched in their national culture. The results of this study have been used in business contexts to understand intercultural interactions and provide expatriates with guidance on how to perform tasks and communicate with people in different cultures.

Hofstede's value-orientations framework

The most widely cited value-orientations framework today is that of Geert Hofstede (1984), a Dutch social psychologist, who published his classic volume *Culture's Consequences* in 1980. Characterizing culture as 'software of the mind', he believes that cultural patterns programme people to behave in particular ways. Much of his work has centred on how values in the workplace are influenced by our cultural programming. For the last few decades, his framework has served as a theoretical model for cross-cultural studies and training in management/business.

Drawing on surveys administered to more than 100,000 IBM employees in 40 countries, Hofstede (1980, 1981) examined the ways in which people from diverse 'national cultures' viewed and interpreted work and approached their social relationships in a work environment. He categorized their responses into the following four dimensions or value orientations of cultural difference: power distance, femininity/masculinity, uncertainty avoidance and individualism–collectivism (a binary first proposed by Kluckhohn and Strodtbeck 1961). Later, he added Confucian dynamism as a fifth value orientation. Let's take a closer look at each dimension.

Power distance

Power distance refers to the degree to which less powerful members of a society or organization expect and accept the unequal distribution of power among members. Small or low power distance cultures have a tendency to stress equality, self-initiative and collaborative problem-solving with supervisors and employees. Punishment and rewards tend to be distributed based on individual performance. In small power distance cultures, it may be normal for a president of a company and a construction worker to be on a first name basis, whereas in high power distance cultures this would be unthinkable. Austria, New Zealand, Denmark and Israel value low power distance, minimizing hierarchies of power. By contrast, countries such as Venezuela, India, China and Mexico are high in power distance; unequal status among members of an organization is accepted and authority figures are expected to make decisions. Relationships between managers and their subordinates are formalized and more distant. High power distance cultures reward rank, status and years of service.

Femininity/masculinity

Femininity/masculinity refers to the extent to which gender roles are valued, and attitudes towards ascribed masculine values (e.g. achievement, ambition). According to Hofstede (2001), **feminine cultures** promote gender equality, interpersonal contact, flexible balancing of life and work and group decision making, whereas **masculine cultures** stress distinct differences in gender roles between men and women in the workplace. Gardiner and Kosmitzki (2010) characterize this dimension as 'working to live' versus 'living to work'. Northern European countries (Sweden, Denmark, Norway) demonstrate a tendency to value the feminine orientation, while Italy, Switzerland, Austria and Japan have a tendency to promote masculine values in the workplace.

Uncertainty avoidance

Uncertainty avoidance refers to the tendency of a culture's members to feel threatened by ambiguous situations and to strive to avoid uncertainty. Countries with low or weak uncertainty avoidance (e.g. Denmark, Singapore, Sweden) tend to be more risk-taking, less rule-governed and more accepting of dissent. Countries with strong uncertainty avoidance (e.g. Japan, Portugal, Greece, Belgium) are more averse to risk-taking; they tend to favour rules and regulations and seek consensus about goals.

Individualism–collectivism

Individualism/collectivism refers to individual versus group orientation. **Individualism** refers to the broad value tendencies of a culture to stress personal over group goals, and tend to have weaker group and organizational loyalty. In New Zealand, Australia and the United States, for example, personal autonomy and individual identities, rights and responsibilities tend to be emphasized. In contrast, **collectivism** refers to the broad value tendencies of a culture to focus on collaboration, shared interests, long-term relationships, traditions, harmony and maintaining face. According to Hofstede's (2001) findings, Arab and Asian countries, Brazil and India tend to be collectivist, that is, emphasis in organizations is placed on the common good (e.g. the needs, interests, and goals of the group).

A fifth dimension: Confucian dynamism

Drawing on the work of cross-cultural psychologist Michael Bond and his colleagues in Hong Kong (Chinese Culture Connection 1987), Hofstede (2001) later added a dimension, **Confucian dynamism**, to account for particular cultural characteristics and behaviours that are prevalent in East Asian nations. The primary values in this fifth orientation are associated with the philosophy and teachings of Confucius (551 to 479 AD), a Chinese philosopher and educator who espoused a practical code of conduct for people in daily life.

The Confucian dynamism orientation emphasizes persistence, personal stability, traditions, frugality, respect for elders, status-oriented relationships, a long-term orientation to time, hard work, a sense of shame and collective face-saving. These Confucian values are often credited with the dramatic economic growth in the Five Dragons (Hong Kong, Taiwan, Japan, Singapore, and South Korea). In these work environments, Hofstede (2001) maintains that employees demonstrate respect for status differences and tend to possess a long-term orientation towards work as well as a strong work ethic. In contrast, a short-term orientation to work is more common in the United States, the United Kingdom and Canada, where the focus is on hard work to gain immediate results and there is less concern about status.

The GLOBE cultural framework

Building on Hofstede's work, researchers in the **GLOBE (Global Leadership and Organizational Behavior Effectiveness)** project have developed surveys to measure the relationship between societal culture, organizational culture and leadership (House *et al.* 2004). Approximately 17,000 middle managers in finance, food processing and telecommunication in more than 60

countries have responded to survey items designed to assess their cultural values and practices based on nine cultural dimensions. Six of the nine **GLOBE dimensions** resemble those
put forward by Hofstede (2001) to address institutional and group collectivism, gender
egalitarianism, power distance, uncertainty avoidance and future orientation. The other dimensions that have been added include: **assertiveness** (the extent to which people in organizations
are strong-willed and confrontational), **performance orientation** (the degree to which an
organization rewards members for their participation and quality of work) and **humane orientation** (the extent to which an organization rewards members for being kind and fair to others)
(House *et al.* 2004).

Researchers used the statistical results of the survey analysis to group countries together
based on levels of similarity and difference. Higher levels of cultural similarity were found
among the following country clusters: Confucian Asia (e.g. Hong Kong, Singapore, Taiwan,
China), Southern Asia (e.g. Indonesia, India, Malaysia, Iran), Latin America (e.g. Ecuador, Bolivia,
Brazil), Nordic Europe (Denmark, Finland, Sweden), Anglo nations (e.g. Australia, Canada, the
U.S.), Germanic Europe (e.g. Austria, the Netherlands, Germany), Latin Europe (e.g. Israel,
Italy, Spain, Portugal), Sub-Sahara Africa (e.g. Zimbabwe, Namibia, Nigeria), Eastern Europe
(e.g. Greece, Hungary, Poland, Russia) and the Middle East (e.g. Egypt, Morocco, Qatar).

When presenting their findings, the researchers drew attention to the degree of cultural
difference between clusters. For example, they maintain that there is a greater cultural difference between Southern Asia and Germanic Europe than between Southern Asia and
Confucian Asia. Similar to Hofstede's (2001) cultural dimensions framework, the Globe
dimensions are used by business professionals to compare home and host cultures, and
predict cultural challenges and potential commonalities.

The impact of the frameworks on global business research, education and practice

Business students and professionals across the globe are still using cultural difference frameworks to identify the core values and assumptions of their own culture as well as the target
or host culture (e.g. international clients from a particular nation). Armed with this awareness
of cultural difference, in theory, business professionals are better positioned to predict
difficulties that might arise when they interact with colleagues and clients from the other
culture. It is believed that this knowledge can help them avoid intercultural misunderstandings
(e.g. by using culture-specific strategies, adjusting their communication style) and more
effectively resolve difficulties or conflicts when they arise.

Among the cultural difference frameworks described above, Hofstede's model (2001) (or
variations of it) continues to dominate intercultural business training as well as communication
research in business and management studies (e.g. cross-cultural marketing surveys of potential customer values, investigations of values impacting on business negotiations in different
countries).

Limitations and dangers of the cultural difference frameworks

Although still widely used in intercultural business education (training) and research, 'culture
difference' frameworks are not without critics. Different understandings of culture, questions
about the methodologies employed in taxonomy studies, perceptions of Western or Eurocentric

bias and the potential for overgeneralizations have resulted in many publications that rally against their use or, at minimum, recommend that users exercise caution when interpreting and applying the findings. Let's take a closer look at these concerns.

Increasingly, as noted in Chapter 2, interculturalists are questioning views of culture as static and shared by all members of a particular nation. Holliday (1999, 2012), for example, distinguishes between the notion of **'large culture'** and **'small culture'**. He warns that the former can lead to 'culturist ethnic, national or international stereotyping' (1999: 237), whereas the latter recognizes 'small social groupings or activities wherever there is cohesive behaviour' (1999: 237). Within a 'large culture' or nation, there are actually many 'small cultures', which can easily be overlooked if solely focused on the broad picture.

Taxonomies of cultural difference are designed to identify the main components of 'national culture', that is, they attempt to describe 'large cultures' across a range of behaviours and values. Piller (2009), Holliday (1999, 2012), Holmes (2012) and many other critics argue that this approach is outdated. In our increasingly globalized world, nations have become much more multicultural and cosmopolitan, and this diversity is often ignored in discussions of national cultural difference. As geographical boundaries become less and less relevant, the notion of 'culture as nation' becomes less plausible. The idea that all people from a particular nation belong to the same culture does not resonate with societies today. Within any nation, there is diversity in terms of social class, accent, age, ethnicity, religion, gender, profession, physical ability and so on.

Frameworks of cultural difference have also been strongly criticized for their Western bias and methodological limitations (e.g. reliance on surveys with no triangulation, that is, no data from other sources or types of data). When describing national cultural characteristics based solely on closed surveys, there is always the risk of overgeneralizations and stereotyping. Consequently, many critics characterize this work as essentialist and reductionist. As has been noted in earlier chapters, **essentialism** refers to an approach in which certain characteristics are linked to a particular cultural group and all individuals categorized as members of this group are assumed to possess these attributes and adhere to similar patterns of behaviour. In other words, they are reduced to one representation. When culture is viewed as a stable feature of an individual or group, multifaceted cultural identities and the dynamic nature of culture are largely ignored. The results of surveys that were administered decades ago are also unlikely to accurately and fully portray the current situation.

ALTERNATIVE APPROACHES TO INTERCULTURAL BUSINESS RESEARCH, EDUCATION AND PRACTICE

Noting the limitations and dangers of cultural difference frameworks, more scholars (e.g. Holliday 2012, Holmes 2012, Scollon *et al.* 2012, Ting-Toomey 2010b) are calling for context-specific analyses of intercultural communication in business contexts (e.g. interpretive, experiential and critical approaches to understanding language and intercultural interactions in the global workplace). In particular, more ethnographic studies, interactional sociolinguistic explorations and critical studies of intercultural business interactions (e.g. critical discourse analyses) are needed to inform practice (e.g. the design and delivery of business intercultural education workshops and courses). Intercultural communication in organizations and businesses does not take place in a power vacuum; nor does it typically involve equal-power relations. More contextualized studies are therefore needed that take into account the power dimension in intercultural interactions whether in domestic or international settings.

Critical intercultural communication scholars recommend the use of locally-relevant methods and tools instead of relying on large-scale surveys developed in Western contexts. More ethnographic studies and discourse analyses are needed that examine the actual use of language and nonverbal codes in intercultural business interactions (e.g. team meetings, supervisor–employee conversations, employee–customer encounters). Building on the earlier work of Gumperz (1979/1990), Newton and Kusmierczyk (2011) advocate the use of recordings of authentic workplace interactions in workplace language programmes (e.g. job-specific English language modules for workers). These theoretical and methodological developments shift the focus away from 'differences between national cultures and the development of universalised competences within international groups, towards multiple identities and particular competences within local groups' (Lund & O'Reagan 2010: 56).

Instead of relying on cultural difference frameworks in business education, critical intercultural educators focus on 'real world' intercultural interactions and experiential modes of learning (e.g. internships in the linguistically and culturally diverse workplace). M.J. Bennett (1998b) argues that trainees should have the opportunity to 'acquire increased self-awareness and other-awareness'. In workplace settings, they need to 'confront emotional and communication challenges and practice context-pertinent communication skills' (Ting-Toomey 2010b: 21) rather than simply be given a list of cultural differences, which can lead to stereotyping and **Otherization (Othering)**, that is, viewing people from other cultures as 'exotic Others'.

ENHANCING INTERCULTURAL COMMUNICATION IN TODAY'S GLOBAL WORKPLACE

Effective global communication requires flexibility, a desire to learn, sensitivity to culture and traditions in a foreign setting, and the ability to apply what you have learned to interactions with others in overseas locations. In addition, combine professionalism, firmness, and business savvy with grace, respect, and kindness. Build appropriate relationships and friendships, and network through international societies and trade groups.

(Krizan *et al.* 2011: 51)

As our workplaces and communities become increasingly diverse and globally-oriented, intercultural competence is becoming more and more important. As noted by Mughan and O'Shea (2010), 'the social context in which we live makes the understanding of intercultural interaction a prerequisite for those who aspire to successful careers' (p. 109). To work more effectively in the multicultural workplace, there are a number of general guidelines that individuals can follow.

Acknowledge diversity in the workplace. First, it is important to recognize and acknowledge the wealth of diversity that exists in work environments today. As noted in this chapter, diversity can take many forms (e.g. differences in age, language, gender, race, ethnicity, physical ability, religion, sexual orientation, social class, etc.). All workplaces are diverse in multiple ways. You do not need to go to a foreign country to experience diversity.

Becoming more knowledgeable about linguistic and cultural dimensions. In today's global workplace, employees must build strong linguistic and cultural awareness in order to enhance their intercultural communication skills and effectiveness at work. It is useful to learn how enculturation influences attitudes, language use, beliefs, **business ethics** (the principles that guide behaviour in business), one's work ethic and style of communication (verbal and nonverbal). It is also vital to recognize that not everyone from a particular cultural background follows the same patterns of behaviour or shares a similar worldview or work ethic. There is diversity *within* cultures. Observe and learn from experience.

Demonstrate second language sensitivity. If you are using your first language with co-workers or customers who are not fully fluent in the language, recognize the advantage you have, especially if you are communicating on the phone. Demonstrate appreciation for the efforts they are making and provide assistance, when necessary. Use explicit comprehension, whenever appropriate, to gauge how your message is being interpreted. You could also learn basic expressions in your co-workers' or clients' first language to make them feel more welcome in the workplace. Becoming aware of how power imbalances impact interactions can help you become a more competent intercultural communicator in the workplace. With linguistic and culture knowledge and sensitivity you are better positioned to engage diversity with more ease and confidence.

Become more self-aware. As well as learning more about other ways of being, it is essential to be mindful of how your own linguistic and cultural socialization and life experiences have shaped your attitudes, perceptions, values, identities and communication behaviours (verbal and nonverbal). Enculturation impacts on how you perceive and interact with people from other cultural backgrounds both in your social life as well as at work. To become more inter-culturally sensitive, it is vital to recognize attitudes and behaviours that are holding you back from adopting a more ethnorelative, inclusive perspective.

Recognize one's biases. The ability to communicate effectively with co-workers or clients who have a different linguistic or cultural background or who differ from you in other ways (e.g. gender, age, physical disability) requires awareness of your personal biases and expectations. For example, realizing that you have learned to value independence and individual responsibility can raise your awareness of the need to be patient in situations where it is considered more important to work cooperatively and not stand out. Recognizing that you have a bias against second language speakers can push you to question the source of your beliefs and make more of an effort to be more understanding of the challenges people face when communicating in another language. Heightened awareness of your stereotypes and biases can pinpoint aspects that you need to work on in order to become more interculturally competent.

Be flexible. In the global workplace, you are bound to encounter different ways of speaking and doing things. Insisting that your way is the only way is not conducive to harmony or productivity. Flexible individuals who demonstrate interest in and respect for other ways of being are far more likely to encourage colleagues from diverse backgrounds to contribute their best efforts in the workplace. Acceptance of new ideas is a characteristic of effective intercultural communicators. Enhance your ability to encourage collaboration and help your organizations and communities leverage the many opportunities that diversity presents.

Expand repertoire of communication/conflict management styles. In today's workforce, you are bound to encounter unfamiliar styles of communication (verbal and nonverbal) and conflict management. Instead of rigidly sticking to familiar habits (e.g. communication patterns), employees who make an effort to develop a wider range of communication strategies and tools can become more effective and appropriate communicators in intercultural situations.They are then better positioned to mediate and resolve intercultural conflict situations in ways that are mutually acceptable. For example, learning face-negotiation strategies that respect the self-identities and dignity of others can enhance interpersonal communication in the workplace.

Be patient and humble. It is natural to commit **faux-pas** (unintentionally violate social norms) when interacting with people from a different linguistic and cultural background in the workplace. Admitting mistakes and showing humility can create goodwill. Being able to laugh at yourself (not other people) and learn from mistakes are vital characteristics of sensitive intercultural communicators.

Keep an open mind and respect diversity. Learn about other ways of being, beliefs and customs and resist the temptation to judge them by your own cultural standards and habits. In other words, make an effort to move beyond an ethnocentric perspective and try to see situations through the eyes of your co-workers or clients who have a different background from you.

Advocate equity in the workplace. Valuing diversity in the workplace means respect and recognition of the unique characteristics and contributions of *all* employees. Strengthen inclusive practices and be an advocate for co-workers or customers who are not treated fairly. Remaining silent signals support for inequity and injustice. (Chapter 12 explores the responsibilities of ethical global citizens.)

SUMMARY

the need for cultural reflection and the building of intercultural competence are increasingly pervasive in our daily professional and private lives, as we are more and more likely to interact and cooperate with people from very different cultural backgrounds.

(Guilherme *et al.* 2010: 243)

This chapter began by discussing the impact of globalization and Englishization on today's workplace. Increasing diversity in the workforce and wider society has profound implications for the way that business is conducted both locally and globally. As noted by Guilherme *et al.* (2010), and many other interculturalists, business professionals and organizations must make changes in order to remain current and competitive. The need has never been greater for employees to possess intercultural competence and bilingual (multilingual) ability or, at minimum, knowledge of an international language.

After examining the benefits and challenges of diversity, we shifted our attention to the impact of 'cultural difference' frameworks on intercultural research, education and practice in business. After reviewing the limitations and dangers of cultural taxonomies, suggestions were made for more interpretive, experiential and critical approaches. Finally, the chapter concluded with general guidelines for enhancing one's intercultural communication and sensitivity in the global workplace.

discussion questions

1 In what ways has globalization influenced intercultural communication and language use in the workplace?
2 Do you agree that English is the de facto language of global business today? Why or why not? Do you think there will be a dominant global language of business in 50 years?
3 Identify four benefits of diversity in the global workplace.
4 What is cultural synergy? How can companies promote synergy in work teams?
5 How might different verbal communication styles and degrees of formality lead to miscommunication at work? Provide examples.
6 In small groups, discuss five challenges of diversity in the global workplace.
7 How can attitudes toward women impact on the intercultural workplace? How are gender and age related to position, status, and power in your home country? Identify other places where the situation is different.
8 What role, if any, does religion play in conducting business in your country? Identify another country where religion is viewed differently in the world of business.
9 How do business introductions vary among cultures? Describe cultural variations in the exchange of business cards and the potential consequences if protocol is not followed.
10 What are some of the established communication protocols that govern business interactions in your environment? How might some of these protocols create a problem when dealing with business representatives from other linguistic and cultural backgrounds? What recommendations would you offer to deal with these problem areas?
11 What actions can people take to become more interculturally and linguistically competent in the workplace?
12 You are responsible for creating an organizational climate that values and embraces diversity. What steps would you take?

further reading

Goodall, H.L. Jr., Goodall, S. and Schiefelbein, J. (2009). *Business and Professional Communication in the Global Workplace*, Boston: Wadsworth.

This accessible book provides an introduction to business and professional communication.

Guilherme, M. *et al.* (eds) (2010) *The Intercultural Dynamics of Multicultural Working*, Bristol: Multilingual Matters.

From theoretical and interdisciplinary perspectives, the chapters in this volume examine intercultural communication in various types of work environments and contexts (e.g. multicultural work teams).

Lauring, J. and Jonasson, C. (2010) *Group Processes in Ethnically Diverse Organizations: Language and Intercultural Learning*, Hauppauge, NY: Nova Science Pub Inc.

This book explores the complex relationship between language, identity and intercultural communication in diverse organizations.

Schmidt, W.V., Conaway, R.N., Easton, S.S. and Wardrope, W.J. (2007) *Communicating Globally: Intercultural Communication and International Business*, Thousand Oaks, CA: Sage.

Integrating intercultural communication theory with the practices of multinational organizations, the authors raise awareness of the potential impact of diverse worldviews in intercultural interactions and suggest ways to enhance intercultural communication in the workplace.

Scollon, R., Wong Scollon, S. and Jones, R.H. (2012) *Intercultural Communication: A Discourse Approach,* 3rd edn, London: Blackwell.

Grounded in interactional sociolinguistics and discourse analysis, this book explores key concepts in intercultural communication with multiple examples of corporate and professional discourse.

CHAPTER 12

Global citizenship and intercultural (communicative) competence

To shift our level of awareness from the ethnocentric to the geocentric, we must challenge ourselves to leave our comfort zone. Whatever narrow identity we were born into, it is time to step out of it and into the larger world. We can still cherish our own heritage, lineage, and culture, but we must liberate ourselves from the illusion that they are separate from everyone else's.

(Gerzon 2010: xxi)

Language clearly plays an important role in the process of developing intercultural competence. Through the study of a foreign language, it becomes easier to enter the cognitive concepts of another culture. However, language learning alone is not sufficient to grasp the complexities of another culture and to finally achieve intercultural competence ... Becoming interculturally competent is a process of changing one's mindset ... It is a process of continuous trans-formation that, ideally, never ends.

(Guilherme *et al.* 2010: 243–44)

You must be the change you wish to see in the world.

Mahatma Gandhi

learning objectives

By the end of this chapter, you should be able to:

1 define global citizenship
2 identify the traits and characteristics of global citizens
3 define what is meant by 'global competency'
4 identify and explain the core elements in the global competence model
5 discuss the ethical obligations of global citizens
6 explain what is meant by 'intercultural competency'
7 define intercultural (communication/communicative) competence and identify fundamental components
8 define what is meant by 'the intercultural speaker' or 'intercultural mediator'
9 discuss intercultural citizenship and its relation to intercultural competence
10 explain the difference between 'culture-specific' and 'culture-general' approaches to intercultural education

11 describe four models of intercultural competence/sensitivity
12 identify and describe the relationship between second language proficiency and intercultural competence
13 identify requisite competencies for today's global society
14 describe ways to enhance one's intercultural competence and intercultural/global citizenry.

INTRODUCTION

In previous chapters, we discussed the many ways in which our world has become globally interdependent and interculturally complex, due, in part, to accelerating globalization, migration and rapid advances in transportation and telecommunications. These changes have impacted on our self-identities and attitudes toward diversity. With more and more intercultural interactions in our home environment and beyond, the potential for miscommunication and conflict is also on the rise, both among individuals and groups. Hence, the need for global, bi(multi)lingual and intercultural competency has never been greater.

As the gap between the rich and poor widens and we compete for limited resources (e.g. food, water, land, wealth, shelter, power, etc.), the importance of global perspectives and peaceful, equitable solutions deepens. The development of a global mindset and the mastery of intercultural communication knowledge and skills are a matter of urgency for both individuals and societies worldwide. It is imperative for all of us to become responsible, ethical members of the global village that we share.

This concluding chapter begins by exploring what is meant by global citizenship, global competency, intercultural competency and intercultural citizenship. We then examine several models of intercultural (communication/communicative) competence and discuss the construct of the 'intercultural speaker' in relation to second language speakers. Attention is drawn to the vital role of language in intercultural competency. We then review the global, linguistic and intercultural competencies that are needed in today's complex world. Finally, we discuss constructive ways to enhance one's intercultural (communicative) competency and take steps toward ethical, global citizenship.

GLOBAL CITIZENSHIP

What is global citizenship and what does it mean to be a global citizen in today's increasingly complex world? What are the qualities and duties of global citizens? How can one acquire the dimensions of global citizenship? In the new millennium, why is it essential to take steps in this direction? What is the relationship between identity, language, global citizenship and ethics? These are just a few of the many questions that preoccupy philosophers, educators, interculturalists, social justice activists and other scholars and students in modern times.

Citizenship

Before we look at definitions of global citizenship, it is necessary to have an understanding of what is meant by citizenship. Throughout the history of humankind, **citizenship** has been linked to an individual's conduct, rights and obligations within a particular society or nation. Most definitions of citizenship focus on people's affiliation with the state and their behaviours or duties in relation to it. In political philosophy, for example, citizenship is generally viewed as a series of rights and responsibilities associated with the individual as a member of a political community. Typically, this includes such aspects as civic, economic, linguistic, political and social rights as well as duties or obligations. Basically, citizenship describes the relationship between the individual and the state, and the need for citizens to understand the economic and political processes, structures, institutions, laws, rights and responsibilities within the system that governs the state (e.g. democracy, communism, socialism, monarchy).

Citizenship and sense of belonging

The mode of governance impacts on perceptions of citizenship as well as an individual's status, duties, rights and freedoms. It influences dimensions of one's identity and sense of belonging within the state (e.g. the strength of one's national identity or affiliation with the state). Within the context of democratic societies, Osler (2005: 12–13) maintains that citizenship involves:

1   a *status* (which confers on the individual the rights to residence, vote and employment)
2   a *feeling* (sense of belonging to a community)
3   *practice* (active participation in the building of democratic societies).

Citizens who feel a deep attachment or connection to their nation are apt to possess a strong national identity, whereas those who are more ambivalent about this bond are likely to have a weak national identity. Increasingly, individuals are developing multiple identities and affiliations that go beyond the local. Second language speakers who master English, for example, may feel a bond with people in other parts of the world who speak this global language. Through this international language, they may forge a global identity, while maintaining a **local self** (e.g. regional or national identity). They may also develop a sense of inbetweenness or hybridity (Jenkins 2007, 2013; McKay & Bokhorst-Heng 2008). (Chapter 6 discusses types of identities, including local, global, national and hybrid identifications and their association with language and culture.) We now take a closer look at the relationship between citizenship and the wider, global community.

Conceptions of global citizenship

There are many definitions of global citizenship. Most stress common values and concerns that unite people who care deeply about the current state of our planet and the quality of life of future generations. As all of us inhabit the same universe, advocates of global citizenry argue that all human beings and communities should work together to solve the major problems facing humanity (e.g. global warming, armed conflicts, border disputes, unequal distribution of wealth and natural resources, natural catastrophes such as earthquakes and tsunamis).

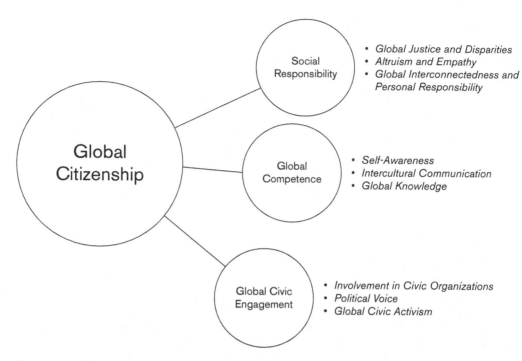

Figure 12.1 Global citizenship conceptual model

For Toh (1996: 185), **global citizenship** entails 'awareness of and commitment to societal justice for marginalized groups, grassroots environment, nonviolent and authentic democracy, environmental care, and North-South relations based on principles of equity, respect, and sharing'. Based on a review of definitions put forward by global scholars from around the world (e.g. Deardorff 2006, 2009; Hunter *et al.* 2006), Morais and Ogden (2011) devised a conceptual model of global citizenship that is depicted in Figure 12.1.

The core elements in this framework are: **social responsibility** (the perceived level of interdependence and social concern for others, the society and the environment), **global competence** ('having an open mind while actively seeking to understand others' cultural norms and expectations and leveraging this knowledge to interact, communicate and work effectively outside one's environment') and **global civic engagement** ('the demonstration of action and/or predisposition toward recognizing local, state, national, and global community issues and responding through actions such as volunteerism, political activism, and community participation (Andrzejewski & Alessio 1999; Lagos 2001; Paige, Stallman, & Josić 2008)') (Morais & Ogden 2011: 448).

Unlike national citizenship, there is no world state or governing body that can grant global citizenship (e.g. global rights, status, responsibilities). Individuals may possess a strong sense of **global consciousness** (concern about the welfare of our planet) and still declare allegiance to the state or region where they have legal citizenship. Put another way, a global identity may coexist with a regional, national or local identity. Tensions may surface, however, when local needs (e.g. deforestation to provide land for an increasing population, expansion of industries that burn fossil fuels) conflict with global concerns (e.g. protection of the environment, climate warming).

What is a global citizen?

For Israel (2012: 79), a **global citizen** is 'someone who identifies with being part of an emerging world community and whose actions contribute to building this community's values and practices'. Instead of seeing oneself as only narrowly connected to a particular region or nation, individuals who identify themselves as global citizens possess a sense of belonging to a world community. As noted by Gerzon (2010: xxi), global citizens may still have fond feelings for their 'heritage, lineage, and culture' but are free of the 'illusion' that their identities are 'separate from everyone else's'. Their sense of self embraces a concern for all humankind and the future of the planet. People with a global identity are also sometimes referred to as **international** or **world citizens**.

The traits and actions of global citizens

A number of traits and behaviours have been linked to global citizens. For Daisaku Ikeda, a Buddhist philosopher, peace builder and educator, the following are essential elements:

- the wisdom to perceive the interconnectedness of all life and living
- the courage not to fear or deny difference; but to respect and strive to understand people of different cultures, and to grow from encounters with them
- the compassion to maintain an imaginative empathy that reaches beyond one's immediate surroundings and extends to those suffering in distant places (Ikeda n.d.).

The attributes of a global citizen have also been carefully considered by Oxfam, a development and relief organization that strives to find solutions to poverty and end suffering around the world. Oxfam views the global citizen as someone who:

- is aware of the wider world and has a sense of his or her own role as a world citizen
- respects and values diversity
- has an understanding of how the world works
- is troubled by social injustice
- participates in the community at a range of levels, from the local to the global
- is willing to act to make the world a more equitable and sustainable place
- takes responsibility for her or his actions
- feels an ethical responsibility to others around the globe (adapted from Oxfam 2006: 3).

Our ethical responsibility

Most scholars emphasize that global citizenship entails a commitment to live responsibly by taking care of the Earth and its inhabitants (e.g. protecting the environment, safeguarding the rights of other human beings). A global citizen is concerned about the welfare of *all* human beings, not just his or her own ethnic, linguistic or national group. Instead of seeking selfish aims (e.g. the sole betterment of one's community or ingroup at the expense of others), global citizens recognize the dignity of every human being and proactively seek the common good for society and the environment. With this in view, Patel, *et al.* (2011) recommend that all of us resolve to:

1   develop an understanding of global interrelatedness and interdependence
2   respect cultural diversity
3   fight racial discrimination
4   protect the global environment
5   understand human rights
6   accept basic social values (adapted from Patel *et al.* 2011: 79).

Martin and Nakayama (2008) concur, arguing that all of us have an ethical responsibility to develop a sense of social justice as we discover more about ourselves and others:

> as members of an increasingly interdependent global community, intercultural commu-
> nication students have a responsibility to educate themselves, not just about interesting
> cultural differences, but also about intercultural conflicts, the impacts of stereotyping and
> prejudice, and the larger systems that can oppress and deny basic human rights—and to
> apply this knowledge to the communities in which they live and interact.
>
> (Martin & Nakayama 2008: 22)

Genuine global citizens are dedicated to fostering a sustainable world that offers promise for all inhabitants. Recognizing the interdependence of communities, global or world citizens are passionate about **social justice** (the fair administration of laws to treat all people as equal regardless of ethnicity, religion, race, language, gender, origin, etc.), **economic justice** (economic policies that distribute benefits equally to all), **human rights** (the fundamental rights and freedoms to which all humans are entitled, such as the right to life and liberty, freedom of thought and expression and equality before the law), **language** or **linguistic rights** (the right to choose the language(s) for communication in private and public places; the right to one's own language in legal, administrative and judicial acts, language education and the media) and **global ethics** (basic shared ethical values, criteria and attitudes for peaceful coexistence among humans). Becoming a global citizen involves much more than travelling to many differ-ent countries and speaking multiple languages. It requires a commitment to bettering our planet. (Later in the chapter, we explore the related construct of 'intercultural citizenship'.)

Global citizenship activism

To build and nurture our emerging world community, global citizens may assume activist roles, which cultivate ethical values, principles, and practices. **Global citizenship activism** can take many forms. For example, individuals or groups may lobby for changes in local, national and international policies and practices that impact the environment. They may join initiatives designed to curb global warming and protect the Earth's ozone level. Activists may also join organizations that aim to solve pressing global problems (e.g. famine, regional conflicts, pollution, economic disparity, unequal opportunities to learn international languages). As well as contribut-ing to worldwide humanitarian relief efforts, individuals may organize and actively participate in activities and events that celebrate global **diversity** (e.g. rich variations in art, language, culture, religion, music, cuisine) and promote equitable, harmonious intercultural interactions. Global citizens may also take an active role in the decision-making processes of global governing bodies and international agencies that strive to make the world a better place, such as the United Nations Educational, Scientific and Cultural Organization (UNESCO), Oxfam (a develop-mental organization), the Global Relief Agency and Medics without Borders, to name a few.

Advocates of global citizenship warn that we need to work together to deal with the many challenges facing our planet. Israel (2012: 79) argues that all citizens should be concerned about 'human rights, environmental protection, religious pluralism, gender equity, sustainable worldwide economic growth, poverty alleviation, prevention of conflicts between countries, elimination of weapons of mass destruction, humanitarian assistance and preservation of cultural diversity'. Linguists also point out that care should be taken to prevent **language death** (language extinction, linguistic extinction or linguicide), a process whereby a language that has been used in a speech community gradually dies out. In this scenario, the level of linguistic competence that speakers possess in a particular language variety decreases to the extent that eventually there are no fluent speakers of that variety left. Some linguists caution that the dominance of global English is leading to the loss of minority languages and linguistic diversity in some parts of the world (Crystal 2000; Nettle & Romaine 2000). The concerns of global citizens are many and varied.

GLOBAL COMPETENCY

There are many definitions of global competence (sometimes referred to as '**transnational competence**') besides the one offered by Morais and Ogden (2011) in relation to their Global citizenship conceptual model (See Figure 12.1). Lambert (1996), for example, defines a **globally competent person** as an individual who has knowledge of current events, the capacity to empathize with others, the ability to maintain a positive attitude, second language competence and an appreciation of foreign ways of doing things. Olson and Kroeger (2001) maintain that a globally competent individual possesses sufficient substantive **global knowledge** (e.g. understanding of cultures, languages, global events and concerns), **perceptual understanding** (e.g. open-mindedness, sophisticated cognitive processing, resistance to stereotyping) and **intercultural communication skills** (e.g. adaptability, **empathy** (concern for others), cross-cultural awareness, intercultural mediation, intercultural sensitivity) to interact appropriately and effectively in our globally interconnected world.

The Stanley Foundation (2003), an American organization that funds research on global education, defines **global competency** as 'an appreciation of complexity, conflict management, the inevitability of change, and the interconnectedness between and among humans and their environment'. The Foundation emphasizes that 'globally competent citizens know they have an impact on the world and that the world influences them. They recognize their ability and responsibility to make choices that affect the future.'

International educators Donatelli *et al.* (2005: 134) cite the following as common traits of global competence:

- general knowledge of one's own culture, history and people
- general knowledge of cultures, histories and peoples other than one's own
- fluency in a world language other than one's native tongue
- cross-cultural empathy
- openness and cognitive flexibility
- tolerance for ambiguity, perceptual acuity and attentiveness to nonverbal messages
- awareness of issues facing the global community (ibid: 134).

Hunter (2004) surveyed senior international educators, transnational corporation human resource managers and United Nations officials to ascertain their perception of the knowledge,

Figure 12.2 Global competence model

skills, attitudes and experiences necessary to become globally competent. For these individuals, a globally competent person is someone who is 'able to identify cultural differences to compete globally, collaborate across cultures, and effectively participate in both social and business settings in other countries' (Deardorff & Hunter 2006: 77). Global competence means 'having an open mind while actively seeking to understand cultural norms and expectations of others, leveraging this gained knowledge to interact, communicate and work effectively outside one's environment' (Hunter 2004: 74).

Based on the findings of his study, Hunter (2004) developed the **global competence model** to provide a framework for international educators to prepare '**global-ready graduates**' (individuals who are adequately prepared for a diverse workforce and society that necessitates intercultural and global competencies). (See Figure 12.2.)

Central to Hunter's (2004) model is the conviction that if one is to achieve global competency, one must recognize that one's own worldview is not universal. In other words, one must move away from an ethnocentric perspective towards a more open stance. His framework emphasizes that '[a]ttitudes of openness, curiosity, and respect are key starting points upon which to build the requisite knowledge and skills' (Deardorff & Hunter 2006: 79). While second language proficiency is not cited in the graphic illustration, it is referred to in articles that explain the model.

INTERCULTURAL COMPETENCY

Many definitions of intercultural competence (e.g. **intercultural effectiveness**) have been developed in the last few decades by speech communication specialists and general education scholars as well as by applied linguists who have a particular interest in the cultural dimension of language learning and use. As noted in Chapter 2, the former have long criticized applied linguists for not paying sufficient attention to the cultural component in language education teaching and research; conversely, second language specialists have rebuked communication specialists for largely ignoring the language component in their studies and theories of intercultural communication.

Many cross-cultural psychologists, anthropologists, international educators, language and social psychologists and scholars from other disciplines have focused their attention on the traits, skills and behaviours of interculturally competent individuals who reside temporarily or permanently in a new culture. Consequently, some of our current understandings of intercultural competence have centred on adaptability and effectiveness in unfamiliar cultural contexts (e.g. intercultural adjustment and adaptation while studying abroad). Other broader, more general conceptions of **intercultural competence** refer to intercultural traits, knowledge and behaviours related to one's interactions in any intercultural situation or context (e.g. in one's home environment or in international settings). (See Chapter 8 for a discussion of intercultural effectiveness in relation to intercultural transitions.)

Much can be learned by examining the perspectives of scholars and practitioners from diverse areas of specialization. In today's complex, globalizing world, whenever feasible, an interdisciplinary approach to intercultural communication is imperative to integrate and build on the strengths of different theories and modes of research. This can help us to better understand the concept of intercultural competency and identify the most effective ways to become intercultural. Let's take a look at various conceptions of intercultural (communication/communicative) competence put forward by scholars from diverse disciplines.

Intercultural (communication) competence

Influenced by their discipline, research and life experience, scholars have used a variety of terms to refer to the competence of individuals in intercultural interactions, including intercultural competence, intercultural communication competence, intercultural communicative competence, cross-cultural competence, multicultural competence, cultural fluency, intercultural sensitivity, cultural intelligence and so on (see Fantini 2012b for a longer list of terms). Let's examine some of the most well-known terms and definitions.

In relation to sojourners and longer-term migrants, Taylor (1994: 154), an adult education specialist, defines **intercultural competency** as 'an adaptive capacity based on an inclusive and integrative world view which allows participants to effectively accommodate the demands of living in a host culture'. 'Interculturally competent persons', according to Chen and Starosta (2006: 357), 'know how to elicit a desired response in interactions and to fulfill their own communication goals by respecting and affirming the worldview and cultural identities of the interactants'. For these communication scholars, **intercultural communication competence** is 'the ability to acknowledge, respect, tolerate, and integrate cultural differences that qualifies one for enlightened global citizenship' (ibid: 357). In Jandt's (2007: 48) view,

> [g]ood intercultural communicators have **personality strength** (with a strong sense of self and are socially relaxed), communication skills (verbal and nonverbal), **psychological**

adjustment (ability to adapt to new situations), and **cultural awareness** (understanding of how people of different cultures think and act).

(Jandt 2007: 184)

For this communication specialist, **intercultural communication competence** requires 'understanding dominant cultural values and understanding how our own cultural values affect the way we perceive ourselves and others. None of these conceptions of intercultural competence deals explicitly with the use of a second language in intercultural interactions.

Intercultural communicative competence

Michael Byram, a foreign language education specialist, observed that many understandings of intercultural competency largely ignore the language component even though language is a core element in intercultural communication and most interactions involve a second language. He prefers to distinguish between intercultural competence and intercultural communicative competence. For Bryam (1997, 2012), the former refers to the skills and ability that individuals draw on to interact in their native language with people from another culture (e.g. first language speakers of English from New Zealand interacting with first language speakers of English from Canada). By contrast, the latter refers to the ability of individuals to interact successfully across cultures while using a second language (e.g. a Taiwanese second language speaker of English interacting with a Malaysian second language speaker of English or a first language speaker of English from Australia).

Intercultural communicative competence focuses on 'establishing and maintaining relationships' instead of merely communicating messages or exchanging information (Byram 1997: 3). This involves 'accomplishing a negotiation between people based on both culture-specific and culture-general features that is on the whole respectful of and favourable to each' (Guilherme, 2004: 297). Within the context of intercultural education, **culture-specific approaches** primarily aim at the achievement of cultural competence in a particular culture. For example, Danish students may prepare for a year-abroad programme in Barcelona by taking Spanish language lessons, reading about Spanish culture and participating in a pre-sojourn course that centres on how to communicate effectively and appropriately in various contexts and situations in Spain.

Culture-general approaches do not focus on a particular culture; instead, they centre on the development of the knowledge, skills and mindset that can help individuals analyse their linguistic and cultural context and engage in successful intercultural interactions, no matter where they are in the world. For example, this intercultural communication text provides examples from many different cultural contexts and is designed to raise awareness of core issues in intercultural relations (e.g. ethnocentrism, intercultural sensitivity, cultural self-awareness). As broad intercultural competence cannot be achieved by focusing on the ability to behave properly in a particular culture, intercultural learning, ideally, should involve a mix of 'culture-specific' and 'culture-general' approaches.

Intercultural communicative competence and the intercultural speaker

The close relationship between language, culture and intercultural competence is conveyed in the notion of the **intercultural speaker**, a term coined by Byram (see Byram & Zarate 1997) to describe foreign language/culture learners who successfully establish intercultural relationships while using their second language. Intercultural speakers

> operate their linguistic competence and their sociolinguistic awareness . . . in order to manage interaction across cultural boundaries, to anticipate misunderstandings caused by difference in values, meanings and beliefs, and . . . to cope with the affective as well as cognitive demands of engagement with otherness.
>
> (ibid: 25)

Intercultural speakers are described as competent, flexible communicators (Byram 2012; Byram & Zarate 1997; Wilkinson 2012) who 'engage with complexity and multiple identities' and 'avoid stereotyping which accompanies perceiving someone through a single identity' (Byram *et al.* 2002: 5). For Guilherme (2004: 298), *critical* **intercultural speakers** are able to 'negotiate between their own cultural, social and political identifications and representations with those of the other', and in the process, become aware of 'the multiple, ambivalent, resourceful, and elastic nature of cultural identities in an intercultural encounter' (ibid: 125). The term 'intercultural speaker' is still widely used today, although some scholars prefer the term '**intercultural mediator**' to emphasize 'the individual's potential for social action rather than the competencies acquired as a consequence of teaching' (Alred & Byram, 2002: 341). When we discuss Bryam's model of intercultural communicative competence, we revisit notions of the intercultural speaker.

Intercultural communicative competence and intercultural citizenship

Byram (2008, 2011a, 2012) has also linked the notion of intercultural communicative competence with citizenship education. In recent publications, he defines the competencies that enable intercultural speakers to take part in community activity and service with people from another country who speak a different first language. To foster the development of '**intercultural political competence**', Byram (2011b: 17) advocates 'the enrichment of citizenship education with an international dimension' coupled with the infusion of a 'political/citizenship dimension' in second or foreign language education. This approach to **intercultural citizenship** brings together 'the general dimensions of attitudes, knowledge and behaviour' common to both citizenship and language education.

> In intercultural citizenship, the question of national or cosmopolitan allegiances is not important; intercultural citizenship is not a matter of creating identifications with state or any other entity. It is rather, the development of competencies to engage with others in political activity across linguistic and cultural boundaries both within and across state frontiers. International 'bonds'—and the reduction of prejudice—are the intended outcomes.
>
> (Bryam 2011b: 19)

Intercultural citizenship, which favours multiculturalism and equality, requires awareness and respect of self and other, the desire to interact across cultures and the acquisition of the knowledge and skills that facilitate constructive, active participation in today's complex, globalized society. For Guilherme (2007: 87), this entails 'the control of the fear of the unknown (at the emotional level), the promotion of a critical outlook (at the cognitive level), as well as the enhancement of self-development (at the experiential level)'. Through education and international experience, Alred *et al.* (2003), Byram (2006, 2008, 2009, 2011a, 2012), Guilherme (2002, 2007, 2012) and other interculturalists maintain that it is possible to cultivate the understanding (e.g. cultural knowledge, open mindset) and skills (e.g. culture-sensitive behaviours, culture-learning strategies) that characterize intercultural communicative competence and cosmopolitan, intercultural citizenship. In the process, this fulfils some of the aims of global citizenship that were discussed earlier in the chapter.

'Effective' and 'appropriate' intercultural communication

Alvino Fantini has also written extensively about intercultural communication in second language situations. For this applied linguist, **intercultural communicative competence** is 'a complex of abilities needed to perform *effectively* and *appropriately* when interacting with others who are linguistically and culturally different from oneself' (Fantini 2007: 9). Implicit in this definition are: individual traits and characteristics (e.g. personality); the domains of relationships, communication and collaboration; the dimensions of knowledge, **attitude** (emotional response to people/things), skills and awareness; proficiency in the host language and a developmental process.

In Fantini's (2007) definition, **_effective_ intercultural communication** relates to one's perception of one's performance in intercultural encounters, drawing on an 'etic' or outsider's view of the host/second language culture. By contrast, the notion of **_appropriate_ intercultural communication** is linked to how one's behaviour is perceived by one's hosts (i.e. an 'emic' or insider's understanding of what is acceptable in the host/second language culture). This conceptualization of intercultural communicative competence acknowledges the importance of the views of *both* interactants (the sender and receiver) in terms of outcomes. In other words, for the communication to be successful, the message must also be received as interculturally sensitive and appropriate, and the meaning should generally be interpreted as intended.

Critical applied linguists Dervin and Dirba (2006) maintain that second language speakers possess intercultural competence 'when they are able/willing to communicate effectively with others, accept their position as "strangers" when meeting others, and realize that all individuals, including themselves, are multicultural and complex (sex, age, religion, status in society, etc.)' (p. 257). For Sercu (2005: 2), an applied linguist, an interculturally competent individual possesses the following traits and skills:

> the willingness to engage with the foreign culture, self-awareness and the ability to look upon oneself from the outside, the ability to see the world through the others' eyes, the ability to cope with uncertainty, the ability to act as a cultural mediator, the ability to evaluate others' points of view, the ability to consciously use culture learning skills and to read the cultural context, and the understanding that individuals cannot be reduced to their collective identities.

A common definition of intercultural competence

By surveying 23 leading intercultural communication experts (e.g. Michael Byram, Janet Bennett, Guo-Ming Chen), Deardorff (2004: 181) aimed to arrive at a common understanding of intercultural competence. The top three elements that the scholars associated with this construct were: 'awareness, valuing, and understanding of cultural differences; experiencing other cultures; and self-awareness of one's own culture' (ibid: 247). After reviewing nine definitions of intercultural competence, the scholars considered the following one as most relevant to their institution's internationalization strategies: 'Knowledge of others, knowledge of self; skills to interpret and relate; skills to discover and/or to interact; valuing others' values, beliefs, and behaviors; and relativizing one's self. Linguistic competence plays a key role' (Byram 1997: 34). Although the majority of the experts surveyed were not language educators, they appeared to recognize the importance of language in intercultural encounters as they gave the highest rating to Byram's (1997) definition, which drew attention to the linguistic dimension.

After analysing the input of the survey respondents, Deardorff (2004: 194) concluded her study by formulating the following broad definition of intercultural competence: 'the ability to communicate effectively and appropriately in intercultural situations based on one's intercultural knowledge, skills and attitudes'. Although the language dimension (e.g. use of a second language) was not made explicit, it is mentioned in related publications.

MODELS OF INTERCULTURAL COMPETENCE

Building on their understandings of intercultural communication and intercultural effectiveness, numerous scholars (e.g. speech communication specialists, applied linguists, interculturalists, international educators) have devised models of intercultural competence. Let's take a look at some of the most widely-known frameworks: Byram's (1997) model of intercultural communicative competence, Chen and Starosta's (2008) model of intercultural communication competence, M.J. Bennett's (1993) developmental model of Intercultural sensitivity and Deardorff's (2004) process model of intercultural competence.

Byram's model of intercultural communicative competence

Byram's (1997) model of intercultural communicative competence has had a profound impact on the teaching of second or foreign languages, especially in European contexts. His conceptual framework draws attention to the need to integrate culture into second language teaching and learning. As illustrated in Figure 12.3, Byram's work builds on notions of communicative competence put forward by Hymes (1966, 1972) and expanded on by other applied linguists in relation to the teaching and learning of foreign languages (e.g. Bachman 1990; Canale & Swain 1980). **Communicative competence** refers to 'what a speaker needs to know, and what a child needs to learn, to be able to use language appropriately in specific social/cultural settings' (Swann *et al.* 2004: 42). Thus, it is linked to notions of first and second language socialization that were discussed in earlier chapters.

In the first part of his model, Byram (1997) cites the following *linguistic* elements as characteristic of an interculturally competent second language speaker (the intercultural speaker or mediator):

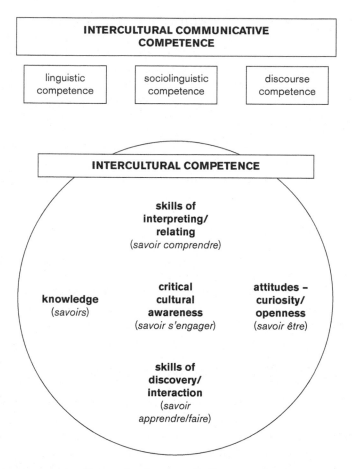

Figure 12.3 The components of intercultural communicative competence

- **Linguistic competence**: the ability to apply knowledge of the rules of a standard version of the language to produce and interpret spoken and written language.
- **Sociolinguistic competence**: the ability to give to the language produced by an interlocutor – whether native speaker or not – meanings that are taken for granted by the interlocutor or are negotiated and made explicit with the interlocutor.
- **Discourse competence**: the ability to use, discover and negotiate strategies for the production and interpretation of monologue or dialogue texts which follow the conventions of the culture of an interlocutor or are negotiated as intercultural texts for particular purposes (Byram 1997: 48).

The second part of this framework identifies five *savoirs* or components that are linked to the *cultural* dimension of the intercultural speaker's competence. The first two are considered prerequisites for successful intercultural/interlingual communication:

- **Intercultural attitudes (*savoir être*)**: curiosity and openness, readiness to suspend disbelief about others cultures and belief about one's own intercultural attitudes.

■ **Knowledge (*savoirs*)**: of social groups and their products and practices in one's own and in one's interlocutor's country.

Finally, the next three components feature the skills deemed necessary for successful communication across cultures and languages:

■ **Skills of interpreting and relating (*savoir comprendre*)**: ability to interpret a document or event from another culture, to explain it and relate it to documents or events from one's own.
■ **Skills of discovery and interaction (*savoir apprendre/faire*)**: ability to acquire new knowledge of a culture and to operate this knowledge in real-time communication.
■ **Critical cultural awareness (*savoir s'engager*)**: an ability to evaluate critically and on the basis of explicit criteria, perspectives, practices and products in one's own and other cultures and countries (Byram *et al.* 2002: 12–13).

This model draws attention to the need for language teachers to integrate a cultural component into their language teaching. With this in view, Byram *et al.* (2002: 6) offer the following advice:

> developing the intercultural dimension in language teaching involves recognizing that the aims are: to give learners intercultural competence as well as linguistic competence; to prepare them for interaction with people of other cultures; to enable them to understand and accept people from other cultures as individuals with other distinctive perspectives, values and behaviours; and to help them to see that such interaction is an enriching experience.

Knowing grammar rules and vocabulary in a second language is not sufficient for one to be interculturally competent. Byram's model of intercultural communicative competence raises awareness of the importance of culture learning for second language learners (e.g. learning about the values and practices of their own and other cultures). After examining the Developmental Model of Intercultural Sensitivity, we delve further into the relationship between second language proficiency and intercultural competence.

Chen and Starosta's model of intercultural communication competence

Speech communication specialists Chen and Starosta (2008) have developed and refined their own model of intercultural communication competence, which emphasizes a 'transformational process of symmetrical interdependence'. Their conceptual framework consists of three 'equally important', interrelated dimensions that work together to create 'a holistic picture of intercultural communication competence': (1) affective or intercultural sensitivity, (2) cognitive or intercultural awareness and (3) behavioural or intercultural adroitness. This model does not, however, deal explicitly with intercultural interactions in a second language.

Intercultural communication competence, in Chen and Starosta's (2008: 223) view, requires **affective** or **intercultural sensitivity**, that is, 'positive emotion that enables individuals to be sensitive enough to acknowledge and respect cultural differences'. This affective process is linked to the following personal elements or characteristics: 'self-concept, open-mindedness, nonjudgmental attitudes, and social relaxation' (ibid: 223). Similar to Byram (1997), these scholars have found that people who are competent intercultural communicators possess higher levels of **cognitive** or **intercultural awareness**, that is, **self-awareness** (e.g. knowledge of one's own personal identities/cultures) and **cultural awareness** (e.g. understanding of how cultures differ). To be competent intercultural communicators, Chen and Starosta (2008: 227) maintain that individuals must also enhance their **behavioural** or **intercultural adroitness** ('message skills, knowledge regarding appropriate self-disclosure, behavioral flexibility, interaction management, and social skills'). These skills and actions, in their view, are vital for world citizens to act effectively in intercultural encounters and 'achieve the goal of multicultural interdependence and interconnectedness in the global village' (ibid: 227).

Recognizing 'the complex multicultural dynamics' of 'our current global society', Chen and Starosta (2008: 227) recommend that measures of intercultural communication competence take into account the multiple perspectives and identities that are now a common feature within communities and cultures:

> The trends of technology development, globalization of the economy, widespread population migration, development of multiculturalism, and the demise of the nation-state in favor of sub- and supranational identifications have shrunk and multiculturalized the world, and traditional perceptions of *self* and *other* must be redefined. The global context of human communication and the need to pursue a state of multicultural coexistence require that we abolish the boundaries separating *me* and *you*, *us* and *them*, and develop a theory of communication competence that takes into account individuals' multiple identities.

Challenging traditional notions of Self and Other, their recommendation is in line with the position of Moon (2008) and other critical theorists (e.g. Dervin 2012; Holliday 2012, Kramsch & Uryu 2012) who rally against homogenizing, static perspectives of culture that adopt a 'culture as nation' perspective and fail to acknowledge the dynamic nature of identities, hybridity within individuals, and diversity within groups.

The developmental model of intercultural sensitivity (DMIS)

While some theorists have focused on describing the behaviours and traits associated with intercultural competence, others have proposed models that aim to depict the *process* of becoming interculturally competent. One such framework is the **developmental model of intercultural sensitivity** (DMIS). The DMIS has had a significant impact on the field of intercultural communication and is widely used in research (e.g. education abroad) and practice (e.g. intercultural education programmes). In relation to this model, Bennett and Bennett (2004) view **intercultural competence** as 'the ability to communicate effectively in cross-cultural situations and to relate appropriately in a variety of cultural contexts' (p. 149), while **intercultural sensitivity** refers to the developmental process that impacts an individual's psychological ability to deal with cultural differences.

Phenomenological in nature, this theoretical framework was developed by Milton Bennett (1993) to explain the observed and reported experiences of individuals in intercultural encounters: 'The underlying assumption of the model is that as one's *experiences of cultural difference* becomes more sophisticated, one's competence in intercultural relations increases' (Bennett & Bennett 2004: 152). The DMIS centres on the constructs of **ethnocentricism** and **ethnorelativism** (Bennett 2009). In the former, 'the worldview of one's own culture is central to all reality' (M.J. Bennett 1993: 30), whereas the latter is linked to 'being comfortable with many standards and customs and to having an ability to adapt behavior and judgments to a variety of interpersonal settings' (ibid: 26).

In this theory, intercultural sensitivity is associated with personal growth and the development of an **intercultural mind**, 'a mindset capable of understanding from within and from without both one's own culture and other cultures' (Bennett *et al.* 2003: 252). M.J. Bennett (1993, 2012) suggests that the development of intercultural sensitivity occurs as the constructs and experiences of cultural differences evolve toward an increased awareness and acceptance of those differences. Specifically, the DMIS theorizes that individuals move from ethnocentric stages where one's culture is experienced as 'central to reality' (denial, defense, minimization), through ethnorelative stages of greater recognition and acceptance of difference (acceptance, adaptation, and integration). People, however, do not necessarily follow a linear progression (e.g. advancing to the next stage in sequence). Due to unpleasant intercultural experiences or acute culture shock, for example, they may retreat to a lower level of sensitivity.

Denial of difference measures a worldview that ignores or simplifies cultural difference. In this stage, one's own culture is experienced as the only real one. **Polarization: defense/reversal** measures a judgmental orientation that views cultural differences in terms of 'us' and 'them', whereby one's own culture (or an adopted one) is experienced as the best way of doing things. In **defense of difference**, 'us' is uncritically viewed as superior, whereas in *reversal* (R), the opposite bias prevails. **Minimization** (M) measures a transitional worldview that emphasizes cultural commonality and universal values. With limited cultural self-awareness, individuals in this phase are still ethnocentric and may not pay sufficient attention to cultural differences, assuming that other cultures are similar to one's own. **Acceptance of difference** measures a worldview that can comprehend and appreciate complex cultural differences, while **adaptation to difference** identifies the capacity to alter one's cultural perspective and adapt one's behaviour so that it is appropriate in a particular cultural context. The DMIS posits that ethnorelative worldviews (**Acceptance, Adaptation**) have more potential to generate the attitudes, knowledge and behaviour that constitute intercultural competence and facilitate adjustment in a new milieu.

In the DMIS, intercultural competence is viewed as a developmental phenomenon, in harmony with Mezirow's (1994, 2000) **transformational learning theory** in adult education. The latter posits that adults who engage in critical reflection and self-examination may experience a dramatic **transformation** (the act or process of change) in response to significant events or difficult stages in their lives (e.g. relocating to another linguistic and cultural environment, taking part in a global internship in a foreign land, moving from secondary school to university).

Within the context of intercultural communication, **critical reflection** is the process of analysing, reconsidering and questioning intercultural experiences with the aim of developing a better understanding of internal and external factors that influenced the outcome. From a transformational learning perspective, **intercultural competence** involves a continuous learning process with 'new or revised interpretations of the meaning of one's experience' (Mezirow 1994: 222). Through intercultural contact, individuals encounter cultural differences (and similarities) and face challenges that may cause them to question their usual ways of doing things. As they deepen their awareness and understanding of these differences, they may adjust their attitudes and mindset (e.g. develop an ethnorelative perspective) and gradually employ new behaviours that help them communicate more effectively and appropriately in intercultural interactions. Mezirow (1994, 2000) suggests that this process has the potential to lead to a life-altering transformation and restructuring of one's sense of self (e.g. identity expansion, identity reconstruction) in some individuals. (See Chapter 6 for a discussion of this phenomenon.)

The DMIS assumes a social construction of identity, positioning it as relational and subject to change. This perspective is aligned with contemporary critical and poststructuralist notions of identity (e.g. Guilherme 2002; Noels *et al.* 2012; Norton 2000), which recognize the fluid, contradictory nature of this construct. In contrast with traditional views of identity as fixed, static and unitary, this perspective allows for the impact of globalization and intercultural contact and the evolution of hybrid, global identities.

In sum, the DMIS offers a theory-based explanation of individual effectiveness in intercultural encounters, capturing the elements that Bhawuk and Brislin (1992: 416) argue are key predictors of success in intercultural contexts: 'To be effective in another culture, people must be interested in other cultures, be sensitive enough to notice cultural differences, and then also be willing to modify their behavior as an indication of respect for the people of other cultures.'

The process model of intercultural competence

Drawing on the input of 23 leading interculturalists, Deardorff (2004: 194), an international educator, also devised a process model. Her graphic representation of intercultural competence, which is presented in Figure 12.4, depicts movement from 'the individual level of attitudes/personal attributes to the interactive cultural level in regard to the outcomes'. It draws attention to the internal shift in frame of reference that is essential for effective and appropriate behaviour in intercultural encounters.

A strength of this process model is that it recognizes the *ongoing* complexity of the development of intercultural competence and the importance of reflection in the life-long journey toward interculturality. Leclerq (2003: 9) defines **interculturality** as 'the set of processes through which relations between different cultures are constructed', whereby '[t]he aim is to enable groups and individuals who belong to such cultures within a single society or geo-political entity to forge links based on equity and mutual respect.'

Similar to Chen and Starosta's (2008) and Byram's (1997, 2006) models, Deardorff's (2004) conceptual framework accentuates the vital role that **attitude** plays in intercultural learning. Significantly, the intercultural experts she surveyed stress that 'the attitudes of open-ness, respect (valuing all cultures), curiosity and discovery (tolerating ambiguity)' are essential for one to become interculturally competent (Deardorff, 2004: 193). Further, in accord with Byram's (1997) *'savoirs'*, her model recognizes that intercultural competence necessitates knowledge and understanding of 'one's own cultural norms and sensitivity to those of other cultures' (Deardorff 2008: 37).

Deardorff's process model (2004, 2006, 2008; Deardroff & Jones 2012) identifies key internal outcomes that may occur as a result of 'an informed frame of reference shift', namely, adaptability, an ethnorelative perspective, empathy and a flexible mindset. Her graphic also specifies desired external outcomes that can be assessed (e.g. 'behaving and communicating appropriately and effectively' in intercultural situations). In Deardorff's (2008: 42) words, her model provides 'a holistic framework for intercultural competence development and assessment'.

All of these models have contributed to our understanding of the multiple factors involved in intercultural competence and the process of gradually moving from an ethnocentric (monocultural) perspective to an ethnorelative or **intercultural mindset**.

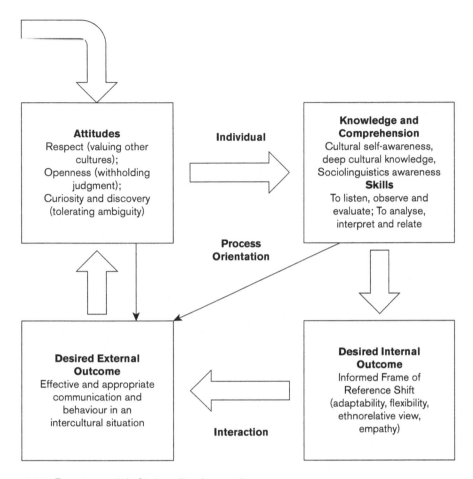

Figure 12.4 Process model of intercultural competence

SECOND LANGUAGE PROFICIENCY AND INTERCULTURAL COMPETENCE

Recently, scholars have attempted to link levels of intercultural competence with proficiency in the second or foreign language (e.g. language of the host community). The development of 'an intercultural mindset', according to Bennett *et al.* (2003: 252), 'resonates positively with communicative competence and proficiency-related theories of language learning'. They hypothesize that there is a 'typical fit between language proficiency levels and developmental levels of intercultural sensitivity' (ibid: 255).

Although language proficiency is not a specific element of the DMIS, the model never-theless supports the view of language learning as a communication endeavor and as a humanistic enterprise. As a communication endeavor, language competence is defined as the ability to use the language as an *insider*. The DMIS creates a parallel to language competence by defining cultural competence as the ability to interpret and behave within culture as an *insider*. As a humanistic enterprise, language learning creates an awareness and appreciation of language itself. The DMIS parallel is that intercultural sensitivity involves an awareness and appreciation of culture itself.

(Bennett *et al.* 2003: 253)

More specifically, they suggest that progression through the stages of the DMIS correlates with advances in one's second language proficiency. In particular, they speculate that learners who have an advanced level of proficiency are apt to be in an ethnorelative stage of cultural development (e.g. Adaptation/Integration). Conversely, those who are novice learners of the language are likely to be in an ethnocentric stage of development (e.g. Denial/Defense). But are intercultural development and second language proficiency necessarily parallel? What evidence has been gathered that supports or refutes this hypothesis?

Thus far, only a few studies have explored this question. In South Korea, Park (2006) examined the relationship between intercultural sensitivity and linguistic competence in 104 pre-service EFL (English as a Foreign Language) teachers. The Intercultural Development Inventory (a cross-culturally validated psychometric instrument) was utilized to measure the participants' level of intercultural sensitivity as outlined in the DMIS. The Michigan English Language Assessment Battery (MELAB) was used to assess their level of language competence. Park (2006) found little correlation between the participants' level of intercultural sensitivity and linguistic competence; those with advanced proficiency in English did not necessarily possess a higher level of intercultural sensitivity. The findings suggest that 'intercultural competence might not naturally grow with the development of linguistic competence'; in fact, it may progress at a much slower rate than proficiency in a second language. Park (2006) recommends that intercultural competence be taught explicitly, as is the case with second or foreign (international) languages (e.g. formal classroom-based instruction).

To better understand the link between linguistic and intercultural development, Edstrom (2005) interviewed 13 American women (second language users of Spanish) living in Venezuela. Employing the DMIS as a theoretical framework, she discovered that the following factors influenced the women's participation in second language conversation: their knowledge of second language (L2) conversational styles, their willingness to accept differences in communication styles and their interest in the topics of conversation. '[A]lthough an appreciation for the complexity of language and an understanding of the relationship between language and culture do not produce proficient, bilingual learners', Edstrom (2005: 32) notes that, 'these concepts may contribute to the formation of informed, tolerant learners who appreciate the difficulty of mastering an L2'.

Similar to Park (2006), Edstrom (2005) recommends that intercultural communication theories and strategies be made explicit in second language education. In particular, she suggests that awareness of cross-cultural differences in conversational styles be incorporated into language teaching along with tasks designed to increase intercultural sensitivity. In her view, 'exploring the role of personal background and intercultural sensitivity in the language learning process does not ensure learners' successful participation in L2 conversation but it does expose them to the complex relationship between language and its users' (ibid: 32). Significantly, Edstrom (2005) was convinced that this awareness 'may serve them longer than their L2 skills' (ibid: 32).

In separate surveys of interculturalists and global education experts, Deardorff and Hunter (2006: 81) found a consensus that 'neither language nor education abroad alone makes someone interculturally or globally competent'. In both studies, the participants argued that 'more language course offerings must include key cultural knowledge that goes beyond the "tip of the iceberg" of food, music, and holidays to explore and understand the deep cultural knowledge of underlying values, norms, and worldviews' (ibid: 81). Consistent with Deardorff's (2004) study, Hunter's (2004) respondents maintain that 'simply studying abroad, learning a L2, or majoring in international relations is no longer enough to prepare students for the global workforce. The approach to preparedness must be comprehensive' (Deardorff & Hunter 2006: 79).

Further, a growing number of study abroad researchers and specialists in intercultural/ second language pedagogy (e.g. Bennett 2009; Jackson 2008; 2010, 2012; Vande Berg *et al.* 2012) concur with Ryan's (2003: 132) observation that '[r]esidence in another country does not automatically produce interculturality'. Simply put, intercultural contact and international travel do not necessarily lead to intercultural communicative competence. As noted by Guilherme *et al.* (2010: 243–44), 'language learning alone is not sufficient to grasp the complexities of another culture and to finally achieve intercultural competence'. Knowing the grammar and vocabulary of another language does not ensure that people will be able to communicate successfully across cultures in that language. With this in mind, Bennett (1997: 16–21) offers the following description of 'a fluent fool':

> A fluent fool is someone who speaks a foreign language well but doesn't understand the social or philosophical content of that language. Such people are likely to get into all sorts of trouble because both they themselves and others overestimate their ability. They may be invited into complicated social situations where they cannot understand the events deeply enough to avoid giving or taking offense. Eventually, fluent fools may develop negative opinions of the native speakers whose language they understand but whose basic beliefs and values continue to elude them . . . To avoid becoming a fluent fool, we need to understand more completely the cultural dimension of language.

While the label 'fluent fool' is rather jarring, Bennett's (1997) admonition raises our awareness of the need to develop intercultural competence along with proficiency in a second or foreign language.

REQUISITE COMPETENCIES FOR TODAY'S GLOBAL SOCIETY

What competencies are necessary for individuals to become responsible, ethical global citizens in today's diverse world? What knowledge, attitudes and skills are vital for success in today's global workforce and society? International educators and scholars from various disciplines have identified a number of requisite competencies of world citizens, which are presented in Figure 12.5.

While this list includes many international/intercultural competencies, it is not exhaustive. Can you identify other items that should be included?

ENHANCING INTERCULTURAL (COMMUNICATIVE) COMPETENCE AND GLOBAL CITIZENSHIP

History shows that we human beings have both the capacity to open our eyes, minds, hearts, and hands—and to close them. We have the capacity to build an interdependent, peaceful global civilization and to splinter and fragment into endless conflict. We can see the world narrowly, or broadly, depending on which parts of ourselves we are able to

Knowledge

Knowledge of world geography, conditions, languages, issues, and events.

Awareness of the complexity and interdependency of world events and issues.

Understanding of historical forces that have shaped the current world system.

Knowledge of one's own culture, language, and history.

Knowledge of effective communication, including knowledge of a foreign language, intercultural communication concepts, international business etiquette, and netiquette.

Sociopragmatic knowledge of a foreign language (e.g., awareness of cultural scripts).

Understanding of the diversity found in the world in terms of values, beliefs, ideas, languages, and worldviews.

Civic knowledge and engagement – local and global.

Attitudes: Personal and social responsibility

Openness to learning and a positive orientation to new opportunities, ideas, languages, and ways of thinking.

Tolerance for ambiguity and unfamiliarity.

Sensitivity and respect for personal, linguistic, and cultural differences.

Empathy or the ability to take multiple perspectives.

Self-awareness and self-esteem about one's own identity, language, and culture.

Appreciation of other ways of being (e.g., diverse communication styles, worldviews).

Ethical reasoning and action.

Skills

Technical skills to enhance one's ability to learn about the world (e.g., research skills, computer literacy).

Critical and comparative thinking skills, including the ability to think creatively and integrate knowledge, rather than uncritical acceptance of knowledge.

Communication skills, including the ability to use another language effectively and interact *effectively and appropriately* with people who have a different cultural background (e.g., well developed sociopragmatic awareness and communication skills).

Teamwork and problem-solving.

Coping and resiliency skills in unfamiliar and challenging intercultural situations.

(Adapted from Association of American Colleges and Universities (AAC&U) (2007); Green and Olson 2003: 106–7; Olson *et al.* 2007).

Figure 12.5 Requisite competencies for today's global citizens

develop. Indeed, wherever we may live, the drama of the Earth itself is occurring within each of us.

If we are willing to open our eyes, minds, hearts, and hands, then every one of us can become a global citizen.

Yes, *everyone.*

(Gerzon 2010: xxiv)

How can each of us develop ourselves as global and intercultural citizens? What actions can we take to overcome ethnocentric tendencies and become more sensitive, effective intercultural communicators? In this chapter, we have reviewed the traits and actions of people who are considered interculturally competent, global citizens. We have examined theories and models of both intercultural competence and global competence. Let's now take a look at some practical steps that you can take to become more globally-minded and intercultural.

Become more self-aware. Throughout this book, the importance of becoming more self-aware has been emphasized. To become an effective intercultural communicator and global citizen, it is imperative to recognize one's strengths and weaknesses in order to have an idea about what to work on. For example, if you have a low tolerance of ambiguity, you can make a concerted effort to reduce your anxiety in unfamiliar or unclear situations. Recognizing your tendency to become quickly frustrated and overwhelmed is the first step to identifying effective coping strategies. If you make snap judgments when meeting people for the first time, you can try to curb this tendency by focusing on the positive. If you discover that you have very little knowledge about your cultural/linguistic background and find it difficult to respond to related questions in intercultural interactions, you can do research in this area. If you feel out of your depth when people are talking about global issues, you can resolve to enhance your knowledge of international affairs.

Become more aware of your preferred self-identities and communication styles and identify the cultural behaviours that seem to annoy or disturb you the most. Then, make an effort to change your attitude so that you approach intercultural situations with a more positive mindset. By developing the habit of critical reflection, you can gain a better understanding of what you need to improve. This process of discovery, reflection and growth can be ongoing throughout your life.

Observe and actively listen. In an unfamiliar cultural context or in intercultural situations in your home environment, carefully observe the verbal and nonverbal behaviours of your communication partners who have a different linguistic and cultural background. Be an active listener. As well as paying attention to what is being said, **active listening** means noticing how and when ideas are conveyed, as well as what is *not* being said. In intercultural interactions, also keep in mind that you may not be interpreting messages in the way that the speaker intended. Consider the possibility of other perspectives and resist the temptation to make quick, negative assumptions about the speaker and his or her linguistic or cultural background. Avoid stereotyping! If you have a negative encounter with someone from a particular background that does not mean that all people who are linked to this language or culture will act or think in the same way.

Cultivate openness. Overcoming ethnocentric tendencies and developing an intercultural or ethnorelative mindset is a critical goal for all citizens. **Ethnocentricism** refers to an attitude that one's ways of being are superior to others. Whereas an ethnocentric individual may regard cultural difference as inferior and unacceptable, an open-minded individual or intercultural person is receptive to new ideas and behaviours.

Effective intercultural communicators strive to understand what lies behind unfamiliar practices and worldviews instead of making quick value judgments. In international intercultural situations, for example, you can demonstrate willingness to try new things (e.g. local cuisine, different communication styles), make an effort to learn the host language and broaden your repertoire of verbal and nonverbal behaviours so that your actions are effective and appropriate for the cultural context. Being intercultural, however, does not mean that you must accept social or culture practices that demean or degrade others (e.g. female mutilation, slavery). As ethical, intercultural and global citizens we should all be concerned about social justice and human rights.

Display respect. There is a fundamental difference between respect and tolerance. The Latin origin of 'tolerance' refers to enduring something and does not convey affirmation or support. Being tolerant suggests an imbalance of power in the relationship, whereby an individual is in the position to grant or refuse permission for the other person to behave in certain ways. In contrast, the Latin word for respect conveys the idea that individuals are equally deserving of honour and mutual regard. Within the context of intercultural communication, **respect** signifies positive regard for an individual from a different cultural background, whereas **tolerance** implies going along with behaviours that one does not necessarily respect or accept. In this regard, tolerance can be viewed as patronizing. For example, tolerating religious diversity suggests that one feels superior to people from other faiths.

Being intercultural also means recognition that the ways in which we express respect for others varies depending on the cultural context. Verbal and nonverbal expressions of respect may work well in one context and be perceived as insincere and inappropriate in another. Cultural knowledge and sensitivity also impact on the effectiveness of your communication in intercultural situations.

Be empathetic (not sympathetic). **Empathy** refers to an individual's ability to convey awareness of another person's feelings, circumstances and experiences. In intercultural interactions, instead of focusing solely on your own message and goals, be aware of and sensitive to your communication partner's needs and feelings. Consider how your message is being received. Effective intercultural communicators have the ability to empathize with the worldviews and situations of people who have a different linguistic and cultural background. **Empathetic behaviours** include nonverbal actions that indicate you are attending to the messages of others (e.g. facial expressions of concern) as well as verbal expressions (e.g. words that convey solidarity).

Learn another language. Mastering another language can enable you to interact with people who do not speak your first language without relying on an interpreter. When studying a second language, it is essential to enhance your cultural knowledge and intercultural communication skills as you develop awareness of grammatical structures and expand your vocabulary. Remember that advanced second language proficiency does not necessarily mean a high level of intercultural competence. Knowledge of grammar does not indicate that you have a high level of **sociopragmatic competence**, the ability to communicate appropriately in social situations in another cultural context. One can be **bilingual** (speak two languages) or **multilingual** (speak more than two languages) and not be **bicultural** (interculturally competent in two cultural contexts) or **multicultural** (interculturally competent in multiple cultural contexts). Just as you need to devote time and attention to language elements, intercultural communication knowledge and skills merit attention.

Intercultural speakers take advantage of opportunities to use their second language. They don't wait for people to approach them; they initiate intercultural interactions and demonstrate a high level of **willingness to communicate** in their second language and enhance their intercultural competence. They make an effort to share their feelings and ideas with people from diverse backgrounds. Bilingualism and biculturalism can both be great assets in today's globalized world.

Seek feedback. Intercultural competence implies effective and appropriate communication with individuals who have a different cultural background. This depends not only on your impression of communicative events but the perceptions of your communication partners. In intercultural interactions, you can get a sense of how effective and appropriate your verbal and nonverbal actions are by paying close attention to their reactions. Of course, it is also possible to misread signals or be unsure of their response so it can be very helpful to get honest and frank feedback from intercultural friends. As well as demonstrating your commitment to becoming a better intercultural communicator, their input can identify areas that you need to improve (e.g. the use of less direct phrases, more appropriate nonverbal behaviours in certain situations, allowing more time for second language speakers to process your speech and respond).

Be engaged in the world. As well as developing intercultural competency and fluency in another language, global citizens take an interest in world affairs. Instead of restricting yourself to local news and events, develop the habit of watching global newscasts (on television or online) on a regular basis or access international reports in newspapers (hard copies or online) in your first or second language. On campus, talk with international students or professors about issues and life in other parts of the world. You could also join a study abroad programme, volunteer abroad, participate in a global internship or undertake service learning in another linguistic/cultural setting. Participate in international associations that aim to make the world a better place (e.g. improve the environment, foster intercultural interactions, celebrate diversity) or campaign for human rights and social justice. Explore opportunities for involvement in your community and beyond. Don't wait for others to come to you with ideas about what you can do. Be proactive! Become interested, informed and involved in local and global issues. Working cooperatively with others, you can make a valuable contribution to your community and our global society. Through your actions you can become a more effective intercultural and global citizen. As well as helping others, your involvement can enrich your life by adding meaning, purpose and diversity.

Be patient. Finally, bear in mind that developing global and intercultural competencies takes time, commitment and energy. Learning a foreign language also requires perseverance and investment. Second language socialization and the acquisition of a global mindset do not happen overnight. Be patient and keep yourself motivated by setting realistic, focused targets. Recognize improvements. Developing intercultural communicative competence is a process of long duration. As noted by Guilherme *et al.* (2010: 244), 'Becoming interculturally competent is a process of changing one's mindset . . . It is a process of continuous transformation that, ideally, never ends'. Changing habits and opening yourself up to other ways of being involve emotions, attitudes and knowledge. A deep level of engagement is required. Change takes time but the rewards can be many.

Developing oneself as a globally-minded, intercultural communicator is best viewed as a life-long process rather than a product. When you are open to new ideas and experiences you will continue to grow and evolve throughout your life. With an intercultural, global mindset, each of us can contribute to making the world a better, more humane place. Each of us has the capacity to make a difference.

SUMMARY

In the twenty-first century, it is imperative that all of us develop intercultural competence and become responsible intercultural, global citizens. Becoming proficient in two or more languages is also important in today's diverse world. Our personal well-being and the future of our communities, and indeed our planet, depend on our ability to meet the challenges of modern life (e.g. linguistic and cultural diversity, intercultural conflicts, pollution, the widening gap between the rich and poor, limited resources, etc.). As our world has become more diverse and interconnected, it is vital for *all* humans to make an effort to respect one another and live in harmony. For life on our planet to flourish, we must transcend regional and national boundaries and reach out to people from different linguistic and cultural backgrounds within our communities and beyond. The future of humankind and the quality of our environment depend on the choices we make. Each of us can make a difference.

With these imperatives in mind, this concluding chapter explored current understandings of global citizenship and discussed what it means to be globally and interculturally competent in today's increasingly diverse and interconnected world. We reviewed several well-known models of intercultural competence and discussed the relationship between language and intercultural sensitivity and intercultural competence. Finally, after reviewing the requisite skills and attributes of globally-minded individuals, we discussed steps one can take to become a more effective intercultural communicator and responsible, ethical global citizen.

discussion questions

1 Offer your own definition of global citizenship. In small groups, share your views.
2 Why does Byram (1997, 2009) distinguish between intercultural competence and intercultural communicative competence? Do you think this distinction is necessary? Why or why not?
3 What does it mean to be an 'intercultural speaker' or 'intercultural mediator'?
4 Describe the relationship between language, culture and intercultural competence.
5 Identify at least one well-known bilingual person whom you consider highly intercultural. What characteristics of this person qualify him or her as an intercultural person?
6 How do you know if you have communicated 'effectively' and 'appropriately' in intercultural interactions?
7 How would you define 'social justice'? How is this concept linked to global competence?
8 How can interculturally sensitive and globally-minded individuals benefit the community on local, national and international levels?
9 What is the relationship between second language proficiency and intercultural competence?
10 Review the list of global, linguistic and intercultural competencies provided in this chapter and identify the ones that you possess. What aspects do you need to work on? How will you accomplish this?
11 Think back to the ideas that you had about intercultural communication when you read Chapter 1. How have your ideas changed? Can you identify more imperatives to develop global-mindedness and intercultural communicative competence today? What are the benefits of becoming bi(multi)lingual in today's globalized world?

further reading

Byram, M. (1997) *Teaching and Assessing Intercultural Communicative Competence*, Clevedon: Multilingual Matters.

This text explores the competencies that are required, how they can be incorporated into foreign language teaching and how the ability to communicate across cultural differences can be assessed. It is based on the premise that foreign and second language teaching should prepare learners to use a language with fluency and accuracy, and also to speak with people who have different cultural identities, social values and behaviours.

Byram, M. (2008) *From Foreign Language Education to Education for Intercultural Citizenship: Essays and Reflections*, Clevedon: Multilingual Matters.

In this monograph, Byram reflects on and further develops his earlier work on the intercultural speaker/intercultural competence and stresses the importance of political dimensions of foreign language education.

Deardorff, D. (ed.) *The SAGE Handbook of Intercultural Competence*, Thousand Oaks, CA: Sage.

Linking theory with research and practice, this handbook raises awareness of the complexity of intercultural communication and draws attention to evolving understandings of what it means to be interculturally competent.

Gerzon, M. (2010) *Global Citizens*, London: Rider.

The author draws attention to the major problems facing the world today and stresses the need for individuals to become responsible global citizens to effect change.

Harden, A. and Witte, T. (ed.) (2011) *Intercultural Competence: Concepts, Challenges, Evaluations*, Berlin: Peter Lang.

The essays in this volume explore a broad range of perspectives on intercultural competence, including theories and applications in the teaching and learning of foreign languages.

Lustig, M. and Koester, J. (eds) (2005) *Among Us: Essays on Identity, Belonging, and Intercultural Competence*, White Plains, NY: Pearson.

This collection presents readings from individuals whose intercultural experiences give insights on how to achieve an effective and fair multicultural society where cultural identities are celebrated and maintained. The essays centre on four themes: Identity, Negotiating Intercultural Competence, Racism and Prejudice and Belonging to Multiple Cultures.

References

Abbott, S.A. (2000) 'Motivations for pursuing an acting career in pornography', in R. Weitzer (ed.) *Sex for Sale: Prostitution, Pornography, and the Sex Industry*, New York: Routledge, pp. 17–34.

Abdallah-Pretceille, M. (2003) *Former en Contexte Hétérogène. pour un Humanisme du Divers*, Paris: Anthropos.

Abigail, R.A. and Cahn, D.D. (2011) *Managing Conflict Through Communication*, 4th edn, Boston: Pearson.

Adams, K., Hean, S., Sturgis, P. and Clark, J.M. (2006) 'Investigating the factors influencing professional identity of first-year health and social care students', *Learning in Health and Social Care,* 5: 55–68.

Adams, R.J., Blieszner, R. and de Vries, B. (2000) 'Definitions of friendship in the third age: Age, gender, and study location effects', *Journal of Aging Studies,* 14: 117–33.

Adler, P. (1975) 'The transitional experience: An alternative view of culture shock', *Journal of Humanistic Psychology,* 15: 13–23.

Adler, R.B., Rosenfeld, L.B. and Proctor II, R.F. (2013) *Interplay: The Process of Interpersonal Communication,* New York: Oxford University Press.

Agar, M. (2006) 'Culture: Can you take it anywhere?' *International Journal of Qualitative Methods,* 5(2): 1–12.

Allan, G. (1989) *Friendship: Developing a Sociological Perspective,* London: Simon and Schuster.

Allport, G.W. (1954) *The Nature of Prejudice,* Cambridge, MA: Addison-Wesley.

Alred, G. and Byram, M. (2002) 'Becoming an intercultural mediator: A longitudinal study of residence abroad', *Journal of Multilingual and Multicultural Development,* 23(5): 339–52.

Alred, G., Byram, M. and Fleming, M. (2003) *Intercultural Experience and Education,* Clevedon: Multilingual Matters.

Alsup, J. (2006) *Teacher Identity Discourses: Negotiating Personal and Professional Spaces,* Mahwah, NJ: Lawrence Erlbaum.

Altman, I. and Taylor, D. (1973) *Social Penetration: The Development of Interpersonal Relationships,* New York: Holt.

American Psychiatric Association (n.d). *LGBT-Sexual Orientation.* Online. Available: www.psychiatry.org/mental-health/people/lgbt-sexual-orientation (accessed 5 November 2012).

Anderson, B. (1983) *Imagined Communities: Reflections on the Origin and Spread of Nationalism,* London: Verso.

Anderson, B. (1991) *Imagined Communities: Reflections on the Origin and Spread of Nationalism,* 2nd edn, London and New York: Verso.

Anderson, M. (1959) What is communication? *Journal of Communication,* 9: 5.

Anderson, P.A., Hecht, M.L., Hoobler, G.D. and Smallwood, M. (2003) 'Nonverbal communication across cultures', in W.B. Gudykunst (ed.) *Cross-Cultural and Intercultural Communication,* Thousand Oaks, CA: Sage, pp. 73–90.

Appadurai, A. (1990) 'Disjuncture and difference in the global cultural economy', in M. Featherstone (ed.) *Global Culture: Nationalism, Globalization and Modernity,* London: Sage, pp. 295–310.

Argyle, M. and Cook, M. (1976) *Gaze and Mutual Gaze*, New York: Cambridge University Press.

Argyle, M. and Trower, P. (1979) *Person to Person: Ways of Communicating*, New York: HarperCollins Publishers.

Arnett, J.J. (2002) 'The psychology of globalization', *American Psychologist*, 57: 774–83.

Arnold, M. (1869) *Culture and Anarchy*, New York: Macmillan.

Arthur, N. (2004) *Counseling International Students: Clients from Around the World*, New York: Springer.

Arundale, R. (2006) 'Face as relational and interactional: A communication framework for research on face, facework, and politeness', *Journal of Politeness Research*, 2: 193–216.

Asante, M., Newmark, E. and Blake, C. (eds) (1979) *Handbook of Intercultural Communication*, Beverly Hills, CA: Sage.

Association of American Colleges and Universities (AAC&U) (2007) *College Learning for the New Global Century: A Report from the National Leadership Council for Liberal Education and America's Promise*, Washington, D.C.: Association of American Colleges and Universities.

Atkinson, D. (2012) 'Intercultural rhetoric and intercultural communication', in J. Jackson (ed.) *Routledge Handbook of Language and Intercultural Communication*, Abingdon: Routledge, pp. 116–29.

Atlas of Student Mobility (n.d.) Online. Available: http://atlas.iienetwork.org/ (accessed 5 September 2012).

Babbitt, L.G. and Sommers, S.R. (2011) 'Framing matters: Contextual influences on interracial interaction', *Personality and Social Psychology Bulletin*, 37: 1233–244.

Bachman, L. (1990) *Fundamental Considerations in Language Testing*, Oxford: Oxford University Press.

Badhwar, N.K. (1993) 'Introduction: The nature and significance of friendship', in N.K. Badhwar (ed.) *Friendship: A Philosophical Reader*, New York: Cornell University, pp. 1–38.

Baldwin, J.R., Faulkner, S. L., Hecht, M.L. and Lindsley, S.L. (eds) (2006) *Redefining Culture: Perspectives across the Disciplines*, Mahwah, NJ: Lawrence Erlbaum.

Baldwin, T.T., Bommer, W.H. and Rubin, R.S. (2013) *Managing Organizational Behavior: What Great Managers Know and Do*, 2nd edn, New York: McGraw-Hill Irwin.

Barak, M.E.M. (2010) *Managing Diversity: Toward a Globally Inclusive Workplace*, Thousand Oaks, CA: Sage.

Barge, J.K. (2006) 'Dialogue, conflict, and community', in J.G. Oetzel and S. Ting-Toomey (eds) *The SAGE Handbook of Conflict Communication: Integrating Theory, Research, and Practice*, Thousand Oaks, CA: Sage, pp. 517–48.

Barker, L.L. and Barker, D.L. (1993) *Communication*, Englewood Cliffs, NJ: Prentice Hall.

Barnlund, D.C. (1975) *Public and Private Self in Japan and the United States: Communication Styles of Two Cultures*, Tokyo: Simile Press.

Barron, T. and Amerena, P. (eds) (2007) *Disability and Inclusive Development*, London: Leonard Cheshire Disability.

Bar-Tal, D. (1996) 'Development of social categories and stereotypes in early childhood: The case of "the Arab" concept formation, stereotype and attitudes by Jewish children in Israel', *International Journal of Intercultural Relations*, 20: 341–70.

Beebe, S.A., Beebe, S.J. and Ivy, D.K. (2010) *Communication Principles for a Lifetime*, 4th edn, Boston: Allyn and Bacon.

Begley, P.A. (2009) 'Dismantling misconceptions about Islam in Egypt', in L.A. Samovar, R.E. Porter and E.R. McDaniel (eds) *Intercultural Communication: A Reader*, Boston: Wadsworth, pp. 162–71.

Beijaard, D., Meijer, P.C. and Verloop, N. (2004) 'Reconsidering research on teachers' professional identity', *Teaching and Teacher Education*, 20: 107–28.

Bell, A. (1984) 'Language style as audience design', *Language in Society*, 13: 145–204.

Bell, A. (2002) 'Back in style: Reworking audience design', in P. Eckert (ed.) *Style and Sociolinguistic Variation*, Cambridge: Cambridge University Press, pp. 139–69.

Bell, A. (2007) 'Style and the linguistic repertoire', in C. Llamas, L. Mullany and P. Stockwell (eds) *The Routledge Companion to Sociolinguistics*, Abingdon: Routledge, pp. 95–100.

Bell, N. (2006) 'Intercultural adjustments in humorous intercultural communication', *Intercultural Pragmatics*, 3(1): 1–28.

Bennett, J.M. (1993) 'Cultural marginality: Identity issues in intercultural training', in R.M. Paige (ed.) *Education for the Intercultural Experience*, Yarmouth, ME: Intercultural Press, pp. 109–36.

Bennett, J.M. (1998) 'Transition shock: Putting culture shock in perspective', in M.J. Bennett (ed.) *Basic Concepts of Intercultural Communication*, Yarmouth, ME: Intercultural Press, pp. 215–24.

Bennett, J.M. (2009) 'Cultivating intercultural competence: A process perspective', in D. Deardorff (ed.) *The SAGE Handbook of Intercultural Competence*, Thousand Oaks, CA: Sage, pp. 121–40.

Bennett, J.M. and Bennett, M.J. (2004) 'Developing intercultural sensitivity: An integrative approach to global and domestic diversity', in D. Landis, J.M. Bennett and M.J. Bennett (eds) *Handbook of Intercultural Training*, 3rd edn, Thousand Oaks, CA: Sage, pp. 145–67.

Bennett, J.M., Bennett, M.J. and Allen, W. (2003) 'Developing intercultural competence in the language classroom', in D. Lange, and M. Paige (eds) *Culture as the Core: Perspectives on Culture in Second Language Learning*, Greenwich, CT: Information Age Publishing, pp. 237–70.

Bennett, M.J. (1993) 'Towards a developmental model of intercultural sensitivity', in R. Michael Paige (ed.) *Education for the Intercultural Experience*, Yarmouth, ME: Intercultural Press, pp. 21–71.

Bennett, M.J. (1997) 'How not to be a fluent fool: Understanding the cultural dimensions of language', in A.E. Fantini (Vol. ed.) and J.C. Richards (Series ed.) *New Ways in Teaching Culture. New Ways in TESOL Series II: Innovative Classroom Techniques*, Alexandria, VA: TESOL, pp. 16–21.

Bennett, M.J. (ed.) (1998a) *Basic Concepts of Intercultural Communication: Selected Readings*, Yarmouth, ME: Intercultural Press.

Bennett, M.J. (1998b) 'Intercultural communication: A current perspective', in M.J. Bennett (ed.) *Basic Concepts of Intercultural Communication: Selected Readings*, Yarmouth, ME: Intercultural Press, pp. 1–34.

Bennett, M.J. (2012) 'Paradigmatic assumptions and a developmental approach to intercultural learning', in M. Vande Berg, R.M. Paige and K.H. Lou (eds) *Student Learning Abroad: What Our Students Are Learning, What They're Not, and What We Can Do about It*, Sterling, VA: Stylus, pp. 90–114.

Berardo, K. (2006) 'The U-curve of adjustment: A study in the evolution and evaluation of a 50-year old model', unpublished master's thesis, University of Bedfordshire, Luton.

Berardo, K. (2012) 'Manage cultural transitions', in K. Berardo and D.K. Deardorff (eds) *Building Cultural Competence: Innovative Activities and Models*, Sterling, VA: Stylus, pp. 183–89.

Berelson, B. and Steiner, A. (1964) *Human Behavior: An Inventory of Scientific Findings*, New York: Harcourt, Brace, and World, Inc.

Berger, C.R. and Calabrese, R.J. (1975) 'Some exploration in initial interaction and beyond: toward a developmental theory of communication', *Human Communication Research*, 1: 99–112.

Berger, P.L. (1969) *The Sacred Canopy: Elements of a Sociological Theory of Religion*, New York: Anchor Books.

Berry, J.W. (1974) 'Psychological aspects of cultural pluralism', *Topics in Culture Learning*, 2: 17–22.

Berry, J.W. (1990) 'The role of psychology in ethnic studies', *Canadian Ethnic Studies*, 12: 8–21.

Berry J.W. (1997) 'Immigration, acculturation, and adaptation', *Applied Psychology: An International Review*, 46: 5–34.

Berry, J.W. (2003) 'Conceptual approaches to acculturation', in K. Chun, P. Balls Organista, and G. Marin (eds) *Acculturation: Advances in Theory, Measurement and Applied Research*, Washington, DC: APA Press, pp. 17–37.

Berry, J.W. (2006) 'Contexts of acculturation', in D.L. Sam and J.W. Berry (eds) *The Cambridge Handbook of Acculturation Psychology*, Cambridge: Cambridge University Press, pp. 27–42.

Berry, J.W., Poortinga, Y.H., Breugelmans, S.M., Chasiotis, A. and Sam, D.L. (2011) *Cross-Cultural Psychology: Research and Applications*, 3rd edn, Cambridge: Cambridge University Press.

Bhawuk, D.P.S. and Brislin, R.W. (1992) 'The measurement of cultural sensitivity using the concepts of individualism and collectivism', *International Journal of Intercultural Relations*, 16: 413–36.

Blackburn, S. (2009) *Ethics: A Very Short Introduction*, Oxford: Oxford University Press.

Blake, R.R. and Mouton, J.S. (1964) *The Managerial Grid*, Houston: Gulf Publishing.

Block, D. (2007) *Second Language Identities*, London: Continuum.

Block, D. (2013) *Social Class and Applied Linguistics*, London: Routledge.

Blum-Kulka, S., House, J. and Kasper, G. (eds) (1989) *Cross-cultural Pragmatics*, Norwood, NJ: Ablex.

Boas, F. (1940) *Race, Language and Culture*, New York: Free Press.

Bochner, S. (2006) 'Sojourners', in D.L. Sam and J.W. Berry (eds) *The Cambridge Handbook of Acculturation Psychology*, Cambridge: Cambridge University Press, pp. 181–97.

Bormann, E.G. (1980) *Communication Theory*, New York: Holt, Rinehart and Winston.

Bourdieu, P. (1986) 'The forms of capital', in J. Richardson (ed.) *The Handbook of Theory and Research in the Sociology of Education*, New York: Greenwood Press, pp. 241–58.

Bourdieu, P. (1991) *Language and Symbolic Power*, Boston: Harvard University Press.

Bradford, L., Burrell, N.A. and Mabry, E.A. (2004) 'Negotiating cultural identity: Strategies for belonging', in M. Fong and R. Chuang (eds) *Communicating Ethnic and Cultural Identity*, Oxford: Rowman and Littlefield, pp. 313–28.

Braithwaite, D.O. and Braithwaite, C.A. (2003) '"Which is my good leg?": Cultural communication of people with disabilities', in L.A. Samovar and R. Porter (eds) *Intercultural Communication: A Reader*, 10th edn, Belmont, CA: Wadsworth Books, pp. 165–76.

Brewer, J.D. (2000) *Ethnography*, Maidenhead: Open University Press.

Brooker, P. (2003) *A Glossary of Cultural Theory*, London: Arnold.

Brown, S. and Eisterhold, J. (2004) *Topics in Language and Culture for Teachers*, Ann Arbor, MI: University of Michigan Press.

Brown, P. and Levinson, S.C. (1978) 'Universals in language usage: Politeness phenomena', in E. N. Goody (ed.) *Questions and politeness: Strategies in social interaction*, Cambridge: Cambridge University Press, pp. 56–311.

Bucholtz, M. (2003) 'Sociolinguistic nostalgia and the authentication of identity', *Journal of Sociolinguistics*, 7(3): 398–416.

Burgoon, J.K. (1978) 'A communication model of personal space violation: Explication and an initial test', *Human Communication Research*, 4: 129–42.

Burgoon, M. (1995) 'Language Expectancy Theory: Elaboration, explication and extension', in C.R. Berger and M. Burgoon (eds) *Communication and social influence processes*, East Lansing, MI: Michigan State University Press, pp. 29–51.

Butler, J. (1990) *Gender Trouble: Feminism and the Subversion of Identity*, New York: Routledge.

Byram, M. (1997) *Teaching and Assessing Intercultural Communicative Competence*, Clevedon: Multilingual Matters.

Byram, M. (2006) 'Language teaching for intercultural citizenship: The European situation', paper presented at the New Zealand Association of Language Teachers (NZALT) conference, University of Auckland, July 2006.

Byram, M. (2008) *From Foreign Language Education to Education for Intercultural Citizenship: Essays and Reflection*, Clevedon: Multilingual Matters.

Byram, M. (2009) 'Intercultural competence in foreign languages: The intercultural speaker and the pedagogy of foreign language education', in D. Deardorff (ed.) *The SAGE Handbook of Intercultural Competence*, Thousand Oaks, CA: Sage, pp. 304–20.

Byram, M. (2011a) 'From foreign language education to education for intercultural citizenship', *Intercultural Communication Review,* 9: 17–36.

Byram, M. (2011b) 'Intercultural citizenship from an internationalist perspective', *Journal of the NUS Teaching Academy,* 1(1): 10–20.

Byram, M. (2012) 'Conceptualizing intercultural (communicative) competence and intercultural citizenship', in J. Jackson (ed.) *Routledge Handbook of Language and Intercultural Communication,* Abingdon: Routledge, pp. 85–97.

Byram, M. and Feng, A. (2004) 'Culture and language learning: Teaching, research and scholarship', *Language Teaching,* 37(3): 149–68.

Byram, M. and Feng, A. (2006) *Living and Studying Abroad: Research and Practice,* Clevedon: Multilingual Matters.

Byram, M., Gribkova, B. and Starkey, H. (2002) *Developing the Intercultural Dimension in Language Teaching: A Practical Introduction for Teachers,* Strasbourg: Council of Europe.

Byram, M., Nichols, A. and Stevens, D. (eds) (2001) *Developing Intercultural Competence in Practice,* Clevedon: Multilingual Matters.

Byram, M. and Parmenter, L. (2012) *The Common European Framework of Reference: The Globalisation of Language Education Policy,* Clevedon: Multilingual Matters.

Byram, M. and Zarate, G. (1997) 'Defining and assessing intercultural competence: Some principles and proposals for the European context', *Language Teaching,* 29: 14–18.

Byrne, D. (1969) 'Attitudes and attraction', in L. Berkowitz (ed.) *Advances in Experimental Social Psychology,* Vol. 4, New York: Academic Press, pp. 36–89.

Byrnes, F.C. (1966) 'Role shock: An occupational hazard of American technical assistants abroad', *The Annals,* 368: 95–108.

Cahn, D.D. (1984) 'Communication in interpersonal relationships in two cultures: Friendship formation and mate selection in the U.S. and Japan', *Communication,* 13: 31–37.

Cai, D. and Fink, E. (2002) 'Conflict style differences between individualists and collectivists', *Communication Monographs,* 69: 67–87.

Cameron, D. (2009) *The Myth of Mars and Venus: Do Men and Women Really Speak Different Languages?* Oxford: Oxford University Press.

Campbell, R., Martin, C.R. and Fabos, B. (2011) *Media and Culture: An Introduction to Mass Communication,* 8th edn, Boston: Bedford/St.Martin's.

Canagarajah, A.S. (1999) *Resisting Linguistic Imperialism in English Language Teaching,* Oxford: Oxford University Press.

Canagarajah, A.S. (2006) 'Negotiating the local in English as a lingua franca', *Annual Review of Applied Linguistics,* 26(1): 197–218.

Canale, M. and Swain, M. (1980) 'Theoretical bases of communicative approaches to second language teaching and testing', *Applied Linguistics,* (1): 1–47.

Carey, J. (1989) *A Cultural Approach To Communication,* New York: Routledge.

Center for Advanced Research on Language Acquisition (CARLA), University of Minnesota (n.d.). *What is Culture?* Online. Available: www.carla.umn.edu/culture/definitions.html (accessed 5 May 2013).

Chen, G.M. (1992) 'Communication adaptability and interaction involvement as predictors of cross-cultural adjustment', *Communication Research Reports,* 9 (1): 33–41.

Chen, G.M. (2010) 'Relational mobility explains between- and within-culture differences in self-disclosure to close friends', *Psychological Science,* 21: 1471–478.

Chen, G.M. (2012) 'A cross-cultural test of the relational turbulence model: Relationship characteristics that predict turmoil and topic avoidance for Koreans and Americans', *Journal of Social and Personal Relationships,* 29: 545–65.

Chen, G.M. and Starosta, W.J. (1998) *Foundations of Intercultural Communication,* Needham Height, MA: Allyn and Bacon.

Chen, G.M. and Starosta, W.J. (2006) 'Intercultural awareness', in L.A. Samovar, R.E. Porter and E.R. McDaniel (eds) *Intercultural Communication: A reader,* Belmont, CA: Wadsworth, pp. 357–66.

Chen, G.M. and Starosta, W.J. (2008) 'Intercultural communication competence: A synthesis', in M.K. Asante, Y. Miike and J. Yin (eds) *The Global Intercultural Communication Reader,* New York: Routledge, pp. 215–37.

Chen, L. (2002) 'Communication in intercultural relationships', in W. Gudykunst and B. Mody (eds) *Handbook of International and Intercultural Communication,* 2nd edn, Thousand Oaks, CA: Sage, pp. 241–57.

Chen, Y.W. and Nakazawa, M. (2009) 'Influences of culture on self-disclosure as relationally situated in intercultural and interracial friendships from a social penetration perspective', *Journal of Intercultural Communication Research,* 38(2): 77–98.

Chen, Y.W. and Nakazawa, M. (2012) 'Measuring patterns of self-disclosure in intercultural friendship: Adjusting differential item functioning using multiple-indicators, multiple-causes models', *Journal of Intercultural Communication Research,* 41(2): 131–51.

Chinese Culture Connection (1987) 'Chinese values and the search for culture-free dimensions of culture', *Journal of Cross-Cultural Psychology,* 18(2): 143–64.

Clyne, M. (1994) *Inter-cultural Communication at Work,* Cambridge: Cambridge University Press.

Coates, J. (2004) *Women, Men, and Language: A Sociolinguistic Account of Differences in Language,* 3rd edn, White Plains, NY: Pearson ESL.

Cole, P.M. (1986) 'Children's spontaneous control of facial expression', *Child Development,* 57: 1309–21.

Coleman, J.A. (2009) 'Study abroad and SLA: Defining goals and variables', in A. Berndt and K. Kleppin (eds) *Sprachlehrforschung: Theorie und Empire, Festschrift fur Rudiger Grotjahn,* Frankfurt am Main: Peter Lang, pp. 181–96.

Coleman, S. and Raider, E. (2006) 'International/intercultural conflict resolution training', in J.G. Oetzel and S. Ting-Toomey (eds) *The SAGE Handbook of Conflict Communication,* Thousand Oaks, CA: Sage, pp. 663–90.

Collier, M.J. (1994) 'Cultural identity and intercultural communication', in L.A. Samovar and R.E. Porter (eds) *Intercultural Communication: A Reader,* 10th edn, Belmont, CA: Wadsworth, pp. 412–29.

Collier, M.J. (1996) 'Communication competence problematics in ethnic friendships', *Communication Monographs,* 63: 314–16.

Collier, M.J. (2002) 'Intercultural friendships as interpersonal alliances', in J.N. Martin, T.K. Nakayama and L.A. Flores (eds) *Readings in Intercultural Communication: Experiences and Contexts,* 2nd edn, Boston: McGraw-Hill.

Connor, U. (2004) 'Intercultural rhetoric research: Beyond texts', *Journal of English for Academic Purposes,* 3: 291–304.

Connor, U. (2008) 'Mapping multidimensional aspects of research: Reaching to intercultural rhetoric', in U. Connor, E. Nagelhout and W. Rozycki (eds) *Contrastive Rhetoric: Reaching toward Intercultural Rhetoric,* Amsterdam: Benjamins, pp. 219–315.

Connor, U. (2011) *Intercultural Rhetoric in the Writing Classroom,* Ann Arbor, MI: University of Michigan Press.

Constable, N. (2005) 'Introduction: Cross-border marriages, gendered mobility, and global hypergamy', in N. Constable (ed.) *Cross-Border Marriages: Gender and Mobility in Transnational Asia,* Philadelphia: University of Pennsylvania Press, pp. 1–16.

Cooper, P.J., Calloway-Thomas, C. and Simonds, C.J. (2007) *Intercultural Communication: A Text with Readings,* Boston: Pearson.

Corbett, J. (2003) *An Intercultural Approach to English Language Teaching*, Clevedon: Multilingual Matters.

Cornes, A. (2004) *Culture from the Inside Out: Travel and Meet Yourself*, Yarmouth, ME: Intercultural Press.

Cortazzi, M. and Jin, L. (1997) 'Communication for learning across cultures', in D. McNamara and R. Harris (eds.) *Overseas Students in Higher Education*, London: Routledge, pp. 76–90.

Cortazzi, M. and Jin, L. (2013) *Researching Cultures of Learning*, Basingstoke: Palgrave Macmillan.

Corvino, J. and Gallagher, M. (2012) *Debating Same-Sex Marriage*, Oxford: Oxford University Press.

Coulmas, F. (2005) *Sociolinguistics: The Study of Speakers' Choices*, Cambridge: Cambridge University Press.

Cruse. D.A. (2006) *A Glossary of Semantics and Pragmatics*, Edinburgh: Edinburgh University Press.

Crystal, D. (2000) *Language Death*, Cambridge: Cambridge University Press.

Crystal, D. (2010) *The Cambridge Encyclopedia of Language*, Cambridge: Cambridge University Press.

Culpeper, J., Bousfield, D. and Wichman, A. (2003) 'Impoliteness revisited: With special reference to dynamic and prosodic aspects', *Journal of Pragmatics,* 35: 1545–579.

Cummins, J. (1994) 'The acquisition of English as a Second Language', in K. Spangenberg-Urbschat and R. Pritchard (eds) *Reading Instruction for ESL Students*, Delaware: International Reading Association, pp. 36–62.

Cupach, W.R. and Spitzberg, B.H. (ed.) (2011) *The Dark Side of Close Relationships*, New York: Routledge.

Cushner, K. and Brislin, R. (1996) *Intercultural Interactions: A Practical Guide*, 2nd edn, Thousand Oaks, CA: Sage.

Dai, Xiaodong (n.d.) *Intercultural Communication Theory in China: Thirty Years Review.* Online. Available: www.hu-berlin.de/aks/PDF/Dai%20Xiaodong%20IC_Theory_in_China%20ppt.pdf (accessed 5 January 2012).

Darwin, C. (1872) *The Expression of Emotion in Man and Animals*, New York: Oxford University Press.

Davies, A. (2005) *A Glossary of Applied Linguistics*, Edinburgh: Edinburgh University Press.

Deardorff, D.K. (2004) 'The identification and assessment of intercultural competence as a student outcome of internationalization at institutions of higher education in the United States', unpublished dissertation, North Carolina State University, Raleigh, NC.

Deardorff, D.K. (2006) 'Identification and assessment of intercultural competence as a student outcome of internationalization', *Journal of Studies in International Education,* 10(3): 241–66.

Deardorff, D.K. (2008) 'Intercultural competence: A definition, model, and implications for education abroad', in V. Savicki (ed.) *Developing Intercultural Competence and Transformation: Theory, Research, and Application in International Education*, Sterling, VA: Stylus, pp. 32–52.

Deardorff, D.K. (2009) 'Synthesizing conceptualizations of intercultural competence: A summary and emerging themes', in D. Deardorff (ed.) *The SAGE Handbook of Intercultural Competence*, Thousand Oaks, CA: Sage, pp. 264–70.

Deardorff, D.K. and Hunter, W.D. (2006) 'Educating global-ready graduates', *International Educator,* 72–83.

Deardorff, D.K. and Jones, E. (2012) 'Intercultural competence: An emerging focus in international higher education', in D.K. Deardorff, H. de Wit, J.D. Heyl and T. Adams (eds) *The SAGE Handbook of International Higher Education*, Thousand Oaks, CA: Sage, pp. 283–304.

Deaux, K. (2001) 'Social identity', in J. Worrell (ed) *Encyclopedia of Women and Gender,* Vol. 2, San Diego, CA: Academic Press, pp. 1059–67.

DeCapua, A. and Wintergerst, A.C. (2004) *Crossing Cultures in the Language Classroom*, Ann Arbor, MI: University of Michigan Press.

Denzin, N. (1996) *Interpretive Ethnography: Ethnographic Practices for the 21st Century*, Thousand Oaks, CA: Sage.

Dervin, F. (2012) 'Cultural identity, representation and othering', in J. Jackson (ed.) *Routledge Handbook of Language and Intercultural Communication*, Abingdon: Routledge, pp. 181–94.

Dervin, F. and Dirba, M. (2006) 'On liquid interculturality. Finnish and Latvian student teachers' perceptions of intercultural competence', in P. Pietilä, P. Lintunen and H.-M. Järvinen (eds) *Language Learners of Today*, Jyväskylä: Suomen soveltavan kielitieteen yhdistyksen (AFinLA) julkaisuja, 64: 257–73.

Diggs, R. and Clark, K. (2002) 'It's a struggle but worth it: Identifying and managing identities in an interracial friendship', *Communication Quarterly*, 50: 368–90.

Digital Buzz Blog (2011) *Facebook statistics, Stats, and Facts for 2011*. Online. Available: www.digitalbuzzblog.com/facebook-statistics-stats-facts-2011/ (accessed 5 September 2012).

Digital Buzz Blog (2012) *Social Media Statistics, Stats, and Facts for 2012*. Online. Available: www.digitalbuzzblog.com/social-media-statistics-stats-2012-infographic/ (accessed 5 March 2013).

Discovery Education (2012) *Web 2.0 Tools*, Online. Available: http://web2012.discoveryeducation.com/web20tools.cfm (accessed 5 April 2013).

Domenici, K. and Littlejohn, S.W. (2006) *Facework: Bridging Theory and Practice*, Thousand Oaks, CA: Sage.

Donatelli, L., Yngve, K., Miller, M. and Ellis, J. (2005) 'Technology and education abroad', in J.L. Brockington, W.W. Hoffa and P.C. Martin (eds) *NAFSA's Guide to Education Abroad for Advisors and Administrators*, Washington, DC: NAFSA: Association of International Educators, pp. 129–50.

Döring, N. (2002) 'Studying online-love and cyber-romance', in B. Batinic, U.-D. Reips and M. Bosnjak (eds) *Online Social Sciences*, Seattle: Hogrefe and Huber Publishers, pp. 333–56.

Duff, P.A. (2010) 'Language socialization', in N.H. Hornberger and S.L. McKay (eds) *Sociolinguistics and Language Education*, Bristol: Multilingual Matters, pp. 427–52.

Duranti, A. (1997) *Linguistic Anthropology*, Cambridge: Cambridge University Press.

Eckert, P. and McConnell-Ginet, S. (1992) 'Think practically and look locally: Language and gender as community-based practice', *Annual Review of Anthropology*, 21: 461–90.

Eckert, P. and Rickford, J. (2001) *Style and Sociolinguistic Variation*, Cambridge: Cambridge University Press.

Edstrom, A.M. (2005) 'Female, nonnative perspectives on second language conversation: Connecting participation with intercultural sensitivity', *Foreign Language Annals*, 38(1): 25–34.

Efron, D. (1968) *Gesture and Environment*, New York: King's Crown Press.

Eitzen, D.S. and Zenn, M.B. (2011) *Globalization: The Transformation of Social Worlds*, Boston: Wadsworth.

Ekman, P. (1972) 'Universal and cultural differences in facial expression of emotion', in J.R. Cole (ed.) *Nebraska Symposium on Motivation 1971*, Vol. 19, Lincoln, NE: Nebraska University Press, pp. 207–83.

Ekman, P. (ed.) (1973) *Darwin and Facial Expression: A Century of Research in Review*, New York: Academic Press.

Ekman, P. (2004) 'Emotional and conversational nonverbal signals', in J.M. Larrazabal and L.A. Pérez Miranda (eds) *Language, Knowledge, and Representation*, Amsterdam: Kluwer Academic Publishers, pp. 39–50.

Ekman, P. (2009) *Become Versed in Reading Faces*. Entrepreneur Media. Online. Available: www.entrepreneur.com/article/200934 (accessed 3 March 2013).

Ekman, P. and Friesen, W.V. (1969) 'The repertoire of nonverbal behavior: Categories, origins, usage, and coding', *Semiotica*, 1: 49–98.

Ekman, P. and Friesen, W.V. (1971) 'Constants across culture in the face and emotion', *Journal of Personality and Social Psychology*, 17: 124–29.

Ekman, P. and Heider, K.G. (1988) 'The universality of a contempt expression: a replication', *Motivation and Emotion*, 12(3): 303–08.

Ekman, P. and Rosenberg, E.L. (eds) (1998) *What the Face Reveals: Basic and Applied Studies of Spontaneous Expression Using the Facial Action Coding System (FACS)*, New York: Oxford University Press.

Elfenbein, H.A. and Ambady, N. (2002) 'On the universality and cultural specificity of emotion recognition: A meta-analysis', *Psychological Bulletin*, 128(2): 205–35.

Emerson, R.W. (1930) *Essays and Lectures: Conduct of Life, Solitude and Society and Other Essays and Addresses*, New York: Three Sirens Press.

Encyclopedia Britannica (n.d.) *Superstition*. Online. Available: www.britannica.com/EBchecked/topic/574567/superstition (accessed 5 May 2013).

Erikson, E.H. (1968) *Identity: Youth and Crisis*, New York: Norton.

Equal Opportunity Unit (2005) *Watch Your Language: Guidelines for Non-discriminatory Language*, University of Melbourne: Melbourne.

Fairclough, N. (2006) *Language and Globalization*, Abingdon: Routledge.

Fantini, A.E. (2007) *Exploring and Assessing Intercultural Competence*, Brattleboro, VT: Federation of the Experiment in International Living.

Fantini, A.E. (2012a) 'Language: An essential component of intercultural communicative competence', in J. Jackson (ed.) *Routledge Handbook of Language and Intercultural Communication*, Abingdon: Routledge, pp. 263–78.

Fantini, A.E. (2012b) 'Multiple strategies for assessing intercultural communicative competence', in J. Jackson (ed.) *Routledge Handbook of Language and Intercultural Communication*, Abingdon: Routledge, pp. 390–405.

Fasching, D., deChant, D. and Lantigua, D.M. (2011) *Comparative Religious Ethics: A Narrative Approach to Global Ethics*, Oxford: Wiley-Blackwell.

Federal Glass Ceiling Commission (1995) *Solid Investments: Making Full Use of the Nation's Human Capital*, Washington, DC: U.S. Department of Labor. Online. Available: www.dol.gov/oasam/programs/history/reich/reports/ceiling2.pdf (accessed 2 April 2013).

Fehr, B.J., Baldwin, M., Collins, L., Patterson, S. and Benditt, R. (1999) 'Anger in close relationships: An interpersonal script analysis', *Personality and Social Psychology,* 25: 299–312.

Fehr, B.J. and Exline, R.V. (1987) 'Social visual interactions: A conceptual and literature review', in A.W. Siegman and S. Feldstein (eds) *Nonverbal Behavior and Communication*, Vol. 2, Hillsdale, NJ: Lawrence Erlbaum, pp. 225–326.

Fella, S. and Ruzza, C. (2013) *Anti-Racist Movements in the EU: Between Europeanisation and National Trajectories,* Basingstoke: Palgrave Macmillan.

Feng, A., Byram, M. and Fleming, M. (eds) (2009) *Becoming Interculturally Competent through Education and Training,* Clevedon: Multilingual Matter.

Filley, A. (1975) *Interpersonal Conflict Resolution*, Glenview, IL: Scott, Foresman.

Floyd, K., Ramirez, A. and Burgoon, J.K. (2008) 'Expectancy violations theory', in L.K. Guerrero, J.A. DeVito and M.L. Hecht (eds) *The Nonverbal Communication Reader: Classic and Contemporary Readings*, 3rd edn, Prospect Heights, IL: Waveland, pp. 503–10.

Folger, J.P., Poole, M.S. and Stutman, R.K. (2013) *Working through Conflict: Strategies for Relationships, Groups and Organizations*, 7th edn, Boston: Pearson.

Fong, M. (2004) 'Identity and the speech community', in M. Fong and R. Chuang (eds) *Communicating Ethnic and Cultural Identity*, Oxford: Rowman and Littlefield, pp. 1–3.

Fong, M. and Chuang, R. (eds) (2004) *Communicating Ethnic and Cultural Identity*, Oxford: Rowman and Littlefield.

Fong, M. and McEwen, K.D. (2004) 'Cultural and intercultural speech uses and meanings of the term *nigga*', in M. Fong and R. Chuang (eds) *Communicating Ethnic and Cultural Identity*, Oxford: Rowman and Littlefield, pp. 165–78.

Forehand, M.R., Deshpande, R. and Reed, A. (2002) 'Identity salience and the influence of differential activation of the social self-schema on advertising response', *Journal of Applied Psychology,* 87(6): 1086–99.

Fortman, J. and Giles, H. (2006) 'Communicating culture', in J.R. Baldwin, S.L. Faulkner, M.L. Hecht and S.L. Lindsley (eds) *Redefining Culture: Perspectives across the Disciplines,* Mahwah, NJ: Lawrence Erlbaum Associates, pp. 91–102.

Forum on Education Abroad (FEA) (2009) *Education Abroad Glossary,* Carlisle, PA: Forum on Education Abroad.

Forum on Education Abroad (FEA) (2011) *Education Abroad Glossary,* 2nd edn, Carlisle, PA: Forum on Education Abroad.

Freadman, A. (2004) *When the King and Queen of England Came to Town: Popular Entertainment, Everyday Life, and the Teaching of 'Culture'.* Inaugural lecture in the University of Melbourne, 23 November 2004. Online. Available: www.fritss.unimelb.edu.au/about/staff/freadman_lecture.html (accessed 10 October 2012).

Funk, T.M. (2010) *Victims' Rights and Advocacy at the International Criminal Court,* Oxford, England: Oxford University Press.

Furnham, A. and Bochner, S. (1986) *Culture shock: Psychological reactions to unfamiliar environments,* New York: Methuen.

Furstenberg, G., Levet, S., English, K. and Maillet, K. (2001) 'Giving a voice to the silent language of culture: The *Cultura* Project', *Language Learning and Technology,* 5(1): 55–102.

Gaines, S.O., Gurung, R.A.R., Lin, Y. and Pouli, N. (2006) 'Interethnic relationships', in J. Feeney and P. Noller (eds) *Close Relationships: Functions, Forms, and Processes,* New York, NY: Psychology Press, pp. 171–87.

Galanti, G.A. (2000) 'An introduction to cultural differences', *Western Journal of Medicine,* 172(5): 335–36.

Gallois, C. and Callan, V. (1997) *Communication and Culture: A Guide for Practice,* Chichester: John Wiley and Sons Ltd.

Gallois, C., Ogay, T. and Giles, H. (2005) 'Communication accommodation theory', in W.B. Gudyunst (ed.) *Theorizing intercultural communication,* Thousand Oaks, CA: Sage, pp. 121–48.

Gamble, T.K. and Gamble, M. (2013) *Communication Words,* 11th edn, Boston: McGraw-Hill.

Gardiner, H.W. and Kosmitzki, C. (2010) *Lives across Cultures: Cross-Cultural Human Development,* 5th edn, Boston: Pearson.

Gareis, E. (1995) *Intercultural Friendship: A Qualitative Study,* New York: University Press of America.

Gareis, E. (2000) 'Intercultural friendship: Five case studies of German students in the USA', *Journal of Intercultural Studies,* 21: 67–91.

Gareis, E. (2012) 'Intercultural friendship: Effects of home and host region', *Journal of International and Intercultural Communication,* 5(4): 309–28.

Gaw, K.F. (2000) 'Reverse culture shock in students returning from overseas', *International Journal of Intercultural Relations,* 24: 83–104.

Gebhard, J.G. (2010) *What Do International Students Think and Feel? Adapting to U.S. College Life and Culture,* Ann Arbor, MI: University of Michigan Press.

Gee, J.P. (2010) *How to do Discourse Analysis: A Toolkit,* Abingdon: Routledge.

Geertz, H. (1973) *The Interpretation of Cultures,* New York: Basic Books.

Gerzon, M. (2010) *Global Citizens: How Our Vision of the World Is Outdated, and What We Can Do about It,* London: Rider.

Giddens, A. (1990) *The Consequences of Modernity,* Stanford, CA: Stanford University Press.

Giles, H., Bonilla, D. and Speer, R.B. (2012) 'Acculturating intergroup vitalities, accommodation and contact', in J. Jackson (ed.) *Routledge Handbook of Language and Intercultural Communication,* Abingdon: Routledge, pp. 244–59.

Giles, H. and Ogay, T. (2006) 'Communication accommodation theory', in B.B. Whaley and W. Samter (eds) *Explaining Communication: Contemporary Theories and Exemplars*, London: Routledge, pp. 293–310.

Giroux, H.A. (1988) *Teachers as Intellectuals: Towards a Critical Pedagogy of Learning*, Granby, MA: Bergin and Garvey.

Goddard, C. (2004) 'Speech-acts, values and cultural scripts: A study in Malay ethnopragmatics', paper presented at the 15th Biennial conference of the Asian Studies Association of Australia, Canberra, Australia. Online. Available: http://coombs.anu.edu.au/SpecialProj/ASAA/biennial-conference/2004/Goddard-C-ASAA2004.pdf (accessed 16 March 2013).

Goddard, V. (2006) 'Ethnopragmatics: A new paradigm', in C. Goddard (ed.) *Ethnopragmatics: Understanding Discourse in Cultural Context*, Cambridge: Cambridge University Press, pp. 1–30.

Goffman, E. (1969) *Strategic Interaction*, Philadelphia, PA: University of Pennsylvania Press.

Goodall, H.L., Goodall, S. and Schiefelbein, J. (2010) *Business and Professional Communication in the Global Workplace*, Boston: Wadsworth.

Goodman, A.H., Moses, Y.T. and Jones, J.L. (2012) *Race: Are We so Different?* Malden, MA: Wiley-Blackwell.

Gordon, R. (1998/99) 'A spectrum of scholars: Multicultural diversity and human communication theory', *Human Communication: Journal of the Asian and Pacific Communication Association*, 2(1): 1–7.

Granello, D. and Young, M.E. (2012) *Counseling Today: Foundations of Professional Identity*, Boston: Pearson.

Green, W. (2013) 'Great expectations: The impact of friendship groups on the intercultural learning of Australian students abroad', in S. Dovic and M. Blythman (eds) *International Students Negotiating Higher Education*, London: Routledge, pp. 211–25.

Green, M.F. and Olson, C.L. (2003) *Internationalizing the Campus: A User's Guide*, Washington, D.C.: American Council on Education, Center for Institutional and International Initiatives.

Gross, J.J. (1998) 'The emerging field of emotion regulation: An integrative review', *Review of General Psychology*, 2: 271–99.

Gudykunst, W.B. (2003) 'Introduction to cross-cultural communication', in W.B. Gudykunst (ed.) *Cross-Cultural and Intercultural Communication*, 2nd edn, Thousand Oaks, CA: Sage, pp. 163–66.

Gudykunst, W.B. (2004) *Bridging Differences: Effective Intergroup Communication*, 4th edn, Thousand Oaks, CA: Sage.

Gudykunst, W.B. (2005) 'An anxiety/uncertainty management (AUM) theory of effective communication: Making the mesh of the net finer', in W.B. Gudykunst (ed.) *Theorizing about Intercultural Communication*, Thousand Oaks, CA: Sage, pp. 281–323.

Gudykunst, W.B. and Kim, Y.Y. (2003) *Communicating with Strangers*, 4th edn, New York: McGraw-Hill.

Gudykunst, W.B. and Nishida, T. (eds) (1989) *Communication in Personal Relations Across Cultures*, Thousand Oaks, CA: Sage.

Guilherme, M. (2002) *Critical Citizens for an Intercultural World: Foreign Language Education as Cultural Politics*, Clevedon: Multilingual Matters.

Guilherme, M. (2004) 'Intercultural competence', in M. Byram (ed.) *Routledge Encyclopedia of Language Teaching and Learning*, London: Routledge, pp. 297–300.

Guilherme, M. (2007) 'English as a global language and education for cosmopolitan citizenship', *Language and Intercultural Communication*, 7(1): 72–90.

Guilherme, M. (2012) 'Critical language and intercultural communication pedagogy', in J. Jackson (ed.) *Routledge Handbook of Language and Intercultural Communication*, Abingdon: Routledge, pp. 357–71.

Guilherme, M., Glaser, E. and Méndez-García, M.C. (2010) 'Conclusion: Intercultural competence for professional mobility', in M. Guilherme, E. Glaser and M.C. Méndez-García (eds) *The Intercultural Dynamics of Multicultural Working*, Bristol: Multilingual Matters, pp. 241–45.

Guirdham, M. (2011) *Communication across Cultures at Work*, Basingstoke: Palgrave Macmillan.

Gullahorn, J.T. and Gullahorn, J.E. (1963) 'An extension of the U-curve hypothesis', *Journal of Social Issues,* 19: 33–47.

Gumperz, J.J. (1979/1990) *Crosstalk* (BBC film). London: National Centre for Industrial Language Training. Online. Video segment available: www.lib.berkeley.edu/ANTH/emeritus/gumperz/gumptalk.html (accessed 1 April 2012).

Gumperz, J.J. (1982a) *Discourse Strategies*, New York: Cambridge University Press.

Gumperz, J.J. (ed.) (1982b) *Language and Social Identity*, Cambridge: Cambridge University Press.

Gumperz, J.J. (1999) 'On interactional sociolinguistic method', in S. Sarangi and C. Roberts (eds) *Talk, Work and Institutional Order*, Berlin: Mouton de Gruyter, pp. 454–71.

Gumperz, J.J. and Cook-Gumperz, J. (2012) 'Interactional sociolinguistics: Perspectives on intercultural communication', in C.B. Paulston, S.F. Kiesling and E.S. Rangel (eds) *The Handbook of Intercultural Discourse and Communication*, Malden, MA: Wiley-Blackwell, pp. 63–76.

Gumperz, J.J. and Hymes, D.H. (eds) (1964) 'The ethnography of communication', *American Anthropologists, (Special issue)* 66: 6.

Gumperz, J.J. and Hymes, D.H. (eds) (1972) *Directions in Sociolinguistics*, New York: Holt, Rinehart, and Winston.

Hall, B.J. (2005). *Among Cultures: The Challenge of Communication*, 2nd edn, Belmont, CA: Wadsworth.

Hall, E.T. (1959) *The Silent Language*, New York: Doubleday.

Hall, E.T. (1963) 'A system for the notation of proxemic behaviors', *American Anthropologist,* 65: 1003–26.

Hall, E.T. (1966) *The Hidden Dimension*, New York: Doubleday.

Hall, E.T. (1968) 'Proxemics', *Current Anthropology*, 9: 83–108.

Hall, E.T. (1976) *Beyond Culture*, 1st edn, New York: Doubleday.

Hall, E.T. (1983) *The Dance of Life: The Other Dimension of Time*, New York: Doubleday/Anchor.

Hall, E.T. (1998) 'The power of hidden differences', in M. J. Bennett (ed.) *Basic Concepts of Intercultural Communication: Selected Readings*, Yarmouth, Maine: Intercultural Press, pp. 53–68.

Hall, E.T. and Hall, M.R. (1990) *Understanding Cultural Differences: Germans, French, and Americans*, Boston: Intercultural Press.

Hall, E.T. and Hall, M.R. (2002) 'Key concepts: Underlying structures of culture', in J.N. Martin, T.K. Nakayama and L. Flores (eds) *Readings in Intercultural Communication: Experiences and Contexts*, 2nd edn, Boston: McGraw Hill, pp. 165–74.

Hall, J. (1969) *Conflict Management Survey: A Survey on One's Characteristic Reaction to and Handling of Conflicts between Himself and Others*, Monroe, TX: Teleometrics International.

Hall, S. (1990) 'Cultural identity and diaspora', in J. Rutherford (ed.) *Identity, Community, Culture, Difference*, London: Lawrence and Wishart, pp. 222–37.

Halualani, R.T. and Nakayama, T.K. (2010) 'Critical intercultural communication studies: At a crossroads', in T.K. Nakayama and R.T. Halualani (eds) *Handbook of Critical Intercultural Communication*, Oxford: Blackwell, pp. 1–16.

Hammer, M. (2004) 'The intercultural conflict style inventory: A conceptual framework and measure of intercultural conflict approaches', paper presented at the IACM 17th Annual conference. Online. Available: http://papers.ssrn.com/sol3/papers.cfm?abstract_id=601981 (accessed 14 February 2013).

Hammer, M. (2005) 'The intercultural conflict style inventory: A conceptual framework and measure of intercultural conflict resolution approaches', *International Journal of Intercultural Relations,* 29: 675–95.

Hammersley, M. and Atkinson, P. (1995) *Ethnography: Principles in Practice*, 2nd edn, New York: Routledge.

Hamon, R.R. and Ingoldsby, B.B. (eds) (2003) *Mate Selection across Cultures*, Thousand Oaks, CA: Sage.

Hampden-Turner, C. and Trompenaars, F. (1998) *Riding the Waves of Culture: Understanding Diversity in Global Business*, New York: McGraw-Hill.

Hannerz, U. (1996) *Transnational Connections: Culture, People, Places*, London: Routledge.

Harlow, L.L. (1990) 'Do they mean what they say? Sociopragmatic competence and second language learners', *The Modern Language Journal,* 74(3): 328–51.

Hart, W.B. (2005) 'Franz Boas and the roots of intercultural communication research', *International and Intercultural Communication Annual,* 28: 176–93.

Headland, T.N., Pike, K.L. and Harris, M. (eds) (1990) *Emics and Etics*, Thousand Oaks, CA: Sage.

Hecht, M.L., Jackson, R.J., II and Pitts, M.J. (2005) 'Culture', in J. Harwood and H. Giles (eds) *Intergroup Communication: Multiple Perspectives*, New York: Peter Lang, pp. 21–42.

Held, D., McGrew, A., Goldblatt, D. and Perraton, J. (1999) *Global Transformations: Politics, Economics, and Culture*, Cambridge: Polity Press.

Hendrickson, B., Rosen, D. and Aune, R.K. (2010) 'An analysis of friendship networks, social connectedness, homesickness, and satisfaction levels of international students', *International Journal of Intercultural Relations,* 34(1): 34–46.

Hertenstein, M.J., Holmes, R., McCullough, M. and Keltner, D. (2009) 'The communication of emotion via touch', *Emotion,* 9(4): 566–73.

Hertenstein, M.J., Keltner, D., App, B., Bulleit, B.A. and Jaskolka, A.R. (2006) 'Touch communicates distinct emotions', *Emotion,* 6(3): 528–33.

Hewings, A. and Hewings, M. (2005) *Grammar and Context*, Abingdon: Routledge.

Hewstone, M. and Brown, R.J. (1986) 'Contact is not enough: An intergroup perspective on the "contact hypothesis"', in M. Hewstone and R. Brown (eds) *Contact and Coflict in Intergroup Encounters*, Oxford: Blackwell, pp. 1–44.

Hickson, M. and Stacks, D.W. (1993) *NVC Nonverbal Communication Studies and Applications*, Dubuque, IA: Wm C. Brown Communications.

Hickson, M., Stacks, D.W. and Moore, N.J. (2004) *Nonverbal Communication: Studies and Applications*, Los Angeles, CA: Roxbury Publishing Co.

Hile, P. (1979) *Language Shock, Culture Shock and How to Cope*. Abilene Christian University Mission Strategy Bulletin 7.2. Online. Available: www.bible.acu.edu/ministry/centers_institutes/missions/page.asp?ID=486 (accessed 27 December 2012).

Hofstede, G.H. (1980) *Culture's Consequences: International Differences in Work-Related Values*, Beverly Hill, CA: Sage.

Hofstede, G.H. (1981) 'Culture and organizations', *International Studies of Management and Organization,* 10(4): 15–41.

Hofstede, G.H. (1984) *Culture's Consequences*, Beverly Hills, CA: Sage.

Hofstede, G.H. (1991) *Cultures and Organizations: Software of the Mind*, London: McGraw-Hill.

Hofstede, G.H. (1997) *Cultures and Organizations: Software of the Mind,* 2nd edn, London: McGraw-Hill.

Hofstede, G.H. (2001) *Culture's Consequences: Comparing Values, Behaviors, Institutions, and Organizations across Nations*, Thousand Oaks, CA: Sage.

Hofstede, G.H. (2003) *Culture's Consequences: Comparing Values, Behaviors, Institutions, and Organizations across Nations,* 2nd edn, Thousand Oaks, CA: Sage.

Hofstede, G.J. (n.d.) *What is Culture?* Online. Available: http://gertjanhofstede.com/culture.htm (accessed 10 May 2013).

Holliday, A. (1999) 'Small cultures', *Applied Linguistics,* 20(2): 237–64.

Holliday, A. (2006) 'Native-Speakerism', *ELT Journal,* 60(4): 385–87.

Holliday, A. (2010) 'Interrogating the concept of stereotypes in intercultural communication', in S. Hunston and D. Oakey (eds) *Introducing Applied Linguistics: Concepts and Skills*, Abingdon: Routledge, pp. 134–39.

Holliday, A. (2011) *Intercultural Communication and Ideology*, London: Sage.

Holliday, A. (2012) 'Culture, communication, context and power', in J. Jackson (ed.) *The Routledge Handbook of Language and Intercultural Communication*, Abingdon: Routledge, pp. 37–51.

Holmes, J. (2001) *An Introduction to Sociolinguistics*, Upper Saddle River, NJ: Pearson.

Holmes, P. (2012) 'Business and management education', in J. Jackson (ed.) *Routledge Handbook of Language and Intercultural Communication*, Abingdon: Routledge, pp. 464–80.

Hopkins, P.E. (2010) *Young People, Place and Identity*, London: Routledge.

House, J. (2012) 'Translation, interpreting and intercultural communication', in J. Jackson (ed.) *Routledge Handbook of Language and Intercultural* Communication, Abingdon: Routledge, pp. 495–509.

House, R.J., Hanges, P.J., Javidan, M., Dorfman, P.W. and Gupta, V. (eds) (2004) *Culture, Leadership, and Organizations: The GLOBE Study of 62 Societies*, Thousand Oaks, CA: Sage.

Hu, W. (1994) *Culture and Communication*, Beijing: Beijing Foreign Language and Teaching Press.

Hu, W. and Grove, C. (1999) *Encountering the Chinese: A Guide for Americans*, Yarmouth, ME: Intercultural Press.

Humboldt, W. von (1836; 2nd edn 1907) 'Über die Verschiedenheit des menschlichen Sprachbaues und ihren Einfluss auf die geistige Entwicklung des Menschengeschlechts', in *Wilhelm von Humboldts Gesammelte Schriften*, Band VII, Berlin: B. Behr's Verlag, pp. 1–344.

Hunter, W.D. (2004) 'Knowledge, skills, attitudes, and experience necessary to become globally competent', unpublished Ph.D. dissertation, Lehigh University, Bethlehem, PA.

Hunter, B., Godbey, G. and White, G.P. (2006) 'What does it mean to be globally competent?', *Journal of Studies in International Education*, 10(3): 267–85.

Hwang, H.S., Matsumoto, D., LeRoux, J.A., Yager, M. and Ruark, G.A. (2010) 'Cross-cultural similarities and differences in emblematic gestures', paper presented at the Biannual Conference of the International Association for Cross-Cultural Psychology, Melbourne, July 2010.

Hymes, D.H. (1966) 'Two types of linguistic relativity', in Bright, W. (ed.) *Sociolinguistics*, The Hague: Mouton, pp. 114–58.

Hymes, D.H. (1972) 'On communicative competence', in J. Pride and J. Holmes (eds) *Sociolinguistics*, Harmondsworth: Penguin, pp. 269–93.

Hymes, D.H. (1974) *Foundations in Sociolinguistics: An Ethnographic Approach*, Philadelphia, PA: University of Pennsylvania Press.

Hymes, D.H. (1986) 'Discourse: Scope without depth', *International Journal of the Sociology of Language*, 57: 49–89.

Intercultural Conflict Style (ICS) (n.d.) *The Intercultural Conflict Style Inventory: An Innovative Tool for Resolving Conflicts across Cultural Boundaries*, 'What is the Intercultural Conflict Style (ICS) Inventory?' Online. Available: www.icsinventory.com/ics_inv.php (accessed 7 May 2013).

Ikeda, D. (n.d.) *Thoughts on Education for Global Citizenship*. Online. Available: www.daisakuikeda.org/sub/resources/works/lect/lect-08.html (accessed 13 May 2013).

Inda, J. Xavier and Rosaldo, R. (2006) 'Introduction: A world in motion,' in J.X. Inda and R. Rosaldo (eds) *The Anthropology of Globalization*, Oxford: Blackwell, pp. 1–34.

International Association for Languages and Intercultural Communication (IALIC) (n.d.) *What is IALIC?* Online. Available: http://ialic.net/?page_id=2 (accessed 5 May 2013).

International Convention on the Elimination of all forms of Racial Discrimination (ICERD) (1989) *CCPR General Comment No. 18*, New York: Office of the High Commissioner for Human Rights. Online.

Available: www.unhchr.ch/tbs/doc.nsf/0/3888b0541f8501c9c12563ed004b8d0e (accessed 22 February 2013).

International Organization for Migration (IOM) (2010) *World Migration Report 2010: The Future of Migration: Building Capacities for Change.* Online. Available: http://publications.iom.int/bookstore/free/WMR_2010_ENGLISH.pdf (accessed 1 April 2012).

International Phonetic Association (n.d.). *The International Phonetic Association (IPA).* Online. Available: www.langsci.ucl.ac.uk/ipa/ (accessed 1 May 2013).

Internet World Stats – Usage and Populations Statistics (n.d.) *Internet Users in the World: Distribution by World Regions 2012 Q2.* Online. Available: www.internetworldstats.com/stats.htm (accessed 16 April 2013).

Ishii, S. (1984) '*Enryo-Sasshi* communication: a key to understanding Japanese interpersonal relations', *Cross Currents,* 11(1): 49–58.

Israel, R.C. (2012) *What Does It Mean to Be a Global Citizen?* Cosmos. Online. Available: www.kosmosjournal.org/articles/what-does-it-mean-to-be-a-global-citizen (accessed 20 February 2013).

Izard, C.E. (1971) *The Face of Emotion,* East Norwalk, CT: Appleton-Century-Crofts.

Jack, G. and Phipps, A. (2005) *Tourism and Intercultural Exchange: Why Tourism Matters,* Clevedon: Channel View Publications.

Jack, G. and Phipps, A. (2012) 'Tourism', in J. Jackson (ed.) *Routledge Handbook of Language and Intercultural Communication,* Abingdon: Routledge, pp. 537–50.

Jackson, J. (2003) 'Case-based learning and reticence in a bilingual context: Perceptions of business students in Hong Kong', *System,* 31(4): 457–69.

Jackson, J. (2008) *Language, Identity, and Study Abroad,* London: Equinox.

Jackson, J. (2010) *Intercultural Journeys: From Study to Residence Abroad,* Hampshire: Palgrave Macmillan.

Jackson, J. (2012) 'Education abroad', in J. Jackson (ed.) *Routledge Handbook of Language and Intercultural Communication,* Abingdon: Routledge, pp. 449–63.

Jackson, J. (2013) 'Adjusting to differing cultures of learning: The experience of semester-long exchange students from Hong Kong', in L. Jin and M. Cortazzi (eds) *Researching Intercultural Learning,* Basingstoke,: Palgrave MacMillan.

Jacobson, C. and Burton, L. (2011) *Modern Polygamy in the United States: Historical, Cultural and Legal Issues,* Oxford: Oxford University Press.

James, C.E. (2001) 'Introduction: Encounters in race, ethnicity, and language', in A. Shadd (ed.) *Talking about Identity: Encounters in Race, Ethnicity, and Language,* Toronto: Between the Lines, pp. 1–7.

Jandt, F. (2007) *An Introduction to Intercultural Communication: Identities in a Global Community,* 5th edn, Thousand Oaks, CA: Sage.

Jandt, F. (2010) *An Introduction to Intercultural Communication: Identities in a Global Community,* 6th edn, Thousand Oaks, CA: Sage.

Jandt, F. (2013) *An Introduction to Intercultural Communication: Identities in a Global Community,* 7th edn, Thousand Oaks, CA: Sage.

Jankowiak, W.R. and Paladino, T. (2008) 'Desiring sex, longing for love: A tripartite conundrum', in W.R. Jankowiak (ed.) *Intimacies: Love and Sex across Cultures,* New York: Columbia University, pp. 1–36.

Jenkins, J. (2007) *English as a Lingua Franca: Attitude and Identity,* Oxford: Oxford University Press.

Jenkins, J. (2013) *English as a Lingua Franca in the International University,* London: Routledge.

Jezewski, M.A. and Sotnik, P. (2001) *Culture Brokering: Providing Culturally Competent Rehabilitation Services to Foreign-born Persons. Center for International Rehabilitation Research Information and Exchange. CIRRIE Monograph Series,* John Stone, Ed. Buffalo, NY: CIRRIE.

Johannesen, R.L., Valde, K.S. and Whedbee, K.E. (2008) *Ethics in Human Communication,* 6th edn, Prospect Heights, IL: Waveland Press.

Jones, G.W., Leng, C.H. and Mohamad, M. (2009) *Muslim-Non-Muslim Marriage: Political and Cultural Contestations in Southeast Asia,* Singapore: Institute of Southeast Asian Studies.

Kachru, B.B. (2005) *Asian Englishes: Beyond the Canon,* Hong Kong: Hong Kong University Press.

Kailin, J. (2002) *Antiracist Education: From Theory to Practice,* Oxford: Rowman and Littlefield.

Kale, D.W. (1991) 'Ethics in intercultural communication', in L.A. Samovar and R.E. Porter (eds) *Intercultural Communication: A Reader,* 6th edn, Belmont, CA: Wadsworth, pp. 421–26.

Kälvermark, T. and van der Wende, M.C. (1997) *National Policies for Internationalization of Higher Education in Europe,* Stockholm: National Agency for Higher Education.

Kanno, Y. (2003) *Negotiating Bilingual and Bicultural Identities: Japanese Returnees and Betwixt Two Worlds,* Mahwah, NJ: Lawrence Erlbaum Associates.

Kaplan, R.B. (1966) 'Cultural thought patterns in intercultural education', *Language Learning,* 16: 1–20.

Kaplan, A.M. and Haenlien, M. (2010) 'Users of the world unite! The challenges and opportunities of social media', *Business Horizons,* 53(1): 59–68.

Kasper, G. (1997) *Can Pragmatic Competence Be Taught?* Online. Available: www.nflrc.hawaii.edu/networks/NW06/ (accessed 2 February 2012).

Kasper, G. (1998) 'Interlanguage pragmatics', in H. Byrnes (ed.) *Learning Foreign and Second Languages: Perspectives in Research and Scholarship,* New York: The Modern Language Association of America, pp. 183–208.

Kawakami, H.S. (2009) 'A history and development of the intercultural communication field in Japan (1950–present)', unpublished PhD thesis, University of New Mexico, Albuquerque, New Mexico.

Kecskes, I. (2012) 'Interculturality and intercultural pragmatics', in J. Jackson (ed.) *Routledge Handbook of Language and Intercultural Communication,* Abingdon: Routledge, pp. 67–84.

Kelly, M. (2012) 'Second language teacher education', in J. Jackson (ed.) *Routledge Handbook of Language and Intercultural Communication,* Abingdon: Routledge, pp. 409–21.

Keltner, D. and Ekman, P. (2003) 'Introduction: Expression of emotion', in R.J. Davidson, K.R. Scherer and H.H. Goldsmith (eds) *Handbook of Affective Sciences,* New York: Oxford University Press.

Kiesling, S.F. (2012) 'Ethnography of speaking', in C.B. Paulston, S.F. Kiesling and E.S. Rangel (eds) *The Handbook of Intercultural Discourse and Communication,* Malden, MA: Wiley-Blackwell, pp. 77–89.

Killian, K.D. (2009) 'Introduction', in T.A. Karis and K.D. Killian (eds) *Intercultural Couples: Exploring Diversity in Intimate Relationships,* New York: Routledge, pp. xvii–xxv.

Kim, M.S. (2002) *Non-Western Perspectives on Human Communication: Implications for Theory and Practice,* Thousand Oaks, CA: Sage.

Kim, M.S. (2007) 'The four cultures of cultural research', *Communication Monographs,* 74(2): 279–85.

Kim, M.S. (2010) 'Intercultural communication in Asia: Current state and future prospects', *Asian Journal of Communication,* 20(2): 166–80.

Kim, M.S. and Ebesu Hubbard, A.S. (2007) 'Intercultural communication in the global village: How to understand "the Other"', *Journal of Intercultural Communication Research,* 36(3): 223–35.

Kim, M.S. and Leung, T. (2000) 'A multicultural view of conflict management styles: Review and critical synthesis', in M. Roloff (ed.) *Communication Yearbook 23,* Thousand Oaks, CA: Sage, pp. 227–69.

Kim, Y.Y. (2001) *Becoming intercultural: An integrative theory of communication and cross-cultural adaptation,* Thousand Oaks, CA: Sage.

Kim, Y.Y. (2005) 'Inquiry in intercultural and development communication', *Journal of Communication,* 55(3): 554–77.

Kim, Y.Y. (2012) 'Beyond cultural categories: Communication adaptation and transformation', in J. Jackson (ed.) *Routledge Handbook of Language and Intercultural Communication*, Abingdon: Routledge, pp. 229–43.

Kincaid, D.L. (ed.) (1987) *Communication Theory: Eastern and Western Perspectives*, NY: Academic Press.

Kinginger, C. (2009) *Language Learning and Study Abroad: A Critical Reading of Research*, Basingstoke: Palgrave Macmillan.

Kitao, K. (1989) 'The state of intercultural communication in the United States: A brief history to the early 1980s', in K. Kitao and S.K. Kitao (eds) *Intercultural Communication: Between Japan and the United States*, Tokyo: Eichosha Shinsha, pp. 3–26.

Kitao, K. and Kitao, S.K. (eds) (1989) *Intercultural Communication: Between Japan and the United States*, Tokyo: Eichosha Shinsha.

Kito, M. (2005) 'Self-disclosure in romantic relationships and friendships among American and Japanese college students', *Journal of Social Psychology*, 145(2): 127–40.

Klopf, D.W. and McCroskey, J. (2007) *Intercultural Communication Encounters*, Boston: Pearson.

Kluckhohn, C. (1949) *Mirror for Man: The Relation of Anthropology to Modern Life*, New York: McGraw-Hill.

Kluckholn, C. and Strodtbeck, F. (1961) *Variations in Value Orientations*, Evanston, IL: Row, Peterson.

Knafo, A., Zahn-Waxler, C., Van Hulle, C., Robinson, J.L. and Rhee, S.H. (2008) 'The developmental origins of a disposition toward empathy: Genetic and environmental contributions', *Emotion*, 8: 737–52.

Knight, J. (2004) 'Internationalization remodeled: Definition, approaches, and rationales', *Journal of Studies in International Education*, 8(1): 5–31.

Knight, J. (2008) *Higher Education in Turmoil. The Changing World of Internationalization*, Rotterdam: Sense Publishers.

Knight, J. and de Wit, H. (eds) (1997) *Internationalization of Higher Education in Asia Pacific Countries*, Amsterdam: European Association for International Education.

Knight, J. and Lee, J. (2012) 'International joint, double, and consecutive degree programs: new developments, issues, and challenges', in D.K. Deardorff, H. de Wit, J.D. Heyl and T. Adams (eds) *The SAGE Handbook of International Higher Education*, Thousand Oaks, CA: Sage, pp. 343–58.

Kohls, R. (2001) *Survival Kit for Overseas Living*, 4th edn, Yarmouth, ME: Intercultural Press.

Kotthoff, H. and Spencer-Oatey, H. (2009) *Handbook of Intercultural Communication*, Berlin: Mouton de Gruyter.

Kozan, M.K. (1997) 'Culture and conflict management: A theoretical framework', *The International Journal of Conflict Management*, 8: 338–60.

Kraidy, M.M. (2005) *Hybridity, or the Cultural Logic of Globalization*, Philadelphia, PA: Temple University Press.

Krajewski, S. (2011) *The Next Buddha May be a Community: Practising Intercultural Competence at Macquarie University, Sydney, Australia*, Newcastle upon Tyne: Cambridge Scholars Publishing.

Kramsch, C. (1993) *Context and Culture in Language Teaching*, Oxford: Oxford University Press.

Kramsch, C. (1998) *Language and Culture*, Oxford: Oxford University Press.

Kramsch, C. (2009) *The Multilingual Subject*, New York: Oxford University Press.

Kramsch, C. and Uryu, M. (2012) 'Intercultural contact, hybridity, and third space', in J. Jackson (ed.) *Routledge Handbook of Language and Intercultural Communication*, Abingdon: Routledge, pp. 211–26.

Krappman, L. (1998) 'Amicita, drujba, shin-yu, philia, freudschaft, friendship: On the cultural diversity of a human relationship', in W.M. Bukowski, A.F. Newcomb and W.W. Hartup (eds) *The Company they Keep: Friendships in Childhood and Adolescence*, Cambridge: Cambridge University Press, pp. 19–40.

Kress, G. (ed.) (1988) *Communication and Culture*, Kensington: New South Wales University Press.

Krizan, A.C., Merrier, P., Logan, J. and Williams, K. (2011) *Business Communication,* 8th edn, Mason, OH: South-Western Cengage Learning.

Kroeber, A.L. and Kluckhohn, C. (1952) *Culture: A Critical Review of Concepts and Definitions*, Cambridge, MA: The Museum.

Kubota, R. (2012) 'Critical approaches to intercultural discourse and communication', in C.B. Paulston, S.F. Kiesling and E.S. Rangel (eds) *The Handbook of Intercultural Discourse and Communication*, Malden, MA: Wiley-Blackwell, pp. 90–109.

Kudoh, T. and Matsumoto, D. (1985) 'Cross-cultural examination of the semantic dimensions of body postures', *Journal of Personality and Social Psychology,* 48(6): 1440–46.

Kuo, E.C.Y. (2010) 'Editorial', *Asian Journal of Communication,* 20(2): 147–51.

Kupka, B. (2008) 'Creation of an instrument to assess intercultural communication competence for strategic international human resource management', unpublished doctoral dissertation, University of Otago, Otago, New Zealand.

La Brack, B. (2003) *What's up with Culture?* Online. Available: www.pacific.edu/sis/culture/index.htm (accessed 5 January 2013).

La Brack, B. (2010) *Theory Reflections: Cultural Adaptations, Culture Shock and the 'Curves of Adjustment',* NAFSA. Online. Available: www.nafsa.org/Resource_Library_Assets/Networks/ICT/Cultural_Adaptation_Culture_Shock/ (accessed 27 December 2012).

La Brack, B. (2011) 'Theory connections, reflections, and applications for international educators', paper presented at the 63rd Annual NAFSA: Association of International Educators conference, Vancouver, Canada.

La Brack, B. and Bathurst, L. (2012) 'Anthropology, intercultural communication, and study abroad', in M. Vande Berg, R.M. Paige and K.H. Lou (eds) *Student Learning Abroad: What Our Students are Learning, What They're Not, and What We can Do About It,* Sterling, VA: Stylus, pp. 188–214.

La Brack, B. and Berardo, K. (2007) 'Is it time to retire the U- and W-curves of adjustment?', paper presented at the Forum on Education Abroad conference, Austin, Texas.

Lamanna, M.A. and Reidmann, A. (2011) *Marriages, Families, and Relationships: Making Choices in a Diverse Society,* 11th edn, Belmont, CA: Wadsworth.

Lambert, R.D. (1996) 'Parsing the concept of global competence,' in R.D. Lambert (ed.) *Educational Exchange and Global Competence*, New York: Council on International Educational Exchange, pp. 11–23.

Langer, E. (1989) *Mindfulness (A Merloyd Lawrence Book)*, Cambridge, MA: Addison-Wesley.

Langer, E. (1997) *The Power of Mindful Learning*, Cambridge, MA: Addison-Wesley.

Lantis, J.S. and DuPlaga, J. (2010) *The Global Classroom: An Essential Guide to Study Abroad*, Boulder, CO: Paradigm Press.

Lave, J. and Wenger, E. (1991) *Situated Learning: Legitimate Peripheral Participation*, Cambridge: Cambridge University Press.

LeBaron, M. (2003) *Bridging Cultural Conflicts: A New Approach for a Changing World*, San Francisco, CA: Jossey-Bass.

LeBaron, M. and Pillay, V. (2006) *Conflict across Cultures: A Unique Experience of Bridging Differences*, Boston: Intercultural Press.

Leclercq, J.M. (2003) *Facets of Interculturality in Education*, Strasbourg: Council of Europe Publishing.

Lee, P.W. (2006) 'Bridging cultures: Understanding the construction of relational identity in intercultural friendship', *Journal of Intercultural Communication Research,* 35(1): 3–22.

Lee, P.W. (2008) 'Stages and transitions of relational identity formation in intercultural friendship: Implications for identity management theory', *Journal of International and Intercultural Communication* (1)1: 51–69.

Leeds-Hurwitz, W. (1990) 'Notes on the history of intercultural communication: The Foreign Service Institute and the mandate for intercultural training', *The Quarterly Journal of Speech*, 76: 262–81.

Leeds-Hurwitz, W. (2011) 'Writing the intellectual history of intercultural communication', in T. K. Nakayama and R. T. Halualani (eds) *The Handbook of Critical Intercultural Communication*, Malden, MA: Blackwell, pp. 21–33.

Lehmiller, J.J. and Agnew, C.R. (2011) '"May–December paradoxes" An exploration of age gap relationships in Western society', in W.R. Cupach and B.H. Spitzberg (eds) *The Dark Side of Close Relationships*, New York: Routledge, pp. 39–64.

Leone, B. (1978) *Racism: Opposing Viewpoints*, Farmington Hills, MI: Greenhaven Press, Inc.

Le Page, R.B. and Tabouret-Keller, A. (1985) *Acts of Identity: Creole-Based Approaches to Language and Ethnicity*, Cambridge: Cambridge University Press.

Leung, C., Harris, R. and Rampton, B. (1997) 'The idealised native speaker, reified ethnicities, and classroom realities', *TESOL Quarterly,* 31(3): 543–60.

Levine, D. (ed.) (1971) *Simmel: On Individuality and Social Forms*, Chicago: Chicago University Press.

Lewis, G. (1998) 'Welfare and the social construction of "race"', in E. Saraga (ed.) *Embodying the Social: Constructions of Difference*, London: Routledge, pp. 85–129.

Lewis, J.J. (n.d.) 'Dorothy Thompson Quotes', *About.Com Women's History.* Online. Available: http://womenshistory.about.com/od/quotes/a/dorothy_thompso.htm (accessed 15 May 2013).

Li, Z.F. (2010) 'Bridging the gap: Intercultural friendship between Chinese and American students', unpublished M.A. thesis, Liberty University, Lynchburg, VA.

Lindsay, R.B., Robins, K.N. and Terrell, R.D. (1999) *Cultural Literacy: A Manual for School Leaders*, Thousand Oaks, CA: Corwin.

Lingard, L., Reznick, R., De Vito, I. and Espin, S. (2002) 'Forming professional identities on the health-care team: discursive constructions of the "other" in the operating room', *Medical Education*, 36: 728–34.

Liu, S., Volčič, Z. and Gallois, C. (2011) *Introducing Intercultural Communication: Global Cultures and Contexts*, London: Sage.

Llamas, C., Mullany L. and Stockwell, P. (2007) *The Routledge Companion to Sociolinguistics*, London: Routledge.

LoCastro, V. (2003) *An Introduction to Pragmatics: Social Action for Language Teachers*, Ann Arbor, MI: University of Michigan Press.

Lorde, A. (1986) *Our Dead Behind Us: Poems*, New York: W.W. Norton.

Lund, A. and O'Reagan, J. (2010) 'National occupational standards in intercultural working: models of theory and assessment', in M. Guilherme, E. Glaser and M.C. Méndez-García (eds) *The Intercultural Dynamics of Multicultural Working*, Clevedon: Multilingual Matters, pp. 41–58.

Lustig, M.W. and Koester, J. (2010) *Intercultural Competence: Interpersonal Communication across Cultures,* 6th edn, Boston: Allyn & Bacon (Pearson).

Lustig, M.W. and Koester, J. (2012) *Intercultural Competence: Interpersonal Communication across Cultures,* 7th edn, Boston: Allyn & Bacon (Pearson).

Lysgaard, S. (1955) 'Adjustment in a foreign society: Norwegian Fulbright Grantees Visiting The United States', *International Social Science Bulletin,* 7: 45–51.

MacIntyre, P.D., Baker, S., Clément, R. and Donovan, L.A. (2003) 'Talking in order to learn: Willingness to communicate and intensive language programs', *Canadian Modern Language Review,* 59: 589–607.

MacIntyre, P.D., Dörnyei, Z., Clément, R. and Noels, K. (1998) 'Conceptualising willingness to com-municate in a L2: A situational model of L2 Confidence and affiliation', *The Modern Language Journal,* 82(4): 545–62.

Mackenzie, D., Falcon, T. and Rahman, J. (2009) *Getting to the Heart of Interfaith*, Woodstock, VT: Skylight Paths.

Mackenzie, I. (2013) *English as a Lingua Franca: Theorizing and Teaching English,* London: Routledge.

Marcoccia, M. (2012) 'The internet, intercultural communication and cultural variation', *Language and Intercultural Communication,* 12(40): 353–68.

Marden, C. and Meyer, G. (1968) *Minorities in America,* 3rd edn, New York: Van Nostrand Reinhold.

Markus, H.R., Kitayama, S. and Heiman, R.J. (1996) 'Culture and "basic" psychological principles', in E.T. Higgins and A.W. Kruglanski (eds) *Social Psychology: Handbook of Basic Principles,* New York: Guilford, pp. 857–913.

Martin, J.N. and Harrell, T. (2004) 'Intercultural reentry of students and professionals: Theory and practice', in D. Landis, J.M. Bennett and M.J. Bennett (eds), *Handbook of Intercultural Training,* 3rd edn, Thousand Oaks, CA: Sage, pp. 309–36.

Martin, J.N. and Nakayama, T.K. (2000) *Intercultural Communication in Contexts,* 2nd edn, Mountain View, CA: Mayfield.

Martin, J.N. and Nakayama, T.K. (2007) *Intercultural Communication in Contexts,* 4th edn, Boston: McGraw-Hill.

Martin, J.N. and Nakayama, T.K. (2008) *Experiencing Intercultural Communication: An Introduction,* New York: McGraw-Hill.

Martin, J.N. and Nakayama, T.K. (2010a) 'Intercultural communication and dialectics revisited', in T.K. Nakayama and R.T. Halualani (eds) *Handbook of Critical Intercultural Communication,* Malden, MA: Blackwell, pp. 59–83.

Martin, J.N. and Nakayama, T.K. (2010b) *Intercultural Communication in Contexts,* 5th edn, New York: McGraw-Hill.

Martin, J.N. and Nakayama, T.K. (2011) *Experiencing Intercultural Communication,* 4th edn, New York, NY: McGraw-Hill.

Martin, J.N., Nakayama, T.K. and Carbaugh, D. (2012) 'The history and development of the study of intercultural communication and applied linguistics', in J. Jackson (ed.) *The Routledge Handbook of Language and Intercultural Communication,* Abingdon: Routledge, pp. 17–36.

Martin, J.N., Nakayama, T.K. and Flores, L.A. (eds) (2002) *Readings in Intercultural Communication: Experiences and Contexts,* Boston: McGraw-Hill.

Matsumoto, D. (1992) 'More evidence for the universality of a contempt expression', *Motivation and Emotion,* 16(4): 363–68.

Matsumoto, D. (2001) 'Culture and emotion', in D. Matsumoto (ed.) *The Handbook of Culture and Psychology,* New York: Oxford University Press, pp. 171–94.

Matsumoto, D. (2009) 'Cultural and emotional expression', in C.Y. Chiu, Y.Y. Hong, S. Shavitt and R.S. Wyer (eds) *Problems and Solutions in Cross-Cultural Theory, Research and Application,* New York: Psychology Press, pp. 271–87.

Matsumoto, D. and Hwang, H.S. (2012) 'Nonverbal communication: The messages of emotion, action, space and silence', in J. Jackson (ed.) *Routledge Handbook of Language and Intercultural Communication,* Abingdon: Routledge, pp. 130–47.

Matsumoto, D., Keltner, D., Shiota, M.N., Frank, M.G. and O'Sullivan, M. (2008) 'What's in a face? Facial expressions as signals of discrete emotions', in M. Lewis, J. M. Haviland and L. Feldman Barrett (eds) *Handbook of Emotions,* New York: Guilford Press, pp. 211–34.

Matsumoto, D. and Kudoh, T. (1987) 'Cultural similarities and differences in the semantic dimensions of body postures', *Journal of Nonverbal Behavior,* 11(3): 166–79.

Maude, B. (2011) *Managing Cross-cultural Communication: Principles and Practice,* Basingstoke: Palgrave MacMillan.

Maya Angelou Quotes (n.d.) *Maya Angelou Quotes.* Online. Available: www.mayaangelouquotes.org/ (accessed 5 May 2013).

McCrosky, J.C. and Richmond, V.P. (1987) 'Willingness to communicate', in J.C. McCroskey and J.A. Daly (eds) *Personality and Interpersonal Communication*, Newbury Park, CA: Sage, pp. 129–56.

McDaniel, E.R., Samovar, L.A. and Porter, R.E. (2009) 'Understanding intercultural communication: The working principles', in E. R. McDaniel, L. A. Samovar and R. E. Porter (eds) *Intercultural Communication: A Reader,* 12th edn, Boston: Wadsworth Cengage Learning, pp. 6–17.

McGrew, A. (1992) 'A global society?', in S. Hall, D. Held and A. McGrew (eds) *Modernity and its Futures*, Cambridge: Polity, pp. 61–102.

McKay, S.L. (2010) 'English as an international language', in N.H. Hornberger and S.L. McKay (eds) *Sociolinguistics and Language Education*, Bristol: Multilingual Matters, pp. 89–115.

McKay, S.L. and Bokhorst-Heng, W.D. (2008) *International English in its Sociolinguistic Contexts: Towards a Socially Sensitive EIL Pedagogy*, New York: Routledge.

Mead, M. (1930) *Growing Up in New Guinea: A Comparative Study of Primitive Education*, New York: Harper.

Mehra, A., Kilduff, M. and Brass, D.J. (2001) 'The social networks of high and low self-monitors: Implications for workplace performance', *Administrative Science Quarterly*, 46(2): 121–46.

Mehrabian, A. (1969) 'Significance of posture and position in the communication of attitude and status relationships', *Psychological Bulletin,* 71(5): 359–72.

Mehrabian, A. (1982) *Nonverbal Communication*, Chicago: Aldine.

Merriam-Webster Online (n.d., a) *Dictionary: Artifact.* Online. Available: www.merriam-webster.com/dictionary/artifact (accessed 5 May 2013).

Merriam-Webster Online (n.d., b) *Dictionary: House.* Online. Available: www.merriam-webster.com/dictionary/house (accessed 3 April 2013).

Meyerhoff, M. (2010) *Introducing Sociolinguistics,* 2nd edn, London and New York: Routledge.

Mezirow, J. (1994) 'Understanding transformative theory', *Adult Education Quarterly,* 44: 222–32.

Mezirow, J. (2000) 'Learning to think like an adult', in J. Mezirow and Associates (eds) *Learning as Transformation: Critical Perspectives on a Theory in Progress*, San Francisco, CA: Jossey-Bass, pp. 3–33.

Miike, Y. (2007) 'An Asiacentric reflection on Eurocentric bias in communication theory', *Communication Monographs*, 74(2): 272–78.

Miike, Y. (2008) 'Toward an alternative metatheory of human communication: An Asiacentric vision', in M.K. Asante, Y. Miike, and J. Yin (eds) *The Global Intercultural Communication Reader*, New York: Routledge, pp. 57–72.

Miike, Y. (2009) 'Harmony without uniformity: An Asiacentric worldview and its communicative implications', in L.A. Samovar, R.E. Porter and E.R. McDaniel (eds) *Intercultural Communication: A Reader*, Belmont, CA: Wadsworth, pp. 36–47.

Miller, A.N. (2005) 'Keeping up with cartography: A call to study African communication', in W.J. Starosta, S. Ting-Toomey and N. Tsukada (eds) *Personal Communication across Cultures*, Washington, DC: NCA, pp. 214–36.

Miller, G.R. (1966) 'On defining communication: Another stab', *Journal of Communication,* 16: 88–98.

Miller, T. (1995) *How to Want What you Have*, New York: Avon.

Moberg, P.J. (2001) 'Linking conflict strategy to the five-factor model: Theoretical and empirical foundations', *International Journal of Conflict Management,* 12: 47–68.

Monaghan, L. (2012) 'Perspectives on intercultural discourse and communication', in C.B. Paulston, S.F. Kiesling and E.S. Rangel (eds) *The Handbook of Intercultural Discourse and Communication*, Malden, MA: Wiley-Blackwell, pp. 19–36.

Moon, D.G. (2002) 'Thinking about "culture" in intercultural communication', in J.N. Martin, T.K. Nakayama and L.A. Flores (eds) *Readings in Intercultural Communication: Experiences and Contexts*, 2nd edn, Boston: McGraw-Hill, pp. 13–21.

Moon, D.G. (2008) 'Concepts of "culture": Implications for intercultural communication research', in M.K. Asante, Y. Miike and J. Yin (eds) *The Global Intercultural Communication Reader*, New York: Routledge, pp. 11–26.

Moon, D.G. (2010) 'Critical reflections on culture and critical intercultural communication', in T.K. Nakayama and R.T. Halualani (eds) *The Handbook of Critical Intercultural Communication*, Oxford: Blackwell Publishing Ltd., pp. 34–52.

Moore, N.J., Hickson, M. and Stacks, D.W. (2010) *Nonverbal Communication: Studies and Applications*, 5th edn, Oxford: Oxford University Press.

Morais, D.B. and Ogden, A.C. (2011) 'Initial development and validation of the global citizenship scale', *Journal of Studies in International Education,* 15: 445–66.

Morgan, M. (2006) 'Speech community', in A. Duranti (ed.) *A Companion to Linguistic Anthropology*, Malden, MA: Wiley-Blackwell, pp. 450–64.

Mort, F. (1989) 'The politics of consumption', in S. Hall and M. Jacques (eds) *New Times. The Changing Face of Politics in the 1990s*, London: Lawrence and Wishart, pp. 160–72.

Mortensen, C.D. (1974) 'A transactional paradigm of social conflict', in G.R. Miller and H.W. Simons (eds) *Perspectives on Communication in Social Conflict*, Englewood Cliffs, NJ: Prentice Hall, pp. 90–124.

Mosby (2009) 'Social Sanctions', *Mosby's Medical Dictionary*, 8th edn, St. Louis, MI: Elsevier. Online. Available: http://medical-dictionary.thefreedictionary.com/social+sanctions (accessed 10 May 2013).

Mughan, T. and O'Shea, G. (2010) 'Intercultural interaction: A sense-making approach', in M. Guilherme, E. Glaser and M. del Carmen Méndez-García (eds) *The Intercultural Dynamics of Multicultural Working*, Bristol: Multilingual Matters, pp. 109–20.

Müller-Jacquier, B. (2004) 'Intercultural communication', in M. Byram (ed.) *Routledge Encyclopedia of Language Teaching and Learning*, London: Routledge, pp. 295–97.

Myers-Scotton, C. (2006) *Multiple Voices: An Introduction to Bilingualism*, Oxford: Blackwell Publishing.

Nakayama, T.K. and Halualani, R.T. (eds) (2010) *The Handbook of Critical Intercultural Communication*, Oxford: Wiley-Blackwell.

Nemoto, K. (2009) *Racing Romance: Love, Power, and Desire among Asian American/White Couples*, New Brunswick, NJ: Rutgers University Press.

Nettle, D. and Romaine, S. (2000) *Vanishing Voices*, Oxford: Oxford University Press.

Neuliep, J.W. (2006) *Intercultural Communication: A Contextual Approach,* 3rd edn, Thousand Oaks, CA: Sage.

Neuliep, J.W. (2012) *Intercultural Communication: A Contextual Approach,* 5th edn, Thousand Oaks, CA: Sage.

Newton, J. and Kusmierczyk, E. (2011) 'Teaching second languages for the workplace', *Annual Review of Applied Linguistics,* 31: 1–19.

Nguyen, A.M.D. and Benet-Martínez, V. (2010) 'Multicultural identity: What it is and why it matters,' in R. Crisp (ed.) *The Psychology of Social and Cultural Diversity*, Hoboken, NJ: Wiley-Blackwell, pp. 87–114.

Niesen, C.C. (2010) 'Navigating reentry shock: The use of communication as a facilitative tool', unpublished M.A. thesis, University of New Mexico, Alberque, New Mexico.

Nobel Women's Initiative (n.d.) *Meet the Laureates.* Online. Available: http://nobelwomensinitiative.org/meet-the-laureates/wangari-maathai/ (accessed 13 May 2013).

Noels, K.A., Yashima, T. and Zhang, R. (2012) 'Language, identity and intercultural communication', in J. Jackson (ed.) *Routledge Handbook of Language and Intercultural Communication*, Abingdon: Routledge, pp. 52–66.

Nolan, R.W. (1999) *Communicating and Adapting across Cultures: Living and Working in the Global Culture*, Westport, CT: Greenwood Publishing Group.

Norton, B. (2000) *Identity and Language Learning: Gender, Ethnicity and Educational Change.* Harlow: Pearson Education Ltd.

Nurmila, N. (2009) *Women, Islam and Everyday Life*, New York: Routledge.

OABITAR (Objectivity, Accuracy, and Balance in Teaching about Religion) (n.d.) 'Rites of birth and death', *Teaching about Religion: In Support of Civic Pluralism.* Online. Available: www.teachingaboutreligion. org/comparerites.html (accessed 5 May 2013).

Oberg, K. (1960) 'Cultural shock: Adjustment to new cultural environments', *Practical Anthropology,* 7: 177–82.

Ochs, E. and Schieffelin, B. (1984) 'Language acquisition and socialization: Three developmental stories and their implications', in R. Shweder and R.A. LeVine (eds) *Culture Theory: Essays on Mind, Self, and Emotion*, New York: Cambridge University, pp. 276–320.

O'Dowd, R. (2001) 'In search of a truly global network: The opportunities and challenges of on-line intercultural communication', *CALL-EJ Online,* 3(1). Online. Available: www.tell.is.ritsumei.ac.jp/ callejonline/journal/3-1/o_dowd.html (accessed 12 December 2012).

O'Dowd, R. (2012) 'Intercultural communicative competence through telecollaboration', in J. Jackson (ed.) *The Routledge Handbook of Language and Intercultural Communication*, London: Routledge, pp. 340–56.

Oetzel, J.G. (1998) 'The effects of self-construal and ethnicity on self-reported conflict styles', *Communication Reports,* 11: 133–45.

Oetzel, J.G. (2009) *Intercultural Communication: A Layered Approach*, Int'l Edition, New York: Vango Books.

Oetzel, J.G. and Ting-Toomey, S. (eds) (2006) *The SAGE Handbook of Conflict Communication: Integrating Theory, Research, and Practice*, Thousand Oaks, CA: Sage.

Olson, C.L., Evans, R. and Schoenberg, R.F. (2007) *At Home in the World: Bridging the Gap between Internationalization and Multicultural Education,* Washington, DC: American Council on Education.

Olson, C.L. and Kroeger, K.R. (2001) 'Global competency and intercultural sensitivity', *Journal of Studies in International Education,* 5(2): 116–37.

Omaggio Hadley, A. (1993) *Teaching Language in Context*, Boston, MA: Heinle and Heinle.

Orbe, M.P. and Everett, M.A. (2006) 'Interracial and interethnic conflict and communication in the United States', in J. G. Oetzel and S. Ting-Toomey (eds) *The SAGE Handbook of Conflict Communication: Integrating Theory, Research, and Practice*, Thousand Oaks, CA: Sage, pp. 575–94.

Orbe, M.P. and Harris, T.M. (2008) *Interracial Communication: Theory into Practice*, Thousand Oaks, CA: Sage.

O'Rioridan, T. (2001) *Globalism, Localism, and Identity,* Abingdon: Routledge.

Osbeck, L.M., Moghaddam, F.M. and Perreault, S. (1997) 'Similarity and attraction among majority and minority groups in a multicultural environment', *International Journal of Intercultural Relations,* 21(1): 113–23.

Osler, A. (2005) 'Education for democratic citizenship: New challenges in a globalised world', in A. Osler and H. Starkey (eds) *Citizenship and Language Learning: International Perspectives,* Stoke-on-Trent and Sterling, US: Trenthamp in partnership with the British Council, pp. 3–22.

Oxfam (2006) *Education for Global Citizenship: A Guide for Schools.* Online. Available: www.oxfam. org.uk/~/media/Files/Education/Global%20Citizenship/education_for_global_citizenship_a_ guide_for_schools.ashx (accessed 1 April 2013).

Park, M. (2006) 'A relational study of intercultural sensitivity with linguistic competence in English-as-a-Foreign-language (EFL) pre-service teachers in Korea', unpublished Ph.D. thesis, University of Mississippi, Oxford, MS.

Parker, P.S. and Mease, J. (2009) 'Beyond the knapsack: Disrupting the production of white racial privilege through organizational practices', in L.A. Samavor, R.E. Porter and E.R. McDaniel (eds) *Intercultural Communication: A Reader,* 12th edn, Belmont, CA: Wadsworth, pp. 313–24.

Patel, F., Li, M. and Sooknanan, P. (2011) *Intercultural Communication: Building a Global Community,* New Delhi: Sage Publications India.

Pauwels, A. (1991) *Non-Discriminatory Language,* Canberra: AGPS.

Peale, N.V. (2007) *A Guide to Confident Living,* New York: Simon and Schuster.

Peck, M.S. (1978) *The Road Less Travelled,* New York: Simon and Schuster.

Peng, F. (2011) 'Intercultural friendship development between Finnish and international students', unpublished M.A. thesis, University of Jyväskylä, Finland.

Pennycook, A.D. (1995) *The Cultural Politics of English as an International Language,* New York: Longman.

Pennycook, A.D. (1998) *English and the Discourses of Colonialism,* New York: Routledge.

Pettigrew, T.F. and Tropp, L.R. (2011) *When Groups Meet: The Dynamics of Intergroup Contact,* New York and Hove: Psychology Press.

Phy-Olsen, A. (2006) *Historical Guides to Controversial Issues in America: Same-Sex Marriage,* Westport, CT: Greenwood Press.

Pilkington, A. (2003) *Racial Disadvantage and Ethnic Diversity in Britain,* Basingstoke: Palgrave MacMillan.

Piller, I. (2007) 'Linguistics and intercultural communication', *Language and Linguistic Compass,* 1(3): 208–26.

Piller, I. (2009) 'Intercultural communication', in F. Bargiela-Chiappini (ed.) *The Handbook of Business Discourse,* Edinburgh: Edinburgh University Press, pp. 317–29.

Piller, I. (2011) *Intercultural Communication: A Critical Introduction,* Edinburgh: Edinburgh University Press.

Piller, I. (2012) 'Intercultural communication: An overview', in C.B. Paulston, S.F. Kiesling and E.S. Rangel (eds) *The Handbook of Intercultural Discourse and Communication,* Malden, MA: Wiley-Blackwell, pp. 3–18.

Pollock, D.C. and Van Reken, R.E. (2009) *Third Culture Kids: Growing Up Among Worlds,* Boston: Nicholas Brealey Publishing.

Prosser, M. (1976) 'The cultural communicator', in H.D. Fischer and J. C. Merrill (eds) *International and Intercultural Communication,* New York: Hastings House Publishers, pp. 417–23.

Puri, J. (2004) *Encountering Nationalism,* Malden, MA: Blackwell.

Pusch, M.D. (2004) 'Intercultural training in historical perspective', in D. Landis, J. Bennett and M. Bennett (eds) *The Handbook of Intercultural Training,* Thousand Oaks, CA: Sage, pp. 13–36.

Putnam, L.L. (2006) 'Definitions and approaches to conflict and communication', in J.G. Oetzel and S. Ting-Toomey (eds) *The SAGE Handbook of Conflict Communication: Integrating Theory, Research, and Practice,* Thousand Oaks, CA: Sage, pp. 1–32.

Rahim, M.A. (1983) 'A measure of styles of handling interpersonal conflict', *Academy of Management Journal,* 26: 369–76.

Rains, L. (2011) 'An exploration of 4 of the most inspiring quotes for travellers', *Flightster Blog,* Online. Available: www.flightster.com/2011/08/25/an-exploration-of-4-of-the-most-inspiring-quotes-for-travelers/ (accessed 13 May 2013).

Rampton, B. (1990) 'Displacing the "native speaker": Expertise, affiliation and inheritance', *ELT Journal* 44(2): 97–101.

Rampton, B. (1995) *Crossing: Language and Ethnicity among Adolescents,* London: New York: Longman.

Reagan, T. and Schreffler, S. (2005) 'Higher education language policy and the challenge of linguistic imperialism: A Turkish case study', in A.M.Y. Lin and P.W. Martin (eds) *Decolonisation, Globalisation: Language-in-Education Policy and Practice,* Clevedon: Multilingual Matters, pp. 115–30.

Redfield, R., Linton, R. and Herskovits, M.J. (1936) 'Memorandum on the study of acculturation', *American Anthropologist,* 38: 149–52.

Renalds, T. (2011) 'Communication in intercultural marriages: Managing cultural differences and conflict for marital satisfaction', unpublished M.A. thesis, Liberty University, Lynchburg, VA.

Reuben, S.C. (2002) *A Nonjudgmental Guide to Interfaith Marriage: Making Interfaith Marriage Work,* U.S.: Xlibris Corp.

Richards, J. and Schmidt, R.W. (2010) *Longman Dictionary of Language Teaching and Applied Linguistics,* 4th edn, London: Longman.

Ritchie, M. (2009) 'Intercultural computer-mediated communication exchange and the development of sociolinguistic competence', unpublished PhD Dissertation, Université du Québec, Canada.

Roberts, C., Byram, M., Barro, A., Jordan, S. and Street, B. (2001) *Language Learners as Ethnographers,* Clevedon: Multilingual Matters.

Rogan, R.G. and Hammer, M.R. (2006) 'The emerging field of crisis/hostage negotiation: A communication-based perspective', in J. Oetzel and S. Ting-Toomey (eds) *The Sage Handbook of conflict communication,* Thousand Oaks, CA: Sage, pp. 457–78.

Rogers, E.M. and Hart, W.B. (2002) 'The histories of intercultural, international, and development communication', in W. B. Gudykunst and B. Mody (eds) *The Handbook of International and Intercultural Communication,* Thousand Oaks, CA: Sage, pp. 1–18.

Rogers, E.M., Hart, W.B. and Miike, Y. (2002) 'Edward T. Hall and the history of intercultural communication: The United States and Japan', *Keio Communication Review,* 24: 3–26.

Rogers, E.M. and Steinfatt, T.M. (1999) *Intercultural Communication,* Prospect Heights, ILL: Waveland Press.

Roloff, M.E. (1981) *Interpersonal Communication: The Social Exchange Approach,* Beverly Hills, CA: Sage.

Roloff, M.E. (1987) 'Communication and conflict', in C.R. Berger and S.H. Chaffee (eds) *The Handbook of Communication Science,* Newbury Park, CA: Sage, pp. 484–534.

Romano, D. (2008) *Intercultural Marriage: Promises and Pitfalls,* 3rd edn, Yarmouth, ME: Intercultural Press.

Rosenblatt, P.C. (2009) 'A systems theory analysis of intercultural couple relationships', in T.A. Karis and K.D. Killiam (eds) *Intercultural Couples: Explaining Diversity in Intimate Relationships,* New York: Routlege, pp. 3–20.

Rothman, J.C. (2008) *Cultural Competence in Process and Practice,* Boston: Pearson, Allyn and Bacon.

Rubin, J.Z., Pruitt, D.G. and Kim, S.H. (1994) *Social Conflict: Escalation, Stalemate, and Settlement,* 2nd edn, Columbus, OH: McGraw-Hill.

Rumbley, L.E., Altbach, P.G. and Reisberg, L. (2012) 'Internationalization within the higher education context', in D.K. Deardorff, H. de Wit, J.D. Heyl and T. Adams (eds) *The SAGE Handbook of International Higher Education,* Thousand Oaks, CA: Sage, pp. 3–26.

Ryan, J. (2013) 'Comparing Learning characteristics in Chinese and Anglophone cultures: Pitfalls and insights', in L. Jin and M. Cortazzi (eds) *Researching Intercultural Learning,* Basingstoke: Palgrave MacMillan, pp. 41–60.

Ryan, P. (2003) 'Searching for the intercultural person', in G. Alred, M. Byram and M. Fleming (eds) *Intercultural Experience and Education,* Clevedon: Multilingual Matters, pp. 131–54.

Ryan, P. (2012) 'The English as a foreign or international language classroom', in J. Jackson (ed.) *The Routledge Handbook of Language and Intercultural Communication,* Abingdon: Routledge, pp. 422–33.

Ryan, S. (2006) 'Language learning motivation within the context of globalization: An L2 self within an imagined global community', *Critical Inquiry in Language Studies: An International Journal,* 3(1): 23–45.

Safdar, S., Friedlmeier, W., Matsumoto, D., Yoo, S.H., Kwantes, C.T. and Kakai, H. *et al.* (2009) 'Variations of emotional display rules within and across cultures: A comparison between Canada, USA, and Japan', *Canadian Journal of Behavioral Science*, 41(1): 1–10.

Safir, L. and Safire, W. (1982) *Good Advice*, New York: Times Books.

Salzmann, Z., Stanlaw, J. and Adachi, N. (eds) (2012) *Language, Culture, and Society: An Introduction to Linguistic Anthropology*, 5th edn, Boulder, CO: Westview Press.

Sam, D.L. and Berry, J.W. (2006) *The Cambridge Handbook of Acculturation Psychology*, Cambridge: Cambridge University Press.

Samovar, L.A., Porter, R.E. and McDaniel, E.R. (2006) *Intercultural Communication: A Reader,* 11th edn, Boston: Wadsworth Cengage Learning.

Samovar, L.A., Porter, R.E. and McDaniel, E.R. (2010) *Communication between Cultures,* 7th edn, Boston: Wadsworth Cengage Learning.

Samovar, L.A., Porter, R.E., McDaniel, E.R. and Roy, C.S. (2012) *Communication Between Cultures*, 8th edn, Boston: Wadsworth Cengage Learning.

Sand-Hart, H. (2010) *Home Keeps moving: A Glimpse into the Extraordinary Life of a 'Third Culture Kid'*, Hagerstown, MD: McDougal Publishing.

Saphiere, D.H., Mikk, B.K. and Devries, B.I. (2005) *Communication Highwire: Leveraging the Power of Diverse Communication Styles*, Yarmouth, ME: Intercultural Press.

Sapir, E. (1921) *Language*, New York: Harcourt.

Sarangi, S. (2012) *Interpreter Mediated Healthcare Consultations*, London: Equinox.

Schacter, S. (1951) 'Deviation, rejection, and communication', *Journal of Abnormal and Social Psychology,* 46: 190–207.

Schirato, T. and Yell, S. (2000) *Communication and Culture: An Introduction*, London: Sage.

Schmidt, W.V., Conaway, R.N., Easton, S.S. and Wardrope, W.J. (2007) *Communicating Globally: Intercultural Communication and International Business*, Thousand Oaks, CA: Sage.

Scholte, J.A. (2000) *Globalization: A Critical Introduction*, London: Palgrave.

Scollon, R. and Wong Scollon, S. (1995) *Intercultural Communication: A Discourse Approach*, Oxford: Blackwell.

Scollon, R. and Wong Scollon, S. (2001) *Intercultural Communication: A Discourse Approach*, 2nd edn, Oxford: Blackwell.

Scollon, R., Wong Scollon, S. and Jones, R.H. (2012) *Intercultural Communication: A Discourse Approach,* 3rd edn, London: Blackwell.

Scovel, T. (1994) 'The role of culture in second language pedagogy', *System,* 22(2): 205–19.

Seargeant, P. (2013) *Exploring World Englishes: Language in a Global Context*, London: Routledge.

Senft, G. (2009) 'Introduction', in G. Senft, J-O Östman and J. Verschueren (eds) *Culture and Language Use*, Amsterdam: John Benjamins, pp. 1–17.

Sensoy, Ö. and DiAngelo, R. (2012) *Is Everyone Really Equal? An Introduction to Key Concepts in Social Justice Education*, New York: Teachers College Press.

Sercu, L. (2005) 'Teaching foreign languages in an intercultural world', in L. Sercu, E. Bandura, P. Castro, L. Davcheva, C. Laskaridou, U. Lundgren, M. del Carmen, M. García and P. M. Ryan (eds) *Foreign Language Teachers and Intercultural Competence: An International Investigation*, Clevedon: Multilingual Matters, pp. 1–18.

Sharifian, F. (2012) 'World Englishes, intercultural communication and requisite competences', in J. Jackson (ed.) *Routledge Handbook of Language and Intercultural Communication*, Abingdon: Routledge, pp. 310–22.

Sharifian, F. and Jamarani, M. (2013) 'Language and intercultural communication: From the old era to the new one', in F. Sharifian and M. Jamarani (eds) *Language and Intercultural Communication in the New Era*, New York/London: Routledge, pp. 1–19.

Schecter, S.R. and Bayley, R. (2002) *Language as Cultural Practice: Mexicanos en el Norte*, Mahwah, NJ: Lawrence Erlbaum.

Shelly, G.B. and Frydenberg, G. (2010) *Web 2.0: Concepts and Applications*, Boston: Course Technology.

Shi, X. and Langman, J. (2012) 'Gender, language, identity, and intercultural communication', in J. Jackson (ed.) *Routledge Handbook of Language and Intercultural Communication*, Abingdon: Routledge, pp. 167–80.

Shi-xu (2005) *A Cultural Approach to Discourse*, Basingstoke: Palgrave Macmillan.

SIETAR India (n.d.) *Welcome to SIETAR India*. Online. Available: www.sietarindia.org/index.html (accessed 10 May 2013).

Simmel, G. (1950) 'The stranger', in K. Wolff (ed. and translator), *The Sociology of Georg Simmel*, New York: Free Press.

Simons, G. (1998) 'Meeting the intercultural challenges of virtual work', *Language and Intercultural Learning*, 16(1): 13–15.

Singh, N.G.K. (2011) *Sikhism: An Introduction*, Cornwall: I.B. Taurus.

Skelton, T. and Allen, T. (1999) 'Introduction', in T. Skelton and T. Allen (eds) *Culture and Global Change*, London: Routledge, pp. 1–10.

Smalley, W. (1963) 'Culture shock, language shock, and the shock of self-discovery', *Practical Anthropology*, 10: 49–56.

Smith, A.G. (ed.) (1966) *Communication and Culture*, New York: Holt, Rinehart and Winston.

Smith, E. and Hattery, A.J. (2009) 'Introduction', in E. Smith and A.J. Hattery (eds) *Interracial Relationships in the 21st Century*, Durham, NC: Carolina Academic Press, pp. 1–10.

Smith, H. (2009) *The World's Religions*, New York: HarperOne.

Smith, P.B., Bond, M.H. and Kağitçibaşi, Ç. (2006) *Understanding Social Psychology across Cultures: Living and Working in a Changing World*, London: Sage.

Smith, S. (2002) 'The cycle of cross-cultural adaptation and reentry', in J.N. Martin, T.K. Nakayama and L.A. Flores (eds) *Readings in Intercultural Communication*, Boston: McGraw-Hill, pp. 246–59.

So, C.Y.K. (2010) 'The rise of Asian communication research: A citation study of SSCI journals', *Asian Journal of Communication*, 20(2): 230–47.

Sorrells, K. (2012) 'Intercultural training in the global context', in J. Jackson (ed.) *Routledge Handbook of Language and Intercultural Communication*, Abingdon: Routledge, pp. 372–89.

Sorrells, K. (2013) *Intercultural Communication: Globalization and Social Justice*, Thousand Oaks, CA: Sage.

Sparrow, L. (2000) 'Beyond multicultural man: Complexities of identity', *International Journal of Intercultural Relations*, 24(2): 173–201.

Spencer, S. and Tuma, K. (eds) (2008) *The Guide to Successful Short-term Programs Abroad*, 2nd edn, Washington, DC: NAFSA: Association of International Educators.

Spencer-Oatey, H. (ed.) (2000) *Culturally Speaking: Managing Rapport through Talk across Cultures*, London: Continuum.

Spencer-Oatey, H. (2005) '(Im)politeness, face and perceptions of rapport: Unpacking their bases and interrelationships', *Journal of Politeness Research*, 1: 95–119.

Spencer-Oatey, H. (2008a) 'Glossary', in H. Spencer-Oatey (ed.) *Culturally Speaking: Culture, Communication, and Politeness Theory*, London: Continuum, 2nd edn, pp. 326–37.

Spencer-Oatey, H. (2008b) 'Face, (im)politeness and rapport', in H. Spencer-Oatey (ed.) *Culturally Speaking: Culture, Communication, and Politeness Theory*, London: Continuum, 2nd edn, pp. 11–47.

Spencer-Oatey, H. (2010) 'Intercultural competence and pragmatics research: Examining the interface through studies of intercultural business discourse', in A. Trosborg (ed.) *Pragmatics across Languages and Cultures*, Berlin and New York: Mouton de Gruyter, pp. 189–216.

Stanley Foundation (2003) *Educator Support Programs.* Online. Available: http://vps.stanleyfoundation. org/programs/esp/gtn.html (accessed 3 March 2013).

Street, B. (1993) 'Culture is a verb: Anthropological aspects of language and cultural process', in D. Graddol, L. Thompson and M. Byram (eds) *Language and Culture*, Clevedon: Multilingual Matters and BAAL, pp. 23–43.

Suler, J.R. (2002) 'Identity management in cyberspace', *Journal of Applied Psychoanalytic Studies,* 4: 455–60.

Sumner, W.J. (1911) *War and Other Essays,* New Haven, CT: Yale University Press.

Swallow, D. (2010) *The Stages of Adjusting to a New Culture.* Online. Available: www.deborahswallow. com/2010/05/14/the-stages-of-adjusting-to-a-new-culture/ (accessed 12 March 2013).

Swann, J., Deumert, A., Lillis, T. and Mesthrie, R. (2004) *A Dictionary of Sociolinguistics*, Edinburgh: Edinburgh University Press.

Synnott, A. (1993) *The Body Social: Symbolism, Self, and Society*, London: Routledge.

Szkudlarek, B. (2010) 'Reentry: A review of the literature', *International Journal of Intercultural Relations,* 34(1): 1–21.

Tajfel, H. (1981) *Human Groups and Social Categories*, Cambridge: Cambridge University Press.

Tajfel, H. (1982) 'Social psychology of intergroup relations', *Annual Review of Psychology,* 33: 1–39.

Tajfel, H. and Turner, J.C. (1979) 'An integrative theory of intergroup conflict', in W.G. Austin and S. Worchel (eds) *The Social Psychology of Intergroup Relations*, Belmont, CA: Wadsworth, pp. 33–53.

Tajfel, H. and Turner, J.C. (1986) 'An integrative theory of intergroup conflict', in S. Worchel and W.G. Austin (eds) *Psychology of Intergroup Relations*, Chicago: Nelson-Hall, pp. 2–24.

Tannen, D. (1995) 'The power of talk: Who gets heard and why', *Harvard Business Review.* Online. Available: http://geoffsurratt.typepad.com/women_who_lead/The%2520Power%2520of%2520 Talk.pdf (accessed 15 March 2012).

Tannen, D. (1996) *Gender and Discourse*, Oxford: Oxford University Press.

Tannen, D. (2001) *You Just Don't Understand: Women and Men in Conversation*, New York: William Morrow.

Taylor, E.W. (1994) 'Intercultural competency: A transformative learning process', *Adult Education Quarterly,* 44(3): 154–74.

Thill, J.V. and Bovée, C.L. (2013) *Excellence in Business Communication,* 10th edn, Upper Saddle River, NJ: Prentice Hall.

Thomas, J. (1983) 'Cross-cultural pragmatic failure', *Applied Linguistics,* 4(2): 91–112.

Thomas, J. (1995) *Meaning in Interaction: An Introduction to Pragmatics*, London: Longman.

Ting-Toomey, S. (1990) *A Face Negotiation Perspective Communicating for Peace*, Thousand Oaks, CA: Sage.

Ting-Toomey, S. (1999) *Communicating Across Cultures*, New York/London: The Guilford Press.

Ting-Toomey, S. (2004) 'Translating conflict face-negotiation theory into practice', in D. Landis, J.M. Bennett and M.J. Bennett (eds), *Handbook of Intercultural Training*, Thousand Oaks, CA: Sage, pp. 217–48.

Ting-Toomey, S. (2005) 'The matrix of face: An updated face-negotiation theory', in W.B. Gudykunst (ed.) *Theorizing about Intercultural Communication*, Thousand Oaks, CA: Sage, pp. 71–92.

Ting-Toomey, S. (2009) 'Intercultural conflict competence as a facet of intercultural competence development: Multiple conceptual approaches', in D. Deardorff (ed.) *The SAGE Handbook of Intercultural Competence*, Thousand Oaks, CA: Sage, pp. 100–20.

Ting-Toomey, S. (2010a) 'Applying dimensional values in understanding intercultural communication', *Communication Monographs,* 77(2): 169–80.

Ting-Toomey, S. (2010b) 'Intercultural conflict interaction competence: From theory to practice', in M. Guilherme, E. Glaser and M.C. Méndez-García (eds) *The Intercultural Dynamics of Multicultural Working*, Bristol: Multilingual Matters, pp. 21–40.

Ting-Toomey, S. (2012) 'Understanding conflict competence: Multiple theoretical insights', in J. Jackson (ed.) *Routledge Handbook of Language and Intercultural Communication*, Abingdon: Routledge, pp. 279–95.

Ting-Toomey, S. and Chung, L.C. (2005) *Understanding Intercultural Communication*, Oxford: Oxford University Press.

Ting-Toomey, S. and Chung, L.C. (2012) *Understanding Intercultural Communication*, 2nd edn, Oxford: Oxford University Press.

Ting-Toomey, S. and Kurogi, A. (1998) 'Facework competence in intercultural conflict: An updated face-negotiation theory', *International Journal of Intercultural Relations*, 22(2): 187–225.

Ting-Toomey, S. and Oetzel, J.G. (2001) *Managing Intercultural Conflict Effectively*, Thousand Oaks, CA: Sage.

Ting-Toomey, S. and Takai, J. (2006) 'Explaining intercultural conflict: Promising approaches and future directions', in J.G. Oetzel and S. Ting-Toomey (eds) *The Sage Handbook of Conflict Communication*, Thousand Oaks, CA: Sage, pp. 691–723.

Ting-Toomey, S., Yee-Jung, K., Shapiro, R., Garcia, W., Wright, T. and Oetzel, J.G. (2000) 'Cultural/ethnic identity salience and conflict styles in four U.S. ethnic groups', *International Journal of Intercultural Relations*, 24: 47–81.

Toh, S.H. (1996) 'Partnerships as solidarity: Crossing north–south boundaries', *The Alberta Journal of Educational Research*, XLII(2): 178–91.

Tompkins, P.S. (2011) *Practicing Communication Ethics: Development, Discernment, and Decision Making*, Boston: Allyn and Bacon.

Tracy, K. (2002) *Everyday Talk: Building and Reflecting Identities*, New York: Guilford.

Trenholm, S. and Jensen, A. (2011) *Interpersonal Communication*, 7th edn, Oxford: Oxford University Press.

Triandis, H.C. (2002) 'Individualism and collectivism', in M. Gannon and K. Newman (eds) *Handbook of Cross-cultural Management*, New York: Lawrence Erlbaum, pp. 16–45.

Trudgill, P. (2003) *A Glossary of Sociolinguistics*, Edinburgh: Edinburgh University Press.

Tubbs, S. (2009) *Human Communication: Principles and Contexts*, Boston: McGraw-Hill.

Tuffley, D. (2011) *Communications for ICT: The Essential Guide*, Seattle, WA: CreateSpace.

Turner, Y. and Robson, S. (2008) *Internationalizing the University*, London and New York: Continuum.

Tylor, E.B. (1871) *Primitive Culture: Researches into the Development of Mythology, Philosophy, Religion, Art, and Custom*, New York: Gordon Press.

United Nations Educational, Scientific and Cultural Organization (UNESCO) (2012) *Global Flow of Tertiary-Level Students*. Online. Available: www.unesco.org/new/en/ (accessed 5 January 2012).

United Nations Enable (n.d.) *Convention on the Rights of Persons with Disabilities*. Online. Available: www.un.org/disabilities/ (accessed 10 May 2013).

United Nations High Commissioner for Refugees (UNHCR) (1992/1979) *Handbook on Procedures and Criteria for Determining Refugee Status under the 1951 Convention and the 1967 Protocol relating to the Status of Refugees*. Online. Available: www.unhcr.org/publ/PUBL/3d58e13b4.pdf (accessed 4 January 2012).

United Nations High Commissioner for Refugees (UNHCR) (n.d.) *Statistics and Operational Data: The Refugee Story in Data and Statistics*. Online. Available: www.unhcr.org/pages/49c3646c4d6.html (accessed 5 May 2013).

United Nations World Tourism Organization (UNWTO) (n.d.) *Understanding Tourism: Basic Glossary*. Online. Available: http://media.unwto.org/en/content/understanding-tourism-basic-glossary (accessed 5 February 2013).

U.S. Department of Health and Human Services (2001) *Mental Health: Culture, Race, and Ethnicity—A Supplement to Mental Health: A Report of the Surgeon General*, Rockville, MD: U.S. Department of Health and Human Services, Substance Abuse and Mental Health Services Administration, Center for Mental Health Services. Online. Available: www.surgeongeneral.gov/library/mental health/cre/sma-01-3613.pdf (accessed 1 April 2012).

van den Besselaar, P. and Heimeriks, G. (2001) 'Disciplinary, multidisciplinary, interdisciplinary: Concepts and indicators', paper presented at the 8th conference on Scientometrics and Informetrics, Sydney, Australia. Online. Available: http://hcs.science.uva.nl/usr/peter/publications/2002issi.pdf (accessed 23 April 2012).

van Meurs, N. and Spencer-Oatey, H. (2010) 'Multidisciplinary perspectives on intercultural conflict: The "Bermuda triangle" of conflict, culture, and communication', in D. Matsumoto (ed.) *APA Handbook of Intercultural Communication*, Washington, D.C.: American Psychological Association and New York: Walter de Gruyter, Inc., pp. 59–77.

Van Oudenhoven, J.P. (2006) 'Immigrants', in D.L. Sam and J.W. Berry (eds) *The Cambridge Handbook of Acculturation Psychology*, Cambridge: Cambridge University Press, pp. 163–80.

Vande Berg, M., Paige, R.M. and Lou, K.H. (2012) 'Student learning abroad: Paradigms and assumptions', in M. Vande Berg, R.M. Paige and K.H. Lou (eds), *Student Learning Abroad: What Our Students are Learning, What They're Not, and What We can Do About It*, Sterling, VA: Stylus, pp. 3–28.

Varner, I. and Beamer, L. (2011) *Intercultural Communication in the Global Workplace*, Boston: McGraw-Hill.

Vela-McConnell, J.A. (2011) *Unlikely Friends: Bridging Ties and Diverse Friendships*, Plymouth: Lexington Books.

Virkama, A. (2010) 'From othering to understanding', in V. Korhonen (ed.) *Cross-Cultural Lifelong Learning*, Tampere: Tampere University Press, pp. 39–60.

Vygotsky, L.S. (1997) 'Genesis of higher mental functions', in R.W. Rieber (ed.) *The Collected Works of L.S. Vygotsky, Volume 4: The History of the Development of Higher Mental Functions*, New York and London: Plenum Press, pp. 97–120.

Wächter, B. and Maiworm, F. (2008) *English-Taught Programmes in European Higher Education: The Picture in 2007 (ACA Papers on International Cooperation in Education)*, Bonn: Lemmens.

Walther, J.B. (1992) 'Interpersonal effects in computer-mediated interaction: A relational perspective', *Communication Research,* 19: 52–90.

Wang, G. and Kuo, E.C.Y. (2010) 'The Asian communication debate: Culture-specificity, culture-generality and beyond', *Asian Journal of Communication,* 20(2): 152–65.

Wang, W. (2012) *The Rise of Intermarriage: Rates, Characteristics Vary by Race and Gender*, PEW Research Social and Demographic Trends. Online. Available: www.pewsocialtrends.org/2012/02/16/the-rise-of-intermarriage/ (accessed 1 February 2013).

Ward, C.A., Bochner, S. and Furnham, A. (2001) *The Psychology of Culture Shock*, London: Routledge.

Ward, C.A., Okura, Y., Kennedy, A. and Kojima, T. (1998) 'The U-curve on trial: A longitudinal study of psychological and sociocultural adjustment during cross-cultural transition', *International Journal of Intercultural Relations,* 22(3): 277–91.

Wardaugh, R. (2006) *An Introduction to Sociolinguistics,* 5th edn, Oxford: Blackwell.

Wardaugh, R. (2010) *An Introduction to Sociolinguistics,* 6th edn, Oxford: Blackwell.

Waters, D. (2005) *One Couple: Two Cultures: 81 Western–Chinese Couples Talk about Love and Marriage*, Hong Kong: MCCM Creations.

Watson, B., Gallois, C., Hewett, D.G. and Jones, L. (2012) 'Culture and health care: Intergroup communication and its consequences', in J. Jackson (ed.) *The Routledge Handbook of Language and Intercultural Communication*, Abingdon: Routledge, pp. 510–22.

Watzlawick, P., Beavin, J. and Jackson, D. (1967) *The Pragmatics of Human Communication*, New York: Norton.

Wellman, C. (1988) *Morals and Ethics,* 2nd edn, Englewood Cliffs, NJ: Prentice Hall.

Wenger, E. (2006) *Communities of Practice: A Brief Introduction.* Online. Available: www.ewenger.com/theory (accessed 23 March 2013).

West, R. and Turner, L.H. (2011a) *Understanding Interpersonal Communication: Making Choices in Changing Times,* Boston: Wadsworth.

West, R. and Turner, L.H. (2011b) 'Technology and interpersonal communication', in K.M. Galvin (ed.), *Making Connections: Readings in Relational Communication,* Oxford: Oxford University Press, pp. 379–86.

Westerhof, G.J. (2008) 'Age identity', in D. Carr (ed.) *Encyclopedia of the Life Course and Human Development,* Farmington Hills, MI: Macmillan, pp. 10–14.

Wetherell, M. and Potter, J. (1992) *Mapping the Language of Racism,* London: Sage.

Whorf, B.L. (1939, 2nd edn, 1956) 'The relation of habitual thought and behavior to language', in J.B. Carroll (ed.) *Language, Thought, and Reality: Selected Writings of Benjamin Lee Whorf,* Cambridge, MA: MIT Press, pp. 134–59.

Whorf, B.L. (1956) *Language, Thought, and Reality,* Cambridge, MA: Technology Press of MIT.

Wiemann, J.M., Takai, J., Ota, H., Wiemann, M O. and Kovacic, B. (eds) (1997) 'A relational model of communication competence', *Emerging Theories of Human Communication,* Buffalo, NY: State University of New York Press, pp. 25–44.

Wierzbicka, A. (2006) *English: Meaning and Culture,* Beijing: Foreign Language Teaching and Research Press and Oxford University Press.

Wilkinson, J. (2012) 'The intercultural speaker and the acquisition of intercultural/global competence', in J. Jackson (ed.) *The Routledge Handbook of Language and Intercultural Communication,* Abingdon: Routledge, pp. 296–309.

Williams, R. (1981) *Culture,* London: Fontana.

Wilmot, W. and Hocker, J. (2010) *Interpersonal Conflict,* Boston: McGraw-Hill.

Winkelman, M. (1994) 'Cultural shock and adaptation', *Journal of Counseling and Development,* 73(2): 121–26.

Wintergerst, A. and McVeigh, J. (2011) *Tips for Teaching Culture: Practical Approaches to Intercultural Communication,* White Plains, NY: Pearson ESL.

Wodak, R. (2008) '"Us and them": Inclusion and exclusion', in G. Delanty, R. Wodak and P. Jones (eds) *Identity, Belonging and Migration,* Liverpool: Liverpool University Press, pp. 54–77.

Wood, J.T. (2005) *Gendered Lives: Communication, Gender, and Culture,* 7th edn, Belmont, CA: Wadsworth.

Wood, J.T. (2009) *Gendered Lives: Communication, Gender, and Culture,* 8th edn, Belmont, CA: Wadsworth.

Wood, J.T. (2013) *Interpersonal Communication: Everyday Encounters,* Boston: Wadsworth.

Wood, P. and Landry, C. (2010) *The Intercultural City: Planning for Diversity Advantage,* London: Earthscan.

World Health Organization (WHO) (2011) *World Report on Disability,* Geneva: WHO.

World Health Organization (WHO) (n.d.) *What Do We Mean by 'Sex' and 'Gender'?* Online. Available: www.who.int/gender/whatisgender/en/ (accessed 5 August 2012).

Xinhua (2010) 316 Confucius Institutes Established Worldwide, Xinhua. Online. Available: http://news.xinhuanet.com/english2010/culture/2010-07/13/c_13398209.htm (accessed 1 April 2012).

Yamada, H. (1997) *Different Games, Different Rules: Why Americans and Japanese Misunderstand Each Other,* Oxford: Oxford University Press.

Yancey, G. and Lewis, R. Jr. (2009) *Interracial Families: Current Concepts and Controversies,* New York and London: Routledge.

Yep, G.A. (1997) 'Intercultural communication in contexts', *Communication Quarterly*, 45(1): 82–84.

Ying, Y.W. (2002) 'Formation of cross-cultural relationships of Taiwanese International Students in the U.S.', *Journal of Community Psychology*, 30(1): 45–55.

Yule, G. (1996) *The Study of Language*, Cambridge: Cambridge University Press.

Yule, G. (2008) *Pragmatics*, Oxford: Oxford University Press.

Zaharna, R.S. (1989) 'Self-shock: The double-binding challenge of identity', *International Journal of Intercultural Relations,* 13: 501–26.

Zenner, W. (1996) 'Ethnicity', in D. Levinson and M. Ember (eds) *Encyclopedia of Cultural Anthropology*, New York: Holt, pp. 393–95.

Zhang, Y.B., Harwood, J. and Hummert, M.L. (2005) 'Perceptions of conflict management styles in Chinese intergenerational dyads', *Communication Monographs,* 72: 71–91.

Zhu Hua (2011) 'Glossary', in Zhu Hua (ed.) *The Language and Intercultural Communication Reader*, Abingdon: Routledge, pp. 418–25.

Zimbler, M. and Feldman, R.S. (2011) 'Liar, liar, hard drive on fire: How media context affects lying behavior', *Journal of Applied Social Psychology*, 41(10): 2492–507.

Glossary

Throughout the text key terms are in **bold**. The explanations of these terms are provided here.

accent The way one pronounces words when one speaks

acceptance of difference According to the developmental model of intercultural sensitivity (DMIS), individuals in this phase accept the existence of culturally different ways of organizing human existence, although they may not like or agree with them

accommodation style This communication style emphasizes an indirect and emotionally restrained approach to dealing with conflict

acculturation The process through which an individual is socialized into a new cultural environment

acculturation strategies The ways that individuals and ethnocultural groups respond to the process of acculturation

acculturative stress A negative psychological reaction to the experiences of acculturation, often characterized by anxiety, depression and a variety of psychosomatic problems

acquaintance A person whom one knows but who is not a particularly close friend

active listening Noticing how and when ideas are conveyed as well as what is *not* being said

adaptation The act or process of adjusting or adapting to a new cultural environment

adaptation to difference According to the developmental model of intercultural sensitivity (DMIS), individuals in this phase can expand their own worldviews to accurately understand other ways of being and are able to behave in culturally appropriate ways

adaptors Gestures or movements that satisfy personal or bodily needs (e.g. scratching, yawning)

additive bilingualism A process whereby one's first language and culture continue to be nurtured as one's second language develops

affect (affective) displays Facial expressions combined with posture, which convey the strength of one's feelings or emotions

affective competence The emotional and motivational capacity to cope with the challenges of living in a new environment

affective conflict A type of conflict that centres on an emotional conflict between parties

affirmative action Education, business, or employment policies that aim to redress the negative, historical impact of discrimination by taking factors such as race, sex, religion, gender or national origin into consideration in hiring/promotion situations

age identity How people feel and think about themselves and others based on age

ageism The stereotyping or discrimination of a person or group of people based on their age

ageist language Language that is used to convey stereotypes of people based on their age

ageist stereotyping The categorizing of individuals into groups according to their age and then ascribing certain characteristics and behaviours to all people of that age group (e.g. teenagers, Generation X, seniors)

anti-discrimination legislation A set of laws that exists to protect the rights of individuals and promote equality among people regardless of their differences (e.g. sex, gender, religion, ethnicity, social class, physical ability)

anti-racist legislation Regulations or laws protecting human rights in certain sectors of society

appearance message The nonverbal signals (e.g. clothing, mannerisms) that facilitate judgments about an individual's personality, abilities and other attributes

appropriate communication Communication that enhances interpersonal relationships

appropriate intercultural communication Communication that enhances intercultural interpersonal relationships from the perspective of both interactants

arbitrary A decision based on random choice rather than reason

articulation The clarity and control of the sounds being produced

artifacts Objects created or shaped by humans, usually for a practical purpose

ascribed identity The identity that others assign to us (or we give to someone else)

ascription The process of ascribing or assigning an identity to someone else

assertiveness The extent to which people are strong-willed and confrontational

assimilation The process whereby immigrants do not retain their original cultural identity and link to their heritage/culture; instead, they seek close interaction with the host culture and adopt the cultural values, norms and traditions of the new society

asylum seeker An individual who is seeking protection as a refugee and is waiting for his or her claim to be assessed by a country that has signed the Geneva Convention on Refugees

asynchronous communication A type of online communication that occurs with time constraints, that is, the receiver of an email message may not read it until several hours or days after it has been sent

attitude An emotional (positive or negative) response to people, ideas and objects

audience design framework A basic structure developed by Allan Bell (1984) that aims to explain observed variations in speech styles

avoidance strategy Deliberate steps taken to avoid uncomfortable situations

avowal The process of conveying what identity(ies) one wishes to be acknowledged by others

avowed identity The identity that an individual wishes to present or claim in an interaction

behavioural (intercultural) adroitness Skills that are needed for one to be interculturally competent, e.g. message skills, knowledge regarding appropriate self-disclosure, behavioural flexibility, interaction management, social skills

behavioural uncertainty One's uncertainty about how one's communication partner will behave

beliefs Learned assumptions and convictions about concepts, events, people and ways of being that are held to be true by an individual or a group

best friend Someone who is especially close to you

bias A personal preference, like or dislike, which can interfere with one's ability to be objective, impartial and without prejudice

bicultural An individual who is culturally competent in two cultural contexts (e.g. his or her original home environment and the host environment)

biculturalism A state that is characterized by proficiency and comfort with both one's original culture and the culture of the new country or region

bilingual Using or able to use two languages with equal or nearly equal fluency

biracial Having parents of two different races

bisexual A person who is sexually attracted to both men and women

bisexuality Romantic or sexual attraction towards males and females

body language A form of human nonverbal communication consisting of body posture, gestures, facial expressions and eye movements (*See* kinesics)

business acumen One's ability to understand business situations and make appropriate decisions in a short amount of time

business ethics Principles that guide behaviour in business

business etiquette Rules that guide social behaviour in workplace situations

business netiquette Guidelines for courtesy in the use of email and the Internet for communication purposes in business

business protocol The discourse, nonverbal behaviour, dress, procedures and social conventions that are expected within a particular company or organization

casual friend *See* acquaintance

casual intercultural dating Individuals from different cultural backgrounds who spend time with each other socially and may have a sexual relationship without necessarily expecting the commitments of a more formal romantic relationship

casual intercultural relationship A physical and emotional relationship between two people from different cultural backgrounds who may have a sexual relationship without necessarily expecting the commitments of a more formal romantic relationship

channel The way in which a message is conveyed from one person to another, e.g. through speech, writing, nonverbal signals

chronemics The study of how people use and structure time

citizenship The relationship between the individual and the state, and the need for citizens to understand the economic and political processes, structures, institutions, laws, rights and responsibilities within the system that governs the state

class identity A sense of belonging or attachment to a group that shares similar economic, occupational or social status

classism Prejudice or discrimination on the basis of social class

close friend Someone who can be relied on to provide emotional support and perhaps lend a hand when needed

co-culture Smaller, coherent collective groups that exist within a larger dominant culture and are often distinctive because of race, social class, gender, etc.

co-habitation Living together in a sexual relationship without being legally married

co-national An individual from one's home nation

code of ethics Guidelines that spell out what is 'right' or 'wrong' behaviour in everyday life as well as in professional contexts

code-mixing The process of mixing the expressions in one language with another

code-switching Changing between different languages when communicating

cognitive awareness Knowledge of one's own personal identities/cultures and understanding of how cultures differ

cognitive competence Knowledge of the host language and culture, history, social institutions and rules or norms of interpersonal conduct in specific situations

cognitive conflict A type of conflict that centres on the completion of a task

cognitive uncertainty Uncertainty about the ways in which an individual's culturally-influenced attitudes and beliefs impact on his or her way of thinking

collaborating style A conflict style in which parties work together cooperatively until a mutually agreeable solution is found

collaboration A process whereby two or more people or organizations work together to realize shared goals

collectivism Interdependence and social cohesion are emphasized so that the needs and wants of groups are given priority over individuals

communication A symbolic, dynamic process by which we create and share meaning with others

communication accommodation theory (CAT) A theory developed by Howard Giles and his colleagues that posits that people in intercultural interactions adjust their language toward or away from their communication partner and in the process may emphasize different aspects of their identities

communication adaptability The ability to modify one's interaction behaviours and goals to meet the specific needs of the situation

communication competence The ability to achieve one's goals in a way that is acceptable to both communication partners

communication style The way individuals or a group of individuals prefer to communicate with others

communicative competence What a speaker needs to know to be able to use language appropriately and effectively in specific social/cultural settings

community of practice (CoP) A group of people who share a concern or a passion for something they do and gradually learn how to do it better through interaction on a regular basis

computer-mediated communication (CMC) Communication that is facilitated by computer technologies (e.g. the use of two or more networked computers)

conflict An expressed struggle between interdependent individuals or groups over perceived incompatible interests, goals, values and resources

conflict face negotiation theory A theory developed by Stella Ting-Toomey, which addresses the ways face-losing and face-saving behaviours influence intercultural conflict situations

conflict facework competence The use of culturally/linguistically appropriate and effective facework negotiation skills in conflict situations

conflict fluency Recognition that conflict is a difference that offers potential growth

conflict interaction style Patterned responses to conflict situations

conflict management The process by which individuals or groups try to find a satisfying outcome in conflict situations

conflict management practices Steps that individuals or groups adopt to resolve conflicts

conflict management style Preferred ways of dealing with conflict situations

conflict negotiation strategies Preferred strategies for negotiating conflicts

conflict script A routinized sequence of verbal and nonverbal actions in a dispute

conflict style A preferred way of behaving in conflict situations

Confucian dynamism A value dimension that aims to account for particular cultural characteristics and behaviours (Confucian values) that are prevalent in East Asian nations, e.g. persistence, a long-term orientation to time (*See also* Hofstede's Value-Orientations Framework)

'conscious' culture Cultural elements that are visible, explicit and able to be sensed

consecutive interpreting Interpreting that takes place after the speaker has finished

constructive communication skills The ability to communicate appropriately and effectively by using skilful language, verbal, and nonverbal behaviours, whether in a first or second language

constructive conflict communication skills The ability to manage a conflict situation appropriately and effectively by way of skilful interpersonal conflict management skills and verbal and nonverbal communication, whether in a first or second language

constructive marginality The development of an integrated multicultural self with the acceptance of an identity that is not based on a single cultural identity

contact hypothesis George Allport's notion that increased contact between different cultural or ethnic groups can lead to mutual acceptance and reduced levels of tension/prejudice provided that certain conditions are met

contested identity Facets or elements of one's identity that are not recognized or accepted by the people one is in contact with

context The overall environment in which communication occurs (e.g. physical, psychological, sociocultural, political, sociorelational, etc.)

contrastive rhetoric The study of how a person's first language and culture influence his or her writing in a second language

convergence The act of adjusting one's speech and stressing particular identities to become more similar to one's addressees in order to emphasize solidarity and reduce social distance

corporate culture The culture of a particular business or organization

crimes against humanity The systemic practice of serious offences against people that are either carried out or condoned by a government (e.g. widespread murder, religious persecution, rapes as a weapon of war, etc.)

critical approach to intercultural communication The impact of power and power relations on intercultural communication are examined bearing in mind the sociopolitical, historical context

critical cultural awareness/political education (*savoir s'engager*) The ability to critically evaluate perspectives, practices and products in one's own and other cultures

critical discourse analysis A form of discourse analysis, which aims to bring about social change by disclosing connections of hidden relationships encoded in language that may not be immediately evident

critical intercultural communication A critical examination of the role of power and positioning in language and intercultural communication within a particular context

critical intercultural speaker An individual (second language speaker) who is able to negotiate between his or her own cultural, social and political identifications and representations with those of the other and, in the process, become critically aware of the complex nature of cultural identities in an intercultural encounter (*See also* intercultural speaker)

critical reflection The process of analysing, reconsidering and questioning intercultural experiences with the aim of developing a better understanding of internal and external factors that influenced the outcome

cross-cultural adaptation The process whereby individuals from one cultural context move to a different cultural context and strive to learn the societal norms, customs and language of the host culture in order to function in the new environment

cross-cultural communication The comparison of communication behaviours and patterns in two or more cultures

cross-cultural communication research Investigations that compare and contrast native discourse and ways of being (e.g. communication styles) in different cultures

cross-cultural pragmatics A branch of pragmatics that focuses on speech acts in different cultures, politeness norms in different languages and cultural/communication breakdowns or pragmatic failures

cultural awareness An understanding of how an individual's cultural background may inform his or her values, behaviour, beliefs and basic assumptions

cultural display rules Cultural rules that influence whether and how to express one's emotions in a particular situation

cultural distance The gap between the culture of two different groups

cultural fluency Recognition that culture profoundly shapes who we are and how we cooperate and engage in conflict

cultural identity A social identity that is influenced by one's membership or affiliation with particular cultural groups

cultural identity formation The formation of a sense of belonging or attachment to a particular cultural group that develops through shared experiences and the teachings of other members of the group

cultural maintenance The effort of immigrants to sustain elements of their culture or heritage by preserving core values, traditions, ways of being, etc. especially when faced with pressure to adopt the ways of the more dominant culture (e.g. the majority group)

cultural membership One's affiliation or sense of belonging to a particular cultural group

cultural norms Shared expectations of appropriate behaviours in certain situations and contexts

cultural relativism The view that beliefs, value systems and social practices are culturally relative, that is, no culture is inherently superior to another

cultural schema A mental structure in which our knowledge and understanding of the world is organized to facilitate our thinking, communication, etc.

cultural script Representations of cultural norms that are widely held in a given society and reflected in language (e.g. a particular sequence of expressions and behaviours in certain situations)

cultural socialization The process through which our primary cultural beliefs, values, norms and worldviews are internalized, to varying degrees

cultural space A physical or virtual place where individuals have a sense of community and culture, e.g. a neighbourhood, region, virtual space

cultural synergy The combined power of people from diverse cultural backgrounds working together to create a greater, stronger effect than if they were separate

culture A community or group that shares a common history, traditions, norms, and imaginings in a particular cultural space (e.g. a neighbourhood, region, virtual space)

culture broker An individual who is tasked with bridging cultural differences

culture brokering The act of bridging or mediating between groups or people who have different cultural backgrounds in order to facilitate communication and reduce conflict

'culture as nation' perspective An orientation towards culture in which nations or communities are viewed as homogeneous and diversity within groups is largely ignored

culture-general intercultural education A form of intercultural education that does not focus on a particular culture; instead, it centres on the development of the knowledge, skills and mindset that can help individuals analyse their linguistic and cultural context and engage in successful intercultural interactions, no matter where they are in the world

culture-sensitive knowledge Awareness of the conceptions, beliefs, values and ways of being of a culture

'culture of learning' The norms, values and expectations of teachers and learners that influence classroom activities in a particular cultural setting

culture shock Disorientation and discomfort that an individual may experience when entering an unfamiliar cultural environment

culture-specific intercultural education A form of intercultural communication that primarily aims at the achievement of cultural competence in a particular culture

cyber friendship A personal connection or affiliation forged between people online

cyber identity A social identity that an Internet user establishes in websites and online communities

cyberculture The culture that develops through the use of computer networks for communication, business and entertainment

decoding The process by which the receiver tries to understand the meaning of a message that is being sent

deculturation The unlearning of cultural habits

deep-level diversity Differences among individuals and groups that are not easily observable such as attitudes, beliefs, knowledge, skills and values or worldviews

defense against difference According to the developmental model of intercultural sensitivity (DMIS), individuals in this ethnocentric phase view their own culture/way of life as the best and overt negative stereotyping is common

defense/reversal According to the developmental model of intercultural sensitivity (DMIS), in this ethnocentric phase one's own culture is devalued and another culture or way of life is romanticized as superior

denial of difference According to the developmental model of intercultural sensitivity (DMIS), individuals in this ethnocentric phase experience their own culture as the only 'real' one and other cultures are either not noticed or are understood in a simplistic way

developmental model of intercultural sensitivity (DMIS) A framework developed by Milton Bennett to depict the process of becoming interculturally sensitive; it describes various ways that individuals perceive and react to cultural differences

dialect A variety of language used in a specific region

direct communication The speaker's intentions and views are made clear by the use of explicit verbal messages and a forthright tone of voice

direct conflict style A verbally direct and confrontational approach to dealing with conflict

direct eye contact Looking into the eyes of the other person

direct language The use of precise, explicit discourse

discourse Written or spoken communication

discourse analysis Investigations of spoken or written language

discourse community A group of people who share common social space and history as well as ways of communicating their values and goals

discourse competence The ability to understand and produce the range of spoken, written and visual texts that are characteristics of a language

discrimination The prejudicial or unequal treatment of individuals based on their membership, or perceived membership, in a particular group or category

discriminatory language Derogatory terms, stereotypes or generalizations about an individual or group (e.g. ethnic, gender, minority, religious, etc.)

discussion style A verbally direct approach to conflict situations that is tempered by an emotionally restrained response

divergence The distancing of oneself from one's interlocutors by accentuating differences in one's speech (e.g. accent, communication style), identities, or nonverbal behaviours (e.g. gestures, personal distance)

diversity Differences among humans in terms of such aspects as culture, language, race, ethnicity, gender, socio-economic status, age, physical/cognitive abilities, national origin, physical attributes, sexual orientation, ethnic affiliation, regional differences, religious beliefs, political beliefs or other ideologies

dual identity Possessing two identities (e.g. a local and global self)

duration (in speech) How long a particular sound is made

dynamic conflict code-switching Adopting one's conflict style to meet the other conflict party's communication approach

dynamic style The use of indirect strategies and emotionally intense expressions to deal with major disagreements or conflicts

economic justice Economic policies that distribute benefits equally to all

education abroad Education outside one's home country (e.g. study abroad, internships, volunteering, directed travel with learning goals)

effective communication Communication that achieves the desired results from the perspective of both the sender and receiver

effective intercultural communication Intercultural communication that achieves the desired results from the perspective of both the sender and receiver

e-identity *See* cyber identity

emblem of identity Markers of one's affiliation with a particular group (e.g. clothing, language, communication style)

emblems (emblematic gestures) Direct nonverbal replacements for words (e.g. OK signal in U.S.)

emic perspective The perspective of an insider (member) in a particular culture

emoticon Pictorial representations of facial expressions and other symbols that are meant to convey particular emotions

emotional display The expression of our emotions

emotional expression Observable verbal and nonverbal actions that convey emotions

emotional intelligence The ability to understand and manage one's own emotions and display sensitivity to others' feelings

emotion regulation The culturally-influenced process of modifying one's emotions and expressions in particular situations and contexts

emotional restraint Controlling the expression of one's emotions

emotionally expressive style A conflict style that is characterized by emotionally confrontational discourse and expression

emotionally restrained style A conflict style that is characterized by emotional restraint and careful word choice

empathetic behaviour Verbal and nonverbal actions that indicate that one is attending to the messages of others

empathy The ability to understand another person's feelings and point of view

employment discrimination Unfair practices in hiring, promotion, job assignment, termination and compensation

encapsulated marginality Intense feelings of loss and inbetweenness that individuals may experience in an unfamiliar environment when they feel torn between different cultural worlds, identities and languages

encoding The process of putting an idea or message into a set of symbols (e.g. words, gestures)

enculturation The primary socialization process in one's home environment whereby one learns the cultural values and rules of behaviour that are prevalent in one's culture

engagement style A conflict style characterized by a more verbally direct and confrontational or direct approach

Englishization The spread of English throughout the world

essentialism The belief that the attributes and behaviour of socially-defined groups can be explained by reference to cultural and/or biological characteristics believed to be inherent to the group (*See also* 'culture as nation', reductionism)

ethics Principles of conduct that help govern the behaviour of individuals and groups

ethnic cleansing The systematic and violent removal of an ethnic or religious group from a particular territory

ethnic group A group of people with the same descent and heritage who share a common and distinctive culture passed on through generations

ethnic group strength The relative status or standing of a particular ethnic group in the context of the surrounding host society

ethnic identity An identity linked to one's perceptions and emotions regarding one's affiliation with one's own ethnic group(s)

ethnicity A socially defined category based on such aspects as common ancestry, cuisine, dressing style, heritage, history, language or dialect, physical appearance, religion, symbols, traditions or other cultural factors

ethnic proximity/distance The gap or degree of closeness between ethnic groups

ethnocentric mindset A way of thinking that holds that one's cultural worldview and way of life are superior to all others

ethnocentricism A point of view that views one's group's standards as the best and judges all other groups in relation to them

ethnographic fieldwork Sustained observation and participation in a cultural setting to develop an understanding of how the members view their social and cultural world and interact with each other

ethnography The study and systematic recording of people in naturally occurring settings to create a detailed, in-depth description of everyday life and practice

ethnography of communication The study of the communication patterns of speech communities

ethnography of speaking *See* ethnography of communication

ethnorelative mindset A way of thinking that tries to view another person's cultural worldview and way of life from that person's perspective

ethnorelativism The ability to understand a communication practice or worldview from another person's cultural frame of reference

etic perspective An outsider's (observer's) perspective on a particular culture

expatriate An individual who is engaged in employment abroad

expectancy violation theory A theory developed by Judee Burgoon that posits that individuals have culturally-based expectations about how people should behave in a communicative event and when they do not perform as expected, miscommunication and negative perceptions may develop

eye contact Direct visual contact with another person's eyes

eye movement The movement of the eye(s) that conveys meaning (e.g. rolling the eyes to convey contempt, direct gaze to convey interest)

face The public self-image that one wants others to recognize and support

face-giving Actions that protect or support an individual's self-image or reputation

face loss Experienced by individuals when they are not treated in a way that respects their preferred self-identities (e.g. position, status, self-image)

face maintenance The desire to project a positive image and avoid appearing weak or foolish

face management Communicating respect and a positive regard for self and others

face-saving Actions that protect or support an individual's self-image or reputation

face threat Challenges to an individual's self-image

face-threatening Actions that cause someone to be humiliated

facework Verbal and nonverbal actions that individuals use to maintain or restore face loss and to uphold and honour face gain

facework strategies Steps taken to manage face

facework style Pattern of behaviours designed to manage face

facial expressions Facial movements that convey one's emotional state

fantasy identity A sense of belonging that centres on characters from science fiction movies, comic books and anime

faux-pas A socially awkward or tactless act, e.g. behaviour that violates accepted social norms, standard customs or the rules of etiquette

feedback Intentional or unintentional verbal or nonverbal signals that receivers give to a speaker to indicate they have processed what the speaker has said

feminine cultures Cultures that promote gender equality, interpersonal contact, flexible balancing of life and work and group decisions

femininity Gender roles that dictate certain roles and behaviours for women (e.g. modesty, tenderness)

field Cultural setting

'friends with benefits' A casual sexual relationship among friends who are not romantically or emotionally involved

friendship A personal connection or affiliation forged between individuals

friendship network A type of social network, includes individuals who are very close personal friends, acquaintances (e.g. those who are more distant), and 'friends of friends'

functional fitness Knowing one's way around in the new environment

functionalism A psychological school of thought concerned with how the conscious is related to behaviour

gay A person attracted to another person of the same sex (homosexual)

gay marriage A marital union between members of the same sex

gaze That act of looking at someone or something

gender One's identification as male, female or, less commonly, both male and female or neither

gender conflict Conflict situations in which gender is a key factor

gender-crossing Beginning life as a male and assuming female behaviours and characteristics (or vice versa)

gender identity Part of one's personal identity that is based on one's gender and society's notions of the role(s) and image of that gender

gender socialization The process of developing gender identities in particular social and cultural contexts

gender stereotyping Simplistic overgeneralizations about the gender characteristics, differences and roles of males and females

gendered identities An acknowledgment that multiple identities are shaped by one's gender and that social identities overlap

generalization A statement about common trends or elements in a group coupled with an understanding that more information is required to determine whether the generalization applies to a particular individual

genocide The targeted killing of a particular ethnic, religious group

gesture A movement or position of the hand, arm, body, head or face that conveys an idea, opinion, or emotion

gift giving The ritual of providing gifts to business clients

glass ceiling An unseen barrier that keeps minorities and women from rising to more senior positions in organizations, regardless of their qualifications or achievements

global business Operations and strategies of businesses designed to serve a world market

global citizen An individual who identifies with being part of an emerging world community and whose actions contribute to building this community's values and practices

global citizenship Awareness of and commitment to societal justice for marginalized groups and care for the environment based on principles of equity, respect and sharing

global citizenship activism Assuming an activist role to cultivate ethical values, principles and practices characteristic of global citizenship

global civic engagement Recognition of local, state, national and global community issues and response through actions such as volunteerism, political activism and community participation

global competence Possessing an open mind while actively seeking to understand different cultural norms and expectations, and using this knowledge to interact, communicate and work effectively outside one's environment

global competency An appreciation of complexity, conflict management, the inevitability of change, and the interconnectedness among humans and their environment (Stanley Foundation 2003)

global competence model A framework developed by W. Hunter (2004) to help international educators prepare individuals for a diverse workforce and society that necessitates intercultural and global competencies

global consciousness Concern about the welfare of our planet

global English The use of English internationally for business negotiations, multinational organizations, scientific communication, diplomacy, academic conferences and international education

global ethics Basic shared ethical values, criteria and attitudes for peaceful coexistence among humans

global identity An identity that affords an individual a sense of belonging in a worldwide culture and is often associated with the use of an international language

global knowledge An understanding of diverse cultures, languages, global events and concerns

globalization The growing tendency towards international interdependence in business, media, and culture

globally competent person An individual who has knowledge of current events, the capacity to empathize with others, the ability to maintain a positive attitude, second language competence, and an appreciation of foreign ways of doing things

global nomads Individuals who have an international lifestyle (e.g. live and work in more than one country for a long period of time), including those who have grown up in many different cultural contexts because their parents have frequently relocated (*See also* third culture kids)

global-ready graduates Individuals who are adequately prepared for a diverse workforce and society that necessitates intercultural and global competencies

global village The term coined by Marshall McLuhan in the 1960s to refer to the way the world is 'shrinking' as people become increasingly interconnected through media and other communication advances

global warming The rising of the temperature in the Earth's atmosphere and oceans that is bringing about droughts and floods

GLOBE cultural framework A framework developed by the Global Leadership and Organizational Behaviour Effectiveness (GLOBE) project to measure the relationship between societal culture, organizational culture and leadership

GLOBE dimensions Cultural differences in societal values and practices identified by the GLOBE project: institutional and group collectivism, gender egalitarianism, power distance, uncertainty avoidance, future orientation, assertiveness, performance orientation and humane orientation

haptics The use of touch in communication, including the type of contact as well as its frequency and intensity

harassment Behaviours of an offensive or threatening nature

hedging The use of cautious or vague language

hegemony Domination through consent whereby the aims, ideas and interests of the dominant class are so engrained that minorities go along with their own subordination and exploitation

heritage Aspects that are inherited or linked to the past (e.g. language, rituals, preferences for music, certain foods, dress)

heritage student A student who studies abroad in a location that is linked in some way (e.g. linguistically, culturally, historically) to his/her family or cultural background

heterosexual orientation Individuals are attracted to persons of the other sex

heterosexuality Sexual attraction to members of the opposite sex

high-contact culture A kind of culture in which people display considerable interpersonal closeness or immediacy

high culture Culture that is linked to the arts (e.g. fine paintings, classical music, literature)

high-context communication A style of communication in which most information is implicitly communicated through indirect, nonverbal and mutually shared knowledge rather than expressed explicitly in words

Hofstede's Value-Orientations Framework The identification of systematic differences in national cultures by Geert Hofstede: power distance (PDI), individualism (IDV), uncertainty avoidance (UAI) and masculinity (MAS), with Confucian Dynamism added later

holocaust A mass slaughter of people (e.g. Jews and Gypsies by the Nazis during WWII)

homogenization The loss of linguistic and cultural distinctiveness through the process of globalization

homosexual orientation A state in which a person is attracted to another person of the same sex

homosexuality Sexual attraction to members of the same sex

honour killing The murder of a young woman by relatives who believe that her actions (e.g. premarital sex, refusal to accept an arranged marriage) have brought dishonour on the family

honourifics Words (e.g. titles) or expressions in some languages that convey respect towards a social superior

horizontal-based facework Informal–symmetrical strategies/equal treatment

host communication competence The ability of a newcomer to decode and encode information in accordance with host cultural communication practices

host conformity pressure The extent to which the host environment challenges newcomers, implicitly or explicitly, to adopt local norms of behaviour

host national A person from the host country

host receptivity The degree to which the host environment welcomes newcomers into its interpersonal networks and offers them support

human migration Physical movement by people from one place to another, sometimes over long distances

human rights The basic rights and freedoms to which all humans are entitled, e.g. the right to life and liberty, freedom of thought and expression and equality before the law

human trafficking The illegal trade of human beings for sexual exploitation or forced labour

humane orientation The extent to which an organization rewards members for being kind and fair to others

humour style The ways individuals use humour in particular contexts and situations

hybrid (mixed) identity A sense of self with elements from multiple cultures

identity An individual's self-concept or sense of self

identity confusion An individual who moves from one environment to another may feel caught between two distinct worlds (*See also* encapsulated marginality)

identity expansion The broadening of one's sense of self through exposure to new ideas and practices

identity intensity The degree of significance of a particular identity

identity labels Terms used to categorize individuals or groups

identity salience The degree to which an identity is prominent in a particular situation

identity shock Confusing and sometimes conflicting self-images that may develop when one moves to a new environment

ideology A system of ideas that promotes the interests of a particular group of people

illustrators Nonverbal actions that shape/illustrate what is being said (e.g. pointing)

imagined community Individuals *assume* that people they associate with their group follow norms, practices and beliefs similar to their own

immigration Moving from one's home country to reside in another

inclusiveness General acceptance and appreciation of differences' within a community or society

independent self-construal A self-perception that puts an emphasis on one's autonomy and separateness from others

indirect communication A style of communication that emphasizes the use of subtle, indirect forms of expression (e.g. hints, suggestions)

indirect conflict style A non-confrontational style of conflict management

indirect language The use of expressions that suggest or hint at ideas

individual racism A person's attitudes, beliefs and actions that support or perpetuate racism

individualism The tendency to emphasize the rights, identities, responsibilities and independent action of the individual rather than the group (*See also* collectivism)

individualistic cultures Cultural groups that stress personal over group goals and self-reliance and individual responsibility, and tend to have weaker group and organizational loyalty

inequality Unequal access to power and resources

information and communications technology (ICT) The role of unified communications and the integration of telecommunication (e.g. wireless signals), computers, middleware as well as necessary software, storage- and audio-visual systems, which allow users to create, access, store, transmit and manipulate information

information technology (IT) The application of computers and telecommunications equipment to store, retrieve, transmit and manipulate data

ingroup   A social or cultural group to which a person psychologically identifies as being a member

ingroup bias   Situations in which people give preferential treatment to those who are perceived to be in the same ingroup

ingroup-favouritism (ingroup bias)   Situations in which people give preferential treatment to those who are perceived to be in the same ingroup

ingroup-favouritism principle   A positive attachment to and predisposition for norms that are related to one's ingroup

ingroup members   People with whom you feel emotionally connected

innate   Existing in one from birth

institutional racism   A kind of racism that can result in differential access to the goods, services and opportunities of society

integration   Immigrants take steps to maintain their cultural heritage and original cultural identity while developing harmonious relationships with host nationals

integration of difference   According to the developmental model of intercultural sensitivity (DMIS), individuals in this phase do not have a definition of self that is central to any particular culture and they are able to shift from one cultural worldview to another

integrative communication theory of cross-cultural adaptation   A theory proposed by Young Yun Kim (2001) to depict an individual's gradual adaption to a new environment

intensity   The importance or strength of something (e.g. identity, value)

intentional communication   Two or more people consciously engage in interaction with a specific purpose in mind

interactional sociolinguistics   A form of micro-sociolinguistics, which investigates the use of language in face-to-face social interaction

interactive communication   A two-way process involving the sending and receiving of messages

intercultural adroitness   *See* behavioural adroitness

intercultural attitudes (*savoir être*)   Curiosity and openness, readiness to suspend disbelief about others cultures and belief about one's own intercultural attitudes

intercultural awareness   *See* cognitive awareness

intercultural citizenship   The development of the competencies necessary to engage in political activity with people who have a different linguistic and cultural background

intercultural communication   Interpersonal communication that involves interaction between people from different cultural (and often linguistic) backgrounds

intercultural communication competence   The ability to communicate appropriately and effectively with individuals who have a different cultural background

intercultural communication research   Investigations of interpersonal interactions involving people who have diverse linguistic and cultural backgrounds (also studies of the adjustment of newcomers in unfamiliar cultural settings)

intercultural communication skills The skills needed to interact appropriately and effectively in intercultural interactions (e.g. adaptability, empathy, cross-cultural awareness, intercultural mediation, intercultural sensitivity)

intercultural communicative competence The abilities needed to communicate effectively and appropriately with people who are linguistically and culturally different from oneself

intercultural competence The ability to communicate effectively and appropriately in intercultural situations based on one's intercultural knowledge, skills and attitudes

intercultural competency An inclusive and integrative worldview which facilitates cross-cultural adaptation

intercultural conflict The perceived or actual incompatibility of cultural values, situational norms, goals, face orientations, scarce resources, styles/processes and/or outcomes in a face-to-face (or mediated) context

intercultural conflict competence The mindful management of emotional frustrations and conflict interaction struggles largely due to cultural, linguistic or ethnic group membership differences

intercultural conflict style model Devised by Mitch Hammer (2004), this model is based on two core dimensions that he maintains are influenced by cultural values and beliefs: (1) the degree of directness when dealing with conflicts and (2) divergent ways of coping with the affective dimension of conflict interaction

intercultural cyber or online romance Romantic relationships formed online

intercultural education Education designed to help prepare students for responsible intercultural citizenship in our global community

intercultural effectiveness The ability to interact with people from a different cultural background in ways that are respectful and appropriate

intercultural facework competence The ability to manage vulnerable identity-based conflict situations appropriately, effectively and adaptively

intercultural friendship A personal connection or affiliation forged between people who have a different cultural background

intercultural gay (lesbian) romance A romantic relationship between two males or two females

intercultural identity orientation An identity that is not rigidly linked to one's home culture or the host culture

intercultural interaction Communication between individuals who have a different cultural background

intercultural interpersonal relationship Friendships, dating, co-habitation, marriages involving people with a different cultural or religious background

intercultural marriage A social union or legal contract between individuals from different cultural backgrounds who may possess differing values, worldviews and personal philosophies

intercultural mediator An individual who is able to interact appropriately and effectively with someone who has a different linguistic and cultural background (*See also* intercultural speaker)

intercultural mind/mindset An open mindset capable of understanding from within and from without both one's own culture and other cultures (*See also* ethnorelativism)

intercultural political competence The ability to take part in community activity and service with people with a different linguistic and cultural background

intercultural pragmatics A branch of pragmatics concerned with how the language system is employed in social encounters between individuals who have different first languages, communicate in a common language and, usually, represent different cultures

intercultural relationship A relationship between individuals who have a different cultural background

intercultural rhetoric The study of the ways in which writers from diverse linguistic and cultural backgrounds construct and negotiate texts

intercultural romance A close interpersonal relationship between individuals from diverse cultural backgrounds who share a romantic love for each other

intercultural sensitivity A positive emotion that enables individuals to acknowledge and respect cultural differences

intercultural speaker A competent, flexible second language speaker who is able to establish positive intercultural relationships by drawing on/recognizing multiple identities and ways of being in intercultural interactions

intercultural transformation A process of change in which border crossers develop a broadened sense of self that is more inclusive and intercultural

interculturality The forging of respectful, equitable links between individuals and groups from different cultural (and linguistic) backgrounds

interdependent self-construal A self-perception that emphasizes one's relatedness to other people

interdisciplinary Scholars from multiple disciplines work together to examine an issue or topic of concern

interethnic conflict (ethnic conflict) A conflict situation between individuals or groups affiliated with different ethnic groups, whereby ethnicity is salient

interethnic marriage Marriage between people with different ethnic backgrounds

interethnic relationship A relationship between individuals affiliated with different ethnic groups

interfaith friendship An interpersonal relationship or friendship bond between individuals who are affiliated with a different religion

interfaith marriage A religious or civil union between partners professing different religions

intergenerational conflict Disputes between individuals or groups from different generations, whereby age is a salient issue

intergroup conflict Disputes that arise between two or more groups of people

intergroup relations Relationships between groups of people (e.g. ethnic, national, religious)

interlanguage pragmatics A sub-branch of pragmatics that focuses on the acquisition and use of pragmatic norms in a second language, e.g. how second language learners produce and understand speech acts, how their pragmatic competence emerges over time

international citizen *See* global citizen

international conflict Disputes between different countries, conflict between people and organizations from different nation-states, intergroup conflicts within a nation that impact other nations

International Criminal Court (ICC) A body established by the United Nations Security Council to try crimes against humanity (*See also* crimes against humanity)

international education Education that takes place outside one's home country

international intercultural relationship The ties that develop between people that bridge national, cultural and citizenship differences

International Phonetic Alphabet (IPA) An alphabetic system of phonetic notation based primarily on the Latin alphabet that serves as a standardized representation of the sounds of spoken language

international relationship The ties that develop between individuals that bridge national cultural and citizenship lines

internationalization Any systematic sustained effort designed to make higher education more responsive to the requirements and demands of an interconnected, global world

'internationalization at home' (IaH) The embedding of international/intercultural perspectives into local education systems to raise the global awareness, cultural understanding and intercultural competence of faculty and students

interpersonal communication A form of communication that involves a small number of people interacting with one another

interpersonal communication skills Communication strategies and techniques that can be enhanced through knowledge, practice, feedback and reflection

interpersonal conflict A conflict or a struggle between two or more people who may or may not have a similar linguistic and cultural background

interpersonal distance The psychological 'bubble' or preferred space that separates individuals from others

interpersonal power The ability to influence another person in the direction we desire

interpersonal relationship A type of human communication that occurs when two individuals interact and try to mutually influence each other, usually for the purpose of managing relationships

interpreter An individual who translates spoken communication

interpreting The act of translating spoken communication

interpretive approach The study of language and intercultural communication in context

interracial communication Interactions between two people in a situational context where racial difference is a salient issue

interracial conflict Individuals in a conflict situation whereby race or racial difference is a source of friction

interracial friendship A relationship between friends who are affiliated with different races

interracial marriage A union between individuals who are regarded as members of different races

interracial relationship A relationship between individuals who are regarded as members of different races

interreligious friendship An interpersonal relationship or friendship bond between individuals who are affiliated with a different religion

interreligious intercultural relationship Interpersonal connections between people with different religious orientations

interreligious or interfaith conflict (religious conflict) Disputes or conflict situations between individuals or groups affiliated with different faiths, whereby religion is a salient issue

intimate intercultural couple A romantic union between partners from different cultural backgrounds who may possess divergent beliefs, assumptions and values

intimate space The closest 'bubble' of space surrounding a person, which is reserved for private situations with those who are emotionally close and if others invade this space, one may feel threatened

intracultural conflict A struggle between individuals with a similar linguistic and cultural background

intracultural interactions The exchange of messages between people who share the same cultural background

intracultural relationship Interpersonal bonds that form between individuals who share the same linguistic and cultural background

intrapersonal communication Language use or thought directed at oneself

intrapersonal conflict The internal struggle that can occur within one's own mind

intraracial relationship Interpersonal relationships between individuals from the same socially-constructed racial group

involuntary migrant An individual who is forced to move to another country or region

kinesics A broad category of nonverbal actions, which encompasses the study of body movement, e.g. body posture, gestures, facial expressions and eye movements

Kluckhohn and Strodtbeck's Cultural Orientation Framework A model developed by Kluckhohn and Strodtbeck (1961), which identifies five problems or challenges that all cultures face

knowledge (*savoirs*) Knowledge of social groups and related products and practices in one's own country as well as in one's interlocutor's country

knowledge industries Organizations that require a workforce with advanced scientific or technological knowledge and skills

language A system comprised of vocabulary and rules of grammar that allows people to engage in verbal communication

language affiliation One's attitudes towards and feelings about the language

language anxiety Degree of nervousness when using a second language

language death A process whereby a language that has been used in a speech community gradually dies out (language extinction, linguistic extinction or linguicide)

language expertise An individual's degree of proficiency in a particular language

language identity The relationship between one's sense of self and the language one uses to communicate

language inheritance Being born into a family or community where the language is spoken

language maintenance The preservation of a language or language variety in a context where there is significant pressure for speakers to use the more prestigious or politically dominant language

language or linguistic rights The right to choose the language(s) for communication in private and public places; the right to one's own language in legal, administrative and judicial acts, language education and the media

language shock The challenge of understanding and communicating in a second language in an unfamiliar environment

language socialization The acquisition of linguistic, pragmatic and other cultural knowledge through social experience

'large culture' Prescribed ethnic, national and international entities

lesbian A woman who is attracted to another woman

lingua franca A language that is used as the medium of communication between speakers who have no native language in common

linguistic anthropology The interdisciplinary study of how language influences social life

linguistic competence The ability to apply knowledge of the rules of a standard version of the language to produce and interpret spoken and written language

linguistic determinism The strong form of the Sapir-Whorf Hypothesis, which argues that the language we speak *determines* our ability to perceive and think about objects

linguistic relativity The weaker version of the Sapir-Whorf hypothesis, which posits that the language one speaks *influences* thinking patterns but does not determine them

linguistic style An individual's speaking pattern, including such features as degree of directness or indirectness, pacing and pausing, word choice and the use of such elements as jokes, sarcasm, figures of speech (e.g. metaphors, irony, hyperbole), stories, questions, silence and apologies

local self A regional or national identity

localism A political philosophy which prioritizes the local (e.g. the local production and consumption of goods, local control of government, promotion of local culture and local identity

long-term relationships An intimate interpersonal affiliation that endures many years

long-term sojourner An individual who lives abroad for many years

loudness The degree of intensity of the voice

low-contact culture Touch occurs in limited circumstances and too much contact is viewed as intruding on an individual's privacy

low-context communication Explicit verbal messages are the norm (e.g. most of the information is in the transmitted message in order to make up for what is missing in the context)

low culture ('popular culture' or 'folk culture') Elements in society that have mass appeal, e.g. the sports, food, dress, manners and other habits of the 'common people' who have limited education, money and sophistication

majority identity An individual's identification with the dominant or majority group

marginality A cultural lifestyle at the edges where two or more cultures meet, which can be either encapsulating or constructive (*see also* constructive marginality, encapsulated marginality)

marginalization An acculturation strategy in which immigrants do not nurture their cultural heritage (e.g. first language, traditions) and also resist interacting with people in the host society

masculine cultures Distinct differences in the gender roles and responsibilities of men and women

masculinity The extent to which gender roles are valued, and attitudes towards ascribed masculine values (e.g. achievement, ambition)

mass media A message created by a person or a group of people sent through a transmitting device to a large audience or market (e.g. television, movies, the Internet)

mediation The settlement or negotiation of a conflict or dispute by an independent person or third party

mediator An independent or third party who facilitates negotiations and dialogue between the disputants

mental ability identity One's sense of belonging, which is linked to one's cognitive abilities (e.g. degree of intelligence) and mental health (e.g. stable, depressed) and ability to function in everyday life

message What is conveyed verbally (e.g. in speech, writing) or nonverbally from one person (the sender) to one or more persons (the receiver(s))

microculture The unconscious aspects of cultural behaviour

micro-term sojourner People who stay abroad for less than three weeks

mindful awareness Recognition of our own cultural ways of knowing and being and their impact on our intercultural interactions

mindful communicator An individual who considers his or her emotional and cognitive reaction and reflects on why someone with a different cultural background may be responding in a particular way

mindful fluency The ability to tune into our own cultural, linguistic and personal habitual assumptions in intercultural interactions

mindfulness Being aware of our own assumptions, ideas and emotions and those of our communication partners

minimization of difference According to the developmental model of intercultural sensitivity (DMIS), elements of one's own cultural worldview are experienced as universal in this phase

minority identity One's sense of belonging to a minority group

misattribution Inaccurate assumptions

mixed-method study A study that incorporates both quantitative and qualitative data

monochronic time orientation A time system in which tasks tend to be done one at a time and time is segmented into precise, small units

monogamy The practice of being married to only one person at a time

multicultural Interculturally competent in multiple cultural contexts

multicultural diversity The cultural variety and diversity that exists in the world

multicultural identity A psychological state of not possessing or being owned by a single culture

multidisciplinary An approach in which scholars from different disciplines investigate an issue separately, with each discipline retaining its own methodologies and assumptions

multilingual The ability to speak more than two languages

multilingual identity A hybrid sense of self linked to the use of multiple languages

multi-national Individuals from other foreign countries

multinational business Operations targeted toward and conducted in two or more countries

multiplex conflict situation Disputes between individuals or groups that cross multiple social and historical boundaries (e.g. ethnic, linguistic, international, racial, social, gender, religion, political)

mutual-face Concern for both parties' images and/or the well-being of the relationship

mutual facework The process of constructing a shared sense of identity

national identity People's affiliation with and sense of belonging to a state or nation

negative face The desire to have autonomy and not be controlled by others

negative facework The degree to which individuals protect their own privacy and freedom from interference

negotiation A process by which individuals or groups resolve a dispute by holding discussions and coming to an agreement that is mutually acceptable

netizens Individuals who actively engage in online interactions

netspeak (chatspeak or cyber-slang) An informal, concise and expressive style

noise (interference) Any disturbance or defect which interferes with or distorts the transmission of the message from one person to another

nonverbal codes All symbols that are not words, e.g. bodily movements, use of space and time, clothing and adornments and sounds other than words

nonverbal communication Communication without words through various communication channels (e.g. gestures, clothing, personal space)

nonverbal cues All potentially informative behaviours that are not purely linguistic in content

nonverbal expectancy violation theory A theory developed by Judee Burgoon (1978), which suggests that during the primary socialization process we build up expectations (mostly subconscious) about how others should behave nonverbally in particular situations and contexts and we respond negatively when people do not conform to these norms

oculesics A subcategory of kinesics, which is concerned with eye behaviour as an element of communication

olfactics (olfaction) The study of how we use and perceive odours (e.g. perfumes, spices, body scent, deodorant)

openness An internal posture that is receptive or open to new practices

operational competence The capacity for individuals in an unfamiliar environment to employ verbal and nonverbal acts that are considered appropriate in specific social transactions

organizational conflict Disputes that can arise within an organization due to competing needs, values, beliefs and interests

organizational identity A sense of attachment to organizations, whether in one's social, educational, religious or professional life

other-face The concern or consideration for the image or 'face' of the other conflict party in the conflict situation

Othering The labelling and degrading of people who are different from oneself

Otherization *See* Othering

outgroup Groups to whom one feels no emotional attachment

outgroup members Individuals from whom one feels emotionally and psychologically detached

outsourcing The contracting out of an internal business process to a third party organization

pacifism An approach in which individuals strive to avoid conflict situations

paradigm Philosophical framework

paralanguage (vocalics) The study of vocal cues, the nonphonemic qualities of language which convey meaning in verbal communication (e.g. accent, emphasis, loudness, rate of speech)

participant observation A method in which the researcher participates in the daily life of the people under study

particularism The application in which individuals may be treated differently depending on interpersonal relationships and obligations

Peace Corps A volunteer programme run by the U.S. government to promote world peace and friendship (initiated by President John F. Kennedy in 1960)

perception Becoming aware of, knowing or identifying by means of the senses through a process involving selection, organization and interpretation

perceptual understanding One's degree of open-mindedness, sophisticated cognitive processing and resistance to stereotyping

performance orientation The degree to which an organization rewards members for their participation and quality of work

peripheral beliefs Beliefs related to personal perceptions and tastes

personal identity An individual's sense of self, which differentiates him or her from others (e.g. our age, personal interests, gender, personality)

personal space The distance most people feel comfortable standing from each other in public

personal strength The quality of an individual's resilience, patience, hardiness and persistence

personality predisposition Interrelated personality resources

personality strength A strong sense of self, resilience and degree of relaxation in social situations

physical ability identity A sense of self that is limited to one's physical capabilities and limitations

physical appearance One's outward appearance (e.g. skin colour, facial features)

physical features Body type, deformities, eye shape, gender, height, skin colour, weight

pitch The range of one's voice during conversation that is linked to the frequency of a sound

platonic intercultural relationship an affectionate friendship between individuals of the opposite sex who have a different cultural background; the connection does not involve sexual relations

pluralistic society A society composed of people from numerous cultural and ethnic backgrounds, whereby cultural diversity among citizens is acknowledged and encouraged

politeness Demonstrating awareness and respect for another person's public self-image/behaving in ways that are deemed socially acceptable in a particular cultural context

polychronic time orientation A system whereby several things tend to be done at once, and a fluid approach is taken to scheduling time

polygamy The practice of having more than one spouse at a time

positive discrimination Education, business, or employment policies that aim to redress the negative, historical impact of discrimination by taking factors such as race, sex, religion, gender or national origin into consideration in hiring/promotion situations (*see also* affirmative action)

positive face A person's desire to gain the approval of other people

positive facework Actions that emphasize the need for acceptance, respect and inclusion

positivity An optimistic outlook that enables individuals to better endure stressful events

posture An individual's bodily stance (e.g. slouching, towering, legs spread, jaw thrust, shoulders forward, arm crossing)

power Authority or strength

power distance The degree to which less powerful members of a society or organization expect and accept the unequal distribution of power among members

power imbalance An individual, group or nation has great influence, control or domination over others

power relations An imbalance of power between individuals or groups

power status One's degree of power in relation to others

pragmatic competence The ability to comprehend and produce communicative acts in a culturally appropriate and effective manner

pragmatic failure The inability to comprehend and produce situationally appropriate language behaviour

pragmatics The study of the relationships between linguistic forms and the users of those forms

prejudice Dislike or hatred of a person or group formed without reason that is often rooted in a person's early socialization

preparedness The degree of readiness of an individual to undertake the process of cross-cultural adaptation

primary socialization The learning and acceptance of social norms, values and practices in one's home environment from an early age (*see also* cultural socialization, enculturation)

private-sector international conflict A type of conflict that is similar to private domestic interpersonal or business conflicts except that it is apt to be more complicated by linguistic and cultural differences

Process model of intercultural competence Darla Deardorff's (1984) model depicting the complexity of the development of intercultural competence

professional identity An individual's sense of belonging to a particular profession (e.g. teaching, nursing, business, etc.)

professional identity formation The developmental process of how individuals develop a sense of what it means to be a member of a particular profession, and how this identity distinguishes them from other professional groups

pronunciation The clarity and control of sounds being produced, the rhythm and the rate of speech

proxemics The social use of space in a communication situation

psychological adaptation Feelings of personal well-being and self-esteem

psychological adjustment The ability to adapt to new situations

psychological health Mental well-being

public space The area of space beyond which individuals perceive interactions as impersonal and relatively anonymous

race A social construction that historically has privileged people in positions of power

racial discrimination The prejudicial or unequal treatment of certain individuals based on their membership, or *perceived* membership, of a particular racial group or category

racial endogamy Marriage within one's own racial group

racial identity An identity linked to one's biological or genetic make-up (e.g. black, white, biracial)

racial quotas Numerical requirements for the selection and promotion of people from a group that is disadvantaged

racial segregation The separation of people into racial groups in daily life

racialization The process of developing racial categorization

racism The belief in the inherent superiority of a particular race and the perceived inferiority of other races

racist discourse Talk that has the effect of sustaining racist practices

racists Individuals who believe that people who have a different skin colour (or ethnicity) are inferior; may convey their hatred and bigotry in their speech (both oral and written) as well as their nonverbal behaviours

rapport Mutual empathy and understanding

rapport-challenge orientation A desire to challenge or impair harmonious relations between interlocutors

rapport-enhancement orientation A desire to strengthen or enhance harmonious relations between interlocutors

rapport-maintenance orientation A desire to maintain or protect harmonious relations

rapport-neglect orientation A lack of concern for the quality of interpersonal relations perhaps because of a focus on the self

'rapport talk' Conversations in which people seek confirmation, offer support and try to reach consensus

receiver The person (or persons) who is receiving a message that is being sent, whether intentional or not

receiver response The verbal or nonverbal reaction, if any, of a receiver after decoding the message

reductionism The tendency to ignore variations within cultures (*see also* essentialism)

reentry The process of returning home after spending time abroad

reentry culture shock The process of readjusting and reacculturating to one's own home environment after living in a different cultural setting for a significant period of time

reflective mindset The ability to revisit and make meaning from one's experience

refugee An individual who flees to another country to escape danger or persecution

regional identity The part of an individual's identity that is rooted in his or her region of residence

register A linguistically distinct variety of a language which is systematically determined by the context

regulators Actions (e.g. hand gestures, head nods) that influence the flow of a conversation

relational bonds The interpersonal connection between individuals, which serves as the basis of social groups and society as a whole

relational identity A privately transacted system of understandings that coordinate attitudes, actions and identities of the parties in a relationship

relational interdependence Mutual dependence or reliance on one other

relational intimacy The closeness one feels and displays towards one's friends

relational maintenance Communication that aims to keep relationships operating smoothly and satisfactorily

religious conflict Disputes or conflict situations between individuals or groups affiliated with different faiths, whereby religion is a salient issue

religious identity One's sense of belonging to a particular religious group

religious identity formation The process by which individuals decide what their relationship to religion will be

religious pluralistic society A society where many different religious beliefs, concepts and ideologies coexist

'report talk' Discourse that transmits information

resilience An individual's ability to cope with stress and adversity

resocialization The process of readjusting one's attitudes and behaviours to feel at ease in one's home environment after a period away

respect The display of positive regard for an individual from a different cultural background

reverse culture shock *See* reentry culture shock

reverse discrimination Perceived unfair treatment of the majority (or group that is generally considered to have more power and privilege) by providing advantages for minorities or those who are deemed underpriviliged

rituals A set of actions or rites performed for symbolic meaning

role shock Lack of knowledge and confusion about the norms of behaviour in a new cultural setting

romantic relationships Intimate interpersonal relationships of a romantic nature

same-sex marriage A marital union between members of the same sex

Sapir-Whorf hypothesis The notion that differences in the way languages encode cultural and cognitive categories significantly affects the way the users of a particular language view the world around them

second language socialization The process by which novices in an unfamiliar linguistic and cultural context gain intercultural communicative competence by acquiring linguistic conventions, sociopragmatic norms, cultural scripts and other behaviours that are associated with the new culture

segregation The acculturation strategy in which individuals strive to maintain their cultural heritage and avoid participation in the larger society of their new country

self-awareness Knowledge about one's identities, strengths and weaknesses

self-conflict *See* intrapersonal conflict

self-disclosure The process of deliberately revealing information about oneself that would not normally be known

self-face Protective concern for one's image when one's face is threatened in a conflict situation

self-presentation Information we disclose about ourselves through our discourse and non-verbal acts (e.g. dress, accent, gestures)

self shock Inconsistent, conflicting self-images, which can involve the loss of communication competence and self-confidence in a new environment

sender The person who is intentionally or unintentionally sending a message (verbally or nonverbally)

separation An acculturation strategy in which individuals strive to maintain their cultural heritage and avoid participation in the larger society of their new country

service learning (community-engaged learning) A structured learning experience that combines community service with guided reflection

sex The biological and physiological characteristics that define men and women

sexism The behaviour, conditions, or attitudes that promote stereotypes of social roles based on gender

sexist language The use of words or phrases that unnecessarily emphasize gender, or ignore, belittle or stereotype members of either sex

sexual harassment Bullying or coercion of a sexual nature

sexual identity How one thinks of oneself in terms of who one is sexually and romantically attracted to

sexual orientation One's desires, fantasies and attachments to sexual partners

short-term relationship An interpersonal relationship that is very brief (i.e. lasting only a few weeks or months)

short-term sojourner An individual who stays abroad for a few months or less

silence The absence of sound

Similarity–Attraction Hypothesis The belief that we are drawn to people we perceive to be similar to us

simultaneous interpreting The act of interpreting while the speaker is talking (e.g. at international business conference or meeting)

skills of discovery and interaction (*savoir apprendre/faire*) The ability to acquire new knowledge of a culture and to operate this knowledge in real-time communication

skills of interpreting and relating (*savoir comprendre*) The ability to interpret a document or event from another culture, to explain it and relate it to documents or events from one's own culture

'small culture' The notion of culture as attached to small social groupings or activities wherever there is cohesive behaviour rather than large groups (e.g. ethnic groups)

social categorization The way we group people into conceptual categories in order to make sense of our increasingly complex social environment

social class A social grouping of people based on common characteristics (e.g. economic resource, educational level) determined by society and reflecting a social hierarchy

social class prejudice Negative personal attitudes towards individuals of another class

social distance The degree of solidarity or closeness between people

social exclusion The barring of individuals or groups from participating in one's activities, strongly discouraging or preventing ingroup members from forming relationships with people who are disabled or from a different social class, etc.

social identity How we identify ourselves in relation to others based on what we have in common

social identity theory (SIT) A theory developed by Tajfel and Turner (1979, 1986) that suggests that individuals tend to categorize people in their social environment into ingroups and outgroups

social inclusion The act of giving all people in society an opportunity to participate regardless of their background or characteristics (e.g. mental or physical disability, race, language, culture, gender, age, social status, etc.)

social justice The fair administration of laws to treat all people as equal regardless of ethnicity, religion, race, language, gender, origin, etc.

social marker An indicator of one's social status or position in society (e.g. accent, material possessions, level and source of education, etc.)

social media Internet-based applications that build on the ideological and technological foundations of Web 2.0 and permit the creation and exchange of content generated by users

social network The multiple web of relationships an individual forms in a society with other people who he or she is bound to directly or indirectly through friendship or other social relationships

social networking sites (SNSs) Web-based services that allow people to develop a public or semi-public profile and communicate with each other (e.g. Facebook, Twitter)

social penetration theory (SPT) A theory proposed by Irwin Altman and Dalmas Taylor (1973), which suggests that as self-disclosure increases in depth (degree of intimacy on a particular topic), amount and breadth (the number of topics about which one self-discloses to one's communication partner), our relationships become more intimate

social responsibility The perceived level of interdependence and social concern for others, the society and the environment

social sanctions The measures used by a society to enforce its rules or norms of acceptable behaviour

social space Formal distance between people or cultural space (e.g. global community)

social status The honour or prestige attached to one's position or standing in society

socialization The process by which individuals internalize the conventions of behaviour imposed by a society or social group (*See also* primary socialization)

sociocultural adaptation Competence in dealing with life in the larger society

socio-emotional support The psychological assistance provided by friendship circles, intra-cultural and intercultural relationships and family members

sociolinguistic competence The ability to understand and use language in a way that is appropriate for the communication situation

sociopragmatic competence The ability to communicate appropriately in social situations in a particular cultural context

sociopragmatic expectancy violation Language usage or nonverbal actions that are perceived to be inappropriate in relation to one's status or role identity in a particular social and cultural context

sociopragmatic norms Rules governing the appropriate use of discourse in social situations

sojourn A period of time spent living in a cultural setting different from one's home environment

sojourner An individual who is in the new environment temporarily for a specific purpose (e.g. study, work, business) and often for a specific length of time (e.g. several days, months or years)

speech act The minimal unit of analysis of conversational interaction

speech community A group of individuals who use the same variety of a language and share specific rules for speaking and for interpreting speech

speech event A set of circumstances in which individuals interact in some conventional way for a particular purpose

speech illustrators Gestures or movements that illustrate or emphasize a verbal message, even though the user may not be conscious of their use

speech style The way we talk (e.g. our use of vocabulary, syntactic patterns, volume, pace, pitch, register, intonation)

speech style preference The speech we are most comfortable using in interactions

stereotype A preconceived idea that attributes certain characteristics (e.g. personality traits, level of intelligence), intentions and behaviours to all the members of a particular social class or group of people

stereotyping A strong tendency to characterize people from other cultural backgrounds unfairly, collectively and usually negatively

stress-adaptation-growth dynamic Young Yun Kim's (2001) notion that acculturative stress (e.g. language and culture shock) can gradually lead to adaptation in border crossers

structuralism A school of thought that sought to identify the components (structure) of the mind (*see* functionalism)

study abroad A subtype of education abroad that leads to progress toward an academic degree at a student's home institution; typically, this may include such activities as classroom study, research, internships, and service learning.

style shifting The process of adjusting or changing from one style of speech to another within the same language

subculture *See* co-culture

subdiscipline A field of specialized study within a broader discipline

subtractive bilingualism A process whereby a second language is added at the expense of the first language and culture (*see also* additive bilingualism)

superstition A belief, half-belief, or practice that does not appear to be based on rational substance

surface-level diversity Differences that are easily recognized through a quick assessment of physical characteristics, e.g. gender, age, race, ethnicity, etc.

symbol An artifact, word(s), gesture, sign, or nonverbal behaviour that stands for something meaningful to individuals in a particular context

synchronous communication Direct communication whereby all parties involved in the communication are present and interacting at the same time (e.g. Skype, chat rooms, internet relay chat)

systemic racism The mistreatment of people on a wide scale

telecommunication Communication at a distance via technological means, e.g. through electrical signals or electromagnetic waves

third-culture building The blending of different cultural identities and practices to form an identity that is unique to the parties involved, i.e. the identity of a multicultural family

third culture kid (TCK) A person who has spent a significant part of his or her developmental years outside the parent's culture (*see also* global nomad)

third gender People who are categorized as neither male nor female, either by themselves or by social consensus

time perception Views about such aspects as punctuality and willingness to wait

tolerance Going along with behaviours that one does not necessarily respect or accept

tolerance of ambiguity One's ability to cope with situations that are not clear

tourism The movement of people to countries or places outside their usual environment for personal, recreational or business/professional purposes

tourist Visitors who usually stay abroad for only a short time (e.g. a few days to several weeks or months) to sight-see, enjoy themselves and get a taste of a different linguistic and cultural environment

traditions The transmission of customs or beliefs from generation to generation

transactive communication People consciously directing their messages to someone else

transformation The act or process of change

transformational learning theory A theory developed by Jack Mezirow (1994, 2000), which posits that adults who engage in critical reflection and self-examination may experience a dramatic transformation

transgender People whose gender identities are different from the expectations and social norms associated with their biological sex

transition shock The state of loss, disorientation and identity confusion that can occur when one enters a new situation, job, relationship or physical location and is confronted with the strain of adjusting to the unfamiliar

translation The act or process of translating from one written language to another

transnational competence *See* global competence

turn-taking The use of nonverbal or verbal means to start and finish a turn in a conversation

U-curve adjustment model A theory of cultural adaption that suggests that border crossers go through several phases as they adjust to a new cultural environment

uncertainty/anxiety management theory (AUM) A theory developed by W. Gudykunst (1985), which suggests that one's level of stress or anxiety subsides as one gains more knowledge and understanding of one's communication partner

uncertainty avoidance Feeling threatened by ambiguous situations, one takes steps to avoid uncertainty

uncertainty reduction theory (URT) A theory developed by Berger and Calabrese (1975) that posits that the greater our ability to predict and explain our communication partners' behaviour, the greater the chance that our relationships will become more intimate

'unconscious' culture Elements that are invisible, nonverbal and unconsciously learned over time

unintentional communication Messages that are unintentionally communicated to a receiver

universal Of, relating to, extending to or affecting the entire world or all within the world; a worldwide phenomenon

universalism The application of the same rules for everyone regardless of their status or relationship

valence The positive or negative nature of something (e.g. values)

value Shared ideas about what is right or wrong

value orientations framework Models that identify, describe and contrast the dominant value system in various cultures

vertical-based facework Formal-asymmetrical strategies/deferential treatment

virtual (cyber) identity *See* cyber identity

vocal characteristics Traits of a speaker's voice, e.g. degree of raspiness or harshness

vocal characterizers Sounds that transmit messages (e.g. belching, crying, gasping, grunting, laughing, sighing, yawning, etc.)

vocal cues The nonphonemic qualities of language that convey meaning in verbal communication (e.g., tone, volume of voice)

vocal qualifiers Volume, pitch, rhythm and tempo

vocalics The study of vocal cues, the nonphonemic qualities of language that convey meaning in verbal communication

voice qualities Characteristics of one's voice including tempo, resonance, rhythm control, articulation

voluntary migrant An individual who willingly chooses to settle abroad

W-curve adjustment model An extended version of the U-curve model of adjustment that suggests that sojourners go through predictable phases when adapting to a new cultural situation and returning home

ways of being The manner or means of a way of life/a way of knowing

Web 2.0 Novel ways of creating, collaborating, editing and sharing user-generated content online

whole person development The nurturing of emotional intelligence and resourcefulness, interpersonal communication skills, intercultural competence, independence and maturity

willingness to communicate (WTC) An individual's readiness to enter into discourse at a particular time with a specific person or persons

work ethic A set of values based on hard work and discipline

workplace discrimination Unfair practices in hiring, promotion, job assignment, termination and compensation

world citizen An individual with a global or international identity

World Englishes Varieties of English in the world

worldview Our overall way of looking at the world, which serves as a filter to help us make sense of humanity

xenophobia An irrational fear of foreigners or strangers

Index

For text that appears within tables or figures, the number span is in **bold**. The use of *italics* denotes specialized terms.